BERLIN

Also by David Clay Large

Between Two Fires:
Europe's Path in the 1930s

Germans to the Front:
West German Rearmament in the Adenauer Era

The Politics of Law and Order:
A History of the Bavarian Einwohnerwehr

Where Ghosts Walked:
Munich's Road to the Third Reich

David Clay Large

A Member of the Perseus Books Group

Published by Basic Books,
A Member of the Perseus Books Group

Illustrations appear by permission of Archiv für Kunst und Geschichte, Berlin; Archive Photos, New York; Bildarchiv preussicher Kulturbesitz, Berlin; Bundesarchiv, Berlin; Hoover Institution, Stanford, Calif.; Landesbildstelle, Berlin; Los Angeles County Museum of Art; Presse- und Informationsamt der Bundesregierung, Berlin; and Ullstein Bilderdienst, Berlin.

Designed by Heather Hutchison

Library of Congress Cataloging-in-Publication Data is available.

ISBN-10: 0-465-02632-X ISBN-13: 978-0-465-02632-6

For Karl

CONTENTS

ILLUSTRATIONS

(AKG = Archiv Für Kunst und Geschichte; BPK = Bilderarchiv preussicher Kulturbesitz; LBS = Landesbiltstelle; Ullstein = Ullstein Bilderdienst)

ACKNOWLEDGMENTS

THIS BOOK HAS BEEN LONG in the making, and before I take my leave of it and move on to something else, I would like to thank (whether or not they would wish to be so thanked) some of the people who assisted me in my labors.

My editor at Basic Books, Don Fehr, believed strongly enough in this project, first to commission it, and then to take it with him as he moved around the New York publishing world. John Kemmerer, also at Basic Books, provided invaluable technical assistance. My agent, Agnes Krup, helped not only with the usual contractual matters but also offered astute suggestions for improving the manuscript. My colleagues Gordon Craig, Peter Gay, Fritz Stern, and Peter Fritzsche shared with me their rich knowledge of Berlin's and Germany's tangled past. Niall Ferguson of Jesus College, Oxford, kindly sent me his insights on Berlin's contemporary situation.

My greatest debt is owed to Karl Baumgart, who over the past twenty years has guided me around Berlin, introduced me to the best (and worst) *Kneipen*, given me a couch to sleep on, and kept me supplied with printed materials on the city when I could not be there to gather them myself. Without him this book could not have been written.

INTRODUCTION

During a stay in West Berlin in the fall of 1989 I decided, as I often did on visits to that city, to take a day's excursion across the Wall to East Berlin. At that time both halves of the "Siamese city" were tense because thousands of East German citizens were demonstrating for greater freedoms, including the right to travel freely to the West; some of the protesters, hoping to settle permanently in the Federal Republic of Germany (FRG), had gone so far as to take refuge in the West German embassies in Budapest, Prague, and Warsaw, refusing to leave without the promise of safe passage to the Federal Republic. To complicate matters, the Soviet president, Mikhail Gorbachev, was scheduled to arrive in the East German capital in a few days to help the German Democratic Republic (GDR) celebrate the fortieth anniversary of its foundation. On that cold early October morning when I took the *S-Bahn* over the Wall to the Friedrichstrasse station there were relatively few passengers on the train. As I handed my passport to a glowering border official I said cheerfully: "It looks like I'm the only one dumb enough to be traveling in this direction." Of course I should have known better than to attempt a lame joke with an East German official—one *never* joked with these fellows—and I was immediately subjected to an extended tongue-lashing for insulting the majesty of the East German state. Then I was made to sit by myself for a while in a small room so that I could contemplate the enormity of my impudence. Only after an hour or so was I allowed to retrieve my passport, pay the fee for a day's visa, and begin my short visit to the "Capital of the GDR." It would have considerably buoyed my spirits that day had I known that the Wall I had just crossed would come down within a matter of weeks and that the state I had just "insulted" would itself collapse a year later.

Of course, I was hardly the only one who did not anticipate the incredible upheaval that was about to transform Berlin, Germany, and Europe. Virtually everyone, including the people who were supposed to know about such things, was caught off-guard by the fall of the Berlin Wall on November 9, 1989. The world was just as astonished by what came next: the reunification of Germany and the disintegration of the Soviet Union. Between these two events the parliament of united Germany made the momentous decision to shift the country's seat of government from Bonn to Berlin, which had been the national capital from 1871 to 1945, and the capital of the GDR from 1949 to 1990.

The fall of the Berlin Wall has appropriately become a kind of shorthand for the entire reorientation of global politics since 1989, but in fact Berlin had stood at the center of European and world events for a much longer period. If Paris was the "Capital of the Nineteenth Century" (in Walter Benjamin's phrase), Berlin became the signature-city of the next hundred years. No other place has so dramatically encapsulated the highs and lows of our modern human experience. "Until 1933," writes the historian Reinhard Rürup, "Berlin had been famed as a symbol of modernity, of the capability and creative power of twentieth century man; from 1933 to 1945 it became a world-wide symbol of injustice and the abuse of power." After 1945, of course, the city took on yet another symbolic role: that of capital of the Cold War. Since the fall of the Wall and the end of the Great Divide, Berlin has come to represent humanity's aspirations for a new beginning, tempered by caution deriving from the traumas of the recent past.

This book is a narrative history of the city of Berlin framed by the two German unifications. These two historical moments harbor some intriguing similarities. Much of Europe watched in trepidation as the Germans marked the establishment of their new nation with a pompous ceremony at Versailles in 1871, and many Europeans shuddered anew when the two Germanys were reunited in 1990. Berlin's elevation to the status of imperial capital under Bismarck and its selection as capital-to-be by the Bundestag in 1991 spawned economic booms, which turned the city into a playground for developers and speculators. Real estate prices shot up as Germans from other parts of the country, along with an influx of foreigners, clamored to gain a toehold on the sandy banks of the River Spree. Among the newcomers in both cases were Jews from Eastern Europe who saw the city as a haven from persecution and an arena of economic opportunity. The city's physiognomy was instantly transformed as old buildings were renovated and new ones thrown up to accommodate the expanding population and new governmental agencies. Old-time residents complained that their town had turned into one huge construction site, overrun by outsiders. Yet while the building sprees seemed to go on interminably, the financial booms that fueled them suddenly lost momentum due to overspeculation, mismanagement, corruption, and economic crises elsewhere in Europe. In each instance, great expectations were quickly replaced by angry disillusionment and a search for scapegoats. Critical commentators, both domestic and foreign, began to assess the city more pessimistically, wondering aloud over its capacity to represent the new nation effectively. Throughout all the hand-wringing and fault-finding, however, Berliners and their backers remained convinced that the Spree city was the crucible of national destiny and the only serious choice for the center of national power.

The similarities between the two unification periods, striking though they are, should not obscure more fundamental differences. Germany's unification by "blood and iron" in 1871, following the successful wars engineered by Bismarck against Denmark, Austria, and France, was attended by an outpouring of national pride, even hubris. The new capital was awash in patriotic demonstrations and chauvinist rhetoric. By contrast, there was little of this kind of thing following reunification in 1990, which of course was achieved not by war but by the disintegration of the Soviet empire and the implosion of East Germany. The ceremonies in reunited Berlin in October 1990 were marked by a restraint befitting the participants' consciousness of the painful history of their nation and the world during the previous century. Because the Germany of 1990 was clearly a different political animal from the one in 1871, the fears on the part of its neighbors soon dissipated. By the time Berlin was designated as the new capital a year later there was little opposition from outside the country to the decision to move back to the place from which Germany's past transgressions had been orchestrated.

Another reason that the rest of the world could be relatively sanguine about the Germany of the 1990s was that its place within the European and world community was very different from that of 1870/71, not to mention 1914 or 1939. Bismarck had been free to play the game of *Grosse Politik*—great power politics—more or less as he saw fit, but Chancellor Helmut Kohl, who presided over German reunification in 1989/90, led a nation that was embedded in a comprehensive set of political, economic, and military constraints. The country's membership in NATO, the European Union, the United Nations, and the Conference on Security and Cooperation in Europe (CSCE), meant that Germany could not follow an independent course in foreign and security policy, which in any event few Germans wanted to do. Most of them welcomed the ties that had helped the "old" Federal Republic establish itself as a trusted and reliable member of the Western community. When the German central government finally opened for business in Berlin in 1999, Gerhard Schröder, the first chancellor to rule from the Spree city since Hitler, hardly needed to point out that *his* Berlin had little in common with the town that had become a byword for vainglorious nationalism and militaristic adventurism in the first half of the twentieth century.

Berlin's evolution during the 130-year period since the first German unification has been marked by jarring discontinuities and a baffling variety of political incarnations. Nonetheless, there are a number of significant themes or trends that can be discerned in the city's modern history. These warrant being outlined here, for they will run like red threads through the story that follows.

Being a latecomer as both a national capital and a major European metropolis, Berlin suffered from a municipal inferiority complex that proved hard to shrug off as the city struggled to catch up with the more established European capitals. Although the Spree metropolis became famous for its cutting-edge modernity, its celebration of the new and the experimental, a fear persisted in some quarters that the town was still "behind" its European rivals when it came to urban sophistication. Berliners might have become infamous within Germany for their swaggering self-assurance, but they worried that Parisians and Londoners might not find them *comme il faut.* Even when the German capital emerged as the most powerful and dynamic city on the Continent, as it did in the early twentieth century, Berliners asked themselves nervously if their town was now truly a *Weltstadt* (world city) like London, which then set the standard for global clout. In the late imperial period and during the Weimar Republic (1918–33), Berliners took justifiable pride in the world-renown of their cultural and scientific institutions, but this glory was short-lived and soon overshadowed by the horrors that emanated from Germany and Berlin after Hitler's seizure of power. The Spree city's political and moral bankruptcy during the Third Reich, its physical devastation in World War II, and its division along the main fault line of the Cold War, reduced the dimensions of Berlin's push for status largely to a battle between East and West. Berliners on both sides of the Wall, however, continued to dream of their city's eventual reemergence as a center of global heft and influence. Now that Berlin has been reunited and has resumed its position as national capital, that aspiration seems within reach, and Berliners are hopeful that *this time* they will finally make the grade.

In their preoccupation with their town's image in the rest of the world, Berliners all too often neglected to polish their reputation at home. From the moment the Spree city became the *Reichshauptstadt* (Reich capital), and then through all the vicissitudes that followed, Berlin inspired ambivalent feelings among the German people as a whole. Some, especially the young, took delight in the city's fast tempo, high energy, and electric atmosphere; many provincial Germans, on the other hand, distrusted Berlin for precisely these qualities—to them the sprawling Spree metropolis was a strange and deeply unsettling place, hardly *German* at all. In this regard Berlin bears comparison with New York City, which has often generated more loathing than love in the American heartland. Americans, however, could take consolation in the fact that New York was not their capital. Germany's many Berlinophobes had to live with the reality of being ruled from a city that they found alien to their own values.

To be fair to the Berliners, the reasons for the widespread distrust of their city were not entirely their fault. Prior to 1871 the German area had been highly decentralized, with regional centers like Munich, Hamburg, Mainz, Cologne, Dresden, Leipzig, and Frankfurt dominating the political and cultural scene. After unification, the citizens of these proud cities feared that their communities would be pushed into the background by the brash new imperial metropolis and by the Prussian state on whose coattails Berlin had risen to political prominence. For generations, Germans from the older cultural centers of the south and west had tended to disparage the Berliners as parvenus whose civilization was hardly more substantial than the Prussian sands on which their town was built. In Munich, the capital of Bavaria, people liked to say of the natives of the Prussian city: "Everyone has to be born somewhere; that poor fellow had the bad luck to be born in Berlin." The citizens of Hamburg, proud of that port-city's openness to the world, imagined Berlin as a benighted prairie outpost, hopelessly provincial and boring. When the French travel writer Jules Huret told a friend from Hamburg in 1907 that he intended to spend two months in Berlin, the Hamburger asked incredulously: "What could you find to do for two whole months in Berlin?" No doubt this question (like most of the regional disparagement of the Prussian city) derived largely from envy, for by that time Berlin was already casting its large shadow over the rest of the Reich.

Whatever the origins of the animus against Berlin, it certainly survived the collapse of the Kaiserreich in 1918. Weimar Berlin's famous avant-garde culture found considerably more resonance outside Germany than within it; indeed, the very cosmopolitanism of that culture hardened the long-standing suspicions in the hinterlands that Berlin belonged more to the world than to Germany. The Nazis, whose top leaders did not hail from Berlin, fully shared these prejudices against the Reich capital, but they consolidated central authority in the city more thoroughly than ever before, thereby exacerbating old regional animosities. Not even Berlin's demise as the capital of a unified nation in 1945, nor its own painful division in the Cold War era, brought an end to this pattern. Both West and East Berlin generated resentment in their respective states, though for somewhat different reasons: West Berlin because it was an expensive and pampered ward of the West German taxpayer; East Berlin because it tried to do on a smaller stage what united Berlin had always done—that is, absorb the lion's share of national resources while exerting an unwelcome dominance over the other cities and regions in the state. The acrimonious debate in 1991 over whether Berlin was fit to become united Germany's capital again showed just how resilient these animosities remained.

Mention of the top Nazis' distrust of Berlin should remind us that this mindset was not limited to ordinary folk but was harbored by the national leadership as well. Indeed, ongoing tensions between the rulers of the nation and the citizens of the Spree metropolis constitute another theme in our story. Like Berlin's problematical image in the popular mind, the city's troubled relationship with its overlords has a long historical pedigree.

From the moment in 1442 when Friedrich ("Iron Tooth") von Hohenzollern, the electoral prince of Brandenburg, established his official residence in Berlin, the privilege of housing ambitious rulers proved a mixed blessing for the Spree city. Before that time the dual settlement of Berlin-Cölln, whose existence was first officially documented in the year 1237, had slowly evolved as a relatively undistinguished trading center, its main distinctions being municipal self-government and membership (since 1391) in the Hanseatic League of mercantile free cities. Iron Tooth's move to the city brought it elevated status as an electoral seat, a measure of protection against marauding robber barons, and an infusion of new trades that catered to the court, but it also meant the subjection of the town's own government to that of the prince, who brooked no insubordination from the citizenry. To enforce his control, Iron Tooth tore down the city's outer wall and erected a stronghold called "Zwing-Cölln" on a small island in the Spree between the twin communities. When, in 1447–48, the citizens revolted in an effort to regain their privileges, the prince brought in troops to crush the uprising. He altered the town's coat of arms, which heretofore had featured a rampant bear, by placing a Brandenburg eagle on the back of a couchant bruin. Lest the bear try to rise again, Iron Tooth garrisoned a good number of armed men within the town. From that time on, soldiers would play a crucial, and often oppressive, role in the life of Berlin. So too would the princely administration, which under Iron Tooth's successors continued his assault on municipal liberties. In 1514 Kurfürst Joachim I demolished the joint town hall on the Long Bridge connecting Berlin and Cölln. In 1538 Berlin was forced to withdraw from the Hanseatic League.

The benefits to Berlin of housing an autocratic court continued to be quite mixed following the elevation of Kurfürst Friedrich to the title of King of Prussia in 1701. Friedrich and his wife Sophie Charlotte enriched the city with some of its most notable buildings and monuments, most of them the work of their brilliant court architect, Andreas Schlüter. These endowments included the baroque palace later called Charlottenburg; extensions to the rambling Royal Palace that was growing up on the site of Iron Tooth's stronghold; completion of a new armory, the Zeughaus, on Unter den Linden; the Berlin Academy; and a magnificent equestrian statue of Kurfürst Friedrich Wilhelm (the "Great Elector"), who had been Friedrich's predecessor. Yet King Friedrich, whom the Berliners cruelly mocked as "crooked Fritz" because of his deformed frame and hunched back, shackled Berlin in a monarchical straitjacket that extended the ruler's prerogatives over the city. He further circumscribed the powers of the city council, whose members all had to be approved by royal authority. The double-edged sword of largesse and regimentation was also wielded by Friedrich's more famous grandson, Friedrich II ("the Great"). Befitting his transformation of Prussia into a great European power, Friedrich ordained the construction of imposing new buildings in his capital, such as the Royal Opera and the Royal Library. To serve his new Silesian subjects the king built a Catholic church, St. Hedwig's. While still crown prince, Friedrich had invited Voltaire to come to the city he described as Europe's "new Athens," and during his reign Berlin indeed became a kind of Athens on the Spree, attracting a host of Enlightenment thinkers and artists. Yet Friedrich's famous flute-playing and devotion to the arts hardly made him a pushover when it came to keeping his subjects, including the Berliners, firmly in their place. His Berlin was as much a latter-day Sparta as an Athens, with some 20,000 soldiers billeted on a population of roughly 100,000. In 1747 he instituted a new municipal administrative code that placed day-to-day authority in the hands of the royal director of police, who served as city president. As if that did not constitute sufficient royal vigilance, the town was also put under the watchful supervision of a city military commander. (It was one of these military officials, Count von der Schulenburg, who famously declared in 1806 that the Berliners' "first duty" as citizens was to remain docile in the face of royal authority.) In the end, Friedrich decided that he did not like Berlin very much after all; he preferred to reside in nearby Potsdam, where he built his magnificent palace, Sanssouci.

With the development of their city into a European center of commerce, finance, and manufacturing in the early nineteenth century, Berliners naturally became increasingly restive under the onerous controls and obligations imposed by the royal court. In many ways, the Hohenzollern capital was outgrowing the dynasty. Simmering resentment over this state of affairs, combined with growing desires for a unified nation based on the will of the people, boiled over into open defiance of the regime during the revolution of 1848. On March 18 of that year a large crowd gathered before the Royal Palace and demanded the withdrawal of the king's soldiers and the creation of a citizens' militia. King Friedrich Wilhelm IV ordered his troops to clear the area with minimal use of force. His officers, however, rode into the crowd with sabers flailing, and the infantry fired off two shots. This was enough to enrage the Berliners. "The king has betrayed us!" they shouted, as they scattered into side streets and erected barricades with any materials that came to hand. Fighting raged across the city that night between the troops and citizens armed with stones, pitchforks, and a few muskets. Unwilling to countenance a full-scale civil war, the king ordered his soldiers to withdraw to their barracks. On the following day, as a further gesture of reconciliation, he rode through the town wearing the red-black-gold colors of the national unity movement and delivered a speech "To my dear Berliners." A few days later he stood with his head bowed as thousands of townspeople marched past the palace on their way to Friedrichshain cemetery to honor the "March Heroes" who had died for the cause of a new Germany, and a new Berlin. The city's moment of triumph, however, was brief. Taking advantage of indecision and discord among the revolutionaries, Friedrich Wilhelm soon regained the initiative. In September 1848 troops under General Friedrich von Wrangel reconquered the city and imposed martial law. As a consequence of the failure of the popular upheaval of 1848, Germany would be unified from above rather than from below, and Berlin would not become the seat of a democratic government until the demise of Hohenzollern power in 1918.

Germany's rulers did not forget Berlin's legacy of unruliness when the city became the imperial capital in 1871. The new emperor, Wilhelm I, who as crown prince had fled Berlin to England during the revolution of 1848, remained distrustful of the town for the rest of his life. So did Bismarck, despite doing more than anyone else to turn the Prussian capital into the imperial capital. The tradition of Berlin-angst was carried on in the imperial era by Kaiser Wilhelm II even though he, like his Hohenzollern predecessors, made many additions to the city's cultural patrimony. While the revolution of 1918 brought an end to the long and complicated relationship between the Hohenzollerns and their capital, it did not put a stop to the tensions between Berlin and the national leadership. During the Weimar era President Paul von Hindenburg made his distaste for the city abundantly clear. His snubs of the capital, however, were of little consequence compared to the ruin that the man he appointed chancellor in 1933, Adolf Hitler, ultimately brought down on the Spree metropolis. Following the postwar division of Germany and its former capital, the Bonn-based Federal Republic helped to keep West Berlin afloat economically, but Bonn's first chancellor, Konrad Adenauer, extended this aid reluctantly, and he took a backseat to no one in his aversion for the big city on the Spree, which he believed was instrumental in bringing on the German catastrophe. As the "Bonn Republic" gradually established itself as a successful democracy—indeed, as the first sustained democracy in German history—Adenauer attributed this achievement partly to the fact that the country was not governed from Berlin. United Germany's new rulers do not share this aversion to the old/new capital, but the fact that they have taken great pains to reassure the world that Berlin presents no threat to peace and stability is a sign that the old anxieties have not died out.

The people who flocked to Berlin in the *Gründerzeit* of the 1870s were often looking for a new beginning in life, and they helped to turn the Spree city into a hothouse of modernity, a place that pursued change like a drug. Of course, other German cities also underwent the jarring processes of rapid urbanization and industrialization, but none embraced the new world more readily than Berlin, or, as a consequence, became such a magnet for the young. The youthful protagonist of Conrad Alberti's novel, *Die Alten und die Jungen* (The Old and the Young, 1889), captured something of the heady atmosphere of the new capital when he rhapsodized about "the nervous, endlessly quivering Berlin air . . . which works upon people like alcohol, morphine, cocaine, exciting, inspiring, relaxing, deadly; the air of the world city."

As Berlin careened from one form of government to the next over the course of the twentieth century, it continued to pride itself on its eagerness to adopt new ways and to throw off the baggage of the old like so much unwanted ballast. In the 1920s Bertolt Brecht claimed that his adopted city's radical spirit derived from a total lack of historical memory. The alacrity with which the city demolished older neighborhoods and buildings to make way for new construction suggests that he had a point.

From the outset, however, the thirst for change was accompanied by an almost equally potent sense of regret for all that was being lost. Nostalgia is as pervasive a theme in Berlin's modern history as the cult of the new. The city had no sooner become Reich capital than local commentators and novelists began writing wistfully about the good old days of the sleepy *Residenzstadt.* In the 1920s, when Berlin touted itself as the capital of modernity, resident intellectuals like Walter Benjamin, Franz Hessel, Siegfried Kracauer, and Arthur Eloesser probed for footholds of psychic continuity in the city while illuminating the ever-changing mores of the fast-moving metropolis. Eloesser wrote that he truly found his "Heimat" only in the "spare remains" that a "merciless progress" had left behind. After the Nazis had snuffed out Weimar Berlin's glories, that era became the stuff of a relentless myth-making that has lasted until our own day. In an interview conducted in 1990, the director of the Berlin Festival claimed that in melding the cultures of East and West, the new Berlin stood in spiritual affinity with the decade before 1933: "Berlin dreams the dreams of the Twenties," he averred. Of course, the dream process in question tends to be selective, filtering out the old nightmares of economic misery and political polarization that brought Weimar down. In addition to the "Golden Twenties," some post-unification Berliners have also found a cherished place in their memory banks for the more recent era of division—a period that one might have thought everybody would be more inclined to forget. As a matter of fact, many *have* forgotten the nastier aspects of this epoch—preferring, in the case of nostalgic West Berliners, to recall the subsidized lassitude of their bohemian idyll rather than the claustrophobic restlessness known as *Mauerkrankheit* (Wall-sickness); and dwelling, in the case of some former GDR citizens, on the claimed community-enhancing benefits of socialism rather than on the atmosphere of fear and suspicion that turned neighbor against neighbor.

In tracing Berlin's history from its role as imperial capital under Bismarck and Wilhelm I to its surprising emergence as capital-redux in the post-reunification Germany of Helmut Kohl and Gerhard Schröder, I have attempted to be as comprehensive as possible without overtaxing the reader's endurance. While the focus here remains on the city of Berlin, I have tried always to examine municipal affairs within the broader framework of Germany, Europe, and the world. Rather than isolating one subplot in this story—say, Berlin's political evolution—I have woven together political, social, economic, and cultural strands in my narrative tapestry. Cultural developments come in for particular attention, for it was largely through culture that Berlin exerted its influence outside Germany—an achievement that many Berlin artists and intellectuals carried on in exile when their city turned hostile to the spirit of free expression.

It has been argued that the repeated efforts by Berlin's rulers to keep the city in check moved the locals to develop their peculiar brand of impudent and subversive wit, the famous *Berliner Schnauze.* No history of Berlin would be complete without reference to this humor, and I have recorded a few choice examples in my narrative. I have also tried, however, to be faithful to Berlin's subversive spirit by engaging in some irreverence of my own with regard to various hoary pieties and comforting myths that have grown up around the city in recent years. A town that has often been critical of its own shortcomings can, one trusts, abide some constructive criticism from the outside.

Berliner Dom (Berlin Cathedral) and Lustgarten, 1900

BERLIN UNDER BISMARCK

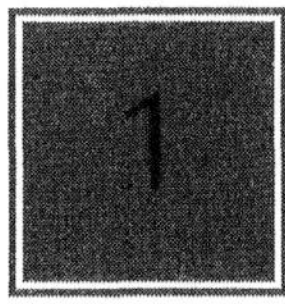

The city wall of Berlin is falling victim to the metropolitan spirit.

—Robert Springer,
***Berlin Wird Weltstadt* (1868)**

WHEN GERMANY BECAME UNIFIED in 1871 following the defeat of France by a Prussian-led coalition of German states, Berlin was transformed from a provincial royal seat into the capital of one of the most powerful nations in Europe. Like the new German nation itself, however, the capital at that point was a work in progress, a far cry from the vibrant cosmopolitan metropolis it would eventually become. As Lord Frederick Hamilton, a young diplomat in Britain's Berlin Embassy, snootily observed: "The Berlin of the 'seventies' was still in a state of transition. The well-built, prim, dull, and somewhat provincial *Residenz* was endeavoring with feverish energy to transform itself into a world city, a *Weltstadt.*" Even some Berliners were doubtful that their rough-edged city had leaped into the ranks of the great European capitals. "Oh Berlin, how far you are from being a true capital," opined the novelist Theodor Fontane. "You have become a capital overnight through political fortuitousness, not through your own devices."

In the course of trying to reinvent itself for its new role, Berlin changed so rapidly that it became difficult to define the essence of the place. Within twenty years, old timers were complaining that they couldn't recognize their town. Yet it was during the great flux following German unification that the leitmotivs that would dominate Berlin's history for the next hundred and thirty years were firmly laid down. Berlin's frantic attempt to catch up with its older and more polished European rivals; its provocation of resentment and envy on the part of Germans from other parts of the country, especially the south and west; its tension-filled relationship with the rulers who governed Prussia and the Reich; its complicated mixture of novelty-worship and nostalgia for a lost, quieter era—all these trends were evident in the nineteen-year period during which Count Otto von Bismarck ran the newly unified German Reich from Europe's newest capital.

Berlin *en Fête*

Germany celebrated its emergence as a unified nation with the largest military parade ever seen in Berlin, a city which over the years had witnessed more than its share of martial displays. On June 16, 1871, a brilliantly clear Sunday, 40,000 soldiers paraded from the Tempelhof Field via the Halle and Brandenburg Gates to the Royal Palace on Unter den Linden. All wore iron crosses on their tunics and many had victory wreaths slung over their shoulders. A contingent of noncommissioned officers bore eighty-one captured French battle flags, some of them in tatters. "The troops looked superb," enthused Baroness von Spitzemberg, the wife of Württemberg's representative in Berlin, "so manly, suntanned, bearded, their traditional Prussian stiffness loosened by the atmosphere of the parade; they were a lovely sight for a patriotic heart."

At the head of the long column rode eighty-seven-year-old Field Marshal Friedrich von Wrangel, a hero of past Prussian victories who had been resurrected from retirement to lead the parade. He was followed by General Albrecht von Roon and Helmuth von Moltke, the latter carrying the field marshal's baton he had just been awarded for his recent victories over France. According to one witness, the grim-faced field marshal looked as though he were planning a new campaign rather than accepting tribute for a war just won. Next to Moltke rode the true genius behind the wars of German unification, Bismarck, who in reward for his services had been made a prince, a title he claimed to disdain. Behind Bismarck and the generals came Germany's new kaiser, William I, his erect posture belying his seventy-four years. "The wonderful old man must have larger-than-life strength to endure the external rigors and inner turmoil so calmly," exulted an awed observer.

The conditions that day were indeed difficult: it was so hot and humid that several riders suffered heatstrokes and fell from their horses. But the heat apparently did not bother the kaiser's grandson, twelve-year-old Wilhelm, who, despite a withered left arm, stayed on his mount throughout the ordeal. Haughtily, he refused to acknowledge a well-wisher in the crowd who addressed him as "Wilhelmkin." "He will never forget this day," said Wilhelm I of the boy who would later rule Germany as Kaiser Wilhelm II.

In accordance with the epochal significance of the occasion, Berlin was decked out as never before in its history. "The *via triumphalis* was about three miles long, through streets as wide and in some cases thrice as wide as Broadway," wrote the American minister George Bancroft. All along the route stood captured French cannon and flagstaffs festooned with oak leaves and evergreens. At important way stations rose enormous allegorical figures made of wood, linen, and straw. A twenty-meter-high statue of Berolina, patron goddess of Berlin, graced the Halle Gate, while two huge female figures, representing the newly acquired cities of Strasbourg and Metz, presided over the Potsdamer Platz. In the Lustgarten next to the Royal Palace loomed an even larger statue: *Mutter Germania,* flanked by her youngest daughters, Alsace and Lorraine. A velarium suspended over Unter den Linden depicted the great military victories that had finally brought Germany its unity.

Upon reaching their destination at the Pariser Platz, next to the Brandenburg Gate, the kaiser and his retinue stood under a canopy while dignitaries from the city of Berlin paid their respects and a maiden in white recited an interminable poem. Princess Victoria, daughter of Queen Victoria and the wife of Crown Prince Friedrich Wilhelm of Germany, had deep reservations about this new Reich born of blood and iron, but even she could not contain her admiration for the victory parade, declaring it "the greatest fête Berlin, and I may say Germany, has ever seen."

Such pomp did not come cheaply. The celebration cost more than 450,000 talers, which had to be raised through a surcharge on all income taxes levied in Berlin. Few Berliners complained, however, for the festivities offered ample opportunity to recoup the tax. Restaurants and taverns added extra tables and dispensed a "Commemoration Beer," which, though the same as the regular beer, cost a few pennies more because of its historical significance. Street vendors hawked a "War and Vic-

Kaiser Wilhelm I enters the Pariser Platz during the victory celebration in Berlin on June 16, 1871

tory Chronicle 1870–71," along with guides to Berlin's nightlife, tickets to tours of the city, coats of arms of famous generals, regimental flags, and fragrant laurel wreaths.

Vantage points from which to watch the proceedings in comfort were in great demand. Merchants with houses or shops along the route rented out viewing space for breathtaking sums. One enterprising store owner on Unter den Linden installed ten "comfortable chairs" in his window "with an unobstructed view of the Pariser Platz." Thousands brought camp-stools to the street or perched atop trees, lamp-posts, and monuments. "No roof was too high, no stool too low that was not occupied by people," wrote the *Vossische Zeitung.* "There was not even any empty space atop the dizzying heights of the Brandenburg Gate. . . . The men and women up there sought to outdo each other with daring poses, all of them showing a contempt for death that was truly astounding."

This moment, with all its bombast and swagger, can be seen as deeply symbolic of Bismarckian Germany and its raw new capital. Apart from its dominant military motif, the triumphal celebration resembled nothing so much as a housewarming party thrown by a newly rich sausage baron upon taking possession of his neo-Renaissance mansion. In subsequent decades the prevailing mood in Berlin would not remain uniformly celebratory, but the city's self-conscious determination to display its prowess and to show the world that it had *arrived* as a great capital remained constant.

The Unloved Capital

Tumultuous as the unification festivities were, they masked disappointment in some quarters that Berlin had become the capital of the new Reich. Given Prussia's crucial role in German unification, Berlin's elevation was no doubt inevitable, but it hardly came without opposition. Wilhelm I would have preferred nearby Potsdam, seat of the Royal Guards and favored residence of Prussia's greatest king, Frederick the Great. Wilhelm had fled Berlin in 1848 to escape the local radicals (see Introduction), and he continued to see the place as potentially unruly and rebellious. Wilhelm's son, Crown Prince Friedrich Wilhelm, known for his liberal inclinations, favored Frankfurt, site of the 1848 parliament that sought unsuccessfully to unify Germany from below. Bismarck quickly quashed objections within the ruling family to Berlin's becoming the German capital by promising that the city's elevation to that status would help ensure Prussian domination of national life.

Yet this Prussian angle was precisely why many Germans in other parts of the country were deeply unhappy with the selection. They resented Prussian power and saw Berlin as a bullying behemoth determined to overwhelm the rights and prerogatives retained by the individual states in the new imperial constitution. That document represented a tortuous compromise between Prussian-based centralism and the particularistic ambitions of semisovereign entities like Saxony and Bavaria. The fact that the national capital was simultaneously the Prussian capital threatened to tip the balance in favor of the centralizers. Many of the smaller states would have preferred Frankfurt, Leipzig, or even little Erfurt. Non-Prussian Germans also objected to Berlin's eastern orientation, decrying it as the "capital of East Elbia," a colonial frontier city on the edges of the Slavic wilderness. The residents of ancient western German cities like Cologne, Aachen, and Trier, which had known the fruits of Roman civilization, fretted about being under the thumb of a city that had been nothing but a bump on the Brandenburg Steppes when these older towns were building cathedrals and hosting lively medieval cultures. Anti-Berlin sentiment was equally strong in the south, especially in Bavaria, whose largely Catholic citizenry saw the Prussian metropolis as a dangerous repository of alien Protestantism.

Concerns about Berlin's new status surfaced even in the imperial capital itself. Municipal officials, whose powers had long been limited by the Prussian government—mayors, judges, and police chiefs all had to approved by the king—would now be subject to yet another higher authority. Berlin's assumption of the capital function made it seem dangerously powerful to non-Berliners, but in reality the municipal government had little authority of its own. The powers of the city assembly, magistrate, and mayor's office were all closely circumscribed by the imperial administration and the authorities of the state of Brandenburg, headquartered in Potsdam. It would be years before local officials even gained control over their own streets and utilities. A determination on the part of Prussian and Reich officials to keep the city politically weak underlay repeated refusals throughout the imperial era to allow Berlin to merge the various suburbs around the historic core into one administrative entity.

Prussian patriots, meanwhile, were concerned that traditional values and customs would be swept aside as the new capital was invaded by alien elements from other parts of Germany and Europe. They worried that their town would become unrecognizable as a result of the demographic and economic changes accompanying Berlin's assumption of imperial-capital status. This view was poignantly illustrated in a popular novel of the day, Ludovica Hesekiel's *Von Brandenburg zu Bismarck* (1873), which lamented the passing of a humble and harmonious "Old Berlin" in the rush to imperial greatness. Having seen her neighborhood around the Wilhelmstrasse totally transformed by national unity, the protagonist, an aging Prussian grande dame, protests: "[My heart] is sick. Let me go home now; the new German sun that is rising into the sky would only blind this old Prussian lady." To Theodor Fontane, who loved Old Prussia, if not necessarily Old Berlin, the capital was becoming just another place in which to get ahead fast. "What does it mean to live in Berlin except to make a career?" he asked in 1884. "The large city has no time for thinking, and, what is worse, it has no time for happiness. What it creates a hundred times over is the 'Hunt for Happiness,' which actually is the same as unhappiness." Fontane's perspective reflected the widely held view in Germany that true creativity was incompatible with the hectic pace of life in a large city like Berlin, where everyone seemed too rushed to think seriously about deep matters of the soul. Contemplating the spread of vice and modernist values in the new capital, the conservative cultural critic Constantin Frantz insisted that Berlin had forfeited its claim "to be the metropolis of the German spirit."

The great Bismarck himself, though largely responsible for Berlin's becoming the German capital, shared some of these prejudices against the city on the Spree. Having grown up as a Junker (the aristocratic, East Elbian landowning class) on an estate in rural Prussia, Bismarck saw Berlin as an ugly concrete jungle full of pallid people and nasty urban smells. "I have always longed to get away from large cities and the stink of civilization," he declared. "I would much rather live in the country," he told the Reichstag members, "than among you, charming though you are." On another occasion he protested that Berlin had "grown too big for me industrially and politically"—a reference to the city's growing manufacturing base and sizable industrial proletariat. He was hardly less wary of Berlin's high society, which he found frivolous and pretentious, and he grew positively contemptuous of its ambitious bourgeois liberals, whose influence he believed was corrupting the Reichstag, making it more difficult for him to control. Speaking before the parliament in 1881, he was quite frank regarding this issue:

> The political disadvantage connected with having the Reichstag in Berlin does not end with the external [security] danger that this poses to the delegates and governmental officials;. . . even more, this has an unfortunate influence on the composition of the Reichstag. . . . The delegates move here and become comfortable here. . . . We have too many Berliners in the Reichstag, which is only natural, since they don't have to travel to meetings.

In the latter part of his reign Bismarck stayed away from the capital as much as possible, preferring to run the nation from the sanctuary of his country estates, Varzin and Friedrichsruh, which had been awarded him for his successful wars of national unification.

Ambivalence about Berlin as imperial capital was further reflected in the haphazard and tentative manner in which the Reich government established its physical presence in the city. Bismarck's bête noire, the Reichstag, did not get a new building of its own until 1894. Until then it had to conduct its business in an abandoned porcelain factory. The structure was so decrepit that its glass ceiling occasionally broke away and fell into the assembly room, slicing up the chairs. Had this ever happened when parliament was in session, observed one member, "a delegate could easily have lost his head, or some other part of his body." Such conditions led to the complaint that "the representatives of the nation are unhoused guests in the new Reich capital." But it was not only the Reichstag that got short shrift. Bismarck's government provided virtually no financial support to the city for logistical and infrastructure improvements. Most of the Reich ministries and administrative agencies initially rented space in private houses or moved into converted palaces on and around the Wilhelmstrasse, where the older Prussian offices were also located. A new building, modeled on the Palazzo Pitti in Florence, was constructed at Wilhelmstrasse Nr. 74 for the Imperial Chancellery. Bismarck, however, did not like the building's style, so he moved his personal residence and office into a neighboring palace at Wilhelmstrasse Nr. 76, and then, in 1878, into a new Chancellery in the former Radziwill Palais at Wilhelmstrasse 77. Meanwhile, the Interior Ministry moved into the building originally designed for the Chancellery. The Foreign Office, increasingly cramped for space, worked out of several different buildings until a new home, modeled after another Florentine palazzo, was built for it on the Wilhelmplatz. Lacking time and preparation to grow gracefully into its new role, Berlin wore its capital vestments like an ill-fitting suit off the rack. For many years after unification, the governmental quarter had a temporary and improvised feel about it, as if the national government were not sure it wanted to be there at all.

Boomtown

The doubts that many Germans harbored about their new capital did nothing to dampen Berlin's physical and economic expansion, which assumed truly frenzied proportions in the period following unification. The city resembled a giant mining camp or gambling casino, luring ambitious newcomers with the promise of instant gains. As many locals feared, rapid growth exacted its price in terms of civic grace and urban aesthetics. Berlin not only felt like a gambling camp, it began to look like one. Moreover, since the steamroller of growth tended to crush any historical impediments to "progress," Berlin seemed increasingly bereft of any coherent identity or sense of continuity. It was settling into what one commentator famously labeled its "modern fate"—that of "always becoming and never managing to be."

At the time of German unification, Berlin's population stood at 865,000. In 1877 it passed the 1 million mark and, after a mere twenty-eight more years, reached 2 million. Berlin's population growth came through large-scale immigration, not through a sudden burst of fecundity on the part of the natives. The newcomers hailed principally from Brandenburg, East Prussia, and Silesia. The Prussian capital had long been a city of immigrants, but now every other person seemed to have just climbed off the train and to radiate that mixture of disorientation and determination typical of recent arrivals. Their prevalence prompted the bon mot "every true Berliner is a Silesian." The rawness, but also the vitality, of Bismarckian Berlin owed much to the influence of its newest residents.

Significantly, a considerable number of the newcomers were Jews from the Prussian provinces or from eastern Europe. In 1860 Berlin had only 18,900 Jews, but by 1880 the figure had risen to 53,900. The so-called *Ostjuden* from eastern Europe were seeking a safe haven from racial persecution in their own countries; for them Berlin was a promised land of religious and economic freedom. The Jews from rural Prussia saw the new capital as a place where they could take maximum advantage of talents honed as a result of past discrimination in the provinces. Having been barred from owning land, practicing many of the traditional crafts, or serving in the bureaucracy and military, the Jews had become experts in commerce, finance, journalism, the arts, and the law, precisely the fields that were most in demand in the modern metropolis. Settling into their new home, the Jews quickly put their stamp on the city, melding their own distinctive style with native traditions of irreverence and caustic wit. Their rise became associated with Berlin's own rise as a major European metropolis. This integration generated much talk of a "Berlin-Jewish symbiosis." Although never merely an illusion, as some commentators would later insist, this partnership was fragile from the outset, and its very seductiveness would tragically prevent all too many Jews from recognizing that fatal moment, some six decades later, when it had broken down altogether. It should be recalled, moreover, that while Berlin's Jews were prominently identified with the city's emergence as a center of cultural and economic modernism, most of the city's modernists were not Jews and most of its Jews were not modernists.

The most pressing problem facing the new arrivals in Berlin was finding a place to live. For years Berlin had experienced housing shortages, but in the dawning imperial era the problem became acute. To accommodate the rising demand for housing, dozens of private *Baugesellschaften* (building societies) began throwing up new structures throughout the city. They covered over vacant lots, urban gardens, and children's playgrounds. To render a large wetland near the Spree buildable, a construction company brought in boatloads of sand and spread it over the bog. Here rose the Hansaviertel, named after the sea-trading league to which Berlin had once belonged. Residents of the district could still experience the sensation of being at sea whenever heavy rains caused the Spree to flood and engulf the surrounding territory.

Much of the new construction took place in suburbs ringing the city, and competition for development sites quickly turned the environs of Berlin into a vast sandbox for real estate speculators. Anticipating the need for expansion, various building societies bought up some of the old Junker estates outside Berlin and subdivided them for private houses and apartment complexes. The former aristocratic holdings of Lichterfelde and Wilmersdorf were urbanized in this way. The potato farmers of Schöneberg became millionaires overnight by selling their fields to the speculators.

State and city officials made some effort to control the growth. There was a plan in place dating from the 1860s that called for grids of apartment blocks intersected by wide streets. The regulations, however, said little about how the units should be constructed, save for limits on height. This deficiency, combined with an entrepreneurial zeal to maximize profits on private plots, resulted in a proliferation of so-called *Mietskasernen* (rental barracks)—sprawling apartment complexes that blighted the poorer suburbs to the north and east of the old city. The "barracks" nickname was apt, for the structures resembled military quarters in their monotonous utilitarianism and disregard for basic human comforts. Typically five stories high, they filled entire blocks in a dense honeycomb of apartments built around inner courtyards just large enough (5.3 meters square) for a fire engine to turn around in. The innermost dwellings, accessible by long passageways from the street, received virtually no sunlight. Flat renters competed for space in the courtyards with small factories and craft shops, ensuring that the pounding of hammers and buzz of saws mixed with the wails of children and chatter of housewives all day long. Everyone who lived and worked in these urban caverns shared communal kitchens and earthen privies. Needless to say, such places were perfect incubators of diseases like cholera, typhus, and smallpox, which periodically swept the city.

Unhealthy and unsightly though they undoubtedly were, the Mietskaserne were by no means mere repositories of gloom; they were centers of genuine social, cultural, and economic vitality. Many an invention was born in those cramped courtyards, which also served as informal stages for popular theater and musical performances. The painter Heinrich Zille would later capture both the misery and liveliness of this scene in his famous drawings of Berliner *Hinterhöfe.* As land values increased after 1871, the Mietskaserne spread from the proletarian districts of Wedding and Luisenstadt to the wealthier districts of Charlottenburg, Schöneberg, and Wilmersdorf. The average number of inhabitants per building lot in the city rose from forty-five in 1860 to sixty in 1880. By contrast, in the 1870s Paris had twenty people per lot, and roomy London only eight. Berlin was on the way to becoming Europe's *Barrakenstadt* par excellence.

Despite increasingly squalid conditions, housing costs in Berlin shot up dramatically in the wake of national unification (as they would again in the early 1990s). Between 1871 and 1873 Berliners were typically paying three times what they had paid two years earlier. Theodor Fontane experienced as a renter the darker side of Berlin's boom. His landlord at Hirschelstrasse 14, where he and his family had lived for nine years, sold the house to a banker in October 1872. The banker increased the rent threefold, though the building was a refuse-strewn wreck, its courtyard "looking like it could infect the entire neighborhood with typhus." Indignant, Fontane moved his family into cheaper quarters at Potsdamerstrasse 134c, but this was not much of an improvement. It was so dilapidated and dirty that cockroaches and other vermin occupied "every nook and cranny."

In shifting quarters to obtain a lower rent, Fontane was hardly alone: 38 percent of Berlin's renters moved at least once in 1871; in 1872 the figure rose to 43 percent. City streets were perpetually clogged with carts bearing the belongings of families in search of affordable housing. This constant coming and going took its psychological toll. A Berliner who counted himself among the "orderly people" reported his shame at having to move around "like a nomad" from one hovel to the next, each worse than the last. He concluded that the old adage that poor lodgings could "kill like an ax" was wrong; rather, they killed "like opium or some slow-acting poison that lames the mind and will."

With the steady increases in rents, more and more Berliners became homeless. Some of them found temporary places in public or private shelters, but by 1872 these institutions were turning people away because of overcrowding. Many cast-outs became *Schlafburschen*—temporary lodgers who rented a patch of floor in someone's apartment for a night or two. But this makeshift arrangement was unworkable for larger families, who were obliged to camp out like Gypsy clans under bridges or on construction sites. Sensing a profit in such desperation, packing-carton manufacturers advertised "good and cheap boxes for habitation." Huge shanty towns sprang up around the Kottbus, Frankfurt, and Landsberg Gates. Occasionally the police moved in and burned out the squatters, pushing them on to other encampments. In summer 1872, when dozens of homeless families rioted against such treatment, mounted soldiers rode in and cut down the demonstrators with their sabers.

Homelessness, destitution, and urban-nomadism, for all their appalling visibility, were hardly the dominant motifs in Boomtown on the Spree. The defining elements were breathtaking commercial expansion, material excess, and municipal hubris. Germany's economic boom of the early 1870s derived primarily from three factors: the elimination of remaining internal tariffs; the liberalization of rules governing banks and joint-stock companies; and a sudden infusion of 5 billion gold marks in war reparations from France. This last factor was especially important: it translated into two carats of gold for every man, woman, and child in the country. Imperial Germany was born with a golden spoon in its mouth.

As the capital, Berlin got a large share of the new riches. Suddenly the city was awash in investment funds, which attracted all sorts of entrepreneurial types with ideas for putting the money to work. As the *Volks-Zeitung* reported in 1873, hardly a week went by without a new company, factory, or bank being established. Between 1871 and 1872, 780 new companies were set up in Prussia, most of them in Berlin. Germany's greatest banks—the Deutsche, Dresdener, and Darmstädter—made their headquarters there. So did the country's newspaper industry. Rudolf Mosse launched his *Berliner Tageblatt* in 1871 with the following characteristic comment: "At a time when the eyes of the world look toward Berlin, we present to the public the *Berliner Tageblatt*. The capital of Prussia has become the capital of Germany, a world city. . . . We must be inspired by the thought that he who writes for Berlin writes for the civilized world."

To make their enterprises more attractive to first-time investors, Berlin entrepreneurs studded their boards of directors with aristocratic names. As a company founder explains in Friedrich Spielhagen's novel *Sturmflut:* "We absolutely need a high aristocratic name. You don't understand our insular patriotism. A Judas goat must go ahead, but then, I tell you, the whole herd will follow. Therefore, a kingdom for a Judas goat!" Bedazzled by titled goats, the herd followed along, and an amazingly inclusive and democratic herd it was, embracing, as one Berliner recalled, "the shrewd capitalist and the inexperienced petty bourgeois, the general and the waiter, the woman of the world, the poor piano teacher and the market woman." All found a new place to worship in Berlin's palatial stock market building on the Neue Friedrichstrasse, an "Everyman's Temple of Temptation."

Among the promoters of Berlin's new wealth could be found a significant number of Jews, who took advantage of the liberalized business climate and full legal rights they achieved with unification to stake out prominent positions in certain branches of the economy. They were particularly prominent in the rise of the department store (the key names here being Wertheim, Tietz, and Israel), the publishing business (Mosse and Ullstein), the stock market, and banking. Jewish families had long been prominent in Prussia's and Berlin's banking scene; in 1808 one-third of Berlin's thirty banks were Jewish-owned, and by 1860 there were twice as many Jewish as non-Jewish banks in Prussia. After unification, Jews controlled about 40 percent of all banks in the Reich, while another one-third were of mixed Jewish and Christian ownership; only one-quarter were in exclusively Christian hands. This phenomenon hardly went unnoticed, and it excited age-old prejudices. Observing the bustling scene around the stock market, one commentator sneered: "Here, too, the Jewish element—no longer restrained, as of old, within particular limits, and today so insolently dominant in Berlin—exercises a continually increasing influence."

Particularly influential was Gerson Bleichröder, Bismarck's personal banker and financial adviser. Bleichröder's father, the son of a gravedigger, had managed to become the Berlin agent of the powerful Rothschild banking dynasty, thereby building a potent banking business of his own. Continuing to exploit the Rothschild connection, and making the most of his ties to Bismarck, Gerson Bleichröder became one of the wealthiest men in the Reich, maintaining a magnificent mansion in the Behrenstrasse and a country estate where he hosted parties that were "great events, Lucullan feasts." While enriching himself he also worked wonders for the financial portfolio of his most illustrious client. (Despite, and partly because of, his vast land holdings, Bismarck was low on capital at the time of German unification; it was up to Bleichröder to make him "a respectable prince.") Bismarck rewarded his banker with useful political tips, access to power, and the first hereditary title awarded a Jew in the new Reich, yet he also told anti-Semitic jokes about him behind his back, as if half-embarrassed by the riches his *Privatjude* had earned him. Bleichröder's story is a kind of morality tale of Bismarckian Berlin. It exemplified (in the words of historian Fritz Stern) "the precariousness of the German plutocracy: they huddled after wealth and status—and discovered that the former did not confer the latter. . . . Berlin was full of plutocratic parvenus; it was full, too, of Jews who were the pariahs among plutocratic parvenus."

The biggest "pariah" of all the Berlin plutocrats was Henry Bethel Strousberg, a Jewish merchant's son from East Prussia who made a fortune by financing railroad construction in Germany and eastern Europe. From there he branched out into manufacturing, mining, and retailing. Although Berlin's aristocrats snubbed him socially, they were happy enough to invest in his enterprises. At the height of his fortunes Strousberg was reputed to be the richest man in Germany. His mansion on the Wilhelmstrasse put Bleichröder's palazzo to shame: adorned with Corinthian columns, it featured an elaborate winter garden replete with an artificial lake. Strousberg also owned over a dozen rural estates to which he traveled by private train or in a four-horse carriage with liveried footmen. To make sure that the Berliners kept up with his exploits, he bought a local newspaper that published regular accounts of his comings and goings.

Strousberg and Bleichröder were hardly the only boomtown entrepreneurs to display their wealth in architectural splendor—or in what they took to be architectural splendor. August Julius Albert von Borsig, heir to his father's industrial fortune, built an imposing neo-renaissance villa on the corner of Wilhelmstrasse and the newly created Vosstrasse. His neighbor was Prince Pless, whose fortune was derived from coal mines and agriculture. Pless was disturbed that his own new home, built in the style of an eighteenth-century French chateau, stood next door to the upstart Borsig's pretentious pile. He therefore put in a stable on the edge of his property, so that "the scent of an older way of life would out-stink the air of the new."

As Berlin's center became congested, more and more of its plutocrats built themselves gaudy palaces in the "New West" of Schöneberg and Charlottenberg. They

Siegessäule, 1930

especially favored the Kurfürstendamm, a broad new avenue, which its promoters, including Bismarck, hoped would surpass the Champs-Elysées in grandeur. The Kurfürstendamm thoroughly transformed western Berlin. Running from the southwestern edge of the Tiergarten to the Grunewald (Berlin's answer to Paris's Bois de Boulogne), it attracted new housing blocks to an area previously occupied by small farms and garden colonies. The heroine of Fontane's novel *Irrungen Wirrungen*, set in the early 1870s, could still walk these fields for miles, but that bucolic world was gone within a decade.

Old Berlin, resolutely spartan and dowdy, had never offered much in the way of luxury shops, restaurants, or hotels. After unification, there was a frantic effort to remedy this deficiency—indeed, to make Germany's new capital the equal of Paris or London in the quality of its urban amenities. Unter den Linden, central Berlin's most famous street, went from being a predominantly residential address for nobles and rich burghers to a commercial thoroughfare lined with fancy shops, restaurants, banks, and hotels. Competing for the attention of passersby, the new stores outdid each other in ornamental facades. The Kaiser-Gallerie, a glass-covered mall modeled after Milan's Galleria Vittorio Emanuelle, opened to great fanfare in 1873. It boasted more than fifty shops, cafés, restaurants, and entertainment facilities. Equally imposing were the new hotels, which were urgently needed, since Berlin was now attracting roughly 30,000 visitors a day, compared to 5,000 before unification. The fanciest of the new hostelries was the Kaiserhof, which featured over three hundred guest suites, numerous conference rooms, and a Viennese-style restaurant, the Café Bauer. Although the Kaiserhof got off to a rocky start, burning down just days after its completion, it was totally rebuilt within three months of the fire.

Up and coming cities, of course, require more than shops and hotels to stake a credible claim to grandeur: they need impressive monuments and public buildings. Berlin's signature monument of the *Gründerzeit* (foundation era) was the Siegessäule (Victory Column), a breathtakingly gaudy shaft dedicated to the military triumphs that had brought Germany its unity. Erected at the western end of Unter den Linden (it was later moved by the Nazis to its present location at the Grosser Stern in the Tiergarten), the fluted column was surrounded with captured French cannon and topped by a golden Victory Goddess. According to the Danish diplomat Georg Brandes, the pillar looked as if it had been commissioned by the King of Siam rather than by a European monarch. The proportions of the crowning Victory Goddess, he noted, were so "unhappy" that Berliners began calling her the "only lady in town without a lover."

Despite all the efforts to make the new German capital a grand and imposing metropolis, *Gründerzeit* Berlin hardly presented itself as the last word in urban sophistication. As one of Bismarck's ministers, Rudolph Delbrück, bluntly declared: "Berlin is frightfully small-townish."

Berlin's railroad stations set the tone for the city. "Pitiful hovels" was the only appropriate description for these structures, lamented Isidor Kastan, a physician who became editor of the *Berliner Tageblatt* in 1872. The Potsdamer Bahnhof, a typical example of the genre, had dark and dingy second-class waiting rooms, while those of first class "assaulted the senses" with mahogany chairs and sofas covered in bright red plush. Travelers were made to feel either like tramps or patrons of a provincial whorehouse.

"One is amazed," wrote the Frenchman Victor Tissot after a visit to Berlin in the early 1870s, "that the center of the new German Reich, the 'city of intelligence,' has much less the character of a capital than Dresden, Frankfurt, Stuttgart, or Munich. Everything here carries the stamp of this new German monarchy that was cut by saber out of the coat of its neighbor and that behaves like the popinjay of lore who bedecked himself with the plumage of a peacock." There was no point to look here for things of spiritual majesty or antiquity, Tissot averred, since to Berlin's Prussian builders "cannons had always meant more than cathedrals." Upon completing his visit, the Frenchman was sure that "Berlin, despite its pretensions, will never be a capital like Vienna, Paris, or London."

Henry Vizetelly, an Englishman who provided a comprehensive, if jaundiced, portrait of Germany's new capital in the Bismarckian era, also scoffed at Berlin's attempts at grandeur. In his two-volume *Berlin under the New Empire* (1879), he wrote:

> Berlin, viewed in comparison with London or Paris, has nothing imposing about it. Its long broad streets commonly lack both life and character. No surging crowds throng the footways, no extended files of vehicles intercept the cross traffic, bewilder one by their multiplicity, or deafen one with their heavy rumbling noise. And until quite recently the best Berlin shops would bear no kind of comparison with the far handsomer establishments in the English and French capitals.

In the 1870s—as would be the case again in the 1990s—Berlin was covered with construction sites. Again to quote Vizetelly:

> In the Prussian capital, scaffoldings and buildings in course of construction constantly arrest the eye. In the outskirts of Berlin new quarters are still being laid out, new streets planned, new houses rising up everywhere. Until quite recently even in the heart of the city so many new structures were in the course of erection that one was led to imagine the capital of the new Empire had been handed over to some Prussian Haussmann to expend a handsome share of the French milliards on its extension and improvement.

Berlin did not install a modern sewer system until the late 1870s. In his memoirs, August Bebel, the Socialist leader, described what Berliners had faced before this reform:

> Waste-water from the houses collected in the gutters running alongside the curbs and emitted a truly fearsome smell. There were no public toilets in the streets or squares. Visitors, especially women, often became desperate when nature called. In the public buildings the sanitary facilities were unbelievably primitive. One evening I went with my wife to the Royal Theater. I was revolted when, between acts, I visited the room designated for the relief of men's bodily needs. In the middle of the room stood a giant tub, and along the sides were chamber pots which each user had to empty himself into the communal pot. It was all very cozy and democratic. As a metropolis, Berlin did not emerge from a state of barbarism into civilization until after 1870.

All European cities smelled badly in the late nineteenth century, but, as Bebel's accounts suggests, Berlin seems to have been in a class of its own—only later would *Berliner Luft* (Berlin air) become a source of pride, rather than of revulsion. "The rankest compound of villainous smell that ever offended the nostril arises on all sides and persistently tracks one's steps," complained Vizetelly. The famed British urban sanitation reformer Edwin Chadwick told Berliners that theirs was "among the foulest smelling capitals in Europe." Claiming that visitors arriving in other cities from Berlin could always be identified by the stink of their clothing, Chadwick urged local and national leaders to attack the problems of stench and unsanitary conditions with the same energy that they applied to "external foes."

Although Berlin's notorious gutters were the prime cause of this malodorousness, they were not the only culprit. The fish, meat, and cheese stalls clustered around the Gendarmenmarkt added their pungent part. Sebastian Hensel, director of the Kaiserhof, recalled:

> I had the opportunity to smell the Gendarmenmarkt in all its glory during Wednesday and Saturday markets. There was a long row of green, slimy, moss-covered fishtanks, with fish floating belly-up in stagnant, reeking water . . . the cadavers were pushed around by women with long paddles in an effort to make them look alive. . . . At the butcher stands along Markgrafenstrasse bottle-flies hummed around moldering carcasses, pools of blood coagulated in the street, and starving dogs fought over bits of gristle and guts. Worse still were the cheese stalls in the passage between Jägerstrasse and Friedrichstrasse. At one o'clock the vendors dumped their garbage into the street. Although a battery of old

> women spend hours mopping up herring tails, cabbage leaves, and cheese wrappings, they couldn't expel the hideous stench.

With its location on the sandy steppes of Prussia, Berlin was also plagued with blowing grit. In dry weather, wrote Vizetelly, one encountered "clouds of sand which . . . rise into the air and envelope everything they encounter in their progress." To prevent the sand from penetrating into houses, housewives kept their windows closed, stifling the occupants. Vizetelly reasoned that blowing grit was the main reason why so many Berliners wore spectacles, just as the men constantly smoked cigars in order to avoid breathing undiluted air.

Like Berlin's physiognomy, the habits and physical features of its inhabitants struck visitors from western European capitals as hopelessly provincial, if not downright gross. Jules Laforgue, a young poet from Paris who was hired by the royal court to read French periodicals to Empress Augusta, was put off by the ugliness of the local shop girls, all of whom seemed to have huge feet and thick ankles. As for their clothes, said the Frenchman, the Berliners were a disaster. Ladies were "slovenliness itself," with not the slightest idea of how to dress. Although the men took care with their suits, their model was the military uniform, so everything was "tight and stiff." And their *manners!* The Berliners' "passion for formality," thought Laforgue, stemmed "from their having so widely been called barbarians and boors." They wanted desperately to be polite like the British and French, but "by working so hard they have put their foot in it." Thus one found in Berlin that the men greeted each other not by slightly nodding their heads but by bending their entire spines and clicking their heels, while women performed a mechanical curtsey. At the same time, Berliners could be shockingly rude. In shops men took off their hats but kept their cigars in their mouths; in restaurants they dumped food into their mouths with their knives and smoked while they ate, scattering ashes everywhere. They stuffed themselves even at theaters and concerts, then belched and farted contentedly. This ensured that the air inside the public places was as foul as that outside.

Another aspect of life in the new capital that caught the attention of visitors was the overwhelming presence of the military and the deferential attitude of the citizenry toward the soldiers. Noting that troops were constantly marching and dragging cannon through the streets, Vizetelly said that the city seemed like one big maneuver field, with "civilian life. . . a mere adjunct to the martial elements." Walking the streets, Laforgue was shocked to see a merchant carrying a pile of hats step off the sidewalk to let a sergeant pass. Similarly, Georg Brandes was amazed at the extent to which soldiers in Berlin were "privileged beings next to whom civilians counted for nothing." The goose-stepping guards in front of the Neue Wache struck him as "ridiculous and barbaric." The British diplomat Charles Harding, on the other hand, found the strutting German officers comical in their vanity. He knew of a young Guards officer who wore his white buckskin breeches "so tight that he could not bend his legs," and had "to be helped up the stairs by two stalwart soldiers from his regiment."

Berliners' popular amusements also struck outsiders as raw and uncouth. Beer-drinking, of course, was prominent among these, the foamy liquid being almost a national religion. It was consumed in innumerable *Bierstuben* and (during warmer months) in raucous outdoor beer gardens. These institutions were studies in informality: men and women of all social classes pressed together on rough benches, quaffing mug after mug of beer and smacking their lips over giant hunks of meat. When not drinking in their beer gardens, Berliners might be found amusing themselves at one of the city's many variety reviews, known locally as *Tingel-Tangel.* These featured small troupes of performers who danced, put on skits, and sang satirical verses lampooning such targets as greedy landlords, the Jesuits, and the French. Visiting a Tingel-Tangel in the Schützenstrasse, Vizetelly witnessed a woman named Alma singing a long song full of animal noises, enthusiastically echoed by the audience, "until one was well able to imagine the kind of existence which Noah and his family must have passed while shut up in the Ark."

Berlin was also known for its "dissolute dancing-places," such as the Orpheum, which boasted erotic frescoes depicting "nudities in postures difficult to describe, but on which Germans gaze through their spectacles without the slightest appearance of being shocked." The women who frequented the Orpheum were mostly prostitutes, strapping Silesians trying very hard to look Parisian. "If these Circes were only as beautiful and seductive as vice is commonly reputed to be," observed Vizetelly, "Berlin youth would run far greater risks of being led astray here." Prostitutes also congregated in large numbers on the corner of Unter den Linden and Friedrichstrasse. To Laforgue, this scene was more depressing than stimulating:

> What a grotesque and heart-breaking spectacle this fast corner provides! On the steps, five or six old crones hunched over the boxes in their laps groan: 'Matches, Matches.' Bums stop you with the same offer, calling out, *'Herr Baron, Herr*

> *Doktor, Herr Professor.*' And then a man slumped on his crutches selling these same matches. And most astonishing of all is a torso enshrined in a crate on wheels moving about with the help of its hands; it wears a long blond beard and glasses and also sells matches. . . . And the demi-mondaine (for Berlin tact has reduced Dumas' word to this level) pounds the pavement incessantly. In the winter it's frightful. Fortunately the lantern of the hot sausage vendor shines in the distance. The ladies help themselves and eat, leaning over the gutter so as not to soil themselves.

From the standpoint of visitors from the great European capitals, then, and even in the eyes of some critically minded locals, Berlin in the first decade or so after German unification was at once rustic and risqué, a strange mixture of backwoods rowdiness and frank sexual openness. It was not yet the bustling hive of up-tempo urban life that it would become at the turn of the century. Pedestrians did not yet have to fear being run over by an auto or bus upon crossing the Potsdamer Platz. On the other hand, the Spree city was already getting that reputation for raunchiness and "decadence" that would persist despite the best efforts of prudish rulers to shape the capital in their own image.

Bust

Berlin's postunification boom had been somewhat shaky from the beginning. Many of the new joint stock companies were little more than hollow fronts whose major function was to bilk unsophisticated investors. The building explosion had been predicated on the illusion that the capital would quickly expand to 9 million souls; parts of the city were thus considerably overbuilt, making it increasingly difficult for landlords to maintain high rents. Railway development in eastern Europe—the basis of Strousberg's empire—was costing far more than it yielded, though this unpleasant fact was covered up for a time by government officials on Strousberg's payroll. Berlin's economy, moreover, was dependent on the health of an international marketplace stretching from Vienna to New York; financial tremors on the Danube or Hudson could wreak havoc on the banks of the Spree.

Even as they threw money into new investment schemes, many Germans were plagued by a sense of unease and guilt. For the Junkers in particular, stock-market speculation clashed sharply with ancient prejudices against commercial capitalism and paper profiteering. Such activities might be acceptable for bourgeois tradesmen and Jews, but these practices had been traditionally off-limits to the titled defenders of Prussian and Christian morality. Yet the aristocrats were as susceptible to greed as anyone, and the increasingly high cost of living was making the old morality seem an unaffordable luxury. As a beleaguered noble protests in Friedrich Spielhagen's novel *Sturmflut:* "A multitude of means which the bourgeois class uses with the most incredible success is denied us because of noblesse oblige. . . . We are supposed to defend our position in state and society and still preserve our moral qualities. This is all too often a difficult thing and sometimes it is impossible: it is nothing but the squaring of the circle." Convinced that changed circumstances were forcing them to join the bourgeoisie at the Temple of Temptation, Berlin's upper classes were on the lookout for scapegoats if anything went wrong.

And something did go wrong. On February 7, 1873, a National Liberal Reichstag deputy named Edward Lasker delivered a three-hour speech in parliament in which he exposed a "Strousberg system of corruption" at the heart of imperial Germany's economic boom. Investors, he said, were living in a giant house of cards erected by shady speculators protected by venal officials. As if Lasker were telling people something they had long suspected, his revelations ignited a wave of selling on the stock market. News that the Vienna market, in which many Berliners had also invested, was on equally shaky ground, compounded the panic. The coup de grâce came with the failure of a major American investment house and the sudden closing of the New York Stock Exchange.

With the collapse of the Berlin *Börse,* sources of investment capital dried up and inadequately secured companies began declaring bankruptcy. In early 1874, 61 banks, 116 industrial enterprises, and 4 railway companies (including Strousberg's) went under. Many of the Berlin building societies also proved vulnerable. The glittering Kaiser-Gallerie on Unter den Linden found itself unable to rent out retail space. Because the investment spree fueling the boom had been so "democratic," the bust was equally inclusive. "The word crash," recalled a Berlin writer, "rang through the palaces of the dukes, the corridors of parliament, the halls of the stock market, the villas of the new rich, and the modest quarters of the fruit and milk vendors."

While the crash exposed the reckless greed of ordinary investors along with the fraudulence of stock-jobbers and their protectors, it did not promote much serious soul-searching; rather, it generated a frenzy of finger-pointing. The outpouring of mutual recrimination engendered by the slump revealed deep fissures in German society, which had been papered over by the euphoria attending national unification.

Anxious to clear themselves of any wrongdoing, Berlin's conservatives pointed their fingers at the liberals, whose laissez-faire doctrines, they claimed, had invited corruption. Noting that some of the leading liberals and bankers were Jews, indignant rightists spoke of an international Jewish conspiracy behind the liberal policies. A popular tract entitled *The Stock Exchange and the Founding Swindle in Berlin* argued that the Jews were attempting to strengthen their own financial empire by destroying the native German middle class. In a series of articles in the middle-brow family magazine *Gartenlaube*, a Berlin journalist named Otto Glagau urged his fellow Christians to take action against Jewish domination of German life, especially in the capital:

> No longer should false tolerance and sentimentality, cursed weakness and fear, prevent us Christians from moving against the excesses, excrescences, and presumption of Jewry. No longer can we suffer to see the Jews push themselves everywhere to the front and to the top, to see them everywhere seize leadership and dominate public opinion. They are always pushing us Christians aside, they put us up against the wall, they take our air and our breath away. . . . The richest people in Berlin are Jews, and Jews cultivate the greatest pretense and the greatest luxury, far greater than the aristocracy and the court. It is Jews who in the main fill our theaters, concerts, opera halls, lectures, etc. . . . It is Jews who primarily engineer the elections to the Diet and the Reichstag. . . . God be merciful to us poor Christians.

On a more elevated plain, Heinrich von Treitschke, doyen of nationalist professors at Berlin University, published an article in the *Preussische Jahrbücher* in which he too railed against the predominance of Jews and their subversion of German values. He claimed that the Jews, by exerting control over key institutions of national life while maintaining a cliquish separateness, were undermining German cohesion. "The Jews are our misfortune," he concluded, coining a phrase that would later be echoed by the Nazis. Another highly influential figure on the Berlin scene, Adolf Stöcker, chaplain at the imperial court, spoke of the need to fight "Jewish supremacy" as part of a crusade to restore "Germanic-Christian culture."

It was not, however, only the conservatives who held the Jews responsible for Germany's plight. Theodor Fontane saw his professed "philosemitism" severely tested by the crash. "I have been philosemitic since my childhood," he wrote a friend. "Nevertheless, I have the feeling of their guilt, their unlimited arrogance, to such an extent, that I wish for them a serious defeat. And of this I am convinced: if they do not suffer it now and do not change now, a terrible visitation will come upon them, albeit in times that we will not live to see."

In their attempts to "explain" the slump, some commentators even faulted Bismarck, accusing him of surrendering economic policy to his influential banker, Bleichröder. Thus the archconservative *Kreuzzeitung*, the voice of Protestant orthodoxy, taxed the chancellor with practicing a shameless *Judenwirtschaft* (Jewish economic policy). Insinuations that Bismarck was under the influence of the Jews were echoed in the conservative Catholic press, which attributed the so-called *Kulturkampf*, the chancellor's anti-Catholic crusade of the 1870s, to an unholy alliance between the national government, the liberals, and the Semites. In Fontane's novel *L'Adultera* (1882) a conservative former official suggests that Bismarck emulated the Jews in his opportunistic political style: "He has something of the plagiarizing quality, he has simply annexed other people's thoughts, both good and bad, and put them into practice with the help of all readily available means."

Smarting from charges that his alleged subservience to the Jews was responsible for the crash, Bismarck embarked on a hasty program of damage control. He convinced Bleichröder to bail out some prominent noble investors who had lost huge sums. However, he did nothing for the little investors; they, as he admitted to the French ambassador, were "left drowning." Through his son Herbert, the chancellor also asked Bleichröder to publicly disavow his close connections to the government. Deeply humiliated, the Jewish banker contemplated leaving Germany altogether. After all, he had given his unswerving support to the German nation in the belief that he himself was fully German and that the state would protect him. Bismarck did not personally join in the vicious attacks against his banker, but he never once offered him his support, nor did he take a public stance against anti-Semitism, which he clearly hoped could be manipulated to deflect the criticism leveled against his own policies. Thus, in addition to cold-shouldering Bleichröder, he turned against the man who had done most to pop the speculative bubble, Edward Lasker, who was conveniently Jewish as well as liberal. Blaming the messenger for the message, Bismarck suggested that the parliamentarian and his colleagues had engineered the crash to embarrass the government. In the wake of the financial debacle, Bismarck saw to it that Germany began to move away from the economic liberalism of the *Gründerzeit* toward a program of high tariffs and state subsidies for hard-pressed manufacturers. Berlin, briefly a center of free trade, now became a bastion of protectionism.

Anti-Semitism—the term was coined by a Berlin journalist named Wilhelm Marr—continued to pollute Berlin society through the Bismarckian era and beyond. Because of anti-Jewish agitation in West Prussia and pogroms in Czar Alexander III's Russia, Jewish immigration to the German capital increased rapidly in the 1880s. This brought calls for measures to keep the *Ostjuden* out. Bismarck himself joined in these efforts, insisting on the need to exclude "undesirable elements." Significantly, some of Berlin's more established Jews also worried about increased Jewish immigration from the East, for they understood that this fanned the flames of local anti-Semitism. To assimilated Jews, moreover, the *Ostjuden* were just as "alien" as they were to German gentiles. Hoping to stem the tide of immigration, a spokesman for the Berlin Jewish community threatened to cut off further financial support to the Alliance Israélite in Paris if it continued to encourage Russian Jews to come to Berlin.

The immigration issue was in fact becoming fodder for conservative politicians in the capital, who now began openly to exploit anti-Semitic themes in electoral politics. As a standard-bearer for the Conservative Party, Adolf Stöcker promised to wrest Berlin away from the Progressive Party, which contained in its ranks prominent Jews like Lasker and Ludwig Bamberger. This development presented a dilemma to conservative Jews like Bleichröder, who could stomach neither the Progressives nor their anti-Semitic antagonists. Following the Berlin municipal election of 1881, in which the Conservatives ran anti-Semitic candidates, Bleichröder wrote despairingly: "I faced the choice between the anti-Semite who reviles me, my birth, and my family in the most shameless fashion and the Progressive. I concluded that I had to abstain from the election." He could only hope that the government would release patriotic Jews from their dilemma by banning the anti-Semitic movement. Such a measure would, he promised in a letter to the kaiser, win the "deepest gratitude" of the Jews and convince them to use "all their energies and means in order to express in the elections their truly patriotic beliefs for Emperor and Reich and Government." As we shall see, the Berlin Jews' perplexity in the face of mounting anti-Semitic agitation, along with their hope for government intervention against this evil, would recur in the late Weimar era when the Nazis began their much more systematic attack on the tattered "Berlin-Jewish symbiosis."

Alarming and dangerous though it was, the anti-Semitic movement failed to make significant gains in Berlin's electoral politics in the Bismarckian period. Certainly it was a less potent force in the German capital than in Vienna, which also had a large Jewish minority (and where Adolf Hitler would later learn about the uses of anti-Semitic demagogy from Vienna's Christian-Social mayor, Karl Lueger). In the Reichstag elections of 1881, Germany's own Christian-Social Party, founded by Stöcker, failed to win any of Berlin's mandates. Moreover, prominent voices in the capital spoke out against the attacks on Jews mounted by Stöcker, Treitschke, Marr, and other anti-Semites. A "Declaration of Notables," signed by university professors, liberal politicians, and a few progressive industrialists, most of them from Berlin, called anti-Semitism a "national disgrace" and warned against reviving this "ancient folly." The liberal notables seemed to believe, or at least to hope, that modern Germany, especially its ethnically diverse capital, was too sophisticated to allow the triumph of such an antiquated idea.

At the time the Declaration of Notables was published, in 1880, Berlin was beginning to recover somewhat from the depression engendered by the crash of 1873. The recovery was assisted by Germany's adoption of the gold standard and (finally) the introduction of a single national currency. Also helpful was the fact that the local economy now became dominated by solid industrial firms like Borsig, Siemens, the German Edison Company, and the chemical giant AGFA. These companies were the mainstays of a "second industrial revolution" that would soon catapult Berlin into world prominence in technology.

Even in the midst of its financial bust, moreover, Berlin had embarked on some much-needed infrastructural improvements. To move Berliners more efficiently across the expanding city, a horse-drawn train on rails was introduced in the 1870s. It was quickly succeeded by a circular steam railway system (the Ringbahn) that followed the course of the old city wall, which had been demolished in 1867/68. In 1882 a new *Stadtbahn*, or city railroad, connected the city center to the outer suburbs, making day-excursions to the Havel lakes possible. Also in the 1880s, electric street lamps were installed along most of the main streets. A central marketplace near the Alexanderplatz replaced the smelly stalls around the Gendarmenmarkt. The municipality bought the private British water company that had previously served the central city and extended service throughout the metropolitan area. Construction of new pumping stations allowed the installation of a subterranean sewer system to replace the pungent gutters. Completed in the late 1870s, this system carried human wastes outside the city to surrounding truck farms, giving Berliners the satisfaction of personally aiding in the growth of their food. The city also built more public bathhouses, which, if nothing else, undoubtedly made it harder to distinguish Berliners when they traveled abroad. (Private baths, on the other hand, remained an anomaly in the city; even the Royal Palace did not have one, so Wilhelm I had to have a tub brought over from the Hotel du Rome.)

In contrast to earlier times, visitors who came to Berlin in the 1880s were often impressed by the urban amenities, especially in public hygiene. Victor Tissot, returning after a ten-year absence, commented on Berlin's "admirable system of drainage," which had replaced "the infectious and muddy gutters running alongside the streets." Mark Twain, who visited Berlin in 1891, was impressed by the "spaciousness and roominess of the city," which had the widest streets, the most ample squares, and the biggest park (the Tiergarten) he had ever seen. Berlin's streets struck him as very well lighted and clean. "They are kept clean," he wrote, "not by prayer and talk and other New York methods, but by daily and hourly work with scrapers and brooms; and when an asphalted street has been tidily scraped after a rain or light snowfall, they scatter clean sand over it."

The result of all these efforts was an increasingly healthy city—one with a death rate of nineteen per thousand, a third less than only fourteen years before. Also noteworthy, especially compared to New York, was a dearth of posters defacing public walls. Berliners owed this blessing to the installation of special sidewalk pillars reserved for the posting of advertisements. Formally known as "Litfass Columns" after their inventor, Ernst Litfass (and popularly called *dicke Damen,* or "fat ladies," by the Berliners), these stout little structures became as characteristic a part of the Berlin scene as the living ladies advertising their charms along the Friedrichstrasse.

Grosse Politik in the Wilhelmstrasse

Although Berlin in the Bismarckian era was not yet the "world city" that many of its citizens thought it to be, Germany's new capital clearly emerged as a major crucible of European politics in the decades immediately following national unification. The creation of a powerful German nation through the victories over Austria and France dramatically altered the European balance of power, establishing a new colossus at the center of the Continent. All eyes now turned to Berlin, or more precisely, to the Wilhelmstrasse, Berlin's governmental quarter, to see how the nation would manage its unprecedented power.

There was considerable trepidation across Europe over Germany's unification. Great Britain, which had always tried to prevent any single power from dominating the Continent, was suddenly confronted with a potent new threat to that principle. Reacting to Germany's humiliation of France, Benjamin Disraeli, then in the opposition, wrote warily of a "new world, new influences at work, new and unknown objects and dangers with which to cope." Although France would have disputed it, Disraeli declared England to be the country most threatened by the new order. Even the Germanophile Sir Robert Morier worried that "the absolute power that the German nation has acquired over Europe" might "modify the German national character, and not necessarily for the better." Anticipating Margaret Thatcher in the 1990s, he foresaw an upsurge of "arrogance and overbearingness." Britain's ambassador to Berlin after 1871, Lord Odo Russell, believed that Bismarck's goal was nothing less than "the supremacy of Germany in Europe and of the German race in the world." France, for its part, having just faced the full force of German "arrogance," proposed that Berlin's "theft" of Alsace-Lorraine was likely to whet its appetite for more French flesh, and perhaps also for tender morsels elsewhere in Europe. Thus Paris warned Russia that Bismarck might try to incorporate ethnic German regions of the Russian empire into the Reich. The Russian foreign minister, Alexander Gorchakov, took this warning firmly to heart. He counseled Czar Alexander II to make clear to Berlin that St. Petersburg would not tolerate any German meddling in Poland or the Baltic states. Similarly, Prussia's old rival, Austria, fretted that Bismarck, having initially opted for the "Little German" route to German unification, might now be inclined to travel the "Great German" road and to pick up all the Habsburgs' German-speaking lands along the way.

Although understandable, such fears were totally unwarranted. In the wake of German unification, Bismarck was preoccupied not with expansion, but with preventing the new empire from being encircled by hostile powers. He knew he could not do much to allay the hostility of France, which could never forget its loss of Alsace-Lorraine. Bismarck's prime concern therefore was to keep France from forming anti-German alliances with any other great power. To achieve this goal, the chancellor worked to shore up Germany's relations with Austria and Russia, two former allies of Prussia's in its wars against Napoleon. In this effort he stressed the threat that French republicanism posed to all the conservative monarchies. He also hoped that the challenge of a common enemy would help reconcile Russia and Austria to the appearance of a powerful new Germany.

Bismarck's message eventually fell on receptive ears in St. Petersburg and Vienna, and not only because of a shared fear of republicanism. Austria and Russia were competing for influence in the Balkans, and each feared that Germany might make an exclusive alliance with the other, thereby giving the rival a signal advantage. A ménage à trois seemed the best way to prevent a dangerous marriage. Thus when Wilhelm I invited Austria's Kaiser Franz Josef to Berlin for alliance talks, Czar Alexander II rushed to secure an invitation for himself as well. Wilhelm, prodded by Bismarck, graciously invited both rulers to a "Three Emperors' Meeting" in the German capital in September 1872.

As in June 1871, Berlin was once again en fête. Vizetelly, who has left us with the most vivid account of this occasion, was not terribly impressed with the city's "outward adorning." There was, he wrote,

> a partial patching up and embellishing of the dingier houses on the Linden, and limited preparations for illuminating. The Russian embassy, which the Czar was to grace with his presence, had a fresh coat of paint given to it, and attempts were made to relieve the tiresome monotony of its long facade by decorating its balconies with flowers and creeping plants, brand new sentry boxes for the guard of honor being posted at the principal entrance.

Some of the grand hotels underwent hasty redecoration, which they could well afford for they would be housing dozens of imperial lackeys traveling on the nineteenth-century equivalent of the expense account.

The Czar arrived at Berlin's Ostbahnhof (Eastern Railway Station) on September 5. The station was festooned with evergreens and the standards of Russia and Germany entwined. On the platform stood Kaiser Wilhelm, hemmed in, observed Vizetelly, "by a motley throng of princes, ministers, and dignitaries of the household, with bright steel and gilt helmets, white plumes and brilliant uniforms, and half the orders in the universe scintillating on their breasts." As was customary, the Germans wore Russian uniforms to honor their guests, while the Russians dressed like Prussians—a "perfect military masquerade" that "rendered it extremely difficult to determine who was who in this complementary exchange of regimentals." After a gushingly affectionate greeting, the two emperors and their suites hastened toward the

Royal Palace in their carriages, though not quickly enough to prevent the Berlin drains from "carrying their vile odours to the nostrils of the imperial visitors."

Kaiser Franz Josef arrived the following evening at the Potsdam station to a similar display of flags, martial salutes, and political cross-dressing. There was "something comical," noted Vizetelly, "in the conceit of the victors in the war of 1866 decking themselves out in the uniform of the vanquished." As if mindful of this black comedy, Franz Josef did not throw himself into the arms of Wilhelm, but merely proffered his hand. The Austrian emperor was also not amused by his hosts' indelicate choice of routes from the station to the palace: it followed the Königgrätzstrasse, named after the decisive Prussian victory in the Austro-Prussian war. Nor were there many Berliners in the streets to greet Franz Josef. According to Vizetelly, "the Berliners still regarded him as a slightly insignificant personage in comparison with the high and mighty austere Russian Czar, before whom they seemed almost disposed to prostrate themselves, while holding their noses high enough in the air in presence of the over-gracious Austrian Kaiser."

While snubbing Franz Josef, the Berliners turned out in droves for the first major spectacle of the Three Emperors' Meeting, a military review on Tempelhof Field. Arriving at the field early in the morning of September 7, Vizetelly found the area already clogged with carriages and vendors selling sausages, butter rolls, and "Das Bier der Drei Kaiser (the Beer of the Three Kaisers)." The sun rose in the clear sky to pour its rays upon the assembled multitudes, "causing the perspiration to stream from beneath the helmets of the mounted police, tanning the complexions of the lovely Jewesses whom one saw on every side, half smothered in gauze and cashmere, and rendering the glossy black carriage horses skittish and irritable, and the poor, broken-down droschken hacks still more weary and dispirited."

People soon forgot the heat, however, as across the sandy plain brilliantly accoutred cavalry began wheeling in formation, their helmets flashing in the sun. Although most of the riders were German, horsemen from Austria and Russia were also in evidence, cantering flank to flank behind the three emperors. "All were intermingled, all pressed together in one compact particoloured mass in which red, blue, green, black, white, and grey, picked out with gold, could be distinguished," observed Vizetelly. In retrospect, of course, this glittering moment can be seen as an innocent harbinger of the rather less harmonious martial entanglement to come a generation later.

That evening Wilhelm I put on a gala banquet at the palace, combining huge amounts of food and drink with extreme punctiliousness of etiquette. Britain's

Queen Victoria, happily ensconced in London, sniffed at the whole business in a letter to her daughter Vicky, who as the wife of Crown Prince Friedrich Wilhelm was obliged to be in attendance. "I pity you indeed to have to be at Berlin for that week of Emperors. . . . *How* ever will you manage between the Kaisers as to rank? . . . Every Sovereign *is alike*—& no one yields to the other. . . . What *will* happen? I should really be amused to hear." In the event, Franz Josef got to sit next to Wilhelm because he had been on the throne longer than the Czar, who was seated next to Vicky. She was not happy with this arrangement, resenting Alexander for having given her teenage son Willy a grenadier uniform, thus encouraging his blossoming militarism. In fact, Vicky was unimpressed with the entire occasion, which she informed her mother was "more like an immense bivouac than anything else."

Present here, as at all the other events during the meeting, was Count Bismarck, the true orchestrator of the affair. Unlike Vicky, who saw nothing but bother in this kind of thing, Bismarck understood how useful it could be politically—at least as long as the imperial guests were kept on a tight leash. "We have witnessed a novel sight today," Bismarck told Odo Russell after the opening banquet.

> It is the first time in history that three emperors have sat down to dinner together for the promotion of peace. I wanted these emperors to form a loving group, like Canova's three graces. I wanted them to stand in a silent group and allow themselves to be admired, but I was determined not to allow them to talk, and that I have achieved, difficult as it was, because they all three think themselves greater statesmen than they are.

The "bivouac" continued that evening with a *Zapfenstreich* (a Prussian military tattoo) on the Opernplatz in the shadow of the statue of Frederick the Great. Columns of guardsmen bearing torches goose-stepped across the square, looking to Vizetelly like "soldiers of the middle ages carrying fire and sword within some doomed city." Suddenly, over the sound of drums and cymbals, came piercing cries of distress, startling the observers but not interrupting the ceremony. Later, it was learned that the Berlin police, anxious to clear curious crowds from the route leading back to the palace, had charged into the throng, pinning hundreds of men, women, and children against buildings and fences. Eight people were killed and ten badly wounded. In this respect, too, the festivities at the Three Emperors' Meeting anticipated ugly events to come.

For the moment, however, Berlin basked in its new status as the "diplomatic navel" of Europe. Bismarck exploited the good will generated by the conference to create the Three Emperors' League, which was formally inaugurated in the following year. Although little more than a declaration of common interest in monarchical principles, the League was certainly a triumph of Bismarckian diplomacy. It was also a triumph for the new German capital, which in hosting the preparatory meeting demonstrated its arrival as a center of *Grosse Politik* in the last third of the nineteenth century.

If the Three Emperors' Meeting in 1872 served as modern Berlin's debut on the lavishly decorated stage of European high politics, a much larger diplomatic gathering, the Congress of Berlin in 1878, confirmed the German capital's centrality to the workings of international affairs. For the first time in its history, Berlin welcomed statesmen from around the world to a full-dress multinational conference. This fact alone, wrote Georg Brandes, showed how much Berlin had come up in the world. Of course, Europe's policymakers did not come to Berlin for its urban amenities, such as they were, but because it was the home turf of Bismarck, who was becoming known as the master of diplomatic arbitration.

Arbitration was called for in 1878 because the so-called Eastern Question—the precipitous disintegration of the Ottoman Empire and the resulting power vacuum in the Balkans—was generating a dangerous pushing and shoving match among the Great Powers. Prodded by pan-Slavs anxious to extend Russia's influence in the region, Russia had gone to war against Turkey in 1877 after the Porte had brutally put down rebellions by Serbs, Montenegrans, and Bulgarians. Emerging victorious, St. Petersburg had forced the Turks, in the Treaty of San Stefano, to accept a Russian presence in the Straits and the creation of an enlarged Bulgaria, which acted as a Russian client state. This development enraged the Austrians, who had their own interests in the Balkans, as well as the British, who regarded Turkey as a valuable protective buffer between their Russian rival and their colonial holdings in the Middle East and India. London and Vienna insisted that the Treaty of San Stefano be revised, threatening war if it was not. Bismarck, seeing his delicate diplomacy in jeopardy, agreed to try to resolve the dispute in hopes of keeping his eastern partners from each others' throats, and from a possible embrace with France. In the chancellor's earthy locution, the problem was simply that "Russia had swallowed too much Turkey, and the powers were trying to get her to relieve herself." By getting Russia to agree to excrete some bits of Turkey, Bismarck wanted to prevent the British from teaming up with Paris to force St. Petersburg to back down. Yet he took up his role as "honest broker" (his words) with some trepidation, aware that he would undoubtedly be blamed by whichever power felt it had gotten the short end of the stick.

In contrast to the Three Emperors' Meeting, Berlin did not dress itself up at all for Bismarck's 1878 conference. Brandes saw this as a sign of maturity: "Berlin has become enough of a metropolis that its citizens are not losing their equanimity by the Congress," he wrote in his diary. By now, he added, Berliners had seen enough foreigners in their midst that they did not automatically turn their heads and gape at exotic-looking strangers. They did not even bat an eye at the colorfully dressed delegations from Japan, China, and Morocco, though there was considerable bafflement regarding the Moroccans' practice of slaughtering animals in their rooms at the Hotel du Rome.

Interestingly, the foreign dignitary who aroused the most curiosity was the aging Benjamin Disraeli, who had resumed the British premiership in 1874. (Disraeli, incidentally, would be the last sitting British prime minister to visit Germany until Neville Chamberlain flew to Berchtesgaden in 1938, where he met with Hitler to begin the sellout of Czechoslovakia that culminated in the Munich Conference later that year.) The great English diplomat was known not only for his extraordinary political gifts but also for his somewhat steamy novels. Berliners were impressed that a Jew with artistic inclinations could have reached such astonishing heights (the only German analogue would be the career of Walther Rathenau, who became foreign minister after World War I, only to be cut down by right-wing assassins in 1922). Disraeli's life, it seemed to the Berliners, might have been the stuff of one of his romantic novels. Everywhere he went in town, ladies pushed flowers into his gnarled hands and men took off their hats. Even Bismarck was impressed: "Der alte Jude, das ist der Mann! (The old Jew, that's the man!)" he declared. Disraeli, in turn, was charmed by the German capital. When asked by Bismarck how he liked Berlin and the "unlovable" Berliners, the Englishman responded that he found the city "better than its reputation" and the inhabitants exceptionally accommodating.

The main business sessions at the Congress of Berlin were held in the new Imperial Chancellery on the Wilhelmstrasse. As noted above, the Chancellery was now housed in the former Radziwill Palais, which had been thoroughly renovated to accommodate the chancellor's office and a private residence. The chancellor's quarters were, in the words of Baroness Spitzemberg, "ordinary and tasteless," but the public rooms were suitably grand, if a bit garish. Bismarck thought that the main receiving room looked like a French bordello, which he considered fitting given the kind of people who frequented it.

The German chancellor, true to his nickname, ran the proceedings at the congress with an iron hand, forcing his colleagues to keep their speeches short and to finish each day's agenda before retiring. When some delegates complained of the pace, he curtly replied: "No one has ever died from overwork."

Bismarck cracked the whip partly because he was anxious to quit Berlin for his annual water-cure at Bad Kissingen, where (much like Helmut Kohl a century or so later) he ritualistically tried, with little success, to purge the effects of months of excess. The chancellor had always been a prodigious eater, drinker, and smoker, fond of consuming six-course dinners washed down with a couple flagons of wine and followed by a seven-inch Havana cigar, one of his half-dozen or so per day. (Cigars were more than a source of pleasure for him; when he was surrounded by boring guests at dinner and wanted to "fog himself in," he resorted to a mighty cigar holder of his own design that allowed him to fire up three Havanas at once.) On workdays the chancellor usually added two bottles of champagne at midday and a few snifters of brandy at night. By the late 1870s he was gaining weight so rapidly that, as he complained, he had to purchase a totally new wardrobe every year. Now tipping the scales at over three hundred pounds, he suffered from acute gastric disorders, gout, shingles, piles, and insomnia. Yet when his doctors advised moderation he dismissed them as "dolts" who made "elephants out of gnats." Moreover, though he frequently complained during the Congress of Berlin about the stress of keeping his colleagues in line and of having constantly to speak French (still the diplomatic language of the day), he refused to change his punishing habits. As he later told a friend:

> Seldom did I sleep before six o'clock [a.m.], often not before eight in the morning, [and then] only for a few hours. Before twelve o'clock I could not speak to anyone, and you can imagine what condition I was in at the sessions. My brain was like a gelatinous, disjointed mass. Before I entered the congress I drank two or three beer glasses filled with the strongest port wine . . . in order to bring my blood into circulation. Otherwise I would have been incapable of presiding.

Disraeli, himself a physical wreck on the verge of collapse (he died three years later), was amused to hear the chancellor's laments. He wrote to Victoria: "Bismarck, with one hand full of cherries, and the other full of shrimps, eaten alternatively, complains he cannot sleep and must go to Kissingen."

To find some diversion during the conference, delegates amused themselves at frequent banquets, balls, receptions, outings, and theatrical performances. Berlin hostesses competed fiercely with each other to snare the most prestigious delegates; winners got the British or French, losers got the Moroccans. For some of the less hardy visitors, these events could themselves be a source of stress. "It is absolutely necessary to go to these receptions," complained Disraeli in a report to the queen, "but these late hours try me. I begin to die at ten o'clock and should like to be buried before midnight." Yet the old man showed no distress at an extravagant dinner party hosted by Bleichröder, where, in contrast to the usual Berlin house parties, Chateau Lafite freely flowed.

Bismarck did not let the many diversions during the conference impede progress on the principal business at hand. Alternatively cajoling and threatening—at one point he confronted the Turkish delegation in full uniform with spiked helmet—he managed to push the affair to a conclusion on July 13, 1878, exactly one month from its opening. The terms of the agreement showed that the chancellor had remained faithful to his promise to be an "honest broker." The major victor was not Germany, but Britain, which gained Cyprus, a reduction in the size of Bulgaria, and the continued closure of the Straits to Russian warships. Turkey retained sovereignty over Macedonia and the coast of the Aegean. In exchange for supporting Turkey, Austria obtained a protectorate over the Porte's Balkan provinces of Bosnia and Herzegovina. Mainly because of pressure from Disraeli, Russia emerged the big loser, having to give up much of what it had gained through the Treaty of San Stefano. Thus, though Bismarck had certainly not set out to humiliate them, the Russians accused him of bias and betrayal. St. Petersburg broke away from its alliance with Berlin and Vienna. The Three Emperors' League, it seemed, had been sacrificed on the altar of honest brokerage.

Berlin hosted one more important, albeit far less grand, diplomatic meeting during the Bismarckian period—the West Africa Conference, which ran, on and off, from November 15, 1884 to February 26, 1885. The purpose of this meeting was to resolve disputes stemming from the "Scramble for Africa," that mad rush for colonial acquisitions in the so-called Dark Continent. Of course, Great Britain, France, and Portugal had already established major holdings in Africa, but at the beginning of the 1870s large sections of central and western Africa were still up for grabs. In the brief period between 1870 and 1900 this hitherto unclaimed part of the continent, along with sizable parts of Asia and the Pacific, were added to the Europeans' imperial domains.

Bismarck's Germany emerged in the mid-1880s as an unexpected player in the frenetic imperial contest. The Reich's participation was unexpected because Bismarck had initially shown little interest in colonial ventures, save for supporting a beleaguered German trading outpost in Samoa. In general the chancellor took the position, as he put it during the Franco-Prussia war, that "for us Germans, colonies would be exactly like the silks and sables of the Polish nobleman, who has no shirt to wear under them." Shortly after unification he told his aide, Baron Holstein, that "so long as I'm chancellor, we shan't pursue a colonial policy." When German explorers began to take an interest in Africa, and urged Bismarck to join in the rush for colonies there, the chancellor pointed to a map of Europe and said: "Here is Russia and here is France, with Germany in the middle. That's my map of Africa." In the three-year period between 1884 and 1886, however, Bismarck acquired a colonial domain five times the size of the Reich itself. The man who supposedly had no interest in expanding German territory put far more land under the German flag than did Kaiser Wilhelm II, who, as we shall see, spoke grandly of *Weltpolitik* and a German "day in the sun."

How does one explain the chancellor's sudden conversion to colonialism? There has been an extensive debate in the scholarly literature over this issue, with some commentators emphasizing domestic considerations, others the traditional "primacy of foreign policy." In the end, it seems, Bismarck was animated both by domestic and foreign political concerns, which in fact were related. He unquestionably came to see the colonial contest as an integral part of the larger game of *Grosse Politik*, which pitted the latecomer Germany against established imperial powers like Britain and France. As far as the Scramble for Africa was concerned, Bismarck hoped that by throwing his hat into this ring he could put London and Paris on notice that they could not continue to expand their colonial holdings on the Dark Continent without taking account of Berlin. Germany, after all, was a Great Power too. Why should it be left out? By stealing a march on the world's greatest imperial power, Britain, Bismarck hoped not only to display the Reich's mettle on the world stage but also to deal a blow against some of his antagonists at home. The rivalry with England was likely to generate a wave of anglophobia in Germany, which would be useful in combating the influence of Crown Prince Friedrich and his English-born wife Vicky, who favored the kind of liberal agenda that the chancellor had come to loathe. The liberal camp as a whole, in fact, might be weakened by a well-publicized colonial campaign, since, as a result of the exploits of explorers and missionaries like Dr. David Livingstone and Henry Morton Stanley, the African bug had infected Germany along with the other European nations. By the early 1880s, Berlin harbored an Africa Society and a German Colonization Society, whose members included the country's leading industrialists, bankers, and academics. Imperial crusaders like Dr. Carl Peters, the moving spirit behind Germany's empire in East Africa, spoke of colonization as a vital test of the nation's virility. Berlin's nationalist newspapers warned that if the Reich did not immediately join the race for territory in Africa there would be none left to grab. Berlin and the rest of Germany were gripped in a *Torschlusspanik* (door-closing panic)—a desperation to act before it was too late. Bismarck reasoned that he could use this colonial fervor as a stick with which to beat the liberals in the Reichstag elections of 1884. This helps to explain the timing of his sudden leap into the imperial scrum. At the beginning of that year he started to amass the Reich's African empire by seizing control of southwest Africa.

This ploy indeed proved effective with the voters, and on the international front it very definitely got the attention of Britain, which was not pleased to see a German colony next door to its own empire in South Africa. As a South African colonial official told Lord Salisbury: "My Lord, we are told that the Germans are good neighbors, but we prefer to have no neighbors at all."

Britain, along with France and Portugal, had designs as well on the Congo Basin in western and central Africa, a vast region that was thought to contain great wealth. Here they ran into a new and extremely resourceful competitor, King Leopold II of Belgium, who dreamed of gaining control over the whole area so that he could corner the lucrative ivory trade there (later he switched his focus to rubber). Of course, Leopold was careful not to announce the precise nature of his plan; rather, he cloaked his rapacious design in the mantle of scientific inquiry, humanitarian improvement, and Christian uplift. Although the king won some allies with his pious verbiage, he knew he needed the help of a major power to realize his dream. Through tireless diplomacy and well-placed bribes he won the backing of the United States, whose white Southern senators hoped to use Leopold's domain as a dumping ground for American blacks. America, however, was not a major player in the African contest and could do the king only limited good. He therefore turned his attention to Bismarck's Germany, which he knew was anxious to throw its own weight around on the Dark Continent.

In the initial phase of his campaign to win German backing for his project, Leopold focused on Bismarck's influential banker, Bleichröder, whom he had met at the fashionable Belgian resort of Ostend. The banker was no fool, yet he seems to have believed in the nobility of Leopold's mission, and, more importantly, he thought that Germany's own economic interests in the Congo region would be best served through an alliance with the Belgian king. To help promote Leopold's project, Bleichröder conveyed a 40,000 franc contribution from the king to Berlin's Africa Society.

Leopold had less success, at least initially, in his attempt to win the backing of Bismarck himself. The chancellor immediately saw through the king's humanitarian pose. In the margins of a royal letter outlining the Belgian's grand plan, Bismarck penciled the word "swindle," and he told an aide that "His Majesty displays the pretensions and naïve selfishness of an Italian who considers that his charm and good looks will enable him to get away with anything." However, as Britain, France, and Portugal began to press into the Congo region, threatening to divide it up among themselves, Bismarck came around to Bleichröder's conviction that Leopold's plan would be beneficial to Germany, since the Reich's trade interests in the area were more likely to find protection under the Belgian king than under any of his rivals. In November 1884, therefore, Bismarck secretly recognized Leopold's so-called "Congo Free State." To help the king gain official recognition for his enterprise, Bismarck agreed to host an international conference on the question in the German capital.

Like the Congress of Berlin seven years earlier, the West Africa Conference took place in Bismarck's Chancellery building on the Wilhelmstrasse. The chancellor was not the official chairman, but, as in the Berlin Congress, he personally guided the proceedings. This time his paunch did not hang over the conference table because he had finally agreed to go on a diet and even to cut his alcohol consumption to a measly two bottles of wine a day, which of course made him more surly than ever. It did not help his disposition that the participants at this conference were not political heavyweights, as in the Congress of Berlin, but mere ambassadors. There was not a single African in attendance, which is hardly surprising, since the European colonizers considered the native Africans no more capable of defining the future of their own lands than American whites believed the Indians were entitled to settle the fate of the American West.

More curious was the absence of Leopold II, the man on whose behalf the conference had been organized. He thought it best to stay away and let the German hosts handle his interests in Berlin. Bleichröder did so by entertaining the delegates with elaborate dinner parties at his mansion. But of course it was Bismarck, once again, who was the crucial figure here, and it was through the diplomatic skill of the German chancellor that Leopold gained what he most dearly wanted: the blessing of the Great Powers for his grand "humanitarian" project in the Congo. Bismarck won Britain's acceptance by promising to support London's interests in Niger against France. He negotiated a complex deal with France and Portugal, whereby those powers were pacified, at least partly, with properties north of the Congo River. The territory that ended up under Leopold's control was not quite as large as he had originally envisaged, but at over a million square miles it was the largest private domain in the history of imperialism.

At the end of the conference, Bismarck delivered a pretty speech in which he spoke of the meeting's glorious successes—freedom of trade in the whole Congo Basin and "careful solicitude" for the moral and physical welfare of the native races. This last claim, of course, was a black farce. By turning the Congo over to Leopold, Bismarck and his colleagues facilitated the creation of a brutal, genocidal regime—the horrific realm evoked in Joseph Conrad's *Heart of Darkness*.

Important as Bismarck's role in this tragic development was, however, it should not be overstated. Because of the West Africa Conference, the myth evolved that the Scramble for Africa was precipitated in Berlin—that "Berlin carved up Africa." In reality, Bismarck only helped to direct and refine the carving, which had begun well before the conference in Berlin. Moreover, while Germany certainly got what it wanted from the meeting, the Reich came across here more as an arbitrator than as a self-aggrandizer.

Indeed, in the African conference, as in the Congress of Berlin, Bismarck showed that the new Germany, far from being a threat to the European and world order, could be a force for peace and stability. He proved that the word "Wilhelmstrasse" could stand for adroit diplomacy rather than rampant militarism. Alas, much like the diplomatic settlement engineered at the Congress of Berlin, this image would turn out to be very short-lived. Already by the turn of the century, mention of Berlin's main governmental street conjured up visions of a rapacious foreign policy acting as a fig leaf for aggression.

Metropolis of Opposition

On May 11, 1878, about a month before the opening of the Congress of Berlin, an imbecilic tinsmith named Max Hödel took three potshots with a pistol at Kaiser Wilhelm I as he was riding down Unter den Linden in an open carriage. None of the shots hit Wilhelm, and Hödel was immediately arrested trying to flee the scene. Two weeks later, again on Unter den Linden, a failed academic with a doctorate in philosophy fired two shotgun blasts at Wilhelm, then turned the gun on himself. ("So much for philosophy," said Queen Victoria, when she heard of the shooting.) Although this time the Kaiser was hit, his injuries were not life-threatening, and he was able to complain as he was rushed to the hospital: "I don't understand why I am always being shot at."

If the Kaiser was puzzled by these cowardly attempts on his life, Bismarck was appalled. For him the assassination attempts were a symbol of the disorder and disrespect for authority that made Berlin such a dangerous place from which to govern. "Here is an old man—one of the kindest old gentlemen in the world—and yet they must try and shoot him!" he exclaimed to former president Ulysses S. Grant, who happened to be visiting Berlin at the time. When Grant proposed that the only thing one could do with such enemies of decency was "to kill them," Bismarck replied: "Precisely so." At the same time, however, the chancellor saw that the attacks on the kaiser could be turned to his advantage. They were, he believed, just the ammunition he needed to launch a campaign against the German Social Democratic Party (Sozialdemokratische Partei Deutschlands, SPD), which had been rapidly gaining followers across the Reich, particularly in Berlin. Although a police investigation revealed that neither of the would-be assassins was directly connected to the SPD, Bismarck suppressed this information and spread the word that both men were part of a Red conspiracy to bring down the monarchy.

Bismarck's campaign against the Social Democrats was focused on Berlin, for the capital had emerged as a hotbed of Marxist activity, due largely to large-scale industrialization. The SPD was headquartered in the Spree metropolis, and twenty-one of Germany's fifty-six Social Democratic periodicals were published there. Berlin even had a Union of Female Socialists, which among other quixotic causes called for the replacement of Christian teaching in the schools with socialist doctrine. Despite constant harassment from the authorities, the Social Democratic movement made steady gains at the polls, winning ever higher percentages of the Berlin vote in national elections. In 1878 August Bebel, one of the party leaders, could declare, "Berlin gehört uns! (Berlin belongs to us!)." And he added: "If Berlin is ours, we can say that Germany also belongs to us; for at Berlin is our great enemy, and there the blow must be struck."

The "great enemy," of course, was Bismarck, but it was he who managed to strike first. In May 1878, following the Hödel attack on Wilhelm, Bismarck brought a bill before the Reichstag to suppress "publications and organizations that pursue the aims of Social Democracy." The bill failed to pass because the National Liberals objected that it was too dictatorial and would only generate sympathy for its targets. Bismarck decided to try again to cripple the Socialists in the wake of the second assassination attempt, which had inspired great indignation across the Reich, including Berlin. Now the chancellor prepared a more sweeping anti-Socialist bill, which he coupled with an order to dissolve the Reichstag and hold new elections. Because he regarded Berlin as the center of the Red danger, he demanded that martial law be imposed on the city and that military regiments patrol the streets "to impress the mob." He also called for measures to inhibit immigration into the capital. His cabinet, however, refused to go along with these last proposals, prompting him to exclaim: "Unless I stage a coup, I can't get anything done."

In the electoral campaign following the Reichstag dissolution, Bismarck attacked not just the Social Democrats, but also the National Liberals and Progressives, whom he accused of coddling the Socialists. The chancellor asked the voters to decide between supporting him, the unifier of the nation and master of European diplomacy, and the various "conspirators" who wished to destroy his work. He was backed by the Conservative Party and its press, which, in the interest of corralling the Socialists, were prepared to forgive Bismarck for his earlier *Judenpolitik*. The *Kreuzzeitung* howled: "Socialism is . . . the worst of the many horrors spawned by liberalism."

The campaign of defamation bore fruit against the liberals, but it did little direct damage to the Socialists. In the Reichstag elections of July 30, 1878, the National Liberals and Progressives both lost significantly, while the SPD declined only slightly nationwide and actually gained in Berlin, climbing from 31,522 to 56,147 votes in the city. This result so shocked the National Liberals that they signaled their readiness to follow the chancellor in his anti-Socialist crusade. The Progressives remained committed to their oppositionist stance, but were too weakened by their electoral defeat to carry much clout in the parliament, which was now dominated by the pro-Bismarckian forces.

The Anti-Socialist Law that was duly passed by the Reichstag in October 1878 was considerably more draconian than the one that had been rejected as too harsh five months earlier. The new law outlawed "socialistic and communistic" organizations on the grounds that they undermined "harmony between the social classes." Publications espousing socialist views were prohibited, as were leftist public assemblies in "endangered districts," such as Berlin. Penalties for transgression included jail, deportation, or "internal exile." The only parts of Bismarck's bill that the parliament refused to pass were proposals to strip current Socialist Reichstag deputies of their seats and to ban any future candidates from running on the Social Democratic ticket. Under the new legislation, Socialists could register for election to the Reichstag, but not actively campaign for a seat. Parliament also restricted the law's validity to two and a half years, after which it would have to be reviewed for possible renewal. (In the event, the law was renewed four times, lapsing only in 1890, when Bismarck was fired.)

The Anti-Socialist Law was applied most vigorously in Berlin, belly of the Red beast. Citing its provisions, local authorities immediately expelled sixty-seven prominent Socialists from the city. Bismarck also tried to jail two Socialist Reichstag deputies, though they successfully invoked their parliamentary immunity. Fortified with an expanded budget, the Berlin police employed an army of informers to ferret out "subversives," which resulted in a wave of denunciations. "One hears daily," wrote Georg Brandes, "of house searches, arrests, and [harsh] penalties. . . . Five years' imprisonment for a murmured curse against the Kaiser is not unusual. . . . A former non-commissioned officer recently got ten years forced-labor because, in a not entirely sober state, he wished death upon the Kaiser. . . . A working-class woman got four years in jail because she laughed at a salute to the Kaiser during an industrial exhibition." Although Berlin's judges were apparently aware of the glaring disproportion between the "crimes" in question and the punishment, they justified their political judgments by citing "the [dangerous] atmosphere of the times."

Socialist Reichstag deputies were allowed to remain in Berlin, but they, like all citizens on the Left, were subjected to constant surveillance and harassment. The police spies, who received two marks a day for their work, followed the delegates wherever they went, and a contingent of informers occupied an entire section of the visitors' gallery in parliament. Once, in the midst of a speech, a Socialist delegate called attention to the bevy of spies, causing them to decamp en masse "like startled crows." "At least you have more shame than those who sent you here," cried the delegate.

Ordinary victims of the persecution campaign responded to it with an intriguing combination of anxious vigilance and resourceful evasion. The writer Max Fretzer recalled how members of a small leftist-oriented "dance club" in Berlin worried that their group had been penetrated by a police spy. Henceforth, they were so wary about what they said that they could take no pleasure in their meetings. At the same time, however, the group got around the banning of Bebel's pamphlet "Die Frau und der Sozialismus" by wrapping it in blank yellow paper and passing it around among colleagues who knew to ask for "the woman in the yellow coat." All across Berlin, Socialist workers held outdoor meetings disguised as picnics and staged demonstrations masquerading as funerals or anniversary celebrations. Every year in March, for example, thousands of workers tramped to the cemetery in Berlin-Friedrichshain, where martyrs of the 1848 revolution were buried.

It soon became apparent that Bismarck's Anti-Socialist Law, designed to break the back of the Social Democratic Party, was serving only to stiffen its spine. A Berlin police report of December 1879 admitted that the party had "lost nothing of its membership, energy, and hope for the future." Denied the basic rights of the other parties, the Socialists pulled more closely together. Decried as anti-Christian, they acted in reality much like the Christians of ancient Rome, drawing strength from their very persecution.

Bismarck's high-handed methods, moreover, also provoked opposition from some elements of the liberal camp, which of course had been tarred with the same "red" brush as the Socialists. Berlin's mayor, Max von Forckenbeck, a National Liberal, opposed his party's kowtowing to the chancellor, whom he accused of trying to run roughshod over parliamentary rights. "Are we not being sucked deeper and deeper into the mire?" he asked in January 1879. "Is not opposition our duty? . . . I for one will under no circumstances swim with the reactionary tide; I'd rather go under." In April 1881 Theodor Fontane thought he detected a "storm" brewing among the people of Berlin against Bismarck, that plague upon the city. Bismarck's popularity in the capital might once have been "colossal," he wrote, but now the chancellor's reputation was sinking like a rock due to the Berliners' growing appreciation for the "smallness" of his character.

Bismarck's failure to curb the opposition, especially in Berlin, was evident in the Reichstag elections of October 27, 1881. In the capital, 45.5 percent of the electorate voted Social Democratic, while the Progressives also fared well. Summing up the result, the left-liberal *Berliner Volks-Zeitung* said it was obvious that the government had not achieved "in the least" what it wanted. The Bismarckian regime, opined the paper, was like a coachman who could not control his horse, and who responded to advice to go easier on the animal by flailing away all the more vigorously with his whip.

In fact, however, the government was beginning to rethink the tough tactics, if not the principles, of its anti-Socialist campaign. In his first speech to the newly elected parliament, Bismarck spoke of a need to heal "social wounds" and suggested that this might be achieved "not only through [continued] containment of Social Democratic excesses, but also through advancing the welfare of the workers." He announced that he would consider new insurance and pension programs for incapacitated and elderly workers. Privately, he admitted that what he had in mind was a scheme "to reconcile the workers to the state." Although expensive, the program would be well worth it if it undercut the influence of the Social Democratic Party and "warded off a revolution." Here then, was a juicy carrot to go along with the government's sharp stick.

Bills providing for illness and accident insurance and old-age benefits accordingly worked their way through parliament and became law in 1884. The government's dubious motives notwithstanding, these measures represented a bold new departure that put Germany in the forefront of the industrialized world in terms of the "social net" it provided its workers. Moreover, the initiatives were combined with a new "mild practice" in the application of the Anti-Socialist Law. The government hoped that German workers, even in unruly Berlin, would now see that the state was their friend.

Like the earlier harsh approach, however, the "mild practice" did not achieve its intended results. Berlin's workers took advantage of the relaxed climate to build trade unions and to mount strikes for higher wages and better working conditions. In summer 1885, 12,000 Berlin masons went on strike. Because their action drew support from other workers, they managed to win a ten-hour workday and a ten-penny-an-hour wage increase.

Faced with developments like this, Bismarck's government reversed its field once again, returning to the hard line. Prussian interior minister Johannes Putkammer instructed the police to apply the full weight of the Anti-Socialist Law against all strikers and to step up expulsions of "agitators" in industrial centers like Berlin. Henceforth, all public assemblies in the capital would require police permission.

Yet, especially in Berlin, the Socialist and trade union movement was now too well entrenched to be uprooted from the scene. The unions continued to grow in the second half of the 1880s and mounted successful strikes despite police intervention. The Berlin ceramics workers, for example, forced employers to grant them a nine-hour workday. As for the Social Democratic party, it increased its vote nationwide by one-third in the Reichstag elections of 1887. It did even better in the capital, where it won 40 percent of the electorate, making it the strongest party in the city.

The Iron Chancellor was not amused. Increasingly, he blamed "the democratic claque that rules Berlin" for the failures of his domestic policy. The parliament, he fumed, had become hopelessly "Berlinized" by its locally based delegates, who had the infuriating habit of attending every session and outmaneuvering their conservative cousins from the provinces. Bismarck now regretted that he had helped to make Berlin the national capital in the first place. In his frustration, he even began toying with the notion of moving the Reichstag to a "healthier" place. After all, as he told his personal physician, Berlin was not Germany. "It would be as great a mistake to confound the Berliners with the Germans as it would be to confound the Parisians with the French—in both countries they represent a quite different people." If the Reichstag were moved away from the Spree metropolis, he reasoned, its delegates would "not have to fear the scandal-mongering press of Berlin."

In a way, it was fitting that Bismarck had become deeply disenchanted with Berlin. By the last decade of the nineteenth century the city had changed significantly, while the Iron Chancellor was reverting to the hidebound views of his youth as a Prussian squire. The reserved and somewhat sleepy Prussian capital that Bismarck had known as a young man, and indeed for much of his career, was beginning to assert itself as an international mover and shaker in commerce, natural science, technology, the arts, and military affairs. At the very moment the Iron Chancellor was cursing the city whose newly prominent stature he had done so much to engineer, the Spree metropolis was getting ready to embark on an even more ambitious course under a new leader, who, though sharing many of Bismarck's reservations about Berlin, was determined to make it into a world capital in every sense of the word.

Reichstag, 1896

WORLD CITY?

Berlin must not only present itself as the largest city in Germany, but must give witness of its energy and progressive spirit in all dimensions of its restless productivity.

—Catalog, Berlin Industrial Exhibition, 1896

"WHAT IS POSSIBLE in other world-cities must also be possible in Berlin." So claimed Martin Kirschner, Berlin's governing mayor, at the turn of the century. The statement suggested pride and insecurity simultaneously—insistence that Berlin had already joined the ranks of world-cities, anxiety that it might yet fall short of greatness in some important way. For the German metropolis, the twenty-six-year period between Kaiser Wilhelm II's ascension to the throne in 1888 and the outbreak of World War I in 1914 brought tremendous change and plenty of cause to boast about urban progress and technological innovation. As the distinguished urbanologist Sir Peter Hall has written, Berlin in the late nineteenth century "could fairly claim the title of high-tech industrial center of the world: the Silicon Valley of its day." But the dizzying changes also brought reasons to reflect on the quality of the city's development and ample justification for concern about how it was handling its demanding role as the capital of a highly volatile young nation.

Parvenopolis

The speed at which Berlin was transformed in the Wilhelmian era pointed up its most salient features: a breathtaking mutability and a "lack of historical consciousness regarding itself." These qualities had been evident in the Prussian capital since the *Gründerzeit* and even before, but the rate of change became even more spectacular in the two and a half decades preceding World War I. During this period Berlin became the most "modern" of European capitals—so up-to-date, in fact, that the most apt comparison seemed to be with that overnight metropolis on the other side of the Atlantic, Chicago. Although Mark Twain famously called Berlin "the German Chicago," he proposed that "Chicago would seem venerable beside it." The French travel writer Charles Huard also considered Berlin "newer even than Chicago, the only city in the world with which one can compare it in terms of the incredible rapidity of its growth." The Berlin industrialist Walther Rathenau, who had a sharp eye for the foibles of his native city, joked about an American inventor from Chicago who when visiting Germany went straight to the capital without stopping at Cologne because he "didn't care for old things" and believed that Berlin was "on the verge of surpassing Philadelphia." It was this preoccupation with making it big fast that led Rathenau to label his hometown "the Parvenu of Great Cities and the Great City of Parvenus."

While Wilhelmian Berlin could undoubtedly be considered (in the words of one contemporary) "the youngest European great city," it remained questionable whether, even now, the German capital could in all respects be classed as a *Weltstadt*, a distinction that many Berliners had been claiming for some time. Although boasting almost 2 million inhabitants in 1900, which made it the fourth largest city in Europe, Berlin lacked the worldwide political and economic power of imperial London, the international cultural resonance of Paris, the global commercial reach of New York, the symbolic heft of Rome or Athens. Between 1900 and 1913 London hosted 536 international conferences, Paris 371, and Berlin only 181. As an economic and cultural magnet for outsiders, Berlin continued to attract primarily other Germans and eastern Europeans. It was certainly not the international melting pot that New York City was at this time. Even within Germany, the capital's influence was much stronger in the north and east than in the west and south, whose citizens still looked to their regional capitals for inspiration.

The physical results of Berlin's rapid modernization were generally not pretty, and the psychological effects could be extremely unsettling. The majority of Berliners seem to have embraced the new age readily enough; indeed, they were very proud of their city's status as "Chicago on the Spree." However, a number of influential social commentators were appalled by Berlin's chaotic "Americanization," with its attendant disregard of aesthetic and spiritual values. In his bitter polemic, *Berlin—Ein Stadtschicksal* (1910), the critic Karl Scheffler called the German metropolis "the capital of German non-culture." He argued that uncontrolled growth and concessions to speculative greed had generated a cluttered amorphousness, while desperate efforts to create an impressive imperial facade had yielded a "barbarian monumentality." The essayist Arthur Eloesser, a native Berliner, lashed out at his city's undiscriminating celebration of the new, its frantic effort to try to overcome the cultural head start of the older European capitals by resorting to "simulations, surrogates, and imitations." He regretted that a Berlin native was likely to feel less at home in his own city than was a newly arrived immigrant, who did not have to "cast off any inhibiting memories or troublesome sentiments in order to jump into the flowing present and swim toward a shoreless future." Even Karl Baedeker's authoritative guide to the city (1903) felt compelled to point out that since "three-quarters of [Berlin's] buildings are quite new, it suffers from a certain lack of historical interest."

Like many contemporary social commentators and travel writers, Berlin's novelists often focused on the negative aspects of rapid growth and hunger for world-class status. As Katherine Roper has pointed out in her study of the novels of imperial Berlin, imaginative writers working at the turn of the century depicted a city wracked by a nervous sickness bordering on collective insanity. They equated Berlin's cult of novelty and need to impress with a generalized collapse of moral integrity. Dilating on the implications of Berlin's dubious distinction as "the parvenu among world cities," a character in one such novel, Theophil Zolling's *Der Klatsch: Ein Roman aus der Gesellschaft*, laments:

> All around us we see and hear the powerful drive of this huge city; here world peace is negotiated, and politics and history are made; here is the center for the intellectual and artistic flowering of our nation. . . . But our civilization has not yet become a noble culture, and our society remains petty, lowly, and mean. . . . Despite all our great men, we will remain barbarians as long as we allow the get-rich spirit, the social fawning, and the back-biting to reign among us.

Max Kretzer's *Meister Timpe* (1888) focuses on the costs that Berlin's rapid industrialization exacted upon its class of small craftsmen. The protagonist, a master wood-turner, sees his world collapse when a furniture manufacturer buys the property next to his shop to build a new factory. One of Timpe's apprentices knows what is coming: "The large factories devour the craft-shops, and in the end nothing remains but workers and factory owners, two-legged machines and steam boilers." Timpe's fate, and that of the city he had known, is foreshadowed when his rapacious neighbor fells some beautiful trees to make space for factory chimneys. To Timpe, what was falling here was nothing less than "the old Berlin, the steady perspective of his childhood, the magical atmosphere of his youth."

Berlin's dramatic growth and bustling modernity did not, in general, make it any more respected in the rest of the country. On the contrary, these developments further alarmed Germans who had believed for some time that the city was too big, too industrialized, too unruly, too "cosmopolitan." In the first decade of the twentieth century Germany's popular press was filled with horror stories about life in the big city. Pamphlets entitled "The Sterile Berlin" (1913) or "The Perverse Berlin" (1910) focused on the soul-killing effects of industrialization and the sinfulness of the capital's nightlife. Operating within a long tradition of agrarian-Romantic hostility to urbanism, the "cultural pessimist" Julius Langbehn identified Berlin as the epicenter of all modern evil. The new capital, he said, was "an abode of rationalism. . . an enemy of creative education," afflicted with a vast "spiritual emptiness." Even Germans who found the place exciting often wondered if it was really suited to be the first city of the nation. There can be no doubt that of the major European capitals, Berlin remained the least loved among its own nationals.

But I Didn't Offer You a Fountain!

When it came to ambiguity about Berlin, Kaiser Wilhelm II himself set the tone. Although he was born and raised in the old Prussian capital, and was rightly seen to have absorbed much of its spirit, he grew to dislike the city profoundly. It has become fashionable lately to write histories of Germany and Berlin in the Wilhelmian era without considering Wilhelm. However, a proper understanding of Berlin's evolution from 1888, when Wilhelm II came to the throne, to the empire's collapse in 1918 surely demands some appreciation of the man who gave his name to the age,

Bismarck with Kaiser Wilhelm II, 1888

and who in many respects personified the city from which he so disastrously ruled his young nation.

On March 9, 1888, old Kaiser Wilhelm I died in his narrow camp bed at Berlin, which had changed so much in his lifetime that he had become increasingly bewildered by the city. His successor, fifty-six-year-old Friedrich Wilhelm, who took the title Friedrich III, did not, as custom dictated, march in his father's funeral procession. Five months earlier he had been diagnosed with throat cancer, and by the time he inherited the throne he was a dying man, scarcely able to speak and certainly in no condition to take a long walk in the cold. Thus he witnessed the funeral procession from a window of Charlottenburg Palace, whispering, as the cortege passed below, "That is where I ought to be now." In fact, he would be there soon enough, but not among the mourners.

The reign of Friedrich III lasted only ninety-nine days. Because his rule was so short, the new monarch could not make much of an impact. His effectiveness was also impeded by the machinations of Bismarck and his ultraconservative chief of staff, Count Alfred von Waldersee. They had long feared that Friedrich, who was known to share some of the liberal sympathies of his English wife, Vicky, would attempt to reform Germany along the constitutional lines prevailing in England. They distrusted him too for his openly friendly attitude toward the Jews, which he had demonstrated by attending a service at a Berlin synagogue dressed in a Prussian field marshal's uniform. Having done their best to undermine his influence when he was crown prince, they now exploited his illness to keep him on the sidelines of the political action in Berlin.

Bismarck and Waldersee had an eager ally in the dying Kaiser's son, Prince Wilhelm, who had become deeply estranged from his father and mother, whose liberal policies he saw as a threat to his own autocratic ambitions. Young Wilhelm's greatest fear was that Friedrich, once he was emperor, would team up with progressive elements in the capital to democratize Germany before he could take control. For the short duration of Friedrich's reign, Wilhelm acted as if his father were already dead, brazenly usurping royal prerogatives and openly siding with the Bismarck faction against his parents. As a member of the British Embassy noted: "There was all through this grim period . . . a conspicuous absence of chivalry in Berlin."

The macabre wait for Friedrich's demise ended on June 15, 1888. True to form, his son and successor hardly bothered to show remorse, shortening the usual period of mourning to only two days and inviting no foreign heads of state to the funeral. Wilhelm even ordered soldiers to cordon off the cortege route so that Berliners would have difficulty paying their last respects to the dead monarch. Wilhelm's object was to banish his father's memory as quickly as possible, so that no one could dwell on the possibility that a more liberal Germany might have emerged had Friedrich III been allowed a long and vigorous rule.

Despite the new emperor's unseemly behavior, most Berliners were excited to have a young, healthy, and energetic monarch on the throne. Wilhelm II seemed cut to order for the city he would rule for the next thirty years. He was restless, dynamic, and openly ambitious. He admired wealth and conspicuous consumption. A study in contradictions, he was at once a stickler for tradition and a crusader for innovation, especially in science and technology. And finally, just like his capital, he was afflicted by an inner self-doubt that he tried to disguise through displays of bombast and strutting pomposity.

Wilhelm's troubled character derived in part from a physical deformity he had incurred at birth. A breach baby, he had been pulled from Vicky's womb with such force that his left arm was wrenched from its socket, severing some ligaments. Ever after, his withered and misshapen limb dangled uselessly at his side. His parents' desperate attempts to correct the malady only made matters worse. Doctors wrapped his arm in the carcasses of freshly slaughtered rabbits, administered electric shock treatments, and made him wear a kind of straitjacket designed to prevent him from turning his head to the left. Most wounding of all, his mother proved incapable of hiding her disappointment in a child who was not perfect in every way. The boy reacted to the lack of maternal affection by searching for affirmation in a much different world: the military garrisons of nearby Potsdam. As an adolescent he spent as much time as he could among soldiers of the imperial guard, an inclination heartily endorsed by his grandfather, whom young Wilhelm had come to worship as a replacement for his parents.

What Berliners did not know when their new emperor took the throne was that he had already developed a certain distaste for the national capital. Early on he had come to associate the city with the dominion of his parents and the political ideas they represented. For his taste, Berlin harbored far too much irreverence toward royal authority, far too much "spirit of rebellion." Despite the conspicuous presence of the military in its streets, Berlin was also, in Wilhelm's eyes, too civilian, and too feminine. In 1878 he wrote to a friend, in his idiosyncratic English: "I never feel happy, really happy, at Berlin. Only Potsdam that is my 'el dorado' . . . where one feels with the beautiful nature around you and such kind nice young men in it."

Wilhelm symbolically registered his disdain for Berlin as soon as he became emperor. In honor of his coronation the city government commissioned a fountain depicting Neptune (the kaiser was known to love the ocean) surrounded by adoring sea goddesses and allegorical representations of the rivers of Europe. When Mayor Max von Forckenbeck and a delegation of notables called upon Wilhelm to present their gift, the emperor refused to shake the mayor's hand or to greet the delegates. These men, after all, were mere civilians, and *liberal* civilians at that. The kaiser's rebuff quickly became the talk of the town; for years afterward Berliners responded to acts of ingratitude with the phrase: "But I didn't offer you a fountain!"

Wilhelm may not have been able to abide the leading politicians of Berlin, but he much admired the father of modern Germany, Count von Bismarck, whom he had been careful to cultivate when he was crown prince. Yet soon after taking power the new kaiser began to fall out with the Iron Chancellor. A divergence of perspectives on social policy was one of the factors in their split. By the late 1880s, Bismarck had concluded that his efforts to reconcile Germany's working classes to the authoritarian state through a mixture of "Butterbrot und Peitsche" (buttered bread and the whip) had failed. Miners in the nation's coalfields were waging devastating strikes for higher wages; the SPD was growing apace and making effective alliances with other opposition parties in the Reichstag. Berlin itself, with its huge working-class population and obstreperous Reichstag delegation, seemed to him like a growing cancer, likely to infect and destroy the political system he had created. In 1890 he decided that the only way to deal with the fractious workers was to throw away the buttered bread and lay on the whip. More specifically, he proposed extending the Anti-Socialist Law indefinitely and, if labor protested, bringing in troops to discipline them. Since the Reichstag was proving increasingly difficult to manage, balking at his efforts to destroy the Socialists, he decided that this body should be abolished and replaced by a chamber beholden to the large landowners and industrialists. He planned, in other words, a kind of state coup against the existing political system, and he was willing to risk a civil war to carry it out.

Kaiser Wilhelm had a different vision. Having as crown prince fallen under the influence of the populist court preacher Adolf Stöcker, Wilhelm fancied himself a man of the people who could win over the workers through additional social reforms. And he certainly could not countenance the prospect of a civil war. "It would be lamentable if I were to color the beginning of my government with the blood of my subjects," he told his ministers. Thus he insisted that the Anti-Socialist Law be allowed to lapse and he rejected Bismarck's call for a dissolution of the Reichstag.

Beyond such matters of policy, Wilhelm and Bismarck also fell out over the fundamental question of who was going to run Germany. Bismarck was used to getting his own way without "interference" from the monarch, but this was a monarch who wanted to rule as well as to reign. Each man resented the other's efforts to make policy independently. Bismarck became extremely vindictive toward the new sovereign, telling all who would listen that Wilhelm was not up to the job of ruling Germany. Berlin, it seemed, was not big enough for both these egocentric personalities.

In the increasingly bitter standoff it was Bismarck who eventually had to go because the system that he had created ordained it: the emperor hired and fired chancellors, even Iron Chancellors. After a series of confrontations in spring 1890, Bismarck offered his resignation (as he had often done in the past), and this time the kaiser accepted it. "My dear prince!" Wilhelm wrote, "It is with the deepest emotion that I see from your request of March 18 that you have decided to resign from the position you have occupied for so many years with incomparable success." As consolation for sacking him, Wilhelm promoted Bismarck to colonel-general of the cavalry, made him Duke of Lauenburg, and gave him a life-sized portrait of the young monarch.

As Bismarck left Berlin to begin his rural retirement, the local citizenry displayed an outpouring of warm sentiment for the old man. People crowded shoulder to shoulder along the route his carriage took from the Chancellery to the Lehrter railway station. Baroness von Spitzemberg recorded in her diary:

> Like a flood the crowd surged toward the carriage, surrounding, accompanying, stopping it momentarily, hats and handkerchiefs waving, calling, crying, throwing flowers. In the open carriage, drawn by the familiar chestnut-colored horses, sat Bismarck, deadly pale, in his cuirassier uniform and cap, [son] Herbert at his side, before them a large black mastiff [popularly dubbed the *Reichshund*]—all three covered with flowers, to which more were constantly being added.

There may have been an element of ambiguity in the cheering, however: after all, the people were cheering a man who was *leaving*. The Berliners' enthusiasm was undoubtedly fueled partly by relief, for it was well known that the old chancellor and the new kaiser could not work effectively together and that Bismarck's standoff with the Reichstag threatened to precipitate a dangerous crisis of state.

It did not take long, however, for the German people, Berliners included, to begin deifying their former chancellor. Once he was safely in retirement, he became a symbol for the inner unity that Germany still so sorely lacked. In the end, as one of his biographers has noted, the Iron Chancellor filled Germans' "need for a romantically conceived national hero, a liberating myth on the order of Siegfried, Frederick Barbarossa, and Frederick the Great capable of elevating them from the mundane routine of daily life and resolving insecurities born of a fast-changing economy and society." To honor the great man, cities and towns throughout Germany named streets or squares after him and staged fawning celebrations on his birthday.

Berlin was quick to join in the Bismarck cult. When the former chancellor passed through the capital on a triumphant "great German tour" in 1892, people once again turned out in their thousands to cheer. The celebrants seemed willing to forget how

Gedächtniskirche (Kaiser Wilhelm Memorial Church), circa 1930

he had castigated the city and worked to emasculate its citizenry. Yet not all were so forgiving. Many workers stayed away from the 1892 celebrations, and the progressive liberals in the city assembly voted to boycott the municipality's birthday greeting. In 1894, the Reichstag voted down a proposal to send birthday salutations to the former chancellor.

Despite their reverence for Bismarck, most Berliners seem to have taken his death in 1898 in stride. According to the drama critic Alfred Kerr, the city hardly paid attention to the great man's passing. People danced "like crazy" and the beer gardens were packed. Kerr attributed this behavior not to a lack of respect for authority but to the people's healthy sense of priorities; after a long day's work they wanted to relax, not to mourn.

The Berliners' nonchalance notwithstanding, Wilhelm II tried to cash in politically on Bismarck's death. He ordered that "Germany's greatest son" be buried in the Berlin Cathedral "by the side of my ancestors." He also proposed a full state funeral, presided over by himself. But it was not to be. Bismarck had left instructions that he was to be buried in a simple ceremony at his country estate Friedrichsruh. Apparently he did not want to be caught dead in Berlin. The kaiser had to content himself with a modest ceremony at which none of the Bismarck family appeared.

I Am Guiding You to Glorious Times!

Although Kaiser Wilhelm II had long shared his vanquished chancellor's distaste for Berlin, he was determined to make his capital worthy of the greatness he expected to bring to Germany. Berlin, he said, must become recognized as "the most beautiful city in the world." It bothered him that visitors from Western Europe tended to consider the German metropolis a significant step down from the older European capitals in terms of elegance and urban amenities. He knew, too, that his own court was often ridiculed for its lack of savoir faire. He blamed this partly on his dutiful but dim-witted wife, Donna, nicknamed "the Holstein." Hoping to raise the sartorial style of Donna's retinue, he appealed to the wife of a British diplomat to invite some of her "smart London friends" to Berlin to "teach my court ladies how to do their hair and put on their clothes." As for the physical makeover of Berlin, he would happily take on that task himself.

Wilhelm pursued his vision of a "representative" Berlin with a dedication not seen in Germany since Bavaria's King Ludwig I redesigned Munich in the first half of the nineteenth century. Like that monarch's bequest to the Bavarian capital, Wilhelm's contribution to Berlin turned out to be truly protean, including governmental buildings, churches, prisons, barracks, and hospitals. His particular love was for monuments, of which he built so many that it became practically impossible to turn a corner in central Berlin without encountering some outsize statue in bronze or marble. Virtually all these architectural additions betrayed their sponsor's conviction that a structure could be impressive only if it were weighted down with heavy historical baggage.

In 1891 Wilhelm dedicated the Gedächtniskirche (Kaiser Wilhelm Memorial Church), built to honor his grandfather. A neo-Gothic monstrosity, the church was a mockery of its namesake's frugality. To make its interior more sumptuous, the

Kaufhaus des Westens (KaDaWe), 1910

kaiser pressed Berlin's richest burghers to donate stained-glass windows in exchange for medals and titles. The building was designed to be the focal point of Berlin's "New West" beyond the Tiergarten, the newly fashionable district that Kerr called "an elegant small town where all the people who can do something, be something, and have something" were determined to live. Close by the Memorial Church was the sprawling Kaufhaus des Westens, or KaDeWe, a glamorous department store that went up in 1912. (Playing on the juxtaposition of these two buildings, Berliners dubbed Wilhelm's pious memorial the *Taufhaus des Westens*—Baptismal House of the West.) The Memorial Church achieved true landmark status only after 1945—as a bombed-out ruin and symbol of the horrors of war. Comparing it as it looks today with photographs from before the war, one can only conclude that this building was improved by the bombing.

Three years later, in 1894, Wilhelm embarked on the construction of another, even larger church, the Berliner Dom. It was built to replace a smaller cathedral that had been recently demolished. A monument of showy piety, it was meant to bedazzle all who saw it, though this was not always the effect it had on discriminating observers. A prominent architectural critic wrote: "What has been achieved here is empty elegance, nothing more. . . . What is the point of the massive triumphal arch over the modest door in the middle? Does it express any sound architectural principle, any clerical ideal, or any genuine feeling whatsoever? No—it shows off, that is all. Hundreds of pillars, pilasters, cornices, arches, gables, statues, and other dressy pieces contrive simply to repeat the impression of emptiness." Such carping notwithstanding, the kaiser was quite pleased with his new Dom. He was convinced that it would become as important to world Protestantism as St. Peter's in Rome was to Catholicism. On the occasion of its dedication in 1905, he declared that Protestantism would soon replace Catholicism as the dominant world religion, and the Berliner Dom would be its headquarters. Of course, the new shrine served also to remind Berlin's Catholics, whose own church, St. Hedwig's, was somewhat shabby, that they were second-class citizens in the German Reich.

The most significant building to be completed in Berlin under Wilhelm II was not commissioned by the kaiser, nor did it win his approval. This was the new Reichstag, started in 1884 and dedicated a decade later. Bismarck had originally proposed that the lower assembly be housed in a simple structure on the Wilhelmstrasse, but a group of Berlin politicians and architects complained that this would hardly be adequate for the parliament of "the newly unified, victorious German nation, on the verge of taking over the leadership of Europe." Searching for an appropriate site, a parliamentary committee recommended a sizable plot on the Königsplatz then occupied by the derelict palace of a Polish-Prussian aristocrat named Athanasius Raczynski. It took over twenty years to arrange for the purchase and demolition of Raczynski's palace and to begin construction on the new building. The structure that finally opened for business in 1894 was, like so many public buildings in the capital, a mixture of styles, something like a cross between the Paris Opera and a Palladian palazzo. Its architect, Paul Wallot, had been charged with capturing the German spirit in stone, and he perhaps unwittingly achieved this through the eclectic confusion of his design. "It was," as historian Michael Cullen has written, "a house that could not decide what it wanted to be." The building's ornate exterior adornments suggested a reverence for Prussian military glory rather than for parliamentary democracy. A twenty-foot-tall statue entitled *Germania in the Saddle* rose above the western facade, while a relief of St. George the Dragon-Slayer,

Siegesallee, circa 1903

bearing the visage of Bismarck, crowned the main entrance. For some, the building's showiness symbolized all too well the lack of substance prevailing inside. In a contemporary novel entitled *Bismarcks Nachfolger* (Bismarck's Successors), the protagonist, a progressive parliamentary representative, laments that the new building was useless for practical political work, "with its front steps only good for parade viewing and its real entrance hidden confusedly in a narrow back street." Another deficiency was a lack of work rooms for the delegates, who thus spent most of their time in the house restaurant, the Fraktion Schulze. Even Kaiser Wilhelm thought the structure "the height of tastelessness," which, given his high tolerance for kitsch, was saying something. He complained loudly over the 22 million marks that had been spent on this "ape house of the Reich." To show his contempt, he entered the building only twice during his entire reign. Wilhelm also vetoed Wallot's proposed inscription over the entrance: *Dem deutschen Volke* (To the German People). The kaiser preferred *Der deutschen Einheit* (To German Unity). Many Berliners, meanwhile, said that more appropriate slogans might be Entry Barred to the German People, or Beware of Pickpockets. The inscription *Dem deutschen Volke* was finally added in 1916 as part of the government's futile effort to maintain morale at home in the face of increasing wartime privations.

The architectural addition to Berlin's topography of which the emperor was most proud was the Siegesallee (1901), an avenue in the Tiergarten lined with the marble busts of Hohenzollern heroes. The kaiser himself provided drawings for the figures, ordering that some of them bear the features of contemporary supporters. Thus the Elector Frederick I, founder of the Hohenzollern dynasty, looked startlingly like Philipp zu Eulenburg, Wilhelm's closest friend. Although Wilhelm firmly believed that his new avenue would raise Berlin's standing in the world, the project merely added to the German capital's reputation for pretentious posturing. Contemplating one of the ensembles, a fountain dedicated to Roland, a foreign diplomat commented that he had not realized that "even flowing water could be made to be ugly." *Simplicissimus*, the Munich humor magazine, ran a cartoon showing a visitor declaring: "My, how beautiful everything is here! Even the bird shit is made of marble!" To many locals, the avenue was a source of embarrassment. They labeled it *die Puppenallee*—avenue of the dolls.

Wilhelm was indignant over the Berliners' mockery of his bequest. He decided to punish the city by denying it his imperial presence for extended periods. "Once the Berliners have gone for some time without seeing the imperial carriage," he said, "they will come crawling back on all fours."

Of course, there *were* plenty of Berliners who pined for a sight of the imperial carriage and who fell over themselves to show their admiration for their emperor. Kaiser-worship was especially pronounced among the city's younger middle-class males, many of whom had their mustaches curled upward at the tips à la Wilhelm. The city's bureaucrats and businessmen often tried to act like mini-kaisers in their dealings with social or professional subordinates. Heinrich Mann brilliantly satirized such behavior via the ludicrous figure of Dietrich Hessling in his novel *Der Untertan* (The Loyal Subject). Upon inheriting the family factory, Hessling declares to his workers: "I have taken the rudder into my own hands. My course is straight and I am guiding you to glorious times. Those who wish to help me are heartily welcome;

whoever opposes me I will smash. There is only one master here and I am he. I am responsible only to God and my own conscience. You can always count on my fatherly benevolence but revolutionary sentiments will be shattered against my unbending will." Imperious before his workers, Hessling becomes grotesquely servile in the presence of the emperor. Spotting the kaiser's carriage, he runs along beside it to catch a glimpse of his hero, only to stumble and fall in the mud. Seeing him lying in a puddle, his legs in the air, the kaiser says to an aide, "There's a royalist for you; there's a loyal subject."

Popular as the kaiser was among Berlin's royalist set, he may well have alienated more citizens through his busybody presence than through his frequent absences. This was a man, Berliners said, who could not attend a funeral without wanting to be the corpse. Few citizens were surprised therefore by a bizarre incident involving their impetuous ruler that occurred during a performance by Buffalo Bill Cody's Wild West Show in Berlin in 1889. As always, the star of the show, Annie Oakley, asked for a volunteer from the audience to smoke a cigar whose ash she would shoot off from a distance of thirty yards. In fact, Annie made this request simply for laughs; her long-suffering husband always stepped forward and offered himself as her human Havana holder. This time, however, the young kaiser himself leaped out of the royal box, strutted into the arena, extracted a cigar from a gold case, and lit it with a flourish. Annie was horrified but could not retract her dare without losing face. She thus paced off her distance, raised her Colt.45, took aim, and blew away the kaiser's ashes. Had she blown away the kaiser instead, the subsequent history of Berlin, Germany, and indeed the entire world might have been very different. (Annie herself realized this later on. During World War I, she wrote the kaiser asking if she could have a second shot.)

Culture Wars

Kaiser Wilhelm II hoped to put his stamp on every aspect of Berlin's artistic and intellectual life. He believed himself especially qualified for this role because in his spare time he liked to draw and write plays. He produced workmanlike renderings of ships and composed a play called *Sardanapal*, featuring a king who immolates himself to avoid being captured by the enemy. So confident was he of his abilities that he made visiting heads of state sit through his play. Among his victims was his uncle Edward VII, who, forced to attend a gala production of *Sardanapal*, promptly fell asleep, only to awaken in the very realistic fire scene and demand that the fire department be called. Wilhelm's efforts to impose his archconservative taste on the capital eventually inspired a backlash among the city's cultural elite. In the end, no figure did more to promote the triumph of the modern spirit in Berlin than this champion of cultural orthodoxy.

The kaiser spelled out his aesthetic philosophy at the dedication of the Siegesallee:

> An art which transgresses the laws and barriers outlined by Me, ceases to be an art; it is merely a factory product, a trade, and art must never become such a thing. The often misused word 'liberty' . . . leads to license and presumption. . . . Art should help to educate the people; it should also give to the lower classes after their hard work . . . the possibility of lifting themselves up to ideals. . . . If art, as so frequently happens now, does nothing more than paint misery more ugly than it is, it sins against the German people. The cultivation of the ideal is, moreover, the greatest work of civilization; if we wish to be and remain an example for other countries, the entire nation must cooperate. If culture is going to fulfill its task, it must penetrate into the greatest layers of the people. This it can do only if it proffers a hand to uplift, instead of to debase.

Germany's capital, the kaiser believed, offered too few examples of cultural uplift and all too many of moral debasement. Berlin's theatrical scene was a case in point, he thought. Although the Royal Theater had traditionally been a bastion of artistic conservatism, theatrical companies outside the royal orbit were busily experimenting with new and innovative forms of drama. "1889 was the year of the German theatrical revolution, just as 1789 was the year of the revolution of humanity," wrote Otto Brahm, founder of Berlin's Free Stage movement. Operating as a private theatrical club, the Free Stage was not subject to the rigid censorship that hamstrung the official state theaters. Thus the first play it produced was Ibsen's *Ghosts*, which heretofore had been banned in Berlin because it dealt with the taboo topic of syphilis. *Ghosts* raised the eyebrows of conservative theatergoers, but the controversy was mild compared to the scandal inspired by the Free Stage's next production, Gerhart Hauptmann's *Before Dawn*, a realistic exploration of daily life among the lower classes. As the play progressed, some members of the audience began yelling catcalls, while others rose to cheer. Soon verbal duels between the rival claques gave way to fisticuffs. Once the smoke had cleared, however, it became evident that the protesters had managed only to assure the play's triumph and to confirm Hauptmann's emergence as the new star of the Berlin theater.

Emboldened by his success with the Free Stage, Brahm acquired a public venue, the Deutsches Theater, and began directly challenging the political establishment with more plays by Hauptmann and other naturalists. In 1894 the Deutsches Theater announced a production of Hauptmann's *Die Weber (The Weavers)*, a bleak depiction of the plight of Silesian textile workers in the 1840s. The Berlin police banned the play on the grounds that it was likely to stir up the lower orders. The ban was soon overturned in court, however, because the judges realized that workers were unlikely to attend an event with a high admission charge. *The Weavers* premiered on September 24, 1894, and enjoyed an enormous success.

Official Berlin was aghast over Hauptmann's rise to prominence. After seeing the playwright's *Hanneles Himmelfahrt*, a chronicle of a poor girl's unsuccessful fight against tuberculosis, Prince Chlodwig zu Hohenlohe-Schillingsfürst, the future chancellor, wrote in his diary: "This evening at *Hannele*. A frightful concoction, Social Democratic–realistic, at the same time full of sickly, sentimental mysticism, uncanny, nerve-rattling, altogether awful. Afterward we went to Borchardt to put ourselves back into a human state of mind with champagne and caviar." To the kaiser, Hauptmann's triumph was a violation of everything the theater should represent. The stage, he said, ought to constitute a "useful weapon against materialism and un-German art." People should leave a dramatic production "not discouraged at the recollection of mournful scenes of bitter disappointment, but purified, elevated, and with renewed strength to fight for the ideals which every man strives to realize." Declaring Hauptmann a willful purveyor of gloom, Wilhelm ordered him arrested for subversion in 1892. When the courts proved unwilling to keep the writer in jail, the kaiser resorted to petty acts of revenge, going so far as to cancel the playwright's award of the Schiller Prize for dramatic excellence and giving the prize instead to one of his favorite conservative hacks, Ernst Wildenbruch.

The kaiser was also unable to stem the rise of Max Reinhardt, a Jew from Austria who arrived in Berlin at the turn of the century to launch an acting career. The city immediately impressed him: "Berlin is veritably a magnificent city," he wrote a friend. "Vienna multiplied by more than ten. Truly metropolitan character, immense traffic, a tendency toward the grandiose throughout, and at the same time practical and upright." Reinhardt failed at acting but showed brilliance as a director when he opened a small cabaret called *Sound and Smoke.* From there he moved on to the legitimate stage, taking over the Deutsches Theater in 1905 and quickly changing it from a stronghold of grim naturalism into an arena of magic and excitement. Although his repertoire ran the gamut from Sophocles to Büchner, everything he produced seemed fresh and modern due to his use of the latest dramaturgical techniques. Reviewing his production of Maxim Gorki's *Nachtasyl (Night Refuge),* a critic enthused: "The production came across like a premier. The public had the impression of seeing it for the first time. Reinhardt treated the piece with such intensity that it seemed as if it had just been written." Unable to do anything to counter Reinhardt's popular success, the kaiser ordered his productions off-limits to the military and, when war broke out in 1914, rejected the playwright's offer to tour the front with his company. Such was the official reception of the artist who more than any other launched Berlin as a world center of modernist drama.

Berlin's musical scene, unlike its theater, commanded international respect well before the imperial era. Its royal orchestra, founded in 1842, was led for a time by Felix Mendelssohn-Bartholdy. In addition, there was a privately funded symphony orchestra directed by a former military bandleader named Benjamin Bilse. His pedigree notwithstanding, Bilse coaxed some brilliant music from his players, and a weekend *bei Bilse* became a regular part of bourgeois life in Berlin during the 1870s and 1880s. In 1882, however, a dissident faction among Bilse's players, tired of being treated like soldiers, defected to create a rival ensemble that they called the Berlin Philharmonic. Performing during its first years in a converted roller-skating rink, the new group did not seem terribly promising. But in 1887 it came under the direction of Hans von Bülow, a brilliant pianist and conductor who combined a mastery of the classics with a commitment to contemporary music. In 1889 Bülow brought his friend Johannes Brahms to Berlin to conduct his D Minor Concerto. Whenever Bülow directed, the Philharmonic sold out.

As might be expected, Bülow's fans did not include the kaiser, who hated modernism in music as much as in any other art. Bülow, for his part, despised Wilhelm, and used the occasion of his last Berlin concert, in 1892, to express his contempt. Noting that the emperor had recently advised his critics to "wipe the German dust from their shoes and vacate the Fatherland with all haste," Bülow took out a silk handkerchief, dusted his shoes, and announced his departure. The orchestra he had led to greatness, however, continued to prosper under his successors, from Arthur Nikisch through Wilhelm Furtwängler, Herbert von Karajan, and Claudio Abbado.

Bülow had long been a champion of Richard Wagner (Wagner rewarded his loyalty by stealing Bülow's wife, Cosima), and a belated infusion of Wagner's music helped to revitalize the Berlin opera scene, which had been moribund since the glory days of Meyerbeer in the 1840s. In the late 1870s and 1880s Wagnerian music-drama became a staple at the Royal Opera. The capital also boasted Germany's largest Wagner Club, which among other services helped raise money for the Master's new theater at Bayreuth. Yet Wagner's success irritated important elements of the political establishment, who, recalling the composer's support for the revolutions of 1848, considered him a dangerous revolutionary. Once again, the kaiser led the opposition. Although he had been a Wagnerian in his youth, he announced soon after ascending the throne that "Glück is the man for me; Wagner is too noisy." This was an odd comment coming from a man who adored John Philip Sousa, and Wilhelm's objections probably stemmed less from a genuine distaste for Wagner's music than from resentment over the splash he was making in Berlin. "What do people see in this Wagner anyway?" he asked. "The chap is simply a conductor, nothing other than a conductor, an entirely commonplace conductor."

Twenty years after Wagner's conquest of Berlin, a new musical revolutionary was storming the gates: Richard Strauss. A protégé of Bülow's, Strauss had made a huge reputation for himself around Germany as a conductor and composer of "tone poems" such as *Don Juan, Tod und Verklärung (Death and Transfiguration), Till Eulenspiegel, Also Sprach Zarathustra (Thus Spoke Zarathustra), Don Quixote,* and *Ein Heldenleben (A Hero's Life).* It is telling that this last piece was a self-portrait. Convinced of his own supremacy, the Bavarian-born Strauss naturally wanted to work in Germany's most important city. He managed to serve as guest conductor of the Berlin Philharmonic in 1894/95. But it took another four years, during which he conducted all over Europe and became the most talked about musician in the world, before he could gain the post he coveted—leadership of the Berlin Royal Opera.

The chief obstacle was Kaiser Wilhelm, who disapproved of Strauss's music except for the bombastic marches that the composer dedicated to His Majesty. Wilhelm finally consented to Strauss's appointment in Berlin only because the musician promised to cooperate with him in guiding the Royal Opera to even greater heights. But once ensconced on the Spree, Strauss continued to write the sort of modernist music the kaiser hated. "I raised a snake in the grass to bite me," fumed

Wilhelm. He told Strauss to his face that he considered his music "worthless." After the empress stalked out of Strauss's *Feuersnot* because it contained erotic themes, Wilhelm ordered the piece banned forever from the Royal Opera. Strauss's much more "decadent" opera, *Salome*, based on a play by Oscar Wilde, could not premier in Berlin due to the court's resistance, and when it finally reached the capital it had to be given an uplifting ending. Similarly, *Der Rosenkavalier* was approved for production in 1912 only after Strauss agreed to cut out sections showing an official of the royal court behaving like a lecher. "An imperial chamberlain should not act like a vulgar fellow," admonished the kaiser.

Although Strauss often deferred to the kaiser's judgment in the interest of promoting his career, he was determined to keep Berlin on the cutting edge of modern music. Because Wilhelm could not be dissuaded from interfering with his work at the Royal Opera, the composer founded a private orchestra, the Tonkünstler, which put on unbowdlerized versions of his own operas as well as works by experimentalists like Bruckner, Elgar, Wolf, and Schönberg. Thus in music as well as in drama, official Berlin was unable to suppress the growing influence of the avant-garde.

Berlin was not Germany's capital of plastic arts at the time of national unification. That distinction was claimed by Munich, which boasted the largest community of painters and sculptors in the nation. But this began to change in the 1880s and 1890s, when artists started scrambling to the new imperial capital in search of money and prestige. The growing concentration of talent also brought bitter internecine battles over commissions and contracts. The divisiveness was exacerbated by the kaiser, who could not resist taking sides, especially in a domain where he considered himself an expert.

Prior to the 1880s, Berlin's best known and certainly most beloved artist was Adolf Menzel, who had moved from his native Breslau to the Prussian capital in 1830 at age 15. In his youth Menzel had been a protomodernist, turning out impressionistic treatments of Berlin's seamier side, its dark streets and primitive factories. Degas was one of his admirers. But by the 1870s he had changed tack both in technique and subject matter, focusing on official Berlin and its historical antecedents. His *The Flute Concert* and *The Round Table* mythologized the court of Frederick the Great. He rendered Kaiser Wilhelm I riding down Unter den Linden on his way to the Franco-Prussian war. Skillful in execution, these paintings con-

The Iron Rolling Mill: Modern Cyclops *by Adolf von Menzel. An example of the painter's realistic depiction of Berlin's factory scene*

veyed an uncritical admiration for Prussian might and glory. Unquestionably, Menzel was anxious to become a part of the court set himself.

And part of it he duly became. Soon the dwarfish and exceptionally ugly painter—he ruefully admitted that on Judgment Day no woman would be able to point to him and say, "You have me on your conscience, old Menzel"—became a fixture in the high society scene, a voyeuristic presence at every party and ball. Ever the attentive observer, he chronicled these occasions in close detail, providing a rich visual history of upper-class Berlin life at the turn of the century. Like his portraits of the Prussian masters, these works tended to be reverential, containing little hint of the grossness under the glitter. As a reward for his piety, Menzel was heaped with titles and medals: he became Professor of Art at the Royal Academy and, on Kaiser Wilhelm II's orders, won the Order of the Black Eagle, Prussia's highest honor.

When he died in 1905, Wilhelm personally marched in the funeral procession; he also ordered the Prussian government to purchase the paintings in Menzel's estate and to display them in the National Gallery.

Another paladin of official art in the new German capital was Anton von Werner, a history painter who glorified the Prussian crown in huge, almost photographically precise, canvases. His *Battle and Victory*, for example, depicted Kaiser Wilhelm I riding in the victory parade of June 16, 1871, with the Brandenburg Gate and a host of fawning subjects in the background. His most famous work, reproduced in thousands of German schoolbooks, was his *Kaiser Proclamation in Versailles*, which recorded the emperor and his generals toasting the foundation of the German Empire in Louis XIV's Hall of Mirrors. Commissioned by Kaiser Wilhelm I as a gift to Bismarck, the painting was put on public display in 1877 and quickly became a national icon. Through his closeness to the imperial court, Werner won accolades similar to Menzel's. He was appointed president of the Academy of Fine Arts in 1875, and chairman of the Association of Berlin Artists and head of the Berlin chapter of the National Union of Artists in the mid-1880s. Upon Wilhelm II's accession, Werner emerged as even more influential, for he had tutored the future emperor in drawing and won his trust as a reliable mentor in all things artistic. After 1888 he served as the new kaiser's unofficial adviser on Royal Academy appointments, museum acquisitions, and official exhibitions. In this capacity he validated Wilhelm's instinctive hatred for modern art. With Werner at his side, Wilhelm vowed to maintain the German capital as a bastion of wholesome and uplifting art.

For all their influence, however, neither the kaiser nor Werner could keep Berlin free of the modernist influences in painting that were sweeping Europe at the turn of the century. In 1892 a progressive faction within the Association of Berlin Artists invited Edvard Munch to mount a one-man show in the German capital. The Norwegian put up fifty-five paintings in the Association's exhibition hall. None of the old guard around Werner knew anything about Munch, and when they saw his works they were horrified. According to the mocking account of a Munch partisan, they gasped in unison: "This is supposed to be art! Oh misery, misery! Why, it's entirely different from the way we paint. It is new, foreign, disgusting, common! Get rid of the paintings, throw them out!" And out they went, via a vote orchestrated by Werner to suspend the show.

Yet while Werner and company were able to expel the foreigner Munch, they could not get rid of Max Liebermann, a native Berliner who became the city's chief

Käthe Kollwitz, circa 1905

crusader for modernist art. Liebermann had made a prominent name for himself in Paris and Munich before returning to his native city in 1884. As the assimilated son of a wealthy Jewish cotton manufacturer, he identified deeply with German culture, without for a moment overlooking the persistent racial and social prejudices around him. When a patronizing acquaintance told him that there would be no anti-Semitism if all Jews were like him, he replied: "No, if all *gentiles* were like me there would be no anti-Semitism. For the rest, I am glad that my face makes it obvious that I am a Jew. I don't need to spell it out to anyone." Nor did Liebermann need to spell out his artistic principles, which were evident in paintings like *The Flax Spinners*, *Views of Workers Eating*, and *Asylum for Old Men*, which exposed contemporary ills in a bold impressionist style.

Liebermann was anathema to Kaiser Wilhelm II. The kaiser had no use for painters who, as he said, "made misery even more hideous than it already is." For a time, Wilhelm and his cultural bureaucrats managed to keep Liebermann from displaying his works in official exhibitions. They could not, however, prevent him from appearing in private shows, such as those organized by "The Eleven," a short-lived offshoot of the Association of Berlin Painters. With time, moreover, Liebermann became so popular that he had to be admitted to the official salon, where he won the Gold Medal in 1897. In that same year he was elected to the Prussian Academy of Art and made a professor at the Royal Academy—both accolades he considered long overdue.

Liebermann's success did not signal a definitive or uncontested triumph for modernist art in Berlin. In 1898 a jury on which he sat recommended that a small gold medal be awarded to Käthe Kollwitz for her brilliant etching cycle *The Revolt of the Weavers*, based on Hauptmann's naturalist drama. Such awards could not be presented without approval of the kaiser, who vetoed the prize with the words, "Please, gentlemen, a medal for a woman, that's really going too far. That would amount to a debasement of every high distinction. Orders and honors belong on the chests of deserving men." Another chest, albeit male, that the kaiser deemed unsuited for a medal belonged to the brilliant landscape artist Walter Leistikow; Wilhelm insisted that as a hunter he knew more about nature than a painter who colored his trees blue.

The Kollwitz affair was the last straw for painters like Liebermann and Leistikow, who had long been frustrated over the attempts by the kaiser and his advisers (especially von Werner) to control the local art scene. In 1898 they launched the Berlin *Sezession* (Secession), a revolt of disaffected artists modeled on earlier secessions in Vienna and Munich. Their chief purpose was to organize exhibitions in which they could display the art they respected. For financial support they relied on donations from wealthy patrons, many of them Jewish. Their most important backers were the Cassirer cousins, Bruno and Paul, who owned a gallery in the Kantstrasse that specialized in modern art. As the Secession's business managers, the Cassirers built a new gallery in 1899 that displayed works by the Berlin group and other leading modernists.

Official Berlin responded predictably to the dissidents' initiative. The kaiser ordered military officers not to attend Secession exhibitions in uniform. He also barred Secession members from serving on juries of the official salon. In alliance

Preparations for the Berlin Secession exhibition in 1904. Members of the exhibition committee (from left to tight): Willy Döring, Bruno Cassirer, Otto Engel, Max Liebermann, Walter Leistifow, Kurt Herrmann, Fritz Klimsch

with the Association of German Artists, Wilhelm managed to exclude the Secession from Germany's exhibition at the 1904 St. Louis World's Fair. When the Cultural Ministry tried to make peace with the Secession by proposing a retrospective show for Liebermann in the Royal Academy's new quarters, the kaiser vetoed the idea. The painter, he said, was "poisoning the soul of the German nation."

Fortunately for the fate of modern art in Germany, such measures did not prevent the Secession from becoming a viable enterprise, one that helped to make the unorthodox and the innovative more culturally acceptable. As Liebermann himself boasted in 1907: "Yesterday's revolutionaries have become today's classics."

But this was precisely the problem for a group of younger artists who had moved to the capital in the early years of the century. Finding the Secession played out and sterile, they embarked on a new artistic path known as expressionism, the first modernist school to be predominantly German. Die Brücke, an expressionist group founded in Dresden in 1905 shifted to Berlin five years later. Its chief spokesman, Herwarth Walden, launched a magazine and art gallery called *Der Sturm*, which became the focal point of the German avant-garde on the eve of the war. Unlike the major Secessionists, these artists turned their attention to the big cities, above all to Berlin. The most important figure here was Ludwig Meidner. The critic Karl Scheffler had argued that it was impossible to love a place as ugly as Berlin, but Meidner insisted that *he* loved it, and urged his fellow artists to love it as well: "We must finally begin to paint our homeland [Heimat], the metropolis, for which we have an infinite love." What Meidner found to love in Berlin was precisely the "unnatural" and "ugly" environment of sprawling tenements, bustling streets, and barely contained chaos. As he wrote in his *Directions for Painting the Big City*: "Let's paint what is close to us, our city world! The wild streets, the elegance of iron suspension bridges, gas tanks which hang in white-cloud mountains, the roaring colors of buses and express locomotives, the rushing telephone wires (aren't they like music?), the harlequinade of advertising pillars, and the night . . . big city night!" Meidner was so fond of metropolitan chaos that many modern critics have interpreted his prewar Berlin studies as an anticipation of the cataclysmic destruction to come.

Another expressionist artist who has been classed retrospectively as a prophet of the apocalypse is Ernst Ludwig Kirchner. His interpretations of Berlin before the war, which feature contorted figures seemingly desperate to escape the confines of the canvas, are said to be "immediately recognizable as pictures of an unnatural, thoroughly dehumanized world." But Kirchner himself saw his Berlin work as a celebration of the raw energy he found in the city's streets and taverns. He said that the "so-called distortions" in his paintings were "generated instinctively by the ecstasy of what is seen." Static representation was impossible, he added, when the subject was in perpetual motion, a blur of light and action. The city required of its artists a new way of seeing, and Kirchner was determined to capture the frantic movement of metropolitan life by abandoning traditional naturalistic, or even impressionistic, techniques.

While at the turn of the century Berlin was just beginning to gain an international reputation for its creative contributions to the visual arts, the Prussian capital had long been known as a solid museum town. In 1830 Karl Friedrich Schinkel had completed the Altes Museum on the small wedge of land flanked by the Spree that came to be known as the Museumsinsel (Museums Island). The Neues Museum, designed by Schinkel's pupil Friedrich August Stüler, was added in 1855, followed by the new National Gallery in 1876. According to Georg Brandes, at the time of national unification the city's museums "played for edification-seeking Berliners a role similar to cathedrals in Gothic countries." In the Wilhelmian era Berlin's museums profited greatly from the efforts of one of Europe's most brilliant collectors, Wilhelm von Bode, who became director of the new Kaiser-Friedrich-Museum when it opened on the Museums Island in 1904. (Two years later Bode was named director-general of all the royal museums, a position he held until 1920, when the museums were no longer royal.) Adept at tracking down hidden treasures around the world, Bode brought to Berlin an amazing collection of Old Masters, including Rembrandt's *Man in a Golden Helmet* and Dürer's *Hieronymus Holzschuher*. For once the kaiser did not interfere; on the contrary, he fully shared Bode's ambition to make Berlin a major repository for the certified classics of European art. To help the curator raise funds, Wilhelm offered titles to wealthy burghers who made sizable contributions to the royal collections. Bode helped his own cause by making allies with anyone who was influential, including Max Liebermann, who painted his portrait.

Berlin's collections, particularly in the realm of classical art, profited also from Germany's belated entry into the international race to loot the Mediterranean and Near East of its remaining ancient treasures. As a latecomer in this field, the Reich was desperate to bring its antiquity collections up to the standards of the great western European museums, especially the British Museum. Fortunately for Berlin, one of the most zealous pillagers of classical art was Heinrich Schliemann, a grocer's son from Mecklenburg who in the early 1870s located and excavated the site of Homer's Troy in western Turkey. It was by no means apparent from the outset that Schliemann would deed the treasures he had found at Troy—most notably a collection of gold articles he claimed had belonged to King Priam—to the German capital. As a self-taught archeologist with no formal degrees, Schliemann had been derided as an impostor by Berlin's classical scholars when he first announced his discoveries. (It was later to be established that he had indeed fabricated details of some of his finds.) Profoundly hurt by this rebuff, he announced, "If I leave it [the

Ludwig Meidner, Apocalyptic Landscape, *1913*

Troy collection] in my will to a German city, it can never be Berlin, for I have never had a single word of appreciation from there and have always been treated with the most odious hostility." Only after he had gained credibility abroad did Berlin finally accept him as a genuine article and launch a campaign to win his loot for the royal collections. Pleased by the attention, Schliemann relented and in 1881 formally willed his Trojan horde to the new Berlin Ethnographic Museum, where a special wing was built to display it.

On the occasion of what Kaiser Wilhelm I called Schliemann's "patriotic gift," imperial Berlin made him an honorary citizen (an honor bestowed heretofore only on Bismarck and Helmuth von Moltke) and threw a lavish dinner party for him at the Town Hall. The menu, written in ancient Greek, showed the Discoverer of Ancient Troy seated on the throne of Priam holding a spade in one hand and a statuette of Victory in the other, while a chastened Berlin bear reposed at his feet. In an official proclamation, Mayor Forckenbeck declared that Schliemann, "by his combination of practical activity with idealism" had become "a pattern for all German citizens." Messages of congratulation came from Kaiser Wilhelm I and Bismarck, both of whom had worked assiduously to stroke the archeologist's bruised ego. In his brief response, Schliemann showed that while he had forgiven Berlin its earlier snubs, he had not forgotten them: "In spite of her former cold treatment, you see that Berlin has done me honor at last. She has three great citizens—Bismarck, von Moltke, and myself."

Schliemann's archeological bug bit Kaiser Wilhelm II, who loved to dig for ancient treasure at his summer estate on Corfu, where, it was rumored, fragments were buried every year by sycophantic aides to facilitate his "discoveries." On his numerous trips abroad he met with foreign potentates to personally press Germany's case for access to the best sites and the right to bring some of the finds back to Berlin. In 1899, for example, he convinced the Turkish sultan to allow German archeologists to claim for Berlin half of what they found at the ancient Greek sites of Priene and Baalbek. Germany thereby gained a great advantage over Britain, France, Russia, and Austria in the exploitation of the cultural riches of the eastern Mediterranean. Germany's cultural warriors brought home the Gate of Milet to add to the fabled Pergamum Altar, which had been placed on display in Berlin in 1880 and touted as Berlin's answer to the Elgin Marbles. In 1902 Kaiser Wilhelm II presided over the dedication of a new space dedicated to the Pergamum treasures. (The famous Pergamum Museum itself was constructed in the period between 1912 and 1929.) With these additions, Berlin indeed rivaled London as a treasure-house of ancient plunder.

Matters were somewhat different when it came to collections of contemporary art. Old Berlin's holdings had not been very distinguished in this domain, and in the imperial era they suffered from the misguided intervention of the kaiser. Wilhelm took a personal interest in acquisitions to the National Gallery, Berlin's major museum for contemporary art; he hoped to weed out works that were too modern in technique or insufficiently edifying in theme. After visiting the National Gallery in 1899, Wilhelm complained to the Cultural Ministry that some "educative" national works had been "replaced by pictures of modern taste, some of them of foreign origin." He demanded that the originals be replaced and the new pictures be "demoted to a less prominent place." He also insisted that henceforth all acquisitions receive his approval.

Wilhelm's censure was aimed primarily at the director of the National Gallery, Hugo von Tschudi, a distinguished scholar with a true appreciation for modern art, particularly for the modern art of France. Doggedly, Tschudi found ways to acquire some important modern pieces for his museum despite the kaiser's guidelines. For example, in 1897 he acquired a painting by Cézanne, becoming the first museum director in the world to do so. (The French state had just refused to include this painter's works in its official collections.) Tschudi failed, however, to slip a major purchase of works by Delacroix, Courbet, and Daumier past the emperor's vigilant eye. Spotting the paintings on a visit to the gallery, Wilhelm indignantly declared that the director "could show such stuff to a monarch who understood nothing of art, but not to *him*." The rebuke infuriated Tschudi, who hated having to defer to a man he considered an art-ignoramus. Thus he gratefully accepted an offer to become the head of Bavaria's royal museums in 1908.

Munich's gain was Berlin's loss. Tschudi's successor, Ludwig Justi, also hoped to open the National Gallery to innovative works, but he lacked his predecessor's dynamism and drive. Visiting the National Gallery in 1912, the distinguished American critic James Huneker wrote that he wanted to gnash his teeth over the plethora of mediocre paintings and the relative dearth of distinguished ones. He was appalled to discover that the museum's French Impressionist works were all hung in a badly lighted room on the top floor. As for the rest: "The sight of so much misspent labor, of the acres of canvas deluged with dirty, bad paint, raises my bile."

Many of the artists and intellectuals who enjoyed the Kaiser's favor were faculty members at the Royal Academy of Art, the Academy of Music, or the University of Berlin. This last institution was the imperial capital's most important center of higher learning. Located on Unter den Linden in a palace built in 1766 by Frederick the Great (but immediately abandoned by the king when he moved his court to Potsdam), the university was established in 1810 to help Prussia revitalize and throw off the domination of Napoleon. Among its founding patrons were the Humboldt brothers, Alexander and Wilhelm, whose organizing principle was the "unity of learning"—the symbiosis of humanism and the natural sciences. In the 1840s bronze statues of the brothers were erected in front of the main building (they are still there today). A century later, when the East German Communists took over the university, they changed the name from Friedrich-Wilhelm-Universität to Humboldt-Universität. They also inscribed in the central hall a famous line from Karl Marx, who had attended the university in the late 1830s: "Philosophers have hitherto explained the world; it is now time to change it."

By the beginning of the imperial period Berlin University was indeed helping to change the world, albeit more through practical learning than through philosophically inspired political action. As an intellectual ally of German industry and government, the university was a key player in Germany's development as a world leader in technology, the natural sciences, and medicine. A brief look at the school's contributions to the disciplines of medicine and physics should suffice to document this point.

Rudolf Virchow, a physician, biologist, and amateur archeologist (he was a friend and supporter of Schliemann) invented the modern discipline of pathology. He also promoted reforms in the meat-processing industry through his discovery of trichina worms in uncooked ham and sausage. He was somewhat less scientific in his approach to tuberculosis, typhus, and cholera; as a radical democrat (about which more below), he argued that these diseases were caused by poverty and overcrowding rather than by microorganisms. His remedies were therefore exclusively social: more rights for the poor rather than quarantine or disinfecting.

Berlin honored Virchow with a new hospital complex named after him. Opened in 1906, the facility was the most modern and technically advanced in the world. Strolling though its buildings and parklike grounds in 1909, Jules Huret found himself feeling ashamed for the dirty old Hotel Dieu in Paris.

> The cleanliness, the order! Nowhere a scrap of paper or any kind of litter. Wastebaskets are placed here and there, and next to the white-painted benches are spittoons filled with antiseptic water. . . . Patients, dressed in blue-and-white-striped suits, wool stockings and leather sandals, freely walk the grounds. . . . Women sit on the benches, reading or knitting. It is the perfect picture of peace and comfort, allowing one to suppress thoughts of the pain contained within these walls. Verily, one wishes that all states would be blessed with such institutions.

Another eminent Berlin physician, Robert Koch, pioneered in the germ theory of disease. He owed his appointment to the medical faculty at Berlin's renowned Charité Hospital to such breakthroughs in bacteriology as the isolation of the anthrax bacillus and his development of a technique for staining bacteria with aniline dyes. In 1882, shortly after taking up his professorship at Berlin, he discovered the tubercle bacillus, thereby dealing a major blow against the greatest killer disease of the nineteenth century. He also isolated the waterborne bacillus responsible for cholera. Intriguingly, Koch's greatest rival, the Bavarian scientist Max Pettenkoffer, did not accept the validity of this discovery, and in a rash effort to discredit it swallowed a sample of cholera-infected water from Koch's lab. Pettenkoffer's attempt to prove the superiority of Bavarian over Prussian science almost killed him. Koch then confirmed Berlin's leadership in epidemiological research by founding the city's renowned Institute for Infectious Diseases. He received the Nobel Prize for medicine in 1905 and, like Virchow before him, was made an honorary citizen of the imperial capital.

Koch's most influential student was Paul Ehrlich, who in 1896 was appointed director of Berlin's new Institute for Serum Investigation. His use of synthetic dyes produced by German industry to analyze tissues was a classic example of the growing and very fruitful collaboration between Germany's industrial and academic communities. Even more important, his discovery in 1909 of salvarsan, an arsphenamine, offered a better treatment for syphilis, that scourge of European cities, including Berlin. For his pioneering work in immunology he too was awarded the Nobel Prize in medicine.

Like its faculty of medicine, Berlin University's physics department was a hothouse of pathbreaking research and a veritable factory of Nobel Prizes. It was here, at the dawn of what Arnold Sommerfeld called "the golden age of German physics," that Newton's world was overturned through the development of quantum theory, thermodynamics, and, after Einstein arrived in 1914, the general theory of relativity. Aside from Einstein, Berlin's recipients of the Nobel Prize for physics included Max Planck, Max Laue, and Walther Nernst. These pioneering scientists, together with their colleagues in medicine and the other natural sciences, confirmed the ascendancy of the empirical sciences over the humanistic disciplines in Berlin.

Most of the professors at Berlin were content enough to make their mark through their scientific work, but a few strayed into the political arena and challenged the policies of the imperial authorities. Virchow was a case in point. As a founder of the Progressive Party and a member of the Reichstag, he had embraced Bismarck's anti-Catholicism and push for national unity under Prussian control. Yet he also demanded greater rights for parliament and protested against the Iron Chancellor's dictatorial tendencies. So persistent was he in this course that Bismarck challenged him to a duel. (Fortunately for the pathologist, who could not demand scalpels as the weapon of choice, the contest never came off.)

The great historian Theodor Mommsen, who taught at Berlin from 1858 until his death in 1903, was world famous for his magisterial history of ancient Rome. In his portrait of the Caesars he had applauded the use of force to spread the power of the empire, and in the 1870s he gave his blessing to Germany's resort to the sword in its push for national unity. But he began to worry about the Reich's political course under Bismarck and Kaiser Wilhelm II, protesting the regime's exploitation of anti-Semitism and the citizens' tendency to cringe before military authority. When told that he should stick to writing history rather than trying to make it, he replied that as a "political animal" he would never abandon his rights.

These academic critics of the kaiser, however, did not set the political tone at Berlin University. On the whole, the professors at that institution were more than happy to endorse Wilhelm's absolutist claims. The university's rector, Emil Du Bois-Reymond, could brag with considerable legitimacy that his faculty was "His Majesty's Intellectual Regiment of the Guards."

Kaiser Wilhelm was very proud of the scientists, engineers, and inventors who were helping to make Berlin a seedbed of technological progress. His conservative tastes in art and architecture notwithstanding, he considered himself a man of the future, and he fully understood that scientific knowledge was a key element in national power. "The new century will be ruled by science, including technology, and not by philosophy as was its predecessor," he declared. The monarch cultivated personal contacts with Wilhelm Röntgen, discoverer of the X ray, and with Count Ferdinand von Zeppelin, the airship pioneer. (Upon Röntgen's discovery of the X ray, Wilhelm telegraphed him: "I praise God for granting our German fatherland this new triumph of science.") At the turn of the century, he prodded Berlin University to open its doors to the graduates of the recently created Realgymnasien, which emphasized natural sciences at the expense of ancient Greek. In 1910, on the one hundredth anniversary of the founding of the Friedrich-Wilhelm-Universität, he announced the creation of a new research complex for the natural sciences, the Kaiser Wilhelm Society, which was situated on royal lands in the western suburb of

Dahlem. The Society was to be Berlin's answer to France's Pasteur Institute and America's Rockefeller institutes, a place where the country's top scientists, funded by private industry and the government, could conduct the basic research necessary to keep Germany on the cutting edge of science and technology.

Bigger, Faster, Newer

In 1892 a group of prominent Berliners proposed to advertise their city's arrival as a world metropolis by staging an international exposition on the model of the recent fairs held in Paris, London, Vienna, and Philadelphia. However, Kaiser Wilhelm, to whom the matter was referred, rejected the plan on the grounds that Berlin was not yet grand enough—not yet transformed enough by *his* hand—to host a World's Fair. "The glory of Paris robs the Berliners of their sleep. Berlin is a great city, a world city (perhaps?), consequently, it has to have a [world's fair]. It is easy to understand why this argument is. . . attractive to the restaurants, the theaters and vaudevilles of Berlin. They would profit from it." But, the kaiser went on,

> Berlin is not Paris. Paris is the great whorehouse of the world; therein lies its attraction independent of any exhibition. There is nothing in Berlin that can captivate the foreigner, except a few museums, castles, and soldiers. After six days, the red book [the Baedeker guide] in hand, he has seen everything, and he departs *relieved*, feeling that he has done his duty. The Berliner does not see these things clearly, and would be very upset were he told about them. However, this is the real obstacle to the exhibition.

Deprived of imperial blessing for a World's Fair, Berlin contented itself with mounting a national Industrial Exposition in 1896. The event may not have had the cachet of an international exposition, but it sought to make up for this in size and glamour. Situated in brand new Treptow Park in the far eastern part of the city, it encompassed a larger area (900,000 square meters) than any previous exposition anywhere in the world. The exhibition halls, built in every imaginable style, showcased the tremendous technological progress made by imperial Germany in recent years. Many of the high-tech marvels on display had been made right in Berlin, which now accounted for 7 percent of the Reich's industrial production. There were hissing steam engines from Borsig, giant cranes from Julius Pintsch, electrical gadgets from Siemens and AEG. Less spectacular in appearance, but every bit as important, were synthetic dyes and photographic materials from AGFA, which later became part of the fabled I. G. Farben chemical trust. In addition to industrial products, there were consumer and luxury goods for the newly rich: Bechstein pianos, electric ovens, bronze desk lamps, a jewel-studded necklace costing 168,000 marks, a porcelain bowl "hand-painted by His Majesty." Then there was the "Hall of Appetite," a shrine to gluttony displaying such wonders as an electric *Wurst* machine that could convert 4,000 swine a year into salami and sausage; and an ensemble of marzipan breakfast items arrayed across a five-meter-long table made entirely of chocolate. When guests grew tried of admiring the displays, they could repair to the many eateries and drinking establishments that dotted the grounds, from luxury restaurants to simple pubs. Fortified with food and drink, they could visit a "Pyramid of Cheops" and view genuine mummies from the royal museums; or stroll through "Cairo in Berlin," a village of "oriental street scenes" whose authenticity was enhanced by genuine dirt on the buildings. To get to the fair, visitors could ride a recently completed extension of the elevated railway to the Treptow Park station or drive on a widened access road across the new Oberbaumbrücke, built to look like a Romanesque castle complete with arches and battlements. The cost of putting all this together was enormous, and despite 5 million visitors the fair was a financial disaster. Berlin never did stage a World's Fair, and, perhaps fittingly, a half-century later Treptow Park became the site of an enormous monument to the victorious Soviet army.

Berlin's Industrial Exposition of 1896 may have been a typical example of Wilhelmian overstretch, but the industrial wizardry displayed at the fair was genuine enough, and there were plenty of other signs that the German capital was a world leader in advanced technology and engineering.

Berlin was a pioneer in urban transportation. As we have seen, the city had a steam railway as early as the 1870s. The world's first electric streetcar had been introduced in Lichterfelde in 1881. By 1900 most of the trolley lines had been electrified; the last horse-drawn car, which ran to the municipal insane asylum in Dolldorf, was taken out of service in 1902. The new *Stadtbahn,* inaugurated in 1882, was Europe's first viaduct railway. It was a kind of city-within-the-city, containing under its brick archways a wealth of shops, storerooms, warehouses, and pubs. Berliners found it distinctly modern to drink a beer while a train rumbled overhead. There was action below ground as well, since construction on a subway system started in

1896, with the first line opening a decade later. Like New York's subway, the Berlin *U-Bahn* was to prove crucial in knitting together the various parts of the sprawling city.

By the turn of the century, Berlin was served by twelve railway lines and boasted ten long-distance train stations. The most impressive of these, Friedrichstrasse, was a far cry from the "pitiful hovels" that had passed for stations when Berlin became the national capital in 1871. A contemporary description of the building reveals the extent to which such structures were becoming icons of a new urban aesthetic:

> Wonderful Friedrichstrasse Station, when one stands on the outside platform over the Spree, where one sees nothing of the 'architecture' but only the huge surface of the glass walls; and the contrast to the shabby confusion of the surrounding buildings is especially lovely when twilight shadows cause the rag-tag environs to merge into a single whole and the many tin windowpanes begin to reflect the setting sun, bringing the whole area to colorful, shimmering life, stretching afar over the dark, low, monstrous cleft out of which the broad-chested locomo-

Bahnhof Friedrichstrasse, circa 1900

> tives threateningly emerge. And then what an intensification when one enters the darkened hall, which is still suffused with hesitant daylight: the huge, gradually arching form indistinct in a murky haze, a sea of gray hues just tinged with color, from the brightness of rising steam to the heavy darkness of the roof-skin and the absolute black of the bellowing engines arriving from the East; but above them, glowing in the murky surface of the glazing like a sharp, red shimmering pinnacle, appears the gable of a building, set luridly ablaze by the evening sun.

If Berlin was enamored with its trains and railway stations, the city also developed a romance with the automobile, which was to transform urban life in the twentieth century even more than the railroads had done in the nineteenth. With time the German capital would become one of the most car-crazy cities in Europe, despite its excellent public transportation system.

Berlin registered its first automobile in 1892 to a department store owner named Rudolf Herzog, who obtained the registration number 1A-1. Unfortunately for Herzog, Kaiser Wilhelm insisted that *his* car, a Daimler he bought in 1898, should carry this distinctive registration. Because Herzog refused voluntarily to cede the number, Wilhelm took him to court to force a transfer. The court rejected the emperor's suit on the ground that obtaining a particular automobile license did not belong to the traditional rights of the sovereign. While this may be taken as a setback for absolutism, the very fact that the case was raised at all showed once again that in modern Berlin the remnants of feudalism remained very much in evidence.

When the kaiser hit the streets of Berlin in his new Daimler, whose horn was tuned to the thunder-motif from Wagner's *Das Reingold*, motor-driven conveyances were just beginning to make headway against traditional horse-drawn vehicles. Most Berliners laughed when the first motor-taxi was introduced in 1899, and six years later there were still 52,000 workhorses in the city. In the first decade of the new century, however, the internal combustion engine began a steady conquest of the streets. In 1905 a motor bus line was in operation on the Friedrichstrasse; hundreds of people gathered at its stops beating one another with umbrellas for a chance to jump aboard. The "luxury bus" service that began in 1909 carrying passengers from the Café Victoria downtown to Luna Park on the Hallensee became a prime attraction for residents and visitors alike. Private cars took a little longer to make their presence felt because they were very expensive, with even the simplest models fetching 2,700 marks. Moreover, at first they were not allowed to go faster than fifteen kilometers per hour, which was the top speed for carriages. Yet by 1913 there were already enough cars on the road that policemen had to be stationed at the main intersections to control the traffic, and after the war Berlin would become the first city in Europe to have a traffic light.

While cars and motor buses were conquering Berlin's streets, an even more spectacular harbinger of the new age, airships, made their first appearance in the skies overhead. When one of the earliest zeppelins, whose construction was financed by public subscription, landed on the outskirts of the capital in 1909, Berliners went wild. Merchants turned the event into a commercial occasion, filling their stores with zeppelin hats, ties, pocket watches, scarves, toys, and cigars. The police warned that people staring up at airships made perfect targets for roving pickpockets, but nothing could detract from the excitement of these amazing machines, which symbolized Germany's technological brilliance.

Fixed-wing aircraft, which were introduced at about the same time, initially encountered some skepticism in Berlin. The local newspapers mocked the Wright brothers when they visited the German capital in 1909 to try to sell their invention to the Prussian War Ministry. The ministry turned them down, saying that airplanes had no future in warfare. But after Orville Wright successfully demonstrated a plane at Tempelhof, attitudes quickly changed, at least among the general populace. One Berlin newspaperman wrote, "The Zeppelin . . . is like a giant bee, a fabulous monster, while the Wright is like a spinning insect, whose wings shimmer in the sunlight and whose delicate skeleton seems transparent. It is something from a fairy tale, a fulfillment of our wildest dreams, a realization of apparent impossibilities." So infectious was the enthusiasm that a sport-flying facility was quickly constructed at Johannisthal outside Berlin, complete with hangers, workshops, and restaurants. From Johannisthal, an aviator named Alfred Frey made the first flight over central Berlin in 1910. Of this historic occasion the *Berliner Tageblatt* wrote: "Everywhere people stood still to observe the flight, shopkeepers and their employees streamed out of the shops, passengers jumped from the trains, all pointing out the air-sailor to one another. Young boys galloped through the streets trying to keep up with the airplane, which, given its great speed, was of course impossible, and some homeowners hurried up to the roof to get a better view." Soon wealthy Berliners were lining up at Johannisthal to go up for joyrides over the city.

During one of the zeppelin overflights in 1911, powerful searchlights illuminated the ship, revealing slogans for various consumer products printed on the sides. Here were two innovations on display simultaneously: flight and electricity. Like airships, electric lighting was a badge of municipal modernity that Berlin wore lavishly and proudly. Berliners called their city "Elektropolis," claiming that it had overtaken Paris as the electrical capital of the world. In addition to pioneering electrified trains and trolleys, Berlin was among the first European cities to replace gas lamps with electric lights in its central streets. In 1910 the first electric advertisement appeared, a sign touting Manoli cigarettes, with the letters revolving in a brightly colored circle. (This immediately yielded a new phrase in Berlin for someone acting weirdly: "He is manoli.") Berliners hoped that electrification would enhance the capital's dubious reputation in Germany. Hans Ostwald, an astute student of life in the big city, wrote that "The profusion of light fills us with wonder. . . . And perhaps as a *Lichtstadt* [city of light], Berlin will win more friends elsewhere in the Reich, will be hailed as a bringer of light." There is no evidence that better lighting made Berlin more popular across Germany, but it did enhance the German capital's reputation as a city of progress. When a delegation of electrical engineers from Melbourne visited Europe in 1912, they beat a path to Berlin as "electrically the most important city."

Another arena in which Berlin competed with Paris involved the department store, a retailing innovation that turned shopping into the quintessential big city experience, a succession of nerve-tingling sensations and rushes of acquisitive fever. The modern department store, observed the Berlin periodical *Die Zukunft*, was a mixture of *Wildness und Weltstadt* (jungle and world city). Wertheim, which opened in 1896 on the Leipzigerstrasse, was Wilhelmian Berlin's most spectacular contribution to this genre. Designed by Alfred Messel, it was a true temple of mass consumption, with a huge central hall lit by chandeliers, upper stories visible through richly carved arches, and row upon row of glass or wooden cases displaying goods from all over the world. Here was the variety of a souk without the discomfort. As the Berlin flaneur Franz Hessel noted, Wertheim and similar Berlin department stores were:

> well organized showplaces that pamper their patrons with a high level of comfort. As we select a meter-long piece of pink elastic cord from one of the circular racks made of bright brass, our gaze rests on marble and mirrors, drifts across glittering parquet floors. In atria and winter gardens we sit on granite benches, our packages in our laps. Art exhibits, which merge into refreshment rooms, interrupt stocks of toys and accouterments for the bath. Between decorative baldachins of silk and satin we wander to the soaps and toothbrushes.

Hessel was surprised that stores like Wertheim, dedicated to mass consumption, did little to accommodate the universal need for kitsch. But there was a good reason for this: the department store was designed to combine convenience with luxury, drawing middle-brow patrons toward a more sophisticated taste. As Hermann Tietz, founder of another retail chain, put it: "The department store hopes to be model and guide for achieving an elevated lifestyle."

Of course, to effect this transformation the stores had first to lure people from the streets into their luxurious web of wares. Thus the new emporia constructed elaborate display windows that rivaled stage sets in their capacity to evoke exotic worlds. The displays often featured mannequins so real looking that passersby were inclined to ask them the time of day. Some of the dummies were even animated, capable of acting out little domestic dramas like dunking a soiled shirt into a basin of soap. Berlin became so taken with this aspect of big-city life that it staged annual window-display contests and christened itself the "city of show windows."

The display windows were models of refined taste compared to another novel means of attracting the attention of Emptor Berlinanus—giant billboards. Entire facades disappeared behind wooden hoardings painted in garish colors. Visiting the city in 1911, the writer Max Brod observed that "All of Berlin is one big placard by [the illustrator] Lucian Bernhard. Doesn't the purple knight with the orange beard fall to his knees on every street corner? Don't prolific hordes of thin greyhounds, lime-green monkeys, cigar-smoking goblins, and tender Gibson girls fill the streets?" Every store, noted another observer, had "its own display, its own illumination, its own mechanical noisemaker" screaming at passersby and turning the streets into "a bewildering mess."

The hordes of people who shopped or worked in Berlin's commercial district needed places to eat that were relatively quick and inexpensive. The department stores installed cafeterias and (another innovation) vending machines so that customers would not have to leave the building to eat or spend too much time doing it. Quick and cheap meals were also available at Aschingers, which may be considered the world's first fast-food chain. At any one of the forty Aschinger branches in the city a hungry patron could get an open-face sandwich for ten pfennigs, or for thirty pfennigs a dish of Loffelerbsen mit Speck, the recipe for which derived from Germany's greatest chemist, Justus von Liebig. Free bread came with every order of beer, a deal that no true Berliner could pass up. Other attractions were spotlessly clean premises and buxom young waitresses dressed in Bavarian-style dirndls, whom Jules Huret found "fresh and appetizing like milkmaids as they stand behind the glass-covered counters."

For those with a little more time and money to spend on a meal, Kempinski in Leipzigerstrasse was the perfect alternative, an "Everyman's Paradise [providing] elegance for all." Most dishes there cost only 75 pfennigs, but for 2 marks 75 pfennigs one could "dine in style with the little lady." Even the kaiser sometimes ate there, which so pleased Kempinski that he placed a bust of His Majesty in the foyer. Later Kempinski opened a second restaurant on the fashionable Kurfürstendamm, where the Hotel Kempinski stands today.

"Man is what he eats," said the philosopher Ludwig Feuerbach. He also is what he reads. At the turn of the century, Berliners read newspapers. They read them so voraciously that the German capital emerged as the newspaper city par excellence, with more papers than London. The media culture helped shape the citizenry, turning legions of freshly arrived country folk into wise-cracking urbanites almost overnight. It also changed the look and feel of the city, as newspaper kiosks sprang up at every major intersection and newspaper vendors prowled the streets shouting the day's headlines.

Among the plethora of new papers founded in the Wilhelmian era, the most important was the *Berliner Morgenpost*, inaugurated in 1898 by the Ullstein press. Aiming at a mass readership, the *Morgenpost* made daily life in the teeming metropolis its main focus. As the paper's first editor declared: "Above all, the *Morgenpost* strives to be a genuinely Berlin paper and as such hopes to be at home in every household in the city. . . . The *Morgenpost* wants to depict Berlin, Berlin as it feels and thinks, as it works and dreams, as it suffers and loves, Berlin the way it really is." To convey this sense of "true Berlin" the paper often employed the distinctive local dialect, turning "g's" into "j's" and "das" into "det," and invented a folksy Ur-Berliner called Rentier Mudicke, who passed on irreverent witticisms in a weekly column. Drawings by Heinrich Zille, the gifted chronicler of Berlin's back streets and tenements, added to the verisimilitude. So too did graphic accounts of murder, rape, suicide, and corruption. As a practical service to its readers, the paper printed streetcar schedules and maps, listed sporting events and cabaret performances, even ran articles on where to find the best meat, butter, and eggs. These and other innovations made the *Morgenpost* an instant success; it boasted 100,000 subscribers after only eight months of operation, and by the turn of the century it was Berlin's largest daily, with almost 200,000 subscribers.

Another new mass circulation paper, *BZ am Mittag*, which first appeared in 1904, relied on street sales rather than home distribution to reach a wide readership. This strategy made good sense because on workdays, when the paper was sold, central Berlin swarmed with pedestrians. On October 1, 1900, some 87,266 people were recorded crossing Potsdamer Platz in the course of a single hour; by 1908 the hourly traffic in the square had risen to 174,000, making it the busiest crossroads in Europe. Aggressive newsboys made sure that no one walked the streets without getting a pitch for the *BZ*.

To grab readers' attention, the *BZ* focused on the more spectacular and colorful dimensions of big-city life. In 1906, for example, it retailed the exploits of a murder suspect named Rudolf Hennig, who had escaped the police by dashing across the rooftops of Prenzlauer Berg, the gritty proletarian district north of the city center. For a full week, the paper kept the story alive with Hennig sightings and mock interviews with the fugitive. Inspired by the *BZ* reports, Hennig imitators donned the green cap and clogs he was reported to favor and began strutting the streets, taunting the cops. A thirteen-year-old boy was shot to death playing the game "Catch Hennig." When the real Hennig was finally run to ground, the paper quickly dropped the story, for it turned out that the notorious criminal was a meek-looking milquetoast totally lacking in gangster charisma.

The Hennig case was still on Berliners' minds when the local papers hit upon an even more piquant tale of life in their city, one that hilariously pointed up the persistent motif of uniform-worship in German society. The story involved an itinerant cobbler named Wilhelm Voigt, who had spent almost half his life behind bars for fraud. One October afternoon in 1906 Voigt donned a Prussian officer's uniform he had bought in a Berlin flea market and began strolling the streets, thinking about how he might obtain a passport so he could emigrate to America. The sudden deference he was accorded in the streets gave him an idea. Spotting a company of soldiers, he commanded them to accompany him by train to the suburb of Köpenick. Upon arriving at the town hall he had his men surround the building while he arrested the mayor "for financial irregularities" and demanded a passport. Informed that the mayor had no authority to issue a passport, Voigt settled for 4,000 marks worth of municipal funds, which he confiscated in the name of the Prussian military, leaving a signed receipt. He then dismissed his guard and disappeared. It took the police several weeks to track him down, and in the meantime the Berlin papers had a new folk hero—the "Captain of Köpenick." Berliners considered the story an excellent joke on fawning suburban officialdom, but of course it was really a joke on the entire city. Kaiser Wilhelm II, a uniform fetishist himself, might have been expected to find this whole business appalling, but instead he found it reassuring: did it not, after all, show that the authoritarian system was alive and well in Berlin despite all the encroachments of urban modernity? When Voigt was returned to prison for fraud, the kaiser arranged a pardon.

BZ am Mittag had taken the lead in turning Wilhelm Voigt into an urban legend, but it failed to exploit the most sensational story of the new century. When a message filtered into the newsroom in the early hours of April 15, 1912, that the liner *Titanic* had gone down off the coast of Newfoundland, the night editor, pressed to get the paper to bed, elected to bury the item on the last page. The Ullstein press prided itself on having a better nose for the drama of modern life than any other newspaper company in the world. With his lapse in judgment that night, the poor editor (in the words of the publisher) "pronounced a death sentence on his career. After that, he never amounted to anything."

For all its urban hustle and trappings of big city life, Berlin at the turn of the century still lacked a key adornment of most major metropolises: first-class hotels that could attract the wealthiest international travelers. The Kaiserhof, which had so impressed Wilhelm I upon its opening in 1875, was already out of date by 1900, and more recently built hotels like the Central at the Friedrichstrasse Station and the Bristol on Unter den Linden were not up to world standards. What the German capital needed was a grand hostelry on the order of Paris's Ritz, Rome's Excelsior, or London's Savoy, but more modern, in keeping with Berlin's obsession with technological innovation.

In the first years of the new century a former carpenter's apprentice from Mainz named Lorenz Adlon set out to repair this deficiency. He had made a fortune in the restaurant business by operating a food concession at the Industrial Exposition of 1896 and by launching Berlin's first genuine French restaurant, the Red Terraces at the Zoo Gardens. Yet such successes had not satisfied this self-made man's lust for wealth and fame; he dreamed of becoming Berlin's own Caesar Ritz. In 1904 he had found an appropriately noble address for his planned undertaking, Nr. 1 Unter den

Hotel Adlon, 1914

Linden, next door to the British Embassy. On the site stood a small palace owned by Count Redern, who was anxious to sell the property in order to pay some gambling debts. But there was a problem with the deal. The Redern Palace had been built by Schinkel and was classed as an historical monument, which protected it from demolition. Luckily for Adlon, Berlin had never been the kind of town to let history stand in the way of progress. Moreover, Kaiser Wilhelm, who knew the entrepreneur, fully shared his dream of bringing a world-class hotel to the German capital. His Majesty and the city fathers saw to it that the legal obstacles impeding the sale and demolition of the Redern Palace were quickly cleared away. "Thank God the old box is finally being torn down," the kaiser is reported to have said. "The thing was a disgrace, blighted my entire Linden. Adlon has promised me to build something more beautiful. My residential city has to become a modern metropolis, don't you think?" As a further act of assistance, the kaiser persuaded the British Embassy to sell part of its garden to create a larger building site.

Lorenz Adlon had promised to build a tour de force of functional magnificence, and this is precisely what he achieved. When the Hotel Adlon opened on October 23, 1907, Berlin's newspapers gushed over suites that were "half-museum, half-living room," bathrooms outfitted with the latest plumbing, and a vast central hall featuring a bust of the kaiser in the style of a Roman emperor. Like no other building in Berlin, the Adlon evoked the pride and power of the new German empire. As one journalist commented, upon entering its stately conference rooms one could easily visualize diplomats redrawing the map of Europe and captains of industry shaping the economic destiny of the world.

The Adlon became a favorite stopover for the globetrotting plutocracy. It was especially popular with Americans, who appreciated its advanced plumbing. Soon other grand hotels sprang up to catch the travel-heavy crowd. The Esplanade, a worthy rival to the Adlon, opened in 1908 on Bellevue Strasse, close to the Potsdamer Platz. It too enjoyed the patronage of Kaiser Wilhelm, for whom one of its grandest reception rooms was named. Like the Adlon, the Esplanade imitated the English fashion of five o'clock tea, during which the jeunesse dorée of Wilhelmian Berlin gathered to gossip and flirt. Slightly less opulent was the Excelsior, which went up across from the Anhalter Bahnhof in 1906–8. According to the snobbish Huret, the public rooms of these grand hotels displayed what passed for "elegance" in imperial Berlin. Here one found "officers with scarred faces, Jewish bankers and their wives, envoys on their way through town, young diplomats on the lookout for rich heiresses, Russian dowagers draped in costly raiment, American ladies wearing flowing veils and gloves running all the way up to their elbows, laughing and talking loudly to the clean-shaven, bespectacled men at their sides."

The new hotels helped to make Berlin a major tourist destination for the first time in its history. In 1913 the number of overnight stays reached 1.4 million, double what it had been in 1896. Between 1909 and 1913 an average of 262,000 foreign guests visited the city annually, of whom 11 percent were Americans and 36 percent Russians. It is noteworthy that Berlin should already have been a favorite among the two nationalities that were to have such a lasting and fateful impact on the German capital.

Berlin Noir

The tourist hordes did not descend on Berlin simply because the hotel situation had improved. The erstwhile capital of Prussian rectitude was finally becoming an amusing place to spend some time, especially at night. Though Berlin was not yet famous around the world for its "decadence," as it would be in the 1920s and early 1930s, Europe's cognoscenti of dissolution were already smacking their lips over the wild things that went on there when the sun went down. After taking several nocturnal tours through Berlin in 1900, the ever-observant Huret could write: "The night life of Berlin is surprisingly lively. Will it surpass even Paris in this respect? Will we have to find a new location for the contemporary Babylon and Nineveh? The carousing continues all night long on Unter den Linden, on the Friedrichstrasse, and around Potsdamer and Leipziger Platz. Many nightspots don't close at all. After the last guests have left, the clubs are quickly cleaned up and then it's time to start all over again." Hans Ostwald, who was an authority on Berlin's seedier side, boasted (a bit prematurely): "If Paris was formerly regarded as the capital of vice and the birthplace of all forbidden pleasures, and if the super-decadent once spoke in hushed tones of the unbeatable delights of Budapest, Cairo, and Rome, today the whole world agrees that it is Berlin which has the most enticing nights."

One of the reasons Berlin's nights were so enticing was that the local authorities, in the interest of promoting tourism and cultivating a reputation for urban flair, did not enforce existing vice laws very strictly. According to a law on the books since 1866, establishments serving alcoholic beverages were supposed to remain closed between 11:00 p.m. and 4:00 a. m., but clubs and bars could apply for special exemption, and they were rarely turned down. Echoing the observation of Monsieur Huret, a police report of 1900 admitted that in the main streets of central Berlin the traditional *Ruhepause* (rest period) in the middle of the night had "almost completely disappeared." Promoters of the "new Berlin" were quick to convey the message that this was a city that did not go to bed. Thus a *Berlin Guide for Connoisseurs* (1912) enthused: "Two o'clock at night. Couples emerge from the Palais de danse and the Moulin Rouge. The glowing red letters at Maxim are extinguished. That is the sign for the lights to go on and the champagne buckets to be set out in the casinos on Unter den Linden, at Toni Grünfeld's club, at Monbijou in the Jägerstraße, in the New Buffet in the Französische Straße, and so forth. . . . This is also the hour of the coquettes, who now, all fresh and frisky, begin their 'day' and completely dominate the milieu."

Dominate indeed. As a garrison town, Berlin had always had plenty of prostitutes, but in the late nineteenth century their numbers exploded as thousands of young women from the countryside gravitated to the big city in search of work.

Well-paying jobs being exceedingly rare for women, many of the girls sold their bodies to make ends meet. Morality crusaders, of which Berlin had its fair share, complained that it was impossible for a gentleman to walk the streets without being constantly accosted by brazen hussies.

In 1891 a sensational murder case cast a lurid light on the prostitution scene in Berlin, bringing calls for an official crackdown. It seems that a pimp named Heinze and his prostitute wife broke into a local church to steal the silver, then killed a night watchman who interrupted their thievery. Arrested and brought to trial, Heinze showed his contempt for the proceedings by swigging from a bottle of champagne in the dock. Indignation over the scandal was so great that the kaiser himself intervened, demanding tougher laws to deal with prostitution and pimping. In response, the imperial government submitted to the Reichstag a law to quarantine prostitutes in brothels supervised by the police. This would, it was claimed, stamp out procurers (not to mention provide a new source of income for the police). Yet to many lawmakers this seemed more like abetting a crime than curtailing it, and the regulation was not instituted nationwide (only Hamburg maintained state-run brothels). In Berlin, street prostitutes and their pimps continued to be a highly visible feature of the nightly scene.

Unable or unwilling to keep prostitutes off the streets, officials in the imperial capital sought to regulate their behavior. All prostitutes were required to register with the police and to submit to regular medical examinations. If a woman was found to be infected with a venereal disease, she was barred from plying her trade until certified as cured. Whores were banned from Unter den Linden and could not solicit business from open carriages. In areas where they were allowed to operate, prostitutes were prohibited from "attracting attention to themselves by standing on curbs or walking up and down in the street"; nor were they allowed to appear in public in the company of their pimps.

These regulations were ineffectual because only a small percentage of the prostitutes paid any attention to them, and the police, many of whom were on the take from pimps, made little effort to enforce them. In 1900 only 1,689 women registered as prostitutes, but the police estimated that over 20,000 were active in the trade. At night they patrolled Unter den Linden as if it were Lovers' Lane, and some of the girls made a specialty of turning tricks in open carriages as they rolled through the Tiergarten. The most heavily infested area was the Friedrichstrasse and the side streets running off it near the Linden. By day this was a busy commercial district, though it was beginning to look a little shabby because some of the better shops were moving to fancier addresses in the "New West." The coffee houses were filled during the afternoons with portly bourgeois ladies stuffing themselves with kuchen, but during the night they catered to parchment-faced men who brought along private supplies of morphine and cocaine. At the corner of Friedrichstrasse and Behrenstrasse stood the Panopticum, a kind of amusement gallery featuring the "fattest and thinnest persons in the world," the "lion-men Lionel and Lentini," and (after 1908) the Captain of Köpenick in person, sitting on a stool in his uniform. By night Wilhelm Voigt and company gave way to hookers so numerous that, as one observer complained, "no decent woman can enter the area without being considered fair game."

The Friedrichstadt also harbored a number of venerable ballrooms that enjoyed a boom at the turn of the century due to the patronage of tourists and naive provincials looking for a hot night on the town. According to a student of the scene, men in frock coats stood inside the doors of these establishments and relieved any innocent-looking visitor of a five-mark cover charge. The rube would then be obliged to order champagne to impress the young woman who instantly materialized at his side. Though he might have preferred an inexpensive domestic brand of drink, the poor provincial would invariably end up with "something French" at eighteen marks the bottle. "Were it not for the tourists and the rustics," noted the observer, "these places could not have survived."

The impresarios of Berlin's raucous nightlife often belonged to underworld societies called *Ringvereine* (sporting associations). These had their origins in an officially sanctioned organization—the Reichsverein ehemaliger Strafgefangener (Reich Association of Former Prisoners)—which was designed to rehabilitate ex-convicts. Almost immediately, the former convicts took over the association and broke it up into smaller groups responsible for drug dealing, smuggling, prostitution, and murder-for-hire. Prospective members of the clubs were required to have served at least two years in prison and to swear an oath to abide by all the group's rules. Dues were stiff, as were the penalties for transgressing any of the codes of conduct. Errant members faced beatings, expulsion, or death, depending on the seriousness of their infraction. In exchange for absolute loyalty, club-brothers enjoyed the right to ply the various criminal trades favored by their group. Should they be arrested, they could count on their club's providing first-rate legal assistance and the funds to bribe witnesses and officials. As masters of their criminal universe, the

Ringvereine were enshrouded in a romantic mythos much like that which later surrounded the Mafia in America.

Berlin Is Not Sodom!

Noting a proliferation in the German capital of *Lustknaben* (young boys catering to male homosexuals) and "women with lesbian tendencies," the author of a pamphlet entitled "Fast-living Nights in the Friedrichstadt" insisted that Berlin had become the "El Dorado of an international rabble spewed out by the other great cities of Europe." As if the city on the Spree did not have enough of its own corruption, this critic fumed, it was "welcoming with open arms the vice-ridden scum from the rest of the world." The rhetoric was a bit hyperbolic, but turn-of-the-century Berlin did harbor an especially sizable homosexual community, many of whose members hailed from other parts of Germany and Europe. In this respect, Wilhelmian Berlin anticipated the "Spree-Babylon" of the Weimar era.

Magnus Hirschfeld, a contemporary authority on this subject and a homosexual himself, argued in a book entitled *Berlins drittes Geschlecht* (Berlin's Third Sex) that the German capital attracted many "persons with other-than-normal sexual inclinations" because they could live there relatively free of interference. Such freedom derived not from official tolerance (male homosexuality was explicitly proscribed by Paragraph 175 of the Prussian Penal Code) but from the opportunity to live unnoticed in the "teeming sea of houses and humanity" that constituted modern Berlin. In the city's labyrinthine apartment complexes, wrote Hirschfeld, "the residents in front rarely know the residents in back, much less care how they live." The capital's internal geography, its varied districts separated by vast distances, allowed people to lead double lives. A Berliner living in the east could meet regularly with a friend in the south without his or her neighbors having a clue. Hirschfeld knew of a buttoned-down gay lawyer with offices in Potsdam who spent his nights at a seedy *Kneipe* in the Friedrichstadt with the likes of "Revolver-Heini, Butcher-Hermann, and Amerika-Franzl." There was a regular round of private dinners and artistic evenings in the gay community, especially among the wealthy. Hirschfeld was invited to an all-male dinner attended exclusively by nobles. While dining on exquisite food, the guests chatted about the latest Wagner performances, "for which practically all educated Berlin homosexuals have a particularly strong sympathy." He also attended a private party at one of Berlin's grandest hotels, which included a performance of *The Merry Wives of Windsor* with an all-male cast. After the performance there was a dance, and "although the wine flowed freely, nothing indecent occurred." Such was probably not the case in an opulent suite at the Hotel Bristol, where Friedrich Krupp, Germany's wealthiest industrialist, regularly entertained young Italian waiters employed at the hotel at his expense. Berlin gays willing to risk attention from the police could frequent well-known "cruising points," such as the exotic postcard shop at the Panopticum or the chestnut grove at the Sing-akademie. Drinking establishments catering to a homosexual clientele also abounded in the city, especially in the Friedrichstadt. On the eve of World War I, Berlin had about forty homosexual bars, and the police estimated that there were between 1,000 and 2,000 male prostitutes.

Although Berlin increasingly took homosexuality in stride as another dimension of life in the modern megalopolis, the city could still be scandalized when gay behavior intersected with high politics. This happened with a vengeance in 1907/8

Magnus Hirschfeld (second from right), founder of the Institute for Sexual Research

when a group of friends of Kaiser Wilhelm II, known as the Liebenberger Circle, were exposed as homosexuals by the muckraking journalist Maximilian Harden. At the center of the storm was Prince Philipp ("Phili") zu Eulenburg, a close confidant of the kaiser, who had served as Berlin's ambassador to Vienna. Eulenburg often entertained His Majesty and other illustrious friends at Liebenberg, his country estate outside the capital. In return, Wilhelm sometimes took Phili along on his ocean cruises. Some of the others caught up in the scandal were Count Kuno von Moltke, commandant of the Berlin garrison; Count Wilhelm von Hohenau, one of the kaiser's aides-de-camp; and Baron Axel von Varnbüler, Württemburg's diplomatic representative in Berlin. None of these men was openly homosexual, for they all understood that they could not acknowledge their predilection without social disgrace and possible legal prosecution. They might have continued to pursue their double lives without interference had not Harden, editor of the Berlin journal *Die Zukunft*, decided that they encouraged the kaiser's illusions of grandeur. Using inside information about the men's intimate affairs supplied by Chancellor Bernard von Bülow, who also considered the Liebenbergers a menace, Harden published two articles calling attention to the group's activities. He did not use the word "homosexual," but everyone knew what he meant.

Berlin was plunged into an uproar over Harden's allegations. All the major dailies covered the story, often adding salubrious details of their own. The only person in town who was unaware of the scandal was the kaiser, who rarely read the newspapers and whose ears were protected from nasty gossip by sycophantic courtiers. His handlers were especially reticent in this instance because they sensed that His Majesty himself harbored homosexual tendencies, albeit deeply repressed. Eventually Crown Prince Wilhelm, fearing that the affair could undermine the monarchy, told his father what was going on. The kaiser was aghast. Telling Eulenburg that he would have to be "cleared or stoned," he ordered his friend to bring legal proceedings against Harden.

Because he knew how damaging a court case could be, Eulenburg refused to take action against the journalist. Kuno von Moltke, however, was not so cautious, and brought an official action for slander in October 1907. Spectators in the court were treated to a detailed exposition of male orgies among Berlin's elite guard regiments. The steamy testimony in the Moltke trial prompted some parliamentarians to raise questions in the Reichstag about the moral character of the army and the imperial court. A Center Party deputy declared that the offenses in question were "reminiscent of pagan Rome." Chancellor Bülow admitted that the case filled him "with disgust and shame," though he insisted that there was no proof that the army was "rotten at heart" or that the kaiser's character was anything but "a fair model to the nation." Berlin "is not Sodom," he added. Bülow's lame defense hardly reassured the kaiser, who was enraged that the "band of rascals" in parliament had had the temerity to discuss this issue at all.

The action shifted back to the legal arena in November when the editor of a magazine for homosexuals suggested that Chancellor Bülow himself was "one of us," his protestations of shame notwithstanding. Bülow promptly sued the magazine for slander. During the course of the trial Eulenburg appeared on behalf of Bülow (he was obviously unaware that the chancellor had been the source of his own humiliating outing) and swore that neither he nor the plaintiff had ever engaged in activities as defined by Paragraph 175 of the Prussian legal code. Although Bülow's case was successful, Eulenburg's testimony proved a disaster for the prince, because in yet another trial, this one engineered by Harden to set up Eulenburg, the writer got two Bavarian working-class men to swear that they had had sex with the statesman. In May 1908 Eulenburg was ordered to stand trial for perjury, but the case was broken off without result when the prince suffered a nervous collapse. Eventually he was allowed to return to Liebenberg, where he lived in seclusion and disgrace until his death in 1921. He had hoped for absolution from the kaiser, but Wilhelm could never forgive him for bringing embarrassment on the royal house. Nor, for that matter, could the monarch forgive "his Berliners" for taking such obvious delight in his humiliation.

Red Berlin

In becoming a modern metropolis, Wilhelmian Berlin also became a *Fabrikstadt* (factory city) par excellence. Walther Rathenau put it best: "What really makes [Berlin] important is our factory-district, which is perhaps the largest in the world though mainly unknown to the inhabitants of the western part of the city. To the north, south, and east the worker-city stretches out its polyp arms and grasps the Westend in an iron grip."

Berlin's factories came in all sizes, but the trend was toward larger and larger establishments. In 1895, 20,000 workers toiled in factories employing fifty workers or more; by 1907 that figure had risen to 70,000. The new mega-factories prided themselves on their rationalized division of labor. Whereas workers in craft shops and small factories often fabricated entire products by themselves, workers at the giant modern plants tended to specialize in one aspect of production, such as milling or lathe operations. These tasks required precision, dexterity, and discipline, and the Wilhelmian factory was a tightly controlled environment, a kind of industrial barracks. The *Werkstatt-Ordnung* (operating procedure) from Siemens und Halske, one of Berlin's largest firms, was typical in its regimentation of the workplace. It required workers to carry identification cards at all times, obey foremen without question, keep exact account of tools (and pay for any that went missing), maintain workstations in an orderly condition, leave their stations only with permission of the foremen, and receive visitors only in cases of emergency. The work itself seems to have provided little compensation for the regimentation. A 1910 survey asked metal workers in Berlin, Solingen, and Idar-Oberstein whether they found any pleasure in their work. A majority (56.9 percent) said they did not, with respondents adding comments like "Making mass-produced articles repulses me"; "I feel like a machine, forced to keep going"; and "I do my work mechanically."

Yet in many ways the conditions of labor in Berlin's factories had improved since the beginning of the Bismarckian era. The average workday had declined from twelve hours in 1870 to nine or ten hours in 1910. In the last years before the war, workers typically got forty-five minutes off for breakfast and about one hour off for lunch. Because employers had to help pay for the national accident-insurance program introduced by Bismarck, safety measures had been inaugurated that significantly reduced the number of industrial accidents. Some employers set up pension plans for their workers, funded awards for good work or long service, and provided employee-families with subsidized housing, schools, and holiday excursions.

One growing segment of the Berlin labor force—females—largely missed out on these benefits. This was because the majority of working women toiled as domestic servants or as seamstresses in the booming garment trade, which remained unregulated. The seamstresses often worked at home, obtaining their materials from large textile companies that provided cloth in exchange for piecework commitments. The women bought their sewing machines from unscrupulous door-to-door salesmen who prowled the proletarian districts. On average, they worked twelve-hour days for about five or six marks per week, which was less than a fourth of the average wage for male factory workers. Wages in the garment industry actually went down in the late Wilhelmian era, due largely to the huge number of women and girls willing to work for next to nothing to help support their families.

The plight of Berlin's female garment workers was the subject of a Home-Work exhibition in 1906, organized by the Christian Home Workers' Association. The exhibition was promoted by a Käthe Kollwitz poster showing a proletarian woman with a wan face and exhausted eyes. Empress Augusta, who was scheduled to open the show, refused to do so until the poster, which she said was depressing, was removed. Visitors who expected to find a celebration of fine handiwork discovered instead a cleverly designed protest against female exploitation. As the middle-brow magazine *Die Gartenlaube* reported: "Whosoever enters [the exhibition] feels at first a disappointment. The items on display suggest neither elegance nor comfort. . . . [We soon realize] that we are not meant to look at the wares but at the little tags that record how much the worker was paid for each piece." The payments were shockingly low, a small percentage of the sums that the garments commanded in the stores. For example, an apron carrying a retail price of two marks fifty pfennigs brought the seamstress only twenty-five pfennigs.

Another exhibition on female labor held six years later sought to tell a different story. The Women at Home and Work Show argued that women could be both good wives and mothers *and* hold responsible jobs outside the home. The focus here was on the female employees who were streaming into Berlin's growing service industry as typists, stenographers, and file clerks. In 1907 women comprised 27 percent of the local service economy, compared to 19.6 percent twelve years earlier. Unlike the seamstresses, the service employees often came from lower-middle-class backgrounds and went to work to gain a measure of freedom from home life. Riding to work on the trains and trolleys, eating at Aschingers with colleagues, and window-shopping in the evening, these women were as integral to Berlin's urban landscape as were the armies of male commuters crisscrossing the city.

Although female labor was proving increasingly essential to Berlin's economy, many social commentators, especially those of a conservative bent, expressed anxiety over the deleterious effects this activity was believed to have on the well-being of the workers and, by extension, on the nation as a whole. Women, it was claimed, were in danger of becoming so debilitated by the pressures of wage labor that they might have difficulty performing their true calling as wives and mothers. An article entitled "The Effect of Sewing Machine Work on the Female Genital Organs" (1897) argued that long hours at the Singer could render a woman unable to conceive children. Other experts insisted that factory labor inhibited lactation. Whatever their physical state, working women had less time to spend caring for their families. Berlin factory inspectors attributed high rates of child mortality and illnesses among infants to neglect by working mothers. Added to these health dangers were the negative moral consequences that female factory labor was said to yield. A report published in 1886 stated that "almost all" the women working in Berlin's linen factories were living "in intimate contact" with men who were not their husbands. Four years later, a Reichstag commission firmly reasserted the traditional wisdom that a woman's place was "at the cradle of her child," not in some factory or office. For once, Kaiser Wilhelm II could only agree with the parliamentarians. Berlin's women, he said, should take his own wife as a model, who had stayed home and produced six sons for the Fatherland. (In private, Wilhelm let it be known that he considered Donna "nothing but a broodhen," and he wanted her to stay at home so she could not embarrass him in public with her provinciality.)

Berlin's working-class women, whether or not they toiled for wages, bore the primary responsibility for managing family budgets, which were always stretched to the limit. The basic necessities of life—housing, food, fuel, and clothing—often required all the income a proletarian family could generate. Affordable housing remained the biggest challenge. At the turn of the century a typical one-room apartment (with kitchen but no bath) in one of the "rental barracks" cost 250 marks a year, or about one-quarter of the annual income of a skilled worker. Fully half of that income generally went for food, the staples being potatoes, bread, sausage, and lard. Another necessity was beer, which typically consumed one-fifth of a worker's annual wages.

If money was always tight, daily life was not uniformly drab for Berlin's working classes. The proletarian districts and suburbs certainly looked grim to outsiders, but they contained pockets of energy and vitality. Aside from hundreds of *Kneipen* (taverns), there were bowling lanes, ice-skating rinks, and makeshift carnivals set up on construction sites. Because the proletarian suburbs were situated on the edge of an expanding city, they magnified the sense of change and flux that characterized metropolitan life. As a novel of the period related, "Buildings change hands three times before they are completed. . . . Where there is a cheese shop today, there will be a shoe store tomorrow, and electric lamps in the window the day after."

The residents themselves were in constant movement, changing apartments, commuting to work across town, and on Sundays and holidays making excursions to lakes, parks, and amusement centers. The Berlin Zoo lowered its entrance fee to twenty-five pfennigs one Sunday each month, allowing working-class Berliners to charge en masse through its famous Elephant Gate. "Today the real Berliner sets the tone! Little people with bag and baggage, and wrapped sandwiches and big hair with all sorts of pins and needles sticking out," observed the *Berliner Illustrierte Zeitung.*

Wilhelmian Berlin's economy was fluid enough to allow working-class types with a strong entrepreneurial spirit to improve their lot in life, perhaps by opening a tavern or running a moving service. The newspapers often ran inspirational stories of upward mobility, offering these success stories as proof that Berlin was the ideal spot for a little man with big ambitions—one need not decamp to America! But there was also plenty of opportunity to move in the other direction and to end up, say, frequenting the municipal shelter at Jannowitzbrücke. Worse, one's name might be added to the growing number of suicide cases reported each week in the newspapers.

Of course, the vast majority of Berlin's workers neither moved up to the bourgeoisie nor leaped into the Spree; rather, they did their best to improve their situation little by little, often by joining the Social Democratic Party and/or a trade union, the two prime sources of organizational clout for industrial workers in imperial Germany.

We have seen that the Socialists were making significant gains in Berlin during Bismarck's time despite the existence of the Anti-Socialist Law. With its repeal in 1890, the party and the affiliated union movement grew even faster. By the turn of the century it became commonplace to speak of the German capital as "Red Berlin." While this development filled local proletarians with pride, it understandably horrified conservative elements among the middle and upper classes, and it added a new dimension to Berlin's problematical reputation in the rest of the Reich. The sprawling capital, it seemed, was a breeding ground not just of moral and cultural corruption but also of political subversion. The "Whore on the Spree" wore a red garter!

In 1890 the SPD built a new headquarters at 69 Lindenstrasse. The massive building, whose 500,000-mark cost was covered by members' dues and local donations, was seen by the Berlin workers as their answer to a recent statement by Kaiser Wilhelm that Social Democracy was a passing phenomenon. The kaiser obviously had his head in the sand. In 1890 the Socialist party counted 100,000 members nationwide, about 10,000 in Berlin. Six years later, the Berlin membership had jumped to 41,700, making it the largest municipal branch in the country. As of 1884, two of Berlin's six Reichstag seats (those serving the proletarian areas in the north and east) were firmly in Socialist hands, and after 1893 three other electoral districts voted consistently for the SPD. In the 1887 Reichstag elections 40.2 percent of Berlin's voters opted for the Socialists; by 1903 the figure was up to 48.5 percent, and in 1912, the high-water mark of Socialist success, 75.3 percent. August Bebel's boast that "Berlin belongs to us," which had been somewhat premature in 1878, now had a good measure of validity, at least with respect to the city's representation in the Reichstag.

The SPD had more difficulty cracking Berlin's city assembly and the Prussian Landtag (state parliament), where Prussia's three-class voting system made electoral clout directly proportional to the amount of taxes a citizen paid. In 1909, for example, each class elected forty-eight delegates to the city assembly, but the first class, whose members paid a minimum annual tax of 42,000 marks, contained only 1,800 voters; the second, paying a minimum of 178 marks, embraced 32,000 voters; and the last class, consisting of all the remaining eligible voters (males over twenty-four), numbered 336,000. Elections for the city assembly and Prussian parliament, moreover, were not direct; voters chose "electoral representatives" who then cast the final votes in a public ballot. As an added hurdle to the Socialists, the city assembly required that one-half of its membership be composed of home owners, which ruled out most workers. Frustration over this rigged system induced many proletarians to abstain from voting in municipal elections; in 1903 some 48 percent of the third-class voters did not go to the polls; in 1907 the figure was 58.5 percent. Yet even here the Socialists managed to gain a foothold; in 1890 they won eleven seats in the assembly and in 1900 doubled that figure to twenty-two (out of 144). They made their first inroads into the Prussian parliament in 1908, when the SPD sent seven representatives (out of 443) to that body, six of them from Berlin.

The SPD's electoral successes in the national capital were due in part to the party's ability to transcend class boundaries. Although socialism remained overwhelmingly a working-class movement, it also attracted bourgeois intellectuals and professionals who dreamed of a truly democratic and socially unified Germany, and who envisaged Berlin as the catalyst for that transformation. Most of the men whom the party sent to the various political bodies came from this group rather than from the working-class rank and file.

Paul Singer, who represented Berlin's fourth district in the Reichstag from 1884 until his death in 1911, was a case in point. The son of a Jewish businessman, he built the family clothing firm on Berlin's Dönhoffplatz into a thriving enterprise. As a political moderate, he worked effectively with his non-Socialist colleagues in the

Karl Liebknecht (middle) and Rosa Luxemburg, 1909

parliament. Singer found theoretical ammunition for his pragmatic approach in the writings of Eduard Bernstein, a Berlin intellectual who called for replacing the Marxian dogma of inevitable social revolution with a policy of practical reformism.

The reformist approach preached by Bernstein and applied by Singer gained momentum within the Socialist movement, especially in Berlin, because the SPD's electoral successes held out the promise of power through ballots rather than through bullets or barricades. On the other hand, the reformists had to admit that increased Socialist representation in the Reichstag would not bring genuine democracy to Germany unless that body itself attained greater clout in the political system. Still, the very act of electoral campaigning was a sign of faith that the system could be changed, and it undoubtedly absorbed energies that might otherwise have gone into revolutionary activism. The radical fervor of the party's rank and file, meanwhile, was gradually blunted by improvements in wages, working conditions, and social welfare. Moreover, Berlin's workers, like those of Germany as a whole, were increasingly proud of their nation's accomplishments. The SPD officially professed loyalty to the international brotherhood of workers, but under the surface its members were often quite patriotic, even nationalistic. In Berlin a typical working-class parlor might display portraits of Bismarck and Moltke side by side with Marx and Engels.

The trade unions to which many Socialist workers belonged also encouraged reformism. The union movement advanced in Berlin along with the city's rapid industrialization. In 1905 the Berlin Union Commission embraced 224,000 members in eighty organizations, of which the metal workers, transport workers, and builders were the largest. Like the Social Democratic Party, the Union Commission built a new headquarters at the turn of the century. Berlin workers called the imposing Gothic-style pile on the Engelufer their "palace," and it looked no different from the heavily ornamented headquarters of the various employers' associations. The union leaders had struggled hard to build up their organization and were disinclined to embrace any measures or ideas that might compromise what they had gained. In essence, they were willing to try to work through the capitalist system in which they had carved a place for themselves.

This policy was anathema to a radical wing of the SPD led by Franz Mehring, Rosa Luxemburg, and Karl Liebknecht. Inspired by the 1905 revolution in Russia, these figures believed that proletarians across Europe must gird themselves for a revolutionary struggle against the possessing classes. Luxemburg was especially adept at preaching the radicals' message to the masses of Berlin. This is ironic, for she was not a Berliner, nor even a German, but a Polish Jew who in 1898 (in the words of one of her biographers) had "descended upon the massive gray city like an exotic colorful bird." Yet it would be a mistake to confuse her prowess as a tub-thumper for genuine influence; her following in Berlin remained quite small.

While Luxemburg and her friends tended to exaggerate their influence, their questioning of the reformists' efforts to work peacefully within the system had some validity. For the most part, Germany's economic and political leadership was disinclined to cooperate with the organized Left, whom the kaiser famously branded "scoundrels without a Fatherland." In the Wilhelmian period the unions did not yet enjoy the unquestioned right to bargain collectively. As often as not, employers simply ignored the unions when they tried to press for higher wages or better working conditions for their members. This left the unions with little option but to strike, which was dangerous given the employers' readiness to bring in strikebreakers and the authorities' willingness to support the bosses, with force if necessary. Berlin, as headquarters both of the German labor movement and of the chief employers' associations, became the country's primary center of labor strife in the decade before World War I.

Every year, it seemed, some faction was in the streets, carrying placards and shouting demands. In 1900 the tram workers went out for several days, throwing the city into chaos. The troops were called out, and Kaiser Wilhelm, who had balked at the prospect of a civil war when he took the throne, told the commanding general that he hoped "five hundred people [among the strikers] might be gunned down." Two years later the German Metal Workers' Association, Berlin's largest union, walked off their jobs to protest the firing of a worker's representative who had been fired for trying to restore the docked wages of a colleague. When the employers brought in strikebreakers, other unions staged sympathy strikes, which shut down the proletarian district of Wedding for fourteen days. The metal workers won that round, but they were less successful when they struck for higher wages in two waves of walkouts in 1905–6 and 1910–12; in every instance, the police came out in force to protect the scabs who broke the strikes.

Economic grievances were not the only cause for work-actions. Berlin's workers tried to use the strike weapon to force the government to liberalize the Prussian electoral system that so patently discriminated against the lower classes. A token reform in 1910, which did nothing to alleviate the basic injustice, prompted a series of Sunday demonstrations in the capital, each larger than the one before. In February the Berlin police president banned the demonstrations on the grounds that the streets were "reserved for the exclusive use of traffic." Wishing both to evade a clash with the police and to score a symbolic victory, on March 6 the SPD announced a "suffrage promenade" to Treptow Park, which drew the forces of law and order to that outlying district. Meanwhile, the real march occurred right in the middle of town and was over by the time the exhausted police arrived to break it up.

This was an impressive display of working-class discipline but also another indication of the SPD's strategic caution. Some of the radicals thought that the strikes and demonstrations in 1910 meant that Berlin's masses were about to rise up and overthrow the kaiser, but they mistook restlessness for revolution. It would take the misery of four years of war, capped by the humiliation of defeat, to turn the capital of German imperialism into the capital of the German revolution.

Kaiser Wilhelm II proclaims war from a balcony of the Royal Palace, August 1, 1914

DISCORD IN THE CASTLE

Berlin, the Reich capital, must and will take the lead in terms of discipline and willingness for sacrifice.

—Anton Wermuth,
Lord Mayor of Berlin, 1914

On August 1, 1914, Kaiser Wilhelm II announced to a cheering crowd of Berliners that Germany was mobilizing for war against Russia. Three days later the cast of enemies also included France and Great Britain, and young men began boarding trains to take them off to battle. After a peace of forty-three years, Berlin was again on a war footing, but this war would be much different from the ones that had turned the Prussian *Residenzstadt* into Europe's newest national capital. World War I, largely the fruit of Germany's desperate desire for world-power status, would destroy the German empire forever and wreck Berlin's bid to match London as a great imperial city. Intended also to pull the nation together and to shore up authoritarian rule at home, the war would divide the country as never before, giving impetus to a revolution that ended five hundred years of Hohenzollern rule in Prussia. As the national capital, Berlin was the nerve center of the German war effort but also the place where social divisions and organizational inadequacies were most sharply revealed. The city would emerge much chastened from the long ordeal—less on the make than on the mend.

A Place in the Sun

Germany had gained its first colonies under Bismarck, but the Iron Chancellor had not thought of the Reich as a global power. It was otherwise with Wilhelm II, who announced on the twenty-fifth anniversary of German unification in 1896 that "The German empire has become a world-empire." As if to prove this assertion, he immediately challenged Great Britain by encouraging South Africa's President Paul Kruger and his Boers in their rebellion against British control of the Cape. Wilhelm's "Kruger Telegram" (1896) provoked indignation in Britain, whose press raged in unison over "German impudence." Queen Victoria chided her grandson for "a very unfriendly gesture" that had "made a most unfortunate impression" in England. But the initiative went down well in Berlin, where the newspapers for once had nothing but good to say about the kaiser's leadership. "Our press is wonderful," exulted State Secretary for Foreign Affairs Baron Adolf von Marschall. "All the parties are of one mind, and even Auntie Voss [the liberal *Vossische Zeitung*] wants to fight."

In the early years of the century Berlin also managed to irritate America, which the kaiser had been trying to woo with flattery and courtly gestures. Seeing America's young president, Theodore Roosevelt, as a Yankee version of his own swaggering self, Wilhelm ordered a medal struck in the president's honor. His government presented the people of the United States with a bronze statue of Frederick the Great, proposing that it be erected on Pennsylvania Avenue. But Germany's actions spoke louder than its awkward gestures of friendship. In 1901 it tried to dislodge America from Samoa, which Germany had colonized in the late 1870s along with the United States and Britain. A year later Berlin sent gunboats to the Caribbean to punish Venezuela for defaulting on some debts. Although Germany disclaimed any intention of occupying Venezuelan territory, Washington was not pleased to see German vessels operating in its "lake." President Roosevelt let it be known that he thought the kaiser a "jumpy" fellow, perhaps even mad. And in view of Germany's sudden incursion into the Caribbean, some Americans proposed that the United States reciprocate Wilhelm's gift of Frederick the Great with a statue of James Monroe for Berlin's Unter den Linden.

Still, it was not Washington but London that was most alarmed by Germany's aggressive new tack. King Edward VII, who took the throne in 1901, was considerably more anti-German than his mother. He considered his German nephew a bully and a coward, "the most brilliant failure in history." He worried that Wilhelm would find extensive support for his bluster among his fellow Germans, who seemed fully to share their monarch's desperate need to make a splash.

Wilhelm was aware of Edward's view and reacted with understandable bitterness. "My uncle never seems to realize that I am a sovereign," he complained, "but treats me as if I were a little boy." Wilhelm resented it, too, that King Edward condescended to visit Berlin only once, though he was always running off to France. Apparently Edward and his English relatives imagined Berlin (in Wilhelm's words) to be "a beastly hole." When the king and his entourage finally did visit Berlin, they expressed surprise, according to an exasperated Wilhelm, at discovering "that Berlin actually had streets on which one could find hotels and big stores. . . . The worthy British seem to have got the impression that they were going to the Eskimos in the farthest backwoods or to the *Botokunden*." The Kaiser's sense of being unjustifiably looked down upon by his English relatives closely matched the feeling that many Germans had about the English. Remarking on Britain's arrogance, Professor Theodor Schiemann at the University of Berlin complained that "England is still the state which has least adjusted to the fact that Germany is an emerging world power. . . . [But Berlin is prepared] to compel that recognition."

Prepared indeed. At the end of the nineteenth century, the Kaiser's government decided to get Britain's attention in the most dramatic way possible, short of laying siege to the Tower of London. The Reich would build a battle fleet potent enough to challenge Britain's supremacy on the high seas.

This represented a major strategic departure for Germany. Prussia had unified the nation with battalions, not boats. During the Franco-Prussian War the entire Prussian navy, consisting of four ironclads, had remained at anchor in Wilhelmshaven, fearful of confronting the French. In the early years of the empire, military spending had been focused on the land army, not on the tiny imperial navy. Few Germans, least of all landlubber Berliners, could have been convinced when their ocean-loving kaiser had suddenly proclaimed, in 1891, "Our future is on the water."

In order to enlighten his people on the need for a strong navy, Wilhelm relied upon the propagandistic genius of his new secretary of the Imperial Naval Office,

Admiral Alfred von Tirpitz. A huge man with a fierce forked beard, Tirpitz was an avid student of the American strategic theorist Admiral Mahan, who held that sea power was the key to world power. Having earned his high rank by winning bureaucratic battles within Germany's military establishment, Tirpitz fully appreciated the challenge inherent in convincing the German people of Mahan's wisdom.

The kaiser's government brought its first major naval spending bill before the Reichstag in 1898. It faced opposition not only from the Social Democrats, who ritually rejected most military outlays, but also from the Conservatives, who preferred to spend money on the army. To muster support for the bill, Tirpitz sought the endorsement of former chancellor Bismarck, but the old man was willing to back only a minor increase in naval power. If the Germans ever had to fight the British, Bismarck believed, they should "slay them with the butt-ends of [their] rifles." Tirpitz had better luck among nationalist academics, whom he wooed with guided tours of Germany's main naval base at Wilhelmshaven. The professors obligingly wrote newspaper articles explaining the life-and-death imperatives of a high-seas fleet. By identifying a large fleet with the nation's economic development, the admiral also won the support of commercial and industrial interests across the Reich, especially in Berlin. As the debates on the naval bill progressed in the Reichstag, Tirpitz made a point of inviting key legislators for chats in his office on Leipzigerplatz. To overcome conservative deputies' reservations about investing in a navy, he pointed out that a big fleet could be a rallying-point for the forces of order against the SPD. As a result of this expert political spadework, the First Naval Bill passed the Reichstag with a vote of 221 to 139. It provided for a naval force of nineteen battleships, twelve large cruisers, thirty small cruisers, and an array of support vessels.

But this was only the beginning. Two years later Tirpitz went back to the Reichstag with a new naval measure that called for doubling the number of battleships to thirty-nine. Without specifically mentioning Britain, the admiral made clear that the larger fleet was necessary to intimidate that island power. This argument, however, was not by itself convincing enough to win the day in the Reichstag. He secured passage of the Second Naval Bill only with some old-fashioned political logrolling. In brief, he promised the Conservatives higher tariffs on grain imports (duly introduced in 1902), while the clerical Center Party was given a larger influence in educational and cultural affairs.

In Berlin the naval buildup quickly caught fire. Self-interest on the part of groups and institutions that stood to profit from it played a significant role here.

The Technical University's department of shipbuilding, created in 1894, added a number of new faculty, all of them eager propagandists for naval expansion. Not to be outdone, the University of Berlin established its own "Institute for Ocean Research." Its faculty worked closely with industrial firms in Berlin that built components for the new vessels. Bankers with investments in overseas trade promoted the fleet expansion in the expectation that it would make their ventures more secure. Yet maritime enthusiasm was not restricted to those who stood to gain directly from the construction of a large fleet. Berlin's chapter of the Navy League was filled with middle-class naval buffs who collected pictures of battleships and thrilled to the idea of the Reich competing with Britain to rule the waves. The League sponsored a Naval Museum in the capital, which opened with much fanfare in 1906. Two years later a large naval and maritime exhibition was held on the grounds of the Berlin Zoo.

Berlin's enthusiasm was matched by London's consternation. Determined that Germany not close the naval gap between the two nations, Britain added significantly to its own great fleet, concentrating on the massive Dreadnought-class battleships, which bore the name of eight previous Royal Navy vessels, the first of which had helped Sir Francis Drake defeat the Spanish Armada. Britain calculated that it would be difficult for Germany to match it ship for ship while simultaneously maintaining a huge land army. In 1904 London also abandoned its long-cherished policy of "splendid isolation" by forging the Entente Cordiale with France, one of its main imperial rivals. As a signal of the new cordiality, Paris renounced its claims in Egypt, while Britain recognized France's dominating interest in Morocco.

This amounted to a major rearrangement of the political chessboard to the disadvantage of the Reich. Alarmed, Germany decided to show Paris that it could not count on its new British partner in a diplomatic crisis. In March 1905, during a pleasure cruise in the Mediterranean, Kaiser Wilhelm disembarked at Tangier to announce that Berlin would protect the independence of Morocco. France immediately protested Berlin's "interference," and London, much to Berlin's chagrin, seconded the protest. Still hoping to isolate France, Germany called for an international conference to determine Morocco's fate. When the conference convened in January 1906 at the Spanish port of Algeciras, only Austria-Hungary sided with the Reich.

Having inadvertently pushed London and France into bed together, Berlin managed to spur another anti-German coupling on the part of Britain and Russia, old colonial rivals in Central Asia and the Far East. Russia had been looking for support in Europe since its humiliating defeat by Japan in 1905. Germany would have been its natural choice as a partner, given the dynastic ties and strong political affinities between the two authoritarian monarchies. Moreover, Berlin banks had provided much of the funding for Russian economic development, and the German capital was a favorite stopping-off point for Russian aristocrats on their way to the great Central European spas. But precisely because there was so much that pulled Russia toward Berlin, Kaiser Wilhelm's government did little to nurture the Russo-German relationship. On the contrary, it let Bismarck's Reinsurance Treaty lapse and gave in to pressures from domestic grain producers for high import tariffs on wheat and rye, which hurt Russian exporters. St. Petersburg thus began working to mend its fences with Britain. The result was the Anglo-Russian Entente of 1907, a pairing so odd that only mutual anxiety over German *Weltpolitik* could have brought it about. As the kaiser himself was obliged to admit, "Yes, when taken all around, [the Anglo-Russian Entente] is aimed at us."

Genuinely concerned and nonplussed over the apparent enmity towards Germany in much of the world, Wilhelm decided to combat the trend through personal diplomacy, starting with England. He would show his friends and relatives there that they had nothing to fear from Berlin. On a state visit to Britain in autumn 1907 he held several informal conversations with a pro-German English grandee named Colonel Edward Stuart Wortley. Among other confidences, Wilhelm informed Wortley that he had personally drafted the plan by which Britain had been able to defeat the Boers. He claimed also that Berlin, despite considerable pressure from France and Russia, had refused to join a continental alliance designed to help the South African rebels. As for the new German navy, that was designed only to protect German trade, especially in the Far East, where the "Yellow Peril" was giving cause for grave concern. Since British interests were also threatened by the Japanese, said the kaiser, London might be damn glad one day that Germany had a big fleet! The final point, then, was that the English were "mad as hatters" to harbor suspicions against Germany.

Wortley, who was rather a dim bulb, thought Wilhelm's remarks would do wonders for Anglo-German relations if they were published in a national newspaper. However, before going ahead with publication, he dispatched a text of the comments to Wilhelm for his approval. The kaiser found everything satisfactory, but just to be on the safe side he turned the manuscript over to Chancellor Bülow for vetting. Busy with other matters, Bülow did not bother to read it, and the "interview" came out in the *Daily Telegraph* in November 1908.

The kaiser's observations served to strengthen the growing fear in Britain that the German ruler was little short of a lunatic. In Berlin, the affair caused even greater dismay. Most Germans had always supported the Boers, and they assumed that the kaiser had too, but now he was claiming to have helped to defeat them! Worse, his boastful assertions harmonized all too perfectly with stereotypes of the Germans as pushy political parvenus striving desperately to impress. Berlin's newspapers, even the promonarchical ones, chastised the ruler for making the entire nation look foolish. Baroness von Spitzemberg aptly summed up the prevailing sentiment in her diary: "[Wilhelm] ruins our political position and makes us the laughing stock of the world. It makes one wonder whether one is in a madhouse." Various parliamentary deputies took up the kaiser's gaffe in the Reichstag, criticizing the monarch with a vehemence unprecedented in German political history. Chancellor Bülow, who was partly responsible for the mess, did nothing to defend his sovereign. Instead, he lamely promised to persuade Wilhelm to act with more discretion in the future.

The kaiser, still smarting from his humiliation in the Eulenburg affair, was thrown into a deep depression by the attacks. "What a wretched man am I!" he penned in the margin of a letter from Bülow. "What crime have I committed that God should punish me by making me ruler of this people?" As often, he focused his bitterness on Berlin, where the attacks had been concentrated. What could one expect, he asked, from the "Jewish press carnival" that dominated the capital? To escape the insults he fled to Max von Fürstenberg's hunting estate at Donau-Eschingen, where some old friends tried to cheer him up by dressing as ballerinas and putting on a dance. Unfortunately, the star of the show, Field Marshal Dietrich von Hülsen-Haeseler, chief of the military cabinet, dropped dead of a heart attack in the middle of the performance. When reports of this macabre spectacle reached the capital, they only heightened the doubts that many Berliners harbored about Wilhelm and his entourage.

Despite all the hand-wringing over Wilhelm's recklessness, however, no substantial political changes emerged from the *Daily Telegraph* fiasco. The Reichstag made no attempt to curb the monarch's powers. Prodded by Bülow, Wilhelm issued a formal statement saying he would "guarantee the consistency of imperial policy by safeguarding constitutional responsibilities." In essence, this was simply a restatement of personal rule: the kaiser, not the lawmakers, would ensure constitutional consistency.

Once the furor over the *Daily Telegraph* affair had died down, Wilhelm felt that he could safely sack Bülow, whom he had come to loathe. In November 1909 he dismissed the chancellor for failing to convince the Conservatives in the Reichstag to accept a raft of new taxes, including death duties, which were necessary for financing his *Weltpolitik*.

Bülow was replaced by Theobald von Bethmann-Hollweg, a ponderous Prussian civil servant who had spent his life slowly climbing the bureaucratic ladder. Although known as a competent administrator, Bethmann lacked the confidence and adroitness to deal effectively with the kaiser. Upon accepting the chancellorship, he said, "Only a genius or a man driven by ambition and lust for power can covet this position, and I am neither." His wife was even more frank: "He can't do it," she declared.

Before ceding his place to Bethmann-Hollweg, Bülow had urged Wilhelm to appoint a strong state secretary of the foreign office to help manage Germany's diplomatic affairs. Wilhelm, however, wanted no competition in this department. "Just leave foreign policy to me," he told Bülow. "I've learned something from you. It will work out fine."

But of course it did not work out fine. Bismarck had once observed that the Kaiser was like a balloon: he drifted all over the place if no one held firmly onto his string. The dangers of erratic and unstable stewardship in Berlin became especially evident over the next three years, which were marked by one international crisis after another. Although the flash points were far from Berlin, the German capital remained at the center of the tension, since it was Germany that believed it had the most to gain by promoting discord among the powers coalescing against it.

The kaiser continued to imagine that Britain was the weak link in the chain of encirclement. Were not London and Berlin, as centers of northern European Protestant culture, natural allies against decadent Latins and boorish Slavs? he asked. The death of King Edward in 1910 added to his hopes for a rapprochement with England. Wilhelm admitted that he was "extremely relieved" when his arrogant uncle departed the scene.

But his relief was short-lived. A new crisis in Morocco in 1911 severely set back Berlin's hopes for better relations with London. In April of that year France occupied Fez, claiming that this was necessary to protect European interests in the wake of an uprising by local tribesmen. Germany branded the move a violation of the Treaty of Algeciras and called for France to pull back. If Paris insisted on staying put, Berlin demanded as compensation the entire French Congo. To add muscle to its demand, the kaiser dispatched the gunboat *Panther* to the Moroccan port of Agadir in July. Wilhelm and his advisers fully expected that this would induce Paris to back down, and that London would remain neutral. But once again Berlin miscalculated. France decried Germany's action as an act of aggression, and Britain immediately expressed solidarity with its ally. David Lloyd George, chancellor of the exchequer and future prime minister, warned that Britain would not accept peace at the price of France's humiliation.

Wilhelm was indignant over Britain's response. All he had done, he protested, was to send "a little ship with only two or three popguns" to support German interests in Morocco. He asked London's ambassador to Berlin why Britain was always so quick to condemn "its only real friend in Europe." But he could do no more than verbally protest. Germany's envisaged weapon of intimidation, its High Seas Fleet, was still only partially built. Bowing to international pressure, Berlin recalled the *Panther*. Shortly thereafter, a settlement was arbitrated whereby France was acknowledged as the dominant power in Morocco, while Germany obtained a large but commercially worthless stretch of swampland in the Congo.

This was obviously another diplomatic defeat for the Reich; and once again it was England that was seen to be standing directly athwart the path of German destiny. As Ernst von Heydebrand und der Lasa, a Conservative delegate to the Reichstag, expostulated:

> Like a flash in the night, this has shown the German people where the enemy is. We now know when we wish to expand in the world, when we wish to have our place in the sun, who it is that lays claim to world-wide domination. . . . Gentlemen, we Germans are not in the habit of permitting this sort of thing and the German people will know how to reply. . . . We shall secure peace, not by concessions, but by the German sword.

Yet many Germans were not so sure that their government would take a tough line. Germany's rulers, especially the kaiser, seemed determined to talk loudly but to carry a little stick. "Have we become a generation of women?" asked the *Berlin Post*. "What is the matter with the Hohenzollerns?" Lamenting that Germany had become more unpopular than ever without acquiring any colonial assets of consequence, Maximilian Harden of *Die Zukunft* declared that the Moroccan settlement was "the last nail in the coffin of German prestige."

But there were still more nails to come. Despite its indignation over Britain's behavior in the Second Moroccan Crisis, Berlin remained ever hopeful of prying London away from its partnership with Paris and St. Petersburg. In February 1912 the German government invited Britain's secretary of war, Lord Richard Burdon Haldane, to come to Berlin to discuss the international situation. Germany wanted a pledge from Britain to remain neutral in case the Reich went to war with a third party—say, France. But Haldane could hardly promise that Britain would stay out of a conflict in which Berlin was the aggressor, nor would London consent to any commitments unless Germany agreed to scale back its fleet construction. As it happened, Tirpitz had submitted a request to the Reichstag for more ships on the very day that Lord Haldane arrived in Berlin. The English lord firmly stated London's case for a smaller German navy, then returned home. In terms of Anglo-German relations, the Haldane Mission was a bust.

Kaiser Wilhelm, who had not played a significant role in the Haldane talks, was convinced that London had acted disrespectfully toward Berlin by making demands that no great power could accept. But he was proud that his government had made no concessions when it came to his precious navy. Moreover, he was sure that a hard line would eventually bring Britain around. "I have shown the English that, when they touch our armaments, they bite on granite. Perhaps by this I have increased their hatred but won their respect, which will induce them in due course to resume negotiations, it is to be hoped in a more modest tone and with a more fortunate result."

Better relations with Britain seemed particularly pressing in 1912–13 because there was serious trouble brewing in the Balkans, where the Germans and their Austrian allies were competing with the Russians to pick up the pieces of the disintegrating Ottoman Empire. Berlin became alarmed when, in 1912, a coalition of Serbs, Montenegrins, Bulgarians, and Greeks pushed the Turks out of their remaining holdings in the Balkan region. These peoples would never have acted so boldly, Berlin believed, without encouragement from St. Petersburg. The upheaval not only imperiled German interests in the region but threatened to compromise the viability of the Habsburg Monarchy, with its huge population of restive Slavs. To Wilhelm, the Slavs posed an even greater danger than the Yellow Peril. "I hate the Slavs," he told Austria's military attaché to Berlin. "I know it's a sin but I cannot help myself. I hate the Slavs." Wilhelm let Austria know that if it saw fit to move against the Serbs, it could count on support from Berlin.

As if to show its resolve, the kaiser's government staged its largest military display to date on Berlin's Tempelhof Field in September 1912. Some 60,000 troops paraded, while two zeppelins and ten airplanes circled overhead. A visiting British official found the event "the most impressive and menacing event I had ever witnessed. . . . The civilian audience seemed almost intoxicated with excitement and the reality of the German menace, with its ever increasing momentum, made the prospects of European peace look more precarious than ever."

The frustrations attending German foreign relations did not prevent the imperial government from indulging in some major celebrations in 1913. On June 15 Kaiser Wilhelm II celebrated the silver anniversary of his ascension as king of Prussia and German emperor. The occasion brought to the capital throngs of loyal subjects, who gaped in wonder at the monuments. The cafés and restaurants were filled with people dancing the tango, the latest imported craze, though officers in uniform were banned from joining in because the kaiser considered the dance immoral. A little later that year, Wilhelm laid the cornerstone of a new sports stadium for the Olympic Games of 1916, which had recently been awarded to Berlin. (Of course, there would be no Olympic Games in 1916, and Berlin would not host this festival until 1936.) In October came the celebrations marking the one hundredth anniversary of the "Battle of Nations" near Leipzig, where Prussian troops had helped to overpower Napoleon, setting him up for his final defeat at Waterloo a year and a half later.

Yet all the celebrations, impressive as they were, could not disguise the fact that Berlin was a city on edge, seething with political and social dissension, full of frustration over diplomatic and military isolation. The most widely discussed book in 1912–13 was General Bernhardi's *Germany and the Next War*, which argued that war was a biological necessity for a healthy young nation surrounded by senile but tenacious adversaries. There was considerable talk among the kaiser's generals about the need for a "preventative war"—a quick strike that could liberate the Reich from its encirclement before its enemies became too powerful to defeat.

It was not only Berlin that was restless. All the European capitals had their "war parties," their eager believers in the notion that if war was inevitable it should come sooner rather than later. Observing all the signs of restless saber rattling during a visit to Europe in summer 1913, Colonel Edward M. House, President Wilson's confidant and emissary, reported worriedly: "The whole of Europe is charged with electricity. Everyone's nerves are tense. It needs only a spark to set the whole thing off."

The Spirit of 1914

Of course, the spark that ignited what came to be known as World War I was the assassination of Austrian Archduke Franz Ferdinand on June 28, 1914, at Sarajevo. The killer was a Serbian terrorist named Gavrilo Princip, who wanted to strike a blow against Austria for annexing Bosnia in 1908. (Princip was later portrayed as a hero by the Yugoslav Communists, who placed a plaque at the spot where he carried out his deed and named a street in his honor. After Bosnia seceded from Serbian-led Yugoslavia in 1992, Muslim officials tore down the plaque and renamed the street.) Franz Ferdinand's death would not have had such far-reaching consequences had the Austrians not known that they had German backing to punish the Serbs. Wilhelm and his advisers believed that a limited war—one confined to the Balkans—could be highly salutary if it rallied folks around the flag while weakening pan-Slavic influences abroad. "Just tread hard on the heels of that rabble," was Wilhelm's advice to Vienna. Thus Bismarck's well-known prediction that the next major war would start in the Balkans was proven correct, though the real source of the explosion was not the Balkans, but Berlin.

On July 23 Austria presented an ultimatum to Serbia, insisting that if its demands were not met in two days, Vienna would declare war. The demands were so far-reaching that Austria was confident that the Serbs would reject them out of hand, giving Vienna the excuse it was looking for to put Belgrade in its place. As it happened, Serbia accepted nearly all the demands, and thus almost denied Vienna its pretext for war.

On the eve of Serbia's reply to Vienna's ultimatum, huge crowds gathered outside the newspaper offices in Berlin, awaiting news of Belgrade's response. According to one witness, the people were quite tense; they had collected in the streets because they were "too excited to remain at home." Chancellor Bethmann-Hollweg was so worried that the Berliners would respond angrily to the Austrian ultimatum that he advised Wilhelm to delay his return to the capital from his annual North Sea cruise. Although the kaiser was always happiest when away from Berlin, he was offended by the chancellor's advice: "Things get madder every minute!" he fumed. "Now the man writes to me that I must not show myself to my subjects!" But Bethmann need not have worried about the Berliners' response to the news of the Serbs' decision. After reading the announcement in the newspaper extras, some citizens cheered "Et jeht los!"—Berlinerisch for "It's on!"—while others went quietly home. Soon another crowd assembled in the city center, this one much more emphatically enthusiastic about the latest developments. The revelers moved down Unter den Linden to the Royal Palace, where they burst into the song *Heil Dir im Siegerkranz* ("Hail to You in Victory Wreath"). Yet another group, mostly university students, trooped to the Austrian Embassy, cheering the ambassador when he made a brief appearance. "German and Austrian, student and soldier, merchant and worker, all feel as one in this deadly serious hour," commented the *Vossische Zeitung*.

Jingoists were not the only ones taking to the streets of Berlin in this hour of crisis. In response to calls from *Vorwärts*, the SPD's newspaper, for antiwar demonstrations, on July 28 thousands of workers marched from the proletarian suburbs toward the center of town chanting "Down with war!" and "Long live Social Democracy!" The police put up roadblocks and rode their horses into the columns, but about 2,000 workers managed to reach the city center. They strolled up Unter den Linden singing internationalist songs, while prowar zealots responded with patriotic refrains.

Whether they were pro- or antiwar, Berliners continued to fill the streets in the last days of July, if for no other reason than to get the latest information regarding the escalating crisis. On July 29 they learned that the czar had mobilized his troops on Russia's border with Austria. This prompted renewed demonstrations of support for Vienna, along with calls for German mobilization against Russia. The kaiser saw Russia's action as the latest episode in a long-running international conspiracy to keep Germany down. Although the order to mobilize was given in St. Petersburg, Wilhelm believed that it had been set in motion by the anti-German policies of his late uncle, King Edward VII. "[Edward] is stronger after his death than I who am still alive," he cried.

Learning on July 31 that Russia had extended its mobilization to the German border, the kaiser announced a state of *drohende Kriegsgefahr*—imminent danger of war. At 5:00 P.M. that day a lieutenant of the Grenadier Guards stood before the statue of Frederick the Great on Unter den Linden and read a proclamation from the Commanding General of Berlin giving him full authority over the city according to the Prussian Law of Siege of 1851. This law suspended civil rights, barred civilians from carrying arms, and granted the military the right to search houses at any time; it amounted, in effect, to granting the military dictatorial control over the capital for the duration of the war.

The announcement of *Kriegsgefahr* prompted widespread jubilation in Berlin. Thousands of men, not just the young and stupid, rushed to enlist in the army. Among them was Count Harry Kessler, a cosmopolitan art connoisseur who in the Weimar era would be identified with liberal internationalism. In 1914, however, he was proud to call himself a conservative nationalist. He spoke for all those crowding Berlin's recruiting centers when he declared, upon ordering his military kit: "One breathes freely, the pressure and cloying closeness fall away, replaced by cool decisiveness." The bellicosity, however, was mixed with signs of fear. Berliners removed their deposits from banks and housewives stormed the stores to stockpile food and supplies. In response, store owners hiked prices. These actions set the tone for an internal struggle for private advantage that would accompany the carnage on the front during the next four years.

On August 1, as the kaiser's government met in the Royal Palace to debate its course of action if Russia refused to rescind its mobilization order, a crowd gathered outside and serenaded the ministers with patriotic songs, accompanied by the band of the Elisabeth Regiment. "The enthusiasm knew no bounds," cabled the Berlin correspondent for the *Frankfurter Zeitung* at 1:55 P.M., "and when as a finale the united will of the masses elicited the *Pariser Einzugsmarsch* [a march celebrating Germany's entry into Paris in 1871] the enthusiasm reached its high point." At about 5:30 P.M. a car rushed out with a General Staff officer inside who shouted one word: "mobilization!" The mob responded with more singing and cries of "We want the kaiser!" Shortly thereafter Wilhelm appeared on a balcony and declared:

> From the depths of my heart I thank you for the expressions of your love, of your faithfulness. In the battle now lying ahead of us, I recognize in my *Volk* no more parties. Among us there are only Germans, and if some of the parties in the course of past differences turned against me, I forgive them all. All that now matters is that we stand together like brothers, and then God will help the German sword to victory.

That evening and the following day nationalist Berliners celebrated the German mobilization with an enormous party. Pubs and beer gardens stayed open all night to accommodate the patriotic revelers, mostly young middle-class men and their girls. Local churches performed some 2,000 emergency marriages for couples soon to be separated by duty at the front. Taking their cue from the kaiser, previously disaffected groups like homosexual rights campaigners and women's franchise crusaders vowed to support the nationalist cause. So did the Association of German Jews, which proclaimed that every German Jew was "ready to sacrifice all the property and blood demanded by duty."

As Germany was now at war with Russia, St. Petersburg's ambassador to Berlin hastened to leave the German capital on August 2. The American ambassador, James W. Gerard, lent his Russian colleague his car for the trip from the Russian embassy to the railway station. As soon as the car pulled out a mob surrounded it and tried to overturn it. People jumped on the running board and struck the ambassador and his family with sticks. Although the ambassadorial party eventually made it to the station, their treatment was an ugly example of the xenophobic frenzy awakened by the prospect of war.

Germany's initial mobilization was aimed only at Russia, but since that nation was deemed too inefficient and backward to mount a quick assault on the Reich, Berlin's battle order, the famous Schlieffen Plan, called for a rapid conquest of France before St. Petersburg could get its military "steamroller" moving. The kaiser summed up this strategy succinctly: "Paris for lunch, dinner in St. Petersburg." To achieve this goal Germany would have to slash toward Paris through Belgium, whose neutrality was guaranteed by Great Britain. On August 1 Britain's foreign secretary, Sir Edward Grey, hinted that London might remain neutral if Germany made no military moves against France or Belgium. The kaiser, ever hopeful of an accommodation with Britain, was prepared to change course and confine opening operations to Russia, but his generals insisted that the Schlieffen Plan could not be altered without producing total chaos. Their insistence upon placing military tactics above questions of statecraft provided a vivid confirmation of Clausewitz's dictum that war is too important to be left to the generals. Taking France's mobilization on August 2 as a casus belli, Germany declared war the following day. At the same time, Berlin chose to ignore a last-minute British ultimatum demanding Germany's respect for Belgian neutrality. As of midnight on August 4, the Reich was also at war with Britain.

Upon learning of London's declaration of war, Wilhelm raged over Britain's "betrayal" of his personal friendship with the English people and Germany's historic ties to the island nation. This was the thanks that the Germans got for helping save the Britons' bacon at Waterloo, he fumed. Many Berliners shared the kaiser's shock and rage over Britain's decision to fight. On August 5 a menacing crowd surrounded the Hotel Adlon, where some British journalists were staying. Another angry mob gathered outside the British embassy and pelted the building with stones. America's Ambassador Gerard became so concerned for the safety of his British counterpart, Sir Edward Goschen, that he drove over to the British compound and offered him sanctuary in the American diplomatic residence. Goschen declined the offer and managed to slip unharmed from the city on the following day. In the meantime, Gerard himself ran into trouble upon leaving the British embassy. As he drove away in his open car a man leaped on the running board and spat on him. Infuriated, Gerard jumped out of the car and chased down his assailant. When the man learned that he had assaulted the American ambassador, rather than the representative of perfidious Albion, he apologized profusely.

The German government made no apologies for rounding up British and French citizens in Berlin and interning them in Spandau Fortress. At the opening of hostilities, Berlin's military command sent out an appeal to the citizenry asking for help in ferreting out spies and rendering "such dangerous people harmless." This was an open invitation to vigilantism, and the results were immediately visible in attacks on foreigners and people who looked foreign. Because she had black hair and exotic features, the Danish-born actress Asta Nielsen was mistaken for a Russian and accosted by a mob. She might have been badly injured had not one of her attackers suddenly recognized her and called off the assault. But she was advised to leave the scene immediately because, as her savior put it, "the people have completely lost their senses."

The kaiser's first official act after war began was to summon members of the Reichstag to the Royal Palace for a kind of pep rally. Here he repeated the phrase: "I no longer acknowledge parties; I know only Germans." While this could be taken as a sign that Wilhelm was anxious to cooperate with all his subjects regardless of party affiliation, he remained deeply suspicious of the SPD, whose leaders were earmarked for immediate arrest if they resisted the war effort.

In the event, the government had no need to arrest the Socialists. On the following day they joined with the other parties in voting for war credits. The party leaders justified this decision on the grounds that Germany was threatened by reactionary Russia, a greater menace to world progress than their own government.

Yet the move also reflected a strong desire to be part of the national consensus at a time of crisis, as well as an undercurrent of patriotism that had long been present in German socialism. In voting to support the war the German Socialists were no different from their counterparts elsewhere in Europe, whose support for their governments' call to arms made a mockery of the Marxist ideal of international proletarian brotherhood. Those German Socialists who wished to remain faithful to the internationalist credo—most notably Karl Liebknecht, Rosa Luxemburg, and Clara Zetkin—were quickly shunted aside. In despair over her party's direction, Luxemburg locked herself in her apartment and wept uncontrollably.

The Socialists' willingness to back the war effort was part of a broader agreement by the major parties and interest groups to suspend their partisan campaigns for the duration of the war. Known as the *Burgfrieden*—"Truce of the Castle"—this arrangement evoked the hallowed tradition whereby the residents of a castle pulled together during a time of siege. In reality, the external threat often accentuated internal differences. Although domestic discord would also be the story in Germany once the pressures of war mounted, the civil truce was touted as another dimension of the Spirit of 1914—added proof that Germany really was, at long last, a unified nation.

For Berlin the outbreak of war brought the proclamation of a mini-*Burgfrieden* and the opportunity to show that the city had overcome all the internal divisions that had plagued it since 1871. Having been a microcosm of German divisiveness, Berlin would, it was declared, become a model of German unity. Officials in the capital also saw the war as a chance to break down some of the hostility toward their city on the part of non-Berliners. As mayor Wermuth declared on August 3: "Berlin, the Reich capital, must and will take the lead in terms of discipline and willingness for sacrifice."

The commitment to unity was relatively easy to make in late summer 1914 because almost everyone thought the war would end quickly. Among the general public, word had it that the war would be over by Christmas, the victory a nice holiday gift. Some of the German troops departing for the front in early August even promised to be home "before the leaves fell." The General Staff, conceding that there might be some delay here and there, prepared for a war that could last as long as six months.

During the first month of fighting it seemed as if the Germans' confidence was not misplaced. True, the invaders encountered resistance from tiny Belgium, forcing them, among other measures, to call up huge Krupp cannons to smash the fortresses around Liège. But Belgian opposition slowed the German advance only by a few days. After taking Brussels the Germans turned south into northern France and were within twenty-five miles of Paris by September 5. The Germans also successfully repressed a French attack into occupied Alsace-Lorraine. Exploiting the breathtaking stupidity of the French commanders, who had ordered their troops to charge without surprise or concealment, the defenders slaughtered over 40,000 Frenchmen in just three days.

On the Eastern Front the Russian steamroller had gotten rolling faster than Germany had expected, and the kaiser worried that Berlin might fall to the Cossacks. Russian generalship, however, proved even more inept than the French, and the czar's soldiers, though numerous, were so poorly equipped that many had to wait for a colleague to fall in order to obtain a rifle. At the end of August, German forces under Paul von Hindenburg and his chief of staff, Erich Ludendorff, who had been hurriedly called east after helping win the victory at Liège, lured a large Russian army into a trap at the Masurian Lakes in East Prussia and annihilated it. Upon learning the news of this great victory, which the Germans named "Tannenberg" in honor of a clash between Teutonic Knights and Slavs in 1410, Berliners breathed a huge sigh of relief; there would apparently be no Cossacks in their city after all.

Indeed, in the wake of all these impressive victories the German capital gave itself over to a mood of festive celebration unmixed with the tension evident on the eve of the war. On August 7, after twenty policemen rode through town bringing news (somewhat prematurely) of the fall of Liège, church bells rang out across Berlin, and cheering crowds paraded up and down Unter den Linden. Among them was a nine-year-old boy named Felix Gilbert, who was later to emigrate to America and become one of its most distinguished historians. In his memoirs Gilbert recalled marching to the Royal Palace and yelling for a member of the royal house to make an appearance. Like other little boys he also celebrated the German victories by playing war games in the streets. Noticing some boys playing such games outside her home, the painter Käthe Kollwitz was amazed to hear one of them plead for mercy from his "captors" by announcing, "I am a father many times over and the only son of my wife."

On August 11, a General Staff officer drove into town to announce "Victory in Alsace," prompting another informal parade, this one led by a Berliner carrying a bust of Kaiser Wilhelm wearing a laurel wreath. The crowd celebrating the Alsatian victory surrounded a column of Prussian troops marching through the Brandenburg Gate and showered them with roses, which the soldiers affixed, in very un-Prussian fashion, to their uniforms and rifles. The celebration extended to the city's working classes, some of whom draped the national colors out their windows. Käthe Kollwitz's family, solid Social Democrats, displayed the imperial flag at their flat in Prenzlauer Berg for the first time in their lives. To a conservative minister living in the proletarian district of Moabit, this phenomenon was "an amazing thing for those who know the conditions. Usually there is not a single flag on, say, the Kaiser's birthday. . . . The Social Democratic worker is proud that he can show his patriotism."

Successive announcements of more victories in Belgium, France, and East Prussia gave Berliners the impression that the war was virtually over. When captured French war material was paraded down Unter den Linden on Sedan Day, September 2, the journalist Theodor Wolff reported that he had never seen Berlin more "excited," more bursting with happy crowds. An old general, recalling the way in which some Berliners had exploited the victory celebration of 1871, admonished home owners "not to rent their windows for the [coming] victory parade at too high a price."

This admonition, of course, proved unnecessary. The massive German drive to take Paris faltered at the Battle of the Marne in September 1914. What was supposed to be a quick victory in the West—the General Staff had allotted only thirty-nine days for the entire campaign against France—degenerated into four years of bitter trench warfare. The Spirit of 1914 had been from the outset part wishful thinking, but as the war dragged on the ideal turned into a necessary mythos, trotted out to help maintain morale in the face of growing despair and internal discord. And just as Berlin had led the nation in cheering the early victories, so it assumed the lead in questioning the war once the conflict had begun to exact its terrible toll on the home front and battlefields alike.

You'll Be Eating Shit for Dessert!

In Berlin, indications that the war might have less than a salutary effect on the economic climate came even before the campaign in the West ran aground. The mobilization of young male workers for the military forced many factories and businesses to shut down or curtail operations. Because the transportation network was turned over to the army for troop movement, firms were suddenly cut off from sources of supply and distant markets. Companies that focused on export suffered the most.

Siemens, for example, lost foreign orders for 5.8 million lightbulbs. Eventually, the task of keeping the insatiable war machine up and running compensated for the loss of foreign markets, but the initial contraction, estimated at 24 percent, produced a sudden upsurge in unemployment. The capital's jobless rate among male trade unionists shot up from 6 to 19 percent in the first two weeks of the war.

Hoping to prevent a breakdown in the civil truce, the government hastily increased unemployment benefits. Berlin added welfare measures of its own, including rent support for war families and a number of new soup kitchens. Because these measures were paid for through borrowing rather than tax increases, they constituted the first steps toward the horrible inflation that would plague the nation in the early Weimar years.

By the end of September there were no more demonstrations or raucous gatherings in the streets of Berlin. Now the largest crowds assembled outside the soup kitchens or in front of the War Academy, where lists of dead, wounded, and missing soldiers were posted. The first such lists went up in Berlin on August 9; new postings appeared approximately every three days for the rest of the war. The newspapers carried similar columns, bordered in black and bearing iron crosses next to the confirmed fatalities.

Käthe Kollwitz was among the Berliners who had reason to grieve in the early months of the war, for she learned on October 30, 1914, that her beloved son Peter had been killed on the Western Front. She admitted to a friend, "There is in our lives a wound which will never heal. Nor should it." For the rest of the war, she kept Peter's room exactly as he had left it. She also embarked on a work of art to commemorate him and the other young volunteers who had died at the front. But it took her until 1931 to complete a memorial with which she was satisfied. It consisted of granite statues of her husband Karl and herself on their knees at their son's grave in Belgium. In 1937 Kollwitz produced another memorial sculpture, a small pietà of a mother mourning her dead child. Sixty years later a larger copy of this work would become part of post-reunification Germany's tortuous effort to memorialize the victims of war and tyranny during a bloody century.

In Germany as elsewhere a high percentage of the early war casualties were middle-class. This was because young bourgeois men were the most active volunteers and as junior officers were most likely to lead charges "over the top." The Kaiser Wilhelm Gymnasium, Berlin's most prestigious high school, lost over a dozen of its recent graduates in the first weeks of war.

As the enthusiasm for volunteering ebbed and conscription became the major source of cannon fodder, peasants and urban workers made up the bulk of the forces at the front. Yet industrial workers (as opposed to farm laborers) remained underrepresented relative to their numbers in society. On average they were less physically fit and therefore more likely to be exempted for health reasons. Also, despite the proclamations of national togetherness, the officer corps was reluctant to recruit a mass army of left-oriented laborers who, the officers feared, might turn their guns against their superiors. Finally, with the need to man the machines at home becoming as important as putting soldiers in the field, highly trained industrial workers were simply too valuable to be expended wholesale in the trenches. Increasingly, industrial workers either received exemptions or were recalled from the front to work at home. A total of 92,400 Berlin workers were recalled over the course of the war. This special treatment inevitably fueled resentment among the urban bourgeoisie and peasantry, leading to accusations that the workers were "shirking" their duty to the Fatherland. Moreover, because Berlin was so heavily working-class, the city mobilized a lower percentage of its males of military age (60 percent) than the national average (80 percent). Here was more fodder for disgruntlement, more reason for citizens across the nation to see the capital as less patriotic than other parts of the Reich.

This perception was all the more problematical because another consequence of the lengthening war was to centralize national power in Berlin even more extensively than had been the case before. Berlin became the headquarters of new bureaucracies designed to coordinate arms production, allocate resources, and distribute manpower. The staffing of these bureaucracies kept another large contingent of capital-dwellers out of the trenches. It did not go unnoticed in the rest of the country that men with cushy jobs far from the front were the very ones making the decisions regarding sacrifices for the war effort. "Why must everything be concentrated in Berlin?" asked a provincial legislator. Berlin's alleged status as a *Kriegslieblingskind* (favored child of the war) fueled calls "to move some of the Reich agencies out of Berlin."

Berlin's emergence as the seat of a centralized war economy was due in part to the influence of Walther Rathenau, the mercurial president of the General Electric Company, one of the city's largest firms. He and his colleague Wichard von Moellendorff knew that, industrially speaking, Germany was not prepared to fight a major war. Not only were there no stockpiles of strategic goods, there was no plan for

Berliners admire a model trench in a local park, 1915

stepping up production or coordinating distribution of needed materials. As early as August 1914, Rathenau prevailed on the War Ministry to establish a Raw Materials Section with himself at the head. He and his group immediately set out to remedy some of the worst deficiencies. Without this agency Germany would not have been able to carry on with the war for more than a few months after the failure of the Marne offensive. Thus the most important figure in keeping the Reich in the conflict was not Hindenburg or Ludendorff, but a Jewish industrialist from Berlin.

Berlin continued to get a large percentage of draft exemptions because its industrial base, already huge at the war's outset, grew even larger as the conflict progressed. Local manufacturing firms exploited their contacts with the war bureaucracies to obtain the most lucrative military contracts. This allowed the companies to pay exceptionally high wages and to lure workers to the capital from other parts of the Reich. The city's many metalworking firms were particularly adept at this game. Once they had recruited thousands of new workers, the firms prevailed upon the War Ministry to issue a decree prohibiting the workers from changing jobs.

The recall of workers from the trenches, however, soon proved insufficient to meet the manpower needs of Berlin's wartime industry. The government responded by recruiting more and more women for jobs normally performed by men. Although this practice was adopted by all the belligerent nations, Germany, and especially Berlin, took the lead in the feminization of industrial labor. Between 1914 and December 1917 the number of female workers increased by 279 percent in Berlin's machine tool industry and by 116 percent in metalworking, which meant that by the end of 1917 over 50 percent of the workers in these fields were female. Other occupations were feminized as well: Ambassador Gerard reported seeing women at work building railroads, driving the city's post carts, even serving as motormen on the tramways.

Berlin's army of workers, like its armies in the field, could not function on empty stomachs. At first there was little worry about this because the citizenry expected soon to be tucking in to caviar and champagne brought back from Paris by German troops. When, instead of bringing back booty, the military began draining away ever greater quantities of food, prices for basic foodstuffs skyrocketed. Pressured by the Social Democrats, who understood that escalating bread prices could undermine workers' morale, the government took control of wheat production and distribution in early 1915. An Imperial Allocation Board in Berlin ordered farmers to sell their grains at a standard price set by the government. Resistance to this order was fierce, especially from heavily agricultural states like Bavaria. Count Georg Friedrich von Hertling, Bavaria's prime minister, complained that the sequestration of wheat amounted to an imposition of "socialist principles."

The hasty creation of centralized war bureaucracies may have helped Germany to stay in the war, but it did not put an end to the bottlenecks and shortages. Germany's armies ran short of ammunition in the late fall of 1914, precluding any new offensives that might have broken the stalemate. The situation got worse in 1915 and 1916. Enormous battles like Verdun and the Somme used up munitions on a scale hitherto unimagined. The ammunition crisis prompted the introduction of the Hindenburg Program, which was supposed to mobilize the entire economy and society for war. It ceded even greater authority to the military, making Hindenburg and Ludendorff virtual dictators, but it by no means enhanced efficiency. On the contrary, the army "governed" by allowing businesses and interest groups to exploit the conflict for their own advantage; the result was "an orgy of interest politics."

Governmental ineptitude and private greed, combined with an increasingly effective British blockade, brought growing deprivation to Germany's cities, including the capital. Shortages of basic foodstuffs became worse despite—and partly because of—the government's assumption of control over distribution. Berlin was obliged to introduce bread rationing as early as February 1915, and other major cities soon followed suit. The rationing was supposed to ensure adequate supplies for all, but its primary effect was to stimulate the growth of a black market that drove up prices as much as 400 percent. Of course, the wealthier classes were often able to obtain items that were supposedly unavailable. The manager of one of the fancy hotels, for example, ordered his chambermaids to give him their butter allowance, which he then sold to rich guests. There was no shortage of fine food at the Adlon, which became home to many of the top war bureaucrats. Because of their presence, recalled Hedda Adlon, "not a room stood empty in our hotel during the entire war."

For the vast majority of ordinary Berliners, who could only dream of dinner at the Adlon, the hunt for sustenance became ever more challenging. Some had relatives in the hinterlands whom they could tap for extra supplies, but many raided surrounding farms and orchards, a tactic that greatly exacerbated old tensions between the capital and its rural environs. Another expedient was to plant vegetables on every conceivable plot of land, no matter how small. Tiny truck gardens sprouted up in vacant lots and along the banks of the Spree; many survive today in the form of *Schrebergärten* (garden colonies).

Urban gardens, however, could hardly cover the growing deficiency in food staples, and Berliners, like other Germans, were obliged to consume vile concoctions containing cheaper ingredients. The first of these innovations was "K-Bread"—the K standing either for *Krieg* (war) or *Kartoffeln* (potatoes), the main component. Felix Gilbert recalled the war bread as "very heavy, very dark," and containing what seemed to be pieces of wood. This stuff confronted him with a dilemma, because he could neither eat it nor discard it at his school, which would have looked unpatriotic. Thus every day on the way to school he surreptitiously dropped his bread ration into the Spree, hoping not to provoke a feeding frenzy among the seagulls, which would have given away his game. But he had no reason to worry: "Even the sea gulls realized that the bread was unpalatable."

By the winter of 1916/17 potatoes, too, were in short supply, so they were replaced by turnips, which Berliners had always regarded as animal fodder. The ubiquity of this bitter-tasting lumpen-vegetable prompted a new title for the national anthem: "Dotschland, Dotschland über Alles" (Turnip-land, Turnip-land Over All). As butter became increasingly scarce, the authorities urged people to spread their K-Bread with jam. But there was no jam to be had either. When an emergency shipment of plum jam failed to arrive in the capital, Berliners suspected that officials of the Ministry of Interior had colluded with speculators to send it elsewhere to make a profit for themselves. They also blamed the government for the proliferation of *Ersatz* (substitute) products, which were designed to mimic the physical appearance, but certainly not the taste, of the goods they replaced. Thus Berlin was inundated with ash masquerading as pepper, extract of fruit pips claiming to be oil, and a mixture of soda and starch pretending to be butter. With the proliferation of ersatz foods, anything natural was prized, including stray cats and even rats. People joked that there would soon be no rats in Berlin, only rat substitute. If a horse died in harness it was unlikely to make it to the knacker. Asta Nielsen recalled seeing a horde of *Hausfrauen* butcher an old

Hungry Berliners carve up a horse cadaver, 1918

nag as soon as it dropped in the street: "They fought each other for the best pieces, their faces and clothing covered in blood. Other emaciated figures rushed over and scooped up the warm blood with cups and napkins. Only when the horse was reduced to a skeleton did the scavengers disperse, anxiously clutching bits of flesh to their hollow breasts." Rumor had it that some Berliners were stuffing the bodies of departed relatives into closets to evade registering the death and losing the deceased's ration card. By the end of 1916 even some of the better-off elements were becoming unfashionably thin. "We are all gaunt and bony now," noted Princess Blücher, "and have dark shadows around our eyes, and our thoughts are chiefly taken up with wondering what our next meal will be."

In their bitterness over the lack of decent food, Berliners often asserted that other parts of Germany, such as Bavaria, had it better. They also complained that refugees were "picking them clean." Not surprisingly, the rest of the nation rejected such complaints as typical Berliner whining. Pointing to a fifty-gram increase in the meat ration for Berlin's industrial workers, Bavarians claimed that it was the capital that was unjustly privileged.

Although Germans might argue over which part of the country suffered the worst shortages, none could dispute the fact that the poor in every major city, including Berlin, suffered the most. Starting in late fall 1914, long lines formed outside bakeries in the capital's proletarian districts; often there was nothing left when people finally got to the counters. Berlin's first serious food riots occurred in the working-class districts of Lichtenberg and Wedding in October 1915. Proletarian women, who bore the responsibility of finding food for their families, led the demonstrations. In one instance a group of them descended on a butter store whose owner had jacked up his prices. When he responded to their complaints by telling them that they'd soon be paying six marks for a pound of butter and "eating shit for dessert," they beat him up and smashed his windows. A little later a mob of women stormed a meeting of the Social Democratic leadership to protest the party's inaction in the food crisis. As the Socialist politician Otto Braun recalled, they threw stink bombs, cursed their leaders as *feige Lumpen* (cowardly rogues), and suggested that they be sent to the trenches. "The comrades from other parts of the Reich got a very graphic demonstration of the unspeakably low level of political discourse in Berlin," commented Braun in his diary.

It was not just food that was in short supply. By 1916/17 Berlin had inadequate stocks of coal, largely because there were too few trains available to transport coal

Elephants from the Berlin Zoo pressed into service during World War I

from the mines to the capital. There was also a lack of horses to pull the coal-carts around the city. As a colorful, but ineffective, replacement, elephants from the Berlin Zoo were pressed into service. To conserve coal for home use, the authorities imposed some restrictions on illuminated advertisements and street lighting, but no efforts were made to curb industrial use or to regulate distribution. The major coal dealers in the capital were more or less free to dispose of their supplies as they saw fit. Here as elsewhere "total mobilization" really meant total freedom to exploit the crisis for private gain.

Wartime Berlin's free-for-all atmosphere often appalled front soldiers who visited the city on furlough or to convalesce from wounds. In addition to price-gouging and black marketeering, the sight of apparently carefree young people strolling the streets at night disgusted the troopers. Their complaints reached the kaiser, who telegraphed from his headquarters on July 16, 1916: "I am indignant that the youth of my Residence is displaying so little sense of decorum in this serious time, when we at the front are showing our metal to the enemy. The young people had better understand that we will not tolerate such behavior. Berlin must manifest in its outward demeanor that it is morally up these difficult times."

Another indignant observer of the wartime Berlin scene was Private First Class Adolf Hitler, who spent a weekend in the capital in October 1916 while recovering from a leg wound at a nearby hospital. This was his first visit to the city, and he found the place a depressing hive of slackers and peace agitators. In the fall of 1917 he returned to the capital on an eighteen-day leave and this time gained a more favorable impression, since he was able to visit the great museums. "The city is tremendous," he wrote in a postcard. "Truly a Weltstadt." In a letter of 1920, Hitler opined that the "mistakes and dark sides" of Berlin were not fundamental to it but stemmed from a local culture dominated by Jews. Although as "Führer" he would dedicate himself to "saving" the German capital from this influence, he never fully lost his sense that Berlin was alien to the true German spirit.

Immer feste druff! (Keep Hittin' 'Em)

The First World War was a war of ideas and images as well as of bullets and bombs. The longer it went on, the more necessary it seemed to enlist the muses in the maintenance of morale at home and on the battlefield. As Germany's cultural capital, Berlin took the lead in mobilizing the nation's artistic, intellectual, and scientific resources for the war effort. Much of what the city produced during this period was virulently chauvinistic and xenophobic, as it was in the other wartime capitals. But the war also brought about some pathbreaking (if not always salutary) departures in art and science, in which Berlin likewise played the leading role.

Berlin fired its first barrage in the cultural war as German troops streamed across Belgium. Professor Adolf von Harnack, head of the Royal Library and a leader of the capital's huge academic community, insisted that Germany had been forced to go to war because its culture, the true bulwark of Western Civilization, was in danger of being blotted out by barbarians from the East backed by unscrupulous predators from the West. Referring to Russia, he spoke of

> the civilization of the tribe, with its patriarchal organization, the civilization of the horde that is gathered and kept together by despots [which] could not endure the light of the eighteenth century, still less that of the nineteenth century, and now in the twentieth century breaks loose and threatens us. This Asiatic mass, like the desert with its sands, wants to gather up our fields of grain.

A little later Harnack joined ninety-two other prominent German cultural figures, many from Berlin, in signing a manifesto designed to repudiate Allied charges of German atrocities. The so-called "Manifesto of the Ninety-three" encapsulated Germany's, and Berlin's, long-standing indignation over Western European caricatures of the Reich as a semicivilized pariah nation. Germany, said the manifesto, was the true home of European Christian culture. In claiming to be the defenders of Western Civilization, the signers hoped to win some understanding and respect from their counterparts in London and Paris. Instead, as any neutral observer could have predicted, their document had the opposite effect, strengthening the distrust that they had set out to break down.

One of the Manifesto signers was the great chemist Fritz Haber. His work in the war was representative of the close and fateful cooperation between the academy—especially that of Berlin—and the military. While working at the Technical University in Karlsruhe in the early years of the century, Haber had discovered the process of fixing nitrogen from the air, a vital breakthrough for industry and agriculture. His achievement was rewarded with a call to Berlin, where in 1911 he became head of the newly founded Kaiser Wilhelm Institute for Physical Chemistry and Electrochemistry. When the war broke out three years later, Haber was quick to place his institute on a war footing, turning it (in the words of Fritz Stern) into a kind of "Manhattan Project before its time." The parallel is apt, for the institute's most important wartime contribution was the development of poison gas, that horrific new addition to mankind's arsenal of evil. Haber found satisfaction in the Germans' surprise deployment of gas at Ypres and on the Eastern Front, though he wished the weapon might have been more effective against the Russians. As he reported: "The panic which the first attack at Ypres caused among the enemy could be observed in the East with the Russians only after repeated attacks at the same place, then, however, regularly." A few years later, the terrible irony of Haber's contribution would become apparent, for the scientist was a Jew. During the war, however, Haber saw nothing untoward about his work for the German military: he was, like so many of his Jewish colleagues, deeply assimilated (in fact, he had converted to Protestantism). His ultimate reward for devoted service was banishment from Germany and death in exile.

One of the few major voices in Berlin's scientific community to oppose the enlistment of the intellect on behalf of the war was Albert Einstein. He had moved to Berlin in April 1914 from Zurich, where he had worked out his Special Theory of

Relativity. Anxious to bring him to Berlin, two of that city's most famous scientists, Max Planck and Walter Nernst, had personally traveled to Switzerland to convince him to make the move. Their task had not been easy, for Einstein deeply distrusted the German Empire as a bastion of militarism and hypernationalism; upon settling in Zurich he had renounced his German citizenship. Planck's and Nernst's most powerful ammunition against Einstein's reservations was Berlin's status as the best possible place for the scientist to carry on his pioneering work. When told once that only a dozen men in the world understood relativity, Nernst had replied: "Eight of them live in Berlin." To sweeten their offer, the Berliners promised Einstein a generous salary with no obligation to teach, the secret fantasy of most academics. After listening at length to their blandishments, Einstein told them to go away for a few days while he made up his mind. They would know his decision when they returned by the color of the rose he carried; if white, he would stay in Zurich; if red, he would go to Berlin. To the immense relief of Planck and Nernst, Einstein showed up to meet them at the train station carrying a red rose.

The behavior of Einstein's new colleagues once war had broken out caused him to wonder if he had made the right decision to come to Berlin. He was horrified by all the war enthusiasm at the university, the Prussian Academy of Sciences, and the Kaiser Wilhelm Institute. As a response to the Manifesto of the Ninety-three (which Planck and Paul Ehrlich had also signed), Einstein coauthored a "Manifesto to Europeans," which among other points chastised the German scientific and artistic communities for behaving, "almost to a man, as though they had relinquished any further desire for the continuance of international relations." They had "spoken in a hostile spirit and failed to speak out for peace." Alas, when this counter-manifesto was circulated among the faculty at the University of Berlin, only three professors, in addition to Einstein, signed it. Frustration over this state of affairs drove Einstein more actively into the political realm. In November 1914, along with Ernst Reuter, who would become mayor of West Berlin after World War II, he helped to establish the Bund Neues Vaterland, which agitated for an early peace. Later, he joined prominent socialists and pacifists from the Allied countries in calling for a cessation of hostilities. Planck, who remained committed to the German war effort, must have wondered if Einstein's selection of a red-colored rose had meant more than just his yes-to-Berlin.

Like Berlin's scientific establishment, the capital's popular entertainment industry placed itself at the service of the nation; its goal was to help justify Germany's cause and to provide diversion in a time of stress. The city's theaters and cabarets had closed at the outbreak of hostilities to show respect for the gravity of the moment, but they soon reopened due to popular demand. As the author of a commentary on Berlin's Wintergarten cabaret noted in November 1914:

> Variety show treats in wartime are perhaps not to every person's taste. God knows, there is much preaching about the seriousness of our times, that the carefree singsong of the dance troupes and the dizzying agility of the acrobats do not seem to fit in. On the other hand: many people believe that occasional diversion is needed precisely for nerves that have been stretched to their limits, that are hounded from one excitement to another.

The diversion was not without its patriotic message. Claire Waldoff, Berlin's most popular cabaret singer, delighted audiences with her number "Immer feste druff!," which contained the stirring refrain: "Der Soldate, der Soldate / ist der schönste Mann bei uns im Staate. / Darum schwärmen auch die Mädchen sehr / für das liebe, liebe, liebe Militär. (Soldier-man, Soldier-man / Prettiest fellow in the land / Thus all the girls go barmy / For the darling, darling army.)" Along with glorification of the home-side came a chorus of contempt for the enemy. An especially popular cabaret ditty, sung also in the schools, was the "Song of Hate against England." It went: "We love as one, We hate as one, / We have one enemy alone: England!" Obviously England was not the only foe, but it was singled out as Enemy Number One because it was seen to be similar to Germany in ethnicity and culture but unwilling to accept the Reich as a peer. Decades of envy and unrequited admiration stood behind this song of hatred and the hundreds of "God Punish England" signs appearing all over Germany. As for France, Berlin's cabaret artists dealt with the motherland of their art form by declaring their independence and wrapping themselves in exclusively national colors. Thus Berlin's Chat noir rechristened itself Schwarzer Kater, and its announcer, previously a "Conférencier," now called himself an "Ansager." The Break-from-France theme was echoed in the fashion industry, which urged that French fashions be vanquished along with French troops, leaving "Berlin [to] take over from Paris the lead in fashion questions."

Foreign influences were not the only taboo in popular theater: so were the traditional gibes at self-infatuated officials and dim-witted officers. Now cabaret skits and musicals, such as Rudolf Nelson's *The Kaiser Called* and *At the Outskirts of Paris,*

Claire Waldoff, Berlin's favorite cabaret artist

lavished sycophantic praise on the monarch and his generals. Performers exhorted audiences to subscribe to war loans, send socks to the troops, and to observe the rationing regulations. In play after play the home front was depicted as a stronghold of patriotic resolve where occasional shortages of food and fuel were shrugged off as temporary inconveniences. In a musical called *Berlin in the War* the chorus intoned the phrase "Laughter too is a civilian service obligation"—a variation on the old Prussian adage that "Quietude is the first duty of the citizen." This suggested that making light of daily deprivations was now a duty almost as solemn as political quiescence. In addition to helping Berliners laugh their way to a stiff upper lip, cabaret and vaudeville performers offered some practical advice to the victims of war. For example, Carl Hermann Unthan, who played the violin with his feet because he had been born without arms, offered to teach soldiers whose hands had been blown off how to substitute the use of their feet for their arms, thereby helping them to regain "their self-confidence and prove to them that they will not be dependent upon the support of their fellow citizens."

Dutifully patriotic as most cabaret artists may have been, the authorities did not trust them to stay on the proper path without supervision, and subjected all their material to precensorship. This opened a new chapter in the old conflict between artists and bureaucrats in Berlin. The government's strict controls provoked protests from some of the performers, who complained that their work, indeed their very ability to assist the war effort, was being compromised. Claire Waldoff was allowed to go ahead with only eight of the fifteen titles she planned to perform at the Metropol Cabaret in January 1915. Among the red-penciled titles was her *Soldaten-Romanze*, which featured a young woman climbing the military ranks, from corporal to general, only to dream upon becoming "Frau General" of starting all over again with the corporal. Herr von Glasenapp, wartime Berlin's chief censor, considered this disrespectful toward the military. When Rudolf Nelson inserted some unauthorized material into one of his musicals, the police warned him that he would be subjected to more stringent controls in the future and might even be banned entirely if he committed any more "irregularities." Conservative elements among the public also put pressure on artists to toe the patriotic line. A newspaper report in August 1916 about a Nelson cabaret program featuring bons vivants swilling champagne and ogling seminude young women while joking about food shortages elicited angry letters from readers, who complained that there was nothing funny about living high at home while German boys were dying for their Fatherland in the battles of the Somme. Furloughed soldiers joined the protest, echoing earlier complaints about idle youth. One group wrote: "We come from the battlefield, where we experience nothing but sorrow, pain, and death, and in the big cities they party into the night. . . . Our wives hardly know how to scrape by with their children, while the others dissipate their money with whores and champagne." A Bavarian soldier, sounding like Private Hitler, declared that "that pack of sows deserves to be hanged, if they're that well off, those unpatriotic bastards." Another Bavarian, even more ominously, saw the Nelson play as evidence of Jewish war-profiteering, a plague that was allowed to ravage the land while "German" women starved and "German" men died in the trenches. The notion that the big cities, especially Berlin, harbored packs of Semitic profiteers persisted through the war and helped to further inflame hatreds during the revolution and Weimar era.

Berlin's nascent film industry, like cabaret, lined up behind the war effort, but instead of being diminished by the experience like vaudeville, it emerged as a much stronger force in popular culture. Before the war Germany's film market was dominated by foreign competitors—French, British, Italian, and, increasingly, American. By 1916, however, all enemy European films were banned, as were American products after Washington's entry into the war in 1917. To accommodate a public hungry for diversion, domestic producers leaped into the breach. The military and the Reich government fostered this development because they had come to understand—largely by watching enemy filmmakers blacken Germany's image—that film could be an invaluable propaganda tool. With the support of Ludendorff, Alfred Hugenberg, a director of the Krupp arms firm, established the Deutsche Lichtbild Gesellschaft (DLG—German Film Corporation) in 1915, which produced short films to celebrate German industry and promote the nation's war aims. A little later, another company, Universum Film A.G. (Universal Film Corporation, or UFA) joined in the cinematic campaign to combat Allied propaganda. Financed by the government, the Deutsche Bank, and heavy industry, UFA soon became the preeminent German film company, a status it retained through the Weimar period.

Like Berlin's film crowd, the city's sizable community of painters, including many members of the avant-garde, put their talents to work for the war, especially in the early stages. Kaiser Wilhelm himself could not have faulted these artists on their patriotism. However, much more than film, painting in Berlin came to reflect the escalating horror of the conflict as it dragged on and on. Moreover, some artists began to focus on the ways in which the war was debasing life on the home front, particularly in the capital.

The artists who founded the Secession and pioneered in the transition to expressionism greeted the opening of hostilities in 1914 with enthusiasm. Lovis Corinth praised the *furor teutonicus*, which he said "showed the enemy that he could not disturb our peaceful existence with impunity." Like so many of Berlin's culturati, he demanded an end to the aping of foreign fashions. Max Liebermann, who had done as much aping as anyone, signed the Manifesto of the Ninety-three, that defense of German aggression in the name of cultural salvation. Paul Cassirer, the Secessionist patron, started a new art magazine in August 1914 called *Kriegszeit* (Wartime), which featured patriotic exhortations and drawings from some of Berlin's best known artists, including Liebermann, Julius Meier-Graefe, Max Beckmann, and Max Slevogt. The first issue contained a lithograph by Liebermann celebrating the spirit of 1914 as well as a declaration from Meier-Graefe saying that artists had to march along with politicians of all factions to the common goal of German victory. The magazine acknowledged Italy's entry into the war on the side of the Allies with a lithograph entitled "Roman Eagle in May 1915"; it showed a vulture perched on Michelangelo's *Moses*.

By 1916, however, Berlin's painters were visibly registering their frustration over a seemingly interminable war that was devouring young lives on the battlefields and engendering widespread misery at home. Cassirer, who returned to Berlin in 1916 after a stint at the front, replaced *Kriegszeit* with a new arts periodical called *Der Bildermann*, which was considerably more critical of the war and its effects on German society. Among other troubling developments, the magazine recorded the escalating deterioration of socioeconomic conditions in the national capital. One of its contributors was Heinrich Zille, whose humorous depictions of lower-class life in Berlin had often tended to mask its misery, but who now offered grim commentaries on despair and loss: whole families getting morosely drunk; a woman and her children in their tenement room reading a letter informing them that the man of the house has been killed in battle. Ottomar Starke, a younger artist, zeroed in on the social cleavages magnified by war: his paintings showed profiteers rich enough to snub old acquaintances; a nouveau riche fop blithely ignoring a beggar wearing an iron cross.

The intensity with which the experience of war could magnify and transform the experience of the big city was exemplified in the work of Max Beckmann. He had lived in Berlin for several years before 1914, joining the expressionist scene but soon coming to dismiss expressionism as too mystical and otherworldly. "My heart beats for a raw average vulgar art," he wrote in his journal in 1909, "which doesn't live between sleepy fairy-tale moods and poetry but rather concedes a direct entrance to the fearful, commonplace, splendid and the average grotesque banality in life." Beckmann's ambition, suggested the art critic Robert Hughes, was to be "a psychological realist in a bad age: the Courbet of the cannibals." The war offered him ample opportunity to realize this ambition. His service as a medical orderly on the Western Front plunged him into a world at once horrific and strangely compelling—the grotesque carnival of spilled intestines and severed limbs, the ethereal beauty of searchlights and fire-belching cannon. After suffering a mental breakdown in 1915, Beckmann returned to Berlin and applied what he had learned at the front to the city, viewing it through the eyes of a survivor of hell who understands that much of the violent, claustrophobic, chaotic life of the trenches can also be found in the industrial metropolis. Out of this understanding came a series of drawings entitled, appropriately, *Hell*, which he worked on through the revolution and published in 1919. Included was a piece called *The Way Home*, showing a maimed war cripple begging in a Berlin street, and *The Family*, featuring Beckmann's own son playing with two hand grenades. Other drawings chronicled the channeling of wartime misery into revolutionary anger. In all these works, as in his extensive Weimar-era oeuvre, Beckmann gave expression to his conviction that it was the artist's duty to live in the large city and help its inhabitants come to grips with the horrors of the present and future. "We must sacrifice our hearts and our nerves to poor deceived humanity's horrible screams of pain. . . . That is the only thing that can motivate our quite superficial and selfish existence. That we give to people a sign of their fate."

Another artist who gave people—especially the people of Berlin—a sign of their fate was George Grosz. Like Beckmann, Grosz had moved to Berlin in the prewar years (1912) and flirted with expressionism. After the sleepy village of Stolp in Pomerania, where he had grown up, and Dresden, where he had attended art school, Berlin seemed exhilarating. As he later wrote: "In Berlin people were progressive . . . there was wonderful theater, a gigantic circus, cabarets and reviews. Beer palaces as big as railway concourses, wine palaces which occupied four floors, six-day [bicycle] races, futuristic exhibitions, international tango competitions. . . . That was Berlin when I arrived there." There were also, of course, dozens of cafés in which a budding artist could while away his time, soaking up the local color. Grosz's favorite was the Café des Westens, known fondly as Café Grössenwahn (Café Grand Illusion). He stood out even among its eccentric clientele by dressing in theatrical checked suits, powdering his face, and carrying a skull-topped cane. It was there that he first revealed his prowess in performance art—by peeing a perfect profile of one of his friends on the bathroom wall.

Although Grosz loved Berlin for its racy glitter, he also appreciated its grime. His prewar drawings, based largely on the toilet graffiti he assiduously studied, exuded a blossoming misanthropy and misogyny, a partiality for *Lustmord*, the sex-murders in which men dispatched whores and wives in creatively grisly fashion. He was just reaching his stride as a chronicler of domestic mayhem when the war broke out. Unlike many of his fellow artists, he did not cheer this development, viewing the whole business as an expression of mass stupidity. He registered his revulsion in a drawing entitled "Pandemonium, August 1914," which depicted prowar revelers as a howling pack of cretinous thugs. Nonetheless, he enlisted in November 1914, apparently convinced that the front could be no more brutal than the rear. He saw no action, though, for a sinus infection soon put him in a military hospital, and he was discharged as unfit for service in late 1915. Returning to Berlin, he found the city

> cold and grey. The frenzied activity of the cabarets and bars contrasted unnervingly with the dark, murky, and unheated places where people lived. The same soldiers who sang, danced and hung drunkenly on the arms of prostitutes could later be seen, ill-tempered, laden with parcels and still muddy from grave-digging duty, marching through the streets from one railway station to the next. How right Swedenborg was, I thought, when he said that Heaven and Hell exist here on earth side by side.

Grosz had always had an eye for the underside of life in Berlin, but now he seemed to see nothing but its stinking nether regions, as if it were the proverbial Asshole of the World. His representations of Germany's capital in wartime seem like an amalgam of Hogarth, Bosch, and Brueghel. In 1917 he described one of his paintings, explicitly Hogarthian, as

> a large picture of Hell—a *Gin Lane* of grotesque corpses and lunatics; there's a lot going on—Old Nick himself is riding on the slanting coffin through the picture out towards the left; on the right a young man is throwing up, vomiting on the canvas all the illusions of youth. . . . A teeming multitude of possessed human beasts—I am totally convinced that this epoch is sailing on down to its own destruction—our sullied paradise. . . . Just think: wherever you step smells of shit.

Six months later Grosz (he had recently changed his name from Georg Gross to document his contempt for Germany) completed a canvas entitled *Widmung an Oskar Panizza* (Dedication to Oskar Panizza). Here the city was a riotous bedlam of flag-waving patriots, strutting generals, and grim priests, along with three grotesque figures representing alcoholism, syphilis, and plague.

One cannot escape the impression that Grosz took a certain perverse pleasure in the depravity he described, that he was proud to live in a place that smelled so thoroughly of shit. But his penchant for wallowing in the dreck did not diminish his work's effectiveness as a searing commentary on life in the beleaguered German capital. In the end, no one was better than Grosz at representing Berlin as a hideous inversion of Germany's vaunted "Peace of the Castle": a place where instead of working harmoniously together people brayed patriotic slogans while fattening themselves at their neighbors' expense, where everyone was fighting over everything from food rations and coal supplies to the anticipated privilege of pouring down boiling oil when the enemy began climbing the walls.

In the last two years of the war, Grosz and another Berlin artist, John Heartfield (he had changed his name from Helmut Herzfelde), began experimenting with a new technique, photomontage, which involved composing parts of photographs into synthetic images seemingly produced by a camera—a very bizarre camera. Their obvious susceptibility for the absurd made Grosz and Heartfield natural converts to a new art movement sweeping up from Zurich: Dada. Invented by an international coterie of war refugees, dada expressed the artists' contempt not just for the "civilized" world at war, but for all the traditional art forms that either failed to point up the absurdity of the war or that opportunistically abetted it. Dada declared war on Art by producing anti-art; it attacked sense with non-sense. "Bevor Dada da war, war Dada da. (Before dada was there was dada there.)" "Aimless of the world unite," declared writer Richard Huelsenbeck, who brought the movement to Berlin. Grosz put this doctrine to practice by performing a tap dance while pretending to pee on a painting by Lovis Corinth. "Art is shit," he cried, and pee made excellent varnish.

Although Dada caught on in many European cities, Berlin became its most important outpost after Zurich. There was method in the madness here: in no other city, after all, was there a greater gap between seemingly rational rhetoric and patently irrational reality; nowhere had the old verities proven so bankrupt. According to Huelsenbeck, the war, like a purging fire, would eventually burn out the rotten underpinnings of Western Civilization, though this would require even more bloodletting. "We were for the war, and Dada is still for the war," he declared. "Everything has to crash together; things are not horrible enough yet by a long shot."

Defeat and Revolution

Things were perhaps not yet bad enough for the Dadaists, but they were fast becoming so for most ordinary Berliners. In the second half of the war the food and coal crisis worsened appreciably, while prices continued to mount. Police reports on morale in the city registered an escalating malaise and "a tense political situation" due to the endless shortages, high prices, and an inequitable distribution of resources. If wealthy people were still able to purchase scarce items through back channels, this was beyond the reach of the poor and even of the middle classes, who complained with justice about the authorities' inability or unwillingness to make life's daily necessities affordable to the general population. As the crisis deepened, Berliners increasingly forgot that quietude was their first duty as citizens. In March 1917 about 500 women stormed a municipal vegetable warehouse in Charlottenburg, demanding an immediate distribution of its contents. Then they marched to the town hall, crying "Hunger, hunger, we want turnips!" It was a bad sign when people started protesting for turnips.

Because the Social Democratic Party, the traditional champion of Berlin's working classes, continued to do little to relieve the suffering, the party leadership lost credibility in the capital. "In no other city does the established Socialist leadership command so little influence as here," reported the Berlin police in March 1917. The capital thus became the natural breeding ground for an internal leftist opposition. Such a movement had surfaced as early as January 1916 with the foundation of the Spartakusbund by Karl Liebknecht and Rosa Luxemburg, who had never reconciled themselves to their party's support of the war. On May Day 1916 the Spartacists organized a demonstration in the center of Berlin against the government and the war; as a result, Luxemburg and Liebknecht were packed off to jail. By early 1917, dissension within the party had reached the point where advocates of an early peace decided to split off from the SPD to form a new entity, the Independent Social Democratic Party (Unabhängige Sozialistische Partei Deutschlands, USPD). The group was strongest in Germany's industrial areas, especially in the Ruhr and Berlin.

Although Berlin was becoming a hotbed of leftist agitation against the war, it also housed an influential contingent of patriotic bitter-enders, which was only natural given its status as the national capital and headquarters of the military-industrial complex. Concerned about growing antiwar sentiment in Berlin and elsewhere, a coalition of military figures, right-wing lobbyists, and nationalist academics published a manifesto in 1916 demanding that Germany fight on until it had achieved an ambitious list of war aims, including domination of the European continent and parity in world affairs with Britain. The following year saw the formation of the Fatherland Party, which lobbied for an expansionist victory abroad and continued authoritarianism at home. As the organizational center of both the militant right and the radical left, Berlin confirmed and expanded its status as cynosure of political polarization in the German Reich.

A key figure in the rightist resurgence was Admiral von Tirpitz, who perhaps wanted to make up in belligerent bluster for the puny wartime performance of Germany's High Seas Fleet, which, with the exception of the Battle of Jutland in 1916, had stayed bottled up in port, reluctant to challenge the British. Only the Kriegsmarine's submarines had made a significant impact on the war by sinking an impressive number of enemy vessels. In February 1917 the decision was made to extend the submarine campaign against neutral shipping, especially American, in hopes of depriving Britain of the supplies it needed to continue the war. According to a police report, Berliners on the whole welcomed this step as the best means of bringing the conflict to a rapid end. The fact that it increased the likelihood of an American declaration of war did not diminish its attractiveness, for few Germans believed that America could make much of an impact before Britain was forced to surrender. However, once the United States had in fact entered the war, Berliners increasingly began to fear that this might be a "fateful" development, after all, which of course it proved to be.

While Berlin's patriots celebrated the declaration of "unrestricted submarine warfare," the city's radical left was encouraged by the collapse of the czarist regime in Russia in spring 1917. In the eyes of the far left, the upheaval in Russia signaled the first crack in the edifice of world capitalism and imperialism. It also undercut the SPD's justification of the war as a defense against czarist reaction. Writing from prison in April, Rosa Luxemburg argued that the events in Russia "faced the German proletariat with a vital question of honor." The radicals, she said, had to step up their campaign against the war or be complicit in a conflict that was "no longer against Czarism, but against the Russian revolution." Russia had liberated itself from an authoritarian regime, she noted, "but who will liberate Germany from military dictatorship, from Junker reaction, from the imperialist slaughter?"

In mid-April 1917 a group of shop stewards from Berlin's metal industry demanded that the German government inaugurate peace talks with the Russian provisional government. To put some muscle behind this demand, and to protest recent cuts in the bread ration, they organized a one-day strike in the city's metalworking plants. According to a police report, some 148,903 workers laid down their tools, though fewer participated in the accompanying mass march mounted by the strike leaders.

Worried that the growing domestic discord might generate more far-reaching disruptions unless some movement was made toward ending the war, a group of moderates in the Reichstag, which heretofore had compliantly backed the government, launched a belated peace offensive in summer 1917. A Center Party representative, Matthias Erzberger, introduced a resolution calling for a compromise peace, without annexations or indemnities. The resolution carried the house but did not significantly

The "Iron Hindenburg" statue on the Königsplatz

affect the government's policy. Germany was not a parliamentary democracy, and Ludendorff and Hindenburg could safely ignore the legislators' appeal. The main result of this initiative was the dismissal of Chancellor Bethmann-Hollweg, whom the generals blamed for not keeping the parliamentarians in line. He was replaced by Georg Michaelis, a Prussian civil servant who was not likely to cause the military any trouble. Upon taking office he said: "I do not consider a body like the German Reichstag a fit one to decide about peace and war on its own initiative during the war."

Committed as it was to ending the war with nothing less than a resounding (and profitable) victory, the German government demanded ever greater sacrifices from the people. Copper was stripped from the roofs of buildings along the Kurfürstendamm to be melted into shell casings. Citizens were urged to turn in pots and pans and used clothing. But the most dramatic symbol of the last-ditch campaign was a huge wooden statue of Field Marshal Hindenburg, which was wheeled out in front of the Reichstag. Patriots were encouraged to purchase nails at a mark apiece to hammer into the flanks of this "Iron Hindenburg." Thousands of people followed the call, but their efforts did little more than turn the effigy into a giant pin cushion. The government also resorted to sending high school students door-to-door to sell war bonds. Felix Gilbert and some of his classmates had the misfortune to be dispatched to Berlin's proletarian districts, where residents generally slammed their doors in the boys' faces. In order not to appear lazy or unpatriotic, Gilbert and his friends shook down their own families for generous donations. This rather pathetic campaign was emblematic of Germany's determination to finance the war by subscriptions, bonds, and other public debt instruments rather than by higher taxes. No social group would suffer more from this decision than the middle-class patriots who dutifully bought war bonds as a sign of their faith in a glorious future.

In November 1917 the Bolsheviks overthrew Russia's provisional government, a development with far-reaching implications for Germany and Berlin. In the short run it benefited the hard-liners because of Lenin's determination to pull Russia out of the war. A truce with Russia would allow Germany to shift men and material from the Eastern to the Western Front, possibly facilitating the long-sought breakthrough in that quarter. In Berlin Lenin's coup was celebrated with the ringing of church bells. Yet the city's radical leftists were also emboldened by the events in Russia, which they hoped to emulate at home. On November 19 the Berlin police reported that the local USPD "stands solidly on the side of Lenin." The police were unsure, however, whether the radicals would choose openly to display their enthusiasm, since in their view most of the leftist leaders lacked "the courage to stage powerful demonstrations."

This assessment proved incorrect. Animated by the growing frustration among Berlin's working classes, the USPD called for a protest march from the proletarian suburbs to the government district on November 26. About 2,000 protesters, many of them women and children, descended on the city center. However, when they sought to march to Unter den Linden via Kaiser-Wilhelm-Strasse, they were turned back by troops wielding sabers.

The government's use of force further alienated the workers. On January 21 a police observer reported increasing talk among the lower classes about an impending upheaval, though he continued to believe that the USPD leadership was unwilling to risk a major test with the authorities. In fact, most of the party leaders hoped to avoid a violent confrontation, fearing that this would result in the group's suppression. Instead of a general strike across the nation, which is what the Spartacists wanted, the

USPD called for a demonstration strike among munitions workers centered in the national capital. On January 28 some 400,000 Berlin workers laid down their tools. The strikers issued a list of demands including a peace without annexations, an end to the Law of Siege, improvements in food distribution, and reform of the Prussian suffrage system. The SPD had not wanted the strike, but it felt obliged to go along with it for fear of totally losing control over the masses.

Enraged by this action, which Ludendorff considered nothing short of treason, the government immediately militarized the striking factories and arrested key strike leaders. One of them, Wilhelm Dittmann, a USPD Reichstag delegate, was sentenced to five years' incarceration by a military court. Strikers with deferments from military service were summarily dispatched to the front, their identity papers stamped with "B-18" (for Berlin 1918) to ensure that they never got a deferment again. On the kaiser's personal orders, a battalion of battle-hardened riflemen patrolled the streets. Such tough measures managed to break the strike movement within one week. The workers' willingness to end their walkout without achieving their demands suggested that they were not (or not yet) truly revolutionary, their fiery rhetoric notwithstanding.

On the other hand, the January strikes, which were most extensive in Berlin, reinforced perceptions of the metropolis as an unruly and unreliable place. The military command decided to limit furloughs to the city in order to prevent contamination of frontline troops. At the same time, guard units there were strengthened with an eye to snuffing out future disturbances with a whiff of grapeshot. Yet even a leader as bullheaded as Ludendorff understood that suppression alone could not contain the growing dissatisfaction; he knew that without victory in the field the discontent at home might become unmanageable. The message from Berlin in early 1918 was that if this victory did not come soon, it might not be possible at all.

Following the signing of the Treaty of Brest-Litovsk on March 3, 1918, by which Soviet Russia formally left the war and ceded huge stretches of territory to Germany, Ludendorff saw fit to launch an ambitious new offensive in the West. The push was accompanied by assurances that it would finally achieve a decisive breakthrough and bring peace with honor. Evidently, many Berliners, despite all the disappointments of the past, were inclined to share this hope. As a police commissar reported, no doubt with some exaggeration: "Now that the highly promising offensive, whose success nobody here doubts, is under way, there is widespread confidence that the war is in its last stage and that peace will come this summer."

After initial gains Ludendorff's great March offensive faltered, as did another push in April. News of the military failures quickly dashed the springtime of hope at home. "The cessation of the offensive in the West has caused much disturbance in the Reichstag," noted one delegate in early May. "Great expectations are replaced by deep and bitter disappointment; certainty of victory gives way to dark pessimism." Hope flickered again in June when Berliners learned of a new thrust to the Marne. The citizenry now believed, said a police report, that victory must certainly come by fall, at the latest. Yet of course this too was an illusion. Germany's lines were overextended and her exhausted soldiers were encountering fresh American troops for the first time. Over the course of the summer the Allies counterattacked and pushed the Germans back. Instead of imminent victory, early fall brought Berliners nothing but bad news, more food shortages, and more names with iron crosses on the tote board of death. "Berlin is indeed a gloomy place," reported Princess Blücher in September. "The news from the front is more and more depressing, there is nothing to eat, and the methods employed to prevent the depression from gaining ground goad the people to fury. Hindenburg has forbidden anyone, whatever his personal feelings may be, to speak of the present position as being anything else than hopeful."

Of course it proved impossible to keep the home front ignorant of what was happening on the battle front. Soldiers on leave told the unvarnished truth about Germany's deteriorating military situation. The generals and their right-wing supporters later insisted that defeatism at home had crucially undermined morale at the front, but it would be more accurate to say that growing demoralization among the frontline troops exacerbated pessimistic sentiments at home. Still, most Germans, most Berliners, believed in the possibility of victory almost to the very end. At worst, they envisaged a negotiated settlement that would not be humiliating for the Reich.

By late September General Ludendorff, the man who had ordered soldiers shot for uttering the word "defeat," became convinced that defeat was inevitable. He further concluded that if the fighting continued much longer, the German army might disintegrate. Backed by Hindenburg, who had reached the same conclusion, he informed the kaiser that it was necessary to appeal for an armistice. Although appalled by this turn of events, Wilhelm agreed to the armistice bid, adding that he had known all along that this was going to happen. The kaiser and his generals, however, were not about to accept personal responsibility for the defeat. They agreed that the onus of arranging an armistice should be handed to civilian politicians, who, in their eyes, had let the army and the monarchy down. As Ludendorff told the General Staff on October 1, 1918, Germany's civilians must "now eat the soup which they have served us." The monarch and the High Command also agreed that the new government undertaking the armistice negotiations would have to be reorganized on a more democratic basis. This would, they hoped, pull the rug out from under the radicals who were calling for a republic.

Thus on October 2, 1918, Kaiser Wilhelm asked his cousin, Maximilian, Prince of Baden, a liberal, to become chancellor and to preside over a belated democratization of the Reich. This move represented a tacit acknowledgment that the four-year effort to preserve undiluted authoritarianism at home through military conquest abroad had failed. The new government hastily drew up a series of reforms making the cabinet responsible to the Reichstag and subordinating the military to civilian control. Max also appealed to President Wilson to broker an armistice based on his Fourteen Points, which, if strictly applied, would have allowed Germany to emerge from the war without losing any of her original territory. (Most Germans, from the kaiser on down, apparently believed that their attempt to steal their neighbors' land should not oblige them to give up any of their own property, since their effort had been unsuccessful.)

Under normal conditions, the constitutional reforms introduced by Prince Max of Baden would have been heralded by progressive-minded Germans as a great breakthrough, but the shock of impending defeat, coming after four years of sacrifice and promises of victory, made the reforms seem paltry. Rather than gratitude, most Germans felt contempt for a regime whose sudden reformist ardor seemed so obviously designed to save its own skin. As for the kaiser himself, Germans understood that he was hated around the world and that his staying on the throne would constitute an impediment to a favorable peace. President Wilson had made it clear that the Allies wished to negotiate with "authentic representatives of the German people," which did not include Wilhelm.

Berlin, which had a long history of troubles with the kaiser, was rife with calls for his ouster. Wilhelm had returned to Potsdam on October 1 to preside over the constitutional revisions. There were rumors that he was not safe in his own capital, and he apparently believed them. Toward the end of the month he left again for the front, not out of fear, but in the mistaken belief that he could convince the troops to help him keep his throne. He would not, he said, allow a few hundred Jews and several thousand workers push him from power. He further declared that after the armistice he would bring his army back to Berlin to restore order.

The reality was that he would never see his capital again. His eleventh-hour visit to the German headquarters at Spa proved to be only a way station on his flight into exile in Holland. Throughout his exile, he persisted in the belief that he owed his ouster largely to the perfidy of Berlin and its Jews. Upon the ex-kaiser's death in 1941, Hitler sought to bring his body back to the Reich capital for a state funeral and burial, which the Führer hoped would allow him to bury the Hohenzollern Monarchy for good along with its last ruler. It turned out, however, that Wilhelm had declared in his will that he would be buried in Berlin only if the Hohenzollern Monarchy had been restored. This not being the case, the kaiser was interred at his exile residence in Doorn, with the Nazi high commissioner for the Netherlands, Arthur Seyss-Inquart, in attendance.

For all the antagonism toward Wilhelm II in Berlin, the revolutionary events that swept him from his throne and into exile began not in the capital but at the naval port at Kiel. In late October the admiral of the fleet stationed there ordered his ships to steam out on a suicidal mission against the British in order to salvage the honor of the German navy. The sailors quite sensibly mutinied. Then they formed a "Sailors' Council," which demanded an immediate end to the war and the abdication of the kaiser. It was somehow fitting that the first decisive actions against Wilhelm's rule were taken in the navy, the branch he had been so keen to develop.

Inspired by the events at Kiel, Workers' and Soldiers' Councils began sprouting up all over Germany. Munich in the south was a major flash point. There, on November 7, the venerable Wittelsbach ruling house fell victim to an uprising orchestrated by a USPD politician named Kurt Eisner. The fact that Eisner was a Jew from Berlin reinforced the conviction among conservative Bavarians that nothing but evil came from the Prussian capital. To a proud Berliner like Harry Kessler, it was a little disconcerting that his hometown was not, for the moment, on the cutting edge of German history. As he wrote in his diary on November 7: "The shape of the revolution is becoming clear; progressive encroachment, as by a patch of oil, by the mutinous sailors from the coast to the interior. Berlin is being isolated and will soon be only an island. It is the other way around from France: here the provinces are carrying revolution to the capital."

But Berlin caught up soon enough. On November 9 a general strike spread through the city, and thousands of workers paraded down Unter den Linden calling for a republic. The Brandenburg Gate was sheathed in red flags, while next door at the Hotel Adlon radical soldiers set up machine guns, as if to make short work of the plutocrats inside. Civilians accosted military officers in the streets and tore off their insignia of rank. Although the assailants looked to Kessler like "schoolboys," their act of military iconoclasm was no trifle in the town that had produced the "Captain of Köpenick."

Alarmed by these signs of rebellion, Max of Baden concluded that the only way to prevent a full-scale revolution—one like that in Russia, where an entire social order was collapsing—was to announce the kaiser's abdication, even without the kaiser's consent. This he did on the morning of November 9, after which he resigned himself and turned power over to Friedrich Ebert, head of the SPD.

Ebert, who had an emotional attachment to the monarchy, if not to the ruling monarch, would have liked to save the institution, perhaps by bringing on one of the kaiser's sons. But it was too late for such an option. At midday Karl Liebknecht, who had been released from prison in October as a goodwill gesture on the part of the new government, appeared on a balcony of the Royal Palace and proclaimed the advent of a socialist republic. Among the crowd below was Princess Blücher, who captured the historic scene in her memoirs:

> Out of the great gateway a rider dashed on horseback, waving . . . a red flag, and at the same moment one of the windows opened on to a balcony in front of the castle, and on the same spot where four and a half years ago the Kaiser made his great appeal to the enthusiastic people, Liebknecht appeared, shouting to the masses that they were now freed from the bondages of the past and that a new era of liberty was opening out before them. History repeats, or rather mimics herself, in a somewhat tasteless way at times.

To the SPD leaders, Liebknecht's act was more than tasteless; it was a direct challenge to their as yet very tenuous grip on power, and it threatened indeed to move Berlin in the direction of Moscow. Determined to prevent a Spartakus takeover, Philipp Scheidemann, the second-ranking member of the SPD executive, ended a speech at the Reichstag by shouting: "The Hohenzollerns have abdicated. Long live the great German Republic!" Scheidemann knew that the first part of this statement was not true, or not true yet, but this was a minor detail when the future of the nation was at stake. What he could not have known was that his and Liebknecht's proclamation of rival republics anticipated Germany's formal division into democratic and communist republics thirty years later.

Soldiers returning from the front march through the Brandenburg Gate, December 1918

THE GREAT DISORDER

"Look at me!" blared the capital of the Reich. "I am Babel, the monster among cities! We had a formidable army; now we command the most riotously wicked night life. Don't miss our matchless show, ladies and gentlemen! It's Sodom and Gomorrah in a Prussian tempo. Don't miss the circus of perversities! Our department store of assorted vices! It's phe-nom-e-nal! An all-out sale of brand new kinds of debauchery!

—Klaus Mann, *The Turning Point*

WHAT REALLY MADE BERLIN extraordinary then was the extent—far greater than that of any other European capital—to which everything that happened there appeared as symptomatic of the crisis in modern civilization." So wrote the British poet Stephen Spender in an article about Berlin in the so-called "Golden Twenties." Spender was not alone in thinking of Weimar-era Berlin as crisis-central, a kind of laboratory of the apocalypse where modern Europeans tested the limits of their social and cultural traditions. People from all over the industrialized world flocked to Berlin to be part of this experiment, if only for a short while. Visitors found the German city to be open, brave, and honest, especially regarding sex. The erstwhile capital of Prussian militarism had become, in Wyndham Lewis's phrase, "the Hauptstadt of vice." According to a character in one of Spengler's novels, *The Temple*, Berlin was a "city with no virgins. Not even the kittens and puppies [were] virgins." But for the Berliners themselves, hosts to this enterprise both in the sense of sponsoring it and being devoured by it, the 1920s were not so much "golden" as red in tooth and claw.

This was especially true of the first years of the postwar decade, which were marked by coup attempts from left and right, devastating inflation, racially motivated riots, strikes, political assassinations, and a general dog-eat-dog rapaciousness. Looking back on this period from the vantage point of the somewhat more stable mid-1920s, the Berlin novelist W. E. Süskind could call it "an extraordinary time, when disorder seemed to be trump."

Sheer Byzantine Conditions!

While much of the world celebrated the end of the war in November 1918, Berlin wallowed in misery. The armistice brought an end to the killing on the front but not to the suffering at home. The Allied blockade remained in place, ensuring continued shortages of food and fuel. Freezing and malnourished, Berliners perished in their thousands in the Spanish influenza epidemic of 1918/19. Over 1,700 died in a single day, their bodies piling up in the morgues. A band of soldiers returning to the city on December 11 was greeted at the Brandenburg Gate by Friedrich Ebert, head of the provisional government, as heroes "unvanquished on the field of battle," but they could hardly have felt like heroes when, as one of them complained, "there was little to buy, and what was available was bad."

The political situation in the capital remained confused, to say the least. Ebert had titular power as head of the People's Commissioners, but the Independent Socialists in his regime had their own ideas on how the nation should be run. So did another body, the National Congress of Workers' and Soldiers' Councils, which convened in Berlin in mid-December and demanded full sovereignty for itself. A third faction, the Spartakus Union, which considered both the Councils and the Independents too tame, persisted in its dream of turning Berlin into another Moscow. The Spartacists had an unruly ally in the form of the People's Naval Division, a motley band of about 3,000 mutinous sailors encamped in the Royal Palace, whose contents they were gleefully destroying or hawking in the streets. Among the items on sale was former Kaiser Wilhelm II's correspondence with Queen Victoria. Berliners could be forgiven for wondering who ran the place.

Anxious to reestablish a modicum of order, Ebert decided in late December to discipline the People's Naval Division. He offered to pay the sailors 125,000 marks back pay if they would reduce the size of their force and vacate the palace in favor of the royal stables next door. They promised to consider this offer if Ebert would pay them another 80,000 marks as a "Christmas bonus." When he balked, they invaded the Chancellery, ransacked several offices, and took Otto Wels, the civilian city commandant of Berlin, as a hostage. "What gives you the right to detain an official of the government?" asked one of Ebert's men. "Our power," was the sailors' answer. In exchange for Wels's release, the sailors demanded not only the 80,000 marks' bonus but official recognition as the permanent garrison of Berlin.

Ebert understood that giving in to the sailors would mean abandoning the capital to chaos, but he also knew that he could not face them down without help from the regular army, and that this would come at a price: carte blanche to deal with the radicals as the military saw fit. Full of qualms, he got on his secret line to military headquarters, now at Kassel. General Gröner's aide, Major Kurt von Schleicher, who thirteen years later would serve as Germany's last chancellor before Hitler, took the call and promised to send a force of Horse Guards from Potsdam to clean up the mess in the capital. A few hours later Ebert got cold feet and tried to cancel the order, but General Gröner informed him curtly that he and Field Marshal Hindenburg were "determined to hold to the plan of liquidation of the Naval Division," and would "see to it that it is carried out."

At about midnight on December 23 the Horse Guards and other government troops set up artillery around the palace and began to shoot. One of the first shells tore away the balcony from which Kaiser Wilhelm had declared that he no longer recognized parties, only Germans. After blowing open the main portal, the Guards swarmed into the building, only to discover that the sailors had fled through a tunnel to the nearby Marstall, or stables. Switching their fire to the Marstall, the Guards kept shooting through the night until the beleaguered sailors, having suffered extensive casualties, put out white flags. It was 9:30 in the morning on the day before Christmas.

Before the government troops could take full control of the situation, thousands of proletarian Berliners, called to action by the Spartacists, appeared on the scene and interposed themselves between the soldiers and their quarry in the Marstall. Unwilling to fire on the crowd, which included women and children, the Guards pulled back. Palace Square now belonged to the radical sailors and their civilian saviors.

Christmas Eve undoubtedly seemed like May Day to Berlin's would-be Bolsheviks, but to most Berliners it was time to celebrate in the traditional holiday fashion, despite, or perhaps because of, all the chaos and continuing deprivations. After strolling the streets of central Berlin, Harry Kessler jotted in his diary:

> The Christmas Fair carried on throughout the blood-letting. Hurdy-gurdies played in the Friedrichstrasse while street-vendors sold indoor fireworks, gingerbread, and silver tinsel. Jewelers' shops in Unter den Linden remained unconcernedly open, their windows brightly lit and glittering. In the Leipziger Strasse the usual Christmas crowds thronged the big stores. In thousands of homes the Christmas tree was lit and the children played around it with their presents from Daddy, Mummy and Auntie dear. In the Imperial Stables lay the dead, and the wounds freshly inflicted on the Palace and on Germany gaped into the Christmas night.

On Christmas day Liebknecht's followers staged a giant march in the center of the city, culminating in their occupation of the *Vorwärts* building, where they ran off red-colored leaflets celebrating the triumph of the "revolutionary sailors' division, the revolutionary proletariat, [and] the international socialist world revolution." Reviewing the situation, Kessler saw that the "core of the problem [for the government] is whether there are anywhere any serviceable and reliable troops available. Or, if not, whether the sailors can be bought and bribed to leave. Sheer Byzantine conditions!"

Aware that he could contend with the radicals in the capital only by bringing in stronger forces from outside, Ebert appointed as his commissioner for war one Gustav Noske, a tough-minded right-wing Social Democrat who was on good terms with the army command in Kassel. The army was in the process of recruiting new volunteer units called Freikorps, which were more than willing to help put down the "rabble" in Berlin. (Later it would become apparent that some of them were also quite prepared to turn against the democratically elected government.)

For Ebert and company, the offer of assistance came none too soon. On January 4, 1919, the simmering conflict between the provisional government and the radical left in Berlin boiled over when Ebert dismissed Chief of Police Emil Eichhorn, an

Revolutionaries man a machine gun atop the Brandenburg Gate, January 1919

Independent Socialist with ties to the Spartacists. The Spartakus Union, which together with some left-wing Independents and Revolutionary Shop Stewards had formed the German Communist Party (Kommunistische Partei Deutschlands, KPD) on January 1, 1919, mobilized the city's restless proletariat for a protest march. The following day some 200,000 demonstrators marched through central Berlin to the police headquarters in Alexanderplatz, where a defiant Eichhorn vowed he would not give up his post. Karl Liebknecht, for his part, urged the masses to complete the German revolution.

Over the course of the next few days bands of radicals seized the capital's main railway stations and newspaper offices, including *Vorwärts*. A red flag appeared atop the Brandenburg Gate, which was occupied by militants taking potshots at people on Unter den Linden. The leftist upheaval, however, was poorly organized; the insurgents failed to take over key government offices, supply depots, and the streetcar system. Nor did the action have the support of all the leading figures on the left. Rosa Luxemburg opposed the uprising as premature. Many of those who joined in the strikes and demonstrations had no clear view of what they wanted, save for food and jobs. Liebknecht was not Lenin, and Berlin was not Moscow, despite all the revolutionary rhetoric.

Noske and his allies in the military, on the other hand, knew precisely what they wanted: to bring "order" to Berlin by smashing the Spartacist upheaval and cutting down its leadership. From his headquarters in a girls' boarding school in Dahlem, Noske, assisted by General Walther von Lüttwitz, military commandant of Berlin, orchestrated assaults on the primary Spartacist outposts. Government forces quickly blasted their way into the *Vorwärts* building and, after accepting the surrender of its occupants, summarily executed a number of prisoners. A similar scenario unfolded at the police barracks in Alexanderplatz, where Noske's men killed defenders who were trying to surrender. The People's Naval Division, which earlier had been rescued from possible slaughter by the intervention of proletarian Berliners, proclaimed its neutrality and remained safely bunkered down in the Marstall throughout the duration of "Spartakus Week."

Most Berliners went about their business as best they could during those chaotic days. Streetcars continued to run, though they sometimes made unscheduled stops to wait out firefights. The city's entertainment industry also continued to function, despite strikes by some performers and a lack of fuel to heat the halls of culture. As the theologian Ernst Troeltsch noted in his *Spektator* newspaper column in mid-January: "The life of the big city went on more or less as usual despite all the horrors. Musicians and actors advertised upcoming performances on every poster-pillar, the theaters were filled to capacity with bullet-dodging crowds—but above all people *danced*, wherever possible, and in total disregard of the lack of heat and light." On January 14, amid signs that the radical upheaval was winding down, Kessler wrote:

> Today the band of the Republican Defense Force stood playing *Lohengrin* among the splintered glass in the courtyard behind the badly battered main gate of Police Headquarters. A large crowd collected in the street, partly to see the damage and partly to hear *Lohengrin*. Nonetheless shooting continues. No spot in the whole city is safe from Spartacist roof-top snipers. This afternoon several shots whistled past me as I was on the Hallische Ufer.

Finally, on January 17, when all was over but the occasional sniper shot, Kessler offered this observation on the effects that the chaos had had on the massive city:

> In the evening I went to a cabaret in the Bellevuestrasse. The sound of a shot cracked through the performance of a fiery Spanish dancer. Nobody took any notice. It underlined the slight impression that the revolution has made on metropolitan life. I only began to appreciate the Babylonian, unfathomably deep, primordial and titanic quality of Berlin when I saw how this historic, colossal event has caused no more than local ripples on the even more colossally eddying movement of Berlin existence. An elephant stabbed with a penknife shakes itself and strides on as if nothing has happened.

At the time Kessler penned these lines the two central figures in the insurrection, Karl Liebknecht and Rosa Luxemburg, were dead. They had been captured on January 15 by the Cavalry Guards Rifle Division and taken to the Guards' headquarters at the Hotel Eden, near the zoo. There they were interrogated under the direction of Captain Waldemar Pabst, a brutal thug who went on to become a Nazi and then a prosperous arms dealer in West Germany. When Pabst was finished with Rosa and Karl he turned them over to his troopers, supposedly for transport to prison in Moabit. A soldier waited by a side door and clubbed them over the head with his rifle as they emerged from the hotel. They were then bundled into two cars. The one with Liebknecht drove to the nearby Tiergarten, where Liebknecht was shot "trying to escape." Luxemburg, almost dead from her clubbing, was finished off in the car by a shot to the head, then pitched into the Landwehr Canal. Her killers later reported that she had been abducted by a mob and carried off to an unknown location. About four months later thirteen-year-old Felix Gilbert joined a small crowd on the bank of the canal and watched a body being fished from its murky waters. It was the barely recognizable corpse of Rosa Luxemburg.

No one was fooled by the official story concerning Luxemburg's and Liebknecht's end, and the brutal murders shocked even jaded Berlin. The left became more sharply divided, since the martyrs' radical followers held Ebert and Noske responsible for the murders. This division in the leftist camp persisted throughout the Weimar Republic, making genuine cooperation impossible even when the challenge of Hitler presented itself. At the same time, the killings helped to make murder an acceptable way of doing political business in Berlin. As one commentator has written, a "direct line runs from these crimes to the murders of the Gestapo."

On January 19, as the last of the red banners and revolutionary posters were cleared away from the city center, Berliners joined the rest of the country in voting for a national assembly that would bring representative government to the nascent republic. On the national level, the SPD emerged as the clear winner in the election, taking 37.9 percent of the vote, while the USDP carried only 7.6 percent. In Berlin, however, the Independents won 27.6 percent, while the SPD totaled 36.4 percent. As under the empire, at the dawn of the republican era the capital was considerably more "red" than most of the rest of the country.

The violence of the January insurrection hardened convictions in other parts of Germany that Berlin was an impossibly unruly place. In an article entitled "Der Geist von Berlin" (The Spirit of Berlin), a commentator for the *Schäbische Merkur* (Stuttgart) complained that the national capital was filled with "visionaries, dreamers, and adventurers" intent upon remaking Germany in their own image. "Germany, be on your guard! The spirit of Berlin is a demon." He went on to protest that the typical Berliner, in his arrogance, believed that

> his and the German horizon are one. *But Berlin is not Germany*. . . . We in southern Germany will not go along with it. We want to have a nation. But now Berlin has forfeited the right to be the capital of the nation and to represent us; it has shown itself unworthy of leading. We must draw a line between Berlin and ourselves, and leave it to its quarrels and its fate. . . . To the spirit of Berlin another must be opposed, *the spirit of Germany!*

The influential Bavarian writer Ludwig Thoma was even more vehement in his denunciation of the Spree city, which for him was the cause of all Germany's problems. If the nation ever hoped to pull itself out of the mire, he said, it would have to look to Bavaria rather than to Berlin: "We in Bavaria know that Berlin is at fault for all of Germany's misery. . . . Berlin is not German, in fact, it's the opposite—it's corrupted and polluted with *galizisch* [i.e., Jewish] filth. Every good man in Prussia knows today where to look for the root-stock of honest Germandom—in Bavaria. No Jew will confuse us on this score."

Because Berlin was perceived as corrupt and dangerous, Germany's leading politicians decided not to hold their deliberations for a new constitution in the capital. Instead, the delegates met in the small city of Weimar, about 150 miles to the southwest in the province of Thuringia. Weimar, whose legacy of Goethe and Schiller seemed a welcome antidote to that of Liebknecht and Luxemburg, could be easily protected by government forces, ensuring that "the voice of the street" did not interrupt the proceedings. Voices from Berlin, however, did briefly disrupt the meeting: a group of Berliners calling themselves the Dadaist Central Committee of World Revolution burst into the hall and dropped leaflets saying, "We will blow Weimar up, Berlin is the place . . . Da . . . Da . . . Nobody and nothing will be spared."

A month after opening their deliberations in Weimar, Germany's constitutional framers felt vindicated in their decision to steer clear of Berlin because the capital erupted once again in political mayhem. On March 3 a coalition of Communists and Independents called a general strike in the city. This time the central figure in the upheaval was the new Communist boss, Leo Jogisches, a Polish-born intellectual and recent lover of Rosa Luxemburg. Like his martyred mistress, Jogisches hoped to engineer a proletarian triumph without excessive violence and bloodshed. But some of the other insurgents were not so fastidious. The People's Naval Division abandoned its neutrality and laid siege to the police headquarters in Alexanderplatz. Bands of young Communists ganged up on lone soldiers and policemen, beating and sometimes killing them. The Ebert-Scheidemann government (Ebert had been elected president by the constituent assembly, and he had chosen Scheidemann as his chancellor) responded with as much force as it could muster. Defense Minister Noske was authorized to call in 42,000 troops armed with tanks, artillery, and flamethrowers.

If Berlin had evaded physical damage during the First World War, it certainly did not do so now, as the troops made ample use of their heavy weapons to smash Communist outposts. Reports of Communist atrocities prompted Noske to issue an order to execute anyone caught in possession of unauthorized weapons. Taking full advantage of this license to kill, troops of the Reinhard Freikorps and the Guard Cavalry Rifle Division ranged through the city rounding up suspected Communists and executing them on the spot. George Grosz, who identified with the Communist cause, managed to elude arrest by sleeping in a different flat each night. A band of soldiers gunned down twenty-four sailors whose only offense had been to demand their back pay. Especially bitter fighting took place in the proletarian quarter of Lichtenberg. The novelist Alfred Döblin, who was then working as a physician in that district, was appalled by the apparent indifference in wealthier parts of the city to the bloodshed in his neighborhood: "I was in Lichtenberg and witnessed the [Communist] putsch and the grisly, unspeakable tactics of the White troops in putting it down. But at the very moment that in our district houses were being demolished and men executed by the score, in other parts of the city people happily danced, there were balls and newspapers. Nobody protested the events in Lichtenberg; even Berlin's thousands of workers kept quiet."

The government's efficiency in putting down the Communist uprising was evident in the final casualty tolls: Noske's forces killed between 1,200 and 1,500 insurgents at a cost to themselves of 75 dead, 150 wounded, and 38 missing. Berlin's central morgue became a very busy place, as relatives of the dead came to collect their loved ones. Käthe Kollwitz recalled the scene: "A dense crowd of people filing by the glass windows, behind which the naked bodies lie. Each has its clothing in a bundle lying upon the abdomen. On top is a number. I read up to number 244. Behind the glass windows lay some twenty or thirty dead. . . . Now and then some of the people waiting would be led out past me to the other room, and I heard loud wailing from that room. Oh, what a dismal, dismal place the morgue is." Noske proclaimed "victory over the enemy at home" on March 12, 1919, but the victory simply papered over gaping social cracks. "In the northern and eastern parts of the city, seething hatred of the 'West' is said to be the preponderant mood," observed Kessler on March 8. He might have said the same thing in 1929—or, for that matter, in 1995.

Berlin was still reeling from this latest flare-up in its civil war when, on May 7, 1919, the Allies presented Germany with their bill for World War I: the Treaty of Versailles. By the terms of the treaty, Germany was to lose all its colonies, 13 percent of its home territory, and 10 percent of its population. The easternmost province of East Prussia would be cut off from the rest of the Reich by the Polish Corridor—a provision that was especially hard on Berlin, which depended on easy access to its agricultural hinterlands in the east. Germany's new army, the Reichswehr, would be limited to 100,000 men, all volunteers, and its famous General Staff was to be disbanded. To guarantee fulfillment of the treaty's military provisions, the Reich's westernmost territory, the Rhineland, was to be occupied by Allied forces for fifteen years and kept demilitarized indefinitely after that. In the notorious "War Guilt Clause," Germany was deemed responsible for the outbreak of the war and therefore liable for all the losses and damages incurred by her enemies; she would have to pay reparations (as yet unspecified) and hand over those of her citizens whom the Allies suspected of having committed acts in violation of the laws and customs of war. Germany was given no opportunity to dicker over these terms, which were handed over to the Reich's representatives at Versailles's Hall of Mirrors, where, forty-eight years before, the German Empire had been proclaimed.

When the German government presented counterproposals, the Allies immediately rejected them and gave Berlin an ultimatum: sign the treaty or face invasion.

Chancellor Scheidemann could not bring himself to comply—"What hand would not wither that binds itself in these fetters?" he cried—and resigned with some others in his cabinet on June 19. President Ebert, convinced that Germany had no recourse but to sign, set about putting together a new government that would be willing to swallow the bitter pill. As he did so, Berlin broke out in new turmoil, with USPD-backed mobs marching in favor of signing, conservative factions demonstrating against. Rumors abounded that various Freikorps groups would stage a putsch if the government signed. On June 21 Ebert finally scraped together a new cabinet, which agreed under protest to sign the treaty two days later, just one hour before the Allied deadline elapsed. The most persuasive voice in favor of compliance was the Center Party politician Matthias Erzberger, who had also signed the armistice in November 1918. Upon learning of Erzberger's role, Kessler wrote in his diary: "I am very much afraid that Erzberger will share Liebknecht's fate. Not undeservedly, like Liebknecht, but self-incurred on account of his pernicious activity." Two years later Erzberger would in fact be gunned down by right-wing assassins.

No group was more outraged over the Versailles Treaty than Germany's military officers. Their anger increased when the Allies insisted upon immediate reductions in personnel to meet the new manpower ceiling of 100,000 men. In response, a group of counterrevolutionaries calling themselves the National Association began plotting to establish a military dictatorship. Among its members was General Ludendorff, who after a brief exile in Sweden found refuge at the Hotel Adlon under a false name, and Wolfgang Kapp, a Prussian civil servant who had been one of the founders of the Fatherland Party during the war. The leader of the group was Walther von Lüttwitz, the commandant of Berlin.

Under increasing pressure from the Allies, in February 1920 the German government ordered the dissolution of several units of the Provisional Reichswehr, among them the so-called Ehrhardt Brigade, led by Captain Hermann Ehrhardt, which in its earlier incarnation as the Ehrhardt Freikorps had earned a reputation for extreme brutality. It was now stationed at Döberitz, about fifteen miles west of Berlin. General Lüttwitz, who insisted that the Ehrhardt Brigade was vital for the protection of Berlin, demanded that the order to disband the brigade be rescinded. When Ebert refused, Lüttwitz ordered Ehrhardt to march on the capital.

An armored truck belonging to the Kapp forces, March 1920

Learning of the rebels' plans, Minister of Defense Noske appealed to the military command to call out the Berlin garrison to defend the city. The army's new commander, General Hans von Seeckt, responded that he could not order one unit of troops to fire on another. Surely, he added, Noske "did not intend that a battle be fought before the Brandenburg Gate between troops who [had] fought side by side against the common enemy." The government would have to deal with this challenge on its own, he said.

On the morning of March 13 Ehrhardt's men, carrying banners with the imperial colors and wearing helmets emblazoned with swastikas, marched into Berlin. They were greeted at the Brandenburg Gate by Ludendorff and Kapp, the latter decked out in top hat and tails, befitting his status as titular head of the new government that now claimed to run Germany.

The legally elected government, meanwhile, fled the city, traveling first to Dresden, then on to Stuttgart, some 250 miles to the southwest. Before leaving the capital, the ministers issued an appeal to the workers of Berlin to resist the rebels by walking off their jobs in a general strike, a tactic that the Ebert government had recently condemned as Bolshevistic. The irony was not lost on Berlin's factory workers, but they knew that a Kapp regime would be far worse than Ebert's, and they accordingly threw down their tools and went home. They were joined by utilities workers, tram drivers, civil servants, sales people, waiters, and even some prostitutes. For the first time in its modern history, Berlin totally shut down. "At night it's completely dark in our neighborhood," wrote Käthe Kollwitz in her diary on March 17. "A darkness like one experiences in the countryside: totally black." The strike was so thorough that the mayor of Berlin was obliged to get around town in an ambulance, disguised as an accident victim.

The putschists were in no way equipped to deal with resistance of this magnitude, and their problems were compounded by their own ineptitude. It took them two days just to find someone to type their manifesto announcing their seizure of power. Other paperwork was delayed because Ebert's officials, in a brilliant act of sabotage, had taken away the rubber stamps necessary to the functioning of any German administration. Lacking money to pay the troops, Kapp ordered Ehrhardt to take the necessary funds from the State Treasury, but the latter refused on the grounds that he was "an officer, not a bank robber." After four days Kapp issued a decree saying he had accomplished all his aims and decamped for Sweden, deeding his "authority" to Lüttwitz. The general had no opportunity to exercise his dubious powers because the military command, seeing that the putsch had failed, forced Lüttwitz to resign his command and called for the return of the legitimate government.

As Ebert and company prepared to reclaim Berlin, Ehrhardt's disgruntled men began their march back to Döberitz. When a young boy mocked them near the Brandenburg Gate, several troopers broke ranks and clubbed him with their rifle butts. Someone in the crowd hissed, whereupon the soldiers fired point-blank into the mass, killing twelve and wounding thirty bystanders. (Ebert later granted the killers an amnesty and paid them the 16,000-mark bonus that Kapp had promised them for marching on Berlin.) Elsewhere in the city, battles between strikers and Freikorps units claimed several hundred casualties.

Although the Kappists had focused their action on the national capital, news of the putsch excited counterrevolutionaries across Germany, including Munich, where Adolf Hitler was working to build up the fledgling Nazi Party. Hoping to ingratiate himself with the putschists, Hitler, accompanied by one of his Munich backers, the racist publicist Dietrich Eckart, flew to Berlin. This was the future Führer's first time aloft, and he was sick throughout the flight. As it turned out, the men landed in Berlin just as the putsch was collapsing and its leaders were fleeing. Disgruntled, they returned to Munich.

Visiting Berlin in the immediate aftermath of the Kapp Putsch, Edwin Embree, an American physician, was struck by how "orderly" the city seemed. Moreover, the food shortages, in his view, had produced some salutary effects. "No longer is the flowing belly and the swine-like neck the predominate feature of the Berliners," he wrote in his diary. "With a diminution of their overfeeding has also come, happily enough, a sharp decline in suffering from cancer and appendicitis." What Embree failed to notice was that Berlin's dearly purchased "order" was highly tenuous and superficial.

Walpurgis Night

"[The Kapp Putsch] has thrown everything achieved so far into question," wrote Ernst Troeltsch on March 23, 1920. So it had. One had to wonder about the loyalty of an army that had chosen to sit on the fence during the coup, and about the long-term viability of a political system that inspired so much hatred among its own citizens. The Kapp Putsch turned out to be the last of the violent postwar insurrections to ravage Berlin, but its failure hardly brought genuine tranquillity, for a new crisis in the form of extreme economic destabilization was fast taking shape.

In the period between 1919 and 1923 the German mark lost virtually all its value, first gradually, then with dizzying speed. With the collapse of the mark a whole way of life disintegrated; old virtues like thrift and saving became suicidal, and wild spending became a national obsession. As the *Deutsche Allgemeine Zeitung* put it in July 1923: "People throw themselves on the stores, buy what is there to buy. They hoard necessary and superfluous things. . . . Illogic, blind emotion, and panic rule the hour." When the insanity had finally run its course in late 1923, millions of people were left destitute. For many Germans, the Great Inflation proved to be a catastrophe they could never overcome or forget. Like the internecine political wars of the immediate postwar era, the experience saddled the young republic and its beleaguered capital with a lasting trauma.

As if in anticipation of the mark's dramatic inflation, Berlin itself inflated at the beginning of the Weimar period. On October 1, 1920, a law combining Old Berlin with its principal suburbs greatly expanded the city's population and area. With the incorporation of eight formerly independent towns—Charlottenburg, Köpenick, Lichtenberg, Neukölln, Pankow, Schöneberg, Spandau, and Wilmersdorf—along with fifty-nine rural communities and twenty-seven estates, Berlin jumped in population to 3,858,000, thereby becoming the third largest city in Europe. In area it increased thirteenfold. Its 878 square kilometers, which embraced lakes and forests in addition to built-up sections, made it the roomiest European city. The municipal officials who engineered this expansion, which had become possible only because of the defeat of the imperial order, were proud of "Greater Berlin's" new status, but many residents of the wealthier boroughs were not at all pleased to be thrown in the same pot with the worker- and immigrant-dominated districts of Old Berlin.

Berlin had always been a difficult city to govern and it became even more so with the expansion, since the various boroughs had considerable autonomy and the city parliament was too fragmented to function effectively. The SPD and USPD controlled the largest number of seats in the city parliament but had to form coalitions with the moderate middle-class parties to achieve governing majorities, which pro-

Gustav Böss, governing mayor of Berlin, 1921–1930

duced endless wrangling. From 1921 to 1930 the lord mayor was Gustav Böss of the Democratic Party. He was a competent administrator and a generous patron of the arts, but the powers of his office were too limited to allow him to exercise much control over the contending factions.

By the time Böss was sworn in as mayor, Berlin was already in economic trouble. Municipal budgets were under increasing strain because local officials had repeatedly given wage hikes to city employees even though tax revenues were down. Another source of financial hemorrhage was unemployment relief, which escalated as thousands of outsiders streamed into the city looking for work. Finding itself strapped for cash, Berlin took out short-term loans with foreign banks payable in foreign currency. Just to service these loans the city had to secure new loans at increasingly unfavorable rates.

In February 1920 the mark stood at 99.11 to the dollar; in November 1921 it stood at 262.96. The Allies accused the German government of willfully pushing the mark down in order to gain concessions in reparations payments, a charge the Germans vehemently denied. The government's deficit spending, mirroring Berlin's on a grander scale, undoubtedly contributed to the inflationary spiral, but the heart of the problem was that the German people increasingly took flight from their own currency either by selling marks abroad or by buying up material goods in anticipation of further depreciation, which of course made such depreciation inevitable.

The mark's uneven slide in the first three years after the war was certainly unsettling, but things got much worse between mid-1922 and November 1923 during the so-called hyperinflation, a currency crash the likes of which the modern world had never seen. At this point Germany's inflation escaped all rhyme or reason, growing like some rampant cancer or jungle-fungus, consuming the body politic.

A series of political crises beginning with the murder of Foreign Minister Walther Rathenau on June 24, 1922, helped propel the inflation into overdrive. Rathenau was killed by right-wing assassins as he drove to work along Berlin's Königstrasse (the death spot is now marked with a plaque, one of many such memorials in the haunted city). To accomplish their mission, the killers pulled up alongside the minister's open car and sprayed him with automatic pistol fire, then tossed in a grenade for good measure. This was Rathenau's reward for being a Jew who had tried to help his nation cope with the demands of the Versailles Treaty and the evils of inflation. Berliners turned out in their thousands to view his body as it lay in state

Walther Rathenau in 1921, a year before his assassination

in the Reichstag (a building he had hated), but they should also have mourned the mark. On the eve of the assassination the German currency had stood at 331 to the dollar; by the end of July 1922 it had dropped to 670. In December 1922, following rumors that the French planned to occupy the Ruhr Valley to punish Germany for defaulting on reparations payments, the mark ballooned to 7368.

The rumors about the French turned out to be true. On January 11, 1923, French and Belgian troops marched into the Ruhr in order to force the Germans to make coal deliveries stipulated in the reparations agreement. This action ignited a storm of patriotic protest across Germany. Berlin was engulfed in anti-French demonstrations; Pariser Platz had to be closed off to prevent attacks on the French embassy.

The German government responded by instituting "passive resistance," encouraging coal companies and railways to shut down and then compensating owners and striking workers with money from the national treasury. Now the mark went into free fall. In early February it hit 42,000 to the dollar, in July 160,000, in August

Money being transported to a Berlin bank during the Great Inflation, 1923

3,000,000. To meet the demand for paper currency more than 2,000 presses worked around the clock churning out bills in ever higher denominations. In September 1923 the Reichsbank issued a 50 million mark note; in October it came out with 1, 5, and 10 billion mark bills; on November 2 a 100 trillion note. The Berlin newspaper publisher Hermann Ullstein, whose presses were requisitioned for the printing, hired elderly women to put newly printed billion-mark bills in neat packages for vigilant Reichsbank officials. "They had to keep an eye on every single billion," he noted. "Officials are so funny sometimes." But why in fact worry about the odd billion when, in late November 1923, one American dollar was worth a mind-boggling 4,210,500,000,000 German marks?

As the mark sprouted zeros, so did the prices for basic necessities. In Berlin a streetcar ride cost 3,000 marks on July 16, 1923; 6,000 marks on July 30; 10,000 on August 6; 50,000 on August 14; and 100,000 on August 20. The price for natural gas shot up from 1,200 marks a cubic meter on July 1, 1923, to 250,000 marks on August 30. In late November, at the height of the Great Disorder, a glass of beer fetched 150 billion marks, a loaf of bread 80 billion, and a pickle 4 billion. Prostitutes were demanding 6 billion marks and a cigarette for the "mistress-slave perversion." At these prices, it made sense to use lower-denomination bills for functions other than trade. Berliners lit their cigars with thousand-mark bills and wiped their bottoms with millions—"filthy lucre" indeed. The dadaists Kurt Schwitters and László Moholy-Nagy used billion-mark notes to make collages of the national symbol, the eagle, which they turned into a vulture.

With the collapse of the mark, many business people insisted upon being paid in goods or services rather than currency. The "most modern city in Europe" was reverting to history's oldest system of trade—barter. Of course, since many daily transactions still had to be conducted in cash, people tried to get rid of their currency as quickly as possible, before it lost further value. They rushed from pay counter to store or bar, often transporting their load of bills in backpacks or even wheelbarrows. By contrast, when it came to settling obligations like taxes, mortgages, and rents, which did not keep pace with inflation, they tried to delay paying for as long as possible. The result was that, for the first time, housing in Berlin became relatively cheap. That was the good news. The bad news was that housing was also more shabby and in shorter supply than ever because builders and landlords had no incentive to put up new structures or to repair the old ones.

As in the First World War, natural products were supplanted by ersatz concoctions. Visiting Berlin in 1920, the Russian writer Ilya Ehrenburg noted: "In the Café Josty where I sometimes went, the wishy-washy so-called 'Mocha' was served in metal coffeepots with a little glove on the handle to prevent the customer from burning his fingers. Sweet cakes were made of frostbitten potatoes. As before, the Berliners still smoked cigars labeled Cuban or Brazilian though in fact they were made of cabbage leaves steeped in nicotine."

Germans did not fare equally under the pressures of inflation. Those with plenty of goods to trade, or, better yet, with access to foreign currency, could do quite well for themselves. The sociologist Leo Lowenthal had enough foreign funds to spend the last days of the hyperinflation in the splendor of the spa at Baden-Baden. Felix Gilbert, having gone off to university in Heidelberg with fifty dollars from his uncle, used the money to buy pots of jam that he sold from time to time when he needed cash. The Berlin director Berthold Viertel was able to buy his own theater with the help of a currency-trader patron. Workers whose unions were able to bargain for steady wage increases got along much better than unorganized civil servants, teachers, doctors, and artists, whose incomes lagged far behind the price curve. Worst off were retired people on fixed incomes and citizens who had conscientiously put their savings in government bonds during the war. Such people, generally middle class, suffered the dual horror of seeing their own living standards plummet while their social inferiors held their own.

Not surprisingly, those who fared the best were those who took ruthless advantage of other people's vulnerability. Berlin had always had its share of economic

German children demonstrating that it takes 100,000 marks to buy one U.S. dollar in early 1923. By the fall of that year the dollar was worth 4.2 trillion marks

predators, but in the inflation era the city became a paradise for profiteers, or *Raffkes*, in popular parlance. With small amounts of foreign currency or stock they bought up the furniture and family heirlooms of desperate widows. They purchased companies for $500 and met their payrolls with worthless marks. The most enterprising *Raffke* of all was Hugo Stinnes, a self-made magnate whom Harry Kessler described as "a cross between a patrician, a commercial traveler, and the Flying Dutchman." Having built up a coal-mining empire with dubious credit, Stinnes turned his coal into foreign currency during the inflation and used that to build one of the largest economic empires the world has ever seen. This complicated operation, however, could be kept going only by the fast footwork of its founder, and when Stinnes died in 1924 his empire collapsed.

Because foreign currency, especially the dollar, was the key to the good life in inflation-ridden Germany, foreigners could live very high off the hog. Ernest Hemingway and his wife Hadley crossed into Germany from France in September 1922 to inspect the scene. For ten francs they received 670 marks, or about ninety cents in Canadian money (Hemingway was then reporting for the *Toronto Daily Star*). "That ninety cents lasted Mrs. Hemingway and me for a day of heavy spending and at the end of the day we had one hundred and twenty marks left!" he reported to the paper. Berlin in particular was overrun with *Ausländer* who went there to enjoy an extravagance that they could never have managed at home. The American writer Djuna Barnes, who spent the summer of 1921 in the Spree city, found "things so cheap for us that you felt almost ashamed to be there. Full of buggers from America who bought boys cheap." In fact, most foreigners felt little shame about their wealth. Flaunting their dollars, pounds, and francs, tourists and expatriates bought up whatever they wanted, from boys to buildings. For one hundred dollars, a classical music fan from Texas rented the entire Berlin Philharmonic for an evening's entertainment. Typical of the new breed of expatriates was the American editor Matthew Josephson, who moved his magazine *Broom* to Berlin because it was cheaper to publish there. According to his friend Malcolm Cowley, who visited him in Berlin in 1923, Josephson was not living the usual life of a little-magazine editor. On his salary of one hundred dollars a month he "lived in a duplex apartment with two maids, riding lessons for his wife, dinners only in the most expensive restaurants, tips to the orchestra, pictures collected, charities to struggling German writers."

The contrast between the foreigners' opulence and the natives' destitution naturally sparked resentment. *Die Weltbühne*, a cosmopolitan journal published in

Berlin, could not disguise its unease over the fact that foreign diplomats—even those from "exotic lands" like the "Nigger Republic of Liberia"—could live much better than their hosts. In his book *Hinterland*, the writer Alfred Polgar took bitter note of American culinary extravagance at a local hotel:

> In the small side room of the hotel there is a table not like other tables. A little flag with the stars and stripes stands in a vase amidst the flowers. A plate overflows with the whitest, wheatiest, sliced bread. Under a glass bell shimmers real butter, golden-yellow. There are unfamiliar boxes and cans, round and square, containing God knows what delicacies. From bowls and bottles waft delicate scents of spices and spirits. The natives at neighboring tables regard this culinary still-life with awe. Here dine the victors, the Americans! Hail to them! It is to their intervention in the war that we owe this peace with its Fourteen Points, these packets of dollars, this democracy, this being-eaten-out-of-house-and-home. We are loving America!

Not just the finest food was going to the visiting victors with their fists full of dollars. Berlin was now crawling with so-called "Valuta Frauen" or "Devisen Damen"—ladies whose motto was: "The man doesn't have to be hard, but the currency does!" Apparently the currency in question need not be in large denominations. In one instance, reported by Hans Ostwald, an American began throwing small change on the floor in a seedy bar, shouting that only naked women were allowed to pick it up. A few girls smirked, but when a fat lady took off her clothes and dropped to her knees, all the others stripped and joined her on the floor in a mad scramble for the Yank's spare change. One of the German men watching this scene was indignant, while another simply shrugged. "What's wrong?" he said. "These women have to work a whole day for one American penny."

"Berlin has become a much rawer place," reported the police in July 1923. As we have seen, the German capital had never been a model of refinement, but the inflation era further roughened its edges. Crime rates rose as the mark fell, and the nature of the criminality tended to match the strange times. A band of thieves swept through the cemeteries and carted away bronze grave markers. Pickpockets working the streetcars eschewed coins and bills in favor of watches and money clips. A new kind of thief called a *Fassadenkletterer* (cat burglar) scaled the sides of apartment buildings and broke into elegant dwellings to steal jewels, furs, and silverware. Professional arsonists were much in demand to torch failing business for their insurance value. Like many branches of criminality, arson-for-hire was controlled by the Berlin *Ringvereine*, which took a percentage of the insurance payments. Another crime of the times was the hoarding of foreign currency, which by law had to be exchanged for German money at the official rate. Of course, no one in his right mind gave up his foreign currency except to buy goods, so the police conducted periodic *Devisenrazzien* (foreign exchange raids) in places where hoarders were known to congregate. A raid in several Berlin coffeehouses in September 1923 netted 3,120 dollars, 36 English pounds, 373 Dutch guilders, and 475 Swiss francs. In addition to foreign currency and precious metals, much of the inflation-era criminality focused on food. Grocery stores and bakeries were robbed so often that owners posted twenty-four-hour guards and fitted their windows with iron bars. When some of Berlin's finest racehorses went missing, it turned out they had been taken to a local slaughter house, where they fetched a fine price. Meanwhile, thousands of Berliners returned to their wartime practice of plundering outlying orchards and farms, but now they carried pistols and hand grenades to deploy against the farmers and their armed guards.

Because the currency collapse brought a demand to live for today as if there were no tomorrow, many Berliners tried to pack their days and nights with as many thrills as possible. Much of the thrill-seeking had a gross, almost sadistic side to it. Barefisted boxing matches became all the rage, the bloodier the better. Another popular attraction was women's mud wrestling, less bloody but more titillating. For those who wanted to mask their prurience with fake aestheticism, there was the famous "Ballet Celly de Rheydt," which featured virtually nude female dancers, some of them in their early teens, performing programs supposedly inspired by classical art. According to Celly's husband, who managed the enterprise, its primary goal was "to bring the ideal of beauty to our shattered people, and to raise it up from its misery." Fully aware that Celly's show was bent on raising something other than the human spirit, and worried that its sold-out houses might undercut Germany's claim to have no money to pay reparations, the police took Celly to court for indecency, but the ensuing trial resulted only in a token fine. Likewise free to follow her muse was a stripper and erotic dancer named Anita Berber, who captivated audiences with her version of the Shimmy, which she did *au naturel.* When she died at age thirty from drug and alcohol abuse, her admirers recalled her as one who "personified the feverish twenties in Berlin, as no one else." Berliners who wanted to see misery disguised as sport could watch the infamous Six-Day Bicycle Races, held in the Sportpalast on the Potsdamerstrasse, where riders whirled around a circular track for six days and nights without interruption. The crowd cheered as some contestants crashed in exhaustion while others went on to win prizes like new suits or bottles of Sekt. Witnessing one of these races, the writer Joseph Roth got the feeling that if he stayed much longer he would take on "the physiognomy of the megaphones used in this mad house to make announcements to the public."

Weimar Berlin's commercial sex scene did not change much in its fundamentals from the imperial era, but the number of folks selling their bodies went up substantially. Police estimated the number of prostitutes at 25,000, but this included only the full-timers. According to one observer, all sorts of young girls "from so-called good families" were turning into whores, and countless marriages had become "a facade for the most wanton sexual chaos." There were 8,000 to 10,000 pimps, most of whom controlled only one or two "spiders," as they called their girls. A famous exception was "Student Willy," who ran a stable of ten. The heart of street prostitution was the *Geile Meile* on the Oranienburger Strasse, a grim strip staked out by strapping Valkyries in fur boas and low-cut frocks. (A new generation of whores, accoutred in Spandex short-shorts and thigh-high boots, patrols the strip today.) If you wanted something on the younger side you went to the Chauseestrasse, which was lined on both sides with preteen girls. The man-and-boy trade was centered in Friedrichstadt or along the Kurfürstendamm, where, according to Stefan Zweig, "powdered and rouged young men," many of them "high school boys out to earn a little extra money," sauntered up and down. The director Josef von Sternberg recalled that Berlin was "full of females who looked and functioned like men." But the reverse was also true. As the actress Anita Loos learned on a visit from Hollywood, "any Berlin lady of the evening might turn out to be a man; the prettiest girl on the street was Conrad Veidt, who later became an international film star." Veidt's favorite hangout was the El Dorado, which attracted gay males and tourists to its famous female impersonation shows. Another popular night spot was "Aleifa," or "Alles eine Familie"—One Big Family. It was indeed ecumenical, welcoming heterosexuals, homosexuals, bisexuals, and people who probably would have been transsexuals had the operation been available. Several clubs, most notably the Resi and the Femina, had telephones at each table, marked with a number, which allowed guests to call each other and make arrangements for the evening.

In the end, Berlin's famous sex clubs were probably not much raunchier than similar places in other cities around the world. What distinguished them from their counterparts in America and in other European cities was their openness, their brazenness. The accessibility of vice was perhaps the main reason behind Weimar Berlin's reputation for singular decadence. Another reason was the desire on the part of visiting foreigners to see the city as super-naughty, since this made them feel more daring. At the same time, however, it also made them feel morally superior to the natives. As Stephen Spender observed, "One of the contributions of Germany to the rest of civilization ever since the time of Tacitus has been to make it feel virtuous in comparison with the Germans."

Among the foreigners attracted to "Babylon on the Spree" in the early twenties was the American writer and publisher Robert McAlmon. As a bisexual and occasional drug-user, McAlmon was in his element. In an autobiographical piece called *Distinguished Air (Grim Fairy Tales)* he recounted his experience during a night of excess in 1921. At a seedy club he met "an American fairy" named Foster, all camped up with waved hair and plucked eyebrows. "I wouldn't look like this in Paris," confided Foster, "but it goes down all right here." Then McAlmon encountered an English homosexual, Carrol, who admitted to being one of the "awful rats who have come to Berlin because of the low exchange." Carrol and his friends could not resist the "lovely window displays" and the smashing shopping, even though they knew the "natives can't buy." McAlmon and his crowd moved on to the Adlon, where they gorged on "cocktails, paté de foie gras, three bottles of wine, pheasant, Russian eggs, pastry, coffee, and several *fines* to round out the meal." Then it was on to the Germania Palast and drinks with a gentleman from San Francisco who had "three automobiles and all the bitches in Berlin trying to keep up with him." For a break they went outside and snorted cocaine. After a stop at a nightclub on the Kurfürstendamm filled with coke addicts, they ended their tour at the Oh la la!, a lesbian bar that did not open until 6:00 A.M. There they watched nude dancers, drank champagne, took some more drugs, and finally vomited it all up on the floor.

McAlmon did not mean for this report to be inspirational; like many visitors, he eventually tired of Berlin's strenuous sleaze and moved on. The sad reality, these foreigners soon saw, was that the German capital could be quite depressing and tawdry under its veneer of glitter. Of course, the foreigners had the luxury of abandoning Berlin when they had had enough of the place; the natives had to stay on and try to survive.

Living in Berlin during the inflation years meant putting up with increasing social disorder. Because farmers refused to sell their produce for depreciated marks, there was a growing shortage of food. Shops in the poorer quarters of town were frequently looted. Strikes in crucial sectors of the economy became endemic as even the better paid workers saw their purchasing power evaporate. In summer 1923 streetcar, elevated train, and gas works employees all walked off the job. In August 1923 workers at the Reich Printing Plant struck, shutting down the production of paper money just as the nation was due to get a much-needed fix of 50 million mark bills.

The strikers, for all their grievances, were better off than the growing legion of unemployed. In mid-September 1923 Berlin had 126,393 registered unemployed. On October 9 the figure had climbed to 159,526, and by late November it was over 360,000. The city was able to provide limited unemployment relief for only 145,000 people. The combination of escalating joblessness, astronomical prices, and the old human need to find a scapegoat for one's misery was too combustible a mix not to blow up, and in early November 1923 the inevitable explosion occurred in the form of deadly rioting with ugly anti-Semitic undertones.

The focus of the action was Berlin's Scheunenviertel—or "barn district"—a poor quarter north of Alexanderplatz that had become a haven for Eastern European Jews fleeing persecution in their homelands. The immediate postwar era had brought a new wave of refugees from Poland and Russia. The majority of Berliners, including assimilated Jews living in the wealthier western and southern districts, tended to shun the Scheunenviertel as alien and possibly dangerous. Venturing into the district in 1920, Joseph Roth found a "strange sad ghetto world" devoid of the racing autos and bright lights of western Berlin. The streets were filled with "grotesque eastern figures" holding "a thousand years of pain in their eyes." While the men shuffled along in black caftans, the women carried their children on their backs "like sacks of dirty laundry." Altogether, the Scheunenviertel Jews seemed like "an avalanche of disaster and dirt, growing in volume and rolling irresistibly from the East over Germany."

Right-wing papers in Berlin had been claiming for some time that the *Ostjuden* in the Scheunenviertel were feeding off the misery of "decent Germans," and the charges were finding a receptive audience among the unemployed. On November 5 a rumor circulated among the jobless that they would get no payments that day

Jews in Berlin's Scheunenviertel, 1929

because Jews from the Scheunenviertel had bought up all the funds to lend at usurious interest rates. Indignant, a mob descended on the Scheunenviertel and began to loot shops. Proprietors who tried to defend their property were pulled into the street and beaten. The owner of a kosher butcher shop was pummeled so badly that he died from his injuries. Jews caught in the streets were often stripped of their clothes, which were thought to contain precious foreign currency sewed inside.

The police did not arrive on the scene until much of the damage had already been done. They closed off parts of the quarter but did not immediately expel the rioters. In fact, the first to be arrested were Jews, who were taken to the police barracks in the Alexanderplatz and made to stand for hours with their hands over their heads. By midnight the district was calm, though full of signs that it had just been a war zone: discarded booty littered the streets, shards of glass from shop windows covered the sidewalks, bonfires smoldered here and there, and some stores sported signs saying "Christian-owned."

Contemporary accounts of the Scheunenviertel rioting interpreted this episode in very different ways. *Vorwärts* argued that it was "a pogrom" orchestrated by the right and the far-left to destabilize the Weimar Republic. The liberal *Vossische Zeitung* charged that Berlin's business barons had fomented the rioting to distract people from the fact that heavy industry was profiting immensely from the collapse of the mark. The rightist *Deutsche Zeitung* insisted that the riots were the spontaneous outgrowth of popular rage over the "unscrupulous profiteering of the Jews in a time of widespread misery." The Jewish community itself was split between those who saw the upheaval as "a fateful signal to German Jewry" and those who believed it was a momentary outpouring of economic frustration, focused solely on eastern Jews. Finally, the Nazi paper, the *Völkischer Beobachter*, claimed on November 8 that the riot proved that the Berliners were coming to their senses regarding the evils of the Jews. "The tumult in Berlin," said the paper, "shows clearly that all the signs today point to a coming storm."

On that very night and the following day Hitler staged his "Beer Hall Putsch" in Munich, which was designed to pave the way for a march on Berlin and the overthrow of the government. As is well known, the putsch failed, and Hitler was forced to put off his seizure of power for almost a decade. The Munich putsch and the Scheunenviertel riot were not directly connected, but both pointed up the widespread malaise and extreme instability of the early Weimar Republic. And in retrospect, of course, we can see that the *Völkischer Beobachter* was correct, if a little premature, about the "coming storm."

In the Jungle of Cities

The Great Inflation did not dull Berlin's cultural and intellectual scene in the early years of the Weimar Republic. On the contrary, the collapse of the mark was one of the factors that helped make Berlin, for the first time in its history, a true world capital of the arts. The city's cultural industry profited from people's need for distraction in a time of general misery. The low cost of living attracted legions of foreign artists for whom the German capital was now a bargain. The climate of social improvisation accompanying the collapse of the economy encouraged experimentation, and there was now no reigning political orthodoxy to impose restraints. Budgetary cuts did hurt the city's great universities and scientific institutes, but these survived the inflation to become even more dominant on the world scene. Of the twenty-five Germans who won the Nobel prize between 1918 and 1944, only two were not associated with Berlin. Chancellor Gustav Stresemann could justifiably call the city "a metropolis of brain power."

Yet Berlin in the early 1920s was anything but an unalloyed paradise for the artists and intellectuals who worked there. As the dramatist Carl Zuckmayer recalled:

> This city hungered after talents and human energies with unprecedented voracity, only to chew them up and spit them out with equal gusto. Like a tornado it sucked in everyone in Germany who wanted to get to the top, the genuine articles as well as the impostors, and at first it showed them all the same cold shoulder. Those who had not yet made it in Berlin spoke of the city as a desirable woman, known for her coldness and coquetry, all the more worthy of curses the less likely she was to yield.

Berlin had certainly "yielded" to Albert Einstein, and in the postwar period he began to yield to her, shedding some of the distaste he had long harbored for his native land. As a democrat, he believed that the Weimar Republic deserved every chance to prosper; if it succeeded, he thought, Germany might become the kind of place in which a citizen of the world would be proud to live. Thus when Max Planck urged him to stay on in the German capital despite tempting offers from Zurich and Leiden, he agreed "not to turn [his] back on Berlin."

Einstein made this decision at a time when he was becoming internationally famous for his general theory of relativity. Few laymen understood this theory, but they knew that it challenged basic assumptions about the structure of the universe. With Einstein becoming the subject of innumerable newspaper and magazine profiles, the world learned that he was the perfect "weird scientist": a Chaplinesque figure with wild hair, luminous eyes, and disheveled clothes. People also learned a little about his nonscientific endeavors—his work on behalf of international understanding, world peace, and Zionism.

The very qualities and ideals that made Einstein a world celebrity made him persona non grata among some elements at home. Right-wing nationalists attacked him as an internationalist Jew who was endangering the interests of German science. In 1920 an anti-Einstein movement calling itself the Study Group of German Natural Philosophers attacked the general theory as a hoax. On August 27, 1920, they rented the Berlin Philharmonic Hall to present their views. Their spokesman, a charlatan named Paul Weyland, claimed that the uproar about relativity was hostile to the German spirit. Einstein himself showed up at the meeting, sitting in the back and giving mock applause to all the inanities. "That was most amusing," he said at the end.

But in reality the matter was not so funny. As the attacks continued Einstein felt obliged to reply to his detractors in a long article in the *Berliner Tageblatt*, an unprecedented gesture that struck some of his friends as demeaning. To such criticism he replied: "I had [to respond in public] if I wanted to remain in Berlin, where every child recognizes me from the photographs. If one is a democrat, one has to acknowledge the claims of publicity." Einstein's stance was not without an element of bravery, for the campaign against him was becoming increasingly vicious. Anti-Semites accosted him outside his apartment, denouncing him as a purveyor of "Jewish science." Rightist students disrupted a lecture he was giving at the university, one of them shouting, "I'm going to cut the throat of that dirty Jew." A racist demagogue offered a reward to anyone who would assassinate the scientist. His family worried that he might meet the same fate as his friend Walther Rathenau. Without his knowing it, his wife hired a bodyguard to watch over him.

Einstein stayed on in Berlin largely because he was committed to Weimar democracy, but he was motivated also by the belief that no other place was so culturally rich. Why should he leave, he asked, when the city was being sought out by some of the most exciting people in the world?

Among the exciting people who settled in Berlin in the early Weimar years was the writer Vladimir Nabokov, who joined an already thriving Russian colony that had gathered in the Spree metropolis in the wake of the Russian revolution. At the time of Nabokov's arrival in 1922 some 200,000 Russian émigrés lived in Berlin, clustered primarily in Charlottenburg, Schöneberg, and Wilmersdorf. Their presence brought dozens of Russian cafés and restaurants, a theater, and over one hundred Russian-speaking taxi drivers. Berliners complained that in parts of Charlottenburg, which they nicknamed "Charlottengrad," one heard only Russian in the streets. One could certainly *read* a lot of Russian: there were eighty-six Russian-language publishing houses and eight Russian newspapers. The largest of the publishers was *Slovo* (Word), which was backed by Ullstein and managed by a colleague of Nabokov's father (also named Vladimir), while the most important paper, *Rul'* (The Rudder) was edited for a time by Nabokov senior. Before moving to Berlin from

Cambridge, where he had studied, young Nabokov insisted that he had no desire to live in Germany. In a way he never did. The Berlin milieu that he inhabited was so thoroughly Russian that he barely learned German and made few German friends. He might have agreed with his fellow émigré, the poet Vladislav Khodasevich, who described Berlin as "the stepmother of Russian cities."

Nabokov's fifteen-year stay in Berlin was blighted at the outset by the accidental death of his father in a botched political assassination. On March 28, 1922, Pavel Miliukov, formerly a minister in the Kerensky government that had briefly ruled Russia between the collapse of the Romanov empire and the Bolshevik revolution, delivered a speech at Berlin's Philharmonic Hall. He had been invited by Nabokov senior, who had also introduced him. Just as he was finishing his speech, a man approached the stage and started firing at the speaker with a pistol. Nabokov threw himself in front of Miliukov and took a bullet to the chest. A second gunman, mistaking him for the former minister, pumped two more rounds into his prostrate body (Miliukov himself remained unscathed). It turned out that the would-be assassins were fanatical czarists then living in Munich. They were captured, tried, and sent to jail, but this was no solace to Nabokov *fils*, who wanted to challenge both the gunmen to duels.

Nabokov wrote his first eight novels in Berlin, and all were set entirely or partly in the German capital. Because of their author's self-imposed ghettoization, however, these works focus almost exclusively on the émigré community, leaving the rest of the city untouched. They deal with people trying to hold on to their former homeland through memory, preferring to live in the past rather than in the present. Berlin, as such, figures mainly as a backdrop of dreary apartment houses, shoddy rented rooms, and parks where one might catch the occasional butterfly. Nabokov later claimed that his Berlin novels could just as well have been written in Naples, Rumania, or Holland. But could they have? Only in a large émigré community such as Berlin's could individual exiles retain so much of their former lives; only in a metropolis so internally fragmented and unsure of itself could they escape the usual pressures to adopt native manners, language, and customs. Nabokov's Berlin oeuvre was the product not of a "melting pot," but of an urban bouillabaisse (or borscht) full of very discrete chunks.

Nabokov believed that during his early years in Berlin he must have ridden the elevated railway with another literary émigré—Franz Kafka. He might indeed have done so, for Kafka, who had moved to the city in September 1923, occasionally took the train from his lodging house in Steglitz to the city center. He had visited Berlin often before the war, and, like so many transplants from the Austrian empire, found the place invigorating compared to Vienna, where he had also lived. "As a city Berlin is so much better than Vienna, that decaying mammoth village," he wrote in 1914. Unlike Nabokov, who could support himself in Berlin by giving tennis and English lessons to wealthy Russians, Kafka was obliged to get by on a tiny pension from the insurance company for which he had toiled in Prague. (Had he not been paid in Czech kronen, he would not have been able to survive at all.) He lived in squalid rooms which he could not afford to heat in the winter. Already seriously sick with the tuberculosis that would soon kill him, he compared his move to Berlin to Napoleon's ill-fated invasion of Russia in 1812. Yet he also saw the big anonymous city as a refuge from the noisy relatives and dreary professional duties that had burdened his days in Prague. Here he wrote his last stories—"The Hunger Artist" and "Josephine, the Singer"—which deal with the eternal opposition between the painstaking artistic craftsman and a public that wants only entertainment and diversion. It is perhaps not accidental that Kafka wrote these stories in Berlin, whose cultural marketplace was as merciless as any in the world.

Unlike Kafka, the Czech journalist Egon Erwin Kisch was drawn to Berlin for its hectic pace, bright lights, busy streets, and technological innovations. "A lot of work and even more amusement, the telephone always ringing, people constantly around, and just enough money"—such was Kisch's Berlin. As an émigré from Prague, Kisch was particularly interested in Berlin's Czech community, whose influence over the local theatrical scene was one of his pet subjects. His only regret in coming to Berlin was the dearth of good Czech food—no decent dumplings, Prague *Selchfleisch*, or genuine *Mehlspeise.*

While residing in the German capital Kisch invented the modern concept of the reporter as part entertainer, part crusader. Although he claimed that "in a world flooded with lies . . . nothing is more amazing than the simple truth . . . nothing is more imaginative than objectivity," he slanted his reportage to fit his own political bias, which was leftist. After the Nazis came to power he was lucky to be deported rather than murdered. His books were among those burned in Berlin in May 1933.

Kisch was friends with Joseph Roth, another refuge from "Kakania"—Robert Musil's term for the Austro-Hungarian empire. Roth was best known as a novelist, but he too worked as a reporter, and his reportage on Weimar Berlin constitutes a perceptive portrait of the republican capital. Like so many outsiders, Roth moved to Berlin with the hopes of making money and building a career. He managed to do both, and in the process to illuminate parts of the city, such as the above-mentioned Scheunenviertel, where few reporters ventured. For him the metropolitan streets were a living stage whose daily dramas were as significant as world events. In a piece entitled "Spaziergang" (A Walk), he wrote of a café terrace "planted with pretty women waiting to be picked," a beggar whose story was notable "precisely because no one notices it," a cripple cleaning his nails with a file dropped by a society lady, "and thereby symbolically leapfrogging a thousand social steps." Roth did not confine himself to such tiny dramas, and his leftist-oriented stories about German politics, like Kisch's, earned him the enmity of the right. In 1932 he decided that it was time for him to escape to Paris. Before leaving Berlin he predicted that the Nazis "will burn our books and mean us."

Like Kisch and Roth, the essayist Franz Hessel was fascinated by Berlin's vibrant street life, which for him constituted a mutable theater of modernity. A native of Stettin, he had spent his childhood in Berlin before moving on to Munich and Paris, where he fell in with Gertrude Stein and her circle. Believing that Berlin, not Paris, harbored the most exciting metropolitan scene, he moved back to the German city after World War I and took a job as an editor at Rowohlt. He considered his real job, however, to be that of observing and recording the urban scene around him, a task he undertook by walking the streets with the "aimlessness" of the flaneur. Hessel fully understood that in a city like Berlin, where everyone was always in a hurry to get someplace fast, the flaneur was regarded as a "suspicious" character: "In this city, you have to 'have to,' otherwise you can't. Here you don't simply go, but go someplace. It isn't easy for someone of our kind." Nonetheless, Hessel persisted in his quiet, slow-paced flanerie, convinced that the city streets could be read like a book. As he wrote in his *Ein Flaneur in Berlin* (1929): "Flanerie is a way of reading the street, in which people's faces, displays, shop windows, café terraces, cars, tracks, trees turn into an entire series of equivalent letters, which together form words, sentences, and pages of a book that is always news. In order to really stroll, one should not have anything too specific on one's mind."

As an urban "reader," Hessel was attracted to those icons of modernity—electric lights, commercial signs and posters, shop windows, train stations. But he also cherished artifacts of the past, and he was profoundly aware that such objects would probably not be around for long in a city that had little tolerance for anachronism. Moreover, if Berlin's streets in the 1920s were not always friendly to the aimless

Romanisches Café, 1925

peregrinations of the flaneur, they would become even less so in the 1930s, when so many public spaces were taken over by the state. Hessel became "suspect" to the new rulers not only as an intensely private observer, but also as a Jew. He chose to stay on in Berlin as long as he could, in order, as he said, "to be close to the fate of the Jews." Finally, in late 1938, he fled the city for Paris, where he joined his friend and fellow flaneur, Walter Benjamin.

Hessel, Kisch, and Roth were regulars at the Romanisches Café, which in the 1920s replaced the old Café des Westens as the primary watering hole for Berlin's cultural arbiters and their hangers-on. The Romanisches Café's name derived from the Romanesque architectural style of the building in which it was housed. Located on a busy corner across from the Gedächtniskirche, it was anything but *gemütlich*. A revolving door, constantly in motion, gave access to two rooms and a gallery. Herr Nietz, the imperious doorman, supervised the traffic. "Artists whom Nietz does not know simply do not exist," averred one customer. The smaller room on the left, called the "swimming pool," was reserved for generous tippers with fat wallets and big names, along with their "little girls" like "Takka-Takka" and "Nadya," famous tarts who had been named in many a divorce suit. The larger room on the right, the "wading basin," accommodated aspiring artists who had not yet learned to stay afloat in the deep end of the cultural pool, as well as writers and painters with prominent names but somewhat thinner wallets. This is where Kisch held court, "conducting excited conversations at all the tables at the same time, reading all the newspapers as well, without neglecting the fascinating gaze he reserves for all the women passing by the pool." Guests who wanted to play chess or simply to stare at the social paddling went up to the gallery, which was reached by a circular staircase. Celebrity-searching tourists, instructed by guidebooks that the Romanisches Café was the best place in Berlin to see famous artists, were confined to a glassed-in terrace outside the main rooms. Günther Birkenfeld, a young writer who frequented the café, aptly captured its unique mixture of banality and brilliance:

> Everybody who was anybody or who hoped to be somebody in the world of culture between Reykjavik and Tahiti assembled here. Just across from the revolving door stood a buffet, which in terms of architectural hideousness and culinary tastelessness was the equal of any Prussian railway waiting room. Over it hung one of those mass-produced wagon wheel chandeliers. And yet this was the place where [Max] Slevogt, [Emil] Orlik, and Mopp [Maximilian Oppenheimer] drank their daily coffee.

Unlike in the old Café des Westens, the regulars at the Romanisches Café did not sit around all day solving the problems of the world. Rather, they typically stayed for just an hour or two, trading gossip and making deals, much like the Hollywood moguls some of them would later become. Impecunious types who, in old-Bohemian fashion, tried to milk a single drink for an entire day's stay received a curt message from the owner saying that they must pay up and leave. The Romanisches Café, in other words, was a perfect mirror of the sink-or-swim cultural milieu that it served.

One Romanisches Café regular who did manage to malinger over his "egg-in-a-glass" (this being the standard sustenance of hard-up artists, inspiring the lines: "Once man was like God, but that has been spoiled. Now man rules alone, on an egg, soft-boiled") was the dramatist Bertolt Brecht. Born and raised in the Bavarian city of Augsburg, and finding nearby Munich too provincial, Brecht visited Berlin often in the immediate postwar era. The capital turned out to be his kind of city: wonderfully vulgar and corrupt. "Everything here is chockfull of tastelessness, but in the greatest dimensions," he reported, adding: "The swindle of Berlin distinguishes itself from all other swindles through its breathtaking shamelessness." Yet the big city was hard to crack, and in pursuit of useful contacts Brecht stayed up all night drinking and playing his guitar, hopping from bed to bed, cultivating people who (in his words) "shove, envy, hate, slander, and grind each other down." The hectic pace took its toll, and Brecht was often obliged to interrupt his ambitious culture-climbing with stays in the Charité. Arnolt Bronnen, a young playwright who fell in (and later out) with Brecht, described a skinny fellow "with a lean, dry, bristly, sallow face; piercing eyes, and short dark bristling hair that fell over his forehead in two curls. A cheap pair of steel-rimmed glasses hung loosely from remarkably shapely ears across the bridge of his sharp and narrow nose. His mouth was extremely delicate, and seemed to be dreaming the dreams that eyes dream."

Brecht tasted his first success not in Berlin but in Munich, the city he was about to abandon. There his play *Drums in the Night*, which dealt with the Spartacist up-

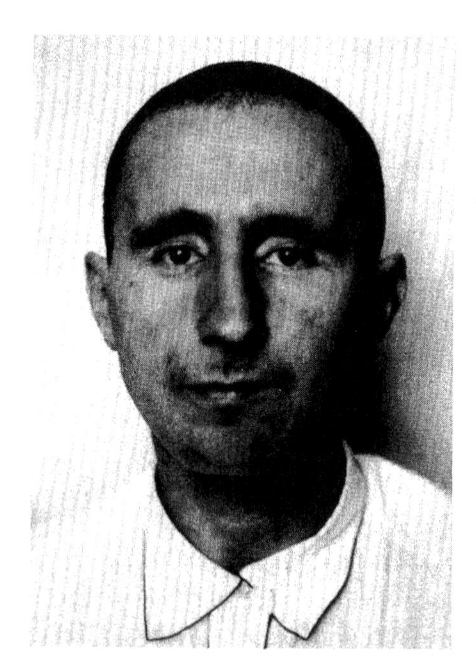

Bertolt Brecht, circa 1925

heaval in Berlin, had its premier in 1922 and won the Kleist Prize. Brecht now turned his intention to another topical work, *In the Jungle of Cities*. Though set in Chicago (which Brecht had never visited), the scene was really the German capital in its postrevolutionary convulsions, fought over by gangster clans. The plot (borrowing heavily from the story of Verlaine and Rimbaud) chronicles the love-hate relationship between a middle-aged merchant (Shlink) and a poor clerk (Garga). At one point Shlink says to Garga: "The infinite isolation of man makes even enmity an unreachable goal. Understanding, even with animals, is not possible." Garga uses his youth and superior street smarts to get the upper hand in his relationship with the older man, ultimately driving him to suicide. He then sets off to find his "freedom" in America's wide-open spaces. Premiering in Munich in May 1923, the play created enough of a *succès scandale* that Brecht could think of settling permanently in Germany's own urban jungle on the Spree.

He made the move a year later and quickly established himself as the *enfant terrible* of Berlin's theatrical scene. Abandoning his wife, he took up with a prominent actress, Helene Weigel, whom he eventually married. Max Reinhardt gave him a job as dramaturg at his Deutsches Theater. Although he now had a little money, Brecht carefully cultivated a proletarian street-tough image, replete with (tailored) work shirt, boots, battered leather jacket, permanent stubble, and semishaved head. Zuckmayer, not entirely taken in by Brecht's pose, said he looked like "a cross between a truck driver, a Black Forest wanderer, and a Jesuit seminarian." The look effectively masked Brecht's true character as a shrewd and ruthless artist-businessman who bargained hard with his employers and played off producers against each other. As one of his biographers noted: "Publishers no more had him on an exclusive basis than any of his lovers." Characteristically, his advice to other artists who wanted to make it in the urban jungle was to remember always that "What is demanded here is chopped beef."

Brecht, by his own account, regularly went to movies during his early days in Berlin. He certainly had a plethora of films from which to choose. Having taken root during the war, Germany's film industry blossomed in the postwar era because its product was the perfect fare for impoverished but diversion-hungry audiences. "At night," reported a New Yorker visiting in Berlin, "everybody flocked to the movies, at least those who couldn't afford seats for *Die Fledermaus* at the classical theater of Reinhardt." By 1919 there were more than one hundred film companies operating in the Friedrichstrasse area alone. In the early 1920s, however, the center of gravity

A scene from The Cabinet of Doctor Caligari, *directed by Robert Wiene*

shifted to a new "film city" in the western suburb of Babelsberg, which was indeed a city unto itself, with its own restaurants, stores, and fire department. This was the headquarters of UFA, now reconstituted as a private company, which in addition to making films operated ten of Berlin's finest movie houses, including the splendid UFA–Palast am Zoo.

Many of the films on display were generic escapist comedies, but the best ones mirrored, even magnified, aspects of the horror-drama playing outside in the streets. F. W. Murnau's *Nosferatu* (1922) features a vampire on the loose, killing innocent people wherever he travels in the world. Fortunately for the world, the vampire dissolves into thin air when he finally confronts someone who does not fear him. Robert Wiene's expressionist *The Cabinet of Doctor Caligari* (1920) tells the story of a maniacal insane asylum director who manipulates a somnambulist to commit murder. Viewing the film at its premier at the Marmorhaus on the Kurfürstendamm,

Kurt Tucholsky wrote: "Not for years have I sat in the cinema so riveted as I was here. This is something quite new." Fritz Lang's *Dr. Mabuse the Gambler* (1922) showcases another evil genius, this one a gangster-mastermind who uses his hypnotic powers to accentuate people's speculative fevers and hunger for sensual pleasure. In one scene, set in a seedy Berlin nightclub, a rich young American is offered the choice between cocaine and cards; choosing the latter, he loses all his money, and then his life, to Dr. Mabuse. The contemporary film critic Siegfried Kracauer observed: "In these films the soul can only choose between tyranny and chaos, a desperate dilemma. For every attempt to cast off tyranny leads straight to chaos. As a result the film creates an all-pervasive sense of horror." Yet it was precisely the nightmarish sense of helplessness conveyed by these films that made them so apt for the times. They reinforced their viewers' masochistic perception of being the playthings of superhuman figures who took cruel pleasure in their powers of manipulation. They also appealed to their audiences' sadistic side. As Ilya Ehrenburg recalled: "I observed [in movie houses] more than once with what rapture pale, skinny adolescents watched the screen when rats gnawed a man to death or a venomous snake bit a lovely girl."

Fritz Lang was clearly the master of this genre, as well as an artist whose own life and career closely mirrored the times. Born and raised in Vienna, Lang moved to Berlin in 1918 to work as a dramaturg for Erich Pommer. In 1919 he wrote the script for a Pommer production entitled *Die Pest in Florenz*, featuring a courtesan who transforms the Tuscan town into a place of debauchery, fratricide, incest, and mass death. In its heady blend of eroticism, crime, and the supernatural, it established a model for Lang's future work as a director. The young Austrian's first real success in this capacity came with *Die Spinnen* (The Spiders), a two-part film depicting a race for buried treasure between an explorer-hero and an evil secret society that leaves deadly tarantulas as its calling card. Along the way the hero must contend with a Chinese temptress, crystal-gazing mirrors, balloon and train chases, Inca sacrificial rites, and giant snakes. *Spiders* Part I was such a success that Pommer offered Lang the job of directing *Dr. Caligari*, but he was too busy with *Spiders* II, and the project passed to Wiene. Lang did, however, make suggestions for changes in the script that became part of the final product. He proposed framing the film with sequences establishing the asylum director as a madman. The film's original authors complained that this alteration undercut their desire to attack authoritarianism as consciously manipulative.

Fritz Lang, photographed in 1945

Lang was becoming something of an authoritarian himself. "Everybody in Berlin was talking about him," recalled a colleague. "He had joined the ranks of the biggest directors overnight because of the films he had made recently, which everyone admired for their striking images. Insiders told real horror stories about his fanatical devotion to work and the huge demands he made on his crew." Needing a pubescent beauty for a floor-show scene in his film *Der müde Tod* (The Tired Death), he scoured Berlin until he found a young lady who was perfect for the part save for her abundance of pubic hair. He demanded that she shave it off. When she refused, protesting that she did not want to hop around on stage "like a sparrow that's molting," Lang insisted that she cover the offensive tuft with flesh-colored adhesive.

As a newly famous director, Lang made a profitable alliance with one of Berlin's leading screenwriters, Thea von Harbou, who also became his mistress. When his wife, Lisa Rosenthal, expressed outrage over the relationship, Lang threatened her with a pistol. Not long thereafter Rosenthal died of a gunshot fired from Lang's Browning. The police ruled the death a suicide but many in Berlin believed that the director had killed his wife to get her out of the way. Whatever the truth of the matter, suicide, false accusations, and inadvertent killings became staple ingredients in his films.

Lang's obsession with his work did not prevent him from becoming a devotee of Berlin's demimonde. Like the pleasure seekers in Dr. Mabuse, he spent his nights flitting from one sex club and drug den to another, dropping devalued marks by the billions. He regularly dined on venison at Horcher's and drank at the bar of the Hotel Adlon. The elegant apartment he shared with von Harbou was crammed with paintings by Egon Schiele, exotic masks, and folk art of a decidedly macabre nature. As he bragged in an interview:

> Innocent visitors who enter our apartment for the first time find themselves confronted with human scalps, petrified but creepily real, with tiny slivers of mother-of-pearl, the last tears of the victim, gleaming in the eyeholes. But once I tell them the story behind these grotesque and beautifully painted heads, they are no longer horrified but are transformed into a similar but completely different state; for, as Goethe would have put it, 'Schaudern ist der Menschheit bester Teil' [The chill of dread is mankind's best quality].

Unluckily for Lang and other German directors, domestic films were experiencing increasing competition from imports, especially from Hollywood. By 1923, the number of American films showing in Germany almost equaled that of the homemade product. German commentators complained about the intellectual vacuity of the American imports, but the German public found these films, with their canned sentimentality, images of fabulous wealth, extreme violence, and wild chase scenes highly compelling. The Hollywood imagination, it seemed, was more closely attuned to German realities than the critics wanted to believe. Within Germany, Hollywood found its most avid audience in Berlin, which after all was Germany's best answer not only to gangster-ridden Chicago but also to the shoot-'em-up Western frontier—Dodge City on the Spree. Local directors were divided over whether they should resist the taste for Americana or cater to it. One film expert, however, had no doubts about the path Germany must follow: "America is currently in style. We must imitate it in order to steal a march on it and should if possible try to be more American than the Americans."

Fritz Lang was among the German directors who became swept up in the American tide. He made his first trip to the United States in 1924 and was overwhelmed

A scene from Lang's Metropolis, *1925–26*

by the sight of the New York skyline. Later he would claim that this vision inspired his brilliant film *Metropolis* (1927). In the end, however, German directors could not stave off American competition by out-Americaning the Americans. In addition to aesthetic reservations, they lacked the capital to keep up. The technology for the new talking pictures was conceived in Germany but a dearth of development capital resulted in the patent's being sold to Fox. Paramount and MGM bought into UFA, ensuring both American influence over German production and a continuing influx of American films. As the capital of the domestic film industry, Berlin remained at the forefront of Germany's "Americanization" during the Golden Twenties.

America, however, was not the model for Berlin's Dada artists. George Grosz, John Heartfield, and Wieland Herzfelde all joined the German Communist Party (KPD) shortly after its founding and trumpeted the Soviet Union as the nation of the future. In their own country they saw that social iniquities—symbolized by crippled war veterans scrambling in the gutter for cigar butts discarded by fat plutocrats—were more crassly evident than ever. To carry on revolutionary propaganda against the Weimar "pseudo-democracy" they founded the Malik-Verlag, which published politically inspired fiction and art books. Their initial production was a journal entitled *Jedermann sein eigener Fussball* (Everyone His Own Football). The first issue featured on its cover a satiric photomontage, "Who Is the Most Beautiful?" with the faces of Noske, Ludendorff, Erzberger, Ebert, and Scheidemann. The publishers distributed some 7,600 copies of their journal during a mock funeral procession through the streets of Berlin, a gesture that turned out to be quite apt, for the police immediately prohibited future numbers. Malik followed with a tract called "Die Pleite" (Bankruptcy), which contained a cartoon by Grosz showing President Ebert as a fat king being served a drink by a capitalist lackey. In the summer of 1920 the Malik circle organized Berlin's First International Dada Fair in a local art gallery. Here the main target was traditional art and bourgeois cultural values. Grosz and Heartfield advertised the show with a placard reading "Art is Dead, Long Live the New Machine Art of Tatlin"—a pitch for Soviet constructivism as the art-

The First International Dada Fair, Berlin, 1920

work of the future. Visitors to the exhibition saw a calculatedly messy assemblage of paintings, prints, and posters parodying Great Art and the bourgeois social order that dutifully worshipped it. One of the posters read: "Dilettantes, Rise Up against Art!" The pièce de résistance was a dummy dressed in a military officer's uniform with a pig's head and a sign hanging from its crotch explaining: "In order to understand this work of art go on a daily twelve-hour exercise on the Tempelhof Field with full backpack and equipped for maneuvers."

For this and other insults to the military the Dada Fair organizers were taken to court. Grosz and Heartfield were fined 300 and 600 marks respectively. But it was not only the conservatives who were outraged. The Communists, whose ideals Grosz and company claimed to represent, were appalled by the Dadaists' wholesale attack on traditional culture. Unlike these anti-artists, the Communists took the great art of the past seriously, believing it could be inspirational for the workers. Echoing Kaiser Wilhelm II's condemnation of modern art, Gertrud Alexander, cultural editor of the KPD's newspaper *Die Rote Fahne*, denounced Dada's "tasteless new barbaric 'paintings'," adding: "The conscious fighter has no need, like Dada, to destroy artworks in order to free himself from 'bourgeois attitudes,' because he is not bourgeois. Those who can do no more than glue together silly kitsch like Dada, should keep their hands off art."

Bertolt Brecht, who would himself later fall afoul of Communist Party guidelines on art, believed he understood why the Dadaists made imperfect Communists: they were animated less by reverence for the proletariat than by contempt for the bloated bourgeoisie. In a letter to Grosz regarding the latter's satirical attack on the plutocracy, *Das Gesicht der herrschenden Klasse* (The Face of the Ruling Class), Brecht proposed that what made the painter "an enemy of the bourgeois was their physiognomy." "You hate the bourgeoisie not because you are a proletarian but because you are an artist," he told Grosz. The same, of course, could have been said of Brecht himself.

In mid-November 1923 the government of Chancellor Gustav Stresemann, which had taken office in August 1923, introduced a new currency, the Rentenmark, to replace the essentially worthless paper marks then in circulation. To buttress the new money, Germany took out a mortgage on itself, putting up all its rolling stock, gold reserves, and public real estate as backing. Hjalmar Schacht, a financial wizard who would later become Hitler's chief banker, was appointed National Currency Commissioner to oversee the transition to the new system. At the same time, Stresemann ended the "passive resistance" policy in the Ruhr, which was draining away 40 million gold marks a day. These measures anchored the Rentenmark at the prewar mark's dollar ratio of 4.2 to 1, a tremendous accomplishment.

The social price, however, was extremely high. The new currency completely swept away whatever paper marks people still possessed, capping, for many Germans, a process of progressive impoverishment. To keep the new currency stable, moreover, the national, state, and municipal governments adopted strict austerity programs, including unprecedented reductions in public spending. In Berlin alone some 39,000 city employees, among them high-level civil servants, lost their jobs. Many never found employment again, ensuring that the jobless rate in the capital would remain dangerously high even during the period of relative prosperity between 1924 and 1929.

The Haller Review at Berlin's Admiralspalast

5

THE WORLD CITY OF ORDER AND BEAUTY

In those days the entire world was watching Berlin. Some with dread, some with hope; in that city the fate of Europe was being decided.

—Ilya Ehrenburg,
Memoirs, 1921–1941

The horrors of the early Weimar era that Berlin's artists so faithfully—and perhaps all too eagerly—recorded did not entirely fade away when the political and economic conditions stabilized in the mid-1920s. The capital's streets were still crowded with underage prostitutes, crippled beggars, and vulgar plutocrats. Yet the city, relying extensively on American loans, now undertook significant modernization and building projects that had been deferred during the Great Inflation. In the process it added between 80,000 and 100,000 new residents a year, pushing the population over the 4 million mark in 1925. Berlin now harbored one-fifteenth of Germany's total population, one-twelfth of its large factories, and one-tenth of its employees. Politically it evolved into a bastion of pro-Republican sentiment: "Weimar," originally posed as a safe alternative to Berlin, became almost synonymous with the capital. The city's cultural life became even more open to outside influences—again from America but also from the young Soviet Union, which offered visions of harmonious social progress to compete with America's survival-of-the-fittest technocracy.

Unfortunately, many progressive-minded Berliners mistakenly assumed that the rest of the nation thought as they did. In reality, however, the industrial concentration, economic rationalization, cultural cosmopolitanism, and pro-Republican politics that shaped Weimar Berlin were not nearly so warmly embraced outside the capital as inside it. The German capital had long been attacked as too big and too foreign, and the attacks escalated over the Weimar period as the city became yet more "alien" in its values. A brochure published in Karlsruhe, for example, denounced the Spree metropolis as a frightening cross between "Chikago und Moskau," a nasty mixture of "Amerikanismus und Bolshevismus." Thus Berlin's claim to stand for Germany seemed more problematical than ever, at least at home. Worried about this gulf between capital and nation, Kurt Tucholsky advised his fellow Berlin intellectuals to "radiate energy in the provinces instead of patting themselves on the back." They should, he said, respond to the provincial outcry against the capital by speaking out "with the power of Berlin, which is light, to the provinces, where it is dark." But what if the provinces preferred it in the dark? And what if the light from Berlin was rather like that cast by the moon: visible only under clear skies and ultimately dependent on an outside source?

The Era of Fulfillment

In August 1923 Gustav Stresemann, with three months still to serve as chancellor, also took up the office of foreign minister, which he held until his death in 1929. It is for his service as foreign minister that he is best remembered. Although he was intent upon restoring Germany's status as a great power, he sought to do so not by saber rattling but by negotiation. By fulfilling Germany's treaty obligations to the Western Powers (he remained hostile to Poland and opposed accepting Germany's revised border with that nation) he hoped to win reductions in reparations and an end to the restrictions on German sovereignty. In 1924 he helped to broker the Dawes Plan, which provided for fixed reparations payments along with generous American loans; he was also the chief German negotiator behind the Locarno Pact (1925), which confirmed the inviolability of the Franco-German and Franco-Bel-

Kempinski Haus Vaterland (center, rear of picture) on the Potsdamer Platz. In the foreground is the clock tower containing Europe's first traffic light

gian borders and the demilitarized zone of the Rhineland; and in 1926 he orchestrated Germany's entry into the League of Nations.

As the son of a Berlin innkeeper and the proud author of a dissertation on the local brewing industry, Stresemann loved the German capital and identified with its prowess. During his reign as foreign minister, the so-called "Era of Fulfillment," Berlin recaptured some of the forward-looking momentum it had lost during the war, revolution, and inflation. For a time the German capital staked a claim to being the most progressive city in Europe, if not the world.

The new direction was nowhere more clearly in evidence than at Tempelhof, the parade ground where generations of Prussian soldiers had marched. In 1924 it became a new civilian airport. With the most advanced transportation facilities in

Europe, Berlin now became a crossroads of European air traffic as well as a great railway hub. Starting in 1926, passengers of the newly formed Deutsche Lufthansa could fly from Berlin to fifteen European destinations. At the same time, construction of a new radio transmitter in western Berlin confirmed the capital's domination of the infant German broadcast industry. The Funkturm, looking like a mini Eiffel Tower, became a much-used symbol in the marketing of the metropolis. Every two years the city sponsored an exhibition showcasing the latest developments in broadcast technology, which in 1929 included the experimental transmission of television signals.

Another symbol of the new Berlin was Kempinski Haus Vaterland, a vast amusement complex on Potsdamer Platz, which opened in September 1928. A kind of proto–Disney World of cinemas, stages, arcades, restaurants, and theme rooms, it employed the latest technology to satisfy age-old cravings for exoticism and sensual pleasure. Roaming through its spacious precincts, visitors could hear flamenco guitar at a Spanish bodega, sip Tokay at a Hungarian inn, sample Heuriger at a Grinzing Weinstube, watch the sun set over the Zugspitze at a Bavarian beer garden, witness an artificial storm at the Rheinterrasse café, pretend to be Tom Mix at the Wild West Bar. (The lack of British and French themes was not accidental: Kempinski, a patriot, could not forgive those nations for their treatment of Germany at Versailles.) At night the whole operation was brilliantly illuminated—a beacon of commercial kitsch on a grand scale. Even visiting Americans were impressed.

To cope with the continuing housing shortage, Berlin's director of building, Martin Wagner, supervised the construction of four huge apartment complexes: Hufeisensiedlung, Weisser Stadt, Siemensstadt, and Onkel-Toms-Hütte. Unlike the hierarchical Mietskaserne of the imperial era, the new developments were rigorously egalitarian: no more bourgeois up front and proletarians in back. But precisely because they catered primarily to low-income people, wealthier neighbors often objected to their presence. For example, the villa owners in Zehlendorf protested vigorously against the construction of Onkel-Toms-Hütte.

The so-called *Grosssiedlungen* were more innovative socially than architecturally. In the mid-Weimar period, however, Berlin did produce a few pathbreaking buildings. Erich Mendelsohn, one of the stars of the new architecture, redesigned the Mosse-Verlag Press House with rounded, futuristic curves. According to one enthusiastic observer, this style reflected "the large modern city, power, confidence, affirmation,

Erich Mendelsohn's "Einstein Tower," Potsdam, 1924

and the rapid pace of work." Mendelsohn's signature building in this period was the so-called Einstein Tower near Potsdam, an astrophysical laboratory that the architect said emerged "from the mystique surrounding Einstein's universe."

Mendelsohn's choice of a tower was deliberate, for, like many architects of his generation, he was fascinated with New York skyscrapers. In 1924 the Mosse press sent him to America on a study trip. He produced a book entitled *Amerika: Bilderbuch eines Architekten* (1926) that added tremendously to the ongoing America-cult in Weimar Berlin. Mendelsohn, Mies van der Rohe, and Ludwig Hilberseimer would have liked to build New York–style skyscrapers in Berlin, but the city's height restrictions prevented such a Manhattan transfer.

To rationalize the public transportation system in the sprawling megalopolis, Berlin consolidated its various streetcar, elevated-train, bus, and subway lines under one administrative roof: the Berlin Transportation Company, or BVG (Berliner-Verkehrs-Betriebe), in 1928. The new enterprise, Berliners liked to boast, was the largest municipal agency in the world, as well as Germany's third largest corporation after the Reichsbahn (which had recently been privatized) and the I. G. Farben

Elevated train at Gitschiner Strasse, 1930

chemical trust. The chairman of the BVG's board of directors, Ernst Reuter, was a leading Social Democratic politician and former Communist who had become an avid proponent of technological modernization. Reuter was also active in the development of Berlin's electrical power system, which needed beefing up to accommodate all the new industries, rail lines, and housing projects. In 1927 the giant Rummelsburg Power Station came on line, followed a year later by the Western Power Station (now the Reuter Station). Both plants were models of functional aesthetics, much photographed by admirers of cutting-edge industrial design.

Cutting-edge was the image that Weimar-era boosters most often propounded for their city, just as their predecessors had done in the imperial era. Now, however, technological modernity was combined with pride in being politically and socially up-to-date. A program entitled "Berlin in the Light" (October 13–16, 1928) heralded the German capital as "Europe's New City of Light," whose nighttime streets, thanks to advanced lighting techniques, had been "transformed into an exciting showplace, an arena for a new nocturnal existence." In the following year the city's newly created Office for Tourism, Exhibitions and Fairs orchestrated a multimedia campaign promoting the message that Berlin was a "World City of Order and Beauty." A promotional poster showing cars with illuminated headlights passing through the Brandenburg Gate carried the slogan: *Jeder einmal in Berlin* (Everyone must go once to Berlin). In 1927 Walter Ruttmann's avant-garde film, *Berlin: Symphonie einer Grossstadt* (Berlin: Symphony of a Metropolis), which projected a symphonic harmony of man and machine in the metropolis, reflected the progressive-republican hope that technological rationalization would translate into political and social advancement.

In 1925 President Ebert died with time left in his term, requiring a new presidential election to replace him. The candidate preferred by most conservatives was former Field Marshal Hindenburg, who, far from losing status because of his role in Germany's defeat, was much admired as an emblem of the imperial era and its proud military class. Prorepublican centrists and liberals could opt for Wilhelm Marx, a colorless former chancellor from the Center Party, while the radical left had Ernst Thälmann, a rabble-rousing Communist. Hindenburg emerged victorious with 48.3 percent of the vote to Marx's 45.3 percent and Thälmann's 6.4 percent. In Berlin, however, Marx outpolled the Hero of Tannenberg by 52.6 percent to 37.0 percent, while Thälmann got 10.4 percent. Hindenburg exacted his revenge on Berlin by delaying for a year and a half his official visit to the governing mayor's office in the "Red City Hall" (so named because of its red-brick facade, not its politics). Although he was obliged to conduct national business in Berlin, he got away as often as he could to his estate in the Prussian countryside, Neudeck, where he felt much more at home.

Mayor Böss took the lead in championing the Weimar order. When, during an official dinner honoring New York's Mayor Jimmy Walker at the venerable Hotel Kaiserhof, hotel officials put out imperial flags rather than the republican colors, Böss refused to attend. Thereafter he kept official functions away from the hotel, which remained on the black list until the ascension of Hitler, who once again made it a center of state occasions.

One of the ironies of Berlin's identification with Weimar is that the capital's financial posture within the German nation and Prussian state was less favorable than it had been in the imperial era. Under republican law, Berlin, like other municipalities, was no longer able to collect a surcharge on national income taxes, which had once been a major source of revenue. This hit the capital hardest because it had to provide extensive services for the various governmental bureaucracies located there. Mayor Böss complained that Berlin could not adequately fulfill its duties as a capital because it was kept on too short a fiscal leash by national and state leaders. His complaints, however, fell on deaf ears. Konrad Adenauer, mayor of Cologne, spoke for many of his colleagues when he observed: "Berlin has an enormous income through corporate taxes because, God knows, everything is concentrated there." As we shall see, when Adenauer served as West Germany's first chancellor between 1949 and 1963, he fully retained his aversion toward the metropolis on the Spree.

Weimar Culture

Mayor Böss was forever in search of new revenues for Berlin because, in addition to sponsoring ambitious housing and social welfare projects, he wished to make the municipal government a major player in the city's cultural life alongside agencies of the Prussian state, which had traditionally dominated the scene. He poured money into a new municipal opera house in the Bismarckstrasse, which competed with the Prussian-backed houses on Unter den Linden and the Platz der Republik, and he funded a new city art museum to supplement the state institutions on the Museum Island. Hoping to convince Max Liebermann to donate one of his paintings to the city collection, he arranged for the artist to be named an honorary citizen of Berlin. During the course of personally delivering this honor to the artist's studio, Böss removed a small oil from the wall and put it in his briefcase—a playful hint, he thought, of the quid pro quo expected from the painter. Liebermann, however, failed to get the joke: he sent the city a bill for 800 marks for the painting.

Böss was justified in focusing so much attention on cultural issues because culture, broadly defined, was the primary arena in which Weimar Berlin was making its name in the world. Although other German cities retained important cultural traditions and attractions, none of them could remotely match the Republican capital's clout on the world stage. Fully aware of this fact, Berliners often disparaged the cultural offerings of other cities, especially those of its old rival, Munich. Writing in 1922, an observer from Berlin argued that Munich, previously "overestimated" as an art center, was now "nothing but a provincial town without an intellectual core." A 1924 article in the Berlin periodical *Das Tagebuch* declared Munich to be "The Dumbest City in Germany" by dint of its reactionary press, xenophobic leaders, and beer-besotted population.

During the Stresemann era Berlin owed its up-to-date cosmopolitan image partly to its continuing absorption of American influences, which, at least in mass culture, set the standard for modernity. Commenting on this trend, Ilya Ehrenburg called Berlin "an apostle of Americanism." Of course, to those Germans who believed that "America" stood for all that was wrong with the modern world, Berlin's ongoing Americanization simply confirmed its status as a trashy and vulgar sink of iniquity. It was on his return from a trip to America that Munich's Cardinal Faulhaber called Berlin the embodiment of "babylonian mongrelism."

Berlin's response to Josephine Baker, the black American dancer who sometimes performed in nothing but a banana skirt, reflected the capital's romance with America, in particular with its Negro culture. Baker arrived in Berlin from Paris in 1925 with her traveling show, *La Revue Nègre*. She instantly took to Berlin, declaring that it had "a jewel-like sparkle, especially at night, that didn't exist in Paris." The huge cafés reminded her "of ocean liners powered by the rhythms of their orchestras." From her own account, the city also took to her. "It's madness, a triumph," she claimed shortly after her first performance on New Year's Eve at the Nelson Theater on the Kurfürstendamm. "They carry me on their shoulders. At a big dance, when I walk in, the musicians stop playing, get up and welcome me. Berlin is where I received the greatest number of gifts." But contemporary assessments of her performances and persona suggest that while there was plenty of fascination there was also a strong undercurrent of racism and cultural condescension. Applauding her dancing as the "victory of negroid dance culture over the Viennese waltz," a reviewer for the *Berliner Tageblatt* added: "In her the wildness of her forefathers, who were transplanted from the Congo Basin to the Mississippi, is preserved most authentically: she breathes life, the power of nature, a wantonness that can hardly be contained." Oscar Bie, the dance critic of the *Berliner Börsen-Courier*, saw in her dance company "the remains of genuine paganism, of idol worship, of grotesque orgies." Baker may have felt welcomed in Berlin, but she was welcomed only as an exotic outsider who provided the thrill of the forbidden without demanding serious or long-term acceptance.

In her Berlin performances Baker was backed by Sam Wooding's all-black eleven-piece jazz band, which also supported another American Negro review that was then big in Berlin, *The Chocolate Kiddies*. Along with the jazz came new American dances like the fox-trot and the Charleston. Like the rock music of the 1960s, this craze was seen to have political implications—to connote a rejection of previous authoritarian ways. As one enthusiast claimed: "If only the Kaiser had danced

Josephine Baker in her famous "banana skirt"

jazz—then all of that [World War I] would never have come to pass." Predictably, however, cultural conservatives were horrified by the American imports. According to the arch-nationalist composer Hans Pfitzner, the "jazz–fox trot flood" represented "the American tanks in the spiritual assault on European culture."

Whatever its spiritual import, jazz turned out to be more than just a temporary fad. In 1926 Deutsche Gramophone created a special label to promote American jazz; this helped to spread its popularity and to give it permanence. So did the proliferation of native (or mostly native) jazz bands, virtually all of which imitated famous American groups like Bix Beiderbecke or Red Nichols. Improvisation did not come easily to classically trained German musicians, and to achieve greater commercial appeal some actually claimed to be American. Such was the case with "Herr Mike Sottnek aus Neuyork," who advertised his outfit as "Die amerikanische Jazz-Tanzkapelle." Eventually the native musicianship improved, and Germany (especially Berlin) developed a thriving indigenous jazz culture.

American influences also helped to reshape Berlin's music hall scene, providing the impetus for a new kind of production, the seminude all-girl chorus line. Admittedly, the "jazz" in question here was no more spontaneous than the Rockettes-style kicklines performed by troupes like the "Tiller Girls," who actually hailed from England. As historian Peter Jelavich has noted, the kicklines represented for the Berliners the technological promise of American society. "Whereas the black entertainers embodied one aspect of America—something spontaneous, wild, uncivilized, unencumbered by European culture—the Girls represented the flip side of the dollar: energy, efficiency, productivity." These acts were choreographed so precisely that their erotic potential was often lost—unless one experienced a masochistic frisson at the prospect of being trampled by a giant millipede. In essence, the kicklines were just body parts in mechanized unison, the show business equivalent of busy hands over a factory conveyor belt.

All-Girl reviews effectively competed with the cinema for mass audiences. For more discriminating tastes, there was the new "jazz-opera." Kurt Weill and Ernst Krenek, two of Weimar Berlin's most important avant-garde composers, consciously incorporated elements of jazz and blues into their operatic works. In his jazz opera *Jonny Spielt Auf* (Johnny Strikes Up), which chronicles the adventures of a black dance band violinist, Krenek fused Duke Ellington with Béla Bartók and Arnold Schönberg, a dazzling combination. Berliners got their first look at *Jonny* on November 21, 1927, at the Städtische Oper (Municipal Opera). In the last act they saw the hero leap up on a train station clock and ride the big hand down playing his violin, while the chorus sang: "The hour of the past has struck, the future is approaching. Don't miss your connection. We are off to the unknown land of the free." Meanwhile, over at the Theater am Schiffbauerdamm, Weill's and Brecht's *Die Dreigroschenoper* (The Threepenny Opera) was beginning its long run. The story derived from John Gay's *Beggar's Opera* of 1728, but the music, once again, drew on American jazz. To perform it, the producers hired a Berlin jazz group with a predictably American name: The Lewis Ruth Band. Reviewing the production, Alfred Kerr thought that Weill's "magnificently simple music" was the only good thing about it. (In fact, the simplicity was deceptive; in the famous "Mack the Knife" song Weill subtly altered the rhythmic patterns and countermelodies in extremely sophisticated fashion.) Kerr noted that Brecht's text had been plagiarized from François Villon's poetry. Later, Brecht blithely confessed to the charge of plagiarism: "I am quite sloppy when it comes to matters of intellectual ownership."

While American jazz was adding new dimensions to Berlin's popular culture, the city's composers and conductors were reworking and reinterpreting the classical tradition. In the 1920s and early 1930s Berlin competed with New York for the title of world capital of classical music. The German city housed twenty classical orchestras and three major opera companies. It boasted two preeminent music schools, the Prussian Academy of Fine Arts and the Academy of Music. Both schools included new forms of composition in their curricula. Arnold Schönberg taught at the Prussian Academy and Paul Hindemith at the Academy of Music.

Like jazz, the new directions in symphonic and choral music inspired a mixture of approbation and revulsion. The premier of Schönberg's *Pierrot Lunaire* on January 5, 1924, at the Academy of Music provoked a riot to rival the famous upheaval at the Paris debut of Stravinsky's *Rite of Spring* in 1913. Appalled conservatives shouted that the piece was "cacophonic garbage" inspired by "Jewish Bolshevism" (Stravinsky was not Jewish, and he hated the Bolsheviks). Two years later Alban Berg's *Wozzeck*, based on a play by Georg Büchner, opened at the old State Opera on Unter den Linden under the baton of Erich Kleiber. This opera employed Schönberg's radical twelve-tone system and unmelodious *Sprechstimme*, a cross between speech and chant. The audience, which consisted almost exclusively of friends of the composer, was predictably enthusiastic, but the reviews were mixed. The SPD's *Vorwärts* hailed the performance as "a historic event" in which the "hard logic [of Büchner's play] was ennobled, humanized, psychologized through the spirit of music." Oddly, the critic for the conservative *Kreuz-Zeitung* found something good to say: "[Berg's] *Tonmalerei* seldom supports the singers with singable melody. . . . But the final act more than makes up for this. Here the composer explores new paths, becomes less harsh in his harmony—indeed, every once in a while he is 'simply old-fashioned pretty' and the listener can relax." The *Berliner Tageblatt*, liberal on political matters but not on high culture, was disdainful: "All those who today purposely create the ugly (dissonant, impoverished, overdone, distorted) are damned to vacuity. It is no accident that their music is boring. . . . Is the State Opera House the right place for such experiments?" The Catholic *Germania* thought it was not: "Pretense! Ingenious pretense, but, in any case, pretense! And this is what 'German' composers, controlled by unseen strings [a reference to Berg's Jewishness] call art. The time is approaching to rebel against giving this inspired methodological nonsense a respectable backdrop."

A similar blend of brilliance and controversy could be found in Berlin's city-owned opera facility, the Municipal Opera House, where *Jonny* had its Berlin premier. It occupied the precincts of the former Deutsches Opernhaus in Charlottenburg, which had gone bankrupt in 1924. Mayor Böss played a key role in getting the city to take it over in 1925. The great Bruno Walter became its first principal conductor, holding that post until 1929. He had established his reputation in Munich but could not abide that city's growing anti-Semitism, its insistence that he, as a Jew, was unfit to conduct the works of German masters like Beethoven and Wagner. He felt much more at home in Berlin during the Stresemann years, which he recalled in his memoirs as "an epoch of hope, hope for the new Europe." Berlin's cultural milieu in this period impressed the conductor for its incredible richness and, again in retrospect, for its precariousness: "It was indeed as if all the eminent artistic forces were shining forth once more, imparting to the last festive symposium of the minds a many-hued brilliance before the night of barbarism closed in."

Although Walter loved being in Berlin and participating in its "symposium of the minds," his brief tenure at the Municipal Opera was by no means harmonious. He found the facility itself to be "the most uninspiring and unmagical of theaters," blighted both by physical ugliness and a lack of history. While he managed to inject some new life into the place, he fought from the outset with the institution's general director, Heinz Tietjen, who also directed the Prussian State Theaters. Tietjen, a competent but ruthlessly ambitious administrator, wanted to fuse the Municipal Opera with the Berlin State Opera on Unter den Linden, and to this end he often shortchanged the former house. For example, he obligated talented young singers, some of whom Walter had discovered, to perform exclusively at the Linden house. Unwilling to tolerate this arrangement, Walter left the Municipal in 1929, though he stayed on in Berlin until 1933, conducting a subscription series at the Philharmonic.

In his short time at the Municipal Opera Walter managed to put it on Berlin's musical map, but it was never as experimental—never as "Weimar," one might say—as the so-called Kroll Opera under Otto Klemperer. This was the primary venue for new opera, as well as for older works performed in new ways. The "Kroll" (thus called because it occupied the old Kroll Theater next to the Reichstag—its official name was Theater am Platz der Republik) opened as a second branch of the Prussian State Opera on January 1, 1924. After the war the facility had been taken over by the Berlin Volksbühne, which hoped to produce socially progressive opera there. But the Volksbühne had run out of money for the project during the inflation era and transferred the property to the state, while holding rights to one-half of the seats. Architectural renovations had produced a technically up-to-date but physically unattractive house. From the beginning the Kroll suffered from a lack of adequate financing (Prussia could not really afford two operas in Berlin) and from the requirement to reserve seats for the Volksbühne, which had become little more than a cut-rate ticket agency with a middle-of-the-road clientele.

The appointment of Otto Klemperer to be principal conductor at the Kroll in 1926 gave the house its moment of brilliance but also added to its problems. Always a risk-taker, Klemperer set the tone for his tenure at the Kroll by including Leoš Janáček's *Sinfonietta* in his opening program. He followed this with a totally new *Fidelio*, replete with cubist sets. This caused an outcry from conservative critics, who regarded Beethoven as sacrosanct. One of them spoke of "German shame everywhere one looks." From Munich, the Nazis' *Völkischer Beobachter* denounced Klemperer as an *Obermusikjude* who could never understand a German genius like Beethoven. Undaunted, the conductor mounted an all-Stravinsky program on an evening when the entire stalls section had been sold to the Association of Berlin Businessmen and Industrialists, who had expected some familiar music and a big-breasted diva. Not surprisingly, they hissed and booed.

And so it continued in subsequent years. While opera-goers with a predilection for the new were making the Kroll their house of choice, more conservative patrons escalated their protest. At a production of Stravinsky's *The Soldier's Tale* in fall 1927 the audience included Einstein, Brecht, Weill, Ernst Bloch, Walter Benjamin, and Gustav Stresemann. All were enchanted. But the Volksbühne subscribers were deeply upset, wondering once again why they weren't seeing *Carmen.* Matters became even worse when Klemperer turned to Wagner, who by the 1920s had been appropriated by the nationalist right as the chief deity of *Deutschtum.* In 1929 the Kroll mounted a futuristic *Flying Dutchman* that did away with all the pious traditionalism that most Wagnerians had come to expect. The (beardless) Dutchman's sailors looked like a gang of dock laborers and Senta came off as an unsubmissive visionary à la Käthe Kollwitz. Fearing that there might be violent protests, the police ringed the hall on opening night. As it happened, there was no violence inside, but plenty of heat in the reviews. The critic Fritz Stege, who later became the Nazis' chief oracle on music, said the performance was "an act of unparalleled cultural shamelessness, with which a sneering grin has reduced a German cultural monument to ruins." Paul Schwers, in the *Allgemeine Musikzeitung,* labeled Klemperer's "proletarianized" *Dutchman* "an artistic betrayal of the people." It was, he added, another example of the way in which the conductor was wasting the public's money and "damaging Berlin's reputation as a cultural center." Either the Kroll's "methods must be changed . . . or it must be shut," he insisted.

While Klemperer was battling for his artistic life at the Kroll, Wilhelm Furtwängler was struggling to establish himself as musical director at the illustrious Berlin Philharmonic. Unlike his beleaguered colleague, however, Furtwängler prevailed and became an institution in his own right. No doubt it helped that Furtwängler saw himself more as a custodian of traditional musical values than as a prophet of the avant-garde.

Not that Furtwängler eschewed the new. On December 2, 1928, he presented Schönberg's *Variations for Orchestra.* Many people in the audience rattled their house keys, which was the upper bourgeoisie's accepted manner of expressing displeasure. The conductor sprinkled other new works through the Philharmonic's programming without occasioning too much protest. He caused more consternation because of his frequent absences, made necessary by the fact that he was also principal conductor of the Leipzig Gewandhaus Orchestra and the Vienna Philharmonic. He also conducted often in New York, even toying with the idea of settling there permanently. But in the end he opted for Berlin as his central base, and his alliance with the Philharmonic became the most solid attachment in his life.

While Berlin's musicians, especially its jazz composers and performers, tended to think of America as the promised land, the city's dramatists often disparaged the world's richest democracy as a rapacious predator. A long-running review entitled "*Oh,*

USA" portrayed Uncle Sam as a bill collector before whom Russia, Germany, and Italy had to bow in submission. America's middle classes were depicted as bigoted and hypocritical, while its workers came across as mere machines. The play was so stridently anti-American that the U.S. embassy lodged a protest with the German government.

Rather than America, Berlin's playwrights turned to the Soviet Union for inspiration. Like Moscow, Berlin spawned a number of theater collectives that produced topical works with a left-wing slant. Among them were the groups led by Erwin Piscator, who in the early 1920s had thrown off the multihued colors of Dada in favor of the solid red drapery of communism. Determined to promote the communist cause via the theater, Piscator staged an agitprop production entitled *Revue Roter Rummel* for the KPD's 1924 election campaign. In the following year he directed a documentary about the German revolution of 1918/19 called *Trotz Alledem*! (In Spite of Everything), a phrase made famous by Liebknecht. It employed film clips along with stage action, a device that became standard in Piscator's documentary theater. While thumping for the KPD, Piscator also worked for the Volksbühne, but quit in disgust when it tried to trim his radical sails. With the support of a newly rich businessman whose wife hoped to act in his plays, the playwright rented the Theater am Nollendorfplatz and launched a "dramaturgical collective" to mount socially progressive works. In 1927/28 he directed four productions, each of which explored new theatrical territory. His production of *Schweik* (based on Jaroslav Hašek's antiwar novel, *The Good Soldier Schweik*) featured two treadmill stages and sets by George Grosz. A play about skullduggery in the oil business called *Konjunktur* included music by Kurt Weill. Among these plays only *Schweik* made money, and the businessman-patron, whose wife never did get to act, withdrew his support. The collective shut down.

In 1929 Piscator was back. Somehow he found the funds to return to the Theater am Nollendorfplatz with a production of Walter Mehring's *Der Kaufmann von Berlin*, a play about an impoverished East European Jew who comes to Berlin and makes millions during the inflation. It had sets by László Moholy-Nagy and songs by Hanns Eisler, a sometime collaborator with Brecht. In one of the numbers, *The Song of the Three Street Sweepers*, the performers do away with some garbage of the inflation era—a pile of currency, a steel helmet, and the corpse of a Freikorps soldier—while singing "Crap: Chuck It Out!" To conservatives in the audience, it was the play that should be chucked out, and it folded after a short run.

Among Piscator's most ardent champions in Berlin was the weekly journal, *Die Weltbühne*, which, in addition to theater, film, and music criticism, offered topical fiction, political commentary, and social satire. At one time or another, it employed just about everyone who was anyone in Weimar Berlin's left-wing literary community. The editor during the later years of the Republic was Carl von Ossietzky, a native Hamburger who had become a passionate pacifist and internationalist before taking a job with the *Berliner Volks-Zeitung* in 1919. In 1927 he took over at the *Weltbühne*, then at the peak of its notoriety. Ossietzky's *Weltbühne* became increasingly purist in its left-wing attachments. In 1929, when the SPD-controlled Berlin police suppressed a Communist May Day demonstration that was designed to embarrass the Socialists, the paper sided completely with the Communists, demanding the dismissal of the Socialist chief of police. This demand was at once obtuse and quixotic, as was the journal's nomination of Heinrich Mann for president of the Republic in 1932, which even Mann rejected as ridiculous. Ossietzky did not get along with *Die Weltbühne*'s best writer, Kurt Tucholsky, who had a much more realistic appreciation of Weimar's political landscape. With his agonized love-hate for his native land, Tucholsky was a kind of latter-day Heinrich Heine. Like that great poet, he was haunted by a sense of futility regarding his effectiveness as a political educator; he worried that he and his paper were having little impact outside a narrow circle of Berlin sophisticates. And, native Berliner though he was, he

Kurt Tucholsky

came to despair for the German capital itself, seeing it as self-satisfied and complacent. "Berlin," he concluded, "combines the disadvantages of an American metropolis and a German provincial city." In the end, Tucholsky understood that *Die Weltbühne*'s relentless carping at Weimar from the left was aiding and abetting those who attacked the Republic from the right. After Hitler's seizure of power he fled to Sweden, where, in despair over his and his colleagues' failure to avert the worst, he took his life.

Die Weltbühne, even in its later stages, retained a certain residue of expressionism in its passionate commitments. But in the mid to late Weimar period the reigning style in literature and painting was *Neue Sachlichkeit* (New Objectivity)—a cool bath of skepticism and sobriety following the effusions of the immediate postwar period. Just as the earlier art and writing had mirrored the chaotic atmosphere of the times, so the new style seemed better suited to the politics of stabilization and accommodation during the second half of the decade.

Writing about the new style in painting, a contemporary critic declared: "The pictures and drawings by the artists of the *Neue Sachlichkeit* read like an account of events in Berlin during the Weimar period. They depict its desires, ideals, and disappointments, its evasions, conflicts, and shortcomings." Most of the painters in question had earlier been identified with Dada or expressionism and had focused on the horrors of war, revolution, and inflation; now they turned a critical but somewhat jaded eye to the scene around them in the "era of fulfillment." In one of his most famous works, *Sonnenfinsternis* (Solar Eclipse, 1926) Grosz depicted President Hindenburg being offered weapons by arms dealers while prisoners rot in jail, a donkey (symbolizing the public) feeds on a newspaper, and a huge dollar sign, Weimar Germany's true source of light, blots out the sun. The major painters also focused attention on themselves and their artist friends as observer-shapers of the cultural scene. Rudolf Schichter painted Brecht in his leather jacket with a stogie and rendered Kisch bare-breasted and covered with menacing tattoos; Grosz depicted writer Max Hermann-Neisse looking like a gnarled troll; Otto Dix drew Sylvia Harden as an emancipated woman, bob-haired and smoking; Max Beckmann did himself in a tuxedo, peering back sardonically at his creator. Such works did not radiate grand visions or overarching beliefs. Hope had shifted to smaller, more attainable aims, such as capturing the essence of an object or a person on canvas with the same no-nonsense precision that went into building a fine car or an airplane.

George Grosz, Selbstporträt *(Self-portrait), 1928*

The young Anglo-Irish painter Francis Bacon arrived in Berlin at this auspicious moment in the city's cultural history, though it was not the local art scene that initially attracted him. He had been expelled from his home in Ireland by his father for showing signs of incipient homosexuality. First he had gone to London and sampled that city's extensive but beleaguered homosexual underground. Hoping yet to reclaim him for traditional morality, his father sent him on a visit to Berlin under the care of a manly uncle. The uncle's virility, however, turned out to be indiscriminate, and young Bacon promptly found himself in bed with his guardian at the Hotel Adlon. Outside their opulent suite beckoned the whole world of "decadent" Berlin, which Bacon began exploring on his own once his uncle had returned to England. He recalled later:

> There was something extraordinarily open about the whole place. . . . You had this feeling that sexually you could get absolutely anything you wanted. I'd never seen anything like it, of course, having been brought up in Ireland, and it excited me enormously. I felt, well, now I can just drift and follow my instincts. And I remember these streets of clubs where people stood in the front of the entrance miming the perversions that were going on inside. That was *very* interesting.

Berlin was a revelation to Bacon in other ways as well. He was struck by the luxury of the Adlon cheek by jowl with the poverty of the Scheunenviertel; the *Unterwelt* of gangsters and their molls; the cinemas playing Fritz Lang's *Metropolis* and Eisenstein's *Battleship Potemkin*; the *Neue Sachlichkeit* exhibition at the Galerie Nierendorf in early 1927; the paintings of Grosz, Pechstein, Beckmann, and Dix, especially the latter's haunting *Big City Triptych*. All this made a lasting impression on the young man and helped shape his own work in the coming decades.

The Berlin world with which Bacon became acquainted through his precocious wanderings and the works of its avant-garde painters was also under intense scrutiny by the city's literary artists, many of whom, like the painters, had passed through Dada and expressionism to the rigors of *Neue Sachlichkeit.*

Alfred Döblin, the physician/writer who in 1919 had been scandalized by bourgeois Berlin's indifference to the brutal repression in proletarian Lichtenberg, gradually shifted from an outraged contempt for Weimar to a more objective, one might say medical, perspective. In 1929 he published his seminal work, *Berlin Alexanderplatz*, a clear-eyed, unvarnished portrait of the postrevolutionary metropolis. Influenced by avant-garde film, newspaper reportage, cabaret reviews, and the works of James Joyce, the novel charts the adventures of a former pimp named Franz Biberkopf as he emerges from prison to begin his life anew in the big city. Accustomed to the security of prison life, Biberkopf finds Berlin a terrifying place, its crowds coalescing into one huge oppressive mass, its inanimate objects acting like dynamic beings. Riding the streetcar and wandering by foot, he notes:

> Outside everything was moving, but—back of it—there was nothing! It—did not—live! It had happy faces, it laughed, waited in twos and threes on the traffic islands opposite Aschinger's, smoked cigarettes, turned the pages of newspa-

Alfred Döblin

> pers. . . . Terror struck him as he walked down Rosenthaler Strasse and saw a man and a woman sitting in a little beershop right at the window: they poured beer down their gullets out of mugs, yes, what about it, they were drinking, they had forks and stuck pieces of meat into their mouths, then they pulled their forks out again and were not bleeding. . . . The cars roared and jangled on, house fronts were rolling along one after the other without stopping. And there were roofs atop the houses, his eyes wandered straight upward: if only the roofs don't slide off, but the roofs stood upright. Where shall I go, poor devil that I am, he shuffled alongside the walls of the houses, there was no end to it.

Falling back among the gangster types of his preprison days, Biberkopf is literally ground down by the big city—he sheds body parts like an aging automobile—but his frightening urban odyssey finally redeems him and allows him to face the metropolis without panic. What emerges in this novel, then, is both a harrowing account of big city anomie and a celebration of the ways in which tough-minded urbanites can find a kind of spiritual sustenance in the daily grind. As one of Biberkopf's mentors, the junky Krause, declares after losing his job and family because of his addiction:

> A wife, a child, it looks as if that were the whole world. I have no regrets. I don't feel any guilt about it, we have to take facts, like ourselves, the way they come. We shouldn't brag about our fate. I'm an enemy of Destiny, I'm not a Greek, I'm a Berliner. . . . I enjoy the Rosenthaler Platz, I enjoy the cop at the Elsasser corner, I like my game of billiards, I'd like anyone to come and tell me that his life is better than mine.

Döblin's Biberkopf had an ally in Jakob Fabian, the protagonist of Erich Kästner's novel of 1920's Berlin, *Fabian. Die Geschichte eines Moralisten.* Like Biberkopf, Fabian explores the seedy underside of Spree-Babylon, but he is too much the "moralist" ever to make his peace with the city, and eventually he returns to his provincial homeland and dies trying to save a drowning child. Before leaving Berlin, Fabian unburdens himself on the subject of the decadent metropolis to a young lady who imagines that it is not much different than her provincial hometown.

> Almost like back home? You're fooling yourself. The moonlight and the smell of flowers, the silence and the small-town kiss in the doorway—those are all illusions. Over there, in that square, is a café where Chinese, nothing but Chinese, are sitting with Berlin whores. In front is a bar where homosexual boys dance with elegant actors and smart Englishmen, strutting their stuff and naming their price, which in the end is paid by a dyed-blond old bag who's allowed to come along and watch. Around the corner on the right is a hotel in which only Japanese reside, next to it a restaurant where Russian and Hungarian Jews rough each other up. In one of the side streets there is a Pension where young schoolgirls sell themselves to pick up a little pocket money. A half year ago there was a scandal that was hard to hush up. An elderly gentleman had rented a room for an assignation with a sixteen-year-old girl, but he found his own daughter waiting for him, which was not what he'd expected. . . . As an expanse of stone this city is more or less like it used to be but with respect to its inhabitants it has long resembled an insane asylum. In the east live the criminals, in the center the

swindlers, in the north there's poverty, in the west vice, and from all directions comes a sense of imminent collapse.

Life Was Not a Cabaret

The Berlin that Kästner described in *Fabian* was already menaced by the Nazis, who had been making their presence felt in the city since 1926, when Joseph Goebbels arrived to take over the Gau (Nazi district) of Berlin-Brandenburg. Before that moment the Berlin branch of the party had been divided and directionless. At first the oily little Rhinelander was not entirely pleased with his assignment. After walking Berlin's nocturnal streets he wrote in his diary: "Berlin last night. A sink hole of iniquity. And I'm supposed to plunge into this?" But plunge he did. Aware, as he put it, that "Berlin needs sensations as a fish needs water," he orchestrated a

Joseph Goebbels, Berlin's Gauleiter, 1932

campaign of violence and intimidation designed to shock even the most jaded sensibilities. He immediately scheduled propaganda marches in working-class districts like Wedding and Neukölln. As they marched, members of the Nazi Sturmabteilung (SA, Stormtroopers) sang "Die Rote Front, schlägt sie zu brei / SA marschiert. Achtung, die Straße frei (Beat the Red Front to a pulp. The SA is marching: keep off the streets)." To further goad the left, Goebbels advertised these marches with huge blood-red posters. Predictably, the Communists sought to defend their turf, resulting in bloody brawls in which both sides made ample use of blackjacks, brass knuckles, iron pipes, and even pistols. On March 21, 1927, a band of 600 to 700 SA men stormed a railway carriage containing twenty-seven Communists at the station in Lichterfelde-Ost. After beating the Communists, the Nazis marched into the center of the city and assaulted Jewish-looking persons on the Kurfürstendamm. In another provocative move, Goebbels founded a weekly newspaper called *Der Angriff* (The Attack), which took aim especially at the Jews. "This negative element must be erased from the German reckoning, or it will always soil that reckoning," declared an editorial. In a piece in his journal on the area around Berlin's Gedächtniskirche, Goebbels blamed the Jews for the capital's "asphalt democracy" and lack of a true German culture: "The eternal repetition of corruption and decay, of failing ingenuity and genuine creative power, of inner emptiness and despair, with the patina of a *Zeitgeist* sunk to the level of the most repulsive pseudoculture: that is what parades its essence, what does its mischief all around the Gedächtniskirche. One would so gladly believe that it is the national elite stealing day and night from the dear Lord on Tauentzien Avenue. It is only the Israelites." The publicity generated by the Nazis' provocations helped attract new members to the movement. The police estimated that in March 1927 the Berlin branch of the Nazi Party had about 3,000 members.

Of course, for all their frenetic activities, the Nazis were far from turning Red Berlin into a brown bastion. In fact, the disruptiveness of their campaign prompted the authorities to ban the organization in Berlin-Brandenburg for an eleven-month period between May 1927 and March 1928. In the May 1928 Reichstag elections the party did poorly across the Reich and especially poorly in Berlin, where it won only 1.5 percent of the vote. Goebbels nonetheless remained determined to prevail in the city, for he knew it was crucial to the Nazis' campaign for control of Germany as a whole. As he wrote in his memoir, *Kampf um Berlin (The Struggle for Berlin)*: "The capital constitutes the center of all political, intellectual, economic, and cultural energies of a country. From it emanate influences which leave no province, small town, or village untouched."

It was precisely those aspects of the cosmopolitan metropolis most despised by the Nazis—homosexuality, avant-garde art, left-wing politics, jazz, lascivious cabaret—which at the end of the decade drew in a pair of young English writers, W. H. Auden and Christopher Isherwood, to the German capital. Both found Berlin simultaneously liberating and depressing. Isherwood would later provide a detailed record of this experience in his famous Berlin novels, *Mr. Norris Changes Trains* and *Goodbye to Berlin*, which served as the basis for the play *I am a Camera* and the musical and movie *Cabaret*. Like so many chronicles of late Weimar Berlin, these works evoke an atmosphere of impending doom, of dancing-on-the-volcano.

Auden was the first to come; he arrived in October 1928 and stayed for ten months. Anxious to escape the "immense bat-shadow of home," he had initially gone to Paris, expecting to spend a full year there. However, he quickly found the French capital too predictable: nothing but (as he put it) "bedroom mirrors and bidets, lingerie and adultery, the sniggers of schoolboys and grubby old men." Wanting something fresh, and believing that aspiring writers should *suffer*, he decamped for "the much grimmer and disturbing uncartesian world of Berlin." Discomfort was hardly Berlin's only attraction. As he excitedly observed: "Berlin is a bugger's daydream. There are 170 male brothels under police control." One of his first stops was Magnus Hirschfeld's Institute of Sexual Research, which maintained an extensive collection of sexual-stimulation devices. Auden was not particularly titillated by this example of Teutonic scholarship, which he dismissed as "a eunuch's pleasure." More genuinely pleasurable were the dozens of gay bars, especially the Cozy Corner in the working-class Hallesches Tor district. John Layard, an English friend of Auden's who also lived in Berlin, described this place as "a very small café, rather scruffy, in which there were always half a dozen boys hanging around drinking beer." Another Englishman, John Lehmann, found the Cozy Corner to be "filled with attractive boys of any age between sixteen and twenty-one . . . all dressed in extremely short lederhosen which showed off their smooth and sunburnt thighs to delectable advantage." When Lehmann excused himself to go to the lavatory, he "was followed in by several boys, who, as if by chance, ranged themselves on either side of me and pulled out their cocks rather to show them off than

W. H. Auden, Christopher Isherwood, and Stephen Spender, 1930

to relieve nature as I was doing." As Lehmann's experience suggests, most of the boys at the Corner were a little rough around the edges, which suited Auden just fine. "Wystan liked being beaten up a bit," wrote Layard. "It would start with pillow-fights and end with blows; then they would go to bed together." Auden himself bragged that one of his boys, whom he described as "a cross between a rugger hearty and Josephine Baker," left him a "mass of bruises."

Berlin for Auden meant not just hard living but also hard thinking—an intellectual as well as carnal liberation. He learned, he claimed, that the traditional wisdom that goodness yields happiness was a dangerous inversion of the truth. "Be happy and you will be good" was his new (equally dubious) motto. Accordingly, most of the poems that he composed during his Berlin days—verses like "From scars where kestrels hover," "Love by ambition," and "Before this loved one"—deal less with the city per se than with the dangers of self-repression and the challenges of love. But he could not help but take notice of the charged political milieu in which he found himself. One of his Berlin-period poems speaks of a young proletarian girl shot through the knees by the police. Another alludes to a fierce battle on May Day

1929 between Communists and the police that left twenty-three people dead in the streets: "All this time was anxiety at night / Shooting and barricades in the street." Later, Auden understood that Berlin had made him politically aware for the first time in his life: "One suddenly realized that the whole foundations of life were shaking."

In early 1929 Auden invited his school friend Christopher Isherwood to visit him in Berlin. Isherwood accepted and ended up staying in the German capital, on and off, until May 1933. Like Auden he was attracted in large part by the wide-open homosexual scene. As he wrote in his autobiography, *Christopher and His Kind:* "Berlin meant boys." But not just any boys. Again like Auden, Isherwood had been sexually inhibited around men of his own social class and nationality and could explore his true self only with the "other": he needed, in short, "a working-class foreigner." He began frequenting the Cozy Corner with Auden and Layard, pleased that this was a proletarian dive and not one of those upscale gay-tourist bars in the West End filled with monocled boys in drag and Eton-cropped girls in dinner jackets playing at being naughty. Looking back later on this scene, Isherwood asked acutely: "Wasn't Berlin's famous 'decadence' largely a commercial 'line' which the Berliners had instinctively developed in their competition with Paris? Paris had long since cornered the straight-girl market, so what was left for Berlin to offer its visitors but a masquerade of perversions?"

Fortunately for Isherwood, the working-class boys who frequented the Cozy Corner were not interested in masquerades. Here he met his first "blue-eyed German boy," Bubi. "By embracing Bubi," Isherwood wrote, "Christopher could hold in his arms the whole mystery-magic of foreignness, Germanness. By means of Bubi, he could fall in love with and possess the entire nation." He took Bubi to restaurants, the zoo, and to movies like Pudovkin's *Storm over Asia* and G. W. Pabst's *Pandora's Box* based on the play by Frank Wedekind. Perhaps inevitably, however, Bubi turned out to be not so possessable after all: just another proletarian kid on the make. Moreover, he was not German at all, but Czech.

Again following Auden, Isherwood made a pilgrimage to Hirschfeld's Sex Institute. He giggled nervously at the high-heeled boots for fetishists, the lacy panties designed for big-crotched Prussian officers, and the trouser legs cut off at the knees and equipped with elastic bands that allowed their wearer to go about town with nothing on but them and an overcoat—perfect for "giving a camera-quick exposure when a suitable viewer appeared." Though somewhat embarrassed by all this, and by the "patients" under Hirschfeld's care, he was forced to admit "a kinship with these freakish fellow tribesmen and their distasteful customs." The "decadence" of Berlin may have been in part a commercial put-on, but there was enough of the genuine article for Isherwood to experience the kind of inner-liberation he could never have managed back home in England.

However enticing Isherwood may have found Berlin's homosexual scene, he was drawn to the city not only by his need for sexual emancipation, but also by the desire to make a gesture of defiance against his native country, which he had come to see as insufferably insular. In the eyes of most Britons, Germany was still the enemy, Berlin the capital of the Huns. Isherwood's father had been killed in the war by the Germans, the very people with whom the son was now choosing to live. By decamping for Berlin, the young writer found the perfect way to cut the strings to family and fatherland.

Another motive for his move to Berlin was his belief that the city would provide a stimulating environment for his work. Like Auden, Isherwood was a serious artist (albeit not so gifted), and he spent considerably less time chasing boys than sitting at his writing table. A telling scene in *Christopher and His Kind* has him leaving a party early in order to be fresh for writing the next morning. "Seldom have wild oats been sown so prudently," he admitted.

The sensibility that Isherwood brought to his work was increasingly shaped by the sociopolitical ambiance of the Spree metropolis as it slipped into depression and chaos. "Here was the seething brew of history in the making—a brew which would test the truth of all the political theories, just as actual cooking tests the cookery books," he wrote later. "The Berlin brew seethed with unemployment, malnutrition, stock market panic, hatred of the Versailles Treaty and other potent ingredients."

Having decided in 1929 to stay on in Berlin, Isherwood moved with one of his lovers to a dingy flat near the Hallesches Tor. Visiting him there in the summer of 1930, Stephen Spender found him living very frugally, eating horse meat and lung soup. After moving briefly to another slum near Kottbuser Tor, Isherwood found more lasting quarters in a flat at Nollendorfstrasse 17. This was middle-class shabby as opposed to slum-shabby. A description of it can be found in his novel, *Goodbye to Berlin*:

> From my window, the deep solemn massive street. Cellar-shops where the lamps burn all day, under the shadow of top-heavy balconied facades, dirty plaster frontages embossed with scrollwork and heraldic devices. The whole district is like

> this: street leading into street of houses like shabby monumental safes crammed with the tarnished valuables and second-hand furniture of a bankrupt middle class.

It was here that Isherwood encountered the figures who would populate his fiction. His landlady was a Fräulein Thurau, who had been ruined in the inflation and was desperate to keep up appearances. As Fräulein Lina Schroeder in the Berlin novels, she waddles about her domain in "a flowered dressing-gown pinned ingeniously together, so that not an inch of petticoat or bodice is to be seen, flicking with her duster, peeping, spying, poking her short pointed nose into the cupboards and luggage of her lodgers." Fond of complaining about the depravity of Berlin, she in fact is nearly unshockable. "How sweet love must be!" she sighs, after listening to "Herr Issyvoo" and one of his boys cavort in the next room. A fellow lodger and English expatriate named Jean Ross served as the model for Sally Bowles, the sometime actress and chanteuse for whom "Life is just a Cabaret, old chum." (The name Bowles, incidentally, was borrowed from the American writer Paul Bowles, who paid a brief visit to Isherwood in 1931. Bowles found Berlin "architecturally hideous," "seething with hatred," and, withal, "the least amusing place I have ever seen, a synonym for stupidity.") Jean Ross, like so many "modern" young women in Weimar Berlin, was determined to burn the candle at both ends even when she lacked the money for candle or matches. She boasted of her many lovers and claimed that she actually made love every night on stage with her partner in a production of Offenbach's *Tales of Hoffmann*. Isherwood, failing to verify this claim with binoculars, believed that it was nothing but braggadocio. The model for "Mr. Norris" was another classic demimonde character: one Gerald Hamilton. On the surface a respectable representative for the London *Times*, Hamilton was in reality an enterprising go-between who fenced stolen paintings, smuggled contraband weapons, and made secret deals with the police. Like Jean Ross, Hamilton ran up bills and bragged incessantly about the titled people he had known, the castles he had visited, the great meals he had consumed. In fact, his major accomplishment was avoiding falling afoul of the Nazis and the Communists, both of whom he served.

Isherwood's works provide a reasonably accurate record of late Weimar Berlin because the frivolity depicted therein masks desperate efforts by the central characters to stay afloat in a sea of trouble. The undercurrent of anxiety and fear was hardly misplaced, for the Great Depression was in its opening phase, and Hitler was on his final march to the gates of power. Recalling those grim days in his memoir *World within World*, Isherwood's friend Stephen Spender was anything but nostalgic:

> In this Berlin, the agitation, the propaganda, witnessed by us in the streets and cafes, seemed more and more to represent the whole life of the town, as though there were almost no privacy behind doors. Berlin was the tension, the poverty, the anger, the prostitution, the hope and despair thrown out on the streets. It was the blatant rich at the smart restaurants, the prostitutes in army top boots at corners, the grim, submerged-looking Communists in processions, and the violent youths who suddenly emerged from nowhere into the Wittembergplatz and shouted: *'Deutschland Erwache!'*

A Touch of Panic

"Let's hope 1929 brings us plenty of struggle, friction, and sparks," wrote the left-wing playwright Friedrich Wolf in late 1928. Wolf got his wish: 1929, of course, was the year of the great stock crash on Wall Street, which had devastating consequences for Germany and Berlin. But 1929 had generated plenty of "sparks" in Berlin even before the October financial fire in New York leaped across the Atlantic to do its damage in Europe. Looking back, we can see that it was the beginning of the end for Weimar democracy.

In early 1929 the police began to accumulate evidence of theft, fraud, and bribery against two high-profile Eastern European Jews, Leo and Willy Sklarek, who owned a textile firm in Berlin that supplied the city with uniforms and other equipment. Classical parvenus, the Sklareks lived in palatial West End villas, drove fancy cars, kept a stable of ponies at the track, and, to ensure a certain freedom in their business dealings, greased the palms of local officials. Apparently they did not spread their bribes quite widely enough, however, for the police eventually arrested them for trafficking in stolen goods. In assembling a case against them, the prosecutors discovered that the brothers had sent Mayor Böss a fur coat for his wife without including a bill. To his credit, the mayor had repeatedly offered to pay for the coat and was eventually billed for 375 marks, which he knew was far too low. He therefore sent the Sklareks an additional payment of 1000 marks, asking that they use the money to buy a painting for his beloved city museum. They did so, but since the actual cost of the coat was 4,950 marks the mayor still seemed to have turned the kind of deal not available to nonofficeholders. When the matter became public in September 1929, all the factions that had long opposed Böss's liberal policies seized upon this issue to vilify him. The Communists called him a typical capitalist crook, while Goebbels's *Der Angriff* branded him a bedmate of the Jews. The mayor happened to be traveling in America when the scandal broke and unwisely did not hasten back to face his accusers. When he finally did return he was accosted by a mob that tried to beat him up. Humiliated and disgusted, he took early retirement from his office, never to return. The Sklareks, for their part, got four years in jail.

Mayor Böss's political career was not the only casualty in this affair. The Prussian Landtag conducted an investigation that treated the case as another example of "Berlin corruption," thus reinforcing images of the city as one big sleeze-factory—*Sklarekstadt.* So tarnished was Berlin's reputation that a circus impresario named Stosch-Sarrasani campaigned to replace Böss with the slogan, "A circus director can become mayor of Berlin, but a mayor of Berlin could never become a circus director." The scandal played an important role in the communal elections of November 17, 1929, which saw the Communists gain at the expense of the SPD, and the Nazis win representation in the city assembly for the first time. Goebbels crowed that with the Nazi showing, his "boldest dreams" had come true. In fact, he was being more than a little hyperbolic, since the Nazis had garnered only 3.1 percent of the vote, a long way from their dream of controlling Berlin. Still, they had made a significant step forward, and every gain for them was a loss for Weimar democracy.

The Weimar Republic suffered another blow on October 3, 1929, with the sudden death of Foreign Minister Gustav Stresemann, architect of the policy of reconciliation between Germany and the Western powers. His last service was the negotiation and ratification of the Young Plan, by which Germany reduced its reparations payments. For this he was reviled by the far right, which rejected reparations payments in principle. In Berlin it was widely understood that his death was a tragedy not just for the nation but for the capital. His funeral was attended by hundreds of thousands of mourners, the largest such turnout since the death of Ebert. Kessler, learning of his friend's demise while on a trip to Paris, mused in his diary: "It is an irreparable loss whose consequences cannot be foreseen. . . . What I fear, as a result of Stresemann's death, are very grave political consequences at home, with a move to the right by [Stresemann's] People's Party, a break-up of the coalition, and the facilitation of efforts to establish a dictatorship."

Less than a month after Stresemann's death came news of the Wall Street crash. Brecht, who despite his Communism admired American economic vitality, wrote a poem entitled "The Late Lamented Glory of the Giant City of New York." But he should also have worried about the giant city of Berlin, which was dependent on steady infusions of American capital. Within weeks of the crash, the Americans not only cut off the flow of loans but began demanding repayment on those that were outstanding. Some Berlin banks also stopped lending money, and a number of companies began laying off workers. Nevertheless, as in the immediate postwar era, Berlin's municipal government continued to spend generously on public programs. In November 1929 officials of the state of Prussia stepped in and mandated reductions in public spending until the city had made progress in clearing away its 400-million-mark deficit. City officials were forced to cancel new building projects, including two *U-Bahn* extensions considered urgently necessary. Nor could the city keep up with the demand for new public housing or hospital beds. The municipality contemplated seeking a loan of $15 million from the American brokerage firm of Dillon, Reed, but the national government disallowed this on the grounds that Berlin's high foreign debt was already a liability for the nation.

Conditions at the national level, however, were no better. Reeling from the economic crisis generated by the Wall Street crash, and unable to agree on necessary fiscal reforms, a coalition cabinet led by Hermann Müller (SPD) gave way in March 1930 to a "cabinet of experts" under Heinrich Brüning. The new chancellor belonged to the right-wing of the Center Party and was known for his strict fiscal conservatism. He decided to contain the spreading depression with a deflationary program of government savings and tax increases. When the parliament refused to pass his program, he received authority from President Hindenburg to rule by decree. Because neither he nor his successors ever returned to parliamentary government, this move can be seen as the end of Weimar democracy per se.

Much of Brüning's austerity package was aimed at Berlin, which was forced to make even deeper cuts in its public spending, thus increasing the number of unemployed. Berliners, along with other Germans, began calling Brüning the "hunger chancellor."

Although the city's extensive culture industry was hit along with the rest of the economy, there were still signs of vitality on this front in the opening year of the

Marlene Dietrich as Lola Lola in The Blue Angel, *1929*

new decade. April 1930 saw the premier in Berlin of the most expensive film Germany had made to date: UFA's *Der Blaue Engel* (The Blue Angel). It was based on a novel by Heinrich Mann entitled *Professor Unrat*, which tells the story of an elderly schoolteacher who becomes infatuated with a cabaret singer and falls into disgrace.

When work began on the screenplay in autumn 1929, the director, Josef von Sternberg, had already secured Emil Jannings, Germany's most famous film star, for the male lead. Jannings had just returned to Berlin from Hollywood, where he had won the first Academy Award ever presented to an actor. Sternberg had also hired Friedrich Holländer, a brilliant songwriter, to provide the incidental music. But he lacked an actress for the crucial part of Lola Lola, the seductress who lures the sanctimonious professor to his ruin in the seedy Blue Angel cabaret. He interviewed dozens of actresses but none of them seemed quite right: among the failures were Leni Riefenstahl, Hitler's future filmmaker, and Trude Hesterberg, Heinrich Mann's mistress. In desperation, Sternberg combed through a trade catalog containing pictures of virtually every actress in Germany until he at last found one who seemed to have the right look. She was Marlene Dietrich, a native Berliner who had heretofore acted in a number of films without making much of a name for herself. Sternberg's assistant, upon studying her picture in the catalog, dismissed her with the comment: "Der Popo ist nicht schlecht, aber brauchen wir nicht auch ein Gesicht? (The ass isn't bad, but don't we also need a face?)" Shortly thereafter, however, Sternberg saw Dietrich in a stage play and was instantly assured, as he later put it, that "here was the face I had sought."

During the filming, which took eight weeks, Sternberg remained convinced that he had made the right choice with Dietrich, though she sometimes tried his patience on the set, playfully flashing more than her beautiful legs at him and poor Jannings. "You sow, pull down your pants! Everyone can see your pubic hair!" he shouted on one occasion. But she was just getting in character, feeling her way into her role as the cock-tease who claims not to be able to help it that men cluster around her "like moths around a flame."

The premier was scheduled for February 1930 but had to be postponed because UFA's new owner, the reactionary press baron Alfred Hugenberg, who had bought up Paramount's and MGM's shares in the company, was unhappy with the film as it stood. Upon screening a rough cut of the film, Hugenberg felt that Sternberg had failed to make absolutely clear that the errant teacher had died at the end, thereby pointing up the wages of sin. Sternberg himself had recently left for America, so Erich Pommer, the producer, was left with the task of pleasing Hugenberg. He did so by adding music by Beethoven to the final scene showing the professor slumped over his classroom desk. Now it was clear that the old man had paid the ultimate price for transgressing against society's norms.

The Blue Angel's premier took place on April 1, 1930, at the Gloria-Palast on the Kurfürstendamm. *Tout* Berlin was there, captains of industry and captains of crime, prominent artists, writers, and actors, including the entire cast of the movie. The general expectation was that the evening would belong to Emil Jannings; after all, he was the film's only true star, and this was his first "talkie" (he had made no sound movies in Hollywood because he could not or would not learn English). But from the moment Lola Lola sang her first song—"Tonight, kids, I'm gonna get a man!"—Marlene Dietrich had the crowd, like Jannings's film character, firmly in her clutches. When the movie ended she took repeated curtain calls.

No one realized that evening that the curtain was actually falling on Dietrich's Berlin career. Thinking that she was simply a vulgar tramp with no talent, UFA's directors had allowed her to sign a contract with Paramount. That very night, with the ovations still ringing in her ears, she boarded the boat train that would take her to America and a new life as a Hollywood legend. She returned to Berlin briefly in 1931—to hear the Nazis denounce *The Blue Angel* as "mediocre and corrupting kitsch"—but she did not come again until after World War II, and then only for a visit.

The Berlin that Dietrich left behind was becoming an increasingly violent place, as Nazis and Communists made the streets a stage for their bloody battles. The brown-shirted SA, though still outnumbered by the Communist Red Front, often took the initiative in these encounters. On May 16, 1930, twelve SA men trampled a Communist to death at the Innsbrucker Platz. Hoping to contain the violence, Minister of the Interior Carl Severing banned the wearing of Nazi brown shirts in public, so the Nazis simply shifted to white shirts and went about their business as usual.

In early 1930 the movement acquired its most important martyr since the Munich Beer Hall Putsch of 1923. The fallen hero was a Berliner named Horst Wessel, chief of the SA branch in proletarian Friedrichshain. The cause for Wessel's martyrdom was utterly banal but perfectly fitting. It seems that he had been trying to avoid paying rent by sharing a flat with his girlfriend, a prostitute. The landlady doubled the rent; and when Wessel refused to pay his share she asked a friend of hers, a Communist Red Front thug, to put some muscle on him. Happy to oblige, the Communist accosted Wessel at his flat and shot him in the mouth. The SA man died a month later. At his funeral a group of Communists showed up with a sign saying "A Last Heil Hitler to the Pimp Horst Wessel." Goebbels, meanwhile, had been busy turning this tawdry affair into the stuff of legend. He put out the story that Wessel had died heroically battling the Communists. At the funeral he eulogized Wessel as a "Christlike socialist," whose deeds proclaimed "Come unto me, and I will redeem you." The SA adopted a song Wessel had written as its fighting hymn: "Oh, raise the flag and close your ranks up tight! / SA men march with bold determined tread./ Comrades felled by Reds and Ultras in fight/ March at our side, in spirit never dead."

In July 1930 Brüning promulgated his new budget by emergency decree, and when the Reichstag demanded that the decree be abrogated he dissolved the body and called new elections, hoping to gain a broader mandate for his austerity policies. Plenty of voices in Berlin and elsewhere warned him of the foolhardiness of holding elections in the midst of a deepening depression, but he was deaf to all objections: he trusted the German people to do the right thing. What they did was to increase the representation of the extremes at the expense of the liberal center and moderate conservatives. The KPD garnered 4,600,000 votes and 77 seats; the Nazis, who had polled only 809,000 in the Reichstag elections of 1928, jumped to 6,400,000 votes and 107 seats. In Berlin, hitherto the strongest bastion of Weimar democracy, the triumph of the extremes was even more striking. The KPD edged past the SPD to compile the highest percentage of the total vote (27.3), while the Nazis became the third largest party in the city with 14.6 percent—four times what they had managed in 1928. Significantly, the Nazi Party did well in all districts, including supposedly "Red" enclaves like Kreuzberg and Köpenick.

On October 13, when the new Reichstag was called into session, the Nazis celebrated their success by terrorizing the center of Berlin. Kessler recorded the scene in his diary:

> Reichstag opening. The whole afternoon and evening mass demonstrations by the Nazis. During the afternoon they smashed the windows of Wertheim, Grünfeld, and other department stores in the Leipzigerstrasse. In the evening they assembled in the Potsdamer Platz, shouting 'Germany awake!' 'Death to Judah', 'Heil Hitler.' Their ranks were continually dispersed by the police, in lorries and on horseback. . . . In the main the Nazis consisted of adolescent riff-raff which made off yelling as soon as the police began to use rubber truncheons. . . . These disorders reminded me of the days just before the revolution, with the same mass meetings and the same Catilinian figures lounging about and demonstrating.

Another witness to the Nazi celebrations was Bella Fromm, a society columnist for the liberal *Vossische Zeitung.* As a Jewess, Fromm has reason to be alarmed at the Nazi electoral success, and to be distressed over the fact that Germany's various Jewish organizations, still sharply divided by philosophical rifts, were unable to agree on which of Hitler's adversaries to support. Now, in the wake of the election results and the Nazi demonstrations in Berlin, Fromm noted in her diary that "There's a touch of panic in certain quarters. Should one leave Germany and wait outside to see what will happen?" But the journalist, like so many deeply assimilated Jews, could not yet fathom the idea of cutting and running. "Surprising," she wrote in her diary, "how many people feel that it [going into exile] might be the prudent thing to do."

A couple of months later the Nazis staged another demonstration in Berlin that signaled their growing confidence and determination to register their influence in the national capital. The occasion was the showing of the American-made film version of Erich Remarque's antiwar novel *Im Westen Nichts Neues* (*All Quiet on the Western Front*). Remarque's book, which graphically captures the horrors of the trench experience and the wrenching psychological separation between the front generation and society at home, had become a phenomenal best-seller, proving that this was a message that readers were ready to hear after a decade of living with the war's consequences. No doubt sales had also been helped by the German publisher Ullstein's aggressive marketing campaign, which included plastering Berlin's Litfass pillars with advertisements and serializing the story in the *Vossische Zeitung*. Predictably, the primary criticism of the book had come from the political extremes, with the Communists deriding it as bourgeois sentimentality and the Nazis attacking it as un-German decadence. Given such glamorous but controversial material, it is not surprising that the film version, which had already won the Academy Award in America, would ignite even greater passions. When it opened at the Mozartsaal on Nollendorfplatz on December 3, there was palpable tension in the air. Somehow, the premier passed without incident. On the next evening, however, 150 Nazis showed up, with Goebbels in the lead. The film had barely begun when mayhem broke out. Leni Riefenstahl, who was in the audience that night, recalled: "Quite suddenly the theater was ringing with screams so that at first I thought a fire had started. Panic broke out and girls and women were standing on their seats, shrieking." They were shrieking because Goebbels and his thugs had thrown stink bombs from the balcony and released white mice in the orchestra. Then they ran up and down the aisles shouting "Jews get out!" and slapping people they assumed were Jewish. The police eventually waded in to clear out the Nazis, but (it was later revealed) 127 members of the police force that had been mobilized at the station refused to participate in the action—a dangerous sign of Nazi infiltration of the Berlin Schutzpolizei.

On the following two evenings the Nazis continued to demonstrate around the Nollendorfplatz, singing their "Horst Wessel Song" and beating up people trying to get into the theater. Hitler himself came up from Munich to "review" a Nazi protest march. Goebbels exulted in his diary: "Over an hour. Six abreast. Fantastic! Berlin West has never seen anything like it." The Berlin police commissioner, Albert Grzesinski, had pledged to protect the film from all disruptions, but after a few more days of nonstop violence he declared that the police could not guarantee public security as long as the film was running. The National Film Board withdrew approval of the movie on grounds that it was a "threat to Germany's honor." On December 16 the Prussian Landtag took up the issue and banned the film in Berlin. Goebbels was understandably elated at this government cave-in, speaking of a victory "that could not have been greater."

The Nazis' assaults notwithstanding, Berlin still struck many Germans and foreign visitors as one of the best places in the world to witness cutting-edge creative work. Like a dying diva who belts out some of her best notes before collapsing on the stage, Berlin put on an exciting cultural show before the brown curtain descended in January 1933. In January 1931 Sergei Tretiakov, the Russian futurist poet and playwright, lectured at the Russischer Hof on "Writers and the Socialist Village." In March Carl Zuckmayer's satirical play *Der Hauptmann von Köpenick*, based on the exploits of that great "Prussian officer" Wilhelm Voigt, opened at the Deutsches Theater. Zuckmayer's and Heinz Hilpert's adaptation of Ernest Hemingway's new novel, *Farewell to Arms*, also played at the Deutsches Theater. (Hemingway himself showed up for the premier and nipped steadily from a hip flask when he wasn't asleep. Taken backstage during the intermission, he asked the leading lady, Käthe Dorsch, how much she charged for the night, adding that he would "pay one hundred dollars and not a cent more.") Meanwhile, the Staatstheater mounted Brecht's *Mann ist Mann* (Man is Man). Although the play's run was brief, Tretiakov hailed it as a masterpiece of radical drama. Brecht also managed to produce his *Die Massnahmen* (The Measures), a long choral piece filled with Communist didacticism that required true ideological commitment and plenty of *Sitzfleisch* to sit through. Over at the Kroll Opera Otto Klemperer conducted the first German performance of Stravinsky's *Symphony of Psalms*. Witnessing it, Paul Hindemith predicted that "a new wave of serious music is on the way." At the Potsdamer Platz a new building, perhaps Weimar Berlin's most innovative structure, was going up: Erich Mendelsohn's Columbushaus office block. With its clean-curved facade, which was illuminated at night by spotlights, the building was a frontal attack on architectural historicism—a floodlit rebuke to all those neoclassical, neo-Renaissance, neo-Gothic, and Romanesque piles that still dominated the Berlin landscape. To the question "What is this place," the architect answered: "future time."

In the year the Columbushaus was completed, 1932, Germany's most innovative design and architectural school, the Bauhaus, moved to Berlin from Dessau. It had been founded in 1919 in Weimar but had relocated to Dessau in 1925 because that city promised a more congenial environment. And so it did, but not for long. In 1932 the Nazis gained control of Dessau's city council and made it their first order of business to attack the Bauhaus as "Jewish-Marxist." The then director, Mies van der Rohe, fled to the capital, setting up shop in an abandoned telephone factory in Steglitz. Mies hoped that the school could do its work relatively undisturbed in the big city, but the local Nazis did their best to prevent that from happening. Goebbels's *Der Angriff* labeled the Bauhaus a "breeding ground of Bolshevism," a clear sign that once the Nazis ran Berlin there would be no place for this innovative institution.

In the meantime, it was not just Nazi pressure that was putting the squeeze on avant-garde culture in Berlin. Other right-wing forces, sometimes in league with the Nazis and sometimes not, took up the fight against the leading figures and institutions of Berlin's progressive cultural scene. At the urging of the military, Carl von Ossietzky, the pacifist editor of *Die Weltbühne*, received an eighteen-month jail sentence for "espionage and treason" because his magazine had exposed secret subsidies from the Reichswehr to Lufthansa, the civilian airline. The Berlin police prevented the radical poet Erich Weinert from reading his poems on grounds of public security. The deepening depression also took its cultural toll, both by drying up revenues and by giving bureaucrats who were anxious to pacify the right an excuse to close down money-losing ventures. In summer 1931 Erwin Piscator's latest radical theater collective went into bankruptcy, inducing the playwright to leave for the Soviet Union. A year later it was the turn of the Kroll Opera, which was afflicted with mounting deficits and a barrage of hostile criticism for its innovative programming. After the final curtain went down, the Berlin critic Oscar Bie wrote a fitting epitaph: "The four years [when Klemperer ran the Kroll] will remain a gleaming chapter in the history of opera, full of art and humanity, with human weaknesses and human error, but with all the grandeur of true endeavor and conscientious labor. May the devil take a time that cannot support that."

The Berlin branch of the Nazi Party, which by the summer of 1931 had grown to 16,000 members, was proud of its disruption of the capital's cultural and political life. Yet the party itself was in a state of turmoil in the first years of the new decade. The local SA was increasingly frustrated with the overall drift of the party, believing that Hitler, in his effort to come to power legally, was cozying up all too closely with establishment reactionaries. The Berlin Brownshirts tended to blame Munich for Hitler's "conservatism": the Bavarian town, in their eyes, was hopelessly provincial, stodgy, and backward-looking. They could not understand why Goebbels, once the champion of a more activist and radical posture, was meekly toeing the Munich line. In August 1930 they made their displeasure evident by smashing up their own party headquarters in the Hedemannstrasse. Goebbels, in fact, shared the SA's frustration, denouncing "the scandalous pigsty in Munich," but he did not include Hitler in his denunciation. When the Führer instructed him to conduct a purge of disruptive elements in Berlin, Goebbels responded: "Whatever you choose to do, I'll back you."

The principal target of the purge was Walter Stennes, chief of the Berlin SA. On April 1, 1931, Stennes was relieved of his post. He responded by staging a full-scale mutiny, taking over party headquarters, occupying the *Angriff* office, and justifying his action by claiming that the Munich leadership had blunted "the revolutionary élan of the SA." Goebbels, who was in Dresden when the mutiny broke out, hastened back to Berlin to restore order. But he needn't have hurried, for the Stennes revolt collapsed on its own due to lack of support from the rest of the Nazi district organizations, which immediately pledged their support to Hitler. Stennes was permanently banned, and Goebbels could report by April 11 that the party apparatus in Berlin was "unshaken" in its commitment to Hitler's policy of legality. This was a pious exaggeration, however; the Stennes revolt served to remind the Nazi leader that Berlin was treacherous ground, where loyalties could never be taken for granted.

In addition to internal problems, the Berlin branch of the Nazi movement had to contend with escalating attacks from the local Communists, who were not about to cede the streets of "their town" to the Brownshirts. There were rumors in summer 1931 that the KPD was about to stage a coup in the capital. No such action occurred, but a group of Communists terrorized Prenzlauer Berg, attacking pubs where Nazis were known to gather and killing two policemen. One of the Communist killers was none other than Erich Mielke, who would later become chief of the infamous East German secret police, the Stasi. These attacks generated some public sympathy for the Nazis, who claimed to be law-abiding victims of Red terror.

But not too law-abiding. On September 12, 1931, the new head of the Berlin SA, a dissolute nobleman named Wolf Heinrich von Helldorf, staged a mini-pogrom in broad daylight on the busy Kurfürstendamm. Driving up and down the boulevard in a car, he directed bands of SA thugs, dressed in normal street clothes, to attack and beat pedestrians who looked Jewish. After about two hours the police intervened and arrested Helldorf, who was obliged to spend a few days in jail. Soon he would be supervising that same jail as chief of police.

Just Kindly Nod, Please

Hindenburg, who had been reelected president in April 1932 (beating out, among other candidates, Adolf Hitler) dismissed Heinrich Brüning from the chancellorship

Franz von Papen (right) at a governmental ceremony, August 1932

at the end of the following month. Brüning's demise was engineered by Kurt von Schleicher, a wily political general who operated from behind the scenes to make and break chancellors in the waning years of the Weimar Republic. Schleicher worked on behalf of a cabal of conservatives who worried that Brüning intended to impose higher taxes on the rich and to settle homeless city-folk on Prussia's large agricultural estates; the conservatives also faulted the chancellor for failing to expand the army and for imposing a ban on public demonstrations by the SA and SS but not on the Reichsbanner, the SPD's paramilitary group.

At Schleicher's suggestion, Brüning was replaced by Franz von Papen, a Catholic nobleman, former Guards officer, and founder of the Herrenklub, an exclusive gentleman's club in Berlin. The general believed that he could control Papen, whom he saw as a man with plenty of background but no backbone, and no brains. When reminded by an associate that Papen did not have a strong head, Schleicher replied, "He doesn't have to. He's a hat." Along with the hat, Papen wore elegant dark suits that some said made him look like an undertaker. The comparison was appropriate, considering Papen's political role in the coming years.

One of Papen's first acts as chancellor was to revoke Brüning's ban on public demonstrations by the SA and SS. The Nazis immediately launched a new campaign of violence, which killed ninety-nine people in four weeks. Much of the action centered on Berlin, where the SA attacked both Communists and the police, hoping thereby to discredit the local Socialist-controlled security forces as protectors of public order.

The tactic paid off. Blaming the SPD-dominated Prussian government for the disorders, Papen deposed the Prussian regime on July 20, 1932, and named a Reich Commissioner to run that state. Twelve years earlier the workers of Berlin had defeated a coup from the right by calling a general strike, but this time there was no significant resistance from the workers or the SPD, which decided not to mobilize the Reichsbanner. When Papen's new officials came to expel Berlin's police president, Albert Grzesinski, and Vice President of Police Bernhard Weiss, the men made no trouble. As a friend of Bella Fromm's noted: "A bullet or two might have changed the picture, but they could not well rebel against the orders of their superior." Nonetheless, their capitulation meant that Berlin was now under the direct control of a national regime committed to an authoritarian course. To strengthen that course, the new Prussian Commissioner declared martial law in Berlin, placing day-to-day administration in the hands of the Reichswehr's regional chief, General Gerd von Rundstedt.

In July 1932 Papen dissolved the Reichstag and called new elections, which Hitler demanded as a price for tolerating the chancellor's conservative "cabinet of barons." If the September 1930 elections were distressing to all those who had hoped to hold Hitler at bay, the results of the poll on July 31, 1932, were a cause for apoplexy. Nationwide, the Nazis won 37.4 percent of the vote and 230 (out of 608) seats in the Reichstag, which made them by far the largest party in the country, almost twice the size of the SPD. In Berlin the Nazis garnered 28.6 percent, significantly less than their national average but almost twice what they had polled in 1930, and almost equal to what they managed in Munich, the movement's birthplace and headquarters. Worrisome too, at least to the beleaguered backers of the democratic ideal, was the continuing rise of the Communists in Berlin, who tied the Socialists' tally of 27.3 percent.

As the leader of the nation's largest party, Hitler now demanded to be named chancellor. He presented his demand to the backroom kingmaker, Schleicher, who told him that if the Nazis were to attain a majority in the Reichstag nobody could stand in his way. Confident that he could form a coalition with the other rightist parties, Hitler assumed that Schleicher had, in effect, promised him the chancellorship. But Schleicher was biding his time, waiting to see if Hitler could indeed craft a majority coalition when the new Reichstag convened in September. In the meantime, he proposed that the Nazi leader make do with the vice-chancellorship under Papen. Exasperated, Hitler paid a second call on Schleicher, demanding full power immediately and threatening to turn the SA loose on Berlin if he was rebuffed. This outburst won him an audience with Hindenburg, but instead of handing him power the president rebuked him for going back on his promise to support Papen and for abandoning all "chivalry" in his political campaigns. This last charge suggested that the old man did not fully understand what Hitler was all about.

George Grosz had a very good understanding of Hitler's intentions, and he knew that Berlin constituted no Red dam against the brown flood. As he later recalled: "I saw the cracks on the floor, and noticed that this or that wall was starting to wobble. I observed my cigar man was overnight wearing a swastika in the same buttonhole where there always used to be a red enamel hammer-and-sickle." Grosz was also depressed by the fact that the art market in Germany had virtually collapsed, making it impossible for him to sell his paintings. In spring 1931 he had received an offer to teach at the Art Students' League in New York, and in May 1932 he boarded an ocean liner for that city, convinced that it was time to put Berlin behind him. He returned to Berlin in late 1932 only to make arrangements for a permanent relocation to America. He sailed back to New York just five days before Hitler was named chancellor, thus averting probable arrest by the new German rulers.

Another political evacuee that year was the left-wing writer Arthur Koestler, who had moved to Berlin from Paris on September 14, 1930, the date of the Nazis' first electoral breakthrough. As he took up his duties as science editor at Ullstein's *Berliner Zeitung am Mittag*, one of his new colleagues asked: "Why on earth didn't you stay in Paris?" His coworkers at the paper confronted the challenge of Nazism in different ways, some saying, "They are too weak, they can't start anything;" others saying, "They are too strong, we must appease them." The Ullstein brothers, though Jewish themselves, attempted a kind of preemptive appeasement by slowly purging Jews from their papers. "The building in the Kochstrasse," recalled Koestler, "became a place of fear and insecurity which reflected the fear and insecurity of the country in general." Editors and writers walked the corridors waiting for the ax to fall. They summed up the situation with a bit of black humor about a famous Chinese executioner of the Ming empire, Wang Lun, whose goal was to sever a condemned man's head so cleanly that the victim didn't realize he'd been decapitated. One day Wang managed to swing his sword with such speed through a man's neck that his head stayed on as he walked up the scaffold. When he reached the top he asked the executioner why he was prolonging his agony. Wang Lun replied: "Just kindly nod, please."

Certain that both his career at Ullstein and Weimar democracy were on the chopping block, Koestler left Berlin immediately after Papen's coup in Prussia. His destination was not New York but Moscow, that other distant lode star in Weimar Berlin's ideological firmament. Of course, horrifying developments were afoot in Moscow as well, and Koestler would soon find himself moving on again, ideologically as well as physically. He wrote his great novel on the Stalinist purges, *Darkness at Noon* (1940), from his new exile in Britain.

Albert Einstein, Germany's most famous scientist, also felt the pressure to leave Berlin as the political, economic, and intellectual climate turned hostile to the kind of creative work he prized. He even had to wonder whether the city that had once enthusiastically adopted him still valued his presence. True, on the occasion of his fiftieth birthday in 1929 the city government had sought to honor him with the gift of a house on the banks of the Havel River. But it turned out that the house was already occupied, obliging the city to come up with a different prospect, which also fell through. The mayor then proposed that Einstein pick out a property he liked, which the city would buy for him. By the time Einstein found a suitable plot in the suburb of Caputh, the depression had settled in, causing the city council to debate whether it could now afford to present him with a gift at all. Understandably miffed, the scientist bought the property in Caputh with his own money and built a house there. He and his wife moved in just in time to see the election results of 1932 make an extended stay there look doubtful. A Nazi delegate to the Prussian Landtag announced that after Hitler had cleaned house in Germany, "the exodus of the Children of Israel will be a child's game in comparison," adding that "a people that possesses a Kant will not permit an Einstein to be tacked on to it." Einstein took the threat seriously, telling a friend in summer 1932 that he believed Papen's military-backed regime would only hasten the advent of "a right-radical revolution." The scientist had been teaching on and off at Cal Tech and Princeton since 1930, and in November 1932, preparing to sail once again to America, he told his wife to take a good look at their dream house outside Berlin. When she asked why, he replied: "You will never see it again."

The Berlin that these illustrious figures left behind still had the capacity to excite and amuse casual visitors. The British writer and diplomat Harold Nicolson, who spent a few days in the city in summer 1932, was impressed, like so many others before him, by the restless movement of cars, trams, flashing lights, even zoo animals pacing in their cages. There was a throbbing air of expectancy, especially at night: "Everybody knows that every night Berlin wakes up to a new adventure." Nicolson also appreciated the city's no-nonsense frankness. If London was like "an old lady in black lace and diamonds," Berlin was "a girl in a pullover, not much powder on her face, Hölderlin in her pocket, thighs like those of Atalanta, an undigested education, a heart that is almost too ready to sympathize, and a

An unemployed man sifts through garbage in search of food, 1930

breadth of view that charms one's repressions from their poison, and shames one's correctitude."

For hundreds of thousands of ordinary Berliners, however, the only adventure to be faced now was the challenge of getting by without regular employment. In April 1932 the city registered 603,000 million unemployed, which constituted over 10 percent of the total unemployment in Germany. Many of these people had long since exhausted their unemployment benefits and had gone on welfare, which was the responsibility of the cities to fund. Berlin's *Sozialhilfe* caseload climbed steadily in 1932, from 316,000 in April to 323,000 in September. Unable to cover the escalating welfare costs, Berlin received some assistance from the Reich, but many citizens were obliged to get by on their own, one way or another.

Christopher Isherwood, delaying his own departure from Berlin to document the growing despair, wrote in late 1932:

> Morning after morning, all over the immense, damp, dreary town and the packing-case colonies of huts in the suburb allotments, young men were waking up

> to another workless empty day to be spent as best they could contrive: selling bootlaces, begging, playing draughts in the hall of the Labour Exchange, hanging around urinals, opening the doors of cars, helping with crates in the markets, gossiping, lounging, stealing, overhearing racing tips, sharing stumps of cigarette-ends picked up in the gutter, singing folk-songs for groschen in courtyards and between stations in the carriages of the Underground Railway.

Conditions for unemployed workers were so grim that many of them preferred to live outside the city in tent-camps. The largest of these was *Kuhle Wampe*, on the shores of the Muggelsee. Brecht made it famous by writing a film about it in summer 1932. Visiting the scene shortly thereafter, the French leftist writer Daniel Guérin was surprised to discover how tidy everything was: "Spread along the lakeshore, under the pines, the tiny dwellings all looked alike: simple wooden posts covered with white or zebra-striped tent canvas. All were well lit, clean, and well kept. The builders rivaled each other in ingenuity and whimsy. Miniature gardens surrounded the most beautiful constructions. At the moment of my arrival, an elderly unemployed couple stood in ecstasy, motionless, watering can in hand, before three still-dripping geraniums." Many of the residents of *Kuhle Wampe* seemed to think of their stay there as a kind of vacation from the horrors of the ravaged metropolis. They told Guèrin: "You see, the air at *Kuhle Wampe* is better than in our neighborhoods, and this is a vacation that doesn't cost a thing. We prefer to cycle to Berlin once a week to pick up our unemployment benefits. And we also want to show that proletarians know how to live an intelligent and liberated life."

While thousands of Berlin's proletarians were fleeing to the countryside to find a more dignified existence, the Nazis were pursuing their destiny in the halls of power in the capital. On September 12, 1932, the newly elected Reichstag, the one in which the Nazis had the largest number of delegates, convened for the first time. In the chair was Hermann Göring, head of the Nazis' parliamentary delegation and new president of the Reichstag. To Daniel Guérin, who was sitting in the visitors' gallery, Göring looked like "a kind of large, beardless doll with a disturbing jaw—half executioner, half clown." But there was nothing clownish about Göring's agenda that day: he intended, with the support of the Communists, to pass a no-confidence resolution against Papen's government and thereby to bring it down. To avert such a scenario, Papen showed up with a presidential decree dissolving the parliament. Göring, however, refused to recognize the chancellor until the Communists' no-

Reichstag president Hermann Göring (left) and two Nazi parliamentary deputies, Wilhelm Frick (middle) and Hans Eugen St. Fabricius, 1932

confidence resolution was voted upon, which went against the government, 512 to 42. Now, when Papen presented his dissolution decree, Göring ruled it constitutionally invalid on grounds that the chancellor had been voted out of office. In fact there was nothing constitutional about Göring's ploy, for parliament could not cashier a chancellor; only the president could do that. Hindenburg did not want to jettison Papen, whom he personally liked and even admired. Thus the dissolution decree was imposed after all, with new elections scheduled for November 6.

Before the new contest could take place, the Nazis and the Communists seized upon another opportunity to raise joint havoc in Berlin. When the government decreed a slight reduction in wages for Berlin's transport workers, Goebbels directed the Nazi employees of the BVG to go out on strike. Goebbels said this would show that the Nazis were serious about offering "a conscious rejection of bourgeois methods." The KPD, not to be outdone by the Nazis, instructed their people in the transport union also to walk off the job. The leader of their strike team was Walter Ulbricht, later to become dictator of East Germany and architect of the Berlin Wall.

On November 2, as the strike began, Nazis and Communists paraded together in front of Berlin's rail yards, beating up scabs and wrecking any busses or streetcars that were still running.

Goebbels realized that this collaboration with the Reds might cost the Nazis some support among bourgeois voters in the upcoming elections, but he remained confident that striking a "revolutionary" posture was the best way to win Berlin in the long run. "After all," he said, "we want to conquer Berlin, and for that it doesn't matter whether one loses a lousy twenty thousand votes or so in a more or less pointless election. Those votes would have no significance anyway in an active revolutionary struggle."

On the day of the election the Berlin transport strike was still in progress, so voters had to walk to the polls. Goebbels's debunking of the contest notwithstanding, he spent the day in "incredible tension." It turned out that his anxiety was justified. Nationwide, the Nazis lost more than 2 million votes (about 4 percent of their previous total) and 34 Reichstag seats. However, they still remained the largest party in the country. In Berlin the losses were less dramatic: a 2.4 percent drop, from 28.6 to 26.2. The Communists' showing was strong nationwide—a gain of 11 seats, making them the third largest party—and even stronger in the capital, where their 31.3 percent of the total put them, for the first time, above the SPD as the largest party in Berlin.

The Nazis' setback in the November elections caused the movement's various opponents to breathe a collective sigh of relief: it seemed that the "brown plague" was receding. The constant campaigning, moreover, had put a huge dent in the party coffers, and contributions were dropping off. Gloating over the Nazis' financial problems, the liberal *Vossische Zeitung* declared it no accident that the number of SA men pleading for donations in the streets was now larger than the population of traditional beggars.

Chancellor Papen could take little comfort in the Nazis' decline because he was fading fast himself. He had done nothing to curb the depression or to restore order. In desperation he cooked up a scheme to eliminate popular sovereignty entirely and to set up a "corporate" state run exclusively by the wealthy elite. Schleicher, still the power behind the throne, would have none of this scheme. He convinced Hindenburg that Papen's plan, if executed, would lead to civil war, with the Nazis and Communists collaborating to overturn the existing order. Reluctantly, Hindenburg asked Schleicher himself to form a new government, and, just as reluctantly (for he truly preferred to stay in the shadows) Schleicher accepted the call. His appointment as chancellor on December 3, 1932, seemed a positive development to many Germans, who reasoned that a military man might be able to put matters right. Even Berlin's liberal press, which had generally been hostile to Schleicher, applauded this step.

Yet there were also voices of pessimism. Karl von Weigand, the Hearst correspondent in Berlin, remained convinced that Hitler would find a way to come to power, by hook or by crook. Weigand knew that Papen, livid over his ouster by Schleicher, was mobilizing his Herrenklub clique against the new chancellor. He worried, correctly as it turned out, that Papen might even try to strike some power-sharing deal with Hitler in order to get back at Schleicher and to regain power himself.

Chancellor Schleicher had his own scheme for dealing with the Nazis. He planned to split the party by offering Gregor Strasser, the popular head of the party's Political Office, the post of vice-chancellor. Knowing that Hitler would not countenance this, Schleicher counted on Strasser to bolt from the party and to bring his many friends with him. The chancellor was proud of this scheme, not the least because it was redolent of the intrigue he so loved.

But the plan was too clever by half. When he got word of the impending deal, Hitler mobilized all his resources to crush Strasser and to drive him from the party. He then replaced Strasser's Political Office with a new central party office under his loyal aide, Rudolf Hess.

Although Strasser's banishment required Schleicher to search for other ways to neutralize the Nazis, he remained confident that he could find such a way. At an intimate dinner party at the chancellor's house on December 28, the society columnist Bella Fromm brought up Karl von Weigand's gloomy prediction of an eventual Nazi victory. Schleicher replied: "You journalists are all alike. You make a living out of professional pessimism. . . . I think I can hold [the Nazis] off."

One is tempted at this point to reinject the story of Wang Lun—to suggest that if Schleicher had only bowed as he expressed his confidence, the true state of affairs would have been revealed. In late December 1932, however, Hitler's triumph was by no means a foregone conclusion. A full month, with much maneuvering and plenty of possibilities for alternative endings, remained before Hitler could indeed grasp power. During that period many Germans, not just Schleicher, remained hopeful that the Nazis could be kept from their prize. This was especially true in Berlin, where the various anti-Nazi forces were strongest. In hindsight we might smile over—but we should not dismiss as hopelessly head-in-the-sand (or head-already-cut-off)—the blissful confidence of a *Berliner Tageblatt* reporter who imagined that some day in the future he would be able to say to his grandchildren: "Everywhere, throughout the whole world, people were talking about—what was his first name?—Adalbert Hitler. Later? Vanished!"

Nazi torchlight parade, January 30, 1933

HITLER'S BERLIN

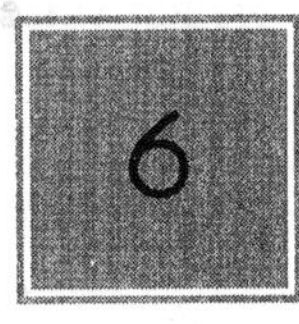

Berlin is the Reich, and the Reich is Berlin.

—Program for Berlin's 700th Anniversary, 1937

ALTHOUGH THE NAZIS invariably identified Weimar Berlin with cultural corruption and political disorientation, once they had established the city as *their* capital they claimed to have turned it into a bastion of order, decency, and correct thinking. Only the National Socialist "revolution," they insisted, had managed to return Berlin to its true self as a "happy and clean city." Yet the Nazis themselves were often unhappy in the great metropolis on the Spree. Most of the top leaders hailed from other parts of Germany, and, despite their best efforts to remake the city in their own image, they continued to find it alien and unsettling—a place from which, as one Nazi writer put it, "countless Germans are spiritually in flight." Hitler hoped to remedy this problem by tearing out the heart of Old Berlin and building a brand new capital in its place, to be called "Germania." Fortunately he was not able to complete much of this project before the onset of World War II forced him to focus on other ambitions. But if the Nazis did not manage to add more than a few new buildings (and, during the war, flak bunkers) to Berlin's urban landscape, they took a great deal away from the city's spirit. As soon as they came to power they began driving into exile or "inner emigration" many of Berlin's most illustrious artists and intellectuals. They also began a campaign to rid the city of its Jews. Their cultural purges and anti-Semitic crusade decimated the capital's economic and intellectual life. No other major city in modern times has suffered such a social and cultural bloodletting.

On the Eve of Power

Munich remained the headquarters of the Nazi Party throughout the Third Reich, but Berlin, not the Bavarian capital, provided the main stage for the complicated maneuvering that finally brought Hitler to power on January 30, 1933. The Nazi leader traveled several times to the Spree metropolis for key meetings with conservative power brokers in the days before he assumed the chancellorship. Ordinary Berliners had little knowledge of what was going on behind the scenes, but they knew that in the streets Nazi and Communist thugs were attacking each other with redoubled fury. On New Year's Eve, 1933, despite a holiday truce, bloody fights broke out across the city. A seamstress walking home in a working-class district was shot dead by an SA man who shouted "Heil Hitler" as he rode away on his bicycle. Three weeks later some 15,000 storm troopers, shouting "We shit on the Jew republic!" held a rally outside KPD headquarters on Bülowplatz. Because the Nazis were protected by a large police guard, the Communists could not drive them away. Goebbels wrote gleefully in his diary: "The Commies raging in the side streets . . . Armored vehicles, machine guns. Police preventing anyone from shooting at us from windows. . . SA men marching in front of Karl Liebknecht House. A fantastic thing! . . . We have won a battle."

They had indeed, but a more important battle was being fought in the elegant rooms where Hitler and the men he hoped to use, and who hoped to use him in turn, held their secret discussions about who should run the country. In January 1933 Hitler met twice with Papen at the Dahlem villa of Joachim von Ribbentrop, a foppish champagne salesman with good connections among Berlin's nouveau riche. The meetings proved unproductive because both men remained insistent on holding the top place in a government that the other would join in a subordinate position.

Meanwhile, the Nazi Party continued on its financial downslide, which threatened its ability to wage further electoral contests. The situation was so precarious that Göring tried to touch the American Embassy for a loan. On top of the financial difficulties, the SA and the SS were at each other's throats, each claiming to be the top enforcement arm of the party. Tired of waiting for their Führer to grab power, some of

Hitler's minions were turning in their brown shirts. Hoping to rally his discouraged troops, on January 20 Hitler delivered a fiery speech at Berlin's Sportpalast, site of the infamous Six-Day Bicycle Races. Like a doughty rider who keeps peddling despite exhaustion, Hitler vowed to continue fighting until he triumphed. He warned Nazism's enemies that they could "strike blows against us but never defeat us."

This might have remained empty rhetoric had not Chancellor Schleicher proved woefully inept at the political intrigue he so loved. He continued to believe that he could bully Hitler into accepting a subordinate political position by mobilizing dissident Nazis against him. In the meantime his own position was becoming precarious because of his deteriorating relationship with Hindenburg. The old man held Schleicher responsible for parliamentary attacks on the East Prussian landowners, who had been accused of using a state fund designed to help them avert bankruptcy to purchase fancy cars and junkets to the French Riviera. At the same time, Schleicher underestimated Papen's vindictiveness, failed to see the extent to which he would go to revenge himself and to regain some measure of power.

Unbeknownst to Schleicher, Papen had now concluded that it would be acceptable to concede the chancellorship to Hitler, provided that he, Papen, retained actual power through his close connection to Hindenburg. With the intention of exploring this possibility, Papen arranged a secret meeting between Hitler, himself, Oskar von Hindenburg (the president's son), and Otto Meissner, Hindenburg's chief of staff. The scene, once again, was Ribbentrop's villa in Dahlem. After an extensive preliminary discussion, Papen let it be known that he would settle for the vice-chancellorship in a cabinet headed by Hitler but dominated by conservatives. Hitler accepted the proposal. Crucially, so did Oskar von Hindenburg and Meissner, who, along with Papen, agreed to try to sell this deal to the president. When presented with this proposal on January 23, the old man countered that Hitler was qualified at most to be postmaster general. But he gradually relented when his son and Meissner joined Papen in promising that Hitler could be used to browbeat the Communists and then discarded when he was no longer useful.

Schleicher soon discovered just how isolated and impotent he had become. Having lost the confidence of parliament, the chancellor asked Hindenburg for authority to dissolve the Reichstag on January 28. The president refused, leaving Schleicher with no option but to resign. That same evening, Berlin's journalistic establishment held its annual Press Ball. Carl Zuckmayer recalled that the atmosphere was tense but determinedly lighthearted, the guests indulging "in a macabre blend of somberness and hectic gaiety." In the Ullstein box the firm's managing director kept refilling the champagne glasses, saying each time, "Drink up, go ahead, who knows when you'll again be drinking champagne in an Ullstein box." The celebrated fighter pilot, Ernst Udet, proposed to Zuckmayer that they "take their pants down and dangle our backsides over the box." But neither was feeling jocular enough to "moon" the ball. Schleicher, who showed up after midnight, did the next best thing: he offered a toast to nothing. Later, commenting on his brief and ill-fated moment in the political spotlight, he said: "I stayed in power only seventy days and on each and every one of them I was betrayed seventy times. Don't ever speak to me of 'German loyalty'!"

Most observers assumed that Schleicher's fall would mean Papen's return to power as chancellor. Harry Kessler, for one, was horrified at this prospect. He wrote in his diary on January 28: "Schleicher has fallen and Papen is to form a new government. He now plays unequivocally the part of presidential minion, for he lacks all other support and has almost the whole nation against him. I feel physically sick at the thought of this mutton-head and gambler ruling us again and apparently acting as Foreign Minister as well."

But what actually transpired was far worse. On January 29 Papen and Hitler worked out the details of their power-sharing arrangement. Hitler's cabinet would include, in addition to Papen as vice-chancellor, Hugenberg as minister of economics, and Franz Seldte, chief of the conservative Stahlhelm veterans' organization, as minister of labor. Only two cabinet posts would go to Nazis: Wilhelm Frick would take the Interior Ministry and Hermann Göring would become minister without portfolio. The Interior Ministry, however, was a crucial post, for it embraced the police. Moreover, Papen consented to Hitler's demand that Göring take over the Prussian Interior Ministry, with similar police functions for that state. These were fateful breaches in the "conservative wall" around Hitler. But Papen remained oblivious to the danger. When a Prussian Junker questioned his wisdom in working with Hitler, he replied: "What do you want? I have the confidence of Hindenburg. In two months we'll have pushed Hitler so far into a corner that he'll squeal."

Hitler was appointed chancellor by Hindenburg at 11:30 in the morning on January 30. Upon moving into the Chancellery, he reportedly said, "No one gets me out of here alive." That evening the Nazis celebrated their victory with a torchlight procession through the streets of Berlin, the first of many such extravaganzas. Having assembled in the Tiergarten, the marchers paraded east through the Brandenburg Gate, crossed the Pariser Platz, then turned down the Wilhelmstrasse. Watching the procession, Theodor Düsterberg of the Stalhelm noticed thousands of townspeople joining the celebration. "The Berliners, usually so level-headed, witty and skeptical were in a state of collective delirium," he reported. According to Hedda Adlon, who watched the procession from her husband's famous hotel, crowds in the Pariser Platz "broke into prolonged applause" when one of the SA bands, upon passing the French embassy, struck up the war-song "Siegreich wollen wir Frankreich schlagen." But not all Berliners were jubilant. As the procession passed his house near the Brandenburg Gate, Max Liebermann was heard to mutter: "Pity one can't eat as much as one wants to vomit."

When the parade reached the presidential palace on the Wilhelmstrasse, Hindenburg appeared at a window and kept time to the music with his cane. As he watched the marchers go by he allegedly turned to Meissner and asked: "Did we really take all these Russian prisoners at Tannenburg?" Hitler received thunderous "Sieg Heils" at a window in the Chancellery next door. Behind him stood the master of ceremonies, Goebbels, for whom the event represented a personal triumph over the "Red Beast," Berlin. As he said over the radio that night: "It is simply moving for me to see how in this city, where we began six years ago with a handful of people, the entire people is now rising up, marching by below me, workers and middle class and peasants and students and soldiers—a great community of the *Volk*, where one no longer asks whether a person is middle-class or proletarian, Catholic or Protestant, in which one asks only: What are you? To what do you belong? To what do you commit yourself in your country?" Goebbels was so impressed by the propagandistic value of his procession that he ordered it reenacted the following evening—this time for newsreel cameras.

Consolidation and Coordination

The new government in Berlin ensured that there would be no disruptions of its inaugural parade by imposing a ban on counterdemonstrations in the center of the city. The SA, however, was anxious to show that the entire town now belonged to the men in brown. Accordingly, on their way home from the march on January 30 a troop from Charlottenburg took a detour down the KPD-dominated Wallstrasse, daring the Communists to show their colors. A firefight broke out, resulting in the death of an SA man. Immediately thereafter, the Berlin police descended on the district and arrested all the Communists they could find.

This episode set the tone for the coming months, which were marked by the Nazis' neutralization of their political enemies across the Reich. For the Nazi leadership, Berlin represented a particularly challenging arena in this campaign, since it harbored the strongest concentration of opponents. Moreover, as the site of diplomatic missions and foreign news agencies, it was prominently in the international spotlight. Now that he was ensconced in the great metropolis on the Spree, Hitler wanted a measure of respectability. But if the Führer hoped to preserve the appearance of legality during his consolidation of power, many of his subordinates were intent on an immediate liquidation of their opponents with no regard for the niceties.

Göring, in his capacity as Prussian minister of interior, issued a directive on February 17 to the police forces throughout the state, including those of Berlin, stating that he would provide administrative cover to all officers who used their firearms in encounters with enemies of the state; policemen who "out of false scruples" failed to act decisively would be punished. On February 22 Göring deputized the SA and SS as *Hilfspolizei* (auxiliary police) in the battle for control of the streets. "My measures," he boasted, quoting Shakespeare, "will not be sicklied o'er by any legal scruples. My measures will not be sicklied o'er by any bureaucracy. It's not my business to do justice; it's my business to annihilate and exterminate, that's all."

Five days later an event occurred in Berlin that greatly facilitated the Nazis' pseudolegal suppression of their enemies. On the night of February 27 the Reichstag was gutted by an enormous fire. Göring, who now resided in the nearby Prussian presidential palace, was the first Nazi leader on the scene; his main concern was to salvage the Gobelin tapestries, which were his personal property. Hitler, dining with Goebbels at the latter's opulent apartment on Reichskanzlerplatz (soon to be renamed Adolf-Hitler-Platz), rushed to the Reichstag upon being alerted by telephone. Upon arriving he was told by Göring that a Communist arsonist had been arrested on the scene; he was a transplanted Dutchman named Marinus van der Lubbe. The obviously addled culprit, who had been found wandering half-naked through the burning rooms, confessed to setting fires in several places in the building with packets of coal lighter, using his gasoline-soaked shirt as tinder. Although van der Lubbe insisted that he had acted alone, the government instantly declared the fire to be the first stage in a planned Communist insurrection. On that

The Reichstag on fire, February 27, 1933

very night Göring put the Berlin police force on highest alert and instituted a roundup of some 4,000 political opponents, most of them Communists. Among those arrested were the writers Egon Erwin Kisch and Carl von Ossietzky.

Because the Reichstag fire suited Hitler's purposes so perfectly, many observers at the time (and many commentators since) assumed that the Nazis themselves started the blaze. More recent scholarship suggests that this was not the case. Although he had contempt for parliamentary government, Hitler liked the Reichstag building, which appealed to his taste for historicist bric-a-brac. On the other hand, he also knew a political opportunity when he saw one, and he privately called the blaze "a God-given signal." On the following day he secured a decree from President Hindenburg to suspend most of the civil liberties guaranteed by the Weimar constitution. The decree also greatly restricted the rights of the various German states, thereby adding to the centralization of power in Berlin. It may seem ironic that the Nazis would enhance the authority of a city they claimed to despise, but they were by nature centralizers, determined to consolidate decisionmaking in the national capital.

On March 5, a week after the Reichstag fire, Berliners went to the polls to elect a new Reichstag. This was the first parliamentary election since Hitler's appointment to the chancellorship, and the regime was anxious to show that the nation stood solidly behind the new order. However, even with extensive intimidation of rival parties, the Nazis fell significantly short of the absolute triumph they had envisaged. Reich-wide they won 43.9 percent of the total vote and in Berlin only 34.6 percent. The Catholic Center and the SPD held their own, while the Communists, despite the recent wave of arrests, managed 12.3 percent nationwide and 24.4 percent in Berlin. To achieve absolute majorities on the national level and in the capital, the Nazis needed to form coalition governments with right-wing conservatives.

Mindful that he still had a way to go to achieve a full dictatorship, Hitler now worked to convince his conservative allies that he needed additional powers to avert a possible leftist resurgence. On March 21 he stood next to President Hindenburg during an elaborate ceremony at Potsdam's Garrison Church, vowing to uphold the traditions of Prussian honor and discipline that the church symbolized. For this occasion Hitler put aside his Nazi uniform for a top hat and tails. Hindenburg was so moved he cried.

This pompous travesty, brilliantly orchestrated by Goebbels, was meant as psychological preparation for a crucial vote by the new Reichstag on an Enabling Act that would allow the regime to dispense entirely with constitutional limitations over the next four years. The fateful session took place on March 23 in the Kroll Opera House. To ensure that the deputies did the right thing, SA men stood outside chanting "We demand the Enabling Act, or there will be hell to pay!" Although the SPD refused to cave in, support from the Center Party allowed the Nazis and their allies to gain the needed two-thirds majority. (All the KPD delegates and some of the Socialists were prevented from attending the vote.) Hitler was now officially dictator of Germany, "created by democracy and appointed by parliament." No wonder Berlin wits began calling the Reichstag, which continued to meet at the Kroll Opera, "the most expensive choral society in the world."

Hitler with President Hindenburg at the "Day of Potsdam," March 21, 1933

Backed by emergency decrees and armed with police-auxiliary status, Berlin's SA forces now turned the streets of the capital into a hunting ground for their political and personal enemies. They focused on the working-class districts, where in the past they had often gotten back as much as they had dished out. They ranged through the massive Mietskasernen, grabbing "subversives" and bundling them off to their various district headquarters, which they converted into ad hoc prisons and torture chambers. The most prominent of these hellholes were the SA barracks in Hedemannstrasse (Kreuzberg) and the SA Field Police post in General-Pappe-Strasse (Tempelhof). Another "wild concentration camp" was located in a squat brick water tower in the district of Prenzlauer Berg. It now bears a plaque attesting to its former function, blithely ignored by the patrons of the hip cafés that have sprouted up around the tower since the fall of the Berlin Wall. Rudolf Diels, the first head of the Gestapo, recalled in his memoirs a visit to the SA barracks in Hedemannstrasse, where he saw men with their faces beaten in and their arms and legs broken. They lay on dirty straw mats, he reported, like "big clumps of mud, funny dolls with dead eyes and wobbly heads."

While the SA was rounding up Communists and Socialists and throwing them in makeshift prisons, the Nazi leadership made a strenuous effort to depict the party as the true protector of the working classes. On May 1, 1933, the workers' traditional day of celebration, Berlin was festooned in swastika banners and signs saying "Only a Strong Germany Can Provide Work for the German Workman." Workers from all over the country were brought to the capital to attend a mass rally in Tempelhof Field, where they heard Hitler promise a war on unemployment through public works and the reduction of interest payments. He also announced a plan for compulsory labor service, whereby every German would be obliged "to gain some experience of manual labor." According to British ambassador Sir Horace Rumbold, who witnessed the speech, Hitler's address generated little enthusiasm among the masses.

In the Berlin region the Nazi terror campaign reached its bloody peak during the infamous Köpenicker Blutwoche (Köpenick Blood Week) in June 1933. In revenge for an anti-Nazi demonstration in that district, Brownshirt gangs rounded up over 500 Communist and Socialist functionaries and threw them into SA prisons. During the following days, ninety-one prisoners were shot or tortured to death. Their mangled corpses were sewn into sacks and dumped into the Havel River, on whose banks they washed up over the course of the summer. The Brownshirts' rival, the SS, also lost no time in imposing itself on the capital. In April 1933 it took control of all the German police forces, including Göring's Berlin-based Secret State Police, or Gestapo. This agency moved into a former applied arts school at Prinz-Albrecht-Strasse 8, while the SS command established its headquarters next door at the Prinz Albrecht Hotel.

Soon the basement of the Gestapo building was so full of political prisoners that a new jail was opened in a former military prison at Tempelhof Airport called "Columbia-Haus." When this facility was exposed in the foreign press as a site of systematic torture and murder, the SS admitted that a few "excesses" might have occurred there, but attributed these to the guards' "bitterness over the crimes committed by the Communists in the wake of the national revolution." As a step toward systematizing the terror campaign, the SS began establishing regular concentration camps around the country, including the Sachsenhausen camp in the northern Berlin suburb of Oranienburg. To counter charges in the foreign press that atrocities were being committed in this place as well, the regime published a picture book on Sachsenhausen showing rows of orderly barracks and fit-looking prisoners. A Berlin

SA leader named Karl Ernst claimed in his foreword to the book that the new concentration camp system was already achieving great successes in "helping misdirected citizens to turn around politically and recover the work-ethic."

While Nazi paramilitary units were seizing control of Berlin's streets, party officials were systematically purging the city's bureaucratic and political institutions. A national "Law for the Reconstitution of the Professional Civil Service," passed on April 7, 1933, provided legal cover for the dismissal of racially or politically objectionable officials. In Berlin the purge cleaned out about one-third of the municipal bureaucracy. Meanwhile, Communist and Social Democratic representatives were barred from taking their places in the new city assembly, which began meeting on April 1, 1933. The then mayor, Heinrich Sahm (Deutschnationale Volkspartei, DNVP), who had been elected in 1931, was allowed for the time being to keep his post because he was a close confidant of Hindenburg's. Like many of his conservative colleagues, Sahm thought he could exercise a restraining influence on the Nazis. Instead he found himself countersigning orders for the dismissal and forced retirement of municipal officials. In November 1933 he presided over a ceremony making Adolf Hitler an honorary citizen of Berlin. On this occasion Sahm insisted that the capital stood behind its Führer "in unconditional loyalty and iron solidarity." Two years later, tiring of his role as a glorified notary, Sahm resigned his office.

While Sahm was useful as a conservative figurehead, the official actually in charge of the administrative purge in Berlin was Dr. Julius Lippert, chairman of the Nazi delegation in the Berlin city assembly. On March 14 he was appointed Reich commissioner of the city of Berlin to help consolidate the regime's control over a capital that, Mayor Sahm's declaration notwithstanding, seemed to be inadequately committed to the new order. Following Sahm's resignation, Lippert folded the functions of mayor into his office as Reich Commissioner, which he held until 1940. The special controls imposed by the new government on Berlin were a testament to the Nazis' distrust of the Spree metropolis.

Despite its dictatorial powers in Berlin and across the Reich, the Nazi leadership continued to feel somewhat uneasy in the saddle. The nation's military, while accepting the change in government, was not yet integrated into the new order. Moreover, Vice-chancellor Papen and some of his conservative friends, having come to realize that they had failed to "tame" Hitler, were demanding a return to constitutional government. On June 17, 1934, Papen delivered a speech at Marburg University in which he accused the Nazis of leading a "revolution against order, law, and church." Papen's initiative convinced Hitler that his efforts to win over the army and the conservative establishment were being undermined by the SA, which was demanding that it, not the Reichswehr, become the primary source of military muscle for the Third Reich. The Führer decided that it was time to discipline the SA. The result of this decision was an orgy of bloodletting known as the Night of the Long Knives.

On June 28, 1934, Hitler ordered Röhm and other top SA leaders to gather at Bad Wiessee, a resort town south of Munich, for a meeting. Two days later, as the SA men frolicked in their hotel, Hitler arrived with a unit of SS guards and placed all the Brownshirts under arrest. The charge was plotting a putsch against the Nazi government. Some of the alleged plotters were killed on the spot. The rest were transported to Munich's Stadelheim prison, where more executions took place. In consideration of their old friendship, Hitler ordered that Röhm be allowed to commit suicide. When the captain refused to do so, he, too, was executed. Later, Goebbels spread the rumor that the SA leader had been captured in bed with a young boy.

Although much of the Long Knives killing took place in Bad Wiessee and Munich, Berlin was also an important stage for this grisly spectacle. Here the targets included leaders of the local SA as well as prominent conservatives. SA Obergruppenführer Karl Ernst, who liked to brag that he "owned Berlin," was about to embark on a honeymoon cruise when he was arrested by the Gestapo in Bremerhaven and flown back to Berlin. Upon arrival at Tempelhof he demanded to be taken to his "good friend," Göring. Instead he was driven to the Lichterfelde Cadet School and promptly shot. His execution was followed in quick succession by that of many other Berlin SA figures, none of whom seemed to understand what they had done to deserve such a fate.

Meanwhile, at the vice-chancellery building, SS killers shot Papen's young assistant, Herbert von Bose, who had allegedly resisted arrest. Also killed was Edgar Jung, a conservative intellectual who had ghostwritten Papen's Marburg speech. Another associate of Papen's who died that day was Erich Klausener, who headed the conservative religious group, Catholic Action. Papen himself was spared, for he had many friends in the foreign diplomatic corps, but he was placed under house arrest while his assistants were being murdered. The experience was sufficiently chastening that he went on to serve the Third Reich as ambassador in Vienna and Ankara.

Gregor Strasser, the Nazi "old-fighter" who had given Hitler trouble on the eve of his seizure of power, was picked up by the Gestapo at his apartment and bundled into a police sedan. He thought he was being taken to Hitler for a reconciliation. His actual destination was Prinz-Albrecht-Strasse 8, where he was shot through a hole in his cell door. The official explanation for his death was suicide.

General Kurt von Schleicher, the former chancellor who had tried to keep Hitler out of power, was spending the morning of June 30 at home in the company of his young wife. At eleven-thirty, five men dressed in long black raincoats walked into his study and shot him to death. When his wife ran into the room, they shot her too. General Kurt von Bredow, a former aide to Schleicher, heard rumors later that day about what had happened to his boss, and he must have guessed that the Nazis were planning something similar for him. Yet instead of fleeing Berlin he showed himself at the Hotel Adlon, a favorite Nazi haunt, and refused a foreign diplomat's offer of sanctuary. The Gestapo arrived at his home that evening and killed him when he answered their knock.

The wave of brazen murders during the Night of the Long Knives inspired a few gasps of outrage from the foreign press and the diplomatic community. American ambassador William Dodd wrote in his diary on July 4: "Our people [in America] cannot imagine such things happening in their country as have happened here." Dodd's French counterpart, André François-Poncet, who was accused in some German newspapers of having engaged in traitorous dealings with Schleicher and Röhm, confided to Dodd that he would "not be surprised to be shot on the streets of Berlin." The new British ambassador, Sir Eric Phipps, had a dinner date with Göring shortly after the killings, and when the Nazi showed up late, explaining that he had just gotten back from shooting, Phipps grunted, "Animals, I hope." None of the ambassadors, however, made any official complaint to the German government regarding the murders.

The vast majority of Germans, meanwhile, accepted Hitler's claim, made in a radio address on July 13, that the government had put down a wide-ranging "mutiny" staged by "enemies of the state." Ordinary citizens had become tired of the rabble-rousing antics of the SA and were pleased to see them "disciplined." The Reichswehr command, overjoyed that the SA had been cut down to size, made no protest over the fact that the regime had also used this occasion to kill two generals. The army leaders might not have been so sanguine, however, had they understood that the SA's diminishment entailed the rise of an even more potent rival: the SS.

In the wake of the killings Hitler worried that President Hindenburg might raise some objections to the bloodletting, but he need not have been concerned—the old man was too senile to appreciate the significance of what had happened. He responded to the news by remarking: "He who wants to make history like Hitler must be prepared to let guilty blood flow and not be soft." About a month later, as Hindenburg lay on his deathbed, Hitler went to see him and was addressed by the president as "His Majesty." This form of address was not entirely inappropriate, because after Hindenburg's death on August 2 Hitler combined the offices of president and chancellor in his own person. Commenting on the old president's passing, the Nazi government acknowledged his "almost incalculable services" to Germany, which included "opening the gates of the Reich to the young National Socialist movement."

Against Decadence and Moral Decay

In June 1940, when the German army paraded down the Champs-Elysées after its stunning victory over France, Jean Cocteau worried about what was going to happen to his favorite opium dens and homosexual haunts. Many Berliners must have wondered the same thing when the Nazis marched down Unter den Linden in the early days of 1933. The city's new rulers quickly closed the most prominent drug palaces and boy bars. Christopher Isherwood, gamely hanging on in the city, lost touch with most of his gay friends. The more prudent ones, he guessed, were lying low, while a few "silly ones fluttered around town exclaiming how sexy the Storm Troopers looked in their uniforms." One pair of homosexual lovers, believing that "Germany was entering an era of military man-love," declared proudly that they were Nazis, only to discover that Nazi Berlin was not the erotic paradise of their dreams. On the contrary, in addition to closing gay bars the Nazis began arresting homosexuals as "social deviants." Meanwhile, the streets of the capital reverberated to the din of radio loudspeakers blaring speeches by Goebbels and Hitler. Berliners (again to quote Isherwood) "sat in front of the cafes listening to [the loudspeakers]—cowlike, vaguely curious, complacent, accepting what had happened but not the responsibility for it. Many of them hadn't even voted—how could they be responsible?"

Another notable sound in the city was the tread of marching men, as in Old Berlin. To facilitate military parades, the Nazis cut down the lime trees in the center of Unter den Linden and paved over the Wilhelmsplatz. Grievous as such barbarities were, however, the Nazis' most crippling assaults on Berlin were aimed not at its physical environment but at its culture. Just as they reshaped the political system to suit their needs, they sought to make over Berlin's cultural life to their specifications. In the process, they also tried to construct a new image of Berlin more in keeping with their own vision of how a great capital should be represented in the world.

Throughout the Weimar period the Nazis had made abundantly clear that they despised the irreverence, diversity, and cosmopolitanism of Berlin's cultural and intellectual scene. The most antiurban and antimodern among them—figures like Alfred Rosenberg, Gottfried Feder, and Walther Darré (who became Hitler's minister of agriculture)—insisted that Berlin was hopelessly irredeemable and did not deserve to be the capital of the Third Reich. In their view, the nation would be better served with its capital in Munich, Hitler's adopted hometown, or in some rustic village that encapsulated the Nazi movement's close-to-the-soil values.

Such "fundamentalists," however, were overruled by Nazi "pragmatists," and above all by Hitler himself. The Führer, despite his ambivalent feelings toward Berlin, never considered moving the capital to another city, much less to a village; in his eyes, Europe's greatest country had to be governed from Germany's greatest city. He contended that Nazi Germany needed the "magical attraction" of its own "Mecca or Rome." Later, in his wartime "Table Talks," he claimed even to have "always liked Berlin," which he said had given his movement more financial support on its road to power than "petite bourgeois Munich." He also believed, however, that it was Berlin's "misfortune" to have been "settled by people of Lower Saxon/Frissian stock," who had failed to create a genuine "cultural foundation." In his view, Berlin's last true cultural leader had been Friedrich Wilhelm IV. Wilhelm I had had "no taste," Bismarck had been "amusical," and though Wilhelm II had had cultural pretensions, his taste was "decidedly bad." Thus there was much that was "ugly" in Berlin, a lot of clutter to be "cast aside" and replaced by new additions that constituted "the best that is possible with today's resources."

The regime began its campaign to reinvent Berlin with a crackdown on the press, which had long been fundamental to Berlin's anarchic and internationalist spirit. In 1933 Berlin had over fifty newspapers, not including the small journals restricted to individual neighborhoods. The Nazis could not summarily eliminate all but their own organs in the city, for at that point they had only two: Goebbels' *Der Angriff* and the recently established Berlin edition of the *Völkischer Beobachter*. Berliners were notoriously dependent on their daily newsprint fix, the sudden withdrawal of which might have shocked them out of that convenient complacency noted by Isherwood. Thus the regime, through the agency of Goebbels' new Ministry for Enlightenment and Propaganda, took a more subtle tack: it initially forbade outright only the Communists' *Rote Fahne* and the Socialists' *Vorwärts*, while forcing other papers to muzzle themselves editorially and to dismiss most of their Jewish and leftist staff. Given the traditional liberal values and strong Jewish presence in the mainstream Berlin press, this amounted to a major purge.

In early 1933 the *Berliner Tageblatt* had to fire its famed chief editor, Theodor Wolff, who as a Jew and outspoken liberal personified in Nazi eyes all that was foul in the Berlin newspaper world. (As an added offense, Wolff had once denied Goebbels a job on the *Tageblatt.*) Deprived of its best personnel, the *Tageblatt* staggered on until 1938, steadily losing money. Its parent house, the Jewish-owned Mosse Verlag, which had declared bankruptcy in late 1932, passed into the hands of a liquidation agency that sold off the profitable parts of the business to well-connected Aryans.

The *Vossische Zeitung*, flagship of the Ullstein Verlag, tried to keep the Nazis at bay by purging most of its Jewish reporters. But Goebbels was not satisfied with partial self-emasculation. In preparation for a planned Reich-wide boycott of Jewish businesses, the *Vossische Zeitung* and other Ullstein papers were forced to print anti-Semitic articles, replete with the slogan, "Die Juden sind unser Unglück (The Jews are our Curse)." Remaining Jewish staff writers, even those who tried hard to adjust to the new circumstances, were soon forced out. Thus society columnist Bella Fromm was informed by her editor in June 1934 that the paper could no longer run articles under her byline. Appeals from her conservative friends Franz von Papen and War Minister Werner von Blomberg failed to persuade Goebbels to reverse this decision. In any event, the *Vossische* was a sinking ship; it went down a year later. Other Ullstein papers suffered a similar fate because many Berliners feared to been seen reading them in public, and many businesses refused to advertise in them. The Ullstein Verlag remained afloat a little longer only because some of its weekly papers and magazines, especially the mass-market *Berliner Illustrierte*, continued to earn a profit. But in 1935 Goebbels imposed a three-month ban on all Ullstein publications, which forced the publisher to liquidate.

Die Weltbühne, that provocative and independent voice on the left, was on uncertain ground as soon as the Nazis came to power. Shortly thereafter, the paper had the temerity to lecture Hitler on how to survive in office. Ossietzky editorialized that the Nazi regime could "last a generation" if it sided with the working class and

Nazi-orchestrated book-burning on Berlin's Opernplatz, May 10, 1933

did not tamper with welfare reforms. But it was the *Weltbühne* journalists whose days were numbered. As we have seen, Ossietzky was arrested on the night of the Reichstag fire; so were two frequent contributors to the journal, Erich Mühsam and Heinz Poll. "Journalists today gaze with envy at the practitioners of such unrisky professions as tightrope walking," lamented a *Weltbühne* writer on February 21, 1933. Two weeks later, on March 7, the SA raided the offices of the journal and confiscated its property.

The right-wing nationalist press made no effort to practice journalistic tightrope walking: its feet were planted solidly on the Nazi line from the beginning. The papers operated by the Scherl Verlag, which was now owned by the Hugenberg empire, continued to earn money for their opportunistic proprietor. Yet Hugenberg and his editors were always aware that their survival depended on never straying too far from the pro-Nazi line that they had so compliantly toed in 1933.

Ironically, the Berlin papers catering exclusively to the Jewish community were given broader latitude than the rest of the city's press. As long as they did not directly attack the regime's policies, papers like *Der Jüdische Rundschau*, *Israelit*, and *Der Nationaldeutsche Jude* were pretty much left alone. The logic here was that the purely Jewish press could not be expected to conform to higher Aryan standards since its writers were racially incapable of doing so. The relative lack of censorship allowed the Jewish papers to be more factually accurate than their "German" competitors. Realizing this, some non-Jewish Berliners began reading the Jewish press. The circulation of the *Jüdische Rundschau* actually increased in the early years of the Third Reich.

In the end, however, even limited diversity in Berlin's newspaper world was unacceptable to the Nazi regime, and more and more papers were forced to close due to political or economic pressures. Between 1933 and 1938 Berlin lost twenty-nine of its papers. By the beginning of World War II, aside from those owned by Hugenberg, only ten papers survived, all of them under direct Nazi control. Berlin's days as Europe's greatest newspaper city were over.

Journalists were the first to feel the heat of Nazi censorship because they obviously shaped public opinion. But imaginative writers, whose influence was less obvious, also had to watch what they wrote if they did not want to end up on the regime's "black list," which at the very least could mean a prohibition on publication. Rather than attempting to conform, a host of novelists and poets left Germany in the early years of the Third Reich, following the example of those who had already emigrated in the waning days of Weimar. Heinrich Mann and Lion Feuchtwanger, who had moved from Munich to Berlin in the mid-1920s to escape the growing influence of *völkisch* barbarism, now quit Germany entirely, decamping first to France, then to America. Their final landing place was Los Angeles, which became the exile home for dozens of other German émigrés: a kind of Berlin-on-the-Pacific. Another prominent German writer who ended up in Los Angeles was Heinrich's brother Thomas. He began his long exile in February 1933 after being branded a traitor by his fellow intellectuals in Munich for allegedly besmirching the good name of Richard Wagner. In addition to Heinrich Mann and Feuchtwanger, the literary hemorrhage from Berlin in the first years of the Third Reich included Kurt Tucholsky, Bertolt Brecht, Walter Benjamin, Walter Hasenclever, Alfred Döblin, Jakob Wassermann, Franz Werfel, Anna Seghers, Arnold and Stefan Zweig—the list reads like a Who's Who of German literature. They constituted the first wave of a cultural exodus that grew with the years until that dreadful moment when it became no longer possible to leave—except in a boxcar. Those who got out in time were the lucky ones, though the dislocation of exile proved too much for some. Among the prominent literary suicides from Berlin were Benjamin, Hasenclever, Stefan Zweig, and Tucholsky.

The Nazis graphically demonstrated their attitude toward "un-German" and "Jewish-Bolshevik" literature by organizing book-burnings in university towns around the country. The one in Berlin, which took place on May 10, 1933, was the largest, befitting the city's status as a center of "literary subversion." In the middle of the Opernplatz, just a few meters from the statues of Alexander and Wilhelm von Humboldt, storm troopers and students built a pile of 20,000 books that they had pillaged from libraries and stores around town. The authors honored in this anti-canon included Marx, Brecht, Feuchtwanger, the Mann brothers, Arnold and Stefan Zweig, Erich Kästner, Erich Maria Remarque, Walther Rathenau, H. G. Wells, Sigmund Freud, Emile Zola, Upton Sinclair, André Gide, Marcel Proust, Ernest Hemingway, and Helen Keller. Also tossed on the pyre was the entire library of Magnus Hirschfeld's Institute for Sexual Research, which the Nazis had recently smashed up and closed. As their fire blazed, the students (and, even more revoltingly, a few professors) chanted the dim-witted dogmas of Nazi cultural politics: "Against decadence and moral decay! For discipline and decency in the family and state!" "Against impudence and arrogance, for respect and reverence toward the immortal German soul!" At midnight Goebbels showed up to address the crowd. He had been somewhat reluctant to attend, fearing that some might recall that he had studied literature with Jewish professors and had once even praised some of the authors now being pilloried. Nonetheless, he managed to bring forth the expected slogans, denouncing the works on the smoldering pile as "the intellectual foundation of the November Republic," now vanquished along with the "era of Jewish hyper-intellectualism."

Aware that such demonstrations and proclamations, however unsubtle, were not enough to ensure conformity, the Nazis established an elaborate bureaucracy to control the nation's cultural life—the Reichskulturkammer (Reich Chamber of Culture), based in Berlin. It contained seven departments individually responsible for radio, theater, film, music, the visual arts, the press, and literature.

Like the other departments, the Reichsschriftumskammer, which dealt with literature, was a kind of government union; writers who did not belong to it were unlikely to get published, at least in Germany. The agency kept publishers and booksellers informed as to which authors were acceptable and which were on its index. Since its writ extended across the entire Reich, it brought a degree of centralization never experienced before (or since) in German literary history. Berlin might be the center of German "decadence," but in culture as in politics it wielded unprecedented authority during the Third Reich.

A few nonconformist writers who were unwilling to flee the country tried to survive by restricting themselves to producing esoteric or specialized works or by writing in a kind of code, which they hoped the Nazi censors were too dim to decipher. This tactic, known as "inner emigration," was hard to pull off in Berlin because the censorship bureaucracy was headquartered there. Thus some writers chose to retreat to the countryside, where they hoped to be left in peace. A prime example was Hans Fallada, whose novel *Kleiner Mann, was nun?* (Little Man, What Now?) chronicles the plight of Germany's petite bourgeoisie squeezed between big labor and big capital. Fallada had thought that as a "nonpolitical man" he had nothing to fear from the Nazis, but they temporarily arrested him in 1933, which convinced him to go to ground in a north German village far from the capital. There he played it safe by writing a novel, *Der Eiserne Gustav* (Iron Gustav), which celebrates a Berlin coachman who refuses to switch to taxicabs. It was not until after the war that he explored antifascist themes in his novel of the Berlin resistance, *Jeder stirbt für sich allein* (Everyone Dies His Own Death). The physician and poet Gottfried Benn, who had initially heralded the triumph of Nazism, was expelled from the Reichsschriftumskammer in 1936 for writing verse with "un-German" imagery. For the rest of the Third Reich he found his own inner immigration as an army doctor in Hanover and on the front. The novelist Ernst Jünger, whose works celebrating trench warfare as a spiritual epiphany had won the admiration of Goebbels, refused to put his talent at the service of the Nazis and abandoned Berlin for the little town of Goslar shortly after Hitler came to power.

The majority of the writers who published actively in Berlin during the Nazi era were hacks or opportunists, grateful for the drop-off in competition. The former bastion of "asphalt literature" was now crawling with *Blut-und-Boden* (blood and soil) writers who celebrated the virtues of race and rootedness. This group included such figures as Hans-Friedrich Blunck, Hans Grimm, Erwin Guido Kolbenheyer, Isolde Kurz, Agnes Miegel, and Hanns Johst (who became head of the Reichsschriftumskammer). Unlike the writers whom they helped to drive away, most of these stars in the Nazi firmament faded from view as soon as the Third Reich collapsed.

While some independent-thinking novelists and poets could continue to do productive work in inner emigration, often in the provinces, playwrights, by dint of the public nature of their craft, found this sort of partial hibernation much harder. They wanted to remain where the action was, and that was Berlin. The Nazis, for their part, were conscious of the Berlin theater's traditional role as conscience and educator of the nation, and they were determined to bend this tradition to their purposes.

The central figure here was Hermann Göring, titular head of all the Prussian state theaters. He once declared that when he heard the word "culture" he got out his gun, but this was just bravado; in reality, he considered himself a connoisseur of the arts. He loved the theater and was himself quite histrionic, a center-stage performer with the girth of Falstaff and the character of Iago. Sometimes he laid aside his beribboned uniforms to dress up in a Robin Hood outfit with leather jerkin and thigh-length boots, or in a Roman toga with jewel-studded sandals. His passion for the theater was also reflected in his choice of a second wife, the actress Emmy Sonnemann, whom he married in 1935 in an elaborate ceremony at the Berlin Cathedral. As chief of the Berlin stage, Göring was no purist: he was prepared to cultivate talented non-Nazi actors and directors as long as they did not try to rewrite the script they had been handed. "It is easier to turn a great artist into a decent National Socialist than to make a great artist out of a humble Party member," he observed.

Göring's chief rival for control over Berlin's theaters was Goebbels, who as head of the Reich Chamber of Culture and minister of propaganda and enlightenment had authority over all the Reich-administered theaters, which in Berlin included the Volksbühne, the Theater am Nollendorfplatz, and the Deutsche Oper (Charlottenburg). It irritated Goebbels that Göring held sway over the Prussian state theaters, for they were far more prestigious than his lot. He tried repeatedly to wrest Göring's "treasure" from him, but to no avail. The Goebbels-Göring feud was typical of the Third Reich's neofeudal structure, its endless battles between rival fiefdoms with overlapping borders.

Göring's prize theater-man was Gustav Gründgens, who became director of the Schauspielhaus in 1934. He had made his reputation in the 1920s in Hamburg, where he had dazzled audiences with his versatility as an actor. In those days he had embraced communism, but only as another role, one he could conveniently drop when he moved to Berlin in the early 1930s to star at the Deutsches Theater. According to Klaus Mann, who had known him in Hamburg (and whose sister, Erika, was briefly married to him), Gründgens won over Göring with a virtuoso performance of Mephistopheles in Goethe's *Faust.* Mann wrote in his memoir, *The Turning Point:* "Göring, completely bedeviled by such a breathtaking display of bold depravity, presently forgave him for all his former slips, including his objectionable marriage.... I visualize my ex-brother-in-law as the traitor par excellence, the macabre embodiment of corruption and cynicism." Klaus Mann was so obsessed with Gründgens that he made him the antihero of his novel *Mephisto*, a meditation on the "prostitution of talent for the sake of some tawdry fame and transitory wealth."

With commanding figures like Gründgens at the Schauspielhaus, Heinrich George at the Schiller-Theater, and Karlheinz Martin, another former revolutionary, at the Volksbühne, Berlin held on to its status as the capital of German drama. Its various theaters continued to mount well-executed productions of the German classics, especially those with an exploitable nationalist message, such as Heinrich Kleist's *Die Hermannschlacht* and Friedrich Hebbel's *Niebelungen.* On the other hand, its new rulers banned works that seemed politically or aesthetically problematical. Thus Nazi Berlin rejected Gerhart Hauptmann's *Die Weber* as too gloomy. Hauptmann himself, however, remained in the city throughout the Third Reich, a valuable cultural show-figure for the regime.

There were no longer any independent theaters in Berlin, unless one counted the small houses operated by the Cultural League of German Jews that were closed to Aryans. Berlin's radical theater movement was decimated by the exodus of its most important practitioners. Erwin Piscator, as we have seen, had left even before the Nazis came to power. Brecht fled on the morning after the Reichstag fire. It is possible that he might have stayed on without being arrested, for the Nazis, especially Goebbels, wanted to retain some of Germany's most famous artists and intellectuals as proof of Berlin's continuing cultural importance. Yet had Brecht stayed on in Berlin he certainly would have been limited in what he (and his unacknowledged female coauthors) could produce, and he thought he could do better in exile, which he did not expect to last long. "Don't go too far away," he advised his friend Arnold Zweig. "In five years we will be back." How could he have known that he would return to Berlin only after a fifteen-year exile in Prague, Vienna, Zurich, Paris, Copenhagen, Helsinki, and Los Angeles?

Berlin's cabaret scene presented the Nazis with a particular challenge because it was central to the city's world-image as a vibrant metropolis and also full of leftist and Jewish entertainers. Although the local cabaret's satirical teeth had grown dull in the Weimar period, it could still bite off its pound of political flesh. The regime moved quickly to shut down Berlin's left-wing agitprop cabaret and to eliminate its chief practitioners. Hans Otto, of the German Workers' Theater League, was murdered at Columbia-Haus; Erich Mühsam, who acted in leftist cabaret in addition to writing for *Die Weltbühne*, was killed at Sachsenhausen. For a brief period Aryan performers were allowed to produce political cabaret as long as they made fun of the right targets. But when Werner Finck of the Catacombs Cabaret began tossing out barbs that were a little too irreverent toward the leadership, his enterprise was shut down. In the same year, 1935, the Tingel-Tangel Cabaret was closed for defaming the National Socialist order with skits celebrating the resilience of "weeds" (dissident thoughts) in a field covered with "manure" (the Nazi state). Unable to cultivate a "positive cabaret" that was economically viable, the regime fell back on pure vaudeville and girlie shows.

Important as live drama was to the Nazis, film was even more so, inasmuch as it had a broader audience and was, along with radio, the perfect propaganda tool. Goebbels, who considered himself a "passionate fan of the cinematic art," insisted that film was an instrument of popular education "at least as influential as the primary school." He was fully aware that Berlin was a major player in the world of film, and he intended to keep it that way. His problem, however, was that Jews were especially prominent in the German cinema. A Nazi tabulation in 1932 claimed that Germany's motion picture distribution companies were 81 percent Jewish-run, and that Jews constituted 41 percent of the screenwriters and 47 percent of the directors.

Although he was determined to end "Jewish domination" of the cinema, Goebbels was willing to tolerate a few renowned Jewish directors and actors in the interest of maintaining Berlin's prominence. He hoped in particular to induce the half-Jewish director Fritz Lang, whose *Siegfried* and *Die Nibelungen* were among his favorite films, to remain in the German capital. Lang later claimed that Goebbels offered to put him in charge of UFA and to make him the "Nazis' Führer of film." This is probably fanciful, but Lang could undoubtedly have stayed and worked in Nazi Berlin had he wanted to. He left the city in 1933 because, like Brecht, he thought he could do better for himself abroad. Unlike Brecht he turned out to be right, for after a few years of exile in France he became a great success in Hollywood, and he was never inclined to return to Berlin.

Another refugee from the Berlin film world who made it big in Hollywood was Billy Wilder. He had moved to Berlin from his native Vienna in 1926, landing jobs as a reporter with the *Nachtausgabe* and *Berliner Zeitung am Mittag.* Chronically broke, he had also picked up a few marks working as a gigolo at the Hotel Adlon, escorting lonely old ladies around the dance floor. "I dance," he wrote, "painstakingly but desireless, joyless, without thoughts, without opinion, without heart, without brain." When he wasn't covering stories or dancing he frequented the Romanisches Café, mingling with the movie people. There he learned about another way to make money: as a "Neger" (ghostwriter) on movie scripts. This turned out to be his unglamorous entrée into the film industry. During the late 1920s he worked on almost fifty scripts, always without credit. His first major writing credit came with a low-budget film called *Menschen am Sonntag* (People on Sunday), a portrait of ordinary Berliners enjoying a Sunday excursion to the Nikolassee. The movie proved a surprising success, both with Berlin audiences and the local critics. *Der Abend* wrote: "Once, Paris was shown to us in an impressive, simple manner; now, we see Berlin without the shine of advertisements in lights and the crazy nightlife of the bars."

But as Wilder's star was rising, so was that of the Nazis—a danger that the director, though Jewish, did not at first take seriously. Only when he witnessed a group of SS men beating up an old Jew did he decide to get out. In his case Goebbels seems to have made no effort to retain him. On the night after the Reichstag fire he and his lover, Hella Hartwig, boarded a train for Paris. Among their neighbors at Paris's Hotel Ansonia were the actor Peter Lorre, the composer Friedrich Holländer, and Wilder's writing partner, Max Kolpe. Wilder saw Paris only as a steppingstone to Hollywood, whose films he had admired for years. In December 1933 he jumped at the chance to go to California to work on a movie called *Pam Pam.* Later he would claim: "My dream all along was to get to Hollywood, which would have happened even without Hitler."

What surely would *not* have happened without Hitler was the transformation of the German film industry into a plaything and instrument of the government. After taking over UFA and expelling most of its Jewish artists, Goebbels worked hard to cultivate the stars who remained. His favorites were the actor Emil Jannings, the director Veit Harlan, and the actress-turned-director Leni Riefenstahl, who he said was "the only one of all the stars who understands us." Goebbels invited his film friends on boating parties on the Havel and to elegant dinners at his Berlin townhouse, located, to his dismay, on Hermann-Göring-Strasse. Although recently married to the blond beauty Magda Quandt, he made a point of personally interviewing all the up-and-coming actresses. Word went out in the Berlin film community that aspiring actresses could get ahead only via the randy little doctor's casting couch.

Goebbels and Hitler were determined to exploit Berlin's renowned film industry for purposes of "enlightenment" and wholesome diversion. Movies would at once mobilize and anesthetize the *Volk*. UFA's giant production facilities at Neu-Babelsberg outside Berlin churned out 1,100 films between 1933 and 1945, about 90 percent of them pure entertainment pictures. Among the latter were a number of films celebrating German nature as a bower for the racially pure soul. Producer Arnold Franck's *Das verlorene Tal* (The Lost Valley) and *Ewiger Wald* (Eternal Forest) fall into this category. UFA also made inspirational films about the Nazi Party. *Hans Westmar, Einer von Vielen*, eulogized the life of Horst Wessel; *SA-Mann Brand* glorified the storm troopers' love for their Führer; and *Hitlerjunge Quex* told the story of a young man from a communist household who dies at the hands of the Reds because of his fierce loyalty to the Hitler Youth. Although these films seem comically sappy today, they went over extremely well in the film palaces of the Third Reich, including those of "cynical" Berlin.

In the early years of the Nazi era, Leni Riefenstahl emerged as the regime's most important maker of propaganda films. It was unusual for a woman to wield such powerful influence in the Third Reich, but Riefenstahl was no ordinary woman. Knee-bucklingly beautiful, she was also firm-willed, skilled in her craft, and a master manipulator of the men who flocked around her. A native Berliner, she had first come to notice in the capital during the early 1920s as a dancer at the Deutsches Theater. She then went on to star in a number of "mountain films," including *The Holy Mountain*, *The White Hell of Piz Polü*, and *The Blue Light*, whose "mystical" portrayal of mountaineering managed to impress both Hitler and Pope Pius XI. Broadening her repertoire, she played a heroic woman pilot in *SOS Iceberg*, one of the first films about the *Titanic* disaster. She undoubtedly would have continued to devote herself exclusively to acting had not Adolf Hitler envisaged another use for her talents.

According to Riefenstahl's own account, Hitler invited her to the Chancellery early in 1933, told her how much he liked her films, and offered to put her "in charge of the artistic aspects of the German cinema," working at the side of Goebbels. She claims to have begged off, pleading lack of experience. In August 1933, she relates, Hitler called her in again, this time to discuss her progress on a documentary film about the Party rally in Nuremberg, scheduled for September. Flabbergasted, she replied that she knew of no such project, whereupon Hitler explained that he had given express orders to Goebbels to recruit her for the film. Although Riefenstahl tried again to say no, pleading that she was not even a Party member, Hitler ordered her to go to Nuremberg and start working on the film. Only a few days in the making, the resulting work, *Victory of the Faith*, was not a success. Goebbels, she says, put all sorts of obstacles in her way despite Hitler's instructions to help her. (It should be noted that Goebbels's diaries, a more reliable source, say nothing about any opposition on his part to Riefenstahl's work.)

The failure of Riefenstahl's first propagandistic venture did not deter Hitler from asking her to direct the filming of the following year's Nuremberg Party rally (1934), for which she was to have much more preparation and a large budget. With a crew of 120 and a battery of thirty-two cameras, Riefenstahl was able to produce one of the most impressive propaganda films of all time, *The Triumph of the Will.* To get the right effects, she used innovative techniques like mobile cameras moving on rails above the action. "I discovered that I had a definite talent for documentaries," Riefenstahl writes. "I experienced the pleasure of a film-maker who gives cinematic shape to actual events without falsifying them."

Without falsifying them, perhaps, but certainly not without glorifying them. Riefenstahl has always maintained that she lacked any commitment to Nazi ideology, but *Triumph of the Will* does not convey an impression of disinterest on the part of its director. It is a veritable hymn to the Nazi *Volksgemeinschaft*, portraying the Party cadres as a tight-knit family, alternately frolicsome and serious, like Boy Scouts high on Wagner. It records only one moment of slight unease, when Hitler, in his speech to the SA and SS, refers briefly to the recent decimation of the Brownshirt leadership.

Triumph of the Will premiered in Berlin at the UFA-Palast on March 28, 1935, with Hitler in the audience. "The end of the film," Riefenstahl recalls, "was greeted by

Leni Riefenstahl directing The Triumph of the Will

long, almost endless applause." Hitler handed her a lilac bouquet. Soon he would also hand her the keys to Berlin as the director of a film on the Nazi capital's greatest show, the 1936 Olympic Games.

Berlin's painters and sculptors, like its filmmakers, were expected to deploy their talents as a "cultural sword" for the ideals of National Socialist Germany. As a Nazi functionary declared: "Only when the artist has become an indispensable contributor to the creative processes of the nation can one call his position a healthy one." An early purge of the visual arts section of the Prussian Academy of Arts resulted in the expulsion of Oskar Kokoschka and Max Pechstein; on their own initiative (but under pressure), Otto Dix, Ernst Barlach, Ernst Ludwig Kirchner, Käthe Kollwitz, and Max Liebermann resigned from the Academy. Then the exodus began in earnest, the flight into exile from the once-favored city of Germany's progressive visual artists. Kirchner went to Switzerland, Max Beckmann to Holland, Kokoschka and John Heartfield to London. Harry Kessler, that great patron of modern art, took refuge in France. Max Liebermann might have left as well had he not been too old and sick; he died in Berlin in 1935.

Rather than fleeing, Käthe Kollwitz went into inner emigration in her Berlin studio. She continued to produce lithographs and small sculptures. In 1936 the regime imposed an unofficial ban on public exhibitions of her work and removed her contributions from that year's Academy exhibit of "Berlin Sculptors from Schlüter to the Present." Nazi pundits occasionally subjected her work to their brand of art criticism. The *Völkischer Beobachter*, for example, complained that "no German mother looks like Kollwitz paints her." But in general the regime left her alone, and she was even able to turn her studio into a clandestine refuge for a circle of young sculptors who produced works that were brilliantly "unhealthy" by Nazi lights.

Despite its purge of the Prussian Academy, the Nazi regime's policy on the visual arts was not unified or consistent in the early years of the Third Reich. Hitler came out against modern art in his speeches on culture at the Nuremberg Party rallies of 1934 and 1935, and Göring, who would later emerge as the Reich's premier art-looter, made clear his preference for traditionalist painting. But Goebbels was partial to some forms of modern art; he kept a Barlach sculpture in his Propaganda Ministry office, hung impressionist paintings in his Gauleitung office, and displayed works by Käthe Kollwitz in his private residence. The propaganda minister fought hard to limit the influence of Alfred Rosenberg, whose rigid *völkisch* anti-modernism he considered primitive and stifling. Aware that Berlin's reputation for artistic creativity was on the line, he stated that, "We guarantee the freedom of art." In mid-1935, however, Goebbels began giving way to Hitler's insistence that art reflect "healthy" German traditions and perform a clear didactic function. The minister's embrace of this view brought to an end what flexibility there had been in the regime's policy on the visual arts.

The emergence of a harder line in this domain was signaled by the appointment in 1936 of Adolf Ziegler as head of the Reichskammer für die bildende Künste (Reich Chamber for the Visual Arts). Known for his startlingly realistic nudes, a specialty that won him the sobriquet Reichsschamhaarpinsler (official pubic hair painter of the Reich), Ziegler was an archconservative of the "blood and soil" school. Along with Goebbels, he organized the Third Reich's infamous Ausstellung entartete Kunst (Exhibition of Degenerate Art), a display of 730 artworks that the Nazis considered representative of "un-German" aesthetic values. The collection, which had been confiscated from galleries and museums around the country, included works by Max Ernst, Paul Klee, Wassily Kandinsky, Oskar Kokoschka, Georg Grosz, Max Beckmann, Ernst Barlach, Otto Dix, and Emil Nolde—to name just a few. The exhibition opened in Munich (Goebbels would have preferred Berlin) in July 1937 and attracted masses of viewers, many of whom undoubtedly wanted to pay their last respects to works that they were not likely to see again in the near future. When the show moved on to Berlin it prompted a similar response.

At the time they opened their display of "degenerate" art, the Nazis also mounted the Great German Art Exhibition. As the name suggests, this show featured works that the regime considered emblematic of the best German traditions. The site was Munich's House of German Art, which was the only new art museum to be built in the Third Reich. The fact that Munich, not Berlin, got this prize reflected Hitler's determination that his favorite city should serve as the "Capital of German Art" during the Third Reich. This role can be seen as compensation for Munich's loss of political clout, a process that continued in the Nazi era despite the Führer's partiality toward his adopted hometown.

In the realm of music, if not in the visual arts, there could be no doubt that Berlin was the German "capital," and its standards of artistic competence remained fairly high despite the departure of some leading figures. Recognizing the importance of music in the German tradition, the Nazis sought to exploit it for their own purposes. Peter Raabe, the second president of the Reichsmusikkammer, declared: "[Music is] to serve a social function, to be clearly defined in subordination to the general aims of National Socialism, and to be denied traditional autonomy." Germans and Jews, it was further argued, could not produce similar musical compositions or even interpret music in the same fashion. As Goebbels proclaimed: "Jewry and German music are opposites; by their very nature they exist in gross contradistinction to each other."

Although it proved difficult for Nazi theorists to define exactly *how* German and Jewish music differed, the regime subjected Jewish musicians to various forms of intimidation based on their supposed alienation from Aryan musical culture. Pressures imposed by the new regime induced four of Berlin's most prominent Jewish musicians to emigrate from Germany in the first months of the Third Reich. Arnold Schönberg, whom the Nazis despised for his atonal music as well as for his race, left for Paris in May 1933 after being dismissed from his teaching position in Berlin.

Kurt Weill also decamped for Paris in spring 1933, leaving behind a newly acquired Berlin house and his former wife, Lotte Lenya, whom he had just divorced. Otto Klemperer, who after his dismissal from the Kroll Opera in 1931 had been conducting at the State Opera, tried to stay in Berlin by proclaiming his "complete agreement with the course of events in Germany." But the Nazis, Hitler in particular, hated him, leaving him little choice but to leave, first for Switzerland and then for America. His colleague Bruno Walter also hoped to stay on in Berlin, but upon learning that his services were no longer required at the Philharmonic he returned to his native Austria, where he remained until 1938. Like so many artist émigrés from Nazi Germany, these four musicians eventually found their way to Los Angeles. Both Walter and Weill prospered in their adopted home. According to Lotte Lenya, whom Weill remarried in exile, her husband avoided the émigré crowd because they were "always talking about the past, how marvelous it was back in Berlin."

Not all of Berlin's major Jewish musicians were forced to flee Germany in the early years of the Third Reich. Fearing that, as one Nazi functionary put it, "our artistic life might soon resemble a giant mortuary," the regime eschewed a wholesale purge in this domain. Among the prominent musical artists who stayed, at least for a time, was Leo Blech, a conductor at the State Opera. Heinz Tietjen, the dramaturg there, insisted that he could not get along without Blech. Moreover, the conductor enjoyed the protection of Hermann Göring, who was intent on retaining high standards in the Prussian cultural empire he oversaw. Blech was even allowed to conduct Wagner, earning a standing ovation for his interpretation of *Die Götterdämmerung* in June 1933. It was not until 1938, when the regime's persecution of Jews became more systematic, that Blech was forced to leave Germany.

Blech was allowed to remain in Berlin because he was a so-called *Günstlingsjude* (favored Jew), but others managed to stay because the process for expelling them from the Reichsmusikkammer, which often precipitated emigration, was cumbersome and sometimes protracted. Musicians were found "unsuitable" for membership on the basis of questionnaires they had to fill out, which could take years. In the meantime, barring intervention from the authorities, they could continue to work.

In addition to bureaucratic inefficiency, the task of weeding out undesirables was deliberately hampered by the Reichsmusikkammer's first president, Richard Strauss, who objected to the entire policy of excluding artists on the basis of race.

Before judging Strauss a paragon of virtue, however, we should note that he accepted his post in the Nazi bureaucracy in order to further his own career; and that by serving the Nazis he helped provide them with much needed cultural legitimacy. During his brief tenure as president of the Reichsmusikkammer he seesawed back and forth between opportunism and efforts to do the right thing by his fellow musicians. He was forced to resign his post in 1935 after the Gestapo discovered that he had written his librettist Stefan Zweig to say that he had taken the Nazi post only to prevent worse things from happening. The deeper reason for his ouster was that his "weakness" on the Jewish question made him impossible as a Nazi cultural bureaucrat. Strauss was happy enough to step down, for he had grown weary of deferring to Goebbels on artistic questions, just as he had once hated toadying to the kaiser. "It is a sad moment," he wrote, "when an artist of my stature has to ask some little upstart of a minister what I may compose and perform. I have joined the ranks of the domestic servants and bottlewashers and am almost envious of my persecuted Jewish friend Stefan Zweig."

Another major musician whose qualified cooperation with the Nazi regime left an enduring stain on his reputation was Wilhelm Furtwängler, the brilliant musical director of the Berlin Philharmonic and the State Opera. Although, like Strauss, he was contemptuous of the Nazi authorities, he consented to become vice president of the Reichsmusikkammer and to stay at his posts in Berlin after Hitler came to power. His expressed reason for staying was to preserve the values of German culture in a perilous time, but he also knew that if he left he was unlikely to find such prestigious posts anywhere else in the world. To his credit, he used his prestige to protect a number of Jewish musicians in the Philharmonic, most notably the concertmaster Simon Goldberg and the cellists Joseph Schuster and Gregor Piatigorsky. As the Nazis' harassment of Jewish musicians grew, Furtwängler wrote a protest letter to Goebbels, who oversaw the Philharmonic, complaining about the regime's anti-Semitic campaign as it applied to music. The grounds for his complaint, however, were pragmatic rather than ethical. "Quotas cannot be placed on music," he wrote, "as they can be for bread and potatoes. If nothing worth hearing is given in concerts, the public will just stay away. For this reason, the quality of music is not merely a matter of ideology. It is a matter of survival." He went on to argue that if the Nazis' campaign against Jewry focused only on those artists who were "rootless and destructive," and who sought to profit "through rubbish and empty virtuosity," the fight would be "justified." Furtwängler's protest was hedged enough that

Wilhelm Fürtwangler and Richard Strauss, 1936

Goebbels ordered it printed in the *Vossische Zeitung* on April 11, 1933. This allowed the minister to convey an illusion of openness without conceding too much ideological ground to a prominent artist who happened to be Hitler's favorite conductor.

Convinced that he enjoyed immunity because of his relationship with Hitler, Furtwängler continued to protest against the regime's cultural dogmatism. In July 1933 he expressed regret over the treatment of Schönberg because the composer was prized by "the Jewish International as one of the most significant musicians of the present." Making him into a "martyr" would only harm the image of Berlin abroad, he argued.

There was no question of reinstating Schönberg, and the Nazi authorities simply ignored Furtwängler's intervention. But they could not turn a blind eye to the conductor's defense of another musician on the Nazis' blacklist, Paul Hindemith. On

March 12, 1934, Furtwängler conducted the premier of three symphonic excerpts from Hindemith's opera *Mathis der Maler*, which brought howls of protest from the nazified press. Alfred Rosenberg denounced the music as kitsch and insisted that the composer, who was married to a Jewess, was unfit to belong to "the highest art institutes of the new Reich." Further performances of *Mathis* were banned. Furtwängler defended Hindemith in the *Deutsche Allgemeine Zeitung*, insisting that no one had done more for the international prestige of German music than this young composer. Many Berliners obviously agreed, for on the evening that Furtwängler's article appeared the audience at the State Opera gave the conductor an extended ovation when he stepped to the podium. Göring, who was in the audience, interpreted the ovation as a challenge to the regime. Seeing an opportunity to strike at Goebbels, who admired both Furtwängler and Hindemith, Göring informed Hitler about the demonstration. Despite his appreciation for the conductor's artistry, Hitler ordered the press to attack Furtwängler. He also insisted on his resignation from the vice presidency of the Reichsmusikkammer. In response, the maestro resigned all his posts and threatened to move to America. Unwilling to lose him, Hitler had Goebbels inform him that if he left he would never be allowed to return. Furtwängler backed down, even issuing a statement that henceforth he would not interfere in the Reich's cultural policy, which he conceded should be made "solely by the Führer . . . and by the expert minister appointed by him." The conductor resumed his post at the Berlin Philharmonic and in 1936 became musical director of the Bayreuth Festival.

The career of Furtwängler's young rival, Herbert von Karajan, showed how quickly an artist could rise if he combined superb technical skill with political opportunism. Born in Austria in 1905, von Karajan joined the Nazi Party in April 1933 in order to smooth his path as an up-and-coming conductor. At that time he was working at the state theater in Ulm, a relatively undistinguished post, but in 1935 he became chief conductor at the Aachen opera. At age twenty-seven, he was the youngest general music director in Germany. He came to the attention of Heinz Tietjen, who brought him to Berlin as guest conductor of the Philharmonic in 1938. His Berlin debut was such a success that he was made a Kapellmeister at the State Opera in the following year. In addition to Tietjen, he cultivated the patronage of Göring, who hoped that his new wunderkind would eclipse Furtwängler in Berlin. Like a Gustav Gründgens of music, von Karajan made excellent use of his contacts. Soon he was challenging Furtwängler for supremacy in Berlin's musical scene. He might have prevailed in this contest were it not for the fact that Hitler considered him an "arrogant fop." Berlin proved barely big enough to accommodate both of these supremely egoistic musicians, and their bitter rivalry pointed up the politicization and Balkanization of the city's cultural life.

In addition to misusing Berlin's renowned musical ensembles for purposes of prestige and propaganda, the Nazi regime founded an orchestra of its own, the National Socialist Symphony Orchestra of the Reich, or NSRSO, as a vehicle to advertise its commitment to high culture. Dressed in brown tailcoats personally designed by Hitler, the NSRSO performed a traditional repertoire of the German Masters. This was a Nazi version of the Boston Pops: easy listening with a message. The band enjoyed much greater popularity in the provinces than in Berlin, whose major soloists refused to perform with it.

While the Nazis' attempt at "popular" orchestral music never made much headway in Berlin, a very different kind of music, jazz, managed to survive in the capital during the Third Reich despite the Nazi leaders' contempt for it. As we have seen, jazz had become well established in the city during the Weimar era—so much so that when the Nazis attacked the perversions of the Kurfürstendamm they included "the death of music in the jazz band." The fact that jazz was an integral part of the invasion of American "nigger culture" made it all the more offensive in Nazi eyes, as did the great popularity in Germany of Jewish-American jazz musicians like George Gershwin and Benny Goodman. Goebbels, who liked to impress his starlets by tinkling on the piano, considered jazz an obscenity. His flunky at the Reichsmusikkammer, Peter Raabe, promised to "remove completely foreign jazz and dance music and to replace it with the works of German composers."

But it was one thing to rail against jazz, quite another to eliminate it—especially in Berlin. After all, the Olympics were coming up in 1936, and it would not do for the German capital to be seen as parochial. Rather than banning jazz outright, the Nazi authorities sought to tame it by expelling the most innovative players (who were often foreign) and by censoring performances in the various jazz venues that were allowed to stay open. Agents of the Reichsmusikkammer combed through the clubs in search of Jews, illegal aliens, and any players lacking the requisite license issued by the chamber. To counter the popularity of jazz broadcasts beamed in from foreign countries, Goebbels allowed some local groups to air their music on the radio. For example, in late 1934 the propaganda minister sanctioned broadcasts by a Nazi-sponsored band called the Golden Seven, which searched for a golden mean between real jazz and the sort of innocuous treacle that prompted young Berliners to break the knobs off their "People's Receivers" dialing back to the BBC. Not surprisingly, the search failed: the Seven's music proved too ersatz for most listeners but "too American" for the authorities, and it went off the air in 1935.

Desperate now to come up with a politically acceptable "German Jazz," the regime sponsored a nationwide contest to identify a band that could swing in lockstep. The final round of the contest, held at the Berlin Zoo in March 1936, featured three regional bands, two that were obviously inept plus a fairly decent group from Hamburg. Most Berliners expected the Hamburgers to win, but the judges, all Nazi hacks, gave first prize to an unknown outfit from Frankfurt because it could make the fox-trot sound like a march. Of course, this band went nowhere, except back to Frankfurt. The authorities eventually abandoned their promotion of nazified jazz, just as they gave up on producing Nazi cabaret. The jazz music that Berliners continued to listen to in the Third Reich was by no means as "hot" as one could hear in New York, but it retained enough soul to disgust the state officials. Fritz Stege, a hard-line cultural bureaucrat, could lament in 1937: "It is true: jazz is still with us, in spite of prohibitions and decrees."

Toward a "Jew-free" Berlin

If certain elements of Weimar culture hung on tenaciously in Berlin during the early years of the Third Reich, so did most of the capital's Jews. The campaign to "aryanize" Berlin's cultural establishment drove away some prominent Jewish artists early on, but the vast majority of the city's sizable Jewish community, which in 1933 numbered 160,564 souls (3.78 percent of the total population), saw fit to remain. Like other groups who were threatened by the new regime, many of Berlin's Jews chose to believe that Nazism was simply a passing storm. "The Nazis will never last," was the hopeful word of the day. In retrospect, such optimism may seem foolhardy, and the Jews who stayed on in Berlin and other German cities were later harshly criticized, especially by pioneering Zionists, for failing to recognize from the outset that they had no future in Nazi Germany. This criticism, while understandable, is unjustified. We must remember that in much of Germany, certainly in Berlin, it was the Nazis, not the Jews (at least not the assimilated native Jews), who were the newcomers, the "foreigners." As the German-American historian Peter Gay, who fled Berlin with his family in 1939, put the matter in his memoir, *My*

German Question: "the gangsters who had taken control of the country were not Germany—*we* were." Recently arrived *Ostjuden*, meanwhile, hoped to find safety in numbers, as did Jews from the German provinces who moved to Berlin in the early years of the Third Reich to escape harsher persecution in their hometowns.

The Nazi regime responded to the Jews' determination to stay put by sharpening discriminatory measures designed to induce emigration. Supposedly in revenge for reports of anti-Jewish persecution in the foreign press, Goebbels called for a Reich-wide boycott of Jewish businesses on April 1, 1933. The campaign was backed by the Kampfbund des gewerblichen Mittelstandes (Fighting Association of the Commercial Middle Class), which hoped to curtail competition from Jewish businesses. Because Berlin had so many thriving Jewish-owned enterprises, the Nazis focused their effort on the capital. Storm trooper thugs scrawled jingles like "Jede

SA man warning Berliners not to patronize a Jewish-owned shop during the Jewish boycott of April 1, 1933

Mark in Judenhand / Fehlt dem deutschen Vaterland (Every mark in a Jew's hand is one less for the fatherland)" on Jewish shop windows and stationed themselves menacingly in doorways. They employed similar tactics at Jewish-run law offices and medical practices. The State Library was closed to Jews, and Jewish students were forbidden to enter the University of Berlin. Litfass Pillars, usually covered with advertisements for plays and concerts, now bore announcements of the boycott. At the Anhalter Railway Station Bella Fromm was shocked to find a group of Brownshirts greeting incoming trains with the cry: "To hell with the Jews! Shameful death to the Jews! We won't have any more Jews!"

The boycott, however, proved a flop, at least in the capital. Many Berliners continued to shop at the stores defaced by anti-Semitic slogans. Whether they did this out of protest against the Nazis, or out of a determination to get the best bargains, is impossible to know. Perhaps in many cases it was a bit of both. In any event, Goebbels was not pleased by the response of "his city" to the Nazi campaign. Clearly, the Berliners needed more "enlightenment" with respect to the Jewish menace.

As if to bring this point home, the regime launched a new series of anti-Jewish measures in the wake of the boycott. In Berlin, all Jewish judges were expelled from the court system and replaced by Aryans. Another measure limited the number of Jewish lawyers allowed to practice in the city to the overall percentage of Jews in the population. This amounted to a major cut, since 73.5 percent of the Berlin lawyers were of Jewish descent. As of August 1933, Jewish law students at the university were banned from taking examinations, thereby shutting them out of the profession. Jewish doctors faced similar discrimination. State Commissar Julius Lippert ordered Berlin's hospitals to fire all its Jewish physicians as soon as possible. By October 1933 the medical purge was complete: the only Berlin hospital that still employed Jews was the Jewish Hospital, which was off-limits to gentiles. The city's preparatory secondary schools, the Gymnasia, were ordered to restrict the number of their Jewish pupils to the percentage of Jews in the population. To strike at the *Ostjuden*, the regime made it illegal for noncitizens to sell goods in the streets or to work as artisans. In 1935 the Berlin police chief, Count von Helldorf, ordered the closure of all Jewish stores on the Kurfürstendamm. In that same year the notorious Nuremberg Laws reclassified Jews as "subjects" rather than as citizens, which reduced their social and political rights. Henceforth Jews could not marry or have sexual relations with German citizens, work as domestics in non-Jewish households, or display the national flag. In Berlin, social segregation between Jews and Germans was furthered by limiting Jewish use of public transport to certain hours and by restricting Jews to out-of-the-way, yellow-painted benches in the Tiergarten. These restrictions applied to all persons of "Jewish blood" whether or not they practiced the Jewish religion or even considered themselves Jewish. In Nazi Germany, it was the regime who decided who was a Jew.

Onerous and intimidating as these measures were, they did not provoke the reduction in the Jewish population that the Nazis had hoped for. In Berlin the number of departing Jews was offset by continuing immigration from the provinces. The Nazi leadership, especially Goebbels, was infuriated by this development, but the regime hesitated to institute even harsher anti-Semitic measures at this point because the country was about to host the 1936 Olympic Games, which offered an opportunity to show the world that Nazi Germany, contrary to many reports in the foreign press, was a humane and civilized place. For Berlin, which was to hold the summer games (the winter events were to take place in Garmisch-Partenkirchen), the spectacle could showcase the Nazi capital as a bastion of order, cleanliness, technological progress, cultural sophistication, social harmony, and rollicking good cheer.

Hitler's Games

The decision to award the 1936 Olympic Games to Germany had been made in 1930 and confirmed at an International Olympic Committee (IOC) meeting in Barcelona the following year. With the rise of the Nazis, however, many in the international sport world questioned this choice. During the 1932 Summer Games, held in Los Angeles, the Belgian president of the IOC, Count Henri de Baillet-Latour, asked a German IOC member to query Hitler regarding his stance on the games. Hitler replied that he contemplated Germany's hosting of the event "with great interest." Yet once the Nazis were in power reservations about allowing the games to take place in Germany increased. As part of its anti-Semitic campaign, the Nazi regime banned Jews from German sports clubs and forbade them to try out for the Olympic teams. The widely respected head of Germany's Olympic Committee, Theodor Lewald, was dismissed from his post because he was half Jewish; his replacement was Reichssportführer Hans von Tschammer und Osten, a Nazi hack whose only connection to sport was his ability to sit handsomely on a horse. These actions prompted demands from some quarters to remove the games from Germany, to boycott them if they were held there, or to cancel them entirely, as had been the case in 1916. Sweden, Holland, Czechoslovakia, and Spain openly threatened to send no teams to Germany (in the end, only the Spanish Republic and Soviet Russia carried through with a boycott).

Initially, the United States played a prominent role in the protest movement. In November 1933 the American Amateur Athletic Union voted to boycott the German games unless Germany changed its policy vis-à-vis Jewish athletes. Avery Brundage, head of the American IOC, raised the possibility of moving the summer games to Rome or Tokyo. Fearful of losing the games, the Germans revoked their ban on Jewish participation on German teams. In June 1934 the national IOC nominated twenty-one Jewish athletes for Olympic training camps. It also invited Helene Mayer, a half-Jewish fencer who had won a gold medal in the 1928 games, to join the German team. These concessions pacified America's Brundage, who now became a passionate supporter of the German games, dismissing lingering opposition as "anti-Olympic" or "Communist-inspired." General Charles Sherrill, an influential member of the American IOC, also declared himself satisfied with the German posture after Mayer had been named to the team. He did not insist that Germany add any more Jews, saying that America had no more business pressing Germany on its Jews than Germany would have in telling America how to treat its Negroes. Anyway, he added, "there was never a prominent Jewish athlete in history."

Meanwhile, on-site plans for the summer games in Berlin were proceeding at a furious pace. The local organizers were determined to put on the most spectacular and best-run games ever. To this end, construction crews thoroughly transformed the western part of the city, putting in new streets, subways, and elevated train lines in addition to elaborate sporting facilities. The most imposing of the new buildings was the main stadium, the Reichssportfeld, the largest structure of its kind to date. The road leading to the entrance of the stadium was lined with monumental statues designed by the pro-Nazi sculptors Arno Breker and Josef Thorak. The area surrounding the stadium was as big as the entire city had been in 1680. A ten-mile route running from the Alexanderplatz to the sporting complex, embracing Unter den Linden and the Charlottenburger Chausee, was dubbed the "Via Triumphalis." It was along this route that the Olympic Torch, designed by German chemists to burn vigorously in wind and rain, traveled its last miles from Greece to the German

Runner carrying the Olympic Torch through the Brandenburg Gate, 1936

capital. On its final leg it was carried by a flaxen-haired Berliner named Schilgen. As he approached the stadium to light the Olympic Flame (a Hollywood touch added for the L.A. Games), SA and SS men raised their arms in the Hitler-salute.

While Nazi iconography was plainly visible around Berlin during the games, signs of the regime's anti-Semitic policies were hardly in evidence. The yellow benches in the Tiergarten had been painted over. Notices forbidding Jewish access to public buildings had been removed. *Der Stürmer*, the Third Reich's most scurrilous anti-Semitic newspaper, was missing from local newsstands. Members of Nazi organizations were instructed to desist from Jew-baiting in the streets during the games.

Additional measures to impress foreign visitors with Berlin's civility included a roundup of beggars and known con-men, as well as a prohibition on price-gouging. Buildings were scrubbed of soot, new lime trees were planted along Unter den Linden, and the Quadriga atop the Brandenburg Gate was regilded. Aware that many guests harbored hopes of finding something of the old "decadent" Berlin, the Nazi authorities reinstated some 7,000 prostitutes whom they had banned from the streets as part of their effort to "clean up" Berlin. Local women, moreover, were allowed to wear their hemlines five centimeters higher than the regime had heretofore permitted. The Nazis also reopened a number of homosexual bars, and Heinrich Himmler instructed the Gestapo not to arrest any foreign gentlemen for transgressing Paragraph 175 of the penal code without first securing written permission from him. *Der Angriff* admonished its readers: "We must be more charming than the Parisians, more easygoing than the Viennese, more vivacious than the Romans, more cosmopolitan than London, and more practical than New York."

The Nazi government, however, had no intention of allowing visitors to forget that Germany was under new management. In addition to plastering Berlin with swastikas, the organizers put out a guide to the city advising guests to visit the Wilhelmstrasse to see where Hitler worked. "Today," bragged the brochure, "the Wilhelmstrasse is once again the center of a goal-oriented national government. It harbors the office of the man whom every visitor wants to see above all: Adolf Hitler!" While touting the city's Christian churches, the Olympic guide carefully omitted any mention of its many synagogues. Jew-baiting was put under wraps during the games, but so were the Jews.

When not watching the Olympic competition or touring the Wilhelmstrasse, visitors could attend dozens of cultural and social events designed to remind them that Berlin was a cosmopolitan and sophisticated metropolis. Very special guests were invited to a garden party at Göring's palatial residence, which, as Ambassador Dodd could not help noticing, was "far larger and more elaborately fitted out than the White House in Washington." Göring's nocturnal party was lit by spotlights stationed on neighboring roofs and by hundreds of lights suspended from trees. "There was hardly anything that modern inventors could have added," commented Dodd. Göring's rival Goebbels, however, threw an even more lavish party on the beautiful Phaueninsel west of the city. Guests reached the island via a newly constructed pontoon bridge and then passed through an "aisle of honor" formed by young female dancers holding torches. The whole place was done up like a movie set and stocked with starlets from UFA, one of whom, the bountiful Lida Baarova, was Goebbels's latest mistress. Although Ambassador Dodd, again dutifully in attendance, was unsettled by fireworks explosions "of a kind that suggested war," he was impressed by the gaudy magnificence of Goebbels's bash, which he guessed "must have cost 40,000 marks of government money." Throughout the games Berlin's museums mounted special exhibitions and its musical ensembles performed gala concerts. For the opening ceremony Richard Strauss directed an all-star orchestra and chorus in renditions of the German anthem, the *Horst Wessel Lied*, and a new "Olympic Hymn" he had written for the occasion.

Some foreign reporters remained skeptical about the show of civility they witnessed during the games. When a group of drunken Brownshirts, forgetting their instructions regarding open displays of anti-Semitism, roamed the streets bawling "Wenn die Olympiade sind vorbei / Schlagen wir die Juden zu brei (When the Olympics are over, we'll beat the Jews to a pulp)," these journalists were not surprised. William Shirer, who reported for CBS News, understood that the Nazis had "put up a very good front for the general visitors." Most of the foreign press, however, was taken in by the friendly atmosphere and organizational virtuosity displayed during the games. Commenting on the American team's reception in Berlin, both the *New York Times* and the *New York Herald Tribune* spoke of a warm welcome surpassing anything the Americans had ever experienced at an Olympic venue. Frederic T. Birchall of the *Times* praised the Olympic stadium as a structure "built for the ages, revealing the far-sighted vision" of its creators. The *British Daily Mail* declared that no festival could be more splendid than the one taking place in Berlin, and gushed that visitors would find the city "magical." The *World of Sports*, also British, proposed that if visitors could forget their "prejudices" and the "rumors" they had heard about Nazi Germany, they would take away an experience of "lasting good" based on "the friendship of the sporting youth of the world." Even journalists from France, which had recently been shocked by Germany's remilitarization of the Rhineland, expressed respect for the cordiality of the German hosts, noting with particular gratitude that Berliners had shouted "Viva la France!" when the French team arrived.

Like the foreign journalists, most foreign visitors to the Berlin games seem to have gotten the impression that the regime had meant them to—namely, that Nazi Berlin was orderly and not nearly so repressive as many critics claimed. Among the prominent American guests, Charles Lindbergh showed himself a Berlin-booster as he toured local airplane factories and sprinted around a practice track at the Olympic Village. The writer Thomas Wolfe fell in love with the city during his Olympic visit, especially since some of the locals mistook him for a competitor. At one point, thoroughly drunk, he staggered down a street hugging the trees and proclaiming his admiration for everything German. He told a reporter for the *Berliner Tageblatt* that if "there were no Germany, it would be necessary to invent one." He pronounced the Olympic stadium to be "the most beautiful and most perfect in its design that had ever been built." As a patriotic American, however, Wolfe rooted for the American team, including its sensational Negro sprinter and jumper, Jesse Owens. "Owens was black as tar," said the Southern writer later, "but what the hell, it was our team and I thought he was wonderful. I was proud of him, so I yelled."

Wolfe's mention of Owens calls to mind the famous story of Hitler's refusal to shake the athlete's hand after his four splendid victories. The story is a myth. To avoid just such an embarrassing possibility, Hitler decided in advance not to congratulate *any* of the athletes publicly. (After the games, he privately honored the German victors.) Owens himself later insisted that Hitler had not been inhospitable. He claimed that he had caught the Führer's eye once in the stadium and that Hitler had waved to him. Owens added: "I think the writers showed bad taste in criticizing the man of the hour in Germany."

Owens's four gold medals were not enough to give America the overall victory in the 1936 Berlin Olympics. With fifty-six medals, the United States came in a distant second to the German team, which won eighty-nine medals, thirty-three of them gold. No doubt the German organizers had taken pains to swell the number of German victories by adding new events, like women's gymnastics and yachting, in which Germany was especially strong. Nonetheless, the host team's victory was impressive—particularly in light of the fact that the Germans had not yet discovered blood-doping.

The Berlin Olympics was the first sporting contest to be televised, though not yet "up close and personal," and not yet in pictures clear enough to be discernible to the tiny viewing audience. A much more celebrated and lasting document of the games was produced by Hitler's court filmmaker, Leni Riefenstahl. As she had with *Triumph of the Will*, Riefenstahl received her commission to make a film about the Berlin Olympics directly from Hitler. The Reich government financed the project and provided extensive organizational support. When the games opened, Riefenstahl was ready with cameras stationed all over Berlin and the Reichssportfeld. Again, her filming techniques were innovative. For example, for aerial shots she sent up balloons fitted with tiny cameras, much like the blimps that would later become ubiquitous at major American sporting events. To film the crew race at Grünau she employed a Luftwaffe zeppelin, but it sprang a leak and dropped into the lake. She also installed cameras in pits in the stadium (Jessie Owens narrowly escaped falling into one), had the marathoners carry cameras during training, and even put cameras on the saddles of competing equestrians. When darkness prevented good shots of the pole vault, she persuaded some of the competitors to jump again for her cameras on the following day. She also persuaded the decathlon champion, the American Glenn Morris, to repeat his 1,500-meter sprint, which she had failed to get on film. Morris was obliging because he was deeply smitten with Riefenstahl. According to her memoir, after one of his victories he accosted her in the stadium, tore off her blouse, and fondled her breasts. She was taken aback but not put off. With his muscular frame and virile good looks, Morris was her kind of man. They embarked on a steamy affair that ended only with Morris's return to America. "Never before had I experienced such a passion," she wrote later.

The resulting film, *Olympia,* is an homage to the male body in action (not surprising, given Riefenstahl's inclinations). The work does not emphasize German victories and does not come across as particularly nationalistic. Yet it is a brilliant propaganda piece nonetheless. Nazi leaders, especially Hitler, appear in the film solely as benevolent sports lovers, cheering when the Germans win, graciously shrugging off defeats. In its technical virtuosity, *Olympia* is a celebration of German creativity and initiative. The German papers made much of the fact that Los Angeles, supposedly the film capital of the world, had produced no film on the 1932 Olympics. As for the city of Berlin itself, it is depicted in *Olympia* as a happy and harmonious place, a *Volksgemeinschaft* open to the world.

The Nazi capital emerged rather differently in another festival a year later: the commemoration of the 700th anniversary of the founding of Berlin. The Hitlerites still had their doubts about their capital: *Der Angriff* frankly admitted in October 1936 that the Nazis had "forced themselves" on Berlin because the majority of the inhabitants had not taken to National Socialism "voluntarily." Thus the regime did not put nearly as much effort into Berlin's birthday party as into the Olympics. The

The German State Library on Unter den Linden decked out for Berlin's 700th anniversary celebration

budget was relatively low, and there were no special preparations for foreign visitors, who were few in number. The focus was on Berlin as the capital of the Nazi Reich, as a uniquely German *Heimat.* Sketchy historical exhibitions betrayed a lack of genuine respect for Berlin's history and traditions, save for those aspects that the Nazis could exploit to their own advantage. Hitler did not even bother to attend the birthday festivities; instead he went to the Wagner festival in Bayreuth. Göring also skipped the affair in order to go on vacation. Goebbels was left to carry the flag for the party. The municipality of Berlin had recently presented its *Gauleiter* (district leader) with a log cabin on a nearby lake. Here, according to the officials' unctuous commentary, "after the strain of his daily work serving the people and the Reich, [Goebbels could] find peace, relaxation, and a place to collect his thoughts." Despite such generosity, Goebbels was not particularly enthusiastic about leading the 700-year celebrations; he cared about Berlin's future, not its past. He sponsored a commemorative parade in which the army played a prominent role—an ominous sign of the direction in which the Nazi regime planned to take the German nation and its capital.

Slouching towards Germania

The Nazi leaders' distaste for Berlin as it stood in the mid-1930s was reflected in their determination to physically transform the city into a capital worthy of the role they expected it to play in coming generations. Berlin was not the only German city earmarked for extensive renovation under the Nazis, but the reconstruction planned for the capital was more far-reaching than anywhere else, even Munich. Of course, the aspiration to reinvent Berlin was nothing new—earlier national leaders had also sought to remake the city—but the Nazi concept was distinguished by a plan to replace the entire city center with a new political stage set of monumental proportions. Berlin would be reborn as "Germania"—the most grandiose capital in the world.

In addition to making Berlin grand, the Nazis saw their urban renewal of the capital as a means to combat their old enemies, the Socialists and Communists. They would "renew" the traditional Red neighborhoods by uprooting their inhabitants and scattering them to the margins of the city. As one party spokesman explained, this would effectively rid the inner city of "asocial and traitorous elements."

Adolf Hitler, who had been fascinated with architecture since his days in Vienna, personally supervised the Nazi plan for Berlin's urban renewal. On September 19, 1933, during a discussion of ways to improve communication between the northern and southern parts of the city, Hitler proposed a new north-south road to complement the east-west axis running through the Brandenburg Gate. He wanted to ensure that ongoing schemes for Berlin's reconstruction were appropriate to "the creation of a capital city of hitherto undreamed-of display . . . [to the creation of] a sublime metropolis."

The Nazis' earliest buildings in Berlin, however, were designed as much for function as for display. Their first major project was an expansion of the Reichsbank (National Bank), which yielded a complex whose long curved facade was rather austere save for the inevitable Nazi eagles. Among the architects who competed for this project were the Bauhaus veterans Mies van der Rohe and Walter Gropius, which suggests that at this point there was no clear National Socialist architectural aesthetic. In 1935/36, when Germany reintroduced military conscription, a huge new building went up on the Wilhelmstrasse: the Reichsluftfahrtministerium (Reich Air Ministry). Designed by Ernst Sagebiel, a pupil of Heinrich Tessenow, the structure was meant to provide much-needed space for a new min-

Model of Hitler's planned north-south axis, including the Arch of Triumph and the domed Hall of the People

istry that was expanding along with the Nazis' military ambitions. Master of this domain was Air Minister Hermann Göring, who ensured that the 400,000-square-foot complex had plenty of heroic reliefs on its facade and in its marbled hallways. Berliners joked that Göring's new quarters reflected the minister's motto: "Pure and simple, and hang the expense." Berlin's civilian airport, Tempelhof, underwent an extensive facelift and expansion in the mid-1930s. Now boasting the largest airport on the continent, Berlin billed itself as the "air hub of Europe." The city's claim to technological superiority was buttressed by a series of new industrial exhibition halls at the Funkturm (Radio Tower), and by an all-purpose building called the Deutschlandhalle, which gave Berlin more exhibition space than any other city in Europe. In addition to serving useful functions, these projects provided jobs for thousands of construction workers, helping thereby to ease the problem of unemployment.

The Reich Air Ministry Building (Göring's headquarters), 1937

These early buildings did not suit Hitler's concept of grandiosity. Ignoring Berlin's real needs, which were for more low-cost housing and retail space, Hitler sketched plans for representational buildings and roads that would dwarf not only the city's existing public buildings but also the great monuments of other world capitals, past and present. The core of his concept, which he began to elaborate in late 1933, involved two gargantuan structures, an arch of triumph and a domed assembly hall, to be connected by his north-south avenue slicing through the center of the city. The projected Assembly Hall, Berlin's answer to St. Peter's, would be many times larger than that structure, just as Berlin's planned Arch of Triumph, 386 feet high and 550 feet wide, would make Paris's equivalent seem Lilliputian. The North-South Axis, while modeled on the Champs-Elysées, would be about seventy feet wider and two and one-half times as long. In July 1934 Hitler proposed to Berlin's municipal authorities an annual budget of 60 million reichsmarks for the next twenty years to complete this scheme; much of the funding was to come from the city's own budget.

Mayor Lippert and his colleagues, though themselves no paragons of architectural taste, were horrified by this plan and sought to replace it with a more modest venture. Calling Lippert "an incompetent, an idiot, a failure, a zero," Hitler had him removed from all responsibility for the reconstruction of Berlin and brought in a young man with whom he believed he could work harmoniously: Albert Speer.

Speer, one of the most complex figures in the leadership of the Third Reich, came from a wealthy Mannheim family that regarded the Nazis as hopelessly plebeian. Befitting his background, Speer was a reserved and diffident fellow who would never think of pummeling Jews in the streets. Yet as an architectural student in Munich and Berlin he became so fascinated with the Nazis that he joined the party, and also the SA, in 1931. He later insisted that this had nothing to do with "politics," as if the Nazis were some kind of hobby club. In fact, from early on Speer was determined to capture Nazi ideals in mortar and stone, though it took him some time to find a consistent "voice." His first political commission in Berlin was to renovate a villa in Grunewald for a Nazi district headquarters. He used Bauhaus-inspired wallpaper even though he feared this might be seen as "communistic." To his relief, the district leader assured him that the Nazis would "take the best they could get from everywhere, even from the Communists." Next, Speer converted a Schinkel-designed palace on the Voßstrasse for use as the Nazi Gauleitung in Berlin. Pleased with the work, Goebbels commissioned him to renovate the propaganda ministry as well as his private townhouse in the city. The speed with which Speer completed these projects impressed Hitler, who was looking for an architect who could make big things happen in minimal time. In the wake of the Night of the Long Knives, he had decided to move the top leaders of the SA to Berlin so he could keep an eye on them. To house them, he wanted to rebuild the Borsig Palace. He assigned the project to Speer, telling him to start at once. When Speer objected that Papen's office was in the Borsig Palace, and that the vice-chancellor would need time to move out, Hitler told him to start working with no consideration for Papen. Speer instructed his workmen to create as much noise and dust as possible, thereby expediting Papen's departure. Hitler was delighted, making jokes about "dusty bureaucrats." During the work, Speer noticed a pool of dried blood on the floor where Papen's assistant, Herbert von Bose, had been gunned down in the Night of the Long Knives. He simply looked away—his response to unpleasant realities during the rest of his career in the Third Reich.

Having passed the Borsig test, Speer now received a much bigger assignment—that of designing a new complex for the Nazi rallies at Nuremberg. For this project he hit on the style that was to become his trademark: a pumped-up neoclassicism. He proposed a knockoff of the Pergamum Altar: "a mighty flight of stairs topped and enclosed by a long colonnade, flanked on both sides by stone abutments." To make space for this monstrous structure, Speer blew up a streetcar depot. Its unsightly wreckage inspired him to propound his "theory of ruin value," according to which all Nazi buildings should be constructed with materials and techniques that would make them look as noble as ancient Roman or Greek ruins when they themselves fell into decay in the distant future. Some Nazi leaders were scandalized by the thought that Third Reich artifacts might ever decay, but Hitler, a Romantic in such matters, gave orders that henceforth all major buildings of the Reich were to be erected in keeping with this "law of ruins."

With his construction of the Nuremberg rally grounds and his staging of the 1934 Party Congress, in which he employed antiaircraft spotlights to create a "Cathedral of Light" around the field, Speer found himself an architectural celebrity, a Nazi Schinkel at age twenty-nine. Unable to tolerate that Speer had worked for Goebbels but not yet for him, Göring hired him to renovate his own palazzo, even though it had just been refurbished. There was no doubt, however, that Speer was Hitler's man above all. The Führer clearly saw an idealized image of himself in the tall, handsome young architect. He decided in 1936 that Speer must be the one to undertake "the greatest of all plans," the reconstruction of Berlin. On January 30, 1937, the fourth anniversary of his coming to power, Hitler named Speer Generalbauinspektor (General Building Inspector) for the Construction of Berlin. The architect would report directly to the Führer, who promised to clear all obstacles in his path. Hitler also made clear that he would brook no small-mindedness in this endeavor. As he told Speer: "Berlin is a big city, but not a real metropolis. Look at Paris, the most beautiful city in the world. Or even Vienna. Those are cities with grand style. Berlin is nothing but an unregulated accumulation of buildings. We must surpass Paris and Vienna."

In discussions with Speer over the next months and years, Hitler steadily expanded on his original ideas. In addition to his domed hall and arch of triumph, he envisaged a new city hall modeled on the neogothic pile in Vienna, but "more beautiful than Vienna's, no doubt about that." He also demanded a new Chancellery, since the existing building was "fit only for a soap company." He would, he noted, "be holding extremely important conferences in the near future," for which he needed "grand halls and salons which will make an impression on people, especially on the smaller dignitaries." When entering the Chancellery, he explained, "one should have the feeling that one is visiting the master of the world." He placed the entire Voßstrasse at Speer's disposal for this project, insisting that it be completed by January 10, 1939. To overcome the municipal administration's reluctance to help finance this and other Nazi works, he proposed threatening to build an entirely new capital elsewhere, perhaps on the plains of Mecklenberg. "You'll see how the Berliners come to life at the threat that the national government may move out," he told Speer.

As Speer and his team took over Hitler's plans for the reconstruction of Berlin, they scrupulously retained the original concept's grandiosity while adding some practical ideas of their own, such as the consolidation of Berlin's railway stations into two northern and southern terminals, and the opening of new urban areas in the east to accommodate the thousands of citizens whose homes in the center were scheduled to be razed. The team planned to construct new airports outside the city to relieve pressure on Tempelhof, which they hoped eventually to convert into an amusement park, like Copenhagen's Tivoli. In the west, bordering the Olympic grounds, Speer planned a huge new university and medical quarter. Hitler went along with these proposals, but he could not work up much enthusiasm for them. All he wanted to talk about was his representational structures, along with plans for new ministries, showrooms for German industry, luxury hotels, and a grand new opera house. Looking back years later on Hitler's vision, Speer found it "rather sinister that in the midst of peacetime . . . [the Führer] was planning buildings representative of an imperial glory which could be won only by war."

This insight should have come earlier, for the most obvious aspect of Hitler's scheme, aside from its derivative monumentality, was its bellicosity, its intimate connection with the Nazi drive for a new German empire. Ironically, it was just this ambition for a new empire that ultimately made the realization of Hitler's Germania impossible, since the demands of war required postponement of most of the building projects. Aside from the Neue Reichskanzlei (New Chancellery) and three large Flak bunkers, the only major part of the Germania program to be completed before the war began was an autobahn ring around the city. Perhaps fittingly, this belt would constitute Berlin's outer line of defenses during the Russian offensive in 1945.

"Tempo, Tempo!"—Berlin Readies for War

While Speer was honing Hitler's plans for a new imperial capital, Hitler himself was laying the diplomatic and military groundwork for Germany's future empire. As in the Kaiserreich, Berlin was the focal point of Germany's quest for world power. It was also the primary arena in which, with the Olympics safely over, the Nazis could reveal more brutally and systematically than ever the domestic dimensions of their ideological agenda.

In September 1937 Mussolini arrived in Berlin on a state visit. He had drifted into his embrace with Hitler following his 1935 invasion of Ethiopia, which had prompted the League of Nations to impose mild sanctions against Italy. Before this contretemps with the West, Mussolini had been a vociferous critic of Hitler, calling the Führer a "horrible sexual degenerate." He feared that the Führer intended to annex Austria (which he eventually did) and tear the South Tyrol from Italy (which he did not). Mussolini had also resented Hitler for challenging his claim to being the biggest bully on the European block. Now, however, as he celebrated the recently concluded "Rome-Berlin Axis" with his visit to the German capital, the Italian leader was all smiles for his new friends. Berlin, in turn, put on a splendid reception for its guest. The route down which Il Duce drove, the "Via Triumphalis," was decorated with pylons displaying alternately the ax and bundle of fascism and the eagle of the Reich. Along Unter den Linden hundreds of columns capped with eagles towered over the recently planted lime trees. At a monster rally near the Olympic Stadium Hitler praised Mussolini as one of those rare geniuses who "are not made by history but make history themselves." He promised that the Italian and German nations together would vanquish the Marxist evil. In halting, barely intelligible German, Mussolini replied by thanking Germany for standing by it in its crusade to bring civilization to Ethiopia. The friendship between Germany and Italy, he declared, would soon change the world. "Tomorrow all Europe will be fascist; one hundred fifteen million men will arise, joined together in an unshakable faith." Just as he said this, a storm erupted and drenched the crowd. France's ambassador, André François-Poncet, later commented: "The very elements warned mankind of what evils the meeting of the dictators was to let loose upon it."

Those evils were not long in coming. In March 1938 Hitler annexed Austria, bringing his native country "home to the Reich." Mussolini meekly accepted this fait accompli, for which the Führer expressed his eternal gratitude. Next, Hitler began putting pressure on Czechoslovakia, insisting that its westernmost region, the Sudetenland, which harbored many ethnic Germans, be joined to the Reich. When the Western powers, which heretofore had reacted to Hitler's transgressions against the Versailles system with mild protests, expressed opposition to the proposed dismemberment of Czechoslovakia, Hitler was furious; war appeared imminent. In Berlin, among other signs of war preparation, an antiaircraft gun was installed on the roof of the I. G. Farben building across from the Hotel Adlon. However, war was averted, at least for a time, by the infamous Munich Conference of September 1938, which turned the Sudetenland over to Germany while "guaranteeing" the sanctity of the rest of Czechoslovakia.

In Berlin the Munich agreement was greeted with cheering in the streets. According to William Shirer, Berliners had shown considerable fear when, at the height of the Czech crisis, a motorized division swept down the Wilhelmstrasse. Now they responded with "delirious joy" at the news that Hitler had once again achieved a foreign policy victory without recourse to arms.

But not everyone was praising the Führer; on the domestic front some of his policies were beginning to occasion resentment and resistance. The Nazi regime's accelerating efforts to "coordinate" the mainstream churches, for example, inspired opposition from certain elements within the clergy and laity. Berlin emerged as a center of religious opposition, especially from the Protestant camp.

A key figure in the Protestant opposition was Martin Niemöller, a former submarine captain who was a pastor in the Berlin district of Dahlem. Alarmed by the Nazis' imposition of an "Aryan paragraph" on the churches, which denied membership in the Christian community to persons of Jewish or other non-Aryan backgrounds, Niemöller formed the Pfarrernotbund (Pastors' Emergency League) to combat racism in the church. The group was careful to call itself "nonpolitical" and to insist that its agenda was purely spiritual. But when Niemöller refused to fill out a questionnaire concerning his own racial background, he was suspended from his position. In response, 600 members of his parish sent telegrams of protest to Reich Bishop Ludwig Müller, the new pro-Nazi head of the Evangelical Church. Hitler personally intervened in the affair, inviting Niemöller to a meeting with him and the church authorities. This resulted in a toe-to-toe confrontation between the pastor and the Führer. When Niemöller continued to preach against the Nazi regime despite warnings to desist, he was packed off to Sachsenhausen as a "personal prisoner of the Führer's."

It must be emphasized that the courageous opposition of Niemöller and other Protestant dissenters like Dietrich Bonhöffer (of whom more below) was by no means typical. The vast majority of Berlin's Protestant community supported the Nazi regime with varying degrees of enthusiasm. In the case of the so-called German Christians, the enthusiasm was very great indeed. They joined the Nazis in condemning "liberalism, Judaism, and Marxism," insisting that it was the Christians' duty to protect the *Volk* against pollution by racial and social inferiors. The German Christians held the majority in every Protestant parish in Berlin except for Dahlem.

A similar pattern of collaboration by the majority and resistance by a minority evolved within Berlin's Catholic community, which constituted only 10 percent of the city's total population. In July 1933 the Hitler regime concluded the Reichskonkordat with the Vatican, which promised the clergy freedom in religious matters in exchange for their political compliance. The chief Vatican negotiator was Papal Nuncio Eugenio Pacelli, who later became Pius XII. As a recent biographer has noted, the treaty that Pacelli helped write represented "a reversal of the situation sixty years earlier, when German Catholics combated and defeated Bismrack's *Kulturkampf* persecutions from the grass roots." Initially, the clergy stuck to its part of the bargain, but increasingly the Nazi regime did not. In 1936 the government banned all Catholic youth groups and mandated Catholic youngsters' participation in the Hitler Youth. Even more grievously, it dissolved all the confessional schools. Catholic papers were forbidden to publish anything but church news. Because some journals ventured beyond this restriction, all the Catholic papers were shut down. Berlin's Bishop Konrad Count von Preysing responded with sermons accusing the regime of violating the Concordat. He received some support from Rome in the form of a papal encyclical, "Mit brennender Sorge" (1937), which chastised the Nazi state for its attacks on the church and its policies on race. Claiming that this papal initiative violated the Concordat, the regime prohibited publication of the encyclical and announced that it would no longer honor its agreement with the church. To show it meant business, the government brought trumped-up charges against a number of priests and nuns for "crimes against morality."

The church fought these measures as best it could, but it carefully limited its struggle to the defense of Catholic interests and individuals. As an institution, the German Catholic church did not take a public stand against Nazi persecution of the Jews. True, a small group of Catholics around Prelate Bernard Lichtenberg at Berlin's St. Hedwig's Cathedral established a "Committee for the Assistance of Catholic Non-Aryans." As the name suggests, however, this initiative was limited to converts to Catholicism. Its primary goal was to help impecunious Catholics of Jewish background assemble the financial wherewithal to emigrate.

Nazi pressure on the Jews of Germany increased dramatically in 1937/38, as the regime stepped up its efforts to drive these people from their country, minus their wealth. In March 1938 the Nazis imposed the "Law Regarding the Legal Status of Jewish Communities," which deprived Jewish congregations of legal protection and forbade them from taxing their own members, thereby reducing them to penury. Shortly thereafter, Jews were ordered to report the value of their property to the regime, a measure obviously intended to make it easier for the government to confiscate their holdings. When Jews applied to emigrate they were required to inform the authorities about what they intended to take with them; valuables of any consequence had to stay in the Reich.

These regulations applied to native Jews whom the Reich wanted to be rid of. As for nonnative Jews, in autumn 1938 the regime suddenly deported some 17,000 Polish Jews to Poland, allowing them to take along no more than ten marks and a few basic necessities. Since Poland at first would not accept the deportees, they were stranded for days in a no-man's-land along the border, without food and shelter. German-born Jews who watched the Poles being rounded up and deported saw a grim preview of their own fate—though many did not yet realize it.

The situation for all Jews in the Reich suddenly became much clearer on the night of November 9/10, 1938, which has gone down in history as Reichskristallnacht, or "Night of the Broken Glass." Having decided that a demonstration of sweeping and spectacular violence was needed to prod the Jews to leave the country, Hitler and his aides were looking for a suitable pretext to launch a modern-day pogrom. This was conveniently delivered with the assassination in Paris of a German embassy official, Ernst vom Rath, by a young Polish Jew who was distraught over the expulsion of his parents from Germany in the recent deportation. When news of Rath's death reached Berlin, the top Nazi officials were assembled in Munich to commemorate the anniversary of the Beer Hall Putsch, as they did every year. After consulting with Hitler, Goebbels declared in a speech on November 9 that if the Rath assassination inspired "spontaneous anti-Jewish riots," the Jews had only themselves to blame.

There was nothing spontaneous about what happened next. Acting on instructions from Goebbels, on the night of November 9/10 Nazi thugs, mainly from the SA, began attacking Jews and Jewish property in cities and villages across the Reich. They burned synagogues, wrecked shops, beat, raped, and murdered Jewish citizens. Some ninety-one Jews died in the attacks, over one hundred synagogues were burned, and about 7,500 shops lay in ruins, their shattered windows scattered in crystals on the sidewalks (hence the oft-used euphemistic term, "crystal night"). About 20,000 Jews were summarily arrested and carted off to concentration camps. Throughout the action, police forces made no effort to intervene, except occasionally to curtail looting; fire departments prevented blazes from spreading to non-Jewish properties, but otherwise kept their hoses coiled.

Although the attacks were especially vicious in rural areas, Berlin, regarded hitherto as something of a refuge for Jews from the provinces, was also very hard hit. In preparation for the action there, Police Chief von Helldorf ordered that gas and telephone lines to Jewish houses and shops be cut off. Barricades were placed around the areas to be targeted. Then, at 2:00 A.M., SA groups received the signal to embark on their "spontaneous" rampage. They immediately set fire to nine of Berlin's twelve synagogues, among them the famed temple in Fasanenstrasse, which was completely gutted. The huge "New Synagogue" in Oranienburgerstrasse, by contrast, received only light damage because a courageous lone policeman held the SA at bay. A handsome red brick synagogue in Wörthstrasse in Prenzlauer Berg was spared because it stood next to valued non-Jewish buildings, including a brewery. Jewish-owned shops around town were stripped of their wares and then wrecked. SA men carried off the loot, joined by townspeople who could not pass up such a bargain. Other targets included Jewish aid organizations and the Zionist headquarters on Meineckestrasse, which was reduced to "splintered wood and mounds of torn records." Thugs invaded Jewish mansions in Grunewald to arrest the men, rape the women, and collect the contents. The Jews who were pulled out of their suburban villas that night belonged to the hundreds of Berliners who were packed off to "protective custody," mainly in Sachsenhausen. In the late af-

Burned-out interior of the Fasanenstrasse Synagogue in the wake of the Night of the Broken Glass

ternoon of November 10, Goebbels went on the radio to announce that the anti-Jewish action had accomplished its "desired and expected purpose," and was now over.

That morning young Peter Gay rode his bicycle on an inspection tour through "a city that seemed to have been visited by an army of vandals." The facades of the Jewish-owned stores along Tauentzienstrasse "had been efficiently reduced to rubble, their huge display windows shattered, their mannequins and merchandise scattered on the sidewalk." Over on Olivaerplatz, a ladies' clothing shop owned by Gay's uncle had obviously provided a night of entertainment for some Nazi thugs:

> Its waist-high glass counters holding stockings, gloves and ladies' underwear had proved irresistible; they had been smashed and their contents savagely torn to pieces. But the wall cabinets had given the wrathful German people avenging the death of vom Rath even more entertaining targets. One of the cabinets, well over five feet tall, with an array of shallow glass-fronted drawers, had held innu-

> merable fine shadings of thread; the other, quite as high and as minutely subdivided, had contained buttons, with a sample sewn onto the front of each drawer. Both had been ripped from the wall and emptied pell-mell, their contents mingling with glass fragments strewn all over the floor. It was as though the store had been swept by a hurricane.

Scholars have suggested that Reichskristallnacht was a "degradation ritual," a sadistic rite designed to let the Jews know that they were pariahs who could expect no protection from the state or their fellow citizens. Although intended primarily to intimidate the Jews, it served also to warn gentile Germans that they had best not show any sympathy for these outcasts. Fortunately for young Peter Gay and his mother, his father got the point. As a consequence of the pogrom, "a determination was born in him to do anything, no matter how illegal, to get the three of us away from the German nightmare."

The response among the capital's non-Jewish citizenry to this night of terror was mixed, as it was in other German cities. Some Berliners joined in the action, or at least took obvious delight in the Jews' distress. Inge Deutschkron, a young Jewish girl living in a fashionable Berlin quarter, recalled a barber calling out to her father "Hey, you Jew!" as Herr Deutschkron inspected the damage to the Fasanenstrasse synagogue. Inge's mother, unintimidated, wheeled on the barber and yelled, "You damn swine!" prompting admonishments from her husband to "keep quiet, for God's sake." Ursula von Kardorff saw some Nazi thugs beat up a young girl who had taken pictures of the pillaging. Nobody intervened to help her. Foreign journalists who witnessed the action reported that some citizens cried "Down with the Jews," while others seemed "deeply disturbed by the events." There were, in fact, plenty of expressions of outrage and shame. Watching the looting, a janitor was heard to remark: "They must have emptied the insane asylums and penitentiaries to find people who'd do things like that!" One group of elderly Berliners fell back in horror when SA looters offered them bottles of wine that they had just stolen from a Jewish-owned restaurant. A gentile shop owner could not understand why the police did not stop some children from throwing stones through the windows of a synagogue: "After all, it is private property."

Expressions like this (and one could quote many more) suggest that much of the public dismay over the Night of the Broken Glass probably derived less from sympathy for the Jews than from outrage over the hooliganism of the perpetrators.

These actions challenged deeply entrenched ideals of order and decorum. Some Berliners reasoned, moreover, that if the Nazis could do this with impunity to the Jews, could they not visit similar indignities on non-Jews? Or might not the Jews themselves find a way someday to punish all Germans for the Nazi crimes? As one woman predicted on the day after Reichskristallnacht: "We Germans will pay dearly for what was done to the Jews last night. Our churches, our houses, and our stores will be destroyed. You can be sure of that."

The Nazi leadership was not uniformly pleased with the pogrom, and not just because of the ambivalent public response. Göring worried that it would be hard to replace all the fine Belgian glass smashed by the looters. Himmler was appalled by the disorderliness of the action, which he was afraid would give Germany a black eye abroad. He also hated to see the SA unleashed so soon after its recent "disciplining" by his SS. Unwilling to hold Hitler responsible for the fiasco, Himmler blamed "that airhead Goebbels," whom he associated with the urban rowdiness and loose morals of the national capital. (Himmler, we should remember, was a Bavarian.)

Hoping to deflect further criticism of the action, especially from abroad, the Nazi leadership argued that the Jews had brought the riot on themselves by inciting "the people's fury." Accordingly, the regime levied a billion mark fine on Germany's Jews to pay for the damages. In Berlin as elsewhere, local Jews were also required to pay for the cleanup following the pogrom. Goebbels called these measures "a nice bloodletting."

But there was more to come. In the immediate aftermath of Reichskristallnacht, the Nazis instituted a new wave of "aryanization" designed to shift Jewish property to gentile hands. In Berlin the hands were eager, if discriminating: 1,200 Jewish firms were put up for auction, but 500 remained unpurchased because, even at rock-bottom prices, they were considered unattractive. Beginning in December 1938 Berlin's Jews were forcibly segregated by a "ghetto decree," which prohibited them from living in the government district or the wealthier western suburbs. One district after another was declared "Jew-free." Jews' movement in the city was further restricted by measures that banned them from theaters, movie houses, concert halls, museums, swimming pools, the exhibition buildings at the Funkturm, the Deutschlandhalle, the Sportpalast, and the Reichssportfeld. Off-limits too was the Wilhelmstrasse from Leipziger Strasse to Unter den Linden; the Voßstrasse from Hermann-Göring-Strasse to the Wilhelmstrasse, and Unter den Linden from the University to the Prussian Armory.

The exterior of Hitler's New Chancellery, designed by Albert Speer, 1939

For many of Berlin's Jews, the Night of the Broken Glass and the subsequent anti-Jewish measures served as a wake-up call, ending the illusion that the Nazis would become more "responsible" once they had been in office for a while, or the hope that the Jews, especially those in Berlin, could remain relatively unmolested if they maintained a low profile. More and more Jews now made the painful decision to leave Germany for one of the foreign lands that would take them—a step made all the more difficult by the tight quotas on Jewish immigration in the Western countries. In early 1937 Berlin still harbored about 140,000 Jews; by July 1939 only about 75,000 remained. Among them was the chief rabbi of the local Jewish community, Leo Baeck. He no longer believed that Berlin constituted a safe haven for Germany's Jews and he no longer advised frightened people to stay in the city. However, as the community's spiritual leader, he felt that he himself must remain at his post to serve those who could not or would not leave. As he told his fellow Berliner, the department store owner Wilfrid Israel: "I will go when I am the last Jew alive in Germany."

On January 8, 1939, two months after the Reichskristallnacht pogrom, Speer's new Chancellery building stood ready for occupancy, forty-eight hours ahead of schedule. It had been completed in record time, an achievement Hitler was very proud of. "This is no longer the American tempo; it has become the German tempo," he declared. But of course "tempo, tempo" had long been the Berlin motto, and there was something very "Berlin" both about the speed with which the Chancellery was built and the grandiosity of its design. Here architectural bombast was carried to extremes. Boasting a front facade some 400 yards long and a main entrance framed in giant square columns, the Neue Reichskanzlei embodied that hyperthyroid neoclassicism which had become Speer's trademark. But if the brutalist exterior sought to impress, the cavernous interior strove to overawe. Visitors arriving for an audience with Hitler drove through the main entrance into a "Court of Honor" ringed with heroic statuary. From there they ascended a staircase leading to a medium-sized reception room, which Hitler rarely used. Passing through double-doors almost seventeen feet high, supplicants entered a long hall clad in mosaic. Another flight of steps took them into a round room with a domed ceiling, from which, with stamina perhaps flagging, they

Hitler's study in the New Chancellery

emerged into a central gallery stretching 480 feet in length. Hitler was delighted with this gallery because it was twice as long as the Hall of Mirrors at Versailles. As we have seen, the Führer loved to contemplate the impression all this would make on visitors: "On the long walk from the entrance to the reception hall they'll get a taste of the power and grandeur of the Third Reich!" he told Speer.

Hitler officially opened the New Chancellery on January 12, 1939, with his annual New Year's reception for the diplomatic corps. On this occasion the Führer was ebulliently hospitable, thrilled to be showing off his Neronian quarters. The foreign guests were reportedly charmed. They would have been less charmed had they been present at the next major function in the Chancellery, a commissioning ceremony for 3,600 lieutenants of the Wehrmacht (as the German military was now called). In his speech to the soldiers, Hitler declared that the German Reich would soon be the dominant power in Europe.

The Nazi leadership spent the following months strengthening Germany's hand in preparation for war. On March 15 Hitler seized the rest of Czechoslovakia on the pretext that "wild excesses" against Germans had taken place in many Czech towns. Although the Western powers made no military moves to reverse this development, they now seemed to grasp that their efforts to placate Hitler had served only to whet his appetite. Britain's ambassador Sir Neville Henderson called the Czech occupation "the final shipwreck" of his appeasement-oriented mission to Berlin, and the British Foreign Secretary Lord Halifax grumbled that while he could "understand Herr Hitler's taste for bloodless victories . . . one of these days he will find himself up against something that will not be bloodless."

Hitler's birthday celebrations in Berlin on April 20 also had a martial air. Tanks and armored personnel carriers rolled down Unter den Linden, while bombers and fighters roared overhead. The Führer's presents included models of ships and planes, and a plaster mockup of his planned Arch of Triumph. On July 26 Berliners practiced an air-raid drill, not perhaps the most hopeful sign for the future. Nor especially hopeful was the introduction in August of ration cards, which imposed weekly limits on meat, sugar, jam, and coffee. Also in August, the Wehrmacht General Staff moved out of its offices in the Bendlerstasse to new headquarters in Zossen, about 25 miles southeast of Berlin. Here they worked on plans for an invasion of Poland, the next course in Hitler's anticipated pan-European banquet.

Although most Berliners did not realize it, the invasion of Poland became a virtual certainty because of an astounding diplomatic development later in August—

the Nazi-Soviet pact. A secret annex to the pact provided for a new partition of Poland by Germany and Russia. For Hitler, this agreement with Stalin ensured that he could attack Poland without having to fear countermeasures from the Soviet Union. Even if the Western powers finally decided that enough was enough and went to war against the Reich, Germany would not have to open hostilities against the West and Russia at the same time, as had been the case in World War I.

Berliners, like most people around the world, were shocked by the Nazi-Soviet pact, but they were also relieved, because they thought it portended yet another reprieve from war. After all, the townspeople reasoned, Hitler would certainly not resort to war if he could get everything he wanted through diplomacy. When the agreement was officially announced on August 24, spontaneous celebrations broke out all over the city.

German troops parade through the Brandenburg Gate following the defeat of France, July 18, 1940

NOW PEOPLE, ARISE, AND STORM, BREAK LOOSE!

Berlin is the world-city of the future.
—***Grieben Travel Guide*, 1939**

The Nazis had held power in Berlin for a little less than seven years when they launched their drive to make Germany a world power. During their brief peacetime rule they had done much to reprovincialize their capital, reducing it from a cosmopolitan metropolis to a chauvinistic enclave hospitable only to Germans (as defined by the regime) and their allies. During the next five years they would transform the city even more—turning it first into the nerve center of their war machine and then, as a consequence of the retaliation that their military crusade provoked, into a field of rubble. While bringing devastation to Berlin, the war also provided the final context for the destruction of the city's Jewish population. A new, albeit divided and much diminished, Berlin would eventually rise from the rubble, but the city could never repair the human damage occasioned by the Nazis' effort to make it the capital of the world and the largest "Jew-free" metropolis in Europe.

All Quiet on the Home Front

Unlike in August 1914, Berliners did not greet the opening of hostilities in September 1939 with celebrations in the streets. People reacted with resignation to the news that the Wehrmacht was "counterattacking" into Poland in response to alleged Polish aggression. "A grey morning with overhanging clouds," wrote CBS correspondent William Shirer in his diary on September 1, 1939. "The people in the street were apathetic when I drove to the *Rundfunk* for my first broadcast at eight fifteen A.M. Across from the Adlon the morning shift of workers was busy on the new I.G. Farben building just as if nothing had happened. None of them bought the extras which the newsboys were shouting."

That evening, at seven o'clock, air-raid sirens wailed across the city, and this time it was not a drill. But no bombs fell that night, and after a brief rush to the shelters Berliners flocked to the cafés, restaurants, and beer halls. The streets were totally dark in accordance with blackout regulations. Though this made for perilous driving and walking, it also yielded a happy surprise: a clear view of the constellations over Berlin. After walking home from a shelter with a friend, Ruth Andreas-Friedrich, a correspondent for Ullstein, wrote in her diary: "On our way we see stars over Berlin for the first time—not paling sadly behind gaudy electric signs, but sparkling with clear solemnity. The moon casts a milky gleam over the roofs of the town. Not a spark of electric light falls upon the streets. 'The metropolis is going back to nature,' [my friend] Andrik smiles. 'It's almost enough to turn one into a romantic.'"

On September 3, Britain and France declared war on Germany, following the Reich's rejection of their ultimatum to withdraw from Poland. Hitler was surprised by the British action, having been assured by his foreign minister, Joachim von Ribbentrop, that London would never go to war against Germany. Shirer was in the Wilhelmplatz at noon when Britain's war declaration was announced. "Some 250 people were standing there in the sun. They listened attentively to the announcement. When it was finished, there was not a murmur. They just stood there as they were before. Stunned." France's declaration came through a couple of hours later. This too elicited "no excitement, no hurrahs, no cheering, no throwing of flowers, no war fever, no war hysteria."

The first weeks of World War II brought no direct threat to the German capital, or indeed to any part of the Reich. Employing its new blitzkrieg tactics, the Wehrmacht smashed through weak Polish defenses, reaching the outskirts of Warsaw by the second week of fighting. On September 17 Russian forces fell upon Poland from the east, expediting that country's collapse, which was complete by early October. In this brief but brutal campaign the Germans and Russians killed over 100,000 Polish soldiers and captured a million; German casualties numbered only about 45,000. Poland's Western European allies did nothing to distract the Wehrmacht from its grim business on the eastern front. Britain and France made no advances against the Reich, electing instead to pursue a purely defensive strategy while they built up their armaments. The result was the so-called "phony war"—*Sitzkrieg* instead of blitzkrieg. For Berliners and other Germans, the lack of action came as a pleasant surprise. They were beginning to wonder, as Shirer reported, "if it's a world war after all."

Berliners certainly *acted* as if there were no war going on. They paid little attention to the victory parade of the troops returning from the Polish campaign. Theaters, operas, and cinemas all stayed open, and all were jammed. In mid-September *Tannhäuser* and *Madama Butterfly* played at the State Opera, while at the Metropole a sister-duo, Margot and Hedi Hoffner, pranced around the stage dressed only in cellophane. Such racy acts were permissible because, as Goebbels explained, in trying times "one must be liberal regarding the exposure of the female body [while forbidding] a degeneration into obscenity." The nightly blackouts, while certainly a bother to most citizens, were a boon to thieves and prostitutes, who did a land-office business in the crepuscular gloom.

Determined to pull the home front into the war effort, the Nazi regime extended its rationing regulations to a broad variety of consumer goods. At the same time, however, it tried not to make the restrictions too harsh, for it hoped to avoid the crippling discontent that had erupted in World War I. To save gasoline, citizens who owned private vehicles were allowed to drive only for work purposes. Some of Berlin's busses were taken out of service or put on shorter schedules. To raise revenue for the war, a 20 percent surcharge was imposed on beer, schnapps, and cigarettes. The government also ordered an end to premiums paid for overtime work, but it quickly rescinded this when the workers protested. In the first year of the war, each citizen was allowed one hundred ration points for the purchase of clothing. The women's ration card was particularly complicated owing to the variety of apparel items and fabrics it covered. For example, a sweater cost nine points, a brassiere ten, a pair of panties or a girdle eight. Because soap was regulated (one bar a month), the air in the Berlin subways soon became quite rank. In early October the government decreed the first Sunday of each month to be "casserole day," meaning no meat. It was announced that the Führer himself shared in this sacrifice—but of course for him it was no sacrifice, since he was a vegetarian.

As in World War I, conscription for the military yielded a "feminization" of Berlin's workforce. By late September some 300 women were employed as streetcar conductors. To fill the places of drafted agricultural workers, teenage Berliners were sent into the fields to help bring in the harvest; they did this without pay, inasmuch as it was considered "patriotic service."

In the winter of 1939/40 Berlin presented a mixed picture. The nightly blackouts and shorter days gave one the impression of living in near-constant darkness. Nor did it help that the temperature dropped to minus fifteen degrees Celsius, and that coal deliveries were curtailed. The American diplomat George Kennan, who had been transferred from Prague to Berlin at the beginning of the war, recalled that winter as "a difficult one. Canals were frozen. Fuel was short. Whole blocks of huge apartment houses could not be heated at all and had to be evacuated in zero weather." Berliners had to put up with incessant requests for "voluntary" donations to the Winter Relief, supposedly a charity for the poor but actually a collection for the war effort. The regime also began collecting paper and metals from the population. Hitler was said to be replacing the bronze doors of the Neue Reichskanzlei with wooden ones as an example of patriotic sacrifice. At the same time, however, the regime eased the rationing regulations at Christmas to promote a happy Yuletide spirit. A pamphlet entitled "Christmas in the Third Reich" featured twelve poems about Hitler, one with the inspiring lines: "Silent night, Holy night / All is calm, all is bright / Only the Chancellor stays on guard / Germany's future to watch and to ward / Guiding our nation aright." Berliners were officially encouraged to patronize the city's cultural and amusement centers. The entertainment on hand that winter was heavily American: the Marmorhaus cinema showed *Südsee-Nächte* (South Sea Nights) with Eleonor Powell and Robert Young, while the Kurbel featured *Micky-Maus* and *Dick-und-Doof* (Laurel and Hardy).

In spring and early summer 1940 the fare in Berlin's cinemas turned more martial, with the *Wochenschau* (weekly news) programs recording the amazing progress of Germany's offensive in the west against Norway, Denmark, the Low Countries, and France. Nevertheless, according to Shirer, the German capital remained blasé. There was "no evidence," wrote the reporter, "that the Berliners, at least, are greatly exercised at the battle for their thousand-year existence." Conquest of the Low Countries and key victories over French and British armies in France elicited similar indifference, though all the Berlin papers carried the stories under banner headlines. According to Kennan, even the announcement of the fall of Paris "was received with the same inscrutable silence and reserve." Instead of victory, the "talk was all of food cards and the price of stockings."

It was only when the Nazi regime staged celebrations in Berlin in July 1940 to mark the victory over France that the citizenry showed much excitement. Tens of thousands turned out to greet their Führer upon his return from a brief victory trip to Paris on July 6. The enthusiasm expressed for Hitler was undoubtedly genuine. On July 18 the 218th Infantry Division marched through the Brandenburg Gate amidst the ringing of church bells and hosannas from the masses. The buildings on Unter den Linden were draped in red and white banners. The mood was all the more festive because the returning troops had brought home all sorts of wonderful booty from the conquered countries: French champagne and cognac, silk stockings, satin underwear, Dutch gin and cigars, silver fox coats from Norway. Another reason for celebrating was the belief that the war might soon be over. With France defeated and the Wehrmacht ensconced on the English Channel, Berliners were sure that Britain would sue for peace.

Fortress Berlin

Instead of suing for peace, Winston Churchill, Britain's new prime minister, went on the air to announce his nation's determination to fight on come what may. Churchill's tenacity infuriated Hitler, hardening his resolve to crush the island kingdom. Like Napoleon, he understood that this might require invading England, but he hoped that air strikes on British shipping would bring the country to its knees. In July 1940 the Luftwaffe began pounding British shipping in the Channel as well as selected ports and harbors. To the dismay of Air Marshal Göring, who had promised a quick victory, the Royal Air Force proved an able match for the Luftwaffe, knocking down high percentages of the German bombers as they struggled to reach their targets. In addition to courageous pilots, the RAF had the advantage of radar, which enabled its Spitfires and Hurricanes to scramble into position just as the Germans reached the English coast. To reporters watching the aerial duels from the White Cliffs of Dover, the sight of British planes holding their own provided the first ray of hope since the beginning of the war. As the American correspondent Vincent Sheean wrote:

> In every such battle I saw, the English had the best of it, and in every such battle they were greatly outnumbered. . . . At Dover the first sharp thrust of hope penetrated our gloom. The battles over the cliffs proved that the British could and would fight for their own freedom, if for nothing else, and that they could do so against colossal odds. . . . The flash of the Spitfire's wing, then, through the mist glare of the summer sky, was the first flash of a sharpened sword; they would fight, they would hold out.

Desperate to neutralize the RAF, the Luftwaffe began in mid-August to focus their attacks on British airfields and radar stations. The new raids were often quite effective, but they came at a high price in terms of lost bombers and airmen. Unaware of just how close they were to breaking the RAF's back, the Germans concluded that they must expand their target list to include strategic installations around London and other large cities. Hitler was resistant to the idea of hitting London itself, fearful that this would strengthen English resolve. On the night of August 24, however, Göring's pilots jettisoned some of their bombs over London on their way home from a raid against Thameshaven and Rochester. The bombs did not do much damage, but by striking the British capital the Germans gave Churchill the opportunity he had been waiting for. "Now that [the Germans] have begun to molest the capital," he minuted the chiefs of his Air Staff on August 25, 1940, "I want you to hit them hard, and Berlin is the place to hit them."

That very night a force of eighty-one Wellington and Hampden bombers made their way toward Berlin. Only about half the planes reached the city, which was covered by dense clouds. Like their German counterparts, they did not inflict much damage, but by blasting away some houses they changed the course of the war. Rather than continuing to concentrate on neutralizing the RAF, which would be necessary if the Reich were ever to invade Britain, Germany now focused on reprisal attacks against English cities, especially London. The British retaliated in kind, with Berlin a favorite target. In an important sense, World War II now turned into a contest to see which of these two great cities could hold out best under the new horror of repeated aerial bombardments.

Hitler's worries about Londoners' resolve notwithstanding, Germany was confident that it could win this contest. Since coming to power the Nazis had preached "air-mindedness," the doctrine that a well-trained and disciplined civilian populace could withstand prolonged assaults from the air. The Reich Civil Defense League, which by the beginning of the war embraced 350,000 citizens, including one out of every six Berliners, held drills on fire suppression and seeking shelter. It appointed thousands of air-raid wardens to supervise civil defense procedures in specific neighborhoods. Armed with their authority, many of these figures became mini-Hitlers, pining for the chance to show that they too could lead the *Volk*. Goebbels promised that Nazi propaganda could handle the situation if bombs ever fell on Berlin. He boasted in 1937:

> The German government . . . will at once master the situation and stimulate the discipline of the people by broadcasting what has taken place in such a way as to electrify every German heart. A message will be broadcast to every home, stating that a dastardly attack on the capital has been made, that whole streets have been demolished, yet the *morale* of the survivors is so superb that tens of thousands of Berliners—men, women, and children, sound and wounded—are standing on the ruins and shouting 'Heil Hitler!'

In reality, Goebbels was worried about how the Berliners would stand up under aerial bombardment. When Berlin actually received its first air attack on August 25, he instructed the Berlin newspapers to report that a few planes had flown over the city and dropped some incendiary bombs, which had damaged one hut. Shirer was amused to note the next day that "there was not a line [in the papers] about the explosive bombs which we all plainly heard." Nor was there any mention about "the three streets in Berlin which have been roped off all day today to prevent the curious from seeing what a bomb can do to a house."

For the people of Berlin the first air raid came as an enormous shock, despite all the "air-conditioning" they had gotten from their leaders. Air Marshal Göring, after all, had long boasted that he would change his name to "Maier" if a single enemy warplane reached German territory. Shirer recorded in his diary on August 26: "The Berliners are stunned. They did not think it could happen. . . . [But] last night the guns all over the city suddenly began pounding and you could hear the British motors humming directly overhead, and from all reports there was a pell-mell, frightened rush to the cellars by the five million people who live in this town."

Four nights later the British returned, and this time they drew blood: ten persons killed and twenty-nine wounded. Some of the bombs landed in the center of the city, close to the Görlitzer railroad station. Mused Shirer: "I think the populace of

Berlin is more affected by the fact that the British planes have been able to penetrate to the center of Berlin without trouble than they are by the first casualties. For the first time the war has been brought home to them. If the British keep this up, it will have a tremendous effect upon the morale of the people here." It was not long before Berliners and other Germans began referring to Göring as "Marshal-Maier."

Hoping to stiffen morale by inflaming hatred for the enemy, Goebbels ordered the papers to decry the "brutality" of the British pilots in attacking defenseless women and children. One paper even accused Churchill of ordering the RAF to "massacre the population of Berlin."

While Churchill certainly had no objection to killing Berliners, the purpose of the Berlin raids, at least at the outset, was less to decimate the population than to take out some of the city's vast array of military and strategic installations. Berlin, it must be remembered, was not just Germany's administrative capital but also the nerve-center of its military-industrial complex. It housed almost one hundred barracks and depots as well as the headquarters of all the service branches. With its rail lines, airports, and canal system, it was the hub of the German communications network. It dominated the national electrical industry with its huge Siemens complex, its ten AEG plants, its Telefunken, Lorenz, and Bosch outlets, all of which made vital military components. The sprawling Alkett factory in Spandau produced self-propelled guns and half of the Wehrmacht's field artillery. Borsig, one of Berlin's pioneer industrial firms, made rolling stock, locomotives, and heavy artillery. A DWM (German Weapons and Munitions) factory in the northern district of Wittenau produced small arms, ammunition, and mortars. Tank chassis rolled off the assembly lines at the Auto-Union factories at Spandau and Halensee. BMW's Berlin branch produced a variety of military vehicles, while Heinkel, Henschel, and Dornier made bombers, attack aircraft, and airplane components.

Fully aware of the capital's crucial strategic significance, the Nazi regime went to great lengths to protect it. Fighter squadrons stationed around Berlin were ordered to intercept enemy planes before they reached the city. Because the flak installations that had been built at the outset of the war were deemed insufficient to cope with the threat of large-scale raids, orders went out in 1940 to erect better defenses. Over the course of the following year a new military-construction agency run by Albert Speer laid out batteries of flak and searchlights in a concentric pattern. The inner ring consisted of three of the largest flak bunkers ever constructed. One was near the Zoological Gardens, another in Humboldthain Park in the north, and another in Friedrichshain Park east of Alexanderplatz. The hulking structures looked for all the world like latter-day Crusader castles, with concrete walls 2.5 meters thick, window slits sheathed in steel, and towers bristling with 128-millimeter antiaircraft guns mounted in pairs. Beneath the roof level were smaller gun turrets housing multibarreled quick-firing "pompom guns" and 37-millimeter cannons for cutting down low-flying aircraft. No wonder British fliers came to regard attacks on Berlin as a nerve-wracking experience. As one Lancaster bombardier put it: "The run-up seemed endless, the minutes of flying 'straight and level' seemed like hours and every second I expected to be blown to pieces. I sweated with fear, and the perspiration seemed to freeze on my body."

In addition to their role as flak platforms, the massive towers also served as air-raid shelters and aid stations. All had their own water supplies, air-conditioning systems, generating plants, and hospitals. Each stored enough food to last its occupants for a full year. The Humboldthain tower had underground passages leading to the

The flak tower in the Tiergarten, photographed in 1945

exceptionally deep Gesundbrunnen subway station, which likewise became a shelter. (Other subway stations and tunnels also served as shelters, but most of the Berlin lines were built so close to the surface that direct hits easily penetrated them.) The zoo tower, the largest of the three bunkers, devoted one entire level to the housing of some of Berlin's most precious art treasures, including the loot Heinrich Schliemann had stolen from Troy.

The Nazis did not rely solely on flak and fighters to protect their capital from enemy "air pirates," as Goebbels called them. They sought to confuse the attackers by camouflaging prime targets and by erecting dummy government buildings on the outskirts of the city. They enshrouded the "Ost-West Axis" under a camouflage net replete with lawnlike greenery and fake fir trees. (The netting, however, did not hold up well; the first big wind tore large holes in it, leaving pieces of wire and canvas dangling from tree branches all over the Tiergarten.) The Victory Column at the Great Star was likewise draped in netting, and the golden goddess on the top was painted a dull brown, which left her looking as if she had just come back from a Caribbean vacation. The Deutschlandhalle, which during the war was used to store grain, disappeared under a giant tent painted to look like a park from the air. Because enemy planes used Berlin's lakes as navigational guides, the authorities covered parts of them with giant wooden rafts designed to give the impression of housing projects. The main government district was "moved" to a vacant lot beyond the Ostkreuz railway station by way of a collection of wooden and canvas structures vaguely resembling well-known buildings. Another major decoy site was established at Staaken on the western approaches to the city; it was built of movie sets from a prewar film studio.

In the end, the elaborate decoys and camouflage probably made little difference. With the heavy flak, frequent cloud cover, primitive bombing sights, and frayed nerves, bombardiers rarely hit what they were aiming at anyway. As late as 1943, an Allied bombing assessment admitted that out of 1,719 bombers so far sent to Berlin, only twenty-seven had managed to drop their bombs within three miles of the target. Assessing one of its raids on Berlin, the RAF's 83rd squadron commented: "The success of the attack was not due to our accurate bombing but to the Germans for building such a large city!"

If the early Berlin raids were not particularly accurate, or, for that matter, particularly deadly—there were only 222 fatalities in 1940, 226 in 1941—they were nonetheless psychologically unsettling. Howard K. Smith, who reported from

Camouflage netting on the East-West Axis (formerly Charlottenburger Chaussee, currently Strasse des 17. Juni), 1941

Berlin for the United Press, noted that "Mornings after raids, people were in a miserable mood from lack of sleep and nervous strain. . . . Friends parting at night created a new farewell term, in place of *Auf Wiedersehen*, wishing one another *Bolona* which is short for *bombenlose Nacht* (bombless night)." Marie Vassiltchikov, a Russian émigré who worked as a secretary in the German Foreign Ministry's Information Department, certainly longed for a *Bolona*. She wrote in her diary on September 16, 1940: "These nightly raids are getting exhausting, as one gets in only three or four hours' sleep." She added on September 9: "Another raid. I slept through the whole thing, hearing neither the siren, nor the bombs, nor the all-clear. This shows how exhausted I am." On March 12, 1941, a single raid did significant damage to the heart of the city, partly wrecking the State Library and Royal Palace, and gutting the State Opera. According to one witness, the fire that ravaged the opera was "so bright that you could read a newspaper by it." Inspecting the remains of the building, Harry Flannery, who replaced Shirer as CBS's man in Berlin after the latter left in December 1940, noticed that the golden eagle of the kaisers, which had once stood atop the royal box, now lay discolored and partly burned under the ruins.

Aggravating as the air raids were, they were probably not the worst feature of life for most Berliners during the second winter of the war. To judge from complaints recorded by the Gestapo and the SPD's underground information network, SOPADE (Sozialdemokratische Partei Deutschlands im Exil), poor food and shortages of coal were the most pressing issues. Now even the Hotel Adlon abided by "Casserole Day," as Marie Vassiltchikov discovered to her dismay when she ate there in December 1940. Flannery saw the first signs of a beer shortage in May 1941. Taverns and restaurants announced that they would serve beer only between 11:30 A.M. and 3 P.M., and from 7 P.M. to 10 P.M. Because vintage wines were in short supply, the Kempinski restaurant on the Kurfürstendamm began a policy of selling Spätlese, Auslese, and Trockenbeerenauslese only to regular customers. As in World War I, ersatz goods began to proliferate. Berliners now ate stuff made from puree of pine needles, powdered chestnut, and ground-up ivy leaves. A new cocktail called the "Razzle-dazzle" consisted of wood alcohol and grenadine. Tobacco was not yet replaced by any vile substitute, although a popular brand called "Johnnies" tasted so bad it was said to contain camel dung, courtesy of General Rommel's Afrika Korps.

Spring 1941 brought relief from the cold and a bit of amusement in the form of one of the most bizarre episodes in the history of the Third Reich. Berliners learned in mid-May that Rudolf Hess, Hitler's personal deputy, had solo-piloted a Messerschmitt to Scotland in a quixotic bid for peace with Britain. Hitler was so horrified that he never allowed Hess's name to be mentioned in his presence again. Göring surmised that Hess was crazy, and this was the thrust of the official communiqué read over Greater German Radio on May 12. "Party Comrade Hess," said the bulletin, had "fallen prey to delusions." In Berlin, where the dour and fanatical Bavarian had never been popular, a new joke made the rounds: "The Thousand Year Reich has now become the One Hundred Year Reich; a zero has just been subtracted."

The efforts of Hess notwithstanding, Britain remained firmly committed to the war, and a month or so after his flight Germany added another potent enemy, the Soviet Union. Of course it had always been merely a matter of time until Hitler exchanged his handshake with the Soviets for a grab to the throat, but the moment of truth came sooner than even he expected. Having given up attempting to invade Britain, Hitler decided that the best way to knock that nation out of the war was to conquer Russia's vast natural resources, which would make the Reich invulnerable to the British blockade.

As far as Berlin was concerned, the opening of a new front in Russia on June 22, 1941, constituted what Howard K. Smith called "The Great Watershed." If the conditions of daily life had started to become more difficult before Operation Barbarossa, they deteriorated rapidly as the Russian campaign sucked resources out of the Reich. With the drain on livestock supplies, meat rations had to be cut, first to 500 grams per person per week, then to 450. Reductions after that were not officially announced, but were effected by providing butchers and restaurants with less meat. The number of meatless days at restaurants became two, then three. On these days the finer establishments substituted a red-colored paste called *Lachs Galantine*, which tasted like "soggy sawdust" to Smith, who estimated that after five months of the war in Russia Germans had given up four-fifths of their weekly meet ration. Trying to keep up appearances, the Kaiserhof Hotel continued to put two meat dishes on the menu, but never served more than one. Fats were also at a premium, as evidenced by the appearance of a *faux* fat product made by filtering edible garbage and adding artificial flavoring. Even potatoes became difficult to find in the winter of 1941/42 due to a bad crop and demands from the army. Berliners were advised not to peel potatoes before boiling them, as this supposedly wasted 15 percent of each potato. Perhaps worse, the beer supply now became so tight that only the big hotels and foreign press club served it on a regular basis. The Adlon Hotel began watering its beer to make supplies last longer. Hard liquor being equally scarce, bars resorted to serving *Himbeergeist*, a raspberry liqueur, or a fake vodka that took the roof off one's mouth. In 1941 wine shops across the city were closed and their contents bought by the government at a fixed price. When Smith left Berlin a month later, he could find no alcohol at all in the German capital. "Against its will, Germany had become, perhaps, the most temperate nation on earth."

Housing had long been tight in Berlin, and it became considerably more so because of an influx of war bureaucrats and workers to man the arms factories. While the population increased by an estimated 25 percent, housing construction remained flat. Thus the legions of newcomers found it extremely difficult to find a single room, much less an apartment, in the overcrowded metropolis. Tex Fischer, an Associated Press correspondent, was forced to live in his office. Even the Crown Prince of Sweden, who showed up unannounced for a visit, was turned away by four big hotels before a fifth one found space for him. Of course, the problem would only become worse later in the war, as Allied bombs blew away more and more residences, and measures like expelling the Jews failed to provide sufficient *Lebensraum* for bombed-out Aryans.

Even before the bombing raids became more effective, Berlin's vaunted public transportation system began falling apart due to lack of spare parts and qualified repair personnel. One bus and tram line after another went out of service. The number of taxis was cut by four-fifths, and those that remained received less than a gallon of fuel a day.

Taxi drivers and repair men could charge whatever they wanted, but many preferred to be paid in goods rather than in cash, since there was a dearth of items in the stores to spend money on. Even the KaDeWe department store, Berlin's premier consumer paradise, now offered little to tempt the buyer. After searching the store for two hours for something of use, a Berliner complained: "That big barn is empty. It is a feat of skill to get rid of fifty pfennigs on all seven floors."

Given these developments, it is not surprising that some of the foreign correspondents in the German capital began to wonder about the Berliners' staying power. Speculation in the foreign press that Berlin might not be able to hold up under sustained bombing infuriated Goebbels, since he shared that fear himself. He countered such talk with accounts of Berliner pluck, citing the case of "one simple man who, after working all night during an air raid, upon going home in the morning, found his home destroyed, his wife and five children dead. Not a word of complaint was forthcoming." This of course left open the possibility that the man in question was too stupefied with grief to complain.

Pity or Regret Is Completely Out of Place Here

In the summer of 1940 there were still about 70,000 Jews in Berlin. Many of them were too old or poor to leave; others continued to hope that they could outlast the evil that had descended upon them. To Goebbels this was a provocation. As long as Jews lived in Berlin, he complained, the city's atmosphere would be polluted. He proposed that they be removed to Poland within a period of eight weeks. He also insisted that Berlin, as the capital, should get preference in the expulsion over other "Jew cities" like Breslau.

To illustrate the perniciousness of the Jewish influence, Goebbels's Propaganda Ministry sponsored the production of a crudely anti-Semitic film, *Jud Süss*, which premiered in Berlin on September 24, 1940. The film's central character, the Jew Oppenheimer, is a parody of dark menace, greed, deceit, and lust; and by raping a blond virgin he adds *Rassenschande* (race defilement) to his many sins. Goebbels, who attended the premier, called it "a brilliant piece of work, an anti-Semitic film as we would wish it." He was pleased that the audience "raved" with enthusiasm.

Yet the majority of the Jews remaining in Berlin still failed to get the message—or, more accurately, continued to refuse to act on a message that was becoming clearer by the day. In the spring of 1941 the Jewish presence in the city had not diminished significantly despite all the intimidation and threats. Surveying the situation on March 20, 1941, Leopold Gutterer, Goebbels's deputy, fumed that it was not right "that the capital of the National Socialist Reich should still harbor such a large number of Jews." Goebbels himself, still pressing for a mass deportation to Poland, believed that Hitler would soon endorse such a "solution." After all, he noted, Hitler's master builder for Berlin, Speer, could certainly use the twenty thousand or so dwellings still occupied by Jews "as a reserve for those rendered homeless by greater bombing damage and later by demolition connected with the revamping of Berlin."

In August 1941 Goebbels received a promise from Hitler that the deportation of Berlin's Jews would begin as soon as the means of transportation became available and arrangements for their expulsion could be worked out. He ordered a survey to determine which Jews might be employed in work crucial to the war effort and which where "ripe" for deportation. In the meantime, in September 1941, the Gauleiter was authorized to make life even more miserable for the capital's remaining Jews by forcing them to wear a yellow Star of David patch on their clothing. Beginning in October 1941, Jews could use Berlin's public transportation system (but not the seats) only with special permission, and in April 1942 they were banned from it entirely. During air raids they were obliged to go to their own shelters, separate from those of the Aryans. They were also barred from shopping in "German" stores or employing the services of "German tradesmen." They could not walk in the public parks or appear in the streets after 8:00 P.M. A decree of December 21, 1941, prohibited Jews from using public telephones. As of early 1942, Jews were required to turn over to the state such "luxury" items as radios, bicycles, typewriters, gramophones, electric stoves, and hand mirrors. To ensure that all Jews would live in the "harsh climate" that the Nazis said they deserved, monthly support payments for the sick and elderly were drastically reduced.

Many Jews evaded the regulations as best they could. Young Inge Deutschkron had no intention of abiding by the restrictions concerning freedom of movement and association. "I wasn't ready to spend my life without occasionally going to a play or concert or for a walk in the park. I couldn't bear the thought of spending all my time in the company of Jews exclusively. All they ever talked of was Nazi persecutions and their own anxieties—a litany of fear, apprehension, and self-torture." Nor did she always wear her stigmata—the Star of David—when out in public. She carried a second jacket without the star and furtively changed into it before riding the subway or entering stores where Jews were not allowed. As she recalled, "I went through my coat-changing routine often, not only because Jews were barred from using public transportation except when going to and from work, but also because our grocer would not have been able to wait on us if I had come in wearing the star; nor would Mrs. Gumz have been allowed to do our laundry or give me the meat she got for us at the butcher's." As Deutschkron's account makes clear, she and other Berlin Jews relied on the help of non-Jewish friends and neighbors to get around some of the Nazi rules. They obtained food beyond their official rations from grocers who slipped them "a little something extra" under the counter. They stored their valuables in the basements or attics of gentile acquaintances.

The number of people affected by the anti-Jewish regulations was finally shrinking significantly, however, for an order to begin the deportation of Berlin's Jews was signed by Kurt Daluege, chief of the city's Order Police, on October 14, 1941. Having waited impatiently for this moment, Goebbels was jubilant. By way of justifying this measure to the public, he recalled Hitler's prophecy, delivered in a speech to the Reichstag in January 1939, that "if the Jews involved in international high finance were to succeed in dragging the peoples of the world into another war, the result would be not the bolshevization of the earth and thereby the victory of Jewry, but rather the extermination of the Jewish race in Europe." The world would now witness the fulfillment of this prophecy, the Gauleiter wrote. He added that if the Jews were in for a "harsh" time, this was simply what they deserved. "Pity or regret is completely out of place here."

Out of place indeed. The ensuing roundup and deportation of Berlin's Jews set a new standard for brutality in a city that had seen its full share of inhumanity. On October 15, 1941, Gestapo men appeared at the homes of the families earmarked for the first "evacuation" and ordered each family to pack one suitcase. The families were held for three days in the partially ruined synagogue in the Levetzowstrasse, where they were cared for by members of the Jewish *Gemeinde* (community). (The Gestapo forced the cooperation of Jewish leaders in the deportation process by threatening even harsher measures in the event of noncompliance.) On October 18 the group set out in heavy rain for the freight railway station at Grunewald—able-bodied men and women marched the entire distance, children and the infirm were transported in open trucks. At Grunewald they were loaded into third-class passenger cars supplied by the Reichsbahn, which charged the SS four pfennigs per adult per kilometer, with kids riding free. Here, too, officials from the Jewish *Gemeinde* proved of assistance, issuing instructions to the deportees "to keep in mind that your demeanor and your orderly compliance with the regulations will contribute substantially to the smooth processing of the transport." According to one witness, the loading proceeded "without crowding or other impositions."

That first transport, carrying about 1,000 Jews, was bound for the ghetto of Lodz in eastern Poland. In subsequent weeks trains carried thousands more to the ghettos and concentration camps being hastily established in the East. For the vast majority of the deportees, work ghettos like Lodz were simply way stations to the killing fields of Auschwitz, Treblinka, and other death camps. The loading ramp at Grunewald was the last patch of Berlin that these people would ever see.

Well after the first transports of Jews from Berlin and other German cities were underway, and well after the mass murder of Jews in the conquered eastern regions had begun, a group of Nazi officials met in the capital to systematize the killing process. The conference took place on January 20, 1942, in a Wannsee villa then serving as a guest house for the SS. The setting could hardly have been more ironic, for Wannsee was Berlin's favorite playground, an idyllic stretch of beach and water invariably crowded on summer days with sunbathers, swimmers, and amateur sailors. Host for the meeting was Reinhard Heydrich, chief of the SD (Sicherheitsdienst—Security Service) of the SS. Participants included officials from Justice Ministry, Interior Ministry, Foreign Ministry, Ministry for Eastern Regions, and the Reich

The Villa Wannsee, site of the Wannsee Conference, January 20, 1942

Chancellery. These men were not known to be fanatical anti-Semites; rather, they were "Technocrats of Death"—bureaucrats dutifully organizing the mechanics of murder as if they were discussing interagency cooperation in the building of a new highway system. The written protocol of the meeting, compiled by Adolf Eichmann, is all the more chilling for its sober, bureaucratic tone. While avoiding reference to extermination or even to camps, it conveys clearly enough what the regime had in mind. One passage reads:

> In the course of the final solution, the Jews will be put to work in appropriate fashion in the East. Large work groups, separated by sex, will be employed in road construction, whereby a significant component will of course fall aside in a natural culling process. Because the surviving elements will doubtless consist of the most resilient types, capable if released of forming the core of a Jewish revival, they will have to be dealt with accordingly. To effect the final solution, Europe will be combed [for Jews] from West to East. . . . The evacuated Jews will be conveyed first to so-called transit ghettos, then transported further into the East.

The bureaucrats at Wannsee may have employed veiled language—perhaps the cruelest euphemisms in history—but the deportation process was open and visible enough to make it improbable that significant numbers of ordinary Berliners were unaware of the action, as many later claimed. Jewish citizens recalled their gentile neighbors observing the loading process from their houses and stores, and crowding around the stations to watch the transports depart. How then did the Berliners react to the horror that was transpiring under their noses? This of course is an integral part of the broader question of how "ordinary Germans" responded to the various stages of the Holocaust. The short answer is that in Berlin, as in other German cities, the majority of the people seem to have accepted this extraordinary development as if it were part of the natural order of events. Some actively welcomed the forced expulsion of a vilified minority, "gloating over the misery that had befallen their fellow citizens," in the words of one witness. Others were ashamed of the deportations; and still others—perhaps as many as 30,000—tried to sabotage the process by hiding or otherwise helping their Jewish neighbors. (There is, alas, no monument in Berlin to this last group.) It is impossible to say exactly how many Berliners had clear knowledge of what was happening to the deportees once they arrived in the East, but by late 1942 accounts of mass killings, sent back by perpetrators and bystanders, were widely circulating in the city. Ruth Andreas-Friedrich wrote in her diary on December 2, 1942: "The Jews are disappearing in throngs. Ghastly rumors are current about the fate of the evacuees—mass shooting and death by starvation, tortures, and gassings." Whatever their knowledge of the situation in the East, those Berliners who were disgusted by the sight of innocent people being dragged from their homes often felt powerless to help the afflicted, much less to thwart the process. At the very outset of the deportations, Ursula von Kardorff, a journalist at the *Deutsche Allgemeine Zeitung*, wrote in a letter to a friend: "The most depressing things are happening here. All Jews under eighty years of age are being transported to Poland. One sees only tearful wretches in the streets. It is horrible and cuts at one's heart. The worst is that one watches it all so helplessly and can do so terribly little to help."

Shameful as the deportations may have seemed to some Berliners, the SS concluded by late 1942 that the Berlin Gestapo was not acting ruthlessly enough in the removal process. Thus the local officials in charge of the operation were replaced by a team from Vienna (recently declared "Jew-free") under the leadership of Alois Brunner, a gnomish Austrian who was quite un-Austrian in his mania for efficiency. Brunner saw his job as showing "those damn Prussian pigs how to handle filthy Jews." Soon capacious moving vans driven by members of Brunner's *Judenpolizei* (Jewish orderlies forced to work with the Nazis on pain of deportation themselves) ranged through the Jewish districts, transporting hundreds of Jews at a time to the collection centers for deportation. The Austrian saw to it that tighter controls were imposed at the predeportation center in Grosse Hamburger Strasse, a former Jewish old folks' home that now replaced the smaller Levetzowstrasse site as Berlin's main collection camp. When, in December 1942, the number of Jews designated for a transport did not materialize at Grosse Hamburger Strasse, Brunner "filled" the quota by shooting officials from the Jewish *Gemeinde.*

In autumn 1942 Jews working in Berlin's vital war industries—some 20,000 of them as of November—were still kept off the deportation lists, but in December Brunner persuaded the Wehrmacht to allow the removal of these individuals if they could be replaced by Poles. On February 27, 1943, Brunner's team and the Gestapo staged a *Fabrikaktion* (factory purge), in which some 5,000 Berlin Jews were pulled from their workplaces and homes for deportation to Auschwitz. Ruth Andreas-Friedrich described the scene on that day:

> Since six o'clock this morning trucks have been driving through Berlin, escorted by armed SS men. They stop at factory gates, in front of private houses; they load in human cargo—men, women, children. Distracted faces are crowded together under the gray canvas covers. Figures of misery, penned in and jostled about like cattle going to the stockyards. More and more new ones arrive, and are thrust into the overcrowded trucks, with blows of gun butts. In six weeks Germany is to be 'Jew-free.'

The number swept up in the *Fabrikaktion* would have been even higher had not some employers, anxious to preserve valued employees, warned their Jewish workers of the impending action. This infuriated Goebbels. "Our plans were tipped off prematurely, so that a lot of Jews slipped through our hands," he wrote. "But we will catch them yet. I certainly won't rest until the capital of the Reich, at least, has become free of Jews." A few weeks later, on June 19, 1943, the Gauleiter claimed that the Nazi purge was indeed complete, and that Berlin was *Judenfrei.* In fact, this was still not the case, and Goebbels knew it, but Berlin's large Jewish community had been reduced to a few thousand souls living in *Judenäuser* (Jewish-only residences), mixed marriages, and underground.

The transports continued to roll east almost to the end of the war, though with smaller and smaller cargoes. The ones in late 1944 averaged one hundred persons. The last shipment from Berlin, which contained 117 people bound for Theresienstadt in Czechoslovakia, departed on March 27, 1945, only about a month before the Russians overran the German capital. That the Nazis continued to employ scarce resources to transport fewer and fewer people was a testament to their fanaticism. In total, 50,535 Berliners were deported from the capital, 35,738 of them to Auschwitz.

The deportations, of course, added a new dimension of horror to the lives of those Jews who remained in Berlin. Everyone in the Jewish community was understandably terrified by this development, though in the first phase of the operation most were apparently unaware of what was happening to the deportees in the East. As Inge Deutschkron observed: "Of course I was afraid of what lay in store for me. We didn't yet know precisely what fate awaited the deportees, but instinct told us that it was sure to be worse than what had gone before. I was also curious. What had happened to those who had already left? What could I expect?" It was not long before she had a clearer idea: "In November 1942 we learned about the gassings and executions for the first time via the BBC. We could not and did not want to believe it. And our ranks were thinning."

Deutschkron watched as her aunt and uncle were taken away in late 1942. She saw what thousands of others were seeing (or choosing not to see):

> Two Jewish orderlies wearing the yellow star went into the house. They reappeared minutes later behind my aunt, who was lugging the heavy backpacks. She walked quickly, as though eager to get it over with. My uncle followed haltingly. They didn't look back as they stepped into the car, not a single backward look at the city that had been their home for almost thirty years. . . . [My mother and I] were the only ones on the street. Strange how the Berliners knew when to make themselves scarce so as not to have to see what was happening in their streets.

Not all of Berlin's remaining Jews chose to wait dutifully for the authorities to come and cart them away. Some abandoned the *Judenhäuser*, threw away their identification papers marked with a "J," and went underground. When these so-called *U-Boote* (submarines) resurfaced, they had to be equipped with forged identification papers and ration cards, or forged *Bombensheine* (bomb certificates) stating that they had lost their papers in a raid. Obviously this made them all the more dependent on assistance and protection from sympathetic gentiles. Although helping Jews was a risky business—if caught, offenders faced imprisonment—enough Berliners took the risk that some 1,321 Jews managed to stay safely submerged in the city until the Nazi collapse.

The number of survivors might have been somewhat higher had not a few Berlin Jews, desperate to save themselves and their relatives, lent their services to the Gestapo in its efforts to bring "submarines" to the surface. Called *Greifer* (grabbers) by their Jewish prey, these figures did not have to wear the yellow star or abide by the various restrictions on movement. As long as they continued to bring in their quota of fellow Jews, they were kept off the deportation lists.

One of the most intrepid of the grabbers was a woman named Stella Kübler (neé Goldschlag), the subject of a searing portrait by journalist/historian Peter Wyden, who interviewed her after the war. A beautiful blond who did not "look Jewish," or, for that matter, *feel* Jewish, Stella deeply resented being subjected to the restrictions imposed on the Jewish community. Like Inge Deutschkron, but much more brazenly, she flaunted the Nazis' regulations, virtually never wearing her yellow star and regularly frequenting popular bars and cafés until the wee hours of the morning. She could not, however, evade being put to work in a Siemens arms factory, which she hated. In spring 1943 she decided to become a "submarine," albeit hardly a deep-diver. Unable to stay away from her beloved *Nachtlokale*, she was spotted by an old friend from her Jewish school, who turned out to be a grabber on the prowl. Stella was arrested and taken to Burgstrasse 26, the Gestapo headquarters for Berlin's central district. According to her later testimony, the authorities tortured her, then offered her the choice between deportation to the East and becoming a grabber herself. The Nazis were especially keen to enlist her because she seemed perfect for the role—a "blond, blue-eyed Jewess who could wiggle her way into any male confidence, who knew the habits, contacts, hiding places, and psychology of the U-boats, who could spot these tenacious resisters on the streets and in the cafes, and who was herself so desperate, so greedy to survive, and tough enough to recover from torture with no visible damage."

So Stella went to work trolling for U-boats, focusing on places like the Swiss embassy and a string of West End cafés where she knew her prey liked to submerge themselves in the crowds. She stayed on the hunt even after her parents were sent

Inmates at Sachsenhausen concentration camp, 1943

to Theresienstadt. Her only drawback as a grabber was that she was well known among the U-boats, who called her "Lorelei," after the legendary Rhine siren who lured river sailors to their deaths on the rocks where she perched. Despite her notoriety, she managed to bag her share of victims and stay in the good graces of her keepers. She pursued this work until the autumn of 1944, when, guessing that the Nazis were likely to lose the war, she began to pull back, pleading that there were no more Jews left to grab. She managed to hold out for the remainder of the war, only to be grabbed herself by Berlin's new rulers after the city fell to the Russians. She was tried and sentenced to ten years in Soviet prisons, which led her to see herself as a "victim of the Jews," on whom she blamed her fate.

Fortunately, types like Stella were an exception in Berlin's Jewish community, and there was always the counterexample of those who sought actively to sabotage the Nazi system. In Berlin a small coterie of Jewish resisters clustered around a charismatic communist named Herbert Baum. All were working-class and passionately leftist in orientation. Intriguingly, a number of them worked at the same Siemens plant that employed Stella Kübler. At first the members of the Baum Group restricted themselves to distributing anti-Nazi propaganda and helping other Jews and leftists escape from the Reich. On May 18, 1942, however, they took the bold step of bombing an anti-Soviet exhibition in the Lustgarten, which resulted in the capture of some members of the organization. Baum himself was arrested and subjected to severe torture, to which he eventually succumbed. Other members of the group were sentenced to death by the People's Court and executed at Plötzensee Prison on the west side of Berlin. As added retribution, the Gestapo shot 250 Jews at the Lichtenfeld Cadet School and dispatched another 250 to Sachsenhausen and other camps.

A rather different instance of resistance involved a protest by the non-Jewish wives of Jewish men and *Mischlinge* (partial Jews) who were being held at a detention center in Berlin's Rosenstrasse. In their determination to make Berlin "Jew-free," the capital's Nazi functionaries had begun to deport a few *Mischlinge* and intermarried Jews at the beginning of 1943. They were also deporting leaders of the Jewish *Gemeinde*, including Leo Baeck, who was sent to Theresienstadt. In February 1943 they planned a "Final Roundup" that would cleanse the city of remaining Jews. The *Fabrikaktion* of February 27, 1943, constituted the first stage of the planned multiday sweep; it included *Mischlinge* and intermarried Jews, as did roundups on subsequent days. On Eichmann's orders, most of these Jews were interned at Rosenstrasse 2-4, a youth and welfare office of the Jewish *Gemeinde*. This measure was designed to make the internees and their relatives think that they would not suffer the same fate as the other Jews caught up in the sweep. Siegbert Kleeman, a functionary of the *Gemeinde*, knew better: "These Jews at Rosenstrasse were supposed to be put on a train, and then no one would have heard from them again," he said.

As word spread via "mouth radio" that intermarried Jews were being detained at the Rosenstrasse center, relatives of the internees began rushing to the scene. Soon a crowd of women gathered across the street from the building. Such public gatherings were strictly illegal, but the authorities hesitated to intervene, preferring to search for the organizers. There were none. This was an entirely spontaneous action—an outburst of love suddenly become desperate. "We want our husbands back!" shouted the women as they walked up and down in the street. The women continued their protest even as an Allied air raid brought buildings crashing down all over the area. Guards at the detention center fled the building after sealing the prisoners inside. Much to the relief of the women, not to mention their interned husbands, Rosenstrasse 2-4 emerged unscathed from the raid.

By early March the regime had decided to wait the women out, expecting that they would soon tire of their protest and go home. But they did not; on the contrary, the crowd grew as more relatives, emboldened by the Nazis' inaction, joined the protest. Threats from the police to shoot into the crowd managed to disperse it momentarily, but within minutes the protesters were back, shouting for their husbands.

With the protest dragging on, Goebbels became convinced that it would be safer for the regime to relent in this case rather than to crack down. He could see that the protesters wanted only to keep their families together, not to challenge the system as such. Moreover, the women involved were non-Jews, and their plight might easily illicit the sympathy of all married women, regardless of their husband's race. Even the Nazis were intelligent enough to understand that stirring up the nation's women was a bad idea. As Hitler himself was to say later: "Women's political hatred is extremely dangerous."

Thus on March 6, 1943, Goebbels gave orders for the release of the Rosenstrasse Jews. He justified this as a temporary concession during a crucial time—a reference to the recent disaster at Stalingrad. He had every intention of including intermarried Jews and *Mischlinge* in future roundups, when progress on the front might make it less imperative to retain the goodwill of working women at home. Of course that time never came, and as early as March 18, 1943, the SS issued an order not to deport any more intermarried Jews pending clarification from Hitler regarding the proper treatment of such cases. This clarification also never came, with the result that the "privileged Jews" of the Rosenstrasse escaped the fate of the unprivileged Jews who died in the camps.

The Rosenstrasse incident illustrates what positive good could come from a courageous stance against a brutal regime, but its significance should not be overstated. To a large degree, this protest was successful because it focused on a relatively narrow issue that did not strike at the core of the system. As one woman admitted later: "We want[ed] our husbands. But only that. We didn't call out for anything else." Moreover, this example did not inspire larger protests on a broader front. As the war dragged on, the Nazi home front was full of malaise, not least in

Berlin, but it held up more or less intact until the Allied armies crushed the Wehrmacht and overran the Nazi state.

Total War

March 1, 1943, the date on which Allied bombs almost claimed the Rosenstrasse center, was the annual "Day of the Luftwaffe." On this date each year Germans were ordered by the Hitler regime to honor the accomplishments of the Nazi air force. By staging a large-scale raid on that day, the enemy intended to help the Germans celebrate. The March raid was part of a bombing campaign against Berlin that was much more extensive and deadly than the raids of 1940/41, which, from the British point of view, had been disappointing. The city was so spread out (900 square miles), and contained so many open spaces, that the bombers had difficulty hitting specific targets or wiping out large contiguous areas. In fact, the early raids had achieved so little by the end of 1941 that the British suspended attacks on Berlin for about a year to concentrate on easier targets and to develop technical improvements that would, they hoped, make it easier to hit the German capital.

As of early 1942 the British Bomber Command was under the leadership of Arthur ("Bomber") Harris, who believed that "area bombing" of large cities and industrial centers could bring an enemy to its knees without the need for a ground invasion. His strategy harmonized with a decision reached at the Anglo-American Casablanca Conference (January 1943) to "wage the heaviest possible bomber campaign against the German war effort," although neither Churchill nor Roosevelt expected bombing alone to win the war. American bombers joined the crusade against Berlin shortly after Casablanca, hitting the city for the first time on January 27, 1943. Interestingly enough, they had practiced for this operation by bombing mock-ups of Berlin apartment houses designed by the modernist architect Erich Mendelssohn, who had gone into exile in the United States. The Combined Bomber Command was now able to deliver a one-two punch, the British (still) flying by night, the Americans by day. Although Allied losses were extensive, the bombers began to do serious damage to the city. In March 1943 alone over 700 Berliners died in raids. There were casualties also at the Berlin zoo, whose terrified animals, along with the city's children, were surely the most innocent victims of a war that had now truly "come home" to the German capital.

The war was coming home more viciously on the battlefront as well, in terms of increased losses of soldiers who hailed from Berlin. During the first year of the war, Berlin had sacrificed its native sons at the rate of 361 per month. In the second year the number went up to 467 per month, and in the third year to 661. Then, in the six-month period between October 1942 and April 1943, soldiers from Berlin died at an average of 1,565 a month.

Some of the losses occurred at the Battle of Stalingrad, which raged from September 1942 to the end of January 1943. The Nazi government predicted a glorious victory in this crucial battle, but on February 1, 1943, the German forces surrendered, marking the Reich's greatest defeat to date. The disaster was so immense that Goebbels's propaganda machine could not ignore it or disguise it as a strategic redeployment. The propaganda minister ordered a three-day period of mourning. At the same time, however, the defeat gave impetus to an initiative that Goebbels had been trying to sell to Hitler for some time: mobilization for "total war" on the home front. Heretofore, the minister insisted, Germany had been fighting with one hand tied behind its back because it had not demanded enough sacrifices from the folks at home. With Hitler's permission, Goebbels staged a huge rally at the Sportpalast on February 18, invoking the "great tocsin of fate" at Stalingrad to call for a new kind of war, one "more total and radical than we can even imagine today." No longer would the Nazi regime be hindered by "bourgeois squeamishness." Every German, high and low, must be made to sacrifice for the common cause. "Now people, arise, and storm, break loose!" he shouted.

In the wake of Goebbels's jeremiad, the regime began closing down businesses not vital to the war effort. All women between seventeen and forty-five were required to register for possible conscription into the labor force. To ensure that the capital was in the vanguard of the new commitment, Goebbels shifted 300 men from his own ministry to the Wehrmacht and replaced them with women. He shut down a number of luxury shops and restaurants, including Horcher's, which had been serving gourmet meals to bigwigs without demanding ration cards. (The Gauleiter took special pleasure in closing Horcher's, because it was Göring's favorite eatery.) Berlin's theaters and cinemas were also ordered closed, but with soldiers coming home on furlough it made sense to maintain some distractions, so these venues were reopened after a few days.

Even as he was demanding greater sacrifices from the populace, Goebbels continued to live high off the hog himself, entertaining his actress friends at the sumptuous villa he had expropriated from a Jewish banker on the Wannsee island of Schwanenwerder, and driving around town in a new armor-plated Mercedes, a Christmas gift from Hitler, who worried that some malcontent might blow up Goebbels in Berlin just as anti-Nazi partisans had assassinated Reinhard Heydrich in Prague in May 1942.

In the event, no one came close to killing Goebbels (a would-be assassin trying to lay a mine at Schwanenwerder was immediately apprehended and executed), but morale in Berlin was badly shaken by the grim news from Stalingrad and the resumption of Allied bombing. The SD, which kept its finger on the pulse of popular opinion, reported increasing signs of defeatism. The myth of Hitler's invincibility was now increasingly "on the defensive." Ursula von Kardorff wrote bitterly in her diary on January 31, 1943: "How gloriously our Führer has saved us from collapse, the Jews, and Bolshevism. In actuality we have Stalingrad, Wornesch, Ladogasee, Illmensee, Rshew [German defeats in Russia], the fleeing Army of the Caucuses. The Jewish deportations. Can one still pray? I cannot do so anymore."

Yet there was worse to come, much worse. In late August and early September 1943 the Allies launched the largest air attacks to date against Berlin. This was the opening phase of the attempt to bomb the Reich into submission. On the night of August 23/24, 1943, the RAF dispatched 719 aircraft to Berlin. The British suffered grievous losses, due mainly to a highly effective fighter defense mounted by the Luftwaffe, but they managed nonetheless to drop 1,706 tons of high explosive and incendiary bombs on the city. As a result, every government office building in the Wilhelmstrasse was at least partially damaged, as were an officer cadet school at Köpenick and the barracks of the Leibstandarte Adolf Hitler in Lichterfelde. A total of 854 people were killed, many of them because they had neglected to seek shelter, a fact that infuriated Goebbels, who threatened to shoot people who did not abide by the air-raid regulations.

Waves of raids over the course of the next three months were deadlier still. A big attack on the night of November 22/23 dumped 2,501 tons of bombs on the city, and subsequent raids in December, including an especially lethal one on Christmas Eve, caused severe damage. These raids killed more than 8,000 people, destroyed 68,226 buildings, and rendered a quarter-million Berliners homeless. Especially hard hit were the city center, Alexanderplatz, and Charlottenburg. Among the prominent buildings to be damaged or destroyed were Speer's War Industry Ministry, the Naval Construction Headquarters, the Charlottenburg

Palace, the "Red Town Hall," the Kaiser Wilhelm Memorial Church, the KaDeWe department store, the Technical University, and the Romanisches Café. Also hit was Hitler's private train, which was parked at a railway siding.

To reduce the human casualties occasioned by the bombing, and to relieve the strain on resources in the capital, Goebbels ordered the evacuation of children, non-working women, and the old. Berlin's designated *Aufnahmegaue* (receiving areas for evacuees) were Mark Brandenburg, East Prussia, and the Wartheland. In order to resettle in one of these areas, Berliners needed to secure a departure certificate, which entitled them to a living allowance and free travel. At first most of the evacuees were children, since women and older Berliners were reluctant to leave their friends and trusted turf. This also irritated Goebbels, for he wanted to rid the city as much as possible of "superfluous eaters." On November 25, 1943, he complained in his diary that the first evacuation train was not full, all too many Berliners preferring to stay "in order to save their most necessary goods and to wait to see what happens next."

What happened next was bad enough to generate a full-scale exodus. In July 1943 about 3,665,000 registered inhabitants remained in the capital (there were thousands more unregistered residents: forced laborers, displaced persons, people in hiding); but by January 1945 the figure had dropped to 2,846,000. Over the course of that period Berlin's schools were shut down, resulting in the wholesale transfer of students and teaching staffs to the hinterlands, whose residents worried about strains on their own resources. Also transferred out of Berlin were many vital industries, including parts of the giant Siemens operation, which were dispersed around the country. This proved to be the beginning of the end of Berlin's dominant place in German heavy manufacturing.

Many of the people who chose to stay in Berlin sought relief from the pressures of steady bombardment by attending cultural events, which remained surprisingly plentiful despite the growing destruction of concert halls, theaters, and cinemas, and the loss of performers to the Wehrmacht or to bombs. It was a testament to the strength of Berlin's cultural heritage—but also to the Nazis' continuing determination to exploit culture for their own political ends—that the city's offerings stayed so rich.

The State Opera, which had been wrecked in an air raid in early 1941, was hastily rebuilt on Hitler's orders as a matter of public urgency. Wilhelm Furtwängler conducted Wagner's *Meistersinger* at the gala reopening on December 12, 1941. To his credit, however, the maestro refused to participate in a Goebbels-sponsored propaganda film about the Berlin Philharmonic entitled *Sinfonie und Liebe* (Symphony and Love). The film claimed that the Nazis alone had made the Philharmonic great, predictably failing to mention any of the Jewish musicians and conductors who in reality had helped to make the orchestra the dominant institution it was.

Furtwängler's bitter rival, Herbert von Karajan, who was kept from the draft on orders from Goebbels, conducted free concerts for wounded soldiers and arms workers with the State Opera orchestra during the 1942/43 season. Over Furtwängler's objections, these performances took place at the Philharmonie on Potsdamer Platz. Although the building was severely damaged by bombs in late 1943, the Philharmonic continued to perform there until January 1945, when further raids destroyed it entirely. Shortly after the Philharmonie was reduced to rubble, the State Opera was wrecked for the second time. Karajan was forced to move to the Beethovensaal, giving his last performance there on February 18, 1945. At that moment he had a visa for Milan in his pocket, which he used to escape the Nazi capital during its final weeks of agony.

In the interest of maintaining morale, the Nazis allowed a number of nightclubs to stay open that featured that officially despised music—jazz. However, only the most dedicated enthusiasts braved the frequent blackouts and bad liquor that were an inevitable part of the wartime jazz scene in the German capital. On the positive side, increasing losses of native musicians to conscription mandated the importation of superior foreign players from the conquered countries and fascist Italy. The Italian tenor sax player Tulio Mobiglia led a hot sextet at the Patria and Posita bars. Berliners could also hear jazz over foreign radio, which they listened to despite an official prohibition. (Cleverly, the British mixed jazz segments with their news broadcasts to Germany.) As he had in the mid-1930s, Goebbels encouraged German stations to play "rhythmic dance music" on the air to combat the influence of the foreign programs. He explained his tolerance for this music by saying that "at war, we need a people that has managed to preserve its good humor." In an effort to provide reliable artistic content for these broadcasts, the regime authorized a new German-style swing orchestra on the model of the defunct Golden Seven. Inaugurated in early 1942, the German Dance and Entertainment Orchestra (Das Deutsche Tanz-und Unterhaltungsorchester, DTU) recruited its players from the best remaining jazz musicians in Germany. The band was based at Berlin's Delphi-Palast, where it gave occasional concerts, but mainly it provided musical fodder for radio broadcasts. Like the Golden Seven, the DTU was forced to wear an artistic straitjacket, all the tighter now because of the war. Improvising was out, as were all American tunes.

For the Nazis, the most important cultural weapon was film, and never more so than during the war, when movies could be used to promote ideals of endurance and togetherness in the face of adversity. Images of Berlin as a bastion of patriotic unity were prominent in a film called *Wunschkonzert* (Request Concert, 1940), which recalled the heady days of the 1936 Olympics. The message it sent was that, by holding together, the Germans could win this new contest just as they had triumphed in 1936. *Die grosse Liebe* (The Great Love, 1942) told the story of a Berlin diva (played by the beautiful Sarah Leander), who through a love affair with a German officer learns the value of keeping up morale, which she demonstrates by singing songs like "I Know That Sometimes a Miracle Will Happen." The Wehrmacht objected to this film because the officer sleeps with the singer, but Göring pointed out that any officer who missed a chance to sleep with Sarah Leander was not fit to serve. Another inspirational film, vastly more expensive to make, was Veit Harlan's *Kolberg*, a reenactment of the heroic Germans' defense of that town against Napoleon's French invaders in 1806/7. To produce this epic, shooting for which commenced in 1943, Goebbels persuaded the Wehrmacht to provide 187,000 soldiers as extras and 6,000 horses. The budget was eight and a half million marks. The film took so long to make—actual fighting got in the way of the staged fighting—that when it finally premiered, in 1945, Berlin lay in ruins.

Even more quixotic was the film *Das Leben Geht Weiter* (Life Goes On), set in a beleaguered Berlin, where in reality the life that went on was mostly underground. While meant to celebrate Berliner pluck, the movie, like *Kolberg*, was an example of hugely misplaced effort. Because most of the buildings on location had been destroyed, UFA built full-scale imitations of them at great expense at its Babelsberg studios. Air raids knocked out electricity and phone lines during the shooting. Eventually production was shifted further west, to Luneberg, but the film was not completed when the British arrived, and none of the footage survives.

In August 1944 Goebbels ordered the closing of Berlin's theaters, this time for good. Even before this time, however, most Berliners were too harried by the escalating air raids to consider an evening at the theater; simple survival provided drama enough. Andreas-Friedrich recorded a night under the bombs on June 21, 1944:

> There is a toppling and crashing, quaking, bursting, trembling. To us it seems as if the floor bounded a yard up in the air. There's a hit. Another. And another. We wish we could crawl into the earth. Biting smoke stings our eyes. Did our neighbors get hit? We have no idea. All we know is that we are poor, naked, and desperately in need of help. . . . [Finally] All clear! Where the next house stood is now a heap of ruins. A woman runs screaming past us. She is wrapped in a horse blanket; terror distorts her face. She is pressing three empty clothes hangers to her breast. Gradually the street comes to life; more and more people appear out of the smoke, the ruins, the ghastly destruction. They say forty-eight bombs hit our block. The dead can't be counted yet; they're under rubble and stone, crushed, annihilated, beyond the reach of help.

Albert Speer, on the other hand, found an element of beauty in the raids. Observing an attack from the roof of one of his flak towers, he had to remind himself

> of the cruel reality in order not to be completely entranced by the scene: the illumination of the parachute flares, which the Berliners called 'Christmas trees,' followed by flashes of explosions which were caught by the clouds of smoke, the innumerable probing searchlights, the excitement when a plane was caught and tried to escape the cone of light, the brief flaming torch when it was hit. No doubt about it, the apocalypse provided a magnificent spectacle.

Looking on the bright side, Speer noted that the Allied bombers were accomplishing much of the demolition work that would be necessary for the realization of Germania, the envisaged Nazi capital of the future.

Speer's boss, Adolf Hitler, witnessed neither the "magnificence" nor the horrors of the Battle of Berlin, for he was away from the city for most of this period. In any event, he had no wish to see the effects of the bombing on German cities; this was too depressing. By late 1943, according to Speer, he was even losing interest in the architectural reconstruction of Berlin. He now preferred to dream about rebuilding his old hometown of Linz, where he expected to retire and be buried. Echoing Bis-

A ruined block of houses in Neue Winterfeldstrasse, 1944

marck and Kaiser Wilhelm II, Hitler said that he did not want to be interred in Berlin. "Even after a victorious war," wrote Speer, "[Hitler] did not want to be buried beside his field marshals in the Soldiers Hall in Berlin."

The Allies hoped through bombing Berlin and other large German cities to generate widespread popular opposition to the Nazi regime. This did not materialize, though there was certainly resentment toward the authorities for bringing home the horrors of war. As Ruth Andreas-Friedrich observed following the raid that wiped out her block, survivors were markedly cool towards the SS salvage squad that came to help clear away the ruins: "'If it weren't for you, there wouldn't be any ruins,' the faces seem to say. 'Why do you come now, when it's too late? Why did you get us into all this in the first place?'"

While resentment towards the regime never translated into mass opposition, a number of resistance circles did emerge in Berlin over the course of the war. We have mentioned the Jewish-Communist Herbert Baum group, which came to grief in August 1942. Other small Communist cells cropped up, taking advantage of the Nazis' distraction by the war and the sheer size and labyrinthine complexity of the capital. Some of the activists had served jail sentences during the early years of the Third Reich, from which they emerged with added hatred for their foe. Because of the Nazi-Soviet Pact, most veteran Communists held back from active resistance until the German invasion of the Soviet Union. During the first phase of the war, the most notable example of Communist resistance in Berlin involved a youth group that distributed fliers urging workers not to produce munitions. Their leader, Heinz Kapelle, was arrested and executed in July 1941—a harbinger of the fate of virtually all active Communist resisters in the city. The exiled KPD leaders in Moscow, anxious to maintain ties in Berlin that they could exploit upon returning to the city after the expected Red Army victory, smuggled a few emissaries into the capital from Sweden. One of them managed fleeting contact with a cell run by the Berliner Robert Uhrig, but Uhrig's group was exposed in February 1942. Moscow did not have ties to a larger resistance group led by Anton Saefkow, which fell to the Gestapo in mid-1944. On the other hand, a leftist officer in the Air Ministry, Harro Schulze-Boysen, along with an official in the Economics Ministry, Arvid Harnack, radioed important military information from Berlin to Moscow. Their spy-operation, which the Nazis called the "Red Orchestra," was broken up in August 1942. Schulze-Boysen was executed on December 22, 1942, leaving behind a verse in his cell that read: "The final judgment is not / Ended by rope or ax / And Judgment Day will give a chance / To get the verdict changed."

The Red Orchestra was dangerous to the Nazis because it operated from inside the government. So did most of the figures involved in the famous conspiracy to assassinate Hitler that culminated in the abortive bombing at his East Prussian headquarters on July 20, 1944. This is not the place for a detailed history of the Twentieth of July movement and the bombing attempt; suffice it here to point up the salient points, highlighting the Berlin dimension.

Although few of the main figures in the plot were native Berliners, the conspiracy was based in the capital because many of the activists were members of military units or bureaucratic agencies headquartered there. Count Claus von Stauffenberg, the man who planted the bomb, was chief of staff to General Friedrich Fromm, commander of the army reserve. Like many of his colleagues, he had originally been attracted to the Nazi movement in the belief that it offered the best hope for a national reawakening. When instead it began covering Germany in shame and leading it toward catastrophic defeat, the count turned passionately against the regime, which he decided could be brought down only if Hitler were eliminated. Yet for all his dedication to the cause of ridding Germany of Nazism, Stauffenberg was ill-equipped for the job of killing Hitler. Having lost his right hand and two fingers of his left hand, along with one eye, in the war, he could not use a pistol and had to resort to the messy and notoriously unreliable method of a time-bomb (a method, incidentally, that had failed to kill Hitler in Munich in 1939).

After a couple of earlier attempts to place bombs near Hitler had not come off, Stauffenberg finally decided to carry out the operation on July 20, 1944, during a staff conference at the Führer's "Wolf's Lair" in East Prussia. Arriving at the complex by plane on the appointed day, he took his bomb package into a bathroom to set the timing, but an interruption, combined with his injuries, prevented him from fusing all his explosives. Once inside the briefing hut he placed his briefcase containing the bomb as close as he could to Hitler before leaving to take a prearranged phone call from Berlin. As luck would have it, the briefcase was kicked behind the leg of a heavy map table just before the bomb detonated. This detail, along with the hut's open windows and flimsy walls, which dissipated the force of the blast, enabled Hitler to survive with only minor injuries.

Stauffenberg and another conspirator, General Erich Fellgiebel, were about 200 hundred yards away from the hut when the bomb went off. Assuming that Hitler was dead, the count asked Fellgiebel to phone Berlin with instructions to go ahead with a preplanned roundup of top Nazis in the capital; then he flew back to Berlin. By the time he arrived the plot was already unraveling, since Hitler let it be known immediately that an unsuccessful attempt had been made on his life. In Berlin a shocked Goebbels enthusiastically launched an investigation into the affair, which he assumed was the work of the "aristocratic generals' clique" he despised. It was not difficult to identify the plotters, for the officers in question, after a brief hesitation, began playing their hand. Their efforts were ill coordinated, and military units loyal to Hitler soon cordoned off the former Oberkommando der Wehrmacht (OKW) headquarters in the Bendlerstrasse, where Stauffenberg and some of the other putschists had barricaded themselves. To deflect suspicion from himself, General Fromm ordered Stauffenberg, General Ludwig Beck, General Friedrich Olbricht, Colonel Mertz von Quirnheim, and Lieutenant Werner von Haeften arrested and conducted to a courtyard in the center of the building. There Stauffenberg, Olbricht, Mertz, and Haeften were promptly shot. Beck was allowed to shoot himself, but, bungling the job, was finished off by a sergeant.

This was only the beginning of the grisly retribution exacted by the Hitler regime against the Twentieth of July movement. In subsequent days and weeks the Gestapo combed the Reich in search of anyone with the slightest connection to the plot. In some cases relatives of the men accused of participating in the action were also taken into custody. Many of the arrests took place in Berlin because of its centrality to the plot. Among the figures caught up in the dragnet was Dietrich Bonhöffer, a Protestant pastor in Dahlem who led a group of dissident theologians called the Confessing Church. In 1942 Bonhöffer had tried to organize foreign support for the German resistance through church contacts in Sweden. Another, very different, arrestee was Count Wolf Heinrich von Helldorf, the rabidly anti-Semitic and morally reprobate chief of police in Berlin. He had turned against the regime out of despair over the course of the war. Count Helmut James von Moltke, an international lawyer and great-nephew of the famous field marshal, was pulled into the net even though he was already in prison when the bombing occurred. The Berlin defendants were tried before the notorious "hanging judge" Roland Freisler at the local branch of the People's Court. Those found guilty in the first trial were executed by hanging at Berlin's Plötzensee Prison, where they were suspended by piano wire from meat hooks attached to a roof beam. Since there was no drop from a scaffold, the victims dangled for several minutes before expiring. Goebbels ordered that the executions be filmed for his and Hitler's later amusement.

Because the Twentieth of July plot failed so disastrously, and because it was so belated, many commentators in later years wrote it off as relatively minor moment in the history of the Third Reich. This is an inaccurate appraisal. There can be no doubt the coup was poorly organized. But with respect to the timing, it has been rightly noted that if the plot had been successful, the loss of additional millions of lives and much physical destruction might have been averted. Taking Germany alone, some 2.8 million people died as a result of the war between September 1, 1939, and July 20, 1944; between the assassination attempt and the end of the war that figure grew to 4.8 million. The mass murder in the death camps in the East, which continued until the Red Army's liberation of Poland, might have ceased. And the hugely destructive ground attacks on German cities, including that against Berlin, were yet to come.

Here Is the Fascist Lair—Berlin

The Twentieth of July conspirators intended to liberate Germany from within. Their failure to do so meant that the country would have to be conquered by its foreign opponents. As we have seen, some Allied strategists had hoped to force a surrender by pounding German cities into rubble. It had become apparent by mid-1944 that this strategy was not going to work. Not only was the Reich holding on, but its industrial capacity was actually increasing despite the bombing. In Berlin, the target of dozens of major raids, many key plants had been damaged and the transportation system was in shambles. However, through rationalization and the relocation of plants to outlying districts, the city's industrial production managed to reach its wartime peak in early 1944.

There being no doubt that Germany would have to be conquered with ground forces, Allied armies pressed their assault on the Reich from west and east. When the Americans managed to cross the Rhine at Remagen in early March 1945, it became urgently necessary to decide how best to organize the push across Germany. A second question was where Berlin would fit in the broader picture. A bitter debate broke out in the Western camp over these issues. General Bernard Montgomery and the British wanted to focus maximum effort on a drive across northern Germany with Berlin as the goal. In their view, this represented not only the fastest way to defeat Germany but had the added advantage of taking Berlin before the Russians could get there. But General Dwight D. (Ike) Eisenhower, the overall commander of the Allied armies, concluded that the most efficacious route to victory lay in destroying large Wehrmacht concentrations in the center and south, a task he believed could be best handled by forces under Generals Omar Bradley and George Patton. Ike also decided to let the Russians take Berlin, which by Allied agreement was designated to lie within the Soviet zone of occupation after the war. For him this was not an overly painful decision: his priority was to defeat the Reich as quickly as possible and with minimal loss of Allied lives. Moreover, he believed that the crucial test would come not in Berlin but in the south of Germany, were the Nazis were rumored to be planning a last-ditch defense in the Alps (the rumors turned out to be false).

Eisenhower was much criticized, especially by the British, for not racing the Russians to Berlin. British officers contemptuously referred to the American general's deference to Stalin as "Have a Go, Joe," a phrase used by London prostitutes seeking GIs' custom during the war. Ike himself later told Willy Brandt that if he had to do it over again, he would have ordered American troops to take the German capital. Yet in the context of the time, he probably made the right decision. In late March, when he reaffirmed his basic strategy, Western armies still stood 250 miles from Berlin, while the Russians were on the Oder-Neisse line, only thirty-three miles from the eastern edge of the city. Asked by Ike to estimate probable Western Allied casualties in an assault on Berlin, Bradley projected a loss of about 100,000 men. "A pretty stiff price for a prestige objective," he said, "especially when we've got to fall back and let the other fellows take over."

The Russians, meanwhile, were gearing up for their push on a city which they considered to be far more than just a prestige objective. "He who controls Berlin controls Germany and whoever controls Germany controls Europe," Lenin once said. The German capital loomed so important in Russian strategy that its prospective conquest ignited a race between two military rivals every bit as fierce as the fabled contest between Montgomery and Patton. In November 1944 Stalin had promised Berlin to Marshal Georgi Zhukov, who had been the principal architect of the Red Army victories so far. But at a staff meeting on April 1, 1945, as the Russians were making their final plans for the Berlin offensive, the Soviet leader allowed himself to be convinced that Berlin could be taken more quickly if General Ivan Konev's First Ukrainian Front pressured the city simultaneously with the forces of Zhukov. Understanding the usefulness of competition, and always willing to play off one subleader against another, Stalin drew up two approach routes to the German capital that stopped just short of the city. After reaching that point, he said, "whoever breaks in first, let him take Berlin."

For a time it appeared that Konev might earn this distinction. Both his and Zhukov's forces crossed the Oder on April 16 with a total strength of 2.5 million troops, 6,250 tanks, and 42,000 artillery pieces and mortars. On the next day Konev was already closing in on Zossen, the new headquarters of the OKW, while Zhukov was held up by tough German resistance at the Seelow Heights on the west bank of the Oder. Frustrated, Zhukov threatened to dismiss any of his officers who did not push forward with total resolution. By April 19 he was able to smash through the German defenses and reach the eastern outskirts of Berlin. With additional backing from General Konstantin Rokossovsky's Second White Russian Front, Zhukov was in a position to give Konev a good run for his money.

The Nazis, for their part, were determined to do their utmost to defend Berlin. On January 16, 1945, Hitler moved back to the city, having decided to direct from there the final phase of what he continued to insist would be a victorious war. However, because Berlin was under constant bombardment, he spent most of his time in an elaborate bunker complex that had recently been built under the Neue Reichskanzlei. Accessible via a spiral staircase leading down from an older and shallower bunker, the new Führerbunker contained eighteen rooms, including a conference room, offices for Goebbels and Martin Bormann (Hess's replacement as Hitler's deputy), valet quarters, a small surgery, a vegetarian kitchen, and the Führer's private accommodations, which consisted of a bedroom, map room, living room, Eva Braun's bedroom, and a bathroom. In Hitler's domain the only decoration was Anton Graf's portrait of Frederick the Great, the Prussian King who had snatched victory from the jaws of defeat in the Seven Years' War. Hitler hoped to repeat this accomplishment.

If a German victory were somehow to be achieved, the national capital could not be allowed to fall. "I must force the decision here, or go down fighting," Hitler told one of his secretaries. On March 9 his government issued a decree setting down the preparations for the defense of "Fortress Berlin." Three rings of defenses were established around the city. The outer ring was some forty kilometers from the city center, the second encompassed the suburbs, and the last followed the *S-Bahn* line around the inner city. Major highways leading into the capital were blocked, and the principal bridges were mined to allow quick demolition if the need arose. A weak point in Berlin's defense system was the manpower on hand within the capital. With most regular troops still on the fronts, the only unit of operational value was the Grossdeutschland Division, which had played a key role in the suppression of the Twentieth of July affair. Smaller flak and *Pak* (antitank) units were also available, as was the Volksturm, a motley collection of the very old and the very young, who had been mobilized at the last minute to sacrifice themselves for the Fatherland. The Volksturm units were untrained and poorly armed, though some of them carried the Panzerfaust, an antitank weapon that could do genuine damage. Hitler

Members of the Volksturm in a maneuver near Potsdam, 1944

had no compunctions about throwing children and old men into battle. "The capital will be defended to the last man and the last bullet," he said.

Perhaps the regime's most potent weapon in the defense of Berlin was the Berliners' fear of what would happen to them if the Russians overran their city. Goebbels's propaganda machine harped on the horrors that would attend a Russian victory, and for once the little doctor was not exaggerating. Nonetheless, morale in Fortress Berlin was hardly of the highest as the Russians approached. Steady bombing had already induced an almost catatonic apathy in many quarters. Ursula von Kardorff likened the population to passengers on a sinking ship, resigned to "a fate that they could not escape."

Some of the inhabitants, on the other hand, were not too apathetic to exploit the chaos around them for private gain. Packs of thieves roamed the ruins, stealing precious food, fuel, and material goods for sale in the thriving black market, which was the only viable market in town. Deserters from the collapsing eastern front filtered into the city and joined in the looting and thievery. Blessed with a bonanza business, funeral directors sold the same coffins over and over, then tossed the dead into mass graves. When one indignant widow complained about this swindle, another responded: "Since the living have no value, why should the dead?" The doorkeeper at the demolished Scherl Press House was heard to advise another widow: "Be happy that [your husband] is buried in a mass grave; at least he'll have company."

As the Russian vise closed on Berlin, Berliner vice resurfaced with a vengeance, but it had a desperate edge to it, as people tried to grab a last bit of pleasure before the anticipated surfeit of pain. There were reports of orgies in the basements and shelters, gluttonous feasts with stolen food, "cellar tribes" anaesthetizing themselves with pilfered medical alcohol and morphine. The physical scene with which the Berliners now had to contend encouraged an abandonment of restraints. With major buildings reduced to piles of rubble, points of orientation had disappeared. Prominent streets and avenues had been replaced by narrow paths winding through the ruins—perfect for muggings and anonymous trysts. As the Berliners said, it was easier to act as if one had just failed the Last Judgment when the world around so closely resembled Hell.

A hell, one should add, with a certain rusticity to it. Due to the loss of their agricultural hinterlands, Berliners had taken to planting vegetable gardens and even grain fields among the ruins. Corn and potatoes grew in the wreckage of the Gendarmenmarkt, between the blasted Schinkel masterpieces. Herds of goats were pastured where cars and busses once zoomed. With its yawning empty spaces, Berlin looked like a semicivilized outpost on the Prussian plain, which of course it once had been. And because transportation and communication between its various districts had broken down, the city also seemed once again to be more a collection of villages than an integrated metropolis. Obviously, this was not what the Nazis had had in mind when they promised to return Berlin to its "true self."

On April 20, 1945, his fifty-sixth birthday, Hitler made a brief appearance above ground. Due to stress and the poisons prescribed by his quack physician, Theodor Morell, Hitler was a physical wreck. His skin was blotchy, his shoulders stooped, his left arm hung loose, and he listed to the right. Obviously uncomfortable outside his troglodyte world, he quickly pinned decorations on some Hitler Youth in the Chancellery garden and then disappeared back into the bunker, where he gave himself over to fantasies about a miraculous victory. He had been indulging in such fantasies for some time. On April 13, when news reached Berlin that President Roosevelt had died, Hitler and Goebbels thought they saw a reprise of Catherine the Great's death during the Seven Years' War, which had allowed Frederick the Great a last-minute victory. Now, they prophesied, Truman would pull the Western forces out of the war, leaving the Reich free to focus on Russia. Hitler also spoke rapturously of "wonder weapons" that would turn the tide: the V-1 and V-2 rockets, a new kind of U-boat, and remote-controlled airplanes. (Ironically—and thankfully—the Germans put little emphasis on developing the most important "wonder weapon" of the Second World War, the atomic bomb.) Down in his map room, Hitler shifted around armies that no longer existed. These forces would fall back on Berlin, he said, creating an impregnable barrier against which the Soviets would throw themselves in vain. Other Nazi forces would then hit the Reds from behind, saving Berlin and opening the way for German counteroffensives across the board. At other moments, however, Hitler could be surprisingly clear-eyed. At a staff conference on April 22 he suddenly announced that the war was lost and that he planned to kill himself.

Blaming his generals for not achieving the fantasy feats he imagined for them, Hitler relieved them of their commands, stripped them of their honors. He fired his best tank commander, Heinz Guderian, for failing to stop the Russians; he sentenced the city commandant of Königsberg to death in absentia for failing to hold that city; and he cursed General Walther Wenck, whose Twelfth Army was situated southwest of Berlin on the Elbe, for not hastening to the rescue of the capital. His fury embraced some of his closest colleagues as well. He ordered Göring arrested for high treason because the Reich Marshal offered to take over leadership of the country in view of Hitler's decision to stay in the bunker in Berlin. Similarly, he ordered Himmler's arrest upon learning that the SS leader had tried to broker a capitulation to the Western powers. Finally, he turned his rage against Berlin itself, ordering the demolition of bridges, waterways, electrical plants, communications installations, and all remaining heavy industry.

Shocked that the man who considered himself the "Savior of Berlin" in the 1930s should now be determined to destroy it, Albert Speer worked during the last weeks of the Reich to prevent this order from being carried out. He also planned—so he claims in his memoirs—to kill Hitler by feeding poison gas into the ventilation shaft of the bunker, only to give up the attempt upon discovering that the ground-level shaft had been replaced by a high chimney. If this story is true (and with Speer, one can never be sure), Hitler's death was deferred not only by the ill-luck of his enemies but also by the irresolution of his disillusioned henchmen.

In late April Hitler was joined in the bunker by Goebbels, his main partner in the conquest of Berlin. Like Hitler, Goebbels vowed to fight on to the bitter end, giving orders that anyone who obstructed the defense of the city should be summarily executed. He too insisted that if the Reich could win in Berlin, the rest of the nation would rally to throw out the invaders. It is impossible to know whether he actually believed such nonsense, but very probably he did: the surreal atmosphere in the bunker, where the sound and shock of Russian shells barely penetrated, encouraged the wildest flights of fancy.

The scene aboveground in the last week of April allowed for few illusions among the defenders, but many nonetheless elected to fight on as their Führer commanded. In addition to battling Soviet troops, SS units and so-called "Werewolf" bands executed Berliners who opted for surrender. Here and there bodies dangled from lampposts with signs reading: "We were too cowardly to defend Berlin from the Bolsheviks. We raised the white flag and thereby betrayed Greater Germany and the Führer. Thus we must die without honor!"

Marshal Zhukov in Berlin, 1945

The German resistance was such that the Russians had to blast their way through the city block by block, house by house. Shells from their tanks and artillery added significantly to the devastation wrought by the years of bombing. After the Soviets had secured a neighborhood, there was often not a single building left intact.

Alas, the Russians left more than physical devastation in their wake. Hungry for revenge against an enemy that had terrorized their own land, Soviet soldiers gave themselves over to an orgy of plunder and rapine. They raped women of all ages, from five to eighty, often dozens of times over. According to the horrified mayor of Charlottenburg, "a woman could not escape being raped unless she kept in hiding." Such behavior violated an order from Stalin to maintain strict discipline when taking Berlin, so as not to alienate the German people. Zhukov, too, admonished his troops to remember that they were in Berlin to destroy Hitlerism, not to humiliate the people. "Soldiers," he said, "make sure that in looking at the hemlines of German girls you don't look past the reasons the homeland sent you here." But in the heat of the moment such admonitions had little currency. Before entering the capital Soviet soldiers had posted signs saying "*Here* it is, the fascist lair—Berlin!" Once inside the city, it was unlikely that that they would try to distinguish between "fascists" and ordinary citizens—at least not until they had slaked their thirst for revenge and garnered the rewards traditionally accorded the conqueror.

By the end of April the Soviets had fought their way to the center of the city. They were pouring artillery fire on the Neue Reichskanzlei, Albert Speer's monumental down payment on the future Germania. When he built this structure, Speer could hardly have known that his theory of "ruin value" would be tested so soon—and be found so sorely lacking.

On April 29 Hitler got word that that there would be no rescue of Berlin from the army under General Wenck, which in fact no longer existed. Aware now that there was no hope of victory, he decided to do what he had often threatened to do in the past: commit suicide. Before doing so, however, he married his mistress Eva Braun, who had joined him in the bunker on April 15. That he waited to wed until the eve of his suicide was perhaps a commentary on his views of married life. As required by Nazi law, he and Eva declared that they were of pure Aryan descent and free of hereditary diseases. After the ceremony, which was performed by a Berlin city councilor, Hitler dictated his Last Will and Testament, in which he blamed the Jews for the sorry plight of the Third Reich. He named Admiral Karl Dönitz as his successor. In a separate document he ordered that his body be "burnt immediately in the place where I have performed the greater part of my daily work during the course of my twelve years' service to the German people."

On the next day, April 30, Hitler took leave of those remaining in the bunker, including Goebbels, and disappeared with Eva Braun into their private quarters. The time was about 3:00 P.M. Although different accounts have been given as to what happened next, the most likely scenario is that Hitler and his bride took cyanide capsules—previously tested on Hitler's dog, Blondi—following which Hitler also shot himself in the head. The bodies were carried by SS men out of the bunker through an emergency exit to the Chancellery garden. They were placed in a shallow crater, doused with gasoline, and set on fire. Because of the steady Russian artillery barrage, however, the SS officers did not stand around and attend the flames, much less stir the ashes to break up any identifiable clumps. Rather, they quickly gave the Nazi salute and ran back in the bunker, returning to the garden only once to pour more gas on the fire. About seven hours later, after nightfall, they emerged a third time to wrap the partially charred corpses in tarps and cover them with a thin layer of dirt. Hitler's instructions regarding the treatment of his remains were therefore not carried out to the letter. The Führer was buried in Berlin after all, if only for a brief time.

Goebbels disobeyed another of Hitler's final orders by remaining in the bunker instead of joining Admiral Dönitz in his rump government northwest of the capital. He sent a telegram to the admiral informing him of the Führer's death, which news the admiral broadcast to the German people on May 1, telling them however that Hitler had died leading his troops in battle. Then, after failing through General Hans Krebs to negotiate a conditional surrender to the Soviets, Goebbels decided that he, too, must die in Berlin, the city of his destiny. He insisted, moreover, that his family, which had recently moved into the bunker, must die along with him. Accordingly, on the day after Hitler's suicide, Goebbels and his wife Magda arranged for the murder of their six children—Helga, Hilda, Helmut, Holde, Hedda, and Heide—with cyanide-laced bedtime chocolates. They then went up to the garden and committed suicide themselves. Their bodies were set on fire, but no one made an effort to bury them. This was not a time to stand on ceremony.

Back in the bunker the atmosphere lightened appreciably now that the master and his chief minion were gone for good. Most of the remaining inhabitants gave little thought to the destruction going on above their heads or even to the macabre

Red Army soldier posing with Soviet flag on the roof of the Reichstag, May 2, 1945

barbecue in the Chancellery garden. In the words of Hugh Trevor-Roper, the first serious student of Hitler's last days, "a great cloud seemed to have lifted from their spirits. The nightmare of ideological repression was over, and if the prospect before them remained dark and dubious, at least they were now free to consider it in a businesslike manner." They were also free to indulge in previously forbidden pleasures, such as smoking and listening to jazz. It is safe to say that the Führerbunker was the only place in Berlin at that moment where people were listening to jazz.

The moment of relief did not last long, however, for on the night of May 1 most of the remaining residents decided to abandon the bunker complex and make a desperate flight through the burning streets of Berlin in hopes of escaping the city. All were killed or captured in the break-out attempt, or run to ground shortly thereafter. For a time it was thought that Martin Bormann might have made it to safety, but he too died in the confines of the capital. Some thirty years later, a skull was found that was identified by pathologists as Bormann's.

On May 2 General Karl Weidling, the city commandant of Berlin, sought out Marshal Zhukov to formally surrender the German capital. To Zhukov's query regarding the whereabouts of Hitler, Weidling told him about the final fate of the Führer and Goebbels. "In my opinion," Weidling then said to Zhukov, "it would be senseless and criminal if [the fighting in Berlin] claimed any more victims." As the orders to end all the firing went out, Russian soldiers climbed to the roof of the ruined Reichstag and hoisted the Soviet flag. There is a famous photograph of this moment, and it might be taken as a fitting pictorial bookend to the photographs of Hitler's SA marching through the Brandenburg Gate on January 30, 1933.

It was also on May 2 that Soviet soldiers, acting on advice from captured German officers, discovered two corpses in the Chancellery garden that were tentatively identified as Joseph Goebbels and his wife, Magda. This was an important find, but the Soviets' primary quarry was Hitler, dead or alive. Two days later, a Russian private, rooting around in the same garden, noticed a pair of legs protruding from a crater. A little digging revealed the charred bodies of a man and a woman. The colonel in charge, having been told by the Germans that Hitler's body was somewhere in the Chancellery building, did not believe that these were the corpses of Hitler and Eva Braun, so he had them reburied. On May 5, still unable to find the Nazi leader's remains, the Russians returned to the garden and dug up the bodies that they had reburied the previous day.

These bodies, along with the putative Goebbels corpses and the suspected remains of General Krebs, who had also killed himself in the bunker, were taken to the headquarters of Soviet Counter Intelligence at Buch, a Berlin suburb. On May 8 autopsies were performed on all the bodies, which indicated that they were indeed those of Joseph and Magda Goebbels, Hans Krebs, Hitler, and Eva Braun. As far as Hitler was concerned, the telling evidence was some bridgework that was identified as his by a dental nurse who had once worked on his teeth.

At first the Soviets kept their discovery and identification of Hitler's body a secret, apparently holding this information in reserve in case somebody claiming to be the Führer showed up and tried to seize power. On June 6, however, they suddenly

Field Marshal Wilhelm Keitel (right) and Admiral Hans-Georg von Friedenburg at the German surrender, Karlshorst, May 9, 1945

announced that they had identified Hitler's corpse, adding that he had died exclusively from poisoning (which was more "cowardly" than shooting). Three days later they retracted this story and suggested instead that he might have escaped from Berlin and gone into hiding.

Why the reversal? It seems that a "live" Hitler was of more use to Moscow than a dead one, for the threat of a Nazi rebirth would allow the Soviets to push for larger reparations from Germany and a stronger role for Russia in Eastern Europe and Berlin. Moscow's duplicity indeed fueled all kinds of rumors regarding Hitler's fate. Many people preferred to believe that the Führer had gotten out of Berlin alive, and Hitler-sightings began cropping up all over the globe. He was seen on an island in the Baltic, a monastery in Spain, a temple in Tibet, a sheep ranch in Patagonia, a Volkswagen repair shop in Buenos Aires, a bandit hideout in Albania, even at an explorer's camp in Antarctica. The sightings continued for decades and with a frequency that rivaled those of the Virgin Mary and Elvis Presley. In November 1989 the *Weekly World News*, an American tabloid, announced that Hitler, now one hundred years old, had been found in the mountains of Chile, where he cared for sick Indian children and enjoyed the status of a "Living God."

In the early hours of May 7, the day before Hitler was autopsied and conclusively identified as the former Führer of the Third Reich, representatives of the rump Nazi regime signed a surrender document at General Eisenhower's headquarters at Reims. The Germans had delayed taking this step for several days in order to allow as many German soldiers as possible to withdraw westward and evade capture by the Russians. The Soviets saw the surrender at Reims as a tactic to deny them their rightful share in the victory. They insisted on a second, and far more elaborate, surrender ceremony in Berlin on May 8. Thus it was that representatives from the Western powers flew to Tempelhof airport and participated along with the Russians in the final surrender of the German forces at the Soviet headquarters in Karlshorst, in the northeastern part of the city. It was appropriate that this momentous event should take place in the demolished Nazi capital, but the recrimination surrounding the German surrender presaged rifts within the Allied camp that would soon result in the division of Germany and Berlin.

An American soldier poses on a flak gun in front of the destroyed Reichstag, 1945

COMING INTO THE COLD

The leaders of the United States are not such idiots as to fight over Berlin.

—Nikita Khrushchev, 1959

AN AIRPLANE CIRCLES over a smashed city in preparation for landing. On board is an American congressional delegation. Looking down on the devastation, a Texas congressman drawls: "Looks like rats been gnawing at a hunk of old Roquefort cheese." The chewed-up mess in question is Berlin, the congressman a character in Billy Wilder's black comedy, *A Foreign Affair* (1948), whose background shots were filmed in the former Nazi capital. The movie features the ex-Berliner Marlene Dietrich in the role of a former mistress of Nazi bigwigs who is now reduced to singing in sleazy bars and sleeping with GIs for her livelihood. In one of her songs, "Black Market," she croons:

I'm selling out, take all I've got—
ambitions, convictions, the works.
Why not?
Enjoy these goods,
for boy, these goods
are hot!

Wilder's film, a story of sexual license, betrayal, and reversal of fortune, brilliantly captures the mood of postwar Berlin. A city that just a few years before had touted itself as the power center of Europe, even of the world, was now reduced to a pile of rubble, ruled over, for the first time since Napoleon, by foreign powers. Foreign rule, of course, also brought division—bisection along the main fault line in the Cold War. The erstwhile capital of Hitler's "Thousand Year Reich" thus became the capital of the Cold War and the site of some of the most dangerous confrontations between the new contenders for control of the post-Hitler world.

Out of the Ruins

In the autumn of 1945, Felix Gilbert, whom we last encountered in this book watching the body of Rosa Luxemburg being fished from the Landwehr Canal, re-

Marlene Dietrich and Jean Arthur in a scene from Billy Wilder's A Foreign Affair, *1948*

turned to Berlin as a member of the American Office of Strategic Services. Hoping to see the apartment building where he had grown up, he drove out to his old neighborhood, only to find it a giant rubble field without a single structure intact. He began climbing over the ruins in an effort to locate some sign of where his house had stood. Suddenly he looked down and saw a pattern of blue and white cobblestones on which he had played hopscotch as a child. Like a macabre version of Proust's madeleine cookies, these dusty cobblestones called to his mind "a remote past because they had played an important role in my childhood."

The Berlin that Gilbert had known as a child and young student was indeed a thing of the past, reduced to a charred and stinking wreck by the years of bombing and the final brutal assault by the Soviets. It had now joined the cities and towns that were grim testimonials to the destructive power of modern warfare: Coventry, Rotterdam, Dresden, Hiroshima. When the war ended about 40 percent of the German capital was destroyed and its population reduced almost by half (though it was soon to rise again because of an influx of refugees). All the major bridges were down, the canal system was clogged with wreckage and dead bodies, the *U-Bahn* tunnels were flooded, water sources were polluted, and rats ran uncontrolled through the streets, feeding on the rotting carcasses of man and beast. Even the famous Berlin Zoo was a scene of carnage; a hippo named Rosa floated dead in her tank with the fin of a shell protruding from her carcass, while in the ape house a gorilla lay dead with stab wounds in his chest.

A vivid picture of the devastation can be gleaned from the accounts of survivors as they climbed out of their cellars and bunkers. One day after Berlin's capitulation the journalist Margret Boveri bicycled across the middle of the city, noting that it offered "a scene of indescribable devastation." Russian soldiers careened drunkenly down streets filled with shot-up tanks and burned autos; dazed refugees shuffled under their enormous burdens; women carrying water buckets lined up patiently at public taps; and escaped horses ran amok. "Haven't [the soldiers] stolen your bike from you yet?" fellow survivors asked Boveri in disbelief. After touring the central city with two friends on May 12, 1945, another dazed survivor, Ruth Andreas-Friedrich, recorded in her diary:

> The final six days of fighting have destroyed more of Berlin than ten heavy air raids. Only occasionally does one spot an intact building. . . .

People with weary faces poke around in the ruins, here and there recovering some battered 'trophy' or charred beam. . . .

A white horse is lying dead among the rubble and ruin of the place where Bruno Walter used to perform. Its body bloated, its eyes black and petrified. Like a gruesome still life it lies spread out under the broken arcades, its stiff legs accusingly pointing in the air. Bernburger Strasse is one huge pile of rubble. . . .

Taking a round-about way, we arrive at Tiergarten Park. Or rather what's left of it. Aghast, I look at the torn-up trees. Smashed, blasted, mutilated beyond recognition. . . . On Charlottenburger Chausee the smell of decaying bodies. On closer inspection we see it is only the skeletons of horses. People living in the neighborhood have cut the meat off the dead animals' bones piece by piece, cooked it in their pots and devoured it greedily. Only the intestines are left to decay between bare bones. . . . Now we are passing the Brandenburg Gate. Pariser Platz is swarming with people. They are carrying furniture out of the Ad-

A Russian soldier relieves a Berlin woman of her bicycle

Russian street signs in the ruins of Berlin, 1945

lon Hotel. Gold-plated mirrors, plush armchairs and mattresses. . . . We turn into Wilhelmstrasse. Ruins and dust. Dust and ruins. Wherever a cellar has remained intact, trophy hunters are at work, struggling up and down the stairs like maggots on cheese. . . . There stands the Chancellery. A battered stone colossus. Cavernous and desolate, its windows look out on the ruins of Wilhelmsplatz. Nothing stirs behind these walls that hold the remains of Adolf Hitler. Before the entrance a Russian soldier is on guard. His gun across his knees, he leans comfortably back in a green silk-covered armchair. In the middle of the Court of Honor, so-called, an image of perfect peace. The sight of it makes us smile. Certainly this is not the sort of guard the Nazis had imagined for their Führer and Chancellor.

Because the Western Allies did not arrive in Berlin until early July 1945, the Soviets had two months of sole control over the city—two months to pillage, plunder, and rape with impunity. Such behavior stemmed in part from pent-up hatred of the Germans, but it was also Stalin's policy to extract as much war booty as possible from Berlin before the Western Allies arrived. Hurriedly the Russians dismantled entire factories and put the equipment on trains heading east; once in the USSR the machines often proved useless because they were incompatible with the local infrastructure. Like the Jews under Nazism, Berlin's citizens were ordered to surrender telephones, radios, and typewriters to the authorities. The pride of Blaupunkt, Telefunken, Philips, and Siemens piled up at various collection points, open to the elements. And just to make sure that the Berliners understood who now ran their town, the Soviets put Berlin's clocks on Russian time and renamed streets and squares after Russian heroes such as General Nikolai Berzarin, the first Soviet city commander. They also erected a memorial to their victory just west of the Brandenburg Gate (it still stands today, minus its guards). "With this memorial," the architectural historian Brian Ladd has aptly noted, "the Soviets staked their claim to the historical landscape: within sight of the Reichstag, astride the former site of the Hohenzollerns' statue-laden Victory Boulevard, and at the point where Speer's north-south and east-west axes were to meet."

For the Soviet soldiers, females of all ages remained fair game in the first weeks after the capitulation. According to one witness, fat women (of whom there cannot have been many) had the most to fear, for "primitive people revere their fat women as symbols of abundance and fertility." Lurid accounts by contemporaries tend to convey the impression that the majority of Berlin women were assaulted and that every other Russian soldier was a rapist. Clearly this was not the case, but abuse of women was indeed widespread during the Soviet occupation, especially in the early phases. Women were violated ten, twenty, sometimes sixty times over. Often they were beaten and maimed in the process. Some who could not live with the experience committed suicide. A twelve-year-old girl who had been raped six times hanged herself on orders from her father, who had been unable to protect her. Desperate to avoid such "dishonor," men hid their womenfolk under piles of coal or bundled them up to look like grannies.

Aware that rape was inflaming German hatred of the Russian army, the Soviet command made efforts to contain the plague after June 1945, going so far as to execute some offenders. The wave of rapine receded somewhat, but the problem did not go away, for each successive contingent of occupation troops wanted to experi-

Central Berlin in ruins, 1945

ence the delights of their predecessors upon encountering the fabled Western metropolis. In any event, the Soviets' belated effort to cultivate an image of "Russian-German friendship" by disciplining their troops did not succeed: memories of the initial occupation were too powerful. Ruth Andreas-Friedrich adumbrated the problem when she wrote on May 29, 1945: "Russia is large. Russia is young, powerful and creative. During the last months under the Nazis nearly all of us were pro-Russian. We waited for the light from the East. But it has burned too many. Too much has happened that cannot be understood. The dark streets still resonate every night with the piercing screams of women in distress. The plundering and shooting, the insecurity and violence aren't over yet."

While Red Army soldiers focused their attention on rape and petty thievery, the Soviet command scoured Berlin for more substantial loot. Stalin's regime was determined to cart away as much industrial and technical equipment as it could, whether or not it was actually usable back home. German workers who had kept the plants running during the war were now forced to help the Soviets dismantle them. The task was huge, for a surprisingly large quantity of machinery had survived the bombing and shelling. In a matter of weeks the Soviets managed to accomplish what the bombs could not: eliminate Berlin as a great industrial city. Between the collapse of Germany in May 1945 and the autumn of that year the Russians removed some 80 percent of Berlin's machine-tool production, 60 percent of its light industrial capacity, and much of its electrical generating capability. Generators from the great Siemens, Borsig, and AEG plants went off to Russia, along with technicians and engineers who "volunteered" to work in Soviet industrial towns. Berlin of course would eventually build new power plants and industrial enterprises, subsidized after 1949 by West Germany, but it would never again be a great manufacturing center or hold the distinction of being Germany's *Fabrikstadt* par excellence.

In addition to industrial equipment, Stalin's government wanted to grab what if could of Berlin's vast monetary and artistic resources, which included parts of the stolen treasure amassed by the Nazis. Prime targets for the "Trophy Teams" that Moscow sent to Berlin in May 1945 were the tons of gold bullion thought to reside in the city's banks and the sacks of foreign currency rumored to have been hidden away by Nazi leaders. The Russians did not get all they had hoped for in this regard, for the Nazis had shipped much of the gold and currency out of the city. The teams had better luck with art, since Hitler had ordered that many of Berlin's collections be kept in the capital as a sign of faith that it would never fall. Only in the last weeks of the war were a number of major works moved to more secure sites in the provinces,

Trümmerfrauen *(rubble women) at work, 1946*

in particular to the giant Kaiseroda-Merkers salt mine in Thuringia. Not only were most of Berlin's art collections still intact, but many pieces were packed up in protective cases, ready to move. The Soviets began their art-plundering even before the German capitulation, focusing their attention first on the parts of Berlin earmarked for Western occupation. They headed straight for the zoo flak tower and its huge repository of crated treasure, which included Schliemann's horde of Trojan gold. Like a bank manager being made by robbers to clean out his safe, the director of the Prehistory Museum was conscripted to help the Russians evacuate the tower. The best items were moved to storehouses in the Soviet zone and then shipped to the USSR; less valuable pieces, including some of Hitler's beloved nineteenth-century kitsch, passed into the possession of individual Trophy Brigade members who fenced them to Berlin shops. Since Berlin's largest art repository, the Museum Island, was safely in the Russian zone, the Soviets could take their time in looting its famous collections. The buildings were in bad shape owing to the bombardment, and some valuable works, such as the Pergamum Altar and the Kaiser-Friedrich-Museum's Ravenna mosaics, had been damaged or destroyed. (The situation could have been even worse, however; German curators had narrowly prevented Berlin's military defenders from using what remained of the Pergamum Altar for a tank barricade.) Over the next months the Soviets took away truckload after truckload of loot from the Museum Island and other sites in their zone, never bothering to leave proper receipts, which scandalized the Germans. Most of this loot ended up in museums in the Soviet Union, where some of it remains to this day.

Berlin also housed Germany's most significant collections of books, manuscripts, and documents, which, though perhaps not as glamorous as artworks or gold, constituted another important category of booty for the Soviets. The Trophy Brigades scoured Berlin's libraries and scientific institutes for historically significant volumes and technical treatises, which they checked out on permanent loan. Less valuable items were carted away by the trainload to serve as decoration and insulation in So-

Performance by the Soviet army's Alexandrov Ensemble at the Gendamenmarkt, 1948

viet apartment houses. The pilfered document collections, which included older Prussian records as well as Nazi-era files, remained in the USSR or went to archives in East Germany—a bane to Western scholars who in coming years would have difficulty gaining access to these materials, if they gained access to them at all.

Taken as a whole, Russia's rapacious romp through Berlin's museums, libraries, and archives significantly reduced the city's status as a center of art and learning. Though by no means the only cause for Berlin's cultural decline in the postwar era, the removals left gaps and holes that proved much harder to fill in than the vacant lots created by the bombing and shelling. Like its industry and commerce, Berlin's artistic and intellectual life—especially in the western sectors—would partially recover with time, but the city would never regain its position of cultural dominance within Germany.

Although the Russians fell on Berlin much in the way that hungry Berliners fell on dead horses in the streets, they also saw the German capital as a stage where they could display the virtues of their own system. As General Berzarin, commander-in-chief of Berlin, stated: "Hitler turned Berlin into a city of chaos. We shall make Berlin a city of progress." Even as some Soviet soldiers continued to loot and rape, the occupiers set about getting things working again. Here the very harshness of their rule was an asset. Just as Berliners were forced to dismantle factories, they were also made to clear rubble from streets, dredge debris from canals, and help repair subway tracks and power lines. Since many of the surviving able-bodied men were either in POW camps or working abroad, much of this labor was done by women—the famous *Trümmerfrauen* (rubble women), who carted away the ruins brick by brick, stone by stone. As early as May 14, 1945, a path had been cleared for the first busses, and a day later the first *U-Bahn* subway line reopened. Meanwhile, Soviet army engineers restored electrical power to some districts and set up standpipes where people could obtain potable water. To avert mass starvation, the city's new rulers handed out food from their own stores and commandeered deliveries from the countryside. As a measure against looting, guards were posted at the few shops that still sold groceries, and purchases were regulated by ration cards.

On the cultural front, too, the Russians sought to repair and rebuild as well as to pillage. Like the Nazis before them, they understood that the arts could serve important psychological and propagandistic functions, especially in a time of stress. Quickly they established a new museum administration to oversee what was left of Berlin's collections, which they reopened to the public in temporary quarters on May 17. A little later, on May 26, the Berlin Philharmonic gave its first postwar concert in a cinema building that had survived the bombing. Fittingly, the program opened with a piece that had been banned in Berlin since 1933: Mendelssohn's incidental music to Shakespeare's *A Midsummer Night's Dream*. At the end of May the Russians licensed Berlin's first postwar newspaper, *Die Tägliche Rundschau*, which Berliners dubbed *Die Klägliche Rundschau* (The Pitiable Review) because it contained only a few lines of genuine news, the rest being articles praising the Soviet system. In July 1945 Johannes R. Becher, a Communist poet who had been living in exile in Moscow, returned to Berlin and founded Der Kulturbund für die demokratische Erneuerung Deutschlands (Cultural League for the Democratic Renewal of Germany), whose task was to help reestablish Berlin as Central Europe's foremost center of "progressive" culture.

It was Berlin's political direction, however, that most preoccupied Moscow in this period. The Soviets wanted to set the course for the first municipal administration that arose amidst the ruins of the vanquished Nazi capital. To achieve this they decided to employ as proxies trusted German Communists who had been living in exile in the USSR. Preparations for the takeover had begun in February 1944 with the creation of a commission of exiles charged with working out the organizational details of a Communist regime. The central figure here was Walter Ulbricht, a pear-shaped and primly goateed Saxon who had served the Communist cause with ruthless efficiency and an unswerving devotion to the party line. After training in the early 1920s at Moscow's Lenin School, he had become a Communist Reichstag deputy in 1928 and District Secretary of the KPD for Greater Berlin in 1929. Escaping Hitler's roundup of Communists by fleeing abroad in 1933, he had worked for the party in Paris and Prague, ever careful to keep his distance from the errant Trotskyites. During the Spanish Civil War he had helped Moscow purge the Republican forces of anti-Stalinist elements, which turned out to be good practice for the internal purges he would later conduct as head of the Socialist Unity Party (Sozialistische Einheitspartei, SED) in East Germany. Ulbricht was often ridiculed for his unimposing exterior, castrato-like voice, and Saxon accent. Yet for all his inadequacies he was clearly a tough survivor, and he was determined to make use of his survivor's talents when appointed by Stalin to head the little group of German exiles dispatched to Marshal Zhukov's headquarters outside Berlin on April 30, 1945.

A colorful personal account of the Ulbricht group's work in Berlin is contained in the memoirs of Wolfgang Leonhard, who at twenty-three was the youngest member of the team. Raised in the USSR and educated at the Comintern School, Leonhard spoke fluent Russian and understood Moscow's ways better than most of the older

Walter Ulbricht (right) with a young Erich Honecker (then chief of the Free German Youth), 1951

exiles. He knew what Berlin meant to the Soviet leaders, and he was honored to be part of their mission to make this former Social Democratic bastion a truly Red—*Moscow* Red—capital of the future. However, none of his ideological preparation in Russia prepared him for what he saw upon entering Berlin with Ulbricht's cadres on May 2, 1945. Having always pictured Berlin as the epitome of civilized order, he now felt as if he had stumbled into a scene from Dante's *Inferno*:

> Our cars made their way slowly through Friedrichsfelde in the direction of Lichtenberg. The scene was like a picture of hell—flaming ruins and starving people shambling about in tattered clothing; dazed German soldiers who seemed to have lost all idea of what was going on; Red Army soldiers singing exultantly, and often drunk; groups of women clearing the streets under the supervision of Red Army soldiers; long queues standing patiently waiting to get a bucketful of water from the pumps; and all of them looking terribly tired, hungry, tense and demoralized.

Undeterred by the desolation around them, Leonhard and the other members of Ulbricht's group set about finding reliable "antifascists" to serve the Soviet military occupation. Needing local lackeys to pass on their orders, Russian commanders had already appointed some native administrators, but their choices had been hurried and often ill advised. Leonhard discovered that one district commander had simply gone into the street and grabbed a passerby whose face he liked, saying "Come here! You now mayor!" In staffing the native administration, Ulbricht and company did not take the stance that only known Communists need apply. On the contrary, in traditional working-class areas like Wedding and Prenzlauer Berg they chose Social Democrats as borough mayors; and in bourgeois districts like Wilmersdorf, Zehlendorf, and Charlottenburg they found veterans of the centrist and liberal parties for these posts. They could afford to appear so evenhanded because the figures they were appointing had no substantive power; real authority was wielded by the borough mayors' deputies and by the holders of key offices like chief of police and head of personnel. *These* men were all trusted Communists who reported directly to their superiors in the Soviet military administration. As Ulbricht defined the strategy: "It's got to look democratic, but we must have everything in our control."

Berlin's new municipal government was in place by May 17. The incoming lord mayor and de facto head of the seventeen-man *Magistrat* (city assembly) was an aged civil engineer named Arthur Werner, who combined unassailable democratic credentials with political timidity and encroaching senility. Werner's lack of mental acuity was just fine with Ulbricht, who, when cautioned by his colleagues that the new mayor was "not all there in the head from time to time," replied: "What's the matter? We've got our deputy." The deputy in question was one Karl Maron, a member of the Ulbricht group who had worked as a journalist in the Soviet Union. After the division of Germany he went on to edit the SED's house newspaper, *Neues Deutschland*, then became head of the secret police. The chief of police in Berlin's first postwar administration was Paul Markgraf, a brutal apparatchik whose previous incarnation as a decorated Nazi officer had ended with his capture at Stalingrad and incarceration in a Soviet POW camp, where he quickly made the appropriate political conversion. Personnel matters in the new government were handled by Arthur Pieck, son of the future president of the GDR, Wilhelm Pieck. Communists also occupied nine seats in the *Magistrat*, just enough to ensure control without it being too obvious.

Revealingly, few of the men around Ulbricht were native Berliners. They brought to their mission in the ruined German capital much of the provincialism and distrust of metropolitan life that had attended the Nazi administration of the city. For the Communists, too, the town's cosmopolitanism, though now much reduced, represented a challenge to ideological conformity and to their prospects for political domination. Talk as they might about making Berlin open to "progress," what they really had in mind was closing the place off to influences that they could not control.

The Beginnings of Four-Power Control

The Soviet military command helped Ulbricht's men establish a pseudodemocracy in Berlin by keeping the Western powers away from the city for as long as possible. The Soviets claimed that uncleared minefields made it unsafe for Western troops to enter; they said that access routes were clogged with refugees and their own troops; and, most importantly, they insisted that the British and Americans withdraw from areas designated for Soviet occupation elsewhere in Germany before joining their Red allies in Berlin.

On June 5 General Eisenhower and Field Marshal Montgomery flew to Berlin to sign the Declaration on the Assumption of Supreme Authority in Germany by the Allies, which eliminated the last vestiges of the Reich's sovereignty and confirmed earlier joint-occupation arrangements for Germany and Berlin. On their way from Tempelhof airport to Marshal Zhukov's headquarters for the signing ceremony, the Americans noted to their horror that the canals were still choked with bloated bodies and that "the odor of death was everywhere." The declaration they signed at the conclusion of their meeting with the Russians stated that questions affecting Germany as a whole would require the unanimous agreement of the occupation powers, but if consensus could not be achieved each zonal commander could act as he saw fit. This was a recipe for the division of Germany, but Ike accepted it in the expectation that the wartime victors would find ways to work together harmoniously. Writing in 1950, General Lucius Clay, American military governor of Germany from 1945 to 1949, declared: "This was a fateful decision which can be fairly judged in its effect only by time and history." Three weeks later, on June 29, Clay returned to the capital and in his capacity as Eisenhower's deputy signed off on an agreement that limited the Western Allies' access to Berlin to one highway, a rail line and two air corridors. He assumed that this restriction was only temporary, but he neglected to gain any written agreement to that effect. Later he admitted that he was perhaps "mistaken in not at this time making free access to Berlin a condition to our withdrawal into our occupation zone."

Having neglected to use the presence of their troops in the projected Soviet zone as a bargaining chip, the Western Allies were unable to gain a foothold in Berlin until early July, and it was a precarious foothold at that. The first British contingent moved into dilapidated barracks in Spandau that had recently been vacated by the Russians, who had removed all the furniture they could carry, as well as lightbulbs, power plugs, door handles, and even water taps. To one British officer the Spandau scene seemed "part of a bad dream" in which "at any moment Dr. Caligari, with his black cloak and his cane, might stump across the Square, a saturnine smile on his lips, to proclaim that he was in charge of all the arrangements." The Americans were no less shocked by what the war had done to this once vibrant city and its famously scrappy citizenry, now shuffling among the ruins like zombies. Wrote Hans Speier, a political officer: "The first impression in Berlin, which overpowers you and makes your heart beat faster, is that anything human among these indescribable ruins must exist in an unknown form. . . . Seeing [the survivors] you almost *hope* that they are not human."

Most Berliners welcomed the Westerners' arrival, seeing it as a liberation from exclusive control by the Russians. When the Americans made their first appearance in the city, Ruth Andreas-Friedrich, who had earlier welcomed the Soviets, gushed in her diary: "The Americans are here! . . . The victors from the West for whom we have waited since the beginning of April. More and more eagerly with each day, and more and more urgently each night." Such eagerness derived not only from fear of the Russians, but from the knowledge that *these* soldiers had money and exotic goodies in their kits. The Western troops, for their part, were surprised at the cheers they received from Berliners as they rolled into town. As one British officer wrote: "Who could have foretold this, the most amazing irony of all, that when we entered Berlin we should come as liberators, not as tyrants, for the Germans."

According to official policy, however, the Western Allies were *not* liberators, but conquerors. Their troops were ordered not to fraternize with the natives, nor even to shake their hands. Many soldiers were happy enough to act like *grand seigneurs* and to treat the erstwhile *Herrenvolk* like *Untermenschen*. General Robert McClure, chief of the American Office of Information Control, used a Nazi flag to cover his sofa and a deluxe edition of *Mein Kampf* as his guest book. The Allies commandeered villas in the wealthy western suburbs, expelling the former owners without compensation. According to the *New York Times*, the American military government rendered 1,000 Berliners homeless by requisitioning 125 homes in the Grunewald district. Flouting their wealth, the occupiers threw parties awash in "unbelievable amounts of Manhattans and Martinis, Creme de Menthe and old French Cognac, Scotch whiskey and the best French champagne." With dollars in their pockets, recalled one officer, occupation soldiers could live in Berlin "as if it were not a pile of ruins but a paradise."

A "sexual paradise," he might have added. The prohibition on fraternization proved unworkable and was soon dropped, leaving the troops free to do what victorious troops traditionally do in vanquished cities. Unlike the impoverished Russians, the Westerners could use material enticements to conquer the women of Berlin. Grateful for this arrangement, the women were often anxious to show their appreciation. As one British officer boasted, the Berlin girls "will take any treatment and they treat you like a king—don't matter if you keep them waiting for half an hour—and they are thankful for the little things, a bar of chocolate or a few fags! It's like giving these girls the moon!" Sometimes the trade of sex for nylons and candy developed into something deeper. As George Clare, another British occupation officer, explained:

> The young, healthy, and well-fed boys from Leeds or Cincinnati were attractive, and the aura of victory gave them added glamour, particularly for German women brought up to believe that winning was the highest military virtue. And to the boys from Leeds or Cincinnati, Northumberland or Wyoming, it was a revelation how German women then looked up to their men, made them the focus of their existence, cosseted them, deferred to them, embraced them often and with an eagerness and warmth for which Anglo-Saxon femininity was not exactly famous. Exposed to such emotional incandescence many a dishonorable intention melted into love, leading to heartbreak or—more rarely—marriage.

Despite the tensions within the conquerors' camp, all the leaders continued to profess qualified confidence that they could cooperate effectively in managing the postwar world. To underscore this determination, and to address various practical problems connected with shaping the new order, the "Big Three"—Truman, Stalin, and Churchill—came together at Potsdam for what turned out to be the last meeting of the Grand Alliance. (Churchill did not stay for the entire conference because he was defeated in the British general election by the Labor candidate Clement Attlee, who replaced him in Potsdam on July 25.) The choice of venue for the meeting was itself significant: by hosting the event in the Soviet zone Stalin could play lord of the manor and suggest ownership of neighboring Berlin as well.

For Truman, who had never been to Germany before, flying to the meeting over the wrecked cities of the Reich in his presidential plane, *The Sacred Cow*, was a sobering experience, and driving through Berlin was even more so. As he recorded later, drawing on his extensive historical reading: "I thought of Carthage, Baalbek, Jerusalem, Rome, Atlantis, Peking . . . of Scipio, Ramses II, Sherman, Jenghis Khan." Truman's headquarters at the conference, an imposing villa in Babelsberg, had a horrible recent history of which the president was not then aware. It had be-

Clement Attlee, Harry Truman, and Josef Stalin at the Potsdam Conference, August 1945

longed to a noted publisher, Gustav Müller-Grote, who two months earlier had been forced to watch Russian soldiers gang-rape his daughters in his living room. The soldiers had then looted and destroyed everything in the house. When they decided to make the place available to Truman for his "Little White House," the Soviets expelled Müller-Grote and his family and brought in new furniture that they had confiscated from other villas. Truman learned of all this later through a letter from one of Müller-Grote's sons. Had he known it at the time, one wonders if he would have "seen no reason," as he said upon his departure for Potsdam, "why we should not welcome [the Soviets'] friendship and give ours to them."

The plenum meetings at the Potsdam Conference took place in a mock-Tudor palace called Cecilienhof, which had been built between 1911 and 1916 for Crown Prince Wilhelm of Prussia and his wife, Cecilia. Its front garden now featured a giant star of red geraniums—a none-too-subtle symbol of the Soviets' proprietary attitude. The long-winded discussions in that gloomy building could hardly have discouraged the Russians in their ambitions for Germany and Berlin. The Potsdam Agreement essentially confirmed the earlier accords, which placed east-central Europe in the Soviet sphere of interest. Poland, still occupied by the Red Army, was

Cecilienhof, site of the Potsdam Conference, 1945

given a new western border on the Oder/Western Neisse Rivers, which put Moscow in effective control of the coal-rich Silesian region, whose former German residents, expelled by the Poles, joined the vast stream of refugees flowing west. While postulating "uniformity of treatment of the German population throughout Germany," the agreement allowed the occupation powers to extract reparations from their zones according to their individual needs. In exchange for shipping food and raw materials to western Germany, Russia was promised 65 percent of the industrial goods in the western zones and another 10 percent free of charge. In accepting these arrangements the Western negotiators unwittingly set the stage for the long-term division of Europe and Germany.

France was not invited to the Potsdam Conference—a reflection, Paris believed, of the Big Three's failure to appreciate the importance of its contribution to the German defeat. But in fact the Anglo-Americans had already decided at Yalta to grant France a role in the postwar administration of Germany, and zones of occupation in western Germany and Berlin had been set aside for her. The British and Americans later had occasion to regret their generosity, for France turned out to be almost as hard to work with as Russia, saying an obstructive *non* to every effort to govern Germany as one unit.

A Berlin woman returning to the city after a successful scavenging trip to the countryside

Assessing the difficulties of the Allied administration of Germany, one British military government officer observed: "The world has never known before a situation in which four peoples lived and tried to cooperate in a country inhabited by a fifth." The challenge was even greater in the relatively confined space of a single city—and a wrecked city at that. The interallied agency established to oversee the administration of Berlin was the Kommandatura, which was composed of the four *Stadtkommandanten,* or city commanders. At its very first meeting on July 11, 1945, the Soviet representative announced that the Russian zone would not be able to send any food to the western sectors. This move was especially pernicious given the existence of widespread hunger and Berlin's dependence on supplies from its agricultural hinterlands. In desperation, Berliners bartered precious household goods for comestibles. It was rumored that some farmers now covered the floors of their cow sheds with Persian carpets. However, as in the First World War, city folk often stole what they wanted, thereby rekindling old hostilities between capital and countryside.

Berlin's situation was all the more desperate because of a massive influx of refugees from the ethnically cleansed regions of Poland and the Baltic states. There were almost 5 million displaced people on the roads in east-central Europe, and for many of them Berlin was the first port of call on the trek west. By the time they got there they were true wretches of the earth, filthy, sickly, emaciated, and, in the case of the women, often suffering the effects of multiple rapes. In an effort to prevent them from putting unbearable pressure on the strained resources of the city, the occupation powers banned them from entering Berlin. Thousands managed to get in anyway. If caught, they were immediately escorted to railway stations and ordered to take the first train out. One of the most haunting images from that era is of refugees huddled in bombed-out depots waiting for transport. Margaret Bourke-White, a *Life* magazine photographer, captured such scenes at the Anhalter Bahnhof. One of her photos shows a train pulling out with emaciated creatures filling every space and even clinging to the sides and top. Her coolly distant commentary reads, in part: "The long train was rushing past now, and the people clinging to the top and sides lost their identity as human beings and began to resemble barnacles. As the train gathered speed it might have been a chain of old boat hulls, whipping into the distance. I turned back to the station platforms and found them as thickly studded with humanity as they had been before the train had carried anyone away." It is easy to see a symbolic symmetry between these overloaded trains and the boxcars that carried Jews out of Berlin in the previous half-decade. But of course, as miserable as these refugees were, most who had made it this far (thousands had died in the initial expulsions) were destined to survive. For them, Berlin was not a gateway to death but a way station on the road to a new, if often difficult, existence.

In an effort to improve conditions for the remaining population in the ruined capital, the Western Allies joined the Russians in rationing food and regulating the sale of necessities like fuel and clothing. Inevitably, this generated a black market—indeed, several black markets scattered across the city. Because just about everything was scarce in Berlin except misery, the markets embraced a vast range of items, from bread and potatoes to caviar, drugs, and fake identity papers. To trade in the markets Berliners used barter, and occasionally their bodies. The main "currency," however, was cigarettes, especially American cigarettes. During a visit to Berlin in November 1945, Hans Speier noticed that a pack of cigarettes was worth one hundred marks (then the equivalent of about ten dollars), with Pall Malls fetching a bit more because they were longer. A nostalgic collection of five photographs of Berlin sights before their destruction was selling for ten cigarettes, a price that Speier's American driver found exorbitant because he could buy a whole pack of smokes at the PX for four cents. The preciousness of cigarettes in the local economy created a new profession: that of *Kippensammler*, or butt collector. Hovering near the entrances to soldiers' clubs and cinemas, the butt snatchers swooped down on discarded fag ends as soon as they hit the pavement. Berlin's waiters also got into the butt business, selling the leavings from ashtrays. At the Café Wien waiters received five dollars for the seventy-five to one hundred butts a day they collected.

Taking full advantage of their enormous buying power, the occupiers became major profiteers of the black market. It was alleged that the wife of General Clay bought up huge quantities of artwork, which she sent back to America in her husband's personal airplane. President Truman's adviser, General Harry Vaughn, bragged that on a trip to Berlin he peddled his spare clothes for "a couple thousand bucks." Berliners resented this exploitation of their vulnerability, but they flocked to the markets themselves, for, as Speier noted, "it enables them to get something additional, for example a package of dried milk in exchange for a valuable glass of crystal."

Recognizing that the black markets were fostering a criminal environment of racketeering and speculation, the occupation authorities threatened to shut them down, but nothing much came of the threats. Moreover, for all the sleazy practices that this economy undoubtedly encouraged, it also provided good training for the budding capitalists of the "economic miracle" of the 1950s and 1960s.

If Berlin's thriving black market pointed up a certain impotence or benign neglect on the part of the occupiers, the same can be said of their policy regarding the political crimes of the recent past. In principle, an interallied program of denazification was supposed to eliminate all vestiges of Nazism in German life and bring surviving offenders to justice. Of course, this policy applied to Berlin along with the rest of the vanquished Reich. But in the capital, as elsewhere, many of the leading Nazi criminals had either died or managed to disappear. Some Nazi functionaries had actually vanished with Allied help, since they had valuable information or talents that they could trade for their freedom. Such was the case, for example, with General Reinhard Gehlen, who had headed the Wehrmacht's intelligence operations against the Red Army during the war. He was flown out of Germany by the OSS, then returned in 1950 to West Germany to run a new American-backed spy agency aimed at the USSR and East Germany.

The Soviets, for their part, had dismissed all Nazi party members from public jobs shortly after taking over the city. Yet within weeks many of these individuals, having changed their political livery from brown to red, were back in positions of trust. The Soviets also revived the Nazi-era network of neighborhood spies, the "block wardens," often employing the same men who had done this job for the Nazis.

The British and Americans tackled denazification in a characteristic Anglo-Saxon way: they sent out *Fragebogen* (questionnaires) asking people to categorize their relationship to the defunct Hitler regime. Respondents were required to state whether they had been members of the Nazi Party or had held positions requiring loyalty to the system. Needless to say, this inspired much creative reworking of curriculum vitae. Berliners with problematical pasts who could not sufficiently cover their tracks, or who were too stupid even to try, had to go through denazification hearings. If they emerged clean from these proceedings they received all-clear certificates that the natives dubbed "Persilscheine," after a popular soap. (For a stiff price, one could obtain a fake Persilschein on the black market.)

Armed with their denazification documents, Berliners descended on the Allied employment offices looking for work. George Clare, who vetted job applications in the British sector, recalled an endless procession of antifascists who claimed to have always admired Churchill and hated Hitler. In light of this procession of virtue, he could not help wondering how it had happened that the Nazis had managed to become the largest party in the Reichstag. Nonetheless, in their haste to hire reasonably competent natives, he and his colleagues generally did not scrutinize the applicants too closely.

The Golden Hunger Years

The wartime Allies' mission to denazify Berlin extended to culture. The plan was not just to purge the local arts scene of politically problematical influences but to impose a whole new culture based on "humanistic" and "democratic" values. But the victors differed when it came to defining exactly what these ideals meant and how the cultural makeover should be achieved.

As we have seen, during their brief tenure as sole occupiers of Berlin the Soviets revived certain segments of the local culture, and they continued to be active in this domain after the Western powers arrived in the city. Aware of the importance that culture held for Berliners, the Russians brought in knowledgeable experts to run their cultural affairs division and allowed them considerable leeway to create programs that would be attractive to the natives. In overall charge of Soviet cultural policy was Colonel Sergei Tulpanov, a bear of a man who resembled Hermann Göring both in his girth and in his ability to mask his political agenda with backslapping bonhomie. His chief assistant was Alexander Dymschitz, a product of the educated bourgeoisie who thoroughly knew his way around German culture. He, like many in the Russian cultural bureaucracy, was of Jewish origin. In setting policy in Berlin the Soviets were not hindered by any pretense of nonfraternization. With their support the above-mentioned Kulturbund sponsored a Writers Congress attended by former "inner emigrants" and political exiles from both East and West. The House of the Culture of the Soviet Union on Unter den Linden organized exhibitions of Russian painting and lectures by noted Soviet authors. The Soviets reopened the renowned Deutsches Theater, which had survived the bombing relatively unscathed, and placed at its head the former avant-garde director Fritz Wangenheim, who promised to enlist the theater "in the broad democratic front of the German renewal."

Three years later Bertolt Brecht returned to Berlin with similar objectives. Anxious to demonstrate his commitment to socialism, Brecht settled in the Soviet sector, where he was placed in charge of the Stadttheater, given a spacious house, and allowed to import a new bevy of mistresses and hangers-on. Soon he would have his own theatrical company, the Berliner Ensemble, and his own theater, the Theater am Schiffbauerdamm. Yet despite all the state-subsidized perks, the like of which no German artist had enjoyed since Wagner, Brecht was often frustrated in East Berlin, which struck him as provincial and small-minded, and he was careful to keep his bank accounts in Switzerland and his citizenship in Austria.

Film was pressed into the Soviets' "cultural renewal" campaign when, with their backing, the old UFA studios in Babelsberg were turned into DEFA, which became the East Germans' main film factory. DEFA's first film, *Die Mörder sind unter uns* (The Murderers Are Among Us, 1946), directed by Wolfgang Staudte, tells the story of a former Wehrmacht doctor who, having failed in the war to prevent his captain from murdering innocent Polish civilians, tracks the man down in postwar Berlin and brings him to justice. Staudte had tried to interest the Americans in this project but was told that the Germans "should not even think of making any films for the next twenty years." In subsequent years a stream of antifascist films flowed out of Babelsberg, most of them stressing the importance of ordinary citizens taking a stand against tyranny.

One might have thought that this was a message that the Soviets would not want to push too strongly, and in fact it was not long before they began to take a harder line in cultural politics, stressing less the value of German traditions than the superiority of Russian and Communist models. Berlin artists whose works did not conform to the ideals of socialist realism were increasingly shut out of the picture, while ideologically correct hacks were rewarded with commissions and prizes. Even Johannes R. Becher, the veteran Communist, was harassed by the Soviet secret police until he produced some poems praising Stalin. (Becher ultimately praised the Soviets so effusively that Berliners called him "Johannes Erbrecher" [vomiter]—a pun on his middle initial and last name.)

Ideological control was also on the agenda at Berlin's chief center of higher learning, the formerly illustrious Friedrich-Wilhelm-Universität on Unter den Linden, which the Soviets reopened on January 29, 1946, as Berlin University. (In 1948, the institution was renamed Humboldt-Universität, the name it carries today.) Claiming that as a former Prussian royal institution the university belonged to Brandenburg rather than to Berlin, the Russians denied their allied partners access to it. Faculty appointments and curriculum decisions were made by the Deutsche Zentralverwaltung für Volksbildung, a Soviet-controlled agency which mandated courses in Russian and Marxism-Leninism. Efforts by the authorities to use the institution as an instrument of party dogma, however, sparked resistance from many of the students, who were sick of having a state ideology crammed down their throats. Berlin University's first years were therefore marked by tension between dissident students and the bureaucracy. It would take some time before the school could be turned into a fully reliable incubator of future party hacks.

The Western occupiers of Berlin were for the most part considerably less knowledgeable about German traditions than the Russians. When George Clare asked Pat Lynch, Britain's officer for theater and music, how he was picked for his job, he replied forthrightly, "Hit or miss!" The American officer in charge of music knew nothing of the great Berlin orchestras and conductors. Yet the Western cultural officers were as determined as the Soviets to use the arts as a way of "reeducating" the Berliners and of spreading their own influence.

As the dominant power among the Western Allies, the Americans took the lead in this endeavor. They responded to the Soviets' early control of the Berlin media with initiatives of their own. They licensed a new newspaper, *Der Tagesspiegel*, which was run on American lines. In August 1945 they launched the American Armed Forces Radio Network (AFN), whose official function was to bolster the morale of the American troops, but whose broader effect was to bolster the mood of the Berliners. A year later, in response to the Soviets' refusal to share access to the Berliner Rundfunk, the U.S. military government set up a new station, RIAS (Radio in the American Sector), which quickly became a crucial voice on the postwar scene. At first its programming was fairly evenhanded and objective, but as the rivalry with the Soviets intensified the station became increasingly ideological, a weapon in the war for the soul of the Berliners.

Another such weapon was the Free University of Berlin, which was founded in the American sector in the borough of Dahlem in 1948 as an alternative to the Communist-controlled Humboldt University on Unter den Linden. (Two years earlier, the British had reopened the Technische Hochschule as the Technische Universität.) It was a group of dissident students from the Berlin University who convinced the Americans to reverse their earlier closing of all higher education institutes in their sector and to sanction the new school. The hope of the Free University's founders was that it would become a model for higher educational reform throughout Germany, and to that end it allowed unprecedented student participation in university governance, promoted closer relations between students and faculty, and outlawed dueling fraternities, which were seen as a legacy of the authoritarian past. The "Berlin Model" in higher education never caught on elsewhere, however, and eventually it faded at the Free University itself. Despite its name, moreover, the Free University in its early days was anything but free of ideological bullying. It fostered its own political orthodoxy, a strident anti-Communism. (Later, from the mid-1960s through the 1970s, the school would become just as doctrinaire in its neoleftist stance.)

The French brought more sophistication and knowledge to the business of cultural tutelage in Berlin than the Anglo-Americans, though they could often be just as high-handed. Watching her countrymen at work in the defeated German capital, Simone de Beauvoir was reminded of the Nazis in Paris during *their* occupation. "It seemed to me that we were just as loathsome as they had been . . . and when one is on the same side as the occupiers, one's sense of discomfort is all the greater." In terms of cultural administration, the French had fewer opportunities to show their superiority because their sector, which consisted of only two boroughs, was relatively devoid of important artistic and intellectual institutions. Reinickendorf and Wedding boasted no theaters, operas, museums, universities, or libraries of note. The French "Mission Culturelle" had to make do with importing French cultural stars such as Jean-Paul Sartre, Hélène Vercors, and Albert Camus. This agency also maintained extensive contacts with German intellectuals across the city, and with the Soviet cultural authorities in the Russian zone. In 1947, when the British and Americans forbade the Soviet-sponsored Kulturbund from operating in their sectors, the French refused to join in the ban. Organizations like the Kulturbund, they insisted, offered excellent opportunities "for developing our influence in Berlin on cultural directives." Felix Lusset, chief of the Mission Culturelle, even held discussions with his Soviet counterpart with an eye to promoting a "Paris-Berlin-Leningrad cultural axis."

While each of the four powers planted its cultural seeds in the former Reich capital, hoping to grow a mini version of itself, the Berliners themselves were intent upon returning their city as soon as possible to its pre-Nazi status as a world-class metropolis of the arts. Visiting Berlin in 1946, Stephen Spender was struck by the locals' hunger for culture and diversion after all the horrors they had just been through. The German capital had reinvented itself often enough in the past, and now it would do so again like a municipal Lazarus rising from the dead. "The strength and the weakness of the Berliners," Spender observed, "was their feeling that they could begin a completely new kind of life—because they had nothing to begin from." Using Berlin's wretched physical conditions as a new frisson, entrepreneurs opened nightclubs and jazz dens in the cellars of bombed-out buildings. Plays were mounted on makeshift stages and operas were performed in torn-up halls. Cabaret made a triumphant comeback and subjected Berlin's recent horrors to characteristic black humor. The Berlin Philharmonic, now under the direction of the Romanian conductor Sergiu Celibidache, put on its concerts at the Titania Cinema. On May 25, 1947, Wilhelm Furtwängler, having just survived a humiliating denazification hearing instigated by the Americans, returned to the orchestra's podium for the first time since the war. For the Berliners, who had seen his trial as an injustice, Furtwängler's return was a hopeful sign that the city was regaining its cultural clout. "Stay here! Stay here!" they shouted to the maestro after the performance.

Driving through Berlin in February 1946, the critic Friedrich Luft was heartened to see placards announcing innumerable plays and concerts. He was also struck by newspaper ads promoting one cultural event after another. "There are at least half a dozen concerts a day—in all parts of the city," he wrote. "Two opera houses are giving regular performances. What other city in the world can say as much?" A tourism-promotion campaign of 1947 entitled "Berlin Lebt—Berlin Ruft!" told the world that Berlin was back in business, as high spirited and cosmopolitan as ever, despite the nasty patch it had just been through. "Berlin may have put on a hard face," said the ad, "but its visage is worldly and lively, and it still displays the constant movement, élan, tempo, noise, and openness beloved of Berliners. The big world is here together, with its newspapers and films, its opinions and ideas, its concerns for peace and understanding cherished by all peoples." For Peter de Mendelssohn, a Berlin intellectual who had returned to his native city as an American occupation officer, the burst of cultural activity meant that the battered German capital was still a force to be reckoned with when it came to the arts: "Berlin is not dead. In many regards it is more alive than Paris," he contended.

More alive, perhaps, but there was reason to question the *quality* of Berlin's culture in this period. Many of the artists and intellectuals who returned from exile were struck by a lack of originality, innovation, and genuine creative power in the art of the time. The dramatist Fritz Kortner, who like Brecht had spent the war years in the United States, was so appalled by the theatrical productions he saw at the Kurfürstendamm-Theater in 1947 that he wanted to flee back to America. Brecht himself complained loudly of "the miserable artistic condition in the theater of the former Reichshauptstadt." Peter Suhrkamp, the publisher, wrote his friend Hermann Hesse in Switzerland about the lamentable "noise" being made by the legions of cultural mice climbing out of their holes and scurrying about the city. Despairing of the local music scene, Wilhelm Furtwängler wrote: "What's going on here now is all passing, insignificant, meaningless. A reign of mediocrity in its truest sense, but which certainly cannot and will not last." The novelist Elisabeth Langgässer found the 1947 Berlin Writers' Conference to be like "a great show of fireworks, and the following morning the parched brown grass was strewn with the charred remains."

It is hardly surprising that Berlin's culture in the immediate postwar period lacked freshness and originality. For the past twelve years the city had been cut off from most of the rest of the world. Berliners understandably wanted to catch up with what had been happening elsewhere during their enforced isolation. Hence the city was inundated by a tide of cultural borrowing, some of it of high quality, but much of it the worst that the wider world had to offer. Another major impulse was to take up culturally where one had left off in 1933, to revive the "Golden Twenties." Alluding to that fabled era, Berliners liked to call the period immediately after World War II the "golden hunger years." To a large degree, the Berlin culture of this time was indeed a throwback to the Weimar culture of the 1920s and early 1930s. But what had once been avant-garde was not so avant any more, and what might have been "golden" in the 1920s now looked merely yellowed.

If Berlin Falls, Germany Will Be Next

In line with their strategy of indirect rule in eastern Germany and Berlin, the Soviets had licensed four political parties in summer 1945: the KPD (Communist Party), the SPD (Social Democrats), the CDU (Christian Democrats), and the LDP (Liberal Democrats). All were essentially "front" organizations, but the KPD, as the party closest to the Soviet military administration, was expected to dominate the political scene. By late 1945 it was clear that this was not happening, especially in Berlin. Precisely because they were perceived as stooges for the Russians, the Communists made little headway in conquering the hearts and minds of the Berliners. The Soviets decided therefore to change tactics and to orchestrate a merger between the KPD and the popular SPD, thereby giving the native Communists a blind behind which to smuggle themselves into a position of control. Stalin once said that imposing communism on the Germans was like trying to fit "a saddle on a cow," but a more appropriate image for the Russian tactic at this juncture was that of the Trojan horse.

The plan might have worked had the SPD in the eastern zone accepted its assigned role, but the majority of the party refused to do so. Over the objections of the Soviet-chosen SPD leadership, rank-and-file Socialists insisted on putting the merger question to a secret vote, which resulted in a landslide victory for the opponents of fusion. Calling the referendum "irrelevant," on April 21, 1946, the leaders of the KPD and eastern SPD went ahead and merged their two parties into the SED (Socialist Unity Party). The bond was sealed by a handshake between the Communist chief Wilhelm Pieck and the Socialist leader Otto Grotewohl. Recognizing this gesture as the headlock it really was, antimerger Socialists refused to join the "unity" group and recast the rump SPD as a rival to the SED. The old division of the German left that had grown out of the First World War and helped to weaken the Weimar Republic was now back in place, courtesy of Soviet bullying. Soon it would segue into the division of Germany and Berlin, with the two leftist parties on opposite sides of the fence.

The SED's ineffectiveness as a political force in the former Reich capital became evident in the first municipal elections of the postwar era, on October 20, 1946. Despite extensive interference by the Soviets, including prohibitions on SPD meetings and publications in the eastern sector, the SED proved no match for its Socialist rival, winning only 19.8 percent of the vote compared to the Socialists' 48.9

Ernst Reuter

percent. The SED did badly even in the Soviet zone and in the working-class districts of the western sectors, where the KPD had once been strong. "The women of Berlin have decided against the Russian lovers," said an SED member sarcastically.

As a result of the elections, the new municipal government that began meeting a month later was dominated by the SPD. The city assembly appointed the Socialist Otto Suhr as its chairman, while another Socialist, Otto Ostrowski, became postwar Berlin's first Lord Mayor. However, because Ostrowski seemed too easily intimidated by the Russians, the *Magistrat* replaced him with yet another Socialist, Ernst Reuter. This was a provocative choice, for Reuter was an ex-Communist who had broken with the party in the early 1920s in protest against its domination by the Soviet Union. Switching to the SPD, he had served in Berlin's city assembly and fought many a political duel with the local Communists. He had returned to Berlin from wartime exile in Turkey with a loathing for all forms of dictatorship, including those that masqueraded as democratic.

Rightly seeing Reuter's appointment as a demonstration of municipal independence, the Soviets used their veto in the Kommandatura to squelch his selection.

Louise Schröder stepped in as acting mayor and did a brilliant job at running the city in this difficult moment. Reuter, meanwhile, continued to oppose Communist policies from his position in the *Magistrat.* Most Berliners considered him their rightful mayor, and he often spoke out on behalf of the city. He would not, however, officially became mayor until 1949, and then only of West Berlin.

Frustrated by their inability to control Berlin through their German marionettes, the Soviets sought to impose their will through repression and terror. In their own sector they heightened censorship and began arresting non-Communists, even members of the front organizations that they themselves had created. Some of the victims ended up in recently liberated Nazi concentration camps like Sachsenhausen and Buchenwald, which slipped almost seamlessly from one dictatorship into another. Hoping to evade the Soviet net, anti-Communist East Berliners began moving to the western sectors, but this was no guarantee of safety, for Russian secret policemen thought nothing of kidnapping people in broad daylight off streets in the West. George Clare reported:

> [The Soviets] began to 'take out' political and human-rights activists who opposed them. It was all over in seconds. A car screeched to a sudden halt, hefty men jumped out, grabbed their victim, bundled him into their vehicle, and before those who witnessed it could comprehend what had happened, they were racing off in the direction of the Soviet sector. There, of course, such dramatics were unnecessary—people just disappeared.

At first the Western Allies seemed impotent in the face of such outrages carried out by their occupation partners—they registered protests with the Soviet administration but otherwise did nothing. However, by early 1947, as it became impossible to deny that Berlin and Germany were fast becoming prime battlegrounds in the emerging Cold War, the Western powers started taking measures to protect "their" Germany. On January 1, 1947, the Americans and British fused their zones economically into "Bizonia" (France, intent upon keeping Germany divided and weak, kept its zone separate). Now the Soviets were prevented from drawing much-needed reparations from the western zones. A few months later, George C. Marshall, the new American secretary of state, announced his famous plan for European economic recovery, the "Marshall Plan," in which he pointedly included western Germany. Thus if the Soviets in 1946/47 were bringing down (in Winston

General Lucius D. Clay

Churchill's famous phrase) an "iron curtain" across Europe, the Western powers were drawing some lines of demarcation of their own.

The Soviets bitterly protested the Western initiatives as violations of the Potsdam Agreement and as steps toward the formal division of Germany. Stalin's aspiration at this point was not to see Germany officially divided but to win control over all of it. Hence the Soviets retaliated in the most effective way they could: by interfering with traffic into Berlin. Claiming "technical difficulties" on the rail lines, they restricted the number of freight trains allowed to pass through their zone, thereby exacerbating the food shortage. In early 1948, with their Berlin garrisons feeling the pinch, the British and Americans launched a small airlift with a few planeloads of supplies, a preview of the much larger lift to come. Although the Kommandatura continued to meet during this crisis, Robert Murphy, political adviser to the American military government, reported that agreement had become impossible "even on the most routine questions." General Clay sensed "a feeling of new tenseness in every Soviet individual with whom we have official relationships." He feared that war might come with "dramatic suddenness."

Yet heightened tensions with the Russians in Berlin did not prevent the Western powers from taking further steps to ensure the political and economic viability of western Germany. In early June 1948 they instructed German officials in the Western zones to draft a constitution for a new federal state "best adapted to the eventual reestablishment of German unity at present disrupted." They also announced that they would begin formulating an "Occupation Statute" to define relations between themselves and the new western German government. Finally, on June 18, the Western military governments announced that a new currency, the Deutsche mark, would replace the inflated Reichsmark as the accepted medium of exchange in their zones. The new Westmarks were not designated for use in Berlin, but when the Soviets tried to impose an East-based currency on the entire city, the Americans, having secretly flown in loads of Deutsche marks in case they might be needed, started issuing the new bills on June 24. Since eastern money was still accepted in the western sectors, Berlin now had competing currencies to go along with its competing ideologies. The Westmarks had a large "B" for Berlin stamped on them, while the Soviet-issued bills bore thumb-sized coupons stuck on with potato glue. No sooner had the Russians introduced their "wallpaper marks" (so named by the Berliners) than their representative on the Kommandatura, Major General Alexander Kotikov, stalked out of the Allied body, allegedly in response to the equally abrupt departure of his American counterpart, Colonel Frank Howley. Now even the pretense of cooperation was gone.

The battle of the bills turned into a full-scale battle for Berlin because the Soviets, citing additional "technical difficulties," stopped most road traffic coming into Berlin from western Germany on June 18, the day the deutsche mark was launched in the western zones. On June 24, they halted barge traffic as well, and they curtailed deliveries of electrical power and coal from the eastern sectors to the West. In the following weeks they also established checkpoints along their sector in Berlin to monitor (but not prevent) the passage of goods and people. The Western powers, it seemed, were about to pay dearly for their failure to guarantee free access to Berlin in early summer 1945, when they still had troops in the Soviet zone.

While the currency imbroglio provided the immediate backdrop for these dramatic measures, it was not the central issue behind the blockade. The Soviets hoped to use their stranglehold over Berlin to force the Allies to rescind their plans for a West German government, which Moscow resolutely opposed. The Soviets also wanted to regain the right to extract reparations from the western zones. These were the immediate goals; down the line they hoped to show the Western powers that it made no sense for them to stay in Berlin at all, deep within the lair of the Bear.

Colonel Howley labeled Russia's decision to impose a blockade "the most barbarous in history since Genghis Khan reduced conquered cities to pyramids of skulls." His comment was quite hyperbolic, ignoring as it did some rather more barbarous decisions of recent vintage. Moreover, contrary to one of the more cherished myths of the Cold War, the Soviets did not even attempt, much less accomplish, a *total* land-blockade of West Berlin in 1948/49. Not only did they neglect to seal off the western sectors of the city from the Russian sector, but they also allowed West Berliners to obtain food and other goods from the surrounding countryside. With Westmarks Berliners could purchase hard-to-get items at special "Free Shops" in the Russian sector—precursors to the famous "Intershops" of the German Democratic Republic (GDR) era. Postal deliveries between western Germany and Berlin continued to function unimpeded, allowing Berliners to receive boxes of food from their friends and relatives in the West. Until September 1948 a steady stream of trucks carrying all manner of goods passed into the western sectors from the Russian zone. Industrial firms close to the Russian sector continued to get electrical power from the eastern grid, and some western factories tapped into the *S-Bahn* lines, which drew current from the East. If this was a blockade, it was one of the leakiest blockades in history.

The reason for all the leaks was simple: the Soviet sector in Berlin was no less dependent on trade with the West than the western sectors were on trade with the East. Manufactured goods from the West were important to the eastern economy, and the introduction of the Westmarks created an insatiable demand for hard currency in the Soviet zone. Politically the Russians might talk tough, but economically they could not afford to stand on their own. Their tactic of building a barricade and simultaneously undermining it was emblematic of the fundamental structural weaknesses in the Soviet empire that would remain in place until its collapse.

For all its holes, however, the Soviet blockade certainly presented added hardships to the 2.1 million people living in the western sectors of Berlin. After all, many of them were still digging out from the rubble, still contending with poor food and chronic shortages. There was also the fear that the blockade might prompt the Western Allies to pull up stakes and leave, allowing the Soviets to reoccupy the entire city. No wonder Berliners cheered when Ernst Reuter called upon the world to help Berlin "in the decisive phase of the fight for freedom."

The Western Allies were in something of a quandary about how to respond to this appeal. Official Washington was caught off guard and full of trepidation. George Kennan, head of the State Department's policy planning staff, recalled: "No one was sure how the Russian move could be countered, or whether it could be countered at all. The situation was dark and full of danger." France wanted to see what action its partners might take before doing anything itself. Only Britain adopted an unequivocal stance immediately. Foreign Secretary Ernest Bevin announced that Britain would neither abandon Berlin nor back away from plans for a separate West German state.

On the scene in Germany, General Clay also appeared steadfast, at least outwardly. Interpreting the Russian move as a bluff designed to frighten the West out of Berlin, he publicly promised that the Americans would not leave. "If Berlin falls," he said, "Germany will be next. If we intend to defend Europe against Communism, we should not budge." In private, however, he worried that if Berlin could not be fed, a starving populace would force the Western powers out in order to get the blockade lifted.

None of the Allied officials contemplated a fight by the tiny Western garrison in Berlin, which in total comprised about 15,000 troops. A possibly more viable option involved breaking the blockade by dispatching an armed convoy from western Germany. Clay was an avid proponent of this gambit, going so far as to lay plans for a 6,000-man task force to storm 110 miles down the autobahn from Helmstedt to Berlin. Clay asked General Curtis LeMay, commander of the U.S. Air Force in Europe, to provide air support in case the Russians started shooting—an eventuality that the fiery LeMay welcomed as a fine opportunity for a preemptive strike on all Russian airfields in Germany. "Naturally we knew where they were," LeMay said. "We had observed the Russian fighters lined up in a nice smooth line on the aprons at every place. If it had happened, I think we could have cleaned them up pretty well, in no time at all."

But of course "it" didn't happen. The State Department considered the convoy option far too risky, while the Pentagon dismissed it as unworkable. As General Omar Bradley, chairman of the Joint Chiefs of Staff, wrote later: "The Russians could stop an armed convoy without opening fire on it. Roads could be closed for repair or a bridge could go up just ahead of you and then another bridge behind you and you'd be in a hell of a fix."

If the Western powers were determined to stay in Berlin, they had to find a way to keep the city better supplied, pending a still hoped for diplomatic solution. In the given circumstances an airlift of some kind seemed the best answer, but at first only Bevin pressed it with any vigor. He argued forcefully that an airlift would at once reinforce the morale of the West Berliners and show Moscow that "we are not powerless but on the contrary possess a wealth of technical ability and spectacular air strength." Clay, having reluctantly given up his convoy idea, soon came around to Bevin's view. But the State Department and Pentagon still dithered, worried that this gambit, too, posed the risk of war. Finally, on June 26, President Harry Truman put an end to all the equivocation by ordering that an airlift to Berlin be made operational as soon as possible. To Secretary of the Army Kenneth Royall's objection that this might mean war, he replied that America would "have to deal with the situation as it developed."

Even if an airlift did not lead to war, there were reasons to worry that it might not be effective with the equipment available in the immediate area. The U.S. Air Force in Europe had only two C-54 Douglas Skymasters, which could ferry about ten tons, and 102 battered C-47's, known as Gooney Birds, each with a three-ton capacity. The British air command in Germany could deploy a total of fourteen Dakotas, their version of the C-47. The French had six Junkers and one Dakota, all derelict. Existing loading and landing facilities were also inadequate. America's primary air base in western Germany, Rhein-Main, had a runway of good length, but its surface was not designed for heavy transport use. The RAF's Wunstorf base in the British zone had little hardstand for parking and loading. At the Berlin end, Tempelhof in the American sector, expanded by the Nazis in the 1930s, had an adequate administrative complex, but its single runway (another was soon added) was surfaced with tire-busting steel planks, and the approach to it from the west required coming in between high apartment buildings and a 400-foot-tall brewery chimney. A cemetery near the field reminded pilots of what would probably happen to them if they miscalculated the approach. Gatow in the British sector was much easier to fly into but lacked a good off-loading area. There were no airfields at all in the French sector, though Paris allowed the Americans to start building a new one at Tegel in July 1948. Because access to Tegel was impeded by transmitting towers belonging to the Soviet-controlled Berliner Rundfunk, France's Berlin commandant asked the Russians to dismantle them. When he refused, the Frenchman ordered them blown up.

As soon as the lift got underway, a call went out for cargo planes from all over the world. In the American case, aircraft arrived from bases as far away as Guam, Alaska, Hawaii, and Panama to make up what was at first labeled the "LeMay Coal and Feed Delivery Service" and later rechristened "Operation Vittles." Although the

Berlin children observe approach of an American transport plane during the airlift

buildup was impressive, the operation at this point was still definitely seat-of-the-pants. "It was a cowboy operation when I got there in July," recalled an American pilot. "It was a joke if you could take off after your buddy and get back to Rhein-Main before he did. It did not matter how you beat him, just so long as you beat him." Loading operations were also chaotic, with trucks sometimes driving into spinning propellers. In the early days, pilots experimented with low-level drops over Berlin's Olympic Stadium to avoid time-consuming landings, but the food ended up as puree, while coal became coal dust. Worse, although the deliveries increased each week, they were not nearly enough to meet Berlin's needs, even in summer. Observing this painful reality, Robert Murphy speculated on July 9 that "within a week or so we may find ourselves faced with a desperate population demanding our withdrawal to relieve the distress."

Clearly, a great leap forward in terms of organizational sophistication was required if West Berlin was to be adequately supplied. Fortunately, even as Murphy was issuing his grim prognostication, measures were being taken to make the operation more viable. Dozens of American C-54s, along with newly arrived British Yorks and Sunderland Flying Boats, which landed on the Havel River, were integrated into the system. The larger aircraft were able to carry bulky items like generators and power plant machinery. As for food, it was now delivered almost exclusively in dehydrated form, which made for less weight and more efficient packaging. So many items arrived as powder that a cartoon showed a stork flying into Berlin with a diapered bundle in its beak—the bundle labeled "Powdered Baby."

The most crucial advances were key technical and logistical innovations introduced by General William H. Tunner, a veteran of the Himalayan "Hump" of World War II, who arrived in July to become commander of the Combined Airlift Task Force. He quickly imposed a rigid routine whereby planes were dispatched according to type, air speed, and cargo loads, which avoided bunching up en route or on the ground. Preestablished flight plans put an end to races through the corridors. Improvements in air-traffic control around Berlin made it possible to bring in planes at very short intervals. A special training facility at Great Falls, Montana, famous for its hostile environment, prepared air and ground crews to work efficiently together in the toughest conditions.

Among the inhabitants of the western sectors, improvements in the airlift did not immediately dispel widespread fears that they would be starved into submission. The first months of the blockade brought significant reductions in daily food rations, which had been meager enough to begin with. Yet by late fall 1948 Tunner's innovations were starting to pay off: Berliners were not starving to death, and the local economy had not ground to a halt. The children of Berlin could take delight in occasional drops of candy attached to tiny parachutes; the kids called the planes *Rosinenbomber* (raisin bombers). At the same time, people understandably worried that the coming winter months might be a very different story, for harsh weather conditions would both increase demand for supplies and make their delivery much more difficult. It was estimated that Berlin required a minimum of 5,650 tons of food and coal per day to survive during the winter months; in Octo-

Berlin children play "airlift"

ber the lift had managed 4,760 and in November 3,800 tons a day—not encouraging statistics.

There was another danger as well. Irritated by the airlift's successes, the Russians were starting to send signals that they might not continue to tolerate this Allied experiment. Soviet planes began staging mock air battles over Berlin, while ground batteries practiced antiaircraft drills in the northern corridor. Red fighters buzzed Allied cargo and passenger planes. In one instance, a Soviet fighter even caused a British transport plane to crash. If these sorties escalated from harassment to actual shooting, the airlift might lead to war after all. As it turned out, however, the Soviet interference, while very dangerous and provocative, did not become more extensive; indeed, it abated somewhat with the onset of winter. As so often in the past, the Russians seemed to be counting on nasty weather to come to their aid.

The Western Allies confronted the approach of winter with a new display of commitment to Berlin. On October 22 President Truman authorized the dispatch of sixty-six more C-54s to Germany, raising the total to 225. In November, the new airport at Tegel became operational, greatly increasing the city's receiving capacity. Meanwhile, advanced radar and improved cockpit instrumentation were making it possible for planes to fly "when birds walked," as the pilots put it. After returning from a trip to Washington, Clay announced: "The airlift will be continued until the blockade is ended."

While the strength of the Western commitment, both material and moral, should not be doubted, the subsequent months turned out to be not quite the white-knuckle experience that everyone had feared. The primary reason is that old General Winter sided this time with Russia's adversaries. January 1949 was a meteorological miracle, with clear skies and no hard frost. During that month the airlift managed an amazing 5,560 tons a day. With relatively mild conditions continuing through March, and daily deliveries sometimes exceeding 6,000 tons, many Berliners in the western sectors found themselves actually *gaining* weight.

At the peak of the Berlin Airlift, in spring 1949, planes were landing every ninety seconds and turning around within six minutes. Many of the planes did not return empty, but "backlifted" goods or ferried out passengers, mainly sick children. It should be noted, however, that the airlift, even with such impressive statistics, never delivered *all* the imports the West Berliners needed. Much of that continued to come through legal East-West trade or through black markets in the eastern sector, which were condoned and even encouraged by the Soviets. The airlift alone might have been able to provide food and fuel for the western-sector population, but it could never have done all that *and* sustained the area's industry, which was heavily dependent on eastern markets and raw materials.

Berliners themselves contributed significantly to the operations of the airlift. Residents of the western zones helped unload planes, worked as ground mechanics, and drove the trucks that distributed food and coal. Young women kept the ground crews supplied with hot coffee as they worked. Perhaps most importantly, Berliners maintained morale by regularly displaying their famous *Schnauze* (irreverent wit). "Aren't we lucky," they joked. "Just think what it would be like if the Americans were running the blockade and the Russians the airlift." A radio program called *Die Insulaner* (The Islanders), beamed by RIAS, featured easily identifiable Berlin types offering a running commentary on life in the beleaguered city. Older Berliners still remember the *Insulaner* theme song, with its description of aircraft noise as "music to the ear" and its longing for the day "when the lights are on and the trains are moving."

All of which is not to say that there was no self-pity or resentment, even toward the Western Allies. Some Berliners claimed that their city would not have fallen into such a fix if the West had not "given" a third of Germany to the Soviets. Others complained about having to pay high prices for dehydrated foods that they didn't like anyway. Yet on the whole, the Berliners were deeply appreciative of the effort being made on their behalf, and they relished the chance to work side by side with the Western powers against the Russians. Perhaps most of all, they delighted in the breathtakingly rapid transformation of their city from "lair of the fascist beast" to the Western world's favorite new symbol of pluck, determination, and hunger for freedom.

The struggle to keep Berlin free received some support from western Germany, including the revenues from a special two-pfennig "Emergency Berlin" stamp and a "Berlin tax" imposed by the new German Economic Council in Frankfurt. Hamburg sent medical supplies, Westphalia candles, and Schleswig-Holstein tree seedlings. But the support was tempered by concern that isolated West Berlin would became a burden on the new West German state. Thus Ludwig Erhard, then an economic administrator in the Bizone, tried to dissuade the Western powers from introducing the Deutsche mark in Berlin, fearing this might weaken the currency, while Ernst Hilpert, a finance expert from Hesse, argued that the Germans should not become too involved in the airlift since this was "a political action of the Americans against the Russians." The Berlin tax, moreover, occasioned howls of protest across the western zones. Exasperated by these signs of ambivalence and even hostility toward the embattled German capital, General Clay asked Max Brauer, the mayor of Hamburg, if he and his colleagues really wanted the Western Allies to stay in Berlin after all.

Western German reservations about Berlin notwithstanding, by spring 1949 the Allied airlift had become so successful that it seemed capable of going on forever. The preparations for a West German state were also proceeding apace, with the drafting of a Basic Law, or constitution, in May. Another epochal creation, the North Atlantic Treaty Organization (NATO), was formalized in April. Short of going to war, there was little that the Soviets could do to impede these developments. They had blockaded Berlin partly to strengthen their hand in the tough poker contest

"Hurrah, we're still alive!" proclaims this sign on the first bus to resume the interzonal route between West Berlin and Hanover following the lifting of the Berlin Blockade, May 12, 1949

over Germany that they were playing with their former partners; now they were dealing themselves out of the game.

The Western powers, moreover, were putting pressure on the Russians through a painful counterblockade of their own. They blocked shipments of crucial raw materials and manufactured goods from the western zones to the east. In addition to hard coal from the Ruhr, they prevented the Soviet zone from receiving key items like electrical motors, diamond drills, and optical equipment. The losses were all the more grievous because the economy in the Russian zone was in terrible shape due to the earlier pillaging and ongoing mismanagement by Sowjetische

Aktiengesellschaften—Soviet-controlled companies known by their apt acronym, SAGS.

Obviously this was not what the Soviets had intended when they launched their blockade, and therefore they decided to bargain. In March 1949, their delegate to the United Nations Security Council, Yakov Malik, began meeting secretly with his American counterpart, Philip Jessup. After lengthy negotiations, the Soviets agreed to lift their blockade if the West consented to hold a Council of Foreign Ministers meeting on Germany some time in the spring. When this deal was announced in early May, many Berliners remained skeptical, fearing a Russian trick. But at one minute after midnight on May 12, 1949, all the lights finally came on in Berlin for the first time in eleven months, and the trains started rolling again between Berlin and western Germany.

Berliners were understandably relieved when the blockade ended. People paraded through the streets, cheering as garland-bedecked trucks entered the city. But the relief was mixed with anxiety. Everyone knew that the Soviets could cut the place off again if they chose to. To drive this point home, the East German newspaper *Neues Deutschland* later threatened: "He who lives on an island should not make an enemy of the sea."

Even before the blockade was lifted, Berlin was effectively split into two sections, with each part increasingly taking on its own character. As of August 1948, the city had two separate police forces. This came about because Police Chief Markgraf, the Soviet appointee, had begun ordering his men to arrest and even to beat up political opponents everywhere in Berlin, including in the western sectors. In response, the Western powers sanctioned a new police force for their half of the city; many of its members were refugees from Markgraf's force. The Berlin city council also split apart. SED thugs had begun harassing Social Democratic delegates when they tried to attend council meetings at the Red City Hall in the eastern sector. Fed up, non-Communist representatives began meeting at the Technical University in the British sector. Later they would switch to the City Hall in the borough of Schöneberg, which became the seat of West Berlin's city government. SED loyalists not only continued to meet in the East, but elected their own mayor, Friedrich Ebert, son of the Weimar president. (Having in his day hated the Communists, Ebert senior would not have been pleased by this development.) The former Reich capital did not yet have a wall running through it, but for all practical purposes it was now a divided city, the most prominent urban casualty of the Cold War.

Division

On May 23, 1949, the West German *Grundgesetz* (Basic Law) was published, providing the legal foundation for the Federal Republic of Germany. In August of that year the West Germans elected their first government, which was headed by the seventy-two-year-old Rhinelander, Konrad Adenauer. Theodor Heuss, of the Free Democratic Party, became the first federal president, a largely ceremonial post. The Bundestag began meeting on September 15. Shortly thereafter, on October 7, 1949, the German Democratic Republic was established on the territory of the Soviet occupation zone in East Germany. The German Reich created by Bismarck and brought to ruin by Hitler was now formally split asunder.

Germany's division inevitably transformed the political status of the former capital, which, as we have seen, was itself now divided into two cities, West Berlin and East Berlin. The Federal Republic hardly wished to have its seat of government in a beleaguered enclave located deep inside a rival state. But physical location was not the only factor behind West Germany's reluctance to make West Berlin its capital. Even before the German division was formalized, there had been considerable opposition in the western zones to retaining Berlin as the national capital (if and when the Allies permitted a new German nation to arise). The most vociferous opponent to Berlin was Konrad Adenauer, the future West German chancellor. He equated Berlin and Prussia with everything he hated: socialism, extreme nationalism, materialism, Protestantism. For him, in fact, the whole of eastern Germany was so unfathomable that it might as well have been in China. Once, when traveling by train through the Mark Brandenburg, he put down the blinds in his compartment so as not to have to see "the steppes." And he liked to say that if he looked a little "Mongolian" himself, this was because he had a grandmother from the Harz Mountains. In one of his postwar speeches he articulated a prejudice shared by many western German Catholics when he said: "Although the Berliners have some valuable qualities, I've always had the feeling in Berlin that I was in a pagan city." As early as 1946, therefore, he pleaded for a shift of power away from Berlin, "even if it were not occupied by the Russians." He was yet more emphatic to his CDU colleague Jakob Kaiser, a native Berliner: "From the standpoint of the German south and west it is completely out of the question that Berlin could be the capital of a newly reconstituted Germany. It makes no difference if and by whom Berlin and the east is occupied." In his opposition to retaining Berlin as Germany's capital,

Adenauer was joined by the British, who preferred that the capital be moved as far away from Russian (and Old Prussian) influence as possible.

Adenauer's major political rivals, the Social Democrats, would normally have resisted his desire to shift Germany's political center of gravity away from Berlin, since that was where their traditional power base lay. But as a result of the forced merger of the eastern SPD and the KPD to form the SED, the rump SPD had moved its headquarters to Hanover and begun to look at Berlin in a new, less favorable, light. As Carlo Schmid, one of the party's leaders from the Southwest, put it in February 1946:

> Berlin centralism has not been good for us Germans; it must not return, and perhaps we must even discuss whether Berlin should remain the capital; for my taste, it lies too close to Potsdam [the heart of Prussian militarism]. . . . In this regard, I know that I'm in agreement with many of our friends in North Germany and also with the Minister-President of Bavaria, [Wilhelm] Hoegner.

But if the West German capital could not be in Berlin, where would it be? For some time, political leaders in the western sectors had been pondering this question, debating the pros and cons of a number of cities, from Hamburg to Munich. By 1948 the race had essentially narrowed to Frankfurt and Bonn. To many Germans, the former city seemed the ideal choice. It was centrally located, cosmopolitan, and it had a rich democratic tradition. Yet for many other inhabitants of western Germany, Frankfurt's very attractiveness, its obviousness as a choice, made it undesirable. The impending Federal Republic was supposed to be a provisional state, a way station on the road to reunification. Frankfurt was too imposing to be the capital of a way station. Bonn did not have this drawback, to put it mildly. With fewer than 100,000 residents in 1948, it was a midsized town, not a real city. Detractors said that the most important event to have happened there was the birth of Beethoven, who had left as soon as he could. On the other hand, with the backing of the state of Rhineland-Westphalia and the British, in whose occupation zone Bonn lay, the Rhineland town won the right to host the parliamentary council, a forerunner to the Bundestag. The British then crucially threw their support behind Bonn's candidacy for the provisional capital, since it was obviously in London's interest to have West Germany's seat of government in its zone. The Americans, in whose zone Frankfurt lay, did not push for the Hessian city over Bonn because they did not wish to pull out of Frankfurt to make room for a new German government.

Important, too, was the pro-Bonn politicking of Adenauer, who came from the area and who regarded the town as the best choice. Mustering all his persuasive power, Adenauer was able to convince a narrow majority of his colleagues in the parliamentary council to see things his way. On May 10, 1949, the council voted thirty-three to twenty-nine to make Bonn the provisional seat of government for the emerging Federal Republic. On November 3, 1950, after the new government had already started to function, that decision was confirmed.

Over the years, Bonn would inspire much derision in its role as capital of a major European nation. In his 1968 spy thriller, *A Small Town in Germany*, John Le Carré described the new capital as "discreetly temporary in deference to the dream, discreetly permanent in deference to the reality." A British envoy in the 1960s said that London's embassy in Bonn was "Her Majesty's only mission in a cornfield." Yet with time Bonn caught on with many foreigners, and, more importantly, with many West Germans. After all, the place seemed the perfect capital for a country that was determined not to make waves, not to fall back into the megalomania of the past. Many Germans hoped that Bonn's lack of a tumultuous past might help the Federal Republic become accepted and even loved. As Adenauer said later: "Bonn didn't have a history; it was a beginning."

What did the creation of the "Bonn Republic" mean politically to the inhabitants of West Berlin? Because Berlin as a whole remained under four-power Allied jurisdiction, West Berlin, though claiming status as a "land" of the Federal Republic, was part of the new nation only in a limited fashion. It could send representatives to the Bundestag, but they could not vote in plenary sessions. Federal laws were not automatically applied to West Berlin; they had to be extended to the city by the local House of Representatives and were subject to veto by the Allied commandants. Likewise subject to Allied veto was the promotion of all policemen in the upper ranks. West Berlin was fully integrated into the Federal Republic's financial and economic system, but the Federal Constitution Court, sitting in Karlsruhe, had no jurisdiction in the city. The Western Allies insisted on these restrictions in order to maintain their own rights in Berlin under the Potsdam Agreement. Thus, not only did the West Berliners no longer reside in the capital of their nation, they were reduced to the status of second-class citizens. Their situation was rendered all the worse by the obvious hostility of the new chancellor, who did not even visit West Berlin until April 1950, when he stayed for a mere forty-eight hours.

The situation for East Berlin was very different. In violation of the Potsdam

Agreement, Moscow allowed the new East German government to establish its capital in the Soviet sector of Berlin. In this way the GDR sought to buttress its claim to being the true Germany, the only legitimate Germany. Of course, the Federal Republic made this claim as well, but while *its* capital was by design provisional, the East German *Hauptstadt* was supposedly in place for the ages. When all of Germany came under Communist rule, as the GDR rulers promised it soon would, there would be no need for the rulers to pack up and move; they were already home.

To reinforce symbolically their claim to the parts of Berlin that they controlled (eight of the twenty districts that had comprised Greater Berlin), the East Germans renamed a large number of streets and squares according to their own political lights. The old Bülowplatz, which under the Nazis had become Horst-Wessel-Platz, did not regain its original name; rather, it became Rosa-Luxemburg-Platz. The Wilhelmstrasse, imperial and Nazi Berlin's premier political address, became Otto-Grotewohl-Strasse, after the East-SPD leader who helped found the SED. Dorotheenstrasse, a major artery in the East, was rechristened Clara-Zetkin-Strasse. As a symbol of its rejection of German militarism, the GDR rulers expunged the names Hindenburg and Ludendorff from the map of East Berlin, while adding that of Carl von Ossietzky, the editor of the *Weltbühne* and the 1936 Nobel Peace Prize winner. Staking their claim to parts of the anti-Nazi resistance legacy that they respected, the East Germans renamed Karl-Friedrich-Strasse in the Mitte district Geschwister-Scholl-Strasse in honor of the Munich University students who were executed for distributing anti-Nazi pamphlets during the war. As part of the Stalinization of East Berlin, the broad Frankfurter Allee was rechristened Stalinallee and totally rebuilt in monumental fashion (about which more below). The name of Stalin's German henchman, Ernst Thälmann, was attached to the former Wilhelmplatz. Lothringer Strasse became Wilhelm-Pieck-Strasse in honor of the GDR's first president. Finally, in a tribute to the founders of the Communist movement, Schlossplatz, the grandest square in the East, and once the center of royal and imperial power, became Marx-Engels-Platz.

The authorities in West Berlin, meanwhile, employed the tactic of name-changing to make some political claims of their own. In June 1949 they renamed the Kronprinzenallee "Clayallee" after the American military governor and hero of the Berlin Airlift. To document their ties to the heritage of Social Democracy, they rechristened Augusta-Viktoria-Platz, in Charlottenburg, Breitscheidplatz, after Rudolf Breitscheid, an SPD leader who was murdered in Buchenwald. In an effort to show that they, too,

Monument to Rosa Luxemburg at the Landewehr Canal

had claims on the revolution of 1918, the West Berliners renamed the Tirpitzufer in the Tiergarten district Reichspietschufer, after Max Reichspietsch, a sailor who had been court-martialed and executed for staging a hunger strike over unjust treatment of the crews in the imperial navy in 1917. (Later, conservatives on West Berlin's city council attempted to rid the city of this association, just as they tried, unsuccessfully, to prevent the erection of a monument to Rosa Luxemburg on the Landwehr Canal.) Unlike East Berlin, West Berlin retained the names of many German military leaders, including Hindenburg, Moltke, and Roon.

As this battle of place-names suggests, the history of Berlin from 1949 on was shaped to a large degree by the competing claims of the two German states. While continuing to worry about West Berlin as a financial drain, the government of the Federal Republic could not turn its back on the city, for it expected (at least in principle) to return there some day, and it hoped to turn this "outpost of freedom" into a living example of Western superiority. The East German government was equally determined to transform East Berlin, which it always referred to as "Berlin—Capital of the GDR," into a showcase of Communist progress and power.

In the first years of the Federal Republic, West Berlin was anything but a model of economic vitality. Stranded within the new East German state, cut off from its traditional markets and sources of supply, and with many of its enterprises outmaneuvered by more efficient Western firms, the city struggled to compete. While West Germany embarked on its "economic miracle," West Berlin suffered a miracle in reverse. In 1950 West Berlin factories, which were working only at 40 percent of capacity, exported DM 997 billion worth of goods to West Germany, while the return trade was worth DM 2,239 billion. In that same year West Berlin registered 31.2 percent unemployment, and a full 40 percent of the population drew public relief. Not until 1954 did unemployment levels dip below 20 percent; it took another two years for them to drop to the level of the preblockade period. West Berlin may have been free, but it was also very poor.

If West Berlin was to recover at all, and not, in effect, be a permanent embarrassment to the West, it would need extensive subsidies from Bonn. Given his feelings for Berlin, Adenauer was not likely to be an avid proponent of aid, but he fell under pressure from the Western powers to help. British high commissioner Sir Brian Robertson warned the German government that he would not tolerate "an insufficient engagement of Bonn for Berlin." In 1950 West Berlin was declared an "emergency area" and granted DM 60 million in assistance. Beginning in 1953, a regular Berlinhilfe (Berlin aid) policy was launched, and two years later various tax breaks and income enhancements were granted to the citizens of the city. Washington earmarked some DM 3,000 million worth of its aid to Germany to West Berlin. Assisted by such measures, West Berliners gradually began to join their countrymen west of the Elbe in prosperity, though their ongoing need for special treatment endowed them with the image of poor cousins living off the largess of their richer relatives.

This was a problem that most East Berliners would have been happy to share. In the first years after Germany's division East Berlin was not appreciably poorer than the western half of the city, but it had fewer prospects for improvement. Its economy was tightly integrated into that of the new East German state, which in turn was wrapped in the Soviets' straitjacket of centralized planning. Small firms were consolidated into huge state-run combines that turned inefficiency into an art form. The Russians, moreover, continued to draw extensive reparations from the GDR. While the Soviets, like the West, might hold out a glorious economic future for their part of Germany, they undercut the chances of achieving this by living hard off the land themselves.

The fierce rivalry between the two German states naturally extended to the realm of urban reconstruction, which provided the most obvious forum for displays of material prowess and contrasting political ideals. Being the point on the map where the two systems most sharply collided, Berlin became the focus of ambitious rebuilding programs—East and West. Of course, the process in both cases involved extensive demolition as well as renovation and reconstruction. What the new German regimes decided to raze tells us as much about them as what they built.

The first plan for the reconstruction of Berlin was not yet caught up in the contention between East and West. In 1945, under the auspices of the *Magistrat*, a committee headed by the well-known architect Hans Scharoun developed an ambitious plan to revamp Berlin according to the most modern urban design principles. In place of the incoherent clutter that had grown up in the Berlin area over the ages, his scheme envisaged a collection of residential/commercial "cells" connected to each other and to outlying industrial complexes by a new network of roads and rail lines. Instead of expanding in concentric rings, which was the old pattern, the new city would follow the course of the Spree River, blending in with the topography and the landscape. Clearly, Scharoun and his colleagues wanted to take advantage of the widespread devastation of Old Berlin to create something completely new. To become reality, however, the plan would have necessitated the total reorganization of Berlin's infrastructure, much of which had survived the war like the foundation of a burned house. Even if the will for such a task had been there, the resources were not, given the need to balance long-term reconstruction against the short-term requirement of putting roofs over peoples' heads. Scharoun was fired in 1946, and his scheme remained a utopian dream. Fifty years later, when a change in political circumstances brought new opportunities for a dramatic shift in urban design, Berlin planners would once again discover how difficult it was to uproot an entrenched infrastructure and to translate innovative schemes into reality.

Given the fact that in divided Germany, East Berlin was a capital and West Berlin was not, it is not surprising that the most ambitious building projects in the first years after the division transpired in the East. The earliest major representational structures to go up there were the work of the Soviet occupiers rather than the East Germans themselves. In Treptow Park the Soviets erected a (still existent) war memorial, much larger than the one near the Brandenburg Gate. Its central structure consists of a thirty-eight-foot-tall figure of a Soviet soldier standing atop a pedestal made from marble reclaimed from the ruins of Hitler's Chancellery. The soldier holds a sword in one hand and cradles a rescued child in the other (Berliners naturally said that it

Stone blocks with Stalin's inscriptions at the Soviet War Memorial, Treptow

would have been more appropriate had he held a ravished woman). On either side of the statue are rows of granite blocks inscribed with uplifting sentiments from Stalin—a kind of Soviet Siegesallee. In a nearby cemetery lie the remains of 3,200 Red Army soldiers who died in the taking of Berlin. The memorial was dedicated on May 8, 1949, four years to the day after the German surrender.

The first major functional building to rise from the ruins of central Berlin was the Soviet embassy, which took up the entire space of the old Russian embassy on Unter den Linden and a neighboring lot as well. Designed by Soviet architects in consultation with Stalin, it was more bombastic than its predecessor, featuring fluted pillars, carved balustrades, and other neoclassical ornamentation. Speer and Hitler might have admired everything about this structure save for its large marble bust of Lenin in the forecourt (now of course long gone).

The Soviet embassy set the standard for the most important representational construction undertaken by the East Germans in their new capital in the early 1950s. While the vogue in the West (including West Berlin) was for trashy functional modernism, the Soviets were pushing a grand historicism that supposedly reflected the heroic spirit of the triumphant masses. As a Russian planning document, dutifully

Stalinallee, shortly after its construction

adopted by the East Germans, explained: "In its structure and architectural form, the city is the expression of political life and the national consciousness of the people."

The East German regime attempted to translate this ideal into practice in the construction of the above-mentioned Stalinallee, an eighty-meter-wide boulevard of six- to seven-story buildings that runs for three kilometers through the working-class district of Friedrichshain. The earliest new buildings on this avenue had been designed in a modernist style, harkening back to the Bauhaus, but Ulbricht complained in 1950 that such modesty diminished the importance of the new socialist capital. When the project commenced in earnest in 1951 monumentalism was the word of the day. Based on designs reflecting Soviet influences (primarily Moscow's Gorky Street) as well as German classicism, the Stalinallee buildings boast facades faced in stone and Meissen tile, along with a plenitude of pillars, balconies, and statuary. At the eastern end of the avenue rise the twin towers of the Frankfurter Tor, a recapitulation of the eighteenth-century church towers flanking Schinkel's Schauspielhaus on the Gendarmenmarkt. The towers' designer, the Bauhaus veteran Hermann Henselmann, later admitted that the Stalinallee bore a certain similarity to Nazi architecture, a view echoed by Western architects like Scharoun, who called it "Speerisch." The similarity is not surprising, given that Speer had also borrowed heavily from Schinkel. In both cases, the German architectural past was coopted for purposes of cultural validation and propagandistic effect. Here was a street, the East Germans said, which fused the most enlightened ideals of German history with the aspirations of modern socialism.

The Stalinallee was meant to be a template for other grand streets in East Berlin, but the boulevard did not prove a lasting influence. Following Stalin's death in 1953 and Khrushchev's subsequent attack on the dictator's legacy, the cultural pendulum swung back toward functionalism, leaving the Stalinallee a white elephant. Its name was changed to Karl-Marx-Allee in 1961, after which it slowly went to seed. Only with German reunification in 1990 did the street gain new life, now at the hands of urban officials and architects from the West, who insisted it be restored as an early version of postmodernism. Westerners began moving into the renovated apartments, and within ten years of the fall of the Wall the "first street of socialism" was firmly in Western hands.

The Stalinallee stood a good distance from the old governmental quarter in Berlin-Mitte, which was the part of the city most devastated by the war. In the first years of its existence, the East German regime did not try to reclaim this quarter for its own headquarters, settling instead in the northern district of Pankow. Yet if the Communists did little building in the city center at this point, they did not hesitate to demolish the quarter's signature structure, the Royal Palace, which during the Weimar era and Third Reich had served primarily as an art museum. Allied bombs had badly damaged parts of the building, but enough of it remained intact for a number of public exhibitions to be held there between 1946 and 1948. The GDR leaders might have made use of this property themselves, much as the Soviets had appropriated the Kremlin, but they had other ideas for the land it occupied. Ulbricht dreamed of building a giant skyscraper on the site to rival the Stalinist towers in Moscow. There was also talk of moving Marx's remains from London's Highgate cemetery to a mausoleum on the former palace square, creating an answer to Lenin's tomb on Red Square. Pending the realization of such grandiose schemes, the area was converted into a stage for mass rallies. As Ulbricht said in a speech in July 1950: "The center of our capital, the Lustgarten and the area of the palace's ruins, must become a grand square for demonstrations, upon which our people's will for struggle and for progress can find expression." A few weeks later the government announced that the palace would be demolished. The announcement prompted widespread protest, even within the GDR. The regime sought to deflect the protest by claiming that the palace had been too badly damaged by "Anglo-American terror-bombers" to be salvaged. But everyone knew that the real issue was the building's political associations. As *Neues Deutschland* editorialized: "May it [the palace] no longer remind us of an unglorious past." The demolition began in September 1950. When it was completed four months later, a gaping void occupied the former center of royal and imperial power. Aside from hosting demonstrations, the area served mainly as a parking lot, with little Trabant cars standing where the masses had once cheered the kaiser.

The public outcry over the demolition of the Royal Palace helped convince the authorities in West Berlin to proceed differently with *their* main Hohenzollern palace, the Charlottenburger Schloss, which had also been heavily damaged in the war. Rather than knock it down, they embarked in 1951 on a long and painstaking restoration process that eventually yielded one of postwar Germany's preeminent historical showplaces. Shortly after the work began, Andreas Schlüter's famous equestrian statue of the Great Elector, which heretofore had graced the Lange Brücke outside the Royal Palace, was installed in the forecourt of the Schloss.

Schloss Bellevue, a beautiful palace on the edge of the Tiergarten, which had been built in the 1780s for Frederick the Great's brother, Prince August Ferdinand, was also restored at this time. Although it had been used by the Nazis as a guest house for foreign dignitaries, the West German authorities decided that it would make an ideal residence for their federal president when he stayed in Berlin. By putting the elegant property to this use, the Federal Republic staked out its first official presence in the divided city.

Of course, the most symbolically significant building in West Berlin—indeed in the whole city—was the Reichstag, which sat just inside the British sector. As we have seen, Hitler had refused to allow the building to be torn down after the fire in February 1933. In the wake of World War II the edifice was in truly sad shape, a rotting hulk of stone and iron, its facade pockmarked with bullet holes and its interior covered in Cyrillic graffiti. The Russians had proposed that it be exploited like a quarry for building projects in the city, but the Berliners preferred to use it for one of their black markets. During the blockade it served as a backdrop for the rallies at which Ernst Reuter hurled his defiance at the Soviets. With the division of Germany, sentiment arose in the West to restore the building as a symbol of the Federal Republic's determination to make Berlin the capital of a reunified nation. In 1949 Jakob Kaiser spoke of it as "a crystallization point for German reunification." But at this stage there was no money for restoration, and the only alteration to be carried out in the 1950s was the demolition of the sagging dome.

While symbolically impressive, restoration of public buildings like Bellevue and the Charlottenburger Schloss was only a tiny part of the huge reconstruction effort that engulfed West Berlin in the 1950s. To clear space for new housing units and commercial districts, the rubble that still clogged much of the city was scooped up and dumped in an enormous pile on the grounds of a former Wehrmacht school in the Grunewald. The mound, which Berliners dubbed the Teufelsberg (Devil's Mountain), eventually grew to a height of 120 meters, high enough for the Americans to place a radar station on its summit. Buried within this artificial Alp were the remains of many partly damaged buildings that had recently fallen victim to the wrecking ball. Some of these, like the still-functioning Anhalter Bahnhof, were of great historical significance. Architectural preservation had never been Berlin's strong suit, but the postwar disregard for treasures of the past was cultural barbarism with a vengeance.

In West Berlin, as in the East, reconstruction was meant to symbolize, even facilitate, political transformation. The West wanted an architectural look that conveyed the Federal Republic's commitment to internationalism, egalitarianism, individualism, and freedom. Unfortunately, the image thought to be most expressive of these values was the bland "internationalist" style that was sweeping across Western Europe and America in the postwar era. The construction materials used in the new buildings also had to be politically correct: in place of stone and brick, one had to use glass and steel. Thus much of West Berlin was covered over in glass boxes touted as "democratic." The Spree metropolis had never been beautiful, but its postwar rebuilders managed, in their pursuit of a progressive new face, to make it even uglier than before.

The new approach to urban housing design was evident in the Hansaviertel, the residential district on the northwestern edge of the Tiergarten that had been built up in the Bismarckian era, only to be knocked flat by Allied bombs during the war. In 1953 the West Berlin Senate announced a competition for the construction of a new housing development in the area that would represent the democratic values of the Federal Republic. Commissions were awarded to a galaxy of international architects, including Le Corbusier, Gropius, Alvar Aalto, Oscar Niemeyer, and

Scharoun. The results of their work were unveiled with great fanfare at an international exhibition, the Interbau, in 1957. In conscious contrast both to Berlin's prewar residential housing and the new Stalinallee in the East, the Hansaviertel featured an assortment of modest structures dispersed in a parklike setting. Each building was unique. While the overall design made the project seem less fortresslike than the eastern housing units, not to mention the old Mietskasernen, the individual buildings turned out to be surprisingly uninspired—just a collection of concrete and glass blocks of varying sizes. The Hansaviertel was nonetheless hailed as an architectural showcase and as a model for future residential building. It might indeed have become so had not its low residential density made it economically impractical once land prices started to go up. Only its blandness carried over into vast new housing beehives like the Otto Suhr Settlement, the Gropiusstadt, and the Märkisches Viertel.

Early commercial reconstruction, meanwhile, focused on the area around Zoo Station and the Kurfürstendamm, whose revival, it was hoped, would help jump-start the local economy. In 1950 the luxurious KaDeWe department store reopened its doors to hordes of shopping-starved citizens. They stormed the place with such zeal that two clerks were injured while trying, in good Prussian fashion, to keep order. An automobile showroom on the "Ku-Damm" proudly displayed that symbol of West Germany's emerging *Wirstschaftswunder* (economic miracle), the Volkswagen Beetle. The most impressive new building on the avenue was the rebuilt Hotel Kempinski, which opened in 1952 on the site of the original hotel, destroyed in 1945. Erected with money from the Marshall Plan, the new hotel was, as the *Tagesspiegel* wrote, a prime symbol for "the faith that's being shown in our city." Such symbols were desperately needed in a town that was already feeling the ill effects of isolation and exclusion from the nexus of political power. Thus the Kempinski was more than just a hotel. It was, in the words of a recent retrospective, "an outpost of glamour in the frightening arena of the Cold War [and] . . . a bridge back to the urbane world of the Twenties, before all the horrors began." The part of West Berlin in which the Kempinski is located was not yet the world famous mecca of consumerism and glitzy entertainment it would become in the 1960s, when its reigning symbol was a revolving Mercedes star atop a high-rise office building, but for many inhabitants of the city, including those who lived in the East, the Zoo/Kurfürstendamm area was now the one place in town where they could feel truly alive—could feel, that is, like *Berliners* again.

The East German Workers' Uprising of June 17, 1953

Worried by the growing attraction of West Berlin, the East German government started taking measures to curtail contacts between the two halves of the city. In early 1952 they cut the telephone links with the West, and a year later they suspended bus and tram service into West Berlin. Now the only public transport between East and West were the *U-Bahn* and *S-Bahn* lines. However, the fact that one could still move at all across the ideological divide in Berlin made the city an anomaly in Germany after May 26, 1952, for on that date the GDR government barricaded its border with West Germany. From this point on the inner-German border became one of Cold War Europe's most menacing frontiers—an 858-mile death-strip of barbed wire fences, control points, watchtowers, mines, and, later, automatic shooting devices. East German citizens living near the border who were considered by their government to be "a risk to the antifascistic, democratic order" were summarily expelled from their homes.

Ulbricht's efforts to isolate the GDR and East Berlin further undermined an economy already burdened by agricultural collectivization, nationalization of industry, neglect of consumer goods, unrealistic productivity quotas, and the huge costs of building up a quasi army, the Kasernierte Volkspolizei. Living standards for the "toilers" plummeted while taxes and other obligations to the state became more onerous. As a result, more and more East Germans chose to move west, which after May 1952 could be accomplished only through Berlin. In the second half of 1952, 48,831 GDR citizens went west; in the first quarter of 1953, the figure rose to 84,034, including 1,836 members of the SED. A high percentage of the refugees were young and well-educated, the kind of people that no state can afford to lose. One would have thought that this situation called for a relaxation of the government's efforts to force the economy toward full communism through increased collectivization and higher production quotas, but Ulbricht and Grotewohl believed it necessary to *raise* the productivity "norms" for industrial and construction workers. Insisting that the most pressing problem of the hour was "to overcome the low work norms," the government decreed on May 28, 1953, a productivity increase of at least 10 percent in state-run operations.

The GDR rulers adopted this policy without backing from Moscow, which in the wake of Stalin's death was reassessing the advisability of trying to impose a fully socialized economy on East Germany. Worried that the East German state was failing as a countermodel to the West, Stalin's successors, most notably Minister for State

Security Lavrenti Beria, proposed a "New Course" for the GDR that called for a suspension of agricultural collectivization and forcefed industrialization. It might seem odd that Beria should have advocated this softer line, for as head of the dreaded NKVD (Soviet secret political police) he had been Stalin's chief hatchet man, helping the Great Leader to purge countless enemies, real and imagined. Yet he was also a realist with a full appreciation for the damage that Stalin's policies had done, not least in East Germany. Because Ulbricht was so closely identified with the hard line, he seemed unlikely to be willing to abandon it. Beria thus began thinking about replacing the SED chief with one of the latter's critics in the East German Politbüro, either Wilhelm Zaisser (minister for state security), or Rudolf Herrnstadt (editor of *Das Neue Deutschland*). In early June Beria ordered Vladimir Semyonov, Soviet Russia's commissioner for German affairs, to instruct Ulbricht to reverse his economic policy or face the consequences.

Ulbricht stood his ground. Aware that his enemies were plotting against him both in Moscow and Berlin, the SED chief coupled his own survival with resisting Beria's New Course. On June 16, 1953, his government announced another 25 percent increase in work norms, along with a warning that workers who failed to meet state quotas could expect pay cuts of up to 35 percent. Stalin might be dead in Moscow, but his German alter ego was alive and well in East Berlin.

Just as alive, however, was a strong current of resentment among the chief victims of Ulbricht's policies, the workers of East Germany. The frustration had been building for some time. On June 13, 1953, during a cruise on the Spree, a group of construction workers decided to call a protest strike. At about nine o'clock in the morning on June 16 workers at the Stalinallee, East Berlin's prestige construction project, threw down their tools and began marching toward the House of Ministries (Göring's former Luftwaffe headquarters) in the Leipziger Strasse. On the way they picked up hundreds more demonstrators from other construction sites and factories. In addition to carrying banners reading "We Demand a Lowering of Norms," some of the marchers called for free elections and the resignation of the current government. "Goatee [Ulbricht], belly [Pieck], and glasses [Grotewohl] are not the will of the masses!" they screamed. Upon arriving at their destination they shouted for goatee and glasses to come out and face the workers of the "workers' state."

Ulbricht and Grotewohl had plenty of experience talking *to* workers, but none talking *with* them. Moreover, demonstrations that were not organized by the state were beyond their ken. In their eyes, this was revolution, or, more accurately, *counter*revolution, undoubtedly instigated by West Germany. Rather than appear before the workers, they cowered in the basement of the House of Ministries, then slipped quietly out a side door. Heinz Brandt, the SED's secretary for agitation and propaganda, was sent out to tell the people that, for the time being, the norm increases would be rescinded.

The gesture came too late. Sensing that they had the government on the run, leaders of the demonstration called for a general strike to begin the following morning. People were instructed to assemble at Strausberger Platz on the Stalinallee. There was, however, no unified or coherent understanding as to what the strike would yield: some simply wanted economic reforms, others apparently hoped for the ouster of Ulbricht and company, while still others seem to have envisaged the end of Communist rule and the reunification of Germany. As the protesters finally left the Ministries building on the night of June 16, no one was certain whether there would be a strike at all on the following day.

Fearing the worst, the government banned any discussion of the protest in the state-run media, but RIAS in West Berlin gave a full account of the demonstration

East Berliners pelt a Russian tank with stones during the uprising of June 17, 1953

and call to action, without explicitly endorsing it. As it turned out, RIAS did not have to provide an endorsement. Despite cold rain and a suspension of public transport, thousands of workers began assembling at Strausberger Platz on the morning of June 17. Demonstrators gathered in other GDR cities and towns as well. All told, almost 400,000 workers threw in with the strike. The first—and, until 1989, the only—uprising against Communist rule in East Germany was about to begin.

In East Berlin, which remained the center of the upheaval, the protesters began marching from the Stalinallee to the center of the city at about ten o'clock. Revealingly, they bore aloft one of the signs that the Soviet occupiers had erected on the border of their sector; it read, "End of the Democratic Sector." As the demonstrators poured down Unter den Linden they sang workers' songs and chanted anti-Ulbricht slogans. Some paused before the Soviet embassy to sing the strictly *verboten* German national hymn, which called for "unity, law, and freedom." Even more provocatively, a gang of youths clambered atop the Brandenburg Gate, tore down the red flag that flew there, and shouted: "We want freedom, we want bread, we will beat all the Russians dead." As the day wore on the crowds became increasingly unruly, smashing windows and overturning cars. Flushed with the confidence that mob action often brings, some of the demonstrators apparently believed that the "first socialist state on German soil" was about to come to an end.

But the GDR leaders were not about to concede defeat. On the previous evening Ulbricht had appealed to Moscow for help, and Beria flew immediately to Berlin to take command of the situation. While the Kremlin blamed Ulbricht for the crisis, it could not afford to let his government fall victim to popular insurrection. This might encourage similar uprisings elsewhere, perhaps even in the USSR itself. Beria therefore ordered the Soviet commandant in East Berlin, Major General Pavel Dibrova, to employ all necessary force to disperse the demonstrators. At noon dozens of T-34 tanks, the same models that had rumbled into Berlin in April 1945, began rolling through the city in the direction of the Brandenburg Gate and the Potsdamer Platz. When a few would-be East German Davids tried to stop the armored Soviet Goliaths by throwing stones at them, the tanks opened fire, killing several courageous but foolhardy young men. Upon reaching the sector border the tanks took up positions to block egress to West Berlin, but did not fire directly into the crowds. At this point the East German Volkspolizei appeared in force and began beating demonstrators with clubs, even shooting people in the back as they tried to flee. (Most observers noted that it was the German police, not the Russians, who were most anxious to draw blood.) After a few hours it was all over. When night fell the only people remaining in the streets were policemen enforcing a strict curfew and martial law. In other East German cities, too, the uprising had been crushed almost before it began.

If one of the weaknesses of the uprising was a lack of clear or unified goals, another was an absence of support from the country's intelligentsia. A few artists and academics joined in the protest, but most preferred to sit on the sidelines, and some even cheered on the regime. Among the latter faction was East Germany's most prominent writer, Bertolt Brecht. When the protest began he dashed off letters of support to the authorities, including one to Ulbricht stating: "Valued Comrade Ulbricht, history will pay its respects to the revolutionary importance of the Socialist Unity Party of Germany. Large-scale discussions with the masses on the subject of the tempo at which socialism is being built would lead to recognition . . . and consolidation of socialist achievements. I need to express to you at this moment my allegiance with the Socialist Unity Party of Germany." As the Russian tanks rumbled into position, Brecht watched from the Brandenburg Gate, waving to the soldiers. During the shooting he was back at the Berliner Ensemble, blaming the uprising on "doubtful elements" from the West. Four days later Ulbricht published Brecht's letter of support, leaving out his advice to negotiate with the workers. This irritated the dramatist, for it was certain to damage his reputation in the West, but he said nothing in public against Comrade Ulbricht. Rather, he privately vented his spleen in a poem written in response to a broadcast from the secretary of the GDR Writers Union admonishing the nation's workers to win back the confidence of their government. The Brecht verse reads:

After the uprising of June 17
the secretary of the Writers' Union
Had leaflets distributed in the Stalinallee
In which it was said that the people
Had lost the government's confidence
Which it would only be able to regain
By redoubling its efforts. In that case, would it
Not be simpler if the government dissolved the people
And elected another?

It would have been nobler had Brecht published this now-famous poem in his lifetime. But in reality it was not so much the GDR government that had disappointed the dramatist, but the East German workers themselves. As he sadly told his friend Hermann Henselmann after listening to some workers complain about their lot: "Hermann, I've seen the true face of the German working class."

Two hundred and sixty-seven people died across East Germany in the June 1953 uprising, twenty-one of them in East Berlin; 4,493 GDR citizens were arrested, most of them workers. Following a series of kangaroo trials, some 200 people were executed, and another 1,400 received life sentences. The number of those disappearing into the East German gulag might have been higher had not thousands of East Germans decided that this was the opportune moment to disappear into West Germany via Berlin.

Although the Soviets and the East German government were quick to dismiss the June 1953 uprising as a "fascist putsch" orchestrated by the West, the affair was profoundly embarrassing to the Communist leaders, especially to those of the GDR. The East German system had been shown to be deeply unpopular with its own working class, the very population it was supposed to benefit. Nonetheless, the Ulbricht regime did not emerge weakened from the uprising, but strengthened. Beria still wanted to get rid of the SED chief, but to do so now would look like a concession to the demonstrators. In any event, Beria's own days as a power broker were numbered, for during his emergency trip to Berlin his enemies at home, led by Khrushchev, had plotted his ouster. On June 26 he was stripped of his powers and arrested. In a political trial much like the ones he had once orchestrated for Stalin he was accused of all manner of offenses, from trying to sabotage the Soviet atomic bomb project to raping little girls. Sentenced to life in prison, he was murdered by his guards before he could serve much time. On July 7 Ulbricht was briefed in Moscow on Beria's purge. Upon returning to Berlin he immediately purged Zaisser and Herrnstadt, the men who would probably have taken his place had Beria stayed in power in Russia.

Contrary to East German accusations that agents provocateurs from the West had fomented the June uprising, Western authorities had done nothing to abet it beyond broadcasting news of the demonstration on June 16. American, British, and French troops in West Berlin stood by and watched as the Russians, still technically their allies in the former Reich capital, helped the East German police beat down the protesters. What the Western Allies seemed to be saying was that the Soviets and GDR authorities had carte blanche in East Berlin, so long as they did not try to push the Western powers out of West Berlin. It was a message that the Soviets, the GDR government, and most of all the East German people, would not soon forget.

West Berliners were understandably appalled by what happened to their fellow citizens in the East on June 17. Some took out their rage on the Soviet war memorial just west of the Brandenburg Gate, but the British troops guarding the site beat them back. Groups from the West placed memorials to the East Germans killed in the uprising, and the West German Senate renamed the boulevard running through the Tiergarten (and past the Soviet memorial) Strasse des 17. Juni—another salvo in the street sign wars.

Like the West Berliners, the government in Bonn was obliged to stand by helplessly as the East German workers' uprising was suppressed. Chagrined by its impotence, but determined to exploit the affair as a propaganda victory for the West, Bonn ordered that June 17 henceforth be set aside as a day of commemoration for the abortive uprising. For years thereafter West German politicians gave speeches praising the courage of the East German workers who—it was claimed—had tried to overturn the tyranny of communism and end the injustice of German division. Yet almost from the beginning, most ordinary West Germans treated this anniversary not as a moment for political reflection but as just another holiday. Dwelling on the problems of the East brought on unwelcome feelings of guilt. As early as 1954, Fritz Stern noted that many West Germans had begun to "resent the East Germans who stand as a muted reproach to their enjoyment of prosperity."

Spy Stories

In July 1954, a little more than a year after the East German uprising, West Germany suffered a humiliation of its own, when Otto John, chief of Bonn's counterintelligence service, the Bundesvervassungsschutz (Office for Constitutional Protection, BfV) slipped from West Berlin into the *Hauptstadt der DDR* and announced that he had changed his loyalties. While John's apparent defection came as a huge shock, no one was surprised that he chose Berlin as his jumping-off point. Standing directly on the Cold War fault line but affording relatively free passage across the ideological divide, Berlin in the 1950s surpassed Vienna as postwar Europe's capital of espionage. Some eighty spy agencies and their various front organizations, disguised as everything from jam exporters to research institutes, worked the city. Spooks were so thick on the ground that a dozen or so of them might find themselves together in the same seedy *Kneipe*, each trying to ignore the presence of the

Markus Wolf, photographed in 1991

others. With spy-story writers and espionage buffs also sweeping down on the city, Cold War Berlin became indelibly associated in the popular imagination with cloak-and-dagger operations carried out in half-lit, half-ruined streets.

Befitting Berlin's importance to the Soviet Union, the biggest espionage player in town was the Soviet state security committee, the Komitet gosudarstvennoĭ bezopasnosti (KGB), which maintained over 800 operatives in 1953, and many more after the East German uprising. Its headquarters was a sprawling former hospital building within the Soviet complex at Karlshorst. From there orders went out to agents all over West Germany and Western Europe to steal sensitive secrets, recruit promising new talent, and, of course, to deal in the appropriate manner with fellow spies who had fallen from the correct path.

The Soviets had plenty of help from their East German clients. Because of language and cultural barriers, Russia's occupation authorities could not maintain surveillance within the GDR or effectively penetrate West Germany on their own. In 1950 Moscow authorized the establishment of a native secret police agency—the

Ministerium für Staatssicherheit, or Stasi—whose primary concerns were monitoring and molding the political climate in the GDR. Over the next forty years the Stasi would evolve into a truly Orwellian organization, weaseling its way into virtually every aspect of East German life. (Tellingly, the Stasi was larger per capita than the Nazi Gestapo, and also maintained a much larger army of informal snoops.) As of 1951, the Stasi had a foreign intelligence component, initially called the Institute for Economic Research, later renamed the Hauptverwaltung-Aufklärung (Main Administration for Intelligence, HVA). Its job was to run spies in the West and to counter enemy spy activity within the GDR.

The Stasi's most brilliant intelligence operative was Markus (Mischa) Wolf, the model for John Le Carré's redoubtable "Karla." As the son of Friedrich Wolf, a well-known Jewish-Communist intellectual, young Markus Wolf had fled with his family to Moscow in 1934. He lived there until 1941, learning Russian and managing to identify with his new home despite the purges that were carrying away many German exiles. When Germany invaded Russia he was evacuated to distant Kazakhstan, then to Bashkira, where in a Comintern school he was trained to promote the international proletarian revolution. After the German defeat he was sent back to his homeland to help Comrade Ulbricht bring the revolution to Berlin. Feeling more Russian than German, he could not understand why the Berliners let the Russian soldiers' orgy of rapine in the city sour their attitude toward the Soviet Union. Nonetheless, he was sophisticated enough to see that the Russians were often out of their depth in the German capital. As an editorial assistant at Berlin Radio, he struggled to convince the Soviet programmers that an exclusive diet of propaganda speeches was driving East German listeners into the arms of RIAS. He began displaying such a keen aptitude for political intrigue that he was made a counselor in East Germany's new embassy in Moscow. In 1951 he was brought back to Berlin to work in the Stasi's Institute for Economic Research, its spy agency. After a little more than one year, Wolf was asked to take over the agency's leadership from its founder, Anton Ackermann, whose advocacy of a separate "German road to Socialism" had alienated Ulbricht.

In the 1950s Wolf's agency smuggled hundreds of agents into West Germany, mainly through Berlin. When the East German refugee stream increased following the 1953 uprising, Wolf ensured that plenty of Stasi spies swam along with the current. Wolf also convinced many West Germans to spy for the Stasi. Some agreed to do so for ideological reasons, while others did it for sex. Though East Germany was a prudish state, the Stasi became expert in the use of the "honeypot"—the sticky-sweet snares set by attractive young women (and sometimes men), who used their sexual skills to coax secrets out of lonely westerners. Since prostitution was illegal in the GDR, an army of out-of-work whores was available as bait for the Stasi love-traps.

Wolf and his colleagues greatly admired the British secret service, which was the first of the Western intelligence agencies to establish regular operations in Berlin. Britain's MI6 set up shop in a building belonging to Hitler's Olympic complex, perhaps an appropriate choice, since some of its native agents were ex-Nazis, among them Klaus Barbie. The homegrown operatives, on the other hand, tended to be recruited via the old-boy network, not necessarily the best way to locate reliable talent. As is well known, some of England's top spooks—the so-called Cambridge spies—turned out to be double agents in the pay of Moscow. The Berlin branch of MI6 under Peter Lunn was relatively efficient, but it was also by no means mole-free.

In the late 1940s Washington's new intelligence organization, the Central Intelligence Agency (CIA), took over the Office of Strategic Services's Berlin Operations Base (BOB) and developed it into the agency's primary European operating post. Berlin was key to the CIA because in the presatellite era it offered the best vantage point in the world from which to snoop on the Soviet Union. As one CIA expert noted, "When the Soviet commandant in Bucharest or Warsaw called Moscow the call went through Berlin." Berlin also afforded American spies their closest proximity to the KGB, their mighty rival. Like missionaries in the bush, the two agencies competed for native souls while trying to convert each other. BOB's first major "turn" was Colonel Pyotr Popov, a Soviet military intelligence operative who betrayed the names of many of his colleagues working in the West. With its deep pockets, the CIA also funded a number of native front organizations whose job was to destabilize the GDR regime. The Kampfgruppe gegen Unmenschlichkeit (Fighting Association against Inhumanity), for example, dropped anti-Communist leaflets from balloons and falsified GDR documents such as postage stamps. Their version of the Ulbricht stamp featured a noose around the dictator's neck.

In 1950 the CIA secretly set up a West German intelligence service, the "Organization Gehlen," to it help it operate more effectively on local turf. The group was named after its chief, Reinhard Gehlen, who, as noted above, had headed the Wehrmacht's espionage operations against the Red Army. Gehlen's agency was based in Pullach near Munich, not in West Berlin, but like its patron it used the Spree city to smuggle agents into East Germany. Shortly after the outfit was launched the London *Daily Express* published a story entitled "Hitler's General

Spies Again—For Dollars"—a blow both to the group's security and its public image. Until 1956, when it was renamed the Bundesnachrichtendienst (BND) and transferred to West German control, it remained little more than an arm of the CIA.

From the outset, Bonn had its own intelligence service in the form of the abovementioned Office for Constitutional Protection, which carried on a bitter rivalry with the Organization Gehlen. The rivalry was fiercest at the top, for Otto John, the BfV's chief, had sided with the anti-Hitler resistance and worked with British intelligence during the war, while Gehlen had remained loyal to the Nazi regime up to the bitter end. After the war, moreover, John had aided the British prosecution at Nuremberg, which hardly endeared him to unreconstructed nationalists like Gehlen.

"Once a traitor, always a traitor," was Gehlen's response when Otto John made his shocking bolt to the East in 1954. The date on which John acted, July 20, 1954, was the tenth anniversary of the ill-starred bombing of Hitler's headquarters at Rastenburg. John had come to Berlin to participate in the annual commemoration of the event at Plötzensee Prison, where some of the conspirators had been executed. In the press conference that he held in East Berlin on the following day, John alluded to the resistance when he said that "Stauffenberg did not die for the Federal Republic." He went on to denounce Adenauer as a tool of the Americans, who, in their "need for war against the East... welcome those who have not learned anything from the catastrophe and are waiting for the moment when they can effect revenge for 1945."

Shifting quickly into damage-control mode, Bonn insisted that John had been kidnapped by the Soviets and forced to spout Red propaganda. This "provocation," they said, was part of a desperate effort to sabotage West Germany's legitimate efforts to bolster its defense by creating an army of its own, the Bundeswehr. John, however, went before the public to claim that his actions had all been voluntary. He then faded from the picture. The Stasi gave him a sinecure at Humboldt University and set him up in a pleasant apartment. They also surrounded him with around-the-clock bodyguards, lest the West try to snatch him back, or he try to go back on his own.

The Stasi's fears were well founded. On December 12, 1955, seventeen months after his bolt to the East, John slipped out of a meeting at the university and, in the company of a Danish journalist, bolted back into West Berlin. Once there he insisted that he had *not* gone freely to the East but had been drugged and kidnapped by his friend, society gynecologist and jazz trumpeter Wolfgang ("Wo Wo") Wolgemuth, who had turned out to be a Soviet agent. He further claimed to have made his press conference comments under duress and in the hope of deceiving his Soviet captors. He had always intended to escape back to the West, he insisted, and had done so as soon as he could. The West German government, having initially blamed the Soviets for John's action, now refused to buy his story. He was tried for conspiracy, convicted, and sentenced to a four-year prison term, of which he served eighteen months. After his release he continued to profess his innocence and to demand rehabilitation, unsuccessfully. He died in 1997.

Was John telling the truth? Even though Soviet archival material on the John case has now become available, much remains murky in a drama that three expert commentators labeled in 1997 "the longest-running mystery play of the Cold War in Germany." For what his testimony is worth, Mischa Wolf is inclined to believe that John never intended to defect. He credits John's contention that his friend Wo Wo, who indeed was a Soviet spy, slipped him a drug in order to get him to East Berlin. But Wolf also believes that Wolgemuth was acting on his own initiative, not under orders from Moscow. Of course, once they had a man like John in their clutches the Soviets extracted maximum propaganda value from his "defection" and coaxed all the information from him that they could, which apparently was not much. They then, in Wolf's words, "dumped the damaged goods on us," allowing the Stasi to take care of John as it saw fit. Whatever the final truth in this bizarre affair, the Otto John story, reeking as it does of deception, betrayal, and political manipulation, is the perfect Cold War espionage tale. All it lacks is technological gadgetry.

There was plenty of gadgetry in the other major Berlin spy story of the 1950s—the saga of "Operation Gold," an ambitious project to eavesdrop on Soviet communications by means of a tunnel bored under the Russian sector. More than the John affair, the now famous Berlin Tunnel operation put the former Nazi capital on the map as espionage-central in the early Cold War era.

The Berlin Tunnel was modeled on an earlier British operation in Vienna code-named "Silver," which had yielded a load of informational ore concerning the Soviet occupation forces in the Austrian capital. Berlin was an even more attractive target than Vienna because, as a CIA man averred, "everything came to Berlin." The Soviets, it seems, had an underground cable running between Karlshorst and their base in Wünsdorf, south of Berlin, which carried extremely sensitive data. In January 1954 CIA chief Allen Dulles gave authorization to build a tunnel between the American and Soviet sectors in Berlin that would allow Western electronic eavesdroppers to tap into the Soviet line and pick up their communications. BOB selected a promising site for the tunnel in the southeastern corner of the American sector, a stone's throw from the Schönfelder Chausee in East Berlin, under which the cable ran. From the outset the operation was conducted jointly with the British, who, given their previous tunneling experience, were thought to be valuable partners.

Digging began in September 1954. To camouflage operations at the tunnel mouth, and to provide space for all the necessary equipment, a warehouse disguised as a radar installation was constructed. As the tunneling progressed, dirt and debris were brought up to the warehouse and packed in cartons prominently labeled "radar equipment." Despite having to pump out ground water as they dug, U.S. Army engineers made good time, finishing the tunnel by the end of February 1955. A month later British electronics experts completed a "tap room" filled with the latest eavesdropping equipment. Anglo-American experts immediately began listening in to everything the Russians passed down their cable. It appeared to be the greatest espionage triumph since the "Ultra" decoding of Nazi naval signals in World War II.

There was only one problem: the Soviets knew all about it. A KGB "mole" in MI6, George Blake, had informed his Russian controllers about the enterprise as soon as it began. This of course enabled the Soviets to precensor the conversations they passed along the tapped cable. Had they wanted to, they could have fed the eavesdroppers nothing but misinformation, but this might have aroused suspicion and compromised Blake. Therefore the Russians tossed the Anglo-Americans a few pieces of useful data from time to time. After about a year, however, they decided to put an end to this unique party line. The trick was to uncover the operation "accidentally," so as not to endanger their mole. A series of heavy rainstorms in spring 1956, which caused some electrical shorts, gave them the pretext they needed to dig up the cable and "discover" the tunnel.

Markus Wolf was with the Soviet team that broke into the tunnel on April 22, 1956. He was amazed by the sophisticated equipment in the "tap" room, which was more advanced than anything the KGB or the Stasi had. Contrary to some contemporary reports, the Soviets did not actually catch any Western technicians red-eared. The eavesdroppers had gotten just enough advance warning of the break-in to scurry out of the tunnel (and, as a little joke, to put up a hand-lettered sign at their end, saying, "You are now entering the American sector"). Wolf found the sign amusing but he was not amused by the fact that the Soviets had told the Stasi nothing about the tunnel operation until the moment they decided to uncover it. As he complained in his memoirs, the Russians had "protected their own conversations, [but] they never told us anything, leaving us unguarded and exposed."

Moscow expected to score a propaganda coup by exposing the Berlin Tunnel, but it did not turn out that way. Rather than writing about how devious the Anglo-

Americans were, most reporters invited to inspect the tunnel praised the West's resourcefulness and ingenuity. The Soviets therefore decided that the less said about this matter, the better. On the other hand, they could hardly put the tunnel out of their minds, for it pointed up their own vulnerability in Berlin. West Berlin might be an isolated Western outpost, but its very existence deep inside the Soviet imperium made it a threat to Russian security—not to mention a pressing challenge to the very integrity of Moscow's East German client.

The Most Dangerous Place in the World

In the late 1950s the Soviets decided to try once again to force the West out of Berlin. On November 10, 1958, Khrushchev told a Soviet-Polish Friendship Rally in Moscow that the "time has clearly come for the Powers which signed the Potsdam Agreement to renounce the remnants of the regime of occupation in Berlin and thus make it possible to create a normal situation in the capital of the GDR." A "normal situation" in Soviet eyes meant control over the entire city by the "sovereign state" of the GDR. Two weeks later, Khrushchev sent notes to Washington, London, and Paris proposing that the "natural solution" in Berlin would be to reunite the city and make it "part of the State on whose land it is situated." But since the Western powers were unlikely to embrace this plan, Khrushchev said he would be willing to discuss turning West Berlin into a "free city" under United Nations protection. If the West was unprepared to accept even this alternative, Moscow would have no choice but to sign a separate peace treaty with East Germany, thereby eliminating the legal justification for the continued Allied occupation of Berlin. The West was given six months to deal satisfactorily with the Soviets, or face being forced out of Berlin by East Germany. Moscow's note also warned against any "reckless threats of force" by the Western powers: "Only madmen can go to the length of unleashing another World War over the preservation of privileges of occupiers in West Berlin."

The Western powers, including the United States, had little inclination to fight over Berlin. No doubt it was a great place from which to spy on the East, but it was not, in the eyes of the Pentagon, of supreme strategic importance to the U.S. defense posture. Nor did the Pentagon have any illusions about being able to defend West Berlin if the Soviets decided to rub it out. On the other hand, the city had taken on great meaning as a political symbol, as a living monument to the West's determination not to give up any more ground to the Communists. Moreover, Washington was under heavy pressure from Bonn to hold the door open in Berlin so that the West Germans would not be shut out of the former German capital. As President Eisenhower grudgingly admitted, Berlin constituted another "instance in which our political posture requires us to assume military postures that are wholly illogical." He might have added the word "ironical," for it would certainly have been perversely ironic if Washington had gone to war against a former ally to "save" a city that, just a few years before, both contenders had been trying to destroy.

Yet it was beginning to look as if Berlin might indeed be the cause of a new war. In his misguided assumption that Washington would abandon Berlin if Russia stepped up the pressure, Khrushchev harangued Ambassador W. Averell Harriman in June 1959:

> We are determined to liquidate your rights in West Berlin. What good does it do for you to have eleven thousand troops in Berlin? If it came to war, we would swallow them in one gulp. . . . You can start a war if you like, but remember, it will be you who are starting it, not we. . . . West Germany knows that we could destroy it in ten minutes. . . . If you start a war, we may die but the rockets will fly automatically.

As a way of removing Germany and Berlin as potential Cold War flash points, Khrushchev proposed to Harriman the withdrawal of all foreign troops from German soil and the reunification of that country as a demilitarized, neutral state. To illustrate his point, the Soviet leader, who was famous for his earthy humor, passed along a "current joke in Russia," which said "that if you look at Adenauer naked from behind, he shows Germany divided, but if you look at him from the front, he demonstrates that Germany cannot stand."

Harriman relayed this cheerful conversation to Eisenhower, who, for all his doubts about Berlin's strategic worth, was not about to back down there. As if to convince himself that Berlin really *was* worth a fight, he envisaged it as the top of a slippery political slope down which the West would surely slide if it abandoned that city, even at the threat of nuclear war. "I'd rather be atomized than communized," he said. The Pentagon, meanwhile, readied a plan of action in case the Russians followed through on their threat to allow the East Germans to curtail Western access in and out of West Berlin. First, America would send a platoon-sized armed convoy across the GDR to Berlin (shades of Clay's plan in 1948); if the East Germans (or Soviets) fired upon this outfit, a division-sized convoy would follow. Should even this force run into trouble, an all-out attack would result in which, as Secretary of State John Foster Dulles told Adenauer, "we obviously would not forego the use of nuclear weapons."

In fact, Pentagon strategy at this juncture called for the U.S. to use its nukes *first*, to get in its best licks before the Russian rockets flew. The plan also envisaged extensive use of tactical atomic weapons against enemy targets in Germany. This would undoubtedly cause some "collateral damage." Dulles admitted to the German chancellor that NATO estimates (based on earlier war games) projected 1.7 million Germans killed and another 3.5 million incapacitated. This grim scenario reduced considerably the chancellor's enthusiasm for a fight to save Berlin, a city which he had never liked anyway. "*For God's sake, not for Berlin!*" he cried.

Officially, the Western powers countered Khrushchev's ultimatum by demanding the retention of the status quo in Berlin for the time being, though they consented to a four-power meeting of the foreign ministers at which the Berlin situation and other German problems would be open to discussion. At this meeting, which was held in Geneva in the summer of 1959, the Soviets repeated their demands for a Western withdrawal from Berlin, while the Western foreign ministers argued that four-power control over Berlin must remain intact until the city became the capital of a reunited Germany. Christian Herter, who had become the new U.S. secretary of state following Dulles's death earlier that year, pointed out that the West Berliners *wanted* the Western troops to stay, which was certainly true. The Berliners' greatest fear, repeatedly articulated by West Berlin mayor Willy Brandt, was that the Western powers might be bullied into believing that they had to trade their stake in Berlin for world peace.

Brandt and the Berliners had reason to be concerned about the steadfastness of British prime minister Harold Macmillan, who warned President Eisenhower that it would "not be easy to persuade the British people that it was their duty to go to war in the defense of West Berlin," and to help a people "who have tried to destroy us twice in this century." Eisenhower privately worried that the same might be true of the Americans. Still hoping for a peaceful way out of the Berlin imbroglio, he invited Khrushchev to visit him at the presidential retreat in Camp David for one-on-one discussions. Such an informal arrangement, he believed, might be more productive than the full-blown summit meeting that Macmillan was lobbying for.

Proud to be the first Soviet leader to be received on U.S. soil by an American president, Khrushchev arrived at what he called the "presidential dacha" in September 1959. The talks were convivial enough, but the only changes in existing positions involved Khrushchev's dropping of the six-month time frame for a Berlin solution and

Eisenhower's concession that the existing Berlin situation was "abnormal." With no substantial progress either at Camp David or Geneva, Eisenhower reluctantly agreed to a four-power summit meeting in Paris in the coming spring on the German problem.

As it turned out, any possible movement at the Paris Summit was scuttled in advance by a momentous event high in the skies over the Soviet Union: the Russians' downing of an American U-2 spy plane on May 1, 1960. Eisenhower had been extremely reluctant to sanction such flights in view of the impending summit, but the CIA convinced him that one last reconnaissance was necessary to check on Soviet intercontinental ballistic missile (ICBM) bases. The Russians were incapable of knocking down a U-2, the CIA promised, and for that very reason unlikely to complain publicly about the flights. As it happened, however, the Soviets succeeded not only in bringing down the plane but in capturing the pilot, Francis Gary Powers, who had disobeyed orders to blow up his aircraft and to kill himself if he ran into trouble. Failing to extract a public apology from Eisenhower for violating Soviet airspace, Khrushchev used the U-2 incident to wreck the Paris Summit, from which in any case he had not expected to extract any substantial gains with respect to Berlin.

Khrushchev had greater hopes on this score following the election of John F. Kennedy to the American presidency. Kennedy was known to be skittish on the Berlin question, which he had barely touched on during his campaign against Vice President Richard Nixon. As the new president himself admitted shortly after being elected, of all his foreign policy problems Berlin had the greatest potential of forcing a choice between "holocaust and humiliation." Khrushchev knew that fear of Russian retaliation against Berlin had been a primary motive for Kennedy's failure to save the Bay of Pigs invasion, his first major humiliation in office. JFK's cut-and-run approach in that instance convinced the Soviet premier that the American leader would also fold if pushed in Berlin, which he gleefully called "the testicles of the West," the place on which he had only to "squeeze" a little when he wanted his adversaries "to scream."

Khrushchev got his chance to squeeze Kennedy on Berlin during their first face-to-face confrontation at the Vienna Summit in June 1961. The meeting had hardly gotten underway when the Soviet premier began to complain about Washington's "impossible" position on Berlin and Germany. But instead of "solving" the problem through the creation of a neutral, reunited Germany, the Soviet leader now called on the West to acknowledge Germany's permanent division by pulling out of Berlin. By staying in West Berlin, remilitarizing West Germany, and feeding Bonn's dreams of reunification, he said, America was creating the preconditions for a new world war. As an interim solution, Khrushchev repeated Moscow's offer to make West Berlin into a "free city" with guaranteed access to the wider world, but without any contractual ties to the West. Glaring at Kennedy, he said that he wanted to reach an agreement "with *you*," but if he could not, he would sign a peace treaty with the GDR. Then "all commitments stemming from Germany's surrender will become invalid. This would include all institutions, occupation rights, and access to Berlin, including the corridors."

Before coming to Vienna, Kennedy had been advised by Allan Lightner, the U.S. minister in West Berlin, to "tell Khrushchev in blunt language" that the "Soviets should keep their hands off Berlin." This, in effect, is what he proceeded to do. While thanking the chairman for being so "frank," he reminded him that "the discussion here is not only about the legal situation but also about the practical facts, which affect very much our national security. . . . This matter is of the greatest concern to the U.S. We are in Berlin not because of someone's sufferance. We fought our way here, although our causalities may not have been as high as the U.S.S.R.'s. We are in Berlin not by agreement by East Germans, but by our contractual rights."

Having expected at least *some* give from the young American president, Khrushchev became increasingly angry, lecturing him like a schoolchild on the stakes at play in Berlin. The former Nazi capital, he said, was "the most dangerous spot in the world." Upping his ante in metaphors, he fumed that his government was determined "to perform an operation on this sore spot, to eliminate this thorn, this ulcer." By signing a peace treaty with East Germany Moscow would "impede the revanchists in West Germany who want a new war." Slamming his hand on the table, he shouted: "*I want peace. But if you want war, that is your problem.*"

Despite a regimen of amphetamines prescribed by a quack doctor for his Addison's disease, Kennedy remained calm under the barrage. "*It is you, and not I, who wants to force a change,*" he replied. America would not abandon Berlin. If as a result Moscow followed through on its threats and signed a peace treaty with East Germany in December, it would be "a cold winter," he said grimly.

Kennedy's calm at Vienna was deceptive. After the meeting he admitted that Khrushchev "just beat hell out of me." More importantly, he unburdened himself in private regarding his actual feelings about Berlin, which were much more ambivalent than he had made out in Vienna. "We're stuck in a ridiculous position," he confided to his aide, Kenneth O'Donnell. "It seems silly for us to be facing an atomic war over a treaty preserving Berlin as the future capital of a reunited Germany when all of us know that Germany will probably never be reunited." Contradicting an earlier assertion that the freedom of Western Europe hinged on the defense of West Berlin, he added:

> God knows I'm not an isolationist, but it seems particularly stupid to risk killing a million Americans over an argument about access rights on an *Autobahn*. . . or because the Germans want Germany reunified. If I'm going to threaten Russia with a nuclear war, it will have to be for much bigger reasons than that. Before I back Khrushchev against the wall and put him to a final test, the freedom of all Western Europe will have to be at stake.

Thinking about the issue from the Communists' point of view, Kennedy could even sympathize with their desire to shut down West Berlin: after all, the place was draining East Germany of vital manpower. "You can't blame Khrushchev for being sore about that," he allowed. But you *could* blame the West Germans and West Berliners for insisting that America do their dirty work for them while they focused on getting rich. Bonn wanted the United States "to drive the Russians out of East Germany. It's not enough for us to be spending a tremendous amount of money on the military defense of Western Europe . . . while West Germany becomes the fastest-growing industrial power in the world. Well, if they think we are rushing into a war over Berlin, except as a last desperate move to save the NATO alliance, they've got another think coming."

As it turned out, Kennedy's private tirade proved to be more predictive of U.S. policy on Berlin than his public stance. He too was hoping for a "change" in the Berlin situation that would eliminate it as a dangerous bone of contention in the Cold War without necessitating a huge sacrifice of Western prestige.

By the spring of 1961, it was clear that some kind of solution would have to be found soon. In 1959 the number of East Germans fleeing to the West through Berlin had dropped somewhat, but since early 1960 the exodus had turned into a veritable flood, increasing from month to month. Factories in the East were curtailing production for want of workers; some shops had closed because their clerks had gone west. The Soviet threat to sign a peace treaty with the East only increased the flight, since people reasoned that they had better get out while they still could. Berlin, to return to Khrushchev's pithy metaphor, might indeed have been the tender testicles of the West, but it was also the loose sphincter of the East.

The People's Army soldier Conrad Schumann leaping to freedom, August 15, 1961

THE DIVIDED CITY

Something there is that doesn't love a wall.
—Robert Frost, "Mending Wall"

DURING THE YEARS when Berlin was divided by its internal barrier, air travelers approaching the city had to strain to see the famous Wall. As Peter Schneider observes in his novel, *Der Mauerspringer* (The Wall Jumper, 1982): "Seen from the air, the city appears perfectly homogenous. Nothing suggests to the stranger that he is nearing a region where two political constructs collide." Once on the ground, however, the differences became very perceptible indeed. East and West Berlin looked different, smelled different, and above all *felt* different. The two halves of Berlin had been growing apart since 1945, but the Wall ensured that the dual cities were more distant from each other than if they had been separated by a continent. Saved by its sealed border from continuing to lose its best people to the West, East Berlin solidified its position as capital of the GDR and show window of East German communism. West Berlin, now cut off more thoroughly from West Germany and the Atlantic world, became a somewhat marginal player in the political and economic framework of the Federal Republic.

Despite their differing fates in the post-Wall world, there were surprising parallels between the two Berlins. Both were lavishly subsidized by their national governments, which were anxious to hold them up as symbols of the superiority of their respective systems. Both thought they had reasons for self-satisfaction: East Berlin touted itself as the most prosperous city in the Eastern bloc; West Berlin saw itself as the only "real city" in the Federal Republic. At the same time, both suffered crises of identity: East Berlin because it had difficulty gaining recognition or respect from the West; West Berlin because its primary function was simply to survive and show the flag. Both claimed to be full of cultural vitality, but in reality the artistic achievements were spotty, illustrating the dilemma of building a first-rate culture through subsidies and government incentives. Dissident elements in both cities claimed to perpetuate Old Berlin's vaunted tradition of opposition to established authority, but in each case the claim was somewhat spurious: in East Berlin antiregime forces remained largely quiescent until the last months of the GDR's existence, while in West Berlin political protest degenerated into sterile and self-indulgent terrorism.

Operation Chinese Wall

On August 11, 1961, the rubber-stamp parliament of the GDR announced, somewhat cryptically:

> The People's Assembly confirms the impending measures to protect the security of the GDR and to curtail the campaign of organized *Kopfjägerei* [head-hunting] and *Menschenhandel* [traffic in human lives] orchestrated from West Germany and West Berlin. The Assembly empowers the GDR Council of Ministers to undertake all the steps approved by the member states of the Warsaw Pact. The Assembly appeals to all peace-loving citizens of the GDR to give their full support to the agencies of their Workers-and-Peasants State in the application of these measures.

Upon learning of this announcement on the following day, West Berlin's mayor, Willy Brandt, spoke of "Ulbricht's Enabling Law," a reference to the blank check for dictatorial measures given to Hitler by the Reichstag in March 1933. Brandt predicted that the ominous pronouncement would dramatically increase the number of

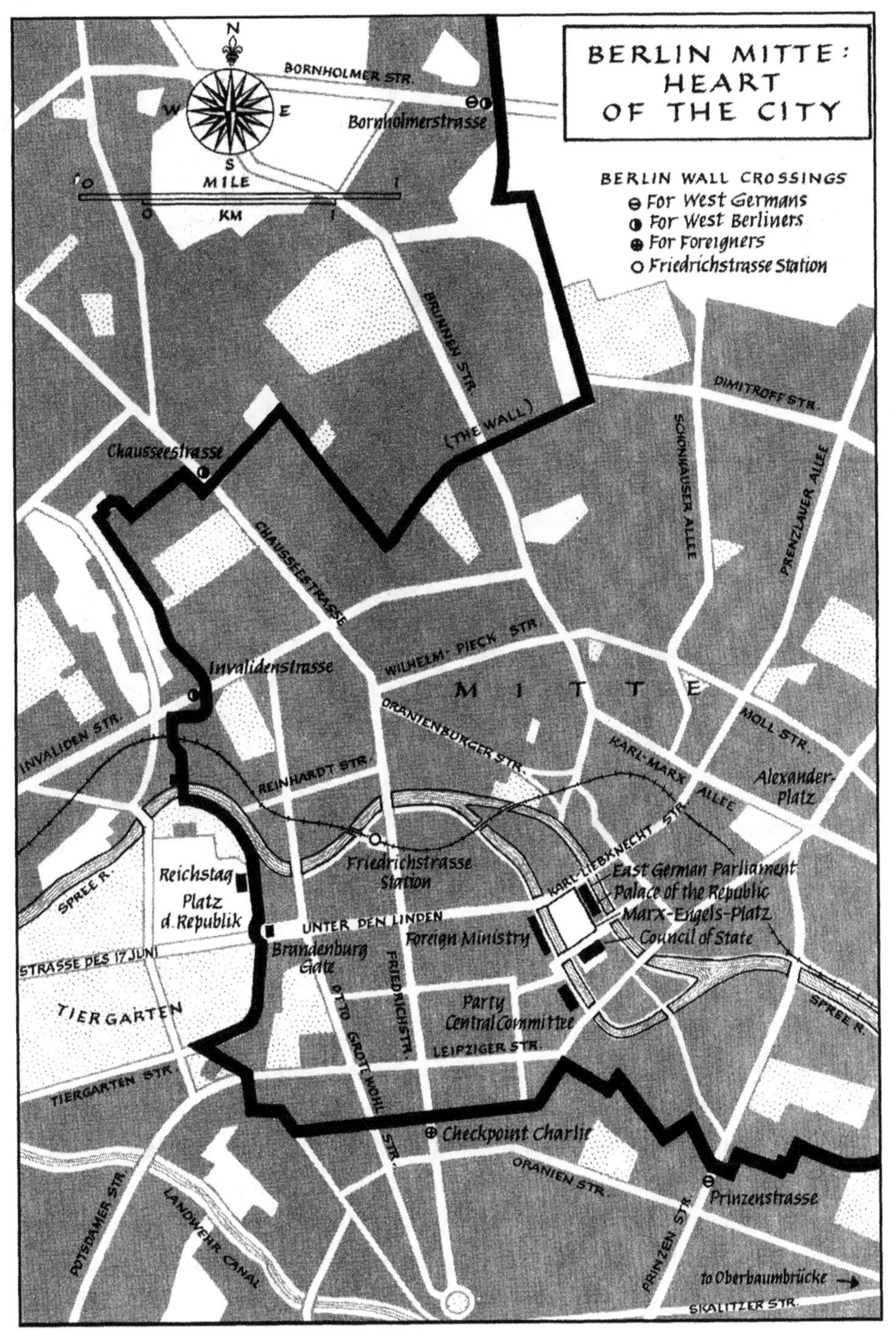

The Berlin Wall

A woman climbs out of her apartment at Bernauer Strasse to freedom in West Berlin

East German citizens fleeing to the West through Berlin. "They will come out of fear that the walls of the Iron Curtain will be cemented shut," he said.

In issuing this dire prediction, Brandt had no idea that it would come to pass so quickly. In the early morning hours of August 13, 1961, a Sunday, East German troops and SED labor gangs began drilling holes and pounding fence posts in the streets along the border between the Soviet and Western sectors of Berlin. Then they strung coils of barbed wire between the fence posts. At the Brandenburg Gate armored cars took up positions between the columns while soldiers installed machine guns around the monument. All the streets running between the eastern and western sectors were blocked off, as were the *U-Bahn* and *S-Bahn* stations in the east. Some parts of the border were difficult to close off. Such was the case at Bernauer Strasse, where the pavement and sidewalks were in the western district of Wedding but the apartment houses on the southern side of the street stood in the district of Mitte in the Soviet sector. Here the houses themselves were made part of the barrier by closing off their entrances and boarding up the windows (at first, only the lower-story ones). The work progressed at a frantic pace, and by Monday morning, as Berliners set out to work, the first phase in what was to become the most infamous edifice of the Cold War was already completed.

Authorization to erect a fortified border in Berlin had officially been given to Ulbricht by Khrushchev at a Warsaw Pact meeting on August 5, 1961. Ulbricht had been pleading for months for permission to build a "Chinese Wall" in Berlin—an analogy he liked because it suggested a defense against intruders rather than a barrier to departure. As recently as March 29, 1961, the Warsaw Pact had voted to deny Ulbricht his wall on the grounds that it might provoke a war. The SED leader nonetheless went ahead with secret preparations to construct a barrier, which he entrusted to one of his favorite satraps, Erich Honecker. At a press conference on June 5 Ulbricht almost let the cat out of the bag by blurting out: "No one intends to build a wall."

Permission to translate Ulbricht's intentions into reality came in the wake of various signals from the Western Allies that they would not go to war to prevent East Germany from sealing its border in Berlin. In a speech on July 25 President Kennedy promised that the United States would do all in its power to protect its position in West Berlin, but he pointedly said nothing about guaranteeing free access between East and West Berlin. In private, as we know, he had expressed sympathy for Khrushchev's predicament in Berlin, musing that a border-closure might be a reasonable solution. Senator J. William Fulbright, chairman of the Senate Armed Services Committee, declared in a speech on July 30: "I don't understand why the East Germans don't close their borders, which I believe they have every right to do." Even with what they took to be a green light from the West, however, the Warsaw Pact leaders were cautious when they gave Ulbricht his go-ahead on August 5: they merely authorized a wire fence, which might become a wall only if the West made no move to knock it down. As an expression of gratitude to Khrushchev for orchestrating this decision, Ulbricht ordered that Stalin's name be removed from

Erich Honecker (middle) with Willi Stoph (left), 1984

East Berlin's showcase-of-socialism boulevard, the Stalinallee, which now became Karl-Marx-Allee. A bronze statue of Stalin that had previously stood on the avenue was broken up and carted away.

Despite many rumors that East Germany and the USSR might undertake drastic measures to stop the flow of refugees fleeing through Berlin, Berliners reacted with stunned disbelief to the events of August 13. Most expected the Western powers to eliminate the offending obstacle immediately, with tanks if necessary. In the meantime, because telephone service between East and West had been suspended, people streamed in their thousands to the border in hopes of catching sight of friends and relatives from whom they had been abruptly cut off. Over the din of post-hole digging they yelled greetings and brave words of encouragement. Tearful lovers waved handkerchiefs and blew kisses across the wire. But it wasn't just greetings and longing looks that were exchanged; some shouted insults and threw stones at the fence-builders.

Willy Brandt was on a campaign trip in West Germany, running as the SPD's candidate for the chancellorship in the upcoming Bundestag elections, when he got the news of what was happening in Berlin. He immediately flew to Tempelhof and rushed to the Potsdamer Platz. As he examined the emerging barrier, one of his aides, Heinrich Albertz, commented: "They are cutting up a city, cutting into living flesh without anesthesia." Although Brandt felt the incision as if it were on his own body, his first concern was to calm the West Berliners. The mayor worried that any attacks on the fence from the western side would give the Soviets a pretext for marching into West Berlin.

Brandt's opponent in the impending elections, Chancellor Adenauer, was considerably less distraught over the events in Berlin. In his view, damming the incoming flood of East Germans, whom he saw as a horde of probable SPD supporters, was hardly a cause for deep distress. As a gesture of solidarity with the city, his aides urged him to fly immediately to Berlin, but having never felt any love for that "pagan" place, Adenauer demurred. After trying to ascertain from the Western powers how they intended to respond, he issued a formal statement containing an appeal for calm: "The need of the moment is to meet this challenge from the East with firmness, but also with deliberation. Nothing should be undertaken that would complicate the situation without improving it."

Adenauer need not have worried that the Western Allies would adopt any precipitous or provocative measures. The leaders of Britain, France, and America saw no reason for alarm in the Soviet/East German action, so long as Western rights in Berlin were not challenged. British prime minister Harold Macmillan, who was hunting in the north of England when the fence went up, refused to hurry back to London to deal with the situation. Charles de Gaulle, weekending at his country house at Colombey-les-deux-Eglises, likewise elected not to return to his capital; the Berlin problem, he felt, could be addressed in the following week. President Kennedy, sailing off Hyannis Port, was not even notified of the events in Berlin until seventeen hours after the action had commenced. "How come we didn't know anything about this?" he asked. (In fact, American intelligence operatives *did* know that something was in the works, but they did not know precisely what would be done, or when.) Upon being assured by Secretary of State Dean Rusk that the Soviets and East Germans were not doing anything to obstruct Allied access to West Berlin, Kennedy approved a statement saying that the "violations of existing agreements will be the subject of vigorous protest through appropriate channels." In the meantime, he instructed Rusk to go as planned to a Yankees-Senators baseball game that afternoon. Later, he explained his sangfroid to his aides: "Why would Khrushchev put up a wall if he really intended to seize West Berlin? There shouldn't be any need of a wall if he occupied the whole city. This is his way out of his predicament. It's not a nice solution, but a wall is a hell of a lot better than a war." As for the some 17 million East Germans who now remained stuck behind that wall, tough luck for them. They had had, Kennedy noted, fifteen years "to get out of their jail."

The West's placid response to the events of August 13 convinced Ulbricht and Honecker that they could begin transforming their wire fence into a concrete wall. On August 15, at the Ackerstrasse, cranes lowered a line of prefabricated concrete blocks into place, five meters to the east of the sector border. These were the first of thousands of blocks that would make up the initial Berlin Wall, which stood about six feet high in most places and ran in a zigzag fashion for twenty-seven miles between the two halves of the city. Another seventy miles of wall separated West Berlin from GDR territory to the north, west, and south.

Ambitious though it was, this structure was a backyard fence compared to the final Berlin Wall that evolved in the 1970s and 1980s—a white concrete monolith some thirteen feet high and capped with a rounded top to thwart the use of grappling hooks. Along much of its eastern side ran a broad "death strip" of raked ground enclosed by a smaller wall or electrified wire fence; anyone caught in this no-man's-land was likely to be fired at by guards posted in watchtowers spaced at regular intervals along the border. At night, spotlights moved across the landscape, lending it a surreal touch. People commonly observed that there was something incongruously "medieval" about the Berlin Wall, but there was nothing medieval about its technology.

As West Berliners watched Ulbricht's barbed wire fence mutate into a concrete wall, they began to get unruly, combining their curses against the East with jeers aimed at the do-nothing West. At a rally outside the Schöneberg Rathaus people hoisted signs saying "Betrayed by the West" and "Where Are the Protective Powers?" Berlin schoolchildren sent Kennedy a black umbrella, reminiscent of the one Neville Chamberlain had carried when he sold out the Czechs at the Munich Conference in 1938. More dangerously, a group of West Germans attacked the Soviet War Memorial that lay in the British sector just to the west of the Brandenburg Gate; the small contingent of Russian guards at the site might have been killed had not British troops intervened and dispersed the attackers.

Willy Brandt did not approve of attacks against Soviets in West Berlin, but he too was livid over the tepid Western response. Originally he had harbored a high regard for Kennedy, with whom he shared a ribald sense of humor and a predatory attitude toward beautiful women, but he now wondered if his admiration was not misplaced. His deep disappointment with Germany's Western Allies in this time of testing shaped the rest of his political career, starting him on a search for accommodation with the East that would culminate in his *Ostpolitik* of the 1970s. For the moment, however, he could not afford to alienate his Western partners, especially the Americans. Hence he dashed off a private letter to Kennedy, warning that West Berliners might flee the city in droves unless the Allies made some significant gesture of support. He recommended reinforcing the Allied garrisons in the city.

While Kennedy was trying to decide how to respond to Brandt, many Berliners were in fact electing to flee, though still from East to West. In its earliest manifestation the Berlin Wall was fairly porous. At the row of houses on Bernauer Strasse people climbed to the upper floors and jumped through windows to the street below. The lucky ones landed on bedsheets held by members of the West Berlin fire department. One who was not so lucky, a young man named Rudolf Urban, became the first fatality of the Berlin Wall when he hit the pavement and broke his neck. Good swimmers braved the treacherous currents of the Spree before the river was effectively sealed off. Still others crawled through drainpipes. Many of the initial escapees were members of the police and military squads guarding the border. A famous picture taken on August 15 shows an East German soldier named Conrad Schumann leaping westward over a coil of wire, gun and all. Between August 13 and the end of the month some 25,605 people made it through the barrier, largely by picking places where there were still gaps.

In response to the wave of escapes, soldiers were given orders to shoot at refugees. Because the original border guards, most of whom hailed from East Berlin, were almost as likely to join the refugees as to shoot at them, replacement guards were brought in from other parts of the country. Many came from a corner of Saxony where Western television signals did not reach; these men were thought to be especially "reliable." On August 24, 1961, twenty-four-year-old Gunter Litfin was shot and killed while trying to swim the across the Humboldthafen on the Spree. His was the first recorded death by shooting at the Wall. Before the barrier fell in 1989 at least eighty more would-be escapees were killed in this fashion, including a young man named Peter Fechter, who on August 17, 1962, was shot while trying to scale the Wall near Checkpoint Charlie. He fell back injured on the eastern side, but rather than rescue him, GDR border police let him slowly bleed to death. This grisly scenario was observed by a group of West Berliners, who pleaded with an American officer on the scene to help the dying man. The Western military forces, however, were under strict orders not to assist escape attempts, and the officer did nothing. As Willy Brandt later noted: "This incident hit the Berliners hard and exacerbated their sense of outrage. Many voiced their disillusionment at the Americans' inability to help a young man who was bleeding to death."

As the Berlin Wall (called by the GDR regime the "Antifascist Protective Barrier") became increasingly difficult to pierce, the escape attempts dropped off in number while becoming more inventive in method. Over the twenty-nine years of the Wall's existence, folks burrowed under it, ballooned over it, slipped through it in hidden compartments in cars, smashed through it in trucks, dove under it in scuba gear, bamboozled their way through it disguised as Soviet officers, and passed through it enclosed in coffins. The most ambitious escape method was tunneling: in all there were twenty-eight different tunnels bored under the Berlin Wall, eighteen of them failures. A total of ninety-seven refugees escaped in this fashion; three were killed and three wounded. In April 1964 a West German pharmacy student named Wolfgang Fuchs (known as "Tunnel-Fuchs"), along with some colleagues from the Free University, began digging a 150-meter long tunnel from Bernauer Strasse in the West to an abandoned house in Strelitzer Strasse in the East. When the work was completed in October 1964, twenty-three men, thirty-one women, and three children fled through it to the West. The oldest escapee was seventy, the youngest three. "Hell isn't really filled with wild animals," observed the three year old upon emerging. More refugees might have escaped through this tunnel had not East German border guards found the opening after three days and closed it off. By the time the Wall finally came down, the West Berlin police had recorded 5,043 successful escapes and about as many known failures. If, as the poet Robert Frost wrote, neither man nor nature loves a wall, no wall in history has been less loved than the one that divided Berlin.

On August 19, the day of the first fatality at the Berlin Wall, Vice President Lyndon Johnson and General Lucius Clay, hero of the Berlin Airlift, arrived in West Berlin with orders from Kennedy to do their best to restore the morale of the West Berliners. On their way to Berlin they had stopped in Bonn as a courtesy to Chancellor Adenauer. At the airport Adenauer pointed out to Johnson an old woman carrying a sign saying "Deeds, Not Words!" With *her*, said *der Alte*, he'd just as soon have neither. Johnson had not been enthusiastic about his Berlin assignment, fearing it might be dangerous, but when he arrived in the city to tumultuous applause he quickly forgot his fears and plunged into the crowds, pressing flesh, kissing babies, and passing out ballpoint pens as if he were on a campaign swing through Texas. His ecstatic welcome, of course, was a sign of the Berliners' desperate need for reassurance in this perilous moment.

That evening Johnson delivered a speech to a huge crowd assembled in front of the Schöneberg Rathaus. Paraphrasing a line from the Declaration of Independence, he intoned: "To the survival and to the creative future of this city we Americans have pledged, in effect, what our ancestors pledged in forming the United States—'our lives, our fortunes, and our sacred honor.' The President wants you to know and I want you to know that the pledge he has given to the freedom of West Berlin and to the rights of Western access to Berlin is firm. . . . This island does not stand alone." These words were greeted with wild applause, though few West Berliners could have been very happy about the prospect of living on an "island" whose borders consisted not of sandy beaches but of an ugly wall. Their unsettling situation was best summed up by the Hungarian composer, György Ligeti, who defined West Berlin as "a surrealist cage: those inside are free."

In addition to delivering his speech, Johnson, along with Brandt, personally welcomed a 1,500-man combat unit that Kennedy had dispatched from West Germany as another gesture of Allied support for Berlin. The convoy had passed through East Germany without incident, which is fortunate, since the commander had not been told how to respond in the event of trouble. Johnson also paid visits to the American garrison and to the Marienfelde Reception Center. He had intended to visit the Wall but never made it. Instead, he did some last-minute shopping, which was difficult since all the stores were closed. Wanting some shoes just like the ones Brandt was wearing, he insisted that the mayor contact the store owner and have the desired items delivered to his hotel suite.

When Johnson flew back to Washington, General Clay stayed behind as Kennedy's personal representative in the city. His presence was meant to demonstrate America's resolve to protect West Berlin. Actually, his presence turned out to be almost *too* demonstrative. Clay was determined to show that the U.S. could still exercise its rights in Berlin despite the new wall. In late October 1961, when the East Germans demanded that American officials show their passports in order to enter East Berlin, Clay sent armed jeeps through Checkpoint Charlie with orders to display nothing but their firepower. On the evening of October 24, U.S. mission chief Allan Lightner was denied entry into East Berlin for not showing his passport.

Clay dispatched troops to escort Lightner across the border. "If the Vopos had started shooting," Lightner later wrote, "we would have had to kill all of them. . . . All hell would have broken loose."

The next day all hell almost *did* break loose. When another group of Americans was stopped at Checkpoint Charlie, Clay came to the rescue with a phalanx of ten M-48 tanks. As might have been predicted, the Soviets responded in kind. Soon the M-48s stood muzzle to muzzle with Russian tanks, the first time in history that American and Soviet armor had ever confronted each other in anger. The tanks on both sides were fully loaded, ready to fire. The American commander on the spot worried that "a nervous soldier might accidentally discharge his weapon," or some tanker might "step accidentally on his accelerator leading to a runaway tank." After seventeen hours, while rumors circulated the globe that Berlin was about to become the flash point for World War III, word came from the Russian command to pull back. It seems that Kennedy, without telling Clay, had called on the Russians to remove their tanks in exchange for future "flexibility" on Berlin. Knowing that with Clay on the scene it would have been hard for the Americans to withdraw first, Khrushchev gave them a graceful way out.

Dean Rusk later dismissed this contretemps as "the silly confrontation at Checkpoint Charlie brought on by the macho inclinations of General Clay." The gesture was certainly macho, but hardly without danger. Had one of those tanks opened fire, the other side would undoubtedly have fired back, and the wartime partners of yesteryear, who sixteen years before had embraced at the Elbe, would have found themselves in a slug-out on the Spree. The next step might well have been all-out war.

The Quarantined City

Instead of bringing war, the Berlin Wall helped to keep the Cold War cold. After it went up, the level of political tension in Europe went down. Berlin, which had been the chief site of contention between East and West since the end of World War II, became something of a backwater in the continuing standoff. The two halves of the divided city went their separate ways with considerably less world attention focused on them.

Although East Berlin did not have a wall around it, it too was isolated in important respects, for it was the capital of a country that (at least early on) the Western nations did not recognize, and its masters were determined to keep it as ideologically distinct from the West as possible. During the first two years after the Wall went up, West Berliners were barred from entering East Berlin altogether. Then, just before Christmas 1963, a complicated arrangement was instituted whereby West Berliners could secure passes for brief visits to East Berlin during the holiday season. As of September 1964 West Berliners could visit their relatives five times during the year. In the immediate post-Wall years East Berliners were allowed to go to the West only on official business. Eventually, pensioners were permitted to move West whenever they wished, since this conveniently shifted the burden of supporting them from the GDR to the Federal Republic.

Because the Berlin Wall removed the possibility of disgruntled GDR citizens fleeing en masse to the West, the Ulbricht government could more resolutely impose its vision of socialist progress on the remaining population. In 1963 the government introduced a "New Economic System of Planning and Leadership." In addition to tightening economic centralization across the board, the plan foresaw extensive development in the field of robotics, which Ulbricht believed was the wave of the future. The SED government promised that the GDR would soon surpass the West in this domain, and in a futile effort to do so it cut spending on housing and consumer-goods production, which had been low to begin with. The money saved on basic consumer necessities, however, turned out to be insufficient to fund the drive for technological supremacy. Ulbricht was forced to go cap in hand to the Soviets for loans. This was not what the Russians had had in mind when they established their East German satellite.

Although East Germany's rulers no longer had to worry that the inadequacies of their system might generate a vast exodus, they feared that frustration with existing conditions might spark popular resistance, even a new version of the 1953 uprising. To nip any "subversion" in the bud, they expanded the size and operational scope of the Stasi. A great deal of time and effort was spent on identifying and punishing GDR citizens who violated the government's ban on contacts with the West. Simply tuning in to Western radio or television was a criminal offense. To ferret out offenders, the Stasi encouraged schoolchildren to inform their teachers about the programs that their parents received at home. Virtually every workplace had its Stasi spies, as did most cultural organizations, sports clubs, and church groups. The East German churches were under especially close supervision because they were considered potential sources of opposition. The information collected by the Stasi agents and their army of "informal collaborators" became so voluminous that the

The Stasi headquarters in East Berlin's Normannenstrasse, photographed in 1990

floors of the agency's headquarters on East Berlin's Normannenstrasse had to be reinforced to hold all the files. What could not be adequately reinforced was the human capacity for making sense of this voluminous data. By recording the tiniest details in the daily lives of millions of people, the Stasi soon began to drown in its own "intelligence."

By the end of 1961, East Germany had more than 10,000 political prisoners in its prisons. Keeping so many "subversives" behind bars, like the process of ferreting them out, was very expensive. It soon occurred to the Stasi leaders that some of these costs might be defrayed by "selling off" selected political prisoners to the Federal Republic. The inspiration for this idea was provided by the exchange of the U-2 spy Francis Gary Powers for the Soviet spy Rudolf Abel in early 1961. The famous exchange took place at the Glienicke Bridge, which connected West Berlin to Potsdam. If the West was willing to barter for spies, might not Bonn be willing to "buy out" some of the political prisoners held in East German jails?

To feel out the West Germans on this proposition, the Stasi called on the services of Wolfgang Vogel, a lawyer who had helped with the Abel-Powers exchange. Immaculately dressed and highly pragmatic, Vogel could just as easily have worked in the West (though he probably would not have made as much money). In early 1963 Vogel began negotiating with West Germany's minister for All-German Affairs, Rainer Barzel, regarding details of the transfers. Although the Stasi was eager to unload some of its prisoners, Vogel was instructed to obtain as high a price as possible for each "sale." The lawyer claimed that the prisoners sent to the West represented a financial loss to the GDR because of the costs invested in their education. "The training of a doctor costs the state 150,000 marks," he declared. Eventually a figure was agreed upon, and in September 1963 eight prisoners were shipped west at a total cost to the West German taxpayers of DM 340,000. Over the next twenty-five years, thousands more would follow. These people did indeed represent a "loss" to the GDR in terms of talent, but their expulsion was also an effective means of ensuring political tranquillity at home. The fact that East Germany could use West Germany as a dumping ground for its dissidents was one of the reasons that East Berlin remained largely quiescent well after other Eastern European capitals became hotbeds of anti-Communist protest.

Along with its campaign to isolate East Berlin and neutralize dissent, the Ulbricht regime stepped up its efforts, begun in the 1950s, to wipe out memories of the presocialist past. As far as Berlin's topography was concerned, this meant replacing some of the city's most prominent historical landmarks with showpieces of the new, forward-looking era. Having demolished the remains of the Royal Palace in the 1950s, GDR wreckers in 1962 blew up Schinkel's Bauakademie, another restorable ruin on the old palace square. They replaced this structure, which many considered Schinkel's masterpiece, with the first of their new governmental buildings, the GDR Foreign Ministry, an eleven-story white slab whose blandness was accentuated by the abstract aluminum sculptures decorating its facade.

The next victim of "socialist renewal" was another historic square, the Alexanderplatz, which in the interwar period had been known for its busy *S-Bahn* station, warren of small shops, bustling marketplace, enterprising crooks, small-time gamblers, and aggressive prostitutes. In place of such bourgeois "decadence," the GDR planners decided to erect a monument to socialist functionalism. In 1958, when planning for the Communist square began, Hermann Henselmann, architect of the Stalinallee, proposed as its centerpiece a 320-meter mast, to be called the "Tower of Signals." This idea was rejected as "Western influenced." However, four years later, after having abandoned an alternative plan to construct a governmental skyscraper, GDR planners revived the tower idea, and in 1969 the 365-meter Television Tower, East Germany's tallest structure, opened for business. Known locally as "the giant asparagus," or "Ulbricht's last erection," the tower featured a glass-covered spheroid near the top containing a restaurant offering grand views in all directions. The most interesting view, however, was of the tower itself at sunset, when the tinted glass ball cast a reflection in the shape of a giant cross. For years GDR architects tried in vain to eliminate this bothersome symbol, which in the West was interpreted as the triumph of Christianity over Communist atheism.

Beneath the tower the new "Alex" spread out like an urban desert. Looking lonely and forlorn in this vast paved-over expanse stood the medieval Marienkirche, which Ulbricht was dissuaded from tearing down because of international protest. Between 1962 and 1970 a series of ungainly concrete boxes went up along the edges of the square. First came the thirty-nine-story Hotel Stadt Berlin, the largest hostelry in the GDR. Next to appear was the Warenhaus Centrum, the GDR's largest department store. With its shoddy goods and near-empty shelves, it was hardly a satisfactory replacement for the old Wertheim store that had once served the area. Other new buildings included the House of Electrical Industry, the House of Health, the Central Administration for Statistics, the House of Publishers, the House of Teachers, and the House of Travel. The education and travel buildings boasted socialist-realist friezes which, according to the government, "match the buildings in size and beauty."

Ich bin ein Berliner

While the Ulbricht regime was seeking simultaneously to quarantine its capital from unsavory influences and to build it up as a showplace of technical progress, the authorities in West Berlin were scrambling to keep their city alive and open to the outside world. At first it seemed that they would get little support in this endeavor from the government in Bonn. Adenauer himself continued to avoid the city. In campaigning for the Bundestag elections in September 1961 he revealed his distaste for Berlin in his attacks against his SPD challenger, Willy Brandt. He charged that Khrushchev had ordered the erection of the Berlin Wall to generate sympathy for West Berlin and to help Brandt win the election. When the new Deutsche Oper opened in West Berlin, five of Adenauer's cabinet ministers saw fit to skip the premier, an obvious snub of the city.

Quite independent of snubs from Bonn, the presence of the Wall threatened to throw West Berlin into terminal doom. The city's senator for popular education ordered the cancellation of the Opera Ball in November 1961 on the grounds that it was "inappropriate to hold an officially sponsored dance-gala at a time when our fellow citizens from the East are risking their lives everyday trying to escape to freedom." Other municipal politicians protested that this policy made no sense. As one senator argued: "Berlin must become . . . the most beautiful, glittering, and modern city in Germany. That goes also for . . . balls." A reporter proposed sarcastically: "Let's also forbid all theater, cinema, sports, and popular dances . . . that's the perfect way to get people to stay in West Berlin."

Getting people to stay in West Berlin was indeed a concern, for by the summer of 1962 folks were leaving the city at the rate of about 300 per day. Most were young and highly trained, the kind of people who before the Wall had been fleeing the GDR. Another danger, at least in the eyes of the Bonn government, was that the West Berliners who remained in the city might become so embittered by their lot that they would look to the East for relief. The West might then lose Berlin after all—not to direct East German annexation but to creeping "defeatism" and "neutralism." As an emergency measure to lift West Berliners' morale, Adenauer asked President Kennedy to pay a personal visit to the beleaguered city.

Aware that he himself had helped to establish the diplomatic preconditions for the Wall, Kennedy was not anxious to comply with Adenauer's request. However, steady pressure from the chancellor, combined with entreaties from his own advisers, convinced him to make the trip. On his way to Berlin Kennedy stopped in Bonn to pick up Adenauer, who did not want to be excluded from this occasion despite his distaste for the venue and the prospect of having to share hosting duties with Willy Brandt. It would be the chancellor's first appearance in West Berlin since the Wall went up.

Kennedy and Adenauer arrived in Berlin on the morning of June 26, 1963. Together with Brandt, they toured the city in an open car. All along the route Berliners cheered and threw flowers. It was not the sour-faced chancellor who was the object of their adoration, nor even Brandt, but the handsome American president. In Brandt's view the homage to Kennedy "contained an element of gratitude towards a former enemy who was demonstrating to the Germans that the West's foremost power had made its peace with them—that they had rejoined the family of nations." Kennedy's tour, unlike Johnson's two years before, included stops at the Berlin Wall. Standing on a platform across from the Brandenburg Gate, which the

President John F. Kennedy, West Berlin Mayor Willy Brandt, and Chancellor Konrad Adenauer during Kennedy's visit to West Berlin, June 26, 1963

East Germans had obscured from view with red bunting, Kennedy got a good sense of the price that the Berliners were paying for the reduction in East-West tension ushered in by the "solution" he had privately welcomed.

Another huge crowd awaited Kennedy at Schöneberg Rathaus, where he was scheduled to deliver a major address on the status of Berlin. As he stepped to the rostrum—looking, in the words of William Manchester, "handsome, virile, and—yes—Aryan"—a mighty roar went up. Recalling that a few short years ago Germans had swooned before another charismatic leader, Adenauer asked Rusk: "Does this mean that Germany can have another Hitler?" Kennedy was not averse to a little demagoguery, and on this occasion he was determined to hit all the emotional high notes. Focusing on the political symbolism of the Berlin Wall, he intoned:

> There are many people in the world who really don't understand, or say they don't, what is the great issue between the Free World and the Communist

> world. *Let them come to* BERLIN! There are some who say that communism is the wave of the future. *Let them come to* BERLIN! . . . And there are even a few who say that it's true that communism is an evil *system,* but it permits us to make economic progress. *Lass' sie nach Berlin kommen.* Let *them* come to Berlin!"

These lines brought spirited applause, but nothing compared to what came next. On the flight over Kennedy had come up with the idea of equating the civic virtue of modern Berlin with that of ancient Rome. He had asked his aide McGeorge Bundy for a German translation of the key phrase, which he had practiced in Brandt's office. Now, lifting one hand in the air, he intoned the famous lines: "Two thousand years ago, the proudest boast was '*Civis Romanus sum.*' Today, in the world of freedom, the proudest boast is '*Ich bin ein Berliner.*'" (Bundy later realized that Kennedy should have said "*Ich bin Berliner,*" since "*ein Berliner*" could mean a doughnut. But given his policy on Berlin, what the President really should have said was "*Ich bin ein West Berliner.*") Hearing Kennedy praise their city in their language, the crowd went into ecstasy, screaming for minutes on end. One of Adenauer's aides later observed that with this one phrase Kennedy had made his audience feel that "he was a great President and friend of the Germans." More to the point, he had made the Berliners feel important again and proud of themselves.

When Kennedy was assassinated five months later, West Berliners went into deep mourning; his death was felt as profoundly on the Spree as on the Potomac. The square in front of Schöneberg Rathaus, where he had given his historic speech, was renamed "Kennedy-Platz." Yet the Berliners' love for Kennedy did not extend in equal measure to later American presidents, who, along with America itself, would soon lose prestige in many (especially younger) Germans' eyes as a consequence of the war in Vietnam and other actions that cast Washington in the role of world policeman.

Life at the Trough

Kennedy's Berlin visit, symbolically important as it was, could not alleviate the structural problems threatening West Berlin's ability to hold its own as the industrialized world's only walled city. As we have seen, logistical obstacles and political crises had undermined the economic viability of the western sectors of the city since the late 1940s, requiring rescue in the form of state subsidies, foreign aid, and special private investments. In the wake of Khrushchev's 1958 Berlin ultimatum, Fritz Berg, president of Bundesverband der Deutschen Industrie, appealed for an "economic bridge" to West Berlin similar to the "air bridge" of 1948/49. After the Wall went up that bridge seemed more needed than ever. The Wall appeared when West Berlin had finally achieved full employment, so there was now an acute shortage of workers. Moreover, the large industries that had already moved their major operations out of Berlin—companies like Siemens and AEG—were not about to return to a city that was so vulnerable to further pressure from the Soviets. West Berlin's political vulnerability also made it off-limits for the production of goods of military significance, including the high-tech gadgetry that was becoming the mainstay of the modern economy.

The Adenauer government was not anxious to pump new subsidies into a city identified so closely with the political opposition, but it felt it had to do so under the circumstances. In 1962 a comprehensive support package was approved, including direct subsidies, investment incentives, and tax breaks for companies operating in West Berlin. The package was renewed in subsequent years, and new subsidies were added. To help deal with the shortage of workers, the government imported thousands of foreign laborers, euphemistically called *Gastarbeiter* (guest workers). To attract native Germans to the city, and to retain those already there, the authorities instituted a host of inducements, including moving subsidies, rent-controlled apartments, automatic pay supplements of 5 percent, and a 30 percent reduction in income taxes. West Berliners called this complex of incentives "our *Zitterprämie*" (jitters premium)—the bribe they got for taking the risk of living on a tiny island in the big Red sea.

To further assist Berlin, several federal agencies were moved to the city. Their employees received a 17 percent "Berlin supplement" on top of their regular salary. In the 1970s, about 40 percent of the city's budget was covered by West German taxpayers; by the mid-1980s, that figure had jumped to 55 percent. At that point Bonn was pumping half a billion marks a year to Berlin in direct subsidies, and another 8 billion yearly in tax breaks, business credits, and salary bonuses. Bonn also paid a portion of the costs of keeping Allied troops and their dependents in the city.

The extensive subsidies stabilized the economic situation in West Berlin, but they could not prevent the city from losing ground relative to other parts of the country. Germany's economic center of gravity shifted more decisively westward and underwent a division of labor: banking was now centered in Frankfurt; heavy industry in Essen and the Ruhr; publishing in Hamburg and Frankfurt; automobile manufacture in Stuttgart and Munich; international commerce in Düsseldorf; moviemaking, arms production, and the high-tech business in Swabia and Bavaria. While the lights of commerce continued to shine in West Berlin after August 1961, their brightness was impressive only when compared to the dim glow on the other side of the Wall.

The barrage of subsidies, moreover, encouraged a "Subventionsmentalität"—a growing sense of entitlement and complacency in the Spree metropolis. Some of the companies that operated there stayed afloat only because of the special support they received. West Berliners who wanted to be where the economic action was continued to abandon the city, leaving behind the less capable and the less ambitious. A city that had once boasted of being faster paced and more dynamic than anywhere else in Germany, if not the world, now took a secret pride in being more relaxed and easygoing than other German cities. Life in the walled island was turning out to be surprisingly *gemütlich.* Now the major fear was not so much that the Communists might disrupt the tranquillity, but that Bonn might cut off the subsidies on which it depended.

West Berlin's political class was not known for its stellar talent. True, the city had a tradition of dynamic mayors, like Ernst Reuter and Willy Brandt, but from the mid-1960s on the best politicians, like the best businessmen, tended to move on rather quickly to higher positions in West Germany after having proven themselves in Berlin. Brandt himself of course left to become foreign minister in 1966. Richard von Weizsäcker, who became West Berlin's mayor in 1981, moved to the federal presidency in 1984. Hans-Jochen Vogel, the SPD's chancellor candidate in 1983, served briefly as a caretaker mayor in West Berlin in 1981.

Vogel was sent to Berlin by Chancellor Helmut Schmidt to rescue the city for the ruling Social Democrats, who since Brandt's departure had succeeded in making the town a byword for political incompetence and corruption. With few demands placed on them aside from staying put, West Berlin's bureaucrats and party hacks got used to doing little real work for their inflated paychecks. When they did stir themselves, it was often to earn additional money in the private sector. Germans call this way of doing things *Filz* (felt), and though one could find it in every German city (in every city in the world, for that matter), West Berlin had turned it into an art form. *Filz*-artists were particularly active in the city's construction industry, whose major companies routinely staffed their boards with municipal politicians.

Sometimes, however, the collusion became too intimate even for Berlin. In early 1981 Mayor Dietrich Stobbe (SPD) approved a 115-million-mark loan to a real estate developer named Dieter Garsky for some construction projects that proved fraudulent. The senator for finance, who had also approved the loan, turned out to be on Garsky's payroll. Stobbe was forced to resign, and Vogel rode in to the rescue. However, neither Vogel nor his successor, Weizsäcker, proved able to root out the deep-seated problems of corruption, feather-bedding, and time-serving mediocrity. West Berlin's *Filz* simply could not be transformed into a wholesome broadcloth.

Not surprisingly, the situation in West Berlin inspired resentment throughout the Federal Republic. West Germans often spoke of the walled city as their "hair shirt." Most had been willing to wear this garment back in the days when West Berlin seemed in imminent danger of being overrun by the Communists, but with the construction of the Wall an odd kind of "normalcy" had set it, and Berlin inspired considerably less empathy. Now it seemed just another big city *am Tropf* (on the drip), with no end in sight to the dependency. In exchange for their subsidies, moreover, West Germans felt that they got little in the way of thanks from West Berlin. West Berliners, for their part, were at once proud and frightened by their alienation from the Federal Republic. They often insisted that only they could solve Berlin's problems, yet when West Germans showed little interest in those problems, they felt snubbed. Increasingly, when West Berliners said *drüben* (over there), they meant West Germany rather than the world just over the Wall.

Little Istanbul

If West Berlin was becoming, at least in the eyes of many West Germans, a shiftless and profligate dependent, the city also seemed to have become unsettlingly foreign, a place where alien cultures and customs were evident at every turn. As we have seen, in former times the German capital had often been regarded as insufficiently "German," but alleged *Überfremdung* (loss of native identity due to an influx of foreigners) emerged as a much more pressing issue with the wholesale importation of foreign workers beginning in the 1960s. West Berlin became especially dependent on foreign laborers because the Berlin Wall cut off its supply of German workers from the East. The walled city went from having virtually no foreign workers in 1960 to having 10 percent of its workforce foreign in 1975. By the early 1980s, 12 percent of the population was non-German. Even though other West German cities, such as Frankfurt and Stuttgart, had higher percentages of nonnatives, West Berlin's dense concentration of foreigners in specific districts made it seem particularly exotic and multicultural.

Turks constituted by far the largest non-German ethnic group in the city. By the late 1970s West Berlin had emerged as the second largest "Turkish city" after Istanbul. Of course this had not been the plan when Turkish laborers were invited to Germany in the early 1960s; they were expected to remain for only a year or two. But many stayed on with extended residency permits and brought their families over from Turkey to join them. Single men married and founded new families in West Berlin. Like immigrant groups before them, they settled in the poorer parts of town, such as Wedding, Neukölln, and above all Kreuzberg. At the turn of the century the streets around Oranienplatz in Kreuzberg had swarmed with Silesians and smelled of cabbage; seventy years later this area, with some 30,000 Turks, smelled (in the words of Turkish writer Aras Oren) "of mutton, thyme, and garlic." Berliners called it "Little Istanbul."

Most of the Turks living in "Little Istanbul" and other heavily Turkish parts of West Berlin did not in fact come from the old Ottoman capital but from villages in central and eastern Anatolia. Accustomed to the rituals and mores of rural village life, they sought to recreate their native environment in the gray streets and crumbling tenements of West Berlin. They established storefront mosques, cafés, restaurants, and countless kabob stands. They tethered their goats in the courtyards of their Mietskasernen. On Sundays they took over entire sections of the Tiergarten for community picnics. They set up small Turkish shops in the abandoned Bülowstrasse *U-Bahn* station and on weekends turned a stretch of the Landwehr Canal into a giant souk. Many Turkish women went around in their traditional garb of head scarves and wide pants under their skirts, a style which in Berlin became known as "Kreuzberg purdah."

In reality, even "Little Istanbul" was not solidly Turkish. Kreuzberg itself, located in the southeastern corner of West Berlin and literally up against the Wall, became famous for its diverse population of punks, skinheads, Sixties radicals, students, and hip artists. It was said that if West Berlin was "the insane-asylum of the Federal Republic," Kreuzberg was its "lock-down room." But while its denizens thought of this scruffy district as the "real Berlin," visitors from other parts of Germany tended to wonder if they hadn't landed on the Bosphorus, or maybe Mars; the place sure didn't look *German* to them. Nor, for that matter, did it seem much like home to conservative West Berliners, who complained about being "overrun" by people with whom they had little in common. Claiming to speak for his fellow citizens, Heinrich Lummer, West Berlin's archconservative interior senator in the early 1980s, said of Kreuzberg: "I'm not in my homeland here; that's been stolen from me by the foreigners. The whole environment is strange to me. The weirdness begins with the look and goes on to the smell." While most Berliners who were bothered by the Turkish presence contented themselves with complaints to the authorities and irate letters to the newspapers, some openly insulted the Turks in the streets, calling them *Kanake.* The city's young hipsters did not resort to such tactics, but even they rarely had anything to do with their Turkish neighbors. The British journalist Adam Lebor, who studied Muslim communities in Europe and America in the 1960s and 1970s, was shocked by the fact that his liberal friends in Kreuzberg "never once introduced me to a Turkish speaker."

Tensions between natives and foreign workers increased dramatically when the German economy plunged into recession following the Arab oil boycott of 1973. As unemployment rates shot up, Turks and other foreigners were accused of holding down jobs that otherwise might have gone to Germans. Following the dictum "The Moor has done his work, the Moor can go," Bonn instructed companies not to renew their *Gastarbeiters'* contracts if German natives applied for these positions. The ruling had little effect, however, because few Germans wanted to take the menial low-paying jobs that the foreigners performed.

In the late 1970s West Berlin's municipal government finally admitted the obvious—namely, that the Turks were there to stay—and instituted programs designed to integrate them into the fabric of German society. But the initiatives were too little and too late. Older Turks had lived too long in their own ethnic ghetto, while the younger ones—those born and raised in Germany—wanted neither to "become German" (even if this were possible) nor to remain Turkish in the fashion of their fathers. The younger generation evolved a hybrid Turkish-German culture suspended between the city in which they lived and the country of their ancestors. They were not willing to turn themselves inside out just to be "accepted" by the Berliners. As one young Turkish rap musician put it: "We are living in Germany and I like Germany. My father has worked here for thirty years. My message to the Germans is that when you want to you can live with me, when you don't want to it's not my problem, it's your problem."

For all their justifiable ambivalence about Germany and Berlin, the Turks were well adapted compared to the illegal immigrants from Africa and Asia who started to enter the city in large numbers in the 1970s and 1980s. Most of them arrived through the courtesy of the East German government, which, in exchange for hefty payments of hard currency, flew them to East Berlin and then dumped them over the Wall. West Berlin's authorities could not prevent this without imposing barriers at the various checkpoints, which would have been tantamount to recognizing the Wall as an international border. But while the illegals were allowed to stay in West Berlin, they were not provided with any of the support systems given to registered asylum seekers and ethnic German *Übersiedler* (settlers) from Eastern Europe. Left to fend for themselves, these people became foot soldiers for prostitution rings, cigarette smuggling operations, and cheap-labor contractors. Their presence added to West Berlin's image as a crime-ridden, foreigner-infested Babel.

The Glittering Thing

In 1966, according to a *Der Spiegel* story entitled "The Glittering Thing," West Berlin had 2.2 million people, 70,000 dogs, 7,000 beehives, 7,000 eating and drinking establishments, hundreds of zoo animals, and Rudolf Hess (now the lone prisoner in Spandau)—all crammed into an area about the size of Andorra. Just about everything had to be imported from West Germany, 150 kilometers away, including milk, which arrived daily in thirty-seven tanker trucks whose drivers had to navigate a strictly controlled route and pass two inspection stations—surely a milk route from hell. In summertime the beach at Halensee, known locally as the "whore's aquarium," boasted "the largest collection of attractive and available women this side of St. Tropez." But the city also had West Germany's highest percentage of old folks: 25 percent of the population was over sixty-five, compared to an average of 11.8 percent in the rest of the Federal Republic. Its suicide rate was double that of the other West German states and one-fifth higher than in East Berlin—a function no doubt of the claustrophobic malaise known as *Mauerkrankheit* (Wall-sickness). Its once-proud football clubs, Hertha BSC and Tasmania 1900, had been dropped from the first federal football league—perhaps another reason for the high number of suicides. Despite all the subsidies, investment in new factories and equipment was 25 percent lower in West Berlin than in the rest of West Germany. On the other hand, the city annually spent 111 marks per capita on its public bureaucracy (compared to 91 marks in Hamburg). Five years after the erection of the Berlin Wall, West Berliners were losing hope that their city might once again serve as "the unified capital of a unified German nation." Some local officials admitted that the atmosphere had become "sticky," and one paper dared to ask if Berlin was a *Weltstadt* at all, or really just an overgrown *Provinz*. Egon Bahr, the Senate's press chief, warned that "Berlin must not be allowed to become the largest small city in the world."

To help prevent it from becoming so, city officials sought to give West Berlin a true "downtown," with trademark buildings, monuments, and a distinctive urban flair. Considerable commercial reconstruction had already commenced in the area around Wittenbergplatz, Zoo Station, and the Kurfürstendamm, so the decision was made to turn this district into West Berlin's Piccadilly Circus or Times Square. At its center stood the ruins of the Gedächtniskirche, slated for demolition since the mid-1950s, but now preserved as a permanent monument to the horrors of war. In addition to shoring up what remained of the building, architect Egon Eiermann echoed its jagged spire with a hexagonal tower honeycombed with dark glass. The idea here was to represent "the new rising from the old," though Berliners spoke deri-

The Gedächtniskirche ruin with its modern addition, photographed in 1998

sively of a broken tooth flanked by a lipstick tube. Admittedly, the ensemble might have been more effective as a monument had not the "renewal" of the area around it been so undistinguished. On the bombed-out site of the old Romanisches Café arose the Europa Center, which featured an eighty-six-meter-high office tower crowned by an enormous revolving Mercedes star. Just as the nearby KaDeWe department store had signaled the victory of mammon over spirit when the Memorial Church was built in the 1890s, so the Europa Center set the tone for the district in the 1960s and beyond.

Although the Europa Center became the anchor of a bustling shopping district, it was quite clear that the walled city could not reestablish itself as a true "world-metropolis" on the strength of this kind of development alone. Because there was little likelihood that the town would regain its former economic or political status any time soon, municipal officials sought to focus their energies on Berlin's other pillar of erstwhile glory: its cultural prowess. Much of that culture would have to be imported and subsidized, since Germany's best artists no longer automatically flocked to the Spree metropolis. Beginning in the 1960s, West Berlin spent more on its culture than did any other West German city, including Munich, West Germany's "secret capital." To shift the frame of reference: by the time the Wall came down, West Berlin was spending DM 620 million on culture, or $365 million, which was more than Washington spent on all cultural projects in the entire United States.

In the 1960s and 1970s, a substantial part of West Berlin's cultural budget went into the construction of new buildings. The city needed new homes for its leading cultural institutions, and it wanted these facilities to make daring architectural statements. The project that embodied this ambition most aggressively was the Kulturforum (Cultural Forum), an array of high-profile buildings that started to take shape in the early 1960s. The construction site, a windswept expanse near the southeastern edge of the Tiergarten, had been littered with partially ruined buildings until the late 1950s, when most of the structures were razed. The erection of the Wall on the eastern periphery of the site added to the sense of desolation. Here the Bremen-based architect Hans Scharoun put up what was to become West Berlin's most famous modern building, the Neue Philharmonie (New Philharmonic Hall). This flamboyant structure, with its upward-sweeping surfaces covered in gold sheeting, looked like a giant tent or beached boat. In accordance with

Scharoun's idea that artistic performance should be a "co-creative experience" uniting performers and their audience, the Philharmonie's interior featured an orchestral stage surrounded by seating space on various levels. As Scharoun explained: "Here you will find no segregation of 'producers' and 'consumers,' but rather a community of listeners grouped around an orchestra in the most natural of all seating arrangements. . . . Here the creation and experience of music occur in a hall not motivated by formal aesthetics, but whose design was inspired by the very purpose it serves. Man, music, and space—here they meet in a new relationship." A nearby companion building, also designed by Scharoun, housed the State Library. Mies van der Rohe, who had reluctantly left Berlin during the Nazi period, returned to design the New National Gallery as another component of the Cultural Forum. The design he used was originally intended for the headquarters of the Bacardi Rum Company in Santiago de Cuba. The Cuban revolution of 1958, however, put an end to this project and left the architect with some unused plans. Unlike Scharoun, Mies did not believe that purpose mandated design: what would work for rum would work for art. Thus, courtesy of Fidel Castro, West Berlin got a new metal and glass box to house parts of its widely dispersed nineteenth- and twentieth-century art collections.

Another addition to West Berlin's cultural landscape, the Deutsche Oper, went up in the Bismarckstrasse in Charlottenburg, where the old Municipal Opera had once stood. The new facility, which opened in September 1961 with a performance of *Don Giovanni,* was architecturally uninspired, but it showed that the cultural bureaucrats in the West were not about to allow the Staatsoper in East Berlin to become the sole venue for grand opera in the divided city.

With generous budgets and no pressure to integrate their work into existing neighborhoods, architects in West Berlin produced some stunning structures, but also much that was hideous. The International Congress Center, completed in the mid-1970s at enormous cost to the taxpayer, fell into the latter category. The architects, Ral Schüler and Ursula Schüler-Wittes, came up with a silver-skinned monstrosity that resembled a jumbo lunch box, or a blown-up version of something a troubled child might have built with his Erector Set.

Of course, no one had to live in this building, which was unfortunately not the case with the two new housing projects constructed in the 1960s and 1970s to accommodate the workers brought in from West Germany. The Gropius-Stadt on the southern edge of the city and the Märkisches Viertel in the north looked as if they

The Neue Philharmonie, designed by Hans Scharoun, 1965

had been dropped on the Brandenburg plain by helicopter. Although more solidly built than their East German equivalent in Marzahn, they functioned better as statements of architectural hubris than as lodgings for human beings. Visiting one of these complexes in 1963, the British writer Ian Fleming spoke of a system that "treats the human being as a six-foot cube of flesh and breathing-space and fits him with exquisite economy into steel and concrete cells." Only in the 1980s, when the city spent additional millions to upgrade these structures and to alter their monolithic appearance, did they become more livable.

While some of West Berlin's new buildings were aesthetically striking, they could not transform the city into a beautiful or harmonious place; on the contrary, they tended to accentuate its ugliness. Yet this in-your-face disharmony was a source of local pride. Many Berliners were pleased that their city had not been tastefully restored, as had so many other West German cities. As the transplanted West Berliner in Peter Schneider's *The Wall Jumper* explains:

> I like Berlin, really, for the ways in which it differs from Hamburg, Frankfurt, and Munich: the leftover ruins in which man-high birches and shrubs have

> struck root; the bullet holes in the sand-gray, blistered facades; the faded ads, painted on fire walls, which bear witness to cigarette brands and types of schnapps that have long ceased to exist. . . . Berlin traffic lights are smaller, the rooms higher, the elevators older than in West Germany; there are always new cracks in the asphalt, and out of them the past grows luxuriantly.

Some Germans also harbored the conviction that Berlin, the former Nazi capital, had no business being pretty or glamorous. In the 1980s the Munich-based filmmaker Margarethe von Trotta, who shot some of her films in West Berlin, argued that Berlin was the only city in Germany that looked like Germany *should* look a half-century after Hitler.

The campaign to make West Berlin into a cultural metropolis of international rank involved, in addition to many new buildings, the creation of an array of artistic and intellectual institutes, think tanks, foundations, festivals, exhibitions, and schools. The institutions endowed by Bonn and other benefactors included the Film and Television Academy, the Institute for Educational Research, the Institute for Advanced Study, the International Institute for Music Studies, the Berlin Academy of Art, the Berlin Literary Colloquium, the Berlin Artists' Program, the Berlin Festival Weeks, and the Berlin Film Festival. Even the Aspen Institute had an outpost in Berlin—on the property where Goebbels's house had once stood.

The cultural institution that stood out from all the others was the Berlin Philharmonic. The orchestra's principal conductor was Herbert von Karajan, who succeeded the beloved Furtwängler in 1954 and reigned over the orchestra like a benevolent (and sometimes not so benevolent) dictator for the next thirty years. During this period he raised the ensemble to the pinnacle of the musical world. Although the conductor was pleased to be performing in such a glorious facility as the Neue Philharmonie, he seems to have had little truck with Scharoun's ideal of an aesthetic sharing between the musicians and their audience. Berliners came to respect von Karajan, but they never loved him the way they had loved Furtwängler. Moreover, as the first jet-set conductor, with posts also in Vienna and Salzburg, Karajan was absent much of the time from Berlin.

Berlin had long been Germany's theater capital, and West Berlin retained this status inasmuch as it boasted the largest number of theaters and the highest theatrical budget in the country. By the 1980s it harbored one-seventh of all the private stages in the Federal Republic and accounted for one-fourth of the nation's private

Herbert von Karajan directs the Berlin Philharmonic, undated photo

theater audience. Yet quantity did not necessarily translate into qualitative dominance. West Germany's theatrical world was now highly decentralized, and many of the best directors preferred to work in cities like Hamburg, Munich, Frankfurt, and Stuttgart. A notable exception was Peter Stein at the Schaubühne. A kind of Bert Brecht of the West, Stein took over the Schaubühne in 1970 and turned it into Germany's foremost venue for experimental, socially critical theater. This being Berlin, Stein's Marxist-oriented theater "collective" had the luxury of biting the hand that generously fed it: 75 percent of its budget came from West German taxpayers. In 1982 the ensemble moved into a state-of-the-art new home amidst the auto showrooms and upmarket boutiques of the Kurfürstendamm.

Like its dramatists, West Berlin's novelists and poets had plenty of opportunity to sup at the public trough. The Berlin Senate, with support from Bonn, established the Berlin Literary Colloquium, which awarded grants to local writers. The German Academic Exchange Service (Deutscher Akademischer Austauschdienst, DAAD)

A scene from the Schiller Theater's production of a musical review based on Hans Fallada's novel Jeder Stirbt Für Sich Allein *(To Each His Own Death), directed by Peter Zadek, 1981*

ran a similar operation, the Artists and Writers in Residence Program, for foreign writers who chose to work in West Berlin. According to the French critic François Bondy, such "subsidized internationalism" effectively reconstituted "Berlin's once spontaneous internationalism." This is doubtful. West Berlin was neither the magnet for writers from abroad nor the national literary capital that it had once been. All kinds of foreign writers passed through the city, but few stayed for long. Many of Germany's own literary luminaries, including Heinrich Böll, Martin Walser, Peter Weiss, and Hans-Magnus Enzensberger, lived elsewhere. In 1980, when the leftist publisher Klaus Wagenbach issued an anthology of cutting-edge German prose for use in German schools, only seven of the thirty authors included in the collection resided in West Berlin.

Among the seven, at least for a time, was Günter Grass, postwar Germany's best-known writer. He chose to live in the walled city because, as he put it, Berliners were "perhaps the only people in Germany to have developed a political sense since the war." Grass's own political sense led him to explore the ways in which Nazism had seduced and corrupted the German petite bourgeoisie. However, his most incisive works—*The Tin Drum*, *Cat and Mouse*, and *Dog Years*—were set not in Berlin but in his native city of Danzig. Only in later works, most notably *The Plebeians Rehearse the Uprising*, *Local Anaesthetic*, and *Too Far Afield*, did he use his adopted town as the setting for an examination of postwar Germany's flawed reckoning with the legacy of Nazism and the more recent challenges of Stalinism and terrorism.

The writer Uwe Johnson, who moved to West Berlin from East Berlin in 1959, became more strongly identified with the walled city than Grass. His central topic was the psychological impact of the German division, for which Berlin provided an excellent laboratory. Johnson offered no solutions to the problem of division. In his most famous novel, *Mutmassungen über Jakob* (Speculation about Jakob), an East German writer is killed by a train after visiting his fiancée in the West. Left unclear is whether he committed suicide or was murdered, and from which direction the fatal train came. In an essay entitled "Berliner Stadtbahn," Johnson captured the growing estrangement between the "two cities of Berlin," where the inhabitants of each half regarded the other half as more "foreign" than a genuinely foreign country. Never feeling entirely at home in West Berlin (which he always wrote in the East German fashion, "Westberlin"), Johnson abandoned the city in 1974 for self-imposed exile in England. After German reunification, the question arose whether his presence in the once and future capital should be acknowledged with a plaque on his former dwelling in the Stierstrasse. One critic urged that it should, adding: "The city is not so rich [in its recent literary heritage] that it can consign Johnson to oblivion."

Because Berlin's once-famed film industry seemed threatened with oblivion, at least in the western part of the city, the Senate created the Berlin Film Academy in 1966. Soon the academy's students could be seen prowling the city with their super-8 cameras, making movies about whores, junkies, *Gastarbeiter*, and lonely GIs. Some of these student films were shown at art houses like the Arsenal Kino. As it did with writers, the DAAD financed sojourns for foreign filmmakers in the city. In an effort to compete with Cannes and Venice, the Senate established the Berlin Film Festival. The city's cultural authorities also transformed UFA's former post-production facility at Tempelhof into a full-scale studio for the shooting of feature films. By the mid-1980s the Berliner Arbeitskreis Film counted over one hundred active filmmakers. Nonetheless, among West Germany's most prominent filmmakers—Alexander Kluge, Völker Schlöndorff, Margarethe von Trotta, Rainer Werner Fassbinder, Edgar Reitz, Werner Herzog, Wolfgang Peterson, and Wim Wenders—only Wenders had his headquarters in West Berlin (and later he moved to Hollywood). On the other hand, with its Wall and highly visible scars of war, the city made a perfect setting for movies, and some of the more notable postwar German films were shot there. They include von Trotta's *Rosa Luxemburg*, Fassbinder's monumental *Berlin Alexanderplatz* (based on Döblin's novel), Wim Wenders's *Himmel über Berlin*, Herbert Ballmann's *Einmal Ku'Damm und Zurück*, Rudolf Thome's *Berlin Chamissoplatz*, and Reinhard Hauff's *Der Mann auf der Mauer*. While Wenders's film deals brilliantly with isolation in West Berlin, Hauff's *Mann auf der Mauer*, which is based on Peter Schneider's *Der Mauerspinger*, features a young man who is trapped in a kind of no-man's-land between the two halves of Berlin: longing, when living in the East, to escape to the West; nostalgic, once deported over the Wall, for life in the East. Influential as such films undoubtedly were in shaping our image of Germany in the modern era, they could not make up for the fact that, when it came to *making* movies, Berlin had been surpassed by Munich as West Germany's new "film capital."

West Berlin was also distinctly second class in the domains of broadcast and print journalism. West Germany's national television station, the ZDF, was headquartered in Mainz, not West Berlin. The two federally funded radio stations, Deutschlandfunk and Deutsche Welle, operated out of Cologne. Given Berlin's former preeminence as a newspaper town, the absence of a paper of national or international importance was striking. None of the daily journals published in West Berlin was on a par with the *Frankfurter Allgemeine Zeitung* or Munich's *Süddeutsche Zeitung*. West Germany's dominant weekly news magazine, *Der Spiegel*, was published in Hamburg, as was its most influential weekly paper, *Die Zeit*. In an era when harboring the principal shapers of mass opinion was crucial to defining a locality's clout, West Berlin's lack of a major hand on this lever surely cast doubt on its status as a *Weltstadt*.

It was not, however, as a would-be world city but as a self-conscious enclave of louche living and neo-Weimar "decadence" that West Berlin exercised its peculiar fascination in the 1970s and 1980s. In a faint echo of the 1920s, the Walled City lured in a small coterie of rebellious foreign artists looking for a life on the margin, on the edge. Punk rockers from Britain and America fetched up in West Berlin because the scene there seemed even grittier and nastier than New York or London, and it had the added frisson of that lovely Wall, the perfect metaphor of dangerous division. Here one could flirt with the ghosts of Goebbels and Hitler and then hop over the border for a little provocative romance with the Commies. "I am waiting for the Communist call," proclaimed the Sex Pistols's Johnny Rotten as he strutted about in West Berlin, decked out in black leather and swastika tattoos. Lou Reed came to the city in the early 1970s to find inspiration for his third solo album, *Berlin*, in which he used images of druggies and derelicts to illustrate his own story of emotional train-wreck. In this record Berlin is a symbol of longing, loss, and stark antinomies, as it was for some of the cabaret artists of the early 1930s. The British punk-crooner David Bowie likewise made the pilgrimage to West Berlin in the 1970s, but in his case he settled in for awhile, consciously emulating Auden and Isherwood. Bowie's decision to move to Berlin reflected not only his Weimar fixation but a fascination for that ultimate abomination, fascism. He prowled the city in search of Nazi relics, taking particular delight in the ruins of the Gestapo headquarters next to the Wall and in Göring's former Air Ministry in East Berlin. À la Isherwood, he found dreary digs in a seedy part of town and frequented gay bars like the Nemesis Café, 1970s Berlin's answer to the Cozy Corner. Accompanied by the American rocker Iggy Pop, who prided himself on being as disgusting off-stage as on, Bowie relentlessly toured the city's nightclubs, favoring the Roxy and above all the infamous Dschungel (Jungle), where coked-out kids moshed to the throbbing beat of West Berlin's techno-pop group, *Kraftwerk*. After their nights on the town the rockers typically took breakfast at Joe's Beer House on the Kurfüstendamm. Friends of Bowie's recall him "upchucking in the alley after a gallon of König-Pilsners" and screaming "Go dick yourself" to fans who asked him for an autograph. No doubt Bowie and company would have acted like asses wherever they were at this stage in their lives, but the city of West Berlin, that open-air theater of the grotesque and the forbidden, seems to have brought out the worst in them.

Although Berlin's chief claim to fame in the Cold War period derived primarily from its brutal division, West Berlin officials downplayed this sad reality in their efforts to market the city to tourists. "*Berlin bleibt Berlin*" (Berlin remains Berlin) was the word of the day. An opportunity to focus attention on the entire city as a destination of historical and contemporary interest came in 1987 with the observation of the city's 750th anniversary. Here was a chance to show the world that both parts of the city, despite a lot of evidence to the contrary, could work together to celebrate a common heritage. This chance was missed, however, because officials in the East rejected the West's proposal for a joint commemoration. Instead of cooperation, the anniversary provided yet another occasion on which the two regimes competed for the title of the "true Berlin."

One of the high points of West Berlin's commemoration was an exhibition on the history of Berlin since its foundation, which took place in the Martin-Gropius-Bau hard by the Wall. To their credit, the organizers did not neglect the less savory side of Berlin's history. Considerable attention was paid to the Nazi period and the exodus of Berlin's Jews, which, as the exhibition catalog correctly noted, "destroyed more [of Berlin's spirit] than the Allied bombing." By devoting so much space to Berlin's place in the Nazi system, the exhibition organizers hoped partially to make up for the city's tendency in the immediate postwar era to "repress its recent history, wipe out historical traces, and demolish the buildings associated with the perpetrators."

Visitors to the Gropius-Bau show who wanted to see physical remnants of the Nazi perpetrators did not have far to go: close by was the site of the Gestapo and SS headquarters, from which the Nazi terror was orchestrated. Surface ruins of the buildings had long been carted away, but plans to cover over the site were shelved in 1985 when excavations uncovered some cells belonging to the Gestapo jail. This provided the impetus for the "Topography of Terror" exhibition, which opened in time for the 750th anniversary commemoration. The exhibition complex included pathways through the weed-infested grounds and signs instructing visitors where the important installations had been. Along the former Prinz-Albrecht-Strasse, now bounded by the Berlin Wall, could be seen some foundations of the Gestapo kitchen and supply rooms. There was also a modest documentation center containing pictures and written records pertaining to the site. The exhibition was meant to be temporary, but popular demand kept it in place after the anniversary commemoration.

A more positive dimension of Berlin's past was displayed in an exhibition called "Reise nach Berlin" (Journey to Berlin) held in the ruins of the Anhalter Bahnhof, the old capital's principal terminal. The show recalled the days when the Spree metropolis was a destination for travelers from all over Europe, and it carried the subtext that Berlin was still "worth a trip." Another exhibition, "Mythos Berlin," examined the ways in which observers, native and foreign alike, had imagined the city. Presciently, one of the displays imagined a reunited Berlin with a linear park marking the path where the Wall had once run.

The most ambitious part of the 750th anniversary celebration was the Internationale Bauausstellung (International Building Exposition, IBA), an architectural competition featuring restoration work and new dwellings by star architects from around the world. Unlike the Hansaviertel project of 1957, the IBA sought to recapture architectural traditions rather than to impose a single modernist vision on Berlin's battered landscape. Rob Krier's small villas in the Tiergarten district and Hinrich Baller's apartment complexes in Kreuzberg were justly touted as "models of modest urban renewal."

The IBA designs won broad approval from the Berlin public, but there was much criticism in conservative circles for another anniversary project, the so-called "Sculpture Avenue" along the Kurfürstendamm. The seven giant sculptures, costing a total of DM 1.8 million, included a pile of police barricades by Olaf Metzel and Wolf Vorstell's montage of two Cadillacs partially embedded in cement. The main point of the Sculpture Avenue, it seemed, was to tell the world that when it came to the outrageous and the provocative, West Berlin was still at the forefront.

Yet once again, the city may have been trying too hard. For all its bold new buildings and artworks, the most provocative and arresting structure in town was still the Berlin Wall. Over the years it had turned into an artwork in its own right. Its western flank was almost entirely covered with graffiti, giving it the look of a very long New York City subway car. There was also some intriguing Wall art, including paintings that sought metaphorically to defeat the structure's purpose by showing holes or zippers on the surface. Viewing platforms along the western side allowed chilling glimpses of the Communist East. It was this infamous structure, not the Neue Philharmonie or the IBA dwellings, that tourists most wanted to see when they came to West Berlin.

Protesters, Terrorists, and Squatters: the "Alternative City"

The visitors who came to West Berlin in the 1970s and 1980s generally did not hail from the other parts of the Federal Republic. True, West German overland visits to the city increased between the early 1970s and the mid-1980s (due largely to reduced hassles on the transit routes), but the vast majority of West Germans still preferred to take their holidays anywhere but in West Berlin. Among their reasons for avoiding this destination was undoubtedly its reputation as the favored turf of Germany's pampered student radicals and riotous *Chaoten* (anarchist crazies). West Berlin might not boast the strongest economy, the brightest politicians, nor even the most accomplished artists in Germany, but it had the most volatile "alternative" scene in the country.

When the Federal Republic created its new army, the Bundeswehr, in the mid-1950s, conscription did not apply to West Berlin because of its continuing status as an Allied protectorate. This meant that thousands of young West Germans moved to West Berlin to dodge the draft. Not surprisingly, they constituted a ready reservoir of protest sentiment in the walled city. West Berlin's higher educational scene, especially the Free University (FU), also provided a breeding ground for antiestablishment politics. Although the founders of the FU had hoped to build a different kind of university, free of old-fashioned hierarchical thinking, the institution soon fell into the same patterns prevailing at other West German schools, with the added disadvantage of extreme overcrowding. The result was a high level of frustration and discontent, fanned by junior faculty who saw little chance for advancement. The FU received considerable financial backing from America, but this created resentment among a new generation of students who regarded the United States as a pernicious influence in world affairs. The fact that America and its wartime allies still functioned as occupation powers in West Berlin added to the sense of grievance, as did the ubiquity of American culture. Initially, U.S. styles had been welcomed as a breath of fresh air, but in the German counterculture of the 1960s and 1970s the American juggernaut was perceived as a corrupting imposition of hypercapitalism, materialism, and kitsch.

The Vietnam War was the crucial factor in bringing these undercurrents of resentment to the surface. From the outset, however, the hostility of West Germany's youthful antiwar protesters was aimed not only at America but also at older Germans who had left the younger generation with a legacy of guilt and shame. Having been too young to protest against National Socialism, the student radicals of the mid-1960s sought the coveted status of "resisters" by campaigning against Washington and the political establishment of their own country, which they accused of repressing or even repeating the crimes of the Nazis.

Berlin's first major anti–Vietnam War demonstration occurred on February 5, 1965. About 2,500 protesters, mainly students, marched through the city along a route preapproved by the authorities. A smaller group split off from the main column and headed for the Amerika Haus. Upon reaching the building they lowered the American flag to half-mast (in honor of the North Vietnamese killed in U.S. bombing raids) and pelted the facade with eggs. They tacked up posters accusing the Bonn government of supporting Washington in its policy of "murder through napalm and poison gas."

The attack on the Amerika Haus horrified local authorities and older Berliners, who continued to see Washington as the free world's primary bastion against communism. Mayor Willy Brandt publicly apologized to the Americans on behalf of his city. Axel Springer, the conservative press baron, accused the students of working hand-in-glove with the East German Communists to undermine the freedom of West Berlin. In response to Springer's intervention, the students added his headquarters to their list of targets.

In the following year West Germany experienced its first major change of government since 1949. (The replacement of Adenauer by his CDU colleague Ludwig Erhard in 1963 did not represent a significant new departure.) In December 1966 a Grand Coalition (CDU-SPD) headed by Kurt Georg Kiesinger, a former member of the Nazi Party, took control in Bonn. As mentioned above, the new foreign minister was Willy Brandt, who gave up his position as mayor of West Berlin. By absorbing the SPD into the ruling coalition, the new government removed the traditional left from the ranks of the opposition, leaving that field open to more radical groups. West Berlin, with its Social Democratic former mayor no longer on the scene as a stabilizing influence, became even more favored by the militant left, who saw their major enemy not on the other side of the Wall but in Bonn and Washington.

In April 1967 Vice President Hubert Humphrey came to West Berlin to reassure its citizens that America, despite its preoccupation with the Far East, was still committed to keeping the city free. In light of the cheers that Lyndon Johnson and President Kennedy had garnered earlier, Humphrey expected to be warmly received. But a leftist collective at the Free University called Kommune I had other ideas. The communards decided to greet the visiting vice president with pudding-filled balloons. To prepare for this action they practiced throwing their missiles at trees in the Grunewald. Somehow the Springer Press got wind of these exercises and, in banner headlines, warned of "Planned Bomb Attacks against U.S. Vice President." The activists were arrested before Humphrey arrived, which spared him the indignity of being covered in *Quark*. He did not, however, come away unscathed, for at every stop he was booed and heckled. He left the city angry and confused—his disillusionment another sign that the postwar love affair between America and West Berlin was losing some of its luster.

For all their provocative gestures, the protest demonstrations in West Berlin remained essentially nonviolent until June 2, 1967, when the Shah of Iran paid a visit to the city. Reza Shah Pahlavi was seen in Berlin's leftist circles as the quintessential American lackey, but it was not enough for the students to denounce him as such. In line with their tendency to equate all contemporary evils with the sins of their parents, they labeled him "Another Hitler." Alerted that there might be trouble during his Berlin visit, the Shah arrived with a large security guard drawn from his dreaded secret police, the Savak. When demonstrators shouted "Shah Murderer" at him during a reception at the Schöneberg Rathaus, the Savak went to work, beating the protesters with clubs. West Berlin police did not intervene. Later that evening, as the Shah and his wife arrived at the Deutsche Oper to attend a gala performance of the *Magic Flute*, another crowd of demonstrators gathered across the street and threw eggs and stones at the imperial couple. Once again the Savak went on the attack, this time assisted by the local police. When the demonstrators dispersed, the police gave pursuit. One protester, a twenty-six-year-old theology student named Benno Ohnesorg, who was participating in his first demonstration, fell to the pavement under a rain of blows. As he lay on the street a police officer shot him in the head—accidentally according to the officer, on purpose according to some witnesses. An hour later Ohnesorg was pronounced dead at Moabit Hospital. The next day Springer's *Bildzeitung* ran a picture of the dead student, declaring that he had been killed by the demonstrators themselves. Günter Grass, on the other hand, called this "the first political murder in the Federal Republic." Upon leaving town the next day, the shah was asked by West Berlin's recently elected mayor, Heinrich Albertz, if he had heard about the fatality. Yes, said the shah, but the mayor should not let the incident get him down; that kind of thing happened in Iran every day.

Of course, the death of a political protester was anything but routine in West Berlin, and the Ohnesorg case provoked an extended bout of soul-searching. Mayor Albertz, who resigned his office in the wake of the shah riots, later argued that the authorities' hard-line reaction to the escalating student demonstrations could best be understood in terms of West Berlin's geopolitical vulnerability.

> In the years after the building of the Berlin Wall we developed an extreme sensitivity to everyone and everything that had contributed to the reality that our city was now walled in. We were fully fixated on the fact that this city, in its current condition, could remain free only through seamless cooperation with the United States. . . . In this situation there suddenly appeared demonstrators with red flags and Ho-Chi-Minh slogans, attacking our guarantor power as a destroyer of humanity and freedom. It was hard to take psychologically.

Albrecht's explanation overlooked the fact that police forces were reacting harshly to student protests in many other parts of the Western world at this time. Yet it was undoubtedly true that West Berlin's unique status as a walled city, with its shut-in population of self-dramatizing students and short-fused police, made it a perfect stage for the bitterly confrontational politics of the era.

Benno Ohnesorg's death convinced some in Berlin's radical scene that the "system" was so rotten that it could not be reformed through the usual parliamentary methods.

One who thought this way was Rudi Dutschke, or "Red Rudi," as he came to be known. Like many who came to play key roles in West Berlin's student movement, Dutschke hailed from the East, having grown up in the small town of Luckenwalde about fifty kilometers southeast of the capital. Independent-minded from the beginning, he had ruined his chances to study at Leipzig University by refusing do "volunteer" service in the new East German army. Since the GDR would not let him study, he moved to West Berlin in 1961 to matriculate at the Free University. No sooner had he gotten there than the Wall went up, marooning him in the West. In order to obtain government funds for the continuation of his studies he registered as a political refugee and renounced his East German citizenship. He earned additional money by working briefly as a sports journalist for the Springer Press (an aspect of his biography that he was later careful to conceal). When not working or studying he often sat in West Berlin cafés frequented by other recent refugees from the East who shared his sense of alienation from the (in their eyes) hypercompetitive, get-rich-quick environment of the West. He began to read Marx, something that he had resisted in the GDR when it was part of the official curriculum. Another influence was Rosa Luxemburg, whose democratically based, humanistic socialism he found preferable to the party-dominated, state socialism of the GDR. In 1963 he drifted into a group calling itself "Subversive Action," which launched Dada-like

"Red" Rudi Dutschke, 1968

"happenings" to mock the career-and-consume society of the Federal Republic of Germany (FRG). But with time Dada did not seem an adequate weapon against the seductive powers of the modern capitalist order, which, according to the neo-Marxist guru, Herbert Marcuse, employed the opiate of consumerism to sedate the people. In 1965 Dutschke joined the Berlin branch of SDS (Sozialistischer Deutscher Studentenbund), a student group dedicated to changing the political order through direct action in the streets. The creation of the Grand Coalition convinced him that the SDS, too, was not an adequate tool of revolutionary change, and in 1967 he established the APO (Ausserparlementarische Opposition), which aimed to replace Bonn's parliamentary system with a "people's democracy" of popular councils elected directly by the masses.

As he established himself as a leading figure in West Berlin's radical leftist scene, Red Rudi became a favored target of local conservatives, including his old employers, the Springer Press. The *Bildzeitung* ran stories calling him a tool of Soviet communism. The radical rightist *Deutsche Nationalzeitung* urged that Dutschke and his ilk be put out of action, "lest Germany become a Mecca for malcontents from all over the world." On April 11, 1968, as Dutschke mounted his bicycle outside the

SDS headquarters on the Kurfürstendamm, a young man named Josef Bachmann shot him several times with a pistol. Dutschke was rushed to a nearby hospital, where doctors performed an emergency operation to remove two bullets from his skull; the intervention was successful, and he survived. As a result of the trauma, however, he suffered from periodic epileptic fits in subsequent years. In December 1979, during the course of one of these seizures, he drowned in the bathtub.

Bachmann, who was quickly arrested, turned out to be a casual laborer whose life had consisted of one failure after another. Upon attending some meetings of the radical rightist NPD (Nationaldemokratische Partei Deutschlands, National-Democratic Party of Germany), he had become convinced that communism was the enemy of honest workers. After his arrest, however, he began to regret his attack on Dutschke, who wrote him letters from prison saying that he, Bachmann, should be directing his anger not at the people who were trying to liberate him but at the "ruling clique" that was oppressing him. Bachmann replied that while he no longer considered Dutschke his enemy, he was puzzled why student radicals demanded a revolution when workers in Germany had never had it so good. This exchange was a telling commentary on the failure of West Germany's university-based left to make headway with the country's working classes.

While Dutschke was being operated on in the hospital, his followers in the SDS, assuming that he was dead, held an emergency meeting to determine how to respond. Although they knew nothing about his assailant, they were unanimous in concluding that the true guilty party was the Springer Verlag. "Murderer! Springer—Murderer! Springer out of West Berlin! *Bildzeitung* also pulled the trigger!" shouted the students. After a short discussion they decided to lay siege to the Springer press building in the Kochstrasse in order to prevent any newspapers from being distributed. That evening over 1,000 students set off down the Strasse des 17. Juni in the direction of the Springer complex. On the way they smashed windows in the Amerika Haus, since in their eyes Washington had also helped to point Bachmann's pistol at Rudi. Upon reaching the press house they found it ringed with police and barbed wire. At first the students did nothing but chant slogans and throw rocks at the gold-tinted windows. Suddenly, a young man named Peter Urbach proposed torching the Springer garage with Molotov cocktails, a supply of which he happened to have with him. The students readily agreed, and soon several delivery trucks were burning. Rudi was revenged! What the firebombers did not know was that their cocktail-supplier was an agent provocateur employed by the BfV.

In the 1970s West Berlin also made headlines as the birthplace and nerve center of political terrorism in the Federal Republic. Newspapers across the country called it the "Hochburg der K-Gruppen"—capital of the Marxist-Leninist fringe groups. Klaus Hübner, West Berlin's new chief of police, warned in 1969 that the city was about to be inundated by "a wave of terrorism" resulting from the "failed revolution" of the 1960s.

West Berlin's terrorist scene did in fact grow out of the failures of the student protest movement. A number of figures associated with the antiwar demonstrations of the late 1960s decided to declare their own private war on a society they considered hopelessly corrupt. Ulrike Meinhof, a pastor's daughter who covered West Berlin for the Hamburg-based radical journal *Konkret*, described her transition from "protester" to "resister" as follows: "Protest is when I say that I don't like a certain state of affairs; resistance is when I say that said state of affairs can no longer be allowed to exist." In 1970 Meinhof came in contact with two other self-appointed "resisters," Andreas Baader and Gudrun Ensslin, who had gone underground in West Berlin after setting fire to a department store in Frankfurt. Baader, born in 1944 in Munich, moved to Berlin at the age of twenty to evade the draft. His mother supported him while he studied art and dabbled in journalism. Although a fixture in Berlin's bohemian scene, he dressed like a high-priced gigolo, favoring silk shirts, Italian shoes, and close-fitting pants. In 1965 he had a child with the wife of his best friend. He seems to have drifted into the radical protest movement less out of conviction than out of a desire for adventure and self-dramatization. Ensslin, like Meinhof a pastor's daughter, had studied German and English at the Free University. For her the epiphany that started her down the road to radical violence was the death of Benno Ohnesorg in 1967. She proclaimed on that occasion: "They'll kill us all—you know what kind of pigs we are up against—that is the generation of Auschwitz we've got against us—you can't argue with people who made Auschwitz. They have weapons and we don't. We must arm ourselves." She fell in love with the dashing Baader, abandoned a son she had had with a previous lover, and joined Baader and Meinhof in their neoromantic quest to right the world of its capitalist wrongs.

Baader was captured in West Berlin in April 1970 and jailed at Tegel Prison. Claiming that he needed to conduct research for a book on the "organization of young people on the fringes of society," he received permission to visit a library in Dahlem under guard. Soon after he arrived at the library, Meinhof and three accomplices freed him under a hail of gunfire, seriously injuring an elderly librarian. The date, May 14, 1970, is generally considered the birthday of the so-called Rote Armee Fraktion (RAF), which, with various related and successor criminal bands, managed to hold the entire country in terror for almost two decades.

According to the RAF's "Concept City Guerrilla Manifesto," the group intended to bring about the Maoist millennium by destroying parliamentary pluralism and the worldwide reign of "American imperialism." Since this could not be accomplished by legal means, the band committed itself to violence and terror. Over the next few years, the RAF placed explosives in U.S. military installations around Germany, bombed the British Yacht Club in West Berlin, robbed banks, bombed the Springer building in Hamburg, and targeted prominent West German business leaders and politicians for kidnapping and murder. Among the early victims of an RAF subgroup calling itself "Movement Second June" (in honor of the martyred Ohnesorg) was the president of the West Berlin Supreme Court, Günter von Drenckmann, who was shot dead at close range in his home.

In 1972 Baader, Meinhof, and Ensslin, along with three other gang members, were run to ground in Frankfurt and imprisoned in Stuttgart. One of the group, Holger Meins, starved himself to death before he could be tried. When news of his death reached West Berlin, sympathizers of the Baader-Meinhof cause went on a violent rampage. As the city's jails filled with arrested rioters, the Movement Second June struck again, this time kidnapping Peter Lorenz, chairman of the West Berlin CDU. The group demanded a collective pardon for the demonstrators and the release of six terrorists from local prisons, including the left-wing lawyer Horst Mahler. Lorenz was released only after the terrorists—minus Mahler, who chose to stay in his cell—were flown to Aden in South Yemen with DM 20,000 each.

Baader, Meinhof, and Ensslin were put on trial in 1975, convicted, and sentenced to life imprisonment in Stammheim (Stuttgart), a maximum security facility built especially for them. On May 9, 1976, Ulrike Meinhof was found hanging by a towel in her cell. She was buried at the Church of the Holy Trinity in West Berlin's Mariendorf district. Thousand of mourners, claiming that she had been murdered by her guards, attended her funeral. Pastor Helmut Gollwitzer, who had also officiated at Ohnesorg's burial nine years before, eulogized Meinhof as "the most significant woman in German politics since Rosa Luxemburg."

The death of Meinhof and the incarceration of the other gang members did not bring an end to the wave of terror that was sweeping over West Germany; on the contrary, in revenge for Meinhof's "murder" and in hopes of forcing the release of Baader and Ensslin, members of the gang staged a series of the most spectacular acts of terror yet. On April 7, 1977, Siegfried Buback, the chief federal prosecutor, was shot dead in Karlsruhe as he drove to work. The killers identified themselves as the "Kommando Ulrike Meinhof." About four months later, on July 30, a young woman named Susanne Albrecht and two accomplices appeared at the Frankfurt-area home of Jürgen Ponto, chief of the Dresdner Bank. Since Albrecht was a good friend of his daughter, Herr Ponto let the trio in. One of them shot him five times as he went to get a vase for the flowers they had brought him. He died shortly thereafter in a Frankfurt hospital. Two weeks later Susanne Albrecht sent a letter to several newspapers saying that Ponto had been executed for having committed crimes of genocide against the peoples of the Third World. In September Hanns-Martin Schleyer, president of the West German Association of Employers, was pulling into the driveway of his Cologne home when five masked figures ambushed his car and an accompanying police vehicle. The attackers killed Schleyer's chauffeur and two policeman before pulling the businessman from his car and racing from the scene. The kidnappers sent the government pictures of Schleyer with a sign on his chest saying "Prisoner of the RAF," along with a note promising to kill him if the RAF prisoners were not released from Stammheim. While German federal police searched frantically for Schleyer, a group of Palestinian terrorists hijacked a Lufthansa plane en route from Palma de Mallorca to Frankfurt with eighty-six people on board. The hijackers likewise demanded the immediate release of "our comrades" in Stammheim, who were "fighting against the imperialist organizations of the world." The plane was forced to fly to Rome, Cyprus, Dubai, and Aden, where the pilot was murdered in cold blood. The saga finally ended on October 17 in Mogadishu, Somalia, when a commando team dispatched by the German government managed in a brilliant operation to rescue the hostages and kill most of the terrorists. Two days later Hanns-Martin Schleyer was found dead in the trunk of a car in the French town of Mulhouse.

The Stammheim inmates kept abreast of the efforts to free them by listening to a transistor radio that had been smuggled into their high-security cell. Within hours after learning about what had happened in Mogadishu, they decided to commit collective suicide. Baader and another prisoner, Jan-Carl Raspe, used smuggled pistols to do the job. Gudrun Ensslin hanged herself with a speaker cable. Irmgard Möller stabbed herself in the chest with a kitchen knife. Alone among the group, Möller survived. Later she insisted that she had not tried to commit suicide, and she questioned whether any of her colleagues had died by their own hand.

News of the deaths at Stammheim provoked violent protest demonstrations across West Germany. The largest and most violent protests occurred in West Berlin, where it had all started. As they had after the alleged "state executions" of Meins and Meinhof, rioters burned cars, looted shops, and attacked police. The violence gave politicians in Bonn another reason—if they needed one—to be relieved that they were not trying to govern the country from the chaotic precincts of the former German capital.

In the wake of the deaths of the Baader-Meinhof leaders, terrorism abated in West Germany, but it did not disappear, especially in West Berlin. In 1982 terrorists blew up the French Cultural House on the Kurfürstendamm. Throughout the 1980s there were bomb scares at American military installations in the city, which led to much tighter security precautions. As one American officer recalled: "They put fences around the PX, and they closed the outpost film theater on one Saturday morning because there was a report that terrorists were going to drive a truckful of explosives into this theater full of American kiddies watching the Saturday matinee. You had to open your trunk and the hood of your car just to get into the PX parking lot." Unfortunately, there was no such tight security on the night of April 5, 1986, at the La Belle discotheque, a popular hangout for U.S. servicemen, especially blacks. On that night a terrorist group with connections to Libya placed plastic explosives in the club. The blast killed a young black GI and a twenty-eight-year-old Turkish woman; 229 people, including seventy-nine Americans and four Arabs, were wounded. Two months later another GI, whose legs had been blown off in the explosion, died from his wounds. In retaliation the Reagan administration ordered air attacks against the Libyan cities of Tripoli and Benghazi, which killed over one hundred people. Berlin seemed unable to escape its association with political extremism and terrorist carnage: now the smashed La Belle disco became a regular stop for tourist busses on their way to the nearby Wall.

Documents that became available after the fall of the Wall revealed that the La Belle bombers had operated out of East Berlin and received assistance from the Stasi. In fact, throughout the 1980s fugitive RAF members found a safe haven in East Germany. The Stasi paid their bills and gave them false identity papers. Among the protected fugitives were Susanne Albrecht, who had helped with the

The La Belle discotheque after the terrorist bombing, April 5, 1986

Ponto murder, and Christian Klar and Silke Maier-Witt, who were involved in the Schleyer kidnapping. The order to provide them sanctuary came directly from Honecker and Mielke, who, according to Markus Wolf, may have been reminded "of their own youth in Germany as underground fighters against the Nazis." However, Wolf believed that the GDR bosses would have been disabused of this fantasy had they actually spent any time with these "hysterical children of mainly upper-middle-class backgrounds. [The young terrorists'] style of combat rarely demanded that they show the bravery and ingenuity that had enabled the Communist Party and its intelligence networks to keep operating in Germany under Hitler."

If the Federal Republic's terrorist movement had its origins and favorite terrain in West Berlin, so did the West German *Hausbesetzer* (squatters) scene of the 1970s and 1980s. Though squatters staked out territory in other cities in the Federal Republic as well, they congregated in greater numbers in West Berlin than anywhere else. In addition to a burgeoning "alternative scene," they found there a large stock of vacant buildings in line for demolition or renovation. Many of these structures were owned by speculators who had evicted the tenants and were holding the properties as tax write-offs. The buildings were generally derelict and squalid, which made them all the more attractive to the squatters. The epicenter of the squat scene was Kreuzberg 36, the scruffier of the two Kreuzberg postal districts. Here the influx of mainly Turkish *Gastarbeiter* in the 1960s had driven out many of the middle-class residents, while the close proximity of the Wall kept property values low. The ur-squat in Kreuzberg was the former Bethanien Hospital, a rambling brick complex that was scheduled for demolition despite having considerable architectural significance. While various citizens' groups struggled to get the demolition order rescinded (which eventually happened), homeless people from the area, along with runaways from all over Europe, moved in and set up house. Dubbing their squat the "Rauhaus," (rough house) they filled it with junk furniture and installed a sign on the roof saying Yankees Go Home!—which did not stop GIs from coming there to buy drugs. Residents of the upper floors had a good view of one of the watchtowers at the Berlin Wall. Some of the women complained that whenever they went to the communal toilet East German guards ogled them through their binoculars. One woman became so irritated by this that she bought a toy machine gun and pointed it at a guard, sending him diving for cover.

From Kreuzberg the squatters' movement spread to other run-down parts of town. In the single year between 1980 and 1981 the number of "occupied buildings" rose from 18 to 150. These structures housed between 2,000 and 3,000 people (there was, of course, no accurate count). Initially, the municipal government tried to find a modus vivendi with the squatters. The city offered easy lease or purchase terms to people willing to renovate their buildings according to code. A few took up this offer, but most spurned it as a devious plot to destroy their "scene." Alarmed at the continuing growth of the squatters movement, which was seen as a further inhibition to investment and yet another stain on the city's image, the authorities began trying to shut down the squats in the late 1970s. The police evicted illegal tenants and sealed off the properties. This of course led to clashes between squatters and the cops and to protest demonstrations by the estimated 10,000 to 15,000 Berliners who sympathized with the evictees. A demonstration in December 1980 turned into a full-scale riot; hooded *Chaoten* looted and vandalized such landmarks of consumer culture as the KaDeWe and the Café Kranzler. Thirty-six demonstrators were arrested and over 200 people injured.

Eight years later another battle between cops and squatters erupted in the so-called Lenné-Dreieck, a small piece of land just to the west of the Wall near Potsdamer Platz. Despite its location it technically belonged to the East and was off-limits to West Berliners. In March 1988 the GDR government agreed to cede the plot to West Berlin in exchange for another piece of land on the western side of the Wall. The transfer was due to take place on July 1, 1988. In the meantime, East Berlin authorities turned a blind eye while West Berlin squatters built a shanty settlement on the land. Since West Berlin's police dared not enter this extraterritorial enclave, the squatters took to launching attacks against police units stationed nearby, then running back to the safety of their "base." This cat-and-mouse game went on for months—providing another object lesson in the bizarre theatricality of West Berlin's protest scene. The game ended in the early morning hours of July 1, when the police stormed the triangle and tore down the shanties. About 200 squatters escaped arrest by jumping over the Wall into the East, where GDR border guards gave them a hot breakfast before slipping them back to the West.

In the 1980s West Berlin's seedier districts, including Kreuzberg, began to show some signs of gentrification—a clothing boutique here, an organic grocery there. Many West Berliners welcomed this development, but the crazies of Kreuzberg did not. They feared that if the trend continued their beloved *Kiez* would end up looking like Charlottenburg—or, much worse, Munich. To prevent such a catastrophe they launched a guerrilla war against the encroaching "schicki-mickies"—their term for anyone who wanted to gentrify their scene. In an ugly culture clash recounted in 1988 by the American journalist Jane Kramer, an artistic couple who had moved to Kreuzberg in the early 1980s ran head-on into the local version of Neighborhood Watch when they tried to open a modestly upscale French restaurant on Oranienstrasse. The wife-chef hoped to raise the tone of her adopted district by teaching the natives to eat *beurre blanc à l'estragon* rather than their beloved *currywurst.* The restaurant, called Maxwell's, opened at Christmas 1985. It was successful enough commercially, though few Kreuzberger came through its doors. When some locals finally did show up, they came not to eat but to trash the place; they also subjected the terrified owners to a *Volksgericht* (people's court), finding them guilty of subverting the "infrastructure" of the neighborhood. Shortly thereafter, a troupe arrived during the dinner hour and emptied buckets of shit all over the restaurant. Maxwell's closed, and the owners moved to Schöneberg.

While the squatters' movement may be said to have constituted the hard core of West Berlin's alternative scene in the 1970s and 1980s, its soft core consisted primarily of the artists, intellectuals, students, teachers, architects, and gallery owners who descended on the city for the high salaries, low rents, and feeling of self-importance they got from living in the hippest place in Germany. Like a kind of bohemian SS, they tended to dress entirely in black. In the firm belief that *mens sana in corpore sano* constituted a contradiction in terms, they smoked and drank heroically, becoming proud wrecks before their time. On any given night they could be found idling in their favorite cafés and *Kneipen*—from the seedy Pinox in Kreuzberg to the chic Paris Bar in Charlottenburg. Those with roots in the student protest movement liked to live in *Wohngemeinschaften*—living collectives that were meant to be models of harmony and sharing, but which in reality often turned out to be war zones of incessant bitching over who ate all the *Quark* in the communal refrigerator or whose dog befouled the floor in the communal foyer. Another source of anxiety was the difficulty of maintaining love relationships beyond a few days. In Peter Schneider's novel *Couplings*, a witty tale about sexual warfare among West Berlin's graying '68ers, the protagonist, a molecular biologist, concludes that "some form of separation virus was raging in the walled city." Although West Berlin's communards lived right next door to a socialist state whose principles they vaguely shared, few actually went there. After all, crossing the Wall meant having to trade in good western marks for near worthless eastern ones, eating mediocre food, breathing heavily polluted air, and listening to East German rock bands earnestly trying to sound like Pink Floyd.

Beginning in the late 1970s, West Berlin's alternative crowd had its own political party, Die Alternative Liste (AL), which was allied with the Green Party. In 1981 the party won 5 percent of the Berlin vote, which gave it the right to representation in the Berlin Abgeordnetenhaus (Assembly), the West German Bundestag, and the European Parliament. This achievement sent shock waves through the older parties, for among other unorthodox ideas the AL supported squatters' rights and the ouster of the Western Allies from West Berlin. In 1985 Petra Kelly, one of the Green Party's founders (and, interestingly enough, half-American), protested in an open letter to the mayor of West Berlin against the "military occupation" of the city by the Allies. "Do not the Berliners, of all people, have the right to decide if and how they are defended in the case of war?" she asked. Her idea of defense was to declare the city a nuclear-free zone.

Real, Existing Socialism

West Berlin's student protesters and apostles of alternative lifestyles had few counterparts on the other side of the Wall, at least during the Ulbricht era. In East Berlin in the 1950s and 1960s the only youth demonstrations allowed by the state were marches for world peace or nuclear disarmament. Ulbricht regarded the West's toleration of unsupervised student activism and its burgeoning alternative culture as signs of weakness.

As the 1960s came to an end, however, Ulbricht was himself in a position of weakness vis-à-vis his masters in Moscow. Leonid Brezhnev, chief of the USSR since 1964, was pushing for closer ties with West Germany in hopes of gaining access to Western technology and expertise. He found a willing partner in the Federal Republic's new chancellor, Willy Brandt, whose *Ostpolitik* aimed at easing tensions with Eastern Europe and facilitating contacts between the two Germanys. Shortly after taking office in 1969, Brandt signed a Nuclear Non-proliferation Treaty with Moscow and tacitly recognized the Oder-Neisse border between the former German Reich and Poland. In March 1970 he met with GDR Council of Ministers chairman Willi Stoph in Erfurt, the first such meeting between top representatives of the postwar German states. On this occasion Brandt breached the Berlin question, insisting that there was no difference between West Berlin and the Federal Republic. "Berlin is in every respect part of us," he declared. Brandt's enthusiastic reception from the people of Erfurt showed how desperate ordinary East Germans were to break down the barriers between the two countries. Ulbricht, on the other hand, stubbornly resisted the East-West rapprochement, fearing that it would undermine the legitimacy of his Communist government. His belief that the GDR could choose its own path in international affairs, combined with the failures of his economic policy, made him a liability for Moscow. In July 1970 Brezhnev confided to Honecker:

> You can believe me, Erich, the situation which has developed in your country disturbs me deeply. Things have reached the stage where they are no longer simply your affair. The GDR is for us a socialist brother-country, an important outpost. It is the result of the Second World War, our conquest, won with the blood of the Soviet people. . . . We must and will react. . . . I tell you quite honestly, we will not permit him to go his own way. . . . After all, we have troops on your soil, Erich. I say this to you frankly, never forget that.

In time Honecker himself would forget who truly ruled the GDR, but for the moment he seemed a reliable replacement for the seventy-eight-year-old Ulbricht, and in May 1971 he was allowed to unseat his former patron with the blessing of Brezhnev. The old Communist warhorse, whose resignation was said to have been based on "health reasons," was put out to pasture with several honorary posts and the job of handing out medals to second-tier heroes of the East German state. He died in 1973.

Honecker's appointment as party leader was greeted with relief in East Berlin, especially among the intellectuals. Unaware of his key role in building the Berlin Wall, many GDR citizens believed him to be something of a liberal and expected him to promote more openness at home and greater contacts with the West. At first these hopes seemed justified. He ended the ban on watching Western television and allowed young people to wear jeans and other "decadent bourgeois" fashions. Boys were permitted to grow their hair long on the grounds that, as the new chief declared, it was more important what was in people's heads than what was on top. At the Eighth SED Party Conference in June 1971 the talk was not so much about obedience and discipline as about variety, tolerance, imagination, and experimentation. Honecker personally stated that the chief goal of the party was to raise the material and cultural standard of living in the GDR, and to that end he endorsed a series of social reforms, including greater support for the old and sick, loans for young married couples, generous vacation pay, free day care for preschool children, maternity leave for pregnant mothers, and free abortions.

In the area of foreign policy, Honecker's regime began with a major change in Berlin's legal status: the Quadripartite Agreement on Berlin, negotiated by the four occupation powers in September 1971 and signed into law in June 1972. While not ending four-power control over the city, the agreement allowed Bonn to represent West Berlin in its external relations. At the same time, the Western powers tacitly recognized East Berlin as the capital of the GDR. (When Washington accorded diplomatic recognition to the GDR in 1974, it carefully described its embassy there as *in* and not *to* East Germany, and it characterized East Berlin as merely "the seat of the GDR government.") Ancillary agreements guaranteed travel and communications between West Germany and West Berlin and stipulated that all future changes in Berlin's status must be achieved through arbitration. Also in 1972, talks between the two Germanys yielded the Basic Treaty, which facilitated inter-German cooperation in such areas as telecommunications, waste disposal, pollution control, and postal services. The FRG and the GDR now formally acknowledged each other's existence, though at the insistence of Bonn, which heretofore had refused to recognize any nation that recognized East Berlin, the mutual acceptance was qualified by the exchange of "permanent missions" rather than full-fledged embassies. Bonn was careful to stipulate that the GDR was a state within the German nation rather than a sovereign foreign nation. With respect to Berlin, the Basic Treaty established more liberal visiting privileges for West Berliners and West Germans wanting to pay visits to the other side of the Wall. Now they could spend up to thirty days a year in East Berlin, provided that they exchanged a certain sum of D-marks—five for West Berliners, ten for West Germans—each day they stayed. (On November 5, 1973, the required exchange went up to ten marks for West Berliners and twenty marks for West Germans.) Some telephone links between the two halves of the city were also restored. The Berlin Wall remained a formidable barrier, but it had developed a few cracks.

It soon transpired, however, that the "openness" touted by Honecker at the beginning of his rule hardly extended beyond such tentative liberalization measures. Indeed, even the modest opening to the West in the early 1970s represented a source of danger for Honecker, since his hopes for promoting the GDR as a fully sovereign state depended in part on the cultivation of a unique East German identity. Bonn's leaders might speak of common German values, but Honecker adopted a policy of ideological apartheid he called *Abgrenzung*. In addition to cracking down on free discussion and artistic expression (about which more below), his regime sought to generate a sense of East German patriotism that might be strong enough to withstand the pressures of increased exposure to Western influences.

Manipulation of history played an important role in this endeavor. Previously the SED regime had eschewed building many bridges to the German past, insisting that the new socialist state represented an abrupt and necessary departure from tainted traditions. In the main, only working-class heroes and martyred Communists had been acceptable as historical models. Under Honecker, however, the state asserted its claim to a host of figures, institutions, and political legacies that heretofore had earned nothing but socialist scorn. Martin Luther, for example, suddenly went from being a lackey of princes to a social rebel and precursor of Marx. Luther's rehabilitation facilitated overtures to the Evangelical (Protestant) Church, which had been rigorously suppressed under Ulbricht. By mending fences with the Evangelical Church, the regime sought to harness its considerable influence and to use it as an agent of social control. The great Protestant composer, Johann Sebastian Bach, was rehabilitated as a musician of the people, while Goethe was found to have championed positive social change. (The GDR regime became so enamored of Goethe that in 1970 it ordered a team of scientists to exhume and inspect his body, in the hope that it might be displayed in a glass case as a poet-saint of the people. The remains proved to be in such bad shape, however, that the scientists simply cleaned up the bones, coated them with chemicals, and returned them to their crypt in Weimar. Needless to say, this creepy operation was conducted in the greatest secrecy.)

As far as Berlin was concerned, the most important historical revision involved Prussia, the political entity through which the old royal capital had risen to prominence. Prussia had been abolished as a state in 1947 by the Allies, but it lived on as an idea, a complex of images, principles, and traditions. On the grounds that Prussia had been the core of German autocracy and militarism, Ulbricht's government had literally blown away some of the most prominent architectural symbols of Berlin's Prussian past. Honecker, on the other hand, hoped to harness the residual power in the Prussian idea by transforming it—after careful sanitation—into a worthy ancestor of the GDR state. Historians were ordered to emphasize the forward-looking side of Prussia's legacy, its contributions to industrial progress and urbanization, its pioneering advances in social legislation. Prussia's most famous king, Frederick the Great, who had been condemned in Ulbricht's era as an archmilitarist, found his way into revised East German history books as an incorruptible servant of the state, champion of tolerance, patron of the arts, and promoter of social and economic progress. As a symbol of Frederick's rehabilitation, the regime returned his bronze equestrian statue from Potsdam, whence it had been banished by Ulbricht, to its former place of prominence on Unter den Linden. Funds were also set aside for the restoration of his grand palace in Potsdam, Sanssouci.

Frederick's return to Unter den Linden was a small part of an ambitious restoration program focused on the historic core of old Berlin, which some thirty years after the war was still dotted with the burned-out skeletons of great buildings and monuments. In an effort to reinvest the Linden with a measure of its former grandeur, the regime restored the Royal Library and rebuilt the Royal Arsenal as a museum of German history. Tellingly, the museum's exhibits emphasized the historical ties between eastern Germany and Prussia, while studiously ignoring events in the West, including West Berlin. The Gendarmenmarkt (renamed Platz der Akademie), also underwent extensive renovation after standing in ruins since the war. In addition to rebuilding the square's two churches, builders painstakingly restored Schinkel's elegant Schauspielhaus, perhaps the most beautiful building in Berlin. Converted into an orchestra hall, the Schaupielhaus was meant to compete with West Berlin's Neue Philharmonie as a center of musical life. At the gala opening ceremony in 1984, one of the architects expressed pride "over a work that finally brought [the GDR capital] recognition from the international musical world."

The restoration program took on particular urgency because of the upcoming 750th anniversary of Berlin's foundation, which, as mentioned above, East Berlin decided to commemorate independently of West Berlin. A brochure published by the tourist office of the GDR stated: "In 1987, Berlin—the capital of the German Democratic Republic—celebrates the 750th anniversary of the first documentation of the city with a year-long salute to its history and culture." Capitalizing on the fact that East Berlin had the lion's share of the old capital's historic buildings, Honecker's men hoped through their restoration efforts to show that their state, not the Federal Republic and West Berlin, harbored the most noble German traditions.

In 1972 a plan was put forth to restore East Berlin's largest surviving ruin, the hulking Berliner Dom. Ulbricht had intended to tear the structure down in the early 1950s, but with so many jobs on his demolition list he never got around to it. Honecker, by contrast, saw the Dom's restoration as a chance both to display reverence for Berlin's Prussian past and to improve relations with the Evangelical Church. The project was enormously expensive, however, and it might not have gotten off the ground had not West Germany's Protestant community agreed to pay most of the costs. By 1983 the church loomed once again in all its bombastic pomposity over the Lustgarten. Renovation of the interior was still going on when the GDR itself passed into history.

Berlin's impending 750th anniversary was also the catalyst for the restoration of the city's oldest district, the Nikolaiviertel, named for its Gothic church, St. Nikolai. In the sixteenth and seventeenth centuries merchants had built row houses along the quarter's narrow streets, and the great humanist writer Gotthold Lessing had lived there in the eighteenth century. World War II, however, had transformed the area into a ruin-field, which is how it had remained for over thirty years. Beginning in 1979, Honecker's architects restored the church and most of the district's housing. The fact that these houses had belonged to merchants presented no problem to the regime, since according to Marxist theory the rise of the bourgeoisie was a necessary precursor to the proletarian revolution. Although the restorers tried to recapture the district's historic flavor, a lack of resources necessitated the use of prefabricated concrete slabs on the facades, which hardly made for authenticity. West German visitors, whom the regime had desperately wanted to impress, condemned the endeavor as an insult to true historical restoration—a piece of pretentious Communist kitsch. Visitors from other parts of East Germany bristled at the expense. They were appalled that large sums of money were being expended on a show-project in the capital while the rest of the country continued to suffer from shortages of every kind.

Similar complaints were raised about another belated grasp for historical legitimacy (not to mention tourists' hard currency): the restoration of the Husemannstrasse in Prenzlauer Berg. This small street was reconstructed in the early 1980s as a "typical workers' neighborhood," complete with historic street lamps, a restaurant called "1900," and a museum devoted to working-class history. In reality, however, Husemannstrasse had never housed many workers, and its solid apartment buildings had remained a bourgeois enclave through the Third Reich. Moreover, the Honecker regime's new theme park of working-class life represented a glaring contrast to the crumbling facades and sagging balconies typical of the genuine working-class streets surrounding it. Rather than highlighting the GDR's proletarian roots, it showed how far the Communist state had yet to go to create a decent living environment for the vast majority of its citizens.

By the late 1970s the East German government was firmly established in the old governmental quarter in central Berlin. Although the Nazis had also ruled from this quarter, their Communist successors did not feel terribly haunted by ghosts in brown sheets; after all, as a "tool of monopoly capitalism," Nazism allegedly had nothing to do with the GDR. Some of the East German ministries even moved into Nazi-era buildings. As we have seen, the House of Ministries was harbored in Göring's vast Aviation Ministry from 1949 on. The only rite of exorcism that the new tenants had performed in that building was to replace a relief of marching Wehrmacht soldiers with a mural depicting the establishment of the GDR, which had taken place there. As of 1959, the SED headquarters was located in the former Reichsbank, one of the central sites of Nazi financial policy. Equally ironic—yet perhaps fitting—was the fact that the GDR elected to house its Government Press Office and Ministry for Media Policy in the former headquarters of Goebbels's Ministry of Popular Enlightenment and Propaganda.

The GDR government took over these Nazi buildings primarily because it was cheaper to refurbish existing structures than to build entirely new ones. From the

A panel from the GDR mural at the House of Ministries (formerly Reich Air Ministry)

beginning, however, East Germany's rulers had hoped to erect at least one governmental structure that could serve as an architectural symbol of the new state. Shortly after taking over from Ulbricht, Honecker decided to build a new home for East Germany's parliament on the site of the former Royal Palace. The choice of this location was at once another reach for historical legitimacy and a symbol of victory over the imperial past. The building that arose in the mid-1970s, and which still stands today (though perhaps not for long), is a squat rectangular structure sheathed in white Bulgarian marble and gold-tinted glass. Inside, the building contains an auditorium that was used for meetings of the GDR's rubber-stamp parliament, a 5,000-seat hall for party congresses and other mass functions, a restaurant and café, and even a bowling alley. At the dedication ceremony on April 23, 1976, the government heralded the Palace of the Republic as a true "house of the people."

At first, many GDR citizens did not see matters this way. Once again, they resented it that their government was sinking millions of marks into a gaudy project in Berlin while a severe housing shortage gripped the nation as a whole. Such critics believed that the new building would serve only the *Bonzen* (party bigwigs); they labeled the new building the "Palazzo Prozzi." With time, however, many East Germans came to feel genuine affection for Palace of the Republic, not least because it turned out to be not just for the *Bonzen* after all. Ordinary citizens were allowed to use its facilities, including its bowling alley. The palace was beloved also because it hosted many of the shows by Western artists that were allowed to appear in East Berlin during the waning years of the GDR. It was here that Carlos Santana and Udo Lindenberg performed, here that the singer Milva brought down the house with the lines: "Wenn der Wind sich dreht, weht er Mauern fort (When the wind changes direction, it blows down walls)."

When GDR television broadcast segments of Milva's concert, it left out the part about walls being blown down. For all the early talk about openness and experimentation, Honecker's regime continued to keep its citizens on a very tight leash. Indeed, Honecker and his colleagues ended up refining and perfecting the police state apparatus they had inherited from Ulbricht. "Real existierender Sozialismus (Real, existing socialism)," as the regime described its system, amounted, in the end, to a real suppression of dissident voices.

The main enforcer of ideological conformity remained the omnipresent Stasi, which grew even more formidable in response to the challenges of East-West détente and increased exposure to the West. By the early 1980s the Stasi had about 85,000 regular employees and about a million and a half full- and part-time informers. (By contrast, the Gestapo at its height had about 15,000 staff employees for a much larger area, and an undetermined, but certainly much smaller, cadre of regular informers.) Although there were Stasi branch offices in every East German town of any consequence, East Berlin remained the center of the agency's operations. The headquarters in the Normannenstrasse bristled with high-tech communications and listening devices, rendered all the more sinister by the complex's false windows, potted geraniums, lace curtains, and innocuous signs. In addition to its over four miles of files, the facility now included thousands of little bottles, called "smell conserves," containing samples of the personal odor of known dissidents. Should the dissidents go underground, the thinking went, their scent could be given to bloodhounds for more effective tracking. Of course, GDR citizens knew that the agency had informers spread throughout the society, but they often could not know precisely who "was Stasi" and who was not. Only after the wall came down and people were allowed to examine the detailed files kept on them by the agency could they find out who among their associates had been working for the Ministerium für Staatssicherheit (Ministry for State Security, MfS).

Western students and scholars who spent extended periods in the GDR also came under surveillance. In 1978 the Oxford historian Timothy Garton Ash, then a Ph.D. student, went to East Berlin to conduct research for his dissertation. As he discovered when he returned to investigate his file fifteen years later, some of his associates and supposed friends had been Stasi informers, busily keeping the agency informed about what he said and whom he saw. The authorities were particularly interested in his ties to members of the Polish Solidarity movement, for the GDR rulers were deeply afraid that their state might catch what they called "the Polish disease"—a thirst for freedom. When, on his return to Berlin in 1993, Ash managed to track down some of the people who had informed on him, none would take personal responsibility for their actions; all blamed the Communist Party, which they said had "forced" them to act as they did.

Such claims sometimes had a measure of validity. The Stasi often recruited its low-level informers with blackmail, offering them a choice of working for the agency or facing punishment for some crime or transgression. However, the surveillance system could not have been as pervasive as it was had not millions of ordinary citizens been willing to help the state enforce ideological orthodoxy. It has been estimated that one out of ten employable East Germans was a Stasi informer.

East Berliners were as active as the rest of their countrymen in enforcing this conformity despite Berlin's vaunted image as a bastion of political irreverence. As "Capital of the GDR," indeed, East Berlin had the highest concentration of party loyalists in the land. The Honecker regime brought to the capital thousands of SED stalwarts from other parts of the GDR, especially from Saxony, Ulbricht's old home turf. (The influx of Saxons was a source of constant aggravation to native East Berliners, who made jokes—but not too openly—about these crude provincials in their midst, calling them "the fifth occupation power.") The classier districts of East Berlin, crammed as they were with ambitious apparatchiks, were among the few parts of the GDR where the citizenry voted solidly SED out of conviction, not just for want of alternatives.

Marzahn housing estate in East Berlin

In addition to prestige, East Berlin offered the best and most numerous perks of power. The city had more than its share of "Intershops," the special hard-currency stores that sold Western goods and other hard-to-find items. Because of the ongoing competition with West Berlin, East Berlin boasted a few "international" restaurants, nightclubs, and even strip joints. Midlevel party and Stasi functionaries had access to decent apartments in the better parts of town, while the top bosses rated detached houses in the government compound near the village of Wandlitz. The compound, like a miniature West Berlin, had a high wall around it.

While East Berlin offered a host of amenities to its party functionaries, most of its citizens had to make do with living conditions that were considerably below Western standards. Rents in the city were low because of government controls, but much of the housing stock was in woeful condition due to years of neglect. Roofs leaked, balconies collapsed, bullet-scarred facades crumbled into dust. The newer housing projects on the outskirts of town, most notably the vast complex at Marzahn, were not much of an improvement, for in addition to being inhuman in scale and drably uniform, they began falling apart almost as soon as they were inhabited—instant slums. As for consumer goods, the Soviet bloc–made domestic appliances that were available in the capital's stores tended to be technologically primitive and aesthetically inelegant by Western standards. This was also true of the East German–made automobiles, the infamous Wartburgs and Trabants, which featured plastic bodies and two-stroke engines that belched noxious fumes. Because production of these machines was as slow as the cars themselves, buyers had to wait several years for delivery after placing an order; on the other hand, the cars did not become dated since there were few design improvements from year to year. East Berlin's grocery stores and butcher shops generally had food on the shelves, though the selection tended to be limited and monotonous. Restaurants served heavy meat dishes and canned vegetables, which one could wash down with good beer or (less good) Bulgarian wine. Cafés featured dry cakes topped with fruit jelly substitute or iced in suspiciously gaudy hues. Fresh fruit was hard to come by, especially exotic items like pineapples and bananas, which many East Berliners knew only from advertisements on West German television. (The lack of bananas inspired one of the many jokes with which East Berliners tried to laugh off the iniquities of life in the Honecker era. To wit: An East Berlin kid and a West Berlin kid face each other across the Wall. "Ha," says the western kid, "I have bananas and you don't." "Phooey," says the eastern kid, "I have socialism and you don't." "So what?" counters the western kid, "we'll get socialism too." "Then you won't have bananas anymore," responds the boy from the East.)

Although East Berliners and other GDR citizens were fully aware that the standard of living in their country was inferior to that of West Germany, they could take consolation in the knowledge that they were generally better off than the citizens of any other East-bloc state. This was an important factor in blunting the development of a strong opposition movement. On the other hand, as the socialist "brother-states" of Poland, Hungary, and even the Soviet Union began to reform and become freer in the 1980s, East Germans were confronted with what Timothy Garton Ash has called a "double contrast": that between their own society and the West, and that between their intransigently repressive system and the suddenly innovative East. It was bad enough to be "behind" the West, but to be behind the Poles was galling in the extreme. To cope with the fears and frustrations of everyday life, many East Germans retreated into the private sphere, a tactic reminiscent of the "inner emigration" of the Nazi era. The GDR advertised itself as a model of social cohesion and community, but in reality it was a *Nischengesellschaft* (society of niches) marked by the protective clinging to one's family and to small groups of kindred spirits.

The consolations of close social ties, low rents, free day care, good beer, and, not to forget, champion Olympic teams (the pharmacological bases of whose successes came out only later) were insufficient to deter a sizable number of GDR citizens from trying to move west, one way or another. They could tender an official application to leave, and under Honecker a few hundred were allowed to emigrate each year provided that they sold their property and valuables to the state at artificially low prices. Of course, people could also attempt to flee illegally, but in addition to the risk of being shot at the border they faced a jail term if captured. Parents caught trying to escape with their children risked having their kids taken away from them and placed with foster parents.

The Stasi maintained a number of prisons around the country specifically for political prisoners. Bautzen II, a high security facility in Saxony, was the most notorious of these. Opened in the early 1950s, it supplemented an existing prison in the same town that had been built in 1904 and used by the Nazis and Soviets before becoming a normal GDR jail. East Berlin itself had three Stasi prisons, each of them a hellhole where torture was a regular part of the "reeducation" process. In a report on his incarceration at Berlin-Pankow and Rummelsburg in the early 1970s, Timo Zilli, an Italian-born socialist, described a regimen of daily beatings, weeks of solitary confinement in a windowless cell, and hours of being hanged by his wrists with his feet barely touching the floor. A Jewish prisoner in Pankow who had spent five years in a Nazi concentration camp made the mistake of addressing his guards as "SS-Gestapo" and giving them the Hitler salute. As the guards beat him senseless, they shouted: "You Jewish swine think you can put on such a show because the Nazis let you survive. . . . We'll finish the job."

The one consolation for GDR political prisoners remained the prospect of being "bought free" by the Federal Republic. This program was expanded under Honecker as a way of bringing in much needed hard currency. In 1977 a covert organization called the "Commercial Coordination Area," or CoCo, which had been set up ten years earlier to help with the human transfers, negotiated a hefty price increase for these transactions. Previously, prisoners serving short sentences went for about 40,000 marks, while long-term cases fetched three times as much. Now Bonn agreed to pay a uniform price of 95,847 marks a head. Occasionally the Stasi also sold prisoners directly to their relatives in the West, but in these cases the price was even higher: around 250,000 marks a head. By the time the Wall fell, almost 34,000 people had reached the West through buy-outs of one kind or another, which earned the GDR over 3 billion marks. This human export turned out to be one of the GDR's most lucrative means of earning hard currency.

Cultural Dissidence: A Sinking Ship?

Of course, not all East German citizens who were disenchanted with conditions at home wanted to move west. Many dissidents continued to have faith in a socialist system whose principles, in their view, were being betrayed by their government. They remained convinced that socialism was fully compatible with, indeed dependent upon, free expression. Rather than abandoning the GDR, they wanted to make it better.

This sentiment was particularly prevalent in the literary community of East Berlin. Having taken seriously Honecker's declaration of 1971 that there would be "no taboos in the area of art and literature" as long as artists proceeded "from the firm position of socialism," writers such as Christa Wolf, Stefan Heym, Heiner Müller, Reiner Kunze, and Ulrich Plenzdorf began exploring the inadequacies of "real, existing socialism" in the daily lives of ordinary East German citizens. They soon discovered that what the government expected from the country's writers was affirmation, not fault-finding. Hermann Kant, president of the GDR Writer's Association, warned his more independent-minded colleagues that they faced expulsion from the association, and hence a ban on publication, if they did not show restraint in their treatment of political subjects.

The regime itself showed some restraint in its dealings with errant artists in the early 1970s because it was then mounting a major campaign for international recognition and could not afford to be seen as disrespectful of human rights. Following the Basic Treaty with Bonn, the GDR, along with West Germany, applied to join the United Nations (UN) and other international bodies. In 1973 both states were admitted to the UN and became signatories to the Helsinki Final Accords. In that same year East Berlin hosted the World Youth Games, another sign of its "arrival" on the international stage. But these very achievements allowed the Honecker government to contemplate a harsher stance vis-à-vis its most difficult intellectuals. In

Wolf Biermann, 1983

this regard, as in so many others, the USSR showed the way by expatriating Aleksandr Solzhenitsyn in 1974. If Moscow could summarily expel one of its best known troublemakers, could not East Berlin do the same?

The GDR's Solzhenitsyn turned out to be the folksinger Wolf Biermann. From a public relations standpoint, Honecker could not have chosen a worse target. The son of a Communist dockworker who had been murdered by the Nazis, Biermann had moved from Hamburg to East Berlin in 1953 to document his preference for the socialist East over the capitalist West. His early songs reflected the fervor of his belief in humanitarian socialism. Yet he also began to chastise the Ulbricht regime for its attacks on intellectual freedom and its disregard for the concerns of ordinary citizens. Singing in a hoarse, off-pitch voice that rendered his biting lyrics all the more poignant, Biermann soon achieved cult status as the troubled conscience of communism. Hoping to muzzle him, the government banned him from performing in public in 1965, but this only increased his standing among local dissidents. Honecker's men found Biermann just as unpalatable as the Ulbricht cadres had, and resolved to kick him out of the country. The opportunity to do so came in November 1976 when the singer received an invitation to perform in Cologne. To his surprise, the authorities not only allowed him to go, but immediately arranged the necessary travel documents. As soon as he was in the West, the GDR government denounced him as an "enemy of socialism," revoked his citizenship, and banned him from returning to East Germany.

If the Honecker regime thought that by expelling Biermann it would silence all questioning of its policies, it was badly mistaken. Immediately after Biermann's expulsion a number of East German writers took the unprecedented step of sending an open letter of protest to the government, claiming that the singer "had never, including in Cologne, left any doubt over which German state he supported." Biermann might be "an uncomfortable poet," the protesters added, but his barbs were just what the GDR needed: "Our socialist state, in line with the words of Marx's *Eighteenth Brumaire*, should criticize itself constantly and must, in contrast to anachronistic forms of society, be able to bear discomfort calmly and in a spirit of reflection." The GDR authorities were indignant over being lectured to in this fashion by mere writers. Konrad Naumann, leader of the Berlin SED youth organization, fumed: "It is interesting to observe who is now creeping out of their rat holes. But the working class has only to stamp down on these vermin to send them scurrying back to their hiding places. We've seen them in the open, and we won't forget their mugs. Those who don't keep their heads down will be crushed."

Yet, tough as it talked, the Honecker regime could not jail or expel *all* its intellectual dissenters, since that would have left East Berlin without any credible culture. Therefore—shades of Nazi policy a generation before—the authorities sought to split the ranks of the dissenters, treating some (like Christa Wolf and Heiner Müller) with relative leniency, proceeding harshly with others in order to set an example. Jurek Becker and Sarah Kirsch were kicked out of the party. Eight prominent figures, including writers Joachim Schädlich and Rolf Schneider, were expelled from the country altogether.

This tactic indeed divided East Berlin's literary community, but it also stimulated a wave of applications from literary artists and other intellectuals to emigrate to the West. Believing that they would cause less harm abroad than at home, the regime allowed many of them to go. Among the émigrés were the writers Reiner Kunze, Jürgen Fuchs, and Sarah Kirsch, the dissident economist Rudolf Bahro, the actors Manfred Krug, Angelica Domröse, and Eva-Maria Hagen, and the producer Götz Friedrich.

Like its literary community, East Berlin's theatrical world suffered severely from ham-handed governmental tutelage. Brecht himself had grown increasingly frustrated with the cultural bureaucrats' interference with the Berliner Ensemble, which functioned as East Germany's unofficial state theater. In the wake of the dramatist's death in 1956 his company fell under the control of his widow, Helene Weigel, and a group of executors appointed by the Ministry of Culture; soon it degenerated into a theatrical mausoleum, mounting mummified productions of Brechtian dramas. (One cannot help but be reminded here of the Bayreuth Festival under Wagner's widow, Cosima.) The Berliner Ensemble performed a few seminal dramas by contemporary writers other than Brecht, but many works critical of the GDR, including some by Heiner Müller, premiered in the West. Nothing more clearly illustrated the hollowness of Honecker's "no taboos" promise than the fact that East Germany's best dramatists were more likely to get their works performed in West Germany than at home.

In an effort to exploit proven cultural traditions and attract tourist revenue, Honecker's government made an effort to revive Berlin's legendary cabaret scene. Government-sponsored cabaret, however, had always been something of a contradiction in terms, as the Nazis had amply proven. The Distel Cabaret, founded in 1953 on orders of the SED, was allowed under Honecker to take a few satirical jabs at the party leadership, but no trenchant criticism was permitted. Attempts to reproduce the famed chorus line productions of the Weimar period proved even more of a farce. The East German dancers who waved their feathered boas at junketing East-bloc visitors were more reminiscent of their Nazi-era predecessors than of the *Tingel-Tangel* girls of the 1920s.

East Berlin's film industry had enjoyed a brief bloom in the early 1970s when filmmakers like Heiner Carow experimented with satires aimed at the GDR's ossified bureaucracy. His *Die Legende von Paul und Paula* (1973) asserted the right of ordinary citizens to a enjoy free and happy romance amidst the prudish restraints of East German society. But the huge popularity of his films made him suspect, and in the wake of the Biermann affair he was warned to proceed more cautiously. Thereafter, he and his colleagues tended to restrict themselves to safer fare, such as adaptations of the German classics.

Painters and art dealers took advantage of Honecker's apparent relaxation of cultural restrictions in 1971 to open new galleries and to create a regional art market. In 1976 an art show entitled "Are Communists Allowed to Dream?" took place in the newly opened Palace of the Republic. The paintings represented in the exhibition, all preapproved by the Ministry of Culture, suggested that the answer to the title question was a qualified "yes," and the surprisingly diverse collection gave evidence of a lively art scene, as lively, perhaps, as that in the West.

Honecker's regime, as noted above, rebuilt Schinkel's Schauspielhaus as a concert hall in hopes of putting East Berlin on the map as a world-class center of classical music. However, the orchestra that regularly performed there, the Berliner Symphonie, which had been founded in 1954, never achieved the international status of the older Berliner Philharmonic, headquartered in West Berlin. East Berlin's Staatsoper on Unter den Linden did enjoy an international reputation, but it could not fully recover from the loss of so many of its best performers following the building of the Berlin Wall.

While classical music was heavily subsidized by the East German government from the beginning, jazz and rock were repressed in the early years of the GDR as an unwholesome influence from the degenerate West. Like Hitler and Goebbels before him, Ulbricht regarded the West's popular music as a cultural Trojan horse that was best kept outside the walls. It proved impossible, however, to prevent East German citizens from listening to such music on West German radio, or from trying to emulate it at home.

Rock in particular caught on with the younger generation, which, even more than in the West, saw it as a protest against the stuffy culture of their elders. During the Ulbricht era aspiring East Berlin rockers were obliged to play at out-of-the-way venues in the rural hinterland, such as the legendary Rübezahl Gasthaus on the Müggelsee, but their concerts nonetheless attracted large and enthusiastic crowds. Having watched his predecessor fail to beat the rock invasion, Honecker decided to join it. His regime attempted to create an official rock 'n' roll culture that could more easily be controlled. The Ministry of Culture gave its blessing to a number of bands—among them the Puhdys, Panta Rhei, the Klaus-Renft-Combo, and Elektra—which were allowed to perform inside the city limits so long as they followed certain guidelines. For example, in order that their music contribute to proper "socialist personality development," the bands were forbidden from singing in English or wearing their hair long unless it was covered in a net. For the officially sanctioned

Die Puhdys, a GDR rock band, in performance in 1986

"Action Rhythm" concert at the Friedrichstadtpalast in 1972, participating groups were required to submit all lyrics for preapproval.

These restrictions, ludicrous even by GDR standards, were soon dropped. In 1982 the GDR's first official rock festival, "Rock for Peace," took place in the Palace of the Republic. The exalted venue showed how far rock had come in terms of official acceptance. Now the regime was even claiming that "young people's dance music"—the official term for rock—was not a Western invention at all but a natural outgrowth of East German culture. As one bureaucrat put it: "The rhythm patterns and sound structures of rock music reflect a sensuousness, a sensuous relation to reality, which, irrespective of all commercial filters, has its social roots in our working-class youth." Official acceptance, however, was very much a Pyrrhic victory for a music that was supposed to be rebellious, and the bands that played at the big state-sanctioned concerts were dismissed by the kids as *Staatsrocker*. Moreover, most East German rock fans still preferred to listen to foreign bands on records and Western radio—or, if possible, live. Whenever major Western groups performed near the Wall in West Berlin, as they sometimes did, hordes of young East Berliners instantly materialized on the other side of the border. During the 750th anniversary celebrations a major riot broke out in East Berlin when the Volkspolizei tried to prevent thousands of young East Germans from listening to a concert near the Reichstag put on by David Bowie, Genesis, and the Eurythmics. The rioting quickly turned political, with the kids shouting, "Die Mauer muss weg (The Wall must go)."

Some of East Berlin's rock bands had their digs in Prenzlauer Berg, the one part of the city that produced a vibrant countercultural scene in the last years of the GDR. If the East German capital had a Greenwich Village or a Haight Ashbury, this was it. The area, bounded by Dunckerstrasse, Lychener Strasse, and Schliemannstrasse, was pitted with places dispensing LSD and hashish. The district boasted seedy *Kneipen* like the Oderkahn, which turned into an informal jazz club after official closing hours. Here were also the classic "scene cafés," the Mosaik and the Wiener Café (known fondly as the "WC"), where intellectuals and artists like Robert Havemann, Grit Poppe, and Bärbel Bohley gathered to discuss ways to give the GDR a "socialism with a human face" (presumably not Honecker's). The "EP Gallerie," which displayed the work of young artists who could not or would not get into the official shows, became a byword for the cool and the forbidden. Yet one should not mythologize Prenzlauer Berg: along with all the bohemian artists and earnest reformers there were plenty of Stasi collaborators, and all too often they were one and the same.

Looking back in 1992 on the cultural hemorrhage from East Berlin that began in the mid-1970s, Wolf Biermann wrote: "One thinks immediately of a sinking ship. The exodus of many writers, actors, painters, and scientists after 1976 was the beginning of the end for the GDR." On the contrary, it is more likely that the exodus of dissident artists and intellectuals helped to *prolong* the life of the GDR. The expulsion of dissident intellectuals, like the sale of political prisoners to Bonn, proved to be an effective way to retard the development of a strong political opposition.

For all its inadequacies—cultural, economic, and political—East Germany seemed in the mid-1980s to be a solid and permanent fixture in the international community. The regime was begrudgingly accepted by the West, even by the new conservative West German government under Helmut Kohl, which like the SPD regimes before it sought to ease tensions over Berlin through extensive negotiations with the GDR. While continually paying lip service to German reunification, Bonn helped to keep the GDR afloat with generous loans. In 1983 a consortium of West

German banks, backed by Bonn, lent the GDR a billion marks on very favorable terms. Franz Josef Strauss, who had brokered the loan, later explained that the German question could no longer be solved with "blood and iron." In that same year West Germany's new president, Richard von Weizsäcker, declared that "the German question will remain unanswered as long as the Brandenburg Gate remains closed." This turned out to be a prophetic pronouncement, but at the time it was made almost no one, probably not even Weizsäcker himself, believed that the Berlin Wall would come down any time soon.

President Richard von Weizsäcker and Foreign Minister Hans-Dietrich Genscher protected by a police cordon during the president's speech at Berlin's Lustgarten, November 8, 1992

FROM BONN TO BERLIN

Did German reunification really occur only five years ago? Are Berlin [West] and Berlin [East], once the ideologically opposed show-windows of the West and East, really one city again?

—Berlin Mayor Eberhard Diepgen, 1995

When Germany was unified under Bismarck in 1871 the selection of Berlin as the national capital displeased many Germans, but that choice had seemed virtually inevitable given the way in which the Reich had been pulled together by the Iron Chancellor. By contrast, there was nothing inevitable about the Bonn parliament's momentous decision in 1991, following the nation's second unification, to move Germany's seat of government back to Berlin. Few decisions in modern German history have been more hotly debated or more divisive. As the newly united Germans set off in the early 1990s on the journey that would put them back in Berlin by the end of the decade, many wished fervently that they could turn back.

Although Berlin emerged as the victor in its bitter battle with Bonn, in some ways it did not seem like a winner. An economic boom that followed immediately upon the fall of the Wall and reunification turned quickly into a bust. Although the city was physically whole again it was by no means *spiritually* whole; on the contrary, it emerged as a microcosm of the famous "Wall in the Head"—that amalgam of social, political, cultural, and psychological barriers that replaced the old concrete wall in keeping eastern and western Germans apart.

The Fall of the Wall

At a ceremony marking the tenth anniversary of the fall of the Berlin Wall, Chancellor Gerhard Schröder declared: "The wall fell from east to west, pushed down by brave and fearless East Germans." This was true enough, but the initial and decisive challenge to Erich Honecker's regime—and to the Berlin Wall that he helped build—came not from within East Germany, certainly not from East Berlin, but from the Soviet Union. Mikhail Gorbachev believed that the Soviet Union could survive as a superpower only if it undertook reforms that might make it more modern, dynamic, and efficient. This was the motivation behind his daring policies of glasnost (openness) and perestroika (economic restructuring). He expected that Russia's renewal would be emulated by the governments of the other East-bloc states, some of which, most notably Poland, Hungary, and Czechoslovakia, were facing serious domestic opposition to communist rule. He was convinced that timely reforms would not only strengthen the communist governments of Eastern Europe but also tie them more tightly to Moscow. At the same time, in an abrupt departure from the "Brezhnev Doctrine," which called for military intervention against antigovernmental insurgencies in the satellite countries, he made it clear that the Soviet Union would not use force to prop up communist regimes that had lost the support of their people. East-bloc nations were now free to map their own path to socialist progress. (This new approach was labeled by Gorbachev's America-expert, Gennady Gerasimov, the "Sinatra Doctrine"—as in "I Did It My Way.") Of course, Gorbachev never dreamed that his plan to strengthen communism at home and abroad through timely reforms from above would ignite a revolt from below that would ultimately bring the whole system down. Like the proverbial Sorcerer's Apprentice, he set in motion a process he could not control.

Erich Honecker wanted no part of Gorbachev's reforms. He instinctively distrusted openness, and he considered economic restructuring unnecessary in his country, which after all was the most prosperous in the East bloc. He believed that the Soviet leader, rather than handing out advice, should be taking pointers from *him*, the "elder statesman" of European communism. The East German leader was

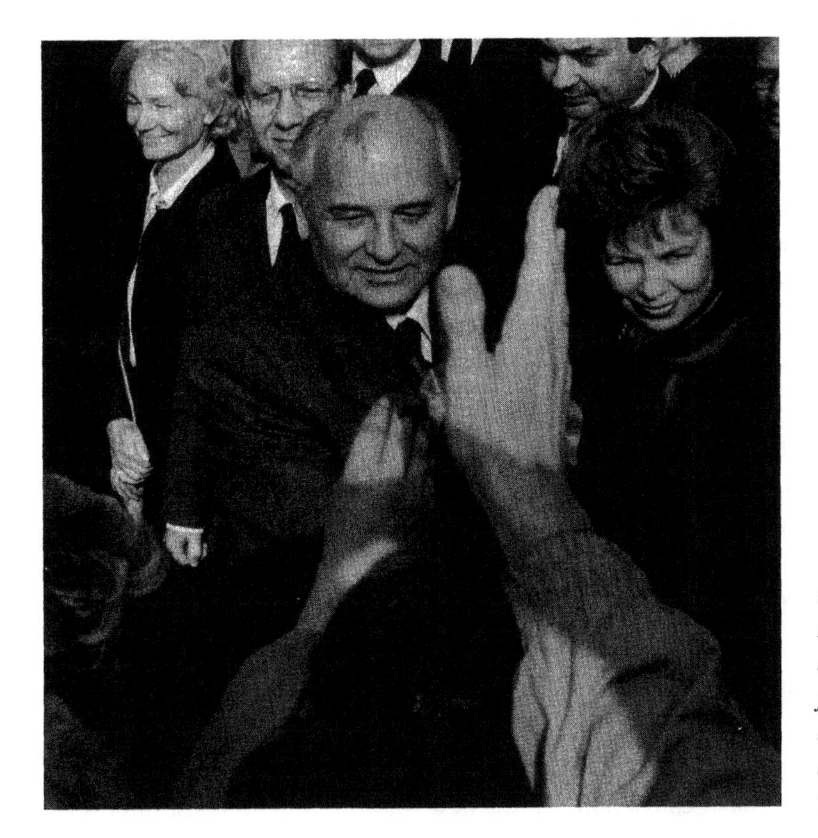

Gorbachev in East Berlin during the GDR's fortieth anniversary celebration, October 6, 1989

confident that he could withstand the challenge from Moscow because he continued to get crucial support from West Germany in the form of loans, trade subsidies, and "buyouts" of political prisoners. Prominent West German politicians, including Franz Josef Strauss, Lower Saxony minister-president Ernst Albrecht, and West Berlin mayor Walter Momper, paid him court. Chancellor Helmut Kohl lent him credibility by welcoming him in Bonn in 1987 as the first chief of the GDR to pay an official visit to the West German capital. Honecker took this opportunity to speak of "the reality . . . of two sovereign German states, independent of each other, with a different social order and opposing alliances."

In addition to financial help from the other German state, Honecker had the advantage of a relatively weak domestic opposition. Unlike some of his Eastern European counterparts, he did not face serious questioning of his party's right to rule. As the self-proclaimed legatee of Germany's leftist resistance to Hitler, the SED stood on a pedestal of historical virtue. Various dissidents might criticize this or that party policy, but they rarely contested the validity of Communist authority. Critics who did go too far, of course, could be sold off to the Federal Republic at a handsome profit to the regime. In the mid-1980s, of all the communist governments ordained by Stalin in the years after World War II, the one in East Germany seemed the most solid.

Nonetheless, Honecker's confidence that East Germany could remain largely unaffected by the new developments in Moscow soon proved illusory. East Germans began demonstrating for reforms similar to those being undertaken in the Soviet Union; when challenged by the police they flashed Soviet badges and pictures of Gorbachev. GDR authorities found themselves in the awkward position of trying to curtail contacts between East German citizens and the mother country of communism. When the Soviet leader visited East Berlin in 1986, the route he took to his official reception was swept clear of would-be greeters. The regime took the extraordinary step of banning notable works of the Soviet reform culture, such as the anti-Stalinist film *Repentance*. The magazines *Sputnik* and *Ogonyok*, which championed liberalization, disappeared from East German newsstands. It was now easier to get contemporary Soviet publications in West Berlin than in East Berlin. All the efforts at repression, however, could not wipe out the "subversion" from the East nor stem the growing popular conviction that the new spirit in Moscow constituted a license to demand similar changes at home.

East German dissidents learned to raise their unwelcome demands at embarrassing moments for the regime. On January 17, 1988, as Honecker and company were reviewing the annual parade in commemoration of the martyrdom of Karl Liebknecht and Rosa Luxemburg, a group of protesters broke into the ranks of the Free German Youth marchers and unfurled banners bearing Luxemburg's dictum: "True Freedom is Always the Freedom of the Non-conformists!" Viewers of the parade were treated to the sight of Stasi agents beating and arresting citizens for brandishing a slogan penned by one of the martyrs being honored. Among those arrested were the dissident artists Bärbel Bohley, Vera Wollenberger, and Werner Fischer. Given the choice of prison or exile abroad, they chose the latter, finding temporary sanctuary in England under the auspices of the Archbishop of Canterbury. The irony of the exiles' situation was not lost on Bohley, who declared later: "Thousands of East Germans were aching for the chance to travel, and here we were, being offered a long holiday in the West by the regime."

As the Honecker government struggled to show that with "real, existing socialism," the GDR had no need to take any reform lessons from Moscow, the nation's Protestant churches emerged as crucial forums for critical debate on the future of the country. The churches played such a central role because they constituted virtually the only public venue—aside from sanctioned state functions or sporting events—where large groups of citizens could congregate. Recognizing this, the Stasi had been careful to infiltrate all the parishes and to enlist some of the clergy as "informal collaborators." Increasingly, however, pastors began using the pulpit to admonish the government to respect basic political and civil rights. During a sermon at East Berlin's Gethsemane Church, Gottfried Forck, the Protestant Bishop of Berlin, pleaded for the release of the over 200 people arrested in connection with the Luxemburg demonstration. In May 1989 Pastor Rainer Eppelmann of the Samaritan parish in East Berlin accused the government of falsifying the results of that month's elections in order to gain its usual near-universal popular endorsement. The pastor proceeded to turn his church into a sanctuary for conscientious objectors and other political dissidents. Tellingly, rather than arresting Eppelmann and throwing him in jail, the regime merely subjected him to increased surveillance. The most important center of Protestant dissidence, however, was not East Berlin but Leipzig, where the congregation of the Nikolaikirche held "prayers for peace" each Monday, followed by silent, candlelit marches through the city. On the night of March 13 the police broke up one of these vigils, but on the next Monday the marchers were back again, and this time they refused to disperse.

While these voices of protest certainly represented a challenge to the Honecker regime, the government probably could have contained the dissension had not a more pressing threat emerged from one of the GDR's "socialist brother states," Hungary. On May 2, 1989, the new reform Communist government of Karoly Grosz in Budapest dismantled the barbed-wire fence on its border with Austria. Budapest assured East Berlin that, for the time being, Hungarian border police would still require East Germans to show GDR exit visas to pass into Austria. Yet this did not prevent thousands of East Germans from heading for the Hungarian-Austrian border in hopes of crossing to the West. When guards turned them back at the regular checkpoints, many simply abandoned their cars in the woods and walked into Austria. Others moved into the West German embassy in Budapest, refusing to leave without a laissez-passer to the West. Tiring of maintaining a "second wall" for a state that seemed incapable of holding the loyalty of its own citizens, the Hungarian government on September 11 formally opened its border with Austria and turned a blind eye when thousands of East Germans poured across the frontier. Honecker's government screamed foul and turned to Moscow for help. The Soviets, however, had gone out of the business of policing their shaky Eastern European empire, and Gorbachev was more interested in fostering good relations with West Germany than in bailing out the GDR. As he told his ambassador to East Berlin: "We support the GDR, but not at the cost of our interests in West Germany and Europe as a whole."

Hungary was not the only escape route for East Germans anxious to leave their country. Thousands drove to Warsaw and Prague, abandoned their Trabis in the streets, and took refuge in the local West German embassies. Like their counterparts in the Budapest embassy, these people refused to leave their sanctuaries until given travel documents enabling them to go west. By the end of September there were over 10,000 East Germans encamped in the Prague complex alone, making it Europe's largest squat. With shelter and sanitation facilities stretched to the limit, the Red Cross warned of an imminent health crisis. Harried embassy officials could not simply evict the refugees because Bonn regarded all East Germans as West Germans-in-waiting, entitled to instant citizenship should they demand it. Finally, on September 30, West German foreign minister Hans-Dietrich Genscher flew to Prague and announced that Bonn and East Berlin had worked out an arrangement allowing the embassy occupiers there and in Warsaw to emigrate to West Germany. As an assertion of GDR sovereignty, Honecker insisted that all the refugees pass through East Germany on their way to the Federal Republic. Officially classed as "expellees," they would be transported in sealed trains and have their GDR identity papers taken from them en route. As they boarded their trains on October 3–4, *Neues Deutschland* sneered that the departing ingrates would not be missed: "Through their [unpatriotic] behavior they have trampled on the moral values of the GDR and isolated themselves. . . . Therefore one should not cry any tears of regret at their departure." But instead of echoing this official verdict, thousands of East Germans came to the railway stations to cheer the refugees as they headed west. At the Dresden station a riot ensued when hundreds of people tried to force their way onto one of the sealed trains. A large police force, backed by units of the National People's Army, beat back the would-be escapees with clubs. Nobody managed to get on the train, but one young man fell under the wheels and lost both legs. Upon reaching the West German border the exhausted but ecstatic refugees were showered with gifts and embraced like long-lost brothers.

In the late summer and early fall of 1989, as the GDR government prepared to commemorate the fortieth anniversary of the state's foundation, the prevailing mood among the populace was anything but celebratory. In cities and villages across the country shop windows and factory gates sported signs advertising for new employees. The place was like a battered old car whose tires were going flat—hardly the sort of conveyance in which one could confidently drive into the bright Communist future. The GDR citizens who chose to stick it out at home insisted that their loyalty be rewarded with genuine reforms, including the freedom to travel when and where they wished. Having been told for so long that theirs was a nation by and for the people, they accompanied their demands for greater freedom with cries of "*We* are the people!"

The largest protest demonstrations were in Dresden and Leipzig, not in East Berlin. Reflecting its status as a bastion of SED loyalty, the East German capital had so far failed to generate large-scale displays of civil courage like the Monday night vigils in Leipzig, where on October 2 over 10,000 citizens demonstrated for freedom. A visitor to the GDR who stayed only in East Berlin might well have agreed with Honecker when he bragged that the Berlin Wall would stand for another one hundred years.

Even Honecker, however, worried that his capital might not put on a properly loyal face during the upcoming anniversary celebration, scheduled for October 6–7. Gorbachev would be the chief guest of honor, and there was reason to fear that his presence might ignite efforts to turn the birthday party into a riotous confrontation with the authorities. The SED chief could imagine a local version of Beijing's Tiananmen Square protests, which, in Honecker's view, the Chinese comrades had let go on for far too long before cracking down. To ensure that his capital remained tranquil during the anniversary celebration he brought in thousands of extra police and Stasi agents; army units were also moved into the city. East Berlin had never been short on signs of official vigilance, but now it resembled a high-security prison, with armed guards on every corner. Surveying the scene on the eve of the anniversary, G. Jonathan Greenwald, political counselor in the American embassy in East Berlin, observed: "There is a body politic odor of nervousness, uncertainty, even fear."

Gorbachev flew in on the morning of the sixth. In order to reduce the size and spontaneity of the welcome, his arrival and schedule were not announced. Only a few shouts of "Gorby! Gorby!" went up as his motorcade proceeded down Unter den Linden. At an official reception one man blurted out "Gorby, help us!", to which the Soviet leader reportedly replied, "Don't panic." Throughout the two-day affair, the police and Stasi managed to prevent significant disruptions, but this required a liberal use of force. In the late afternoon of October 7, about 400 young people gathered in the Alexanderplatz shouting "Gorbachev! Freedom!" When the crowd moved toward the Palace of the Republic, where the final reception was in progress, the police herded the marchers into side streets and made arrests by the score. On the night of October 8 hundreds of people gathered in the streets around the Gethsemane Church in Prenzlauer Berg. They waved pictures of Gorbachev and called for the dismantling of the Berlin Wall. The police closed off the area and attacked the demonstrators with clubs, which succeeded only in making the demonstrators more resolute. As one protester recalled: "I never knew how hard a billy-club was. And in that moment I thought, 'It's right for me to be here.'" For another demonstrator, the police behavior made what the regime called *Staatsfeindlichkeit*—being an enemy of the state—"not just a question of political temperament, but a matter of morality."

The authorities' ready use of force stood in stark contrast to the nonviolent tactics of the protesters. A visitor from West Berlin, an aging '68er, scoffed to Counselor Greenwald about the passivity and small size of the East Berlin demonstrations compared to the legendary anti-Shah riot in West Berlin in June 1967. What would the East Berlin "pigs" have done, the West Berliner wondered, if they had been faced with the large numbers and tough tactics that *his* generation had employed? Greenwald, who actually knew something about the East German authorities, was understandably irritated by such puffed-up naïveté. "These police are not like those you played against as students," he replied. "There is a chance for real change here, but if the old men feel their state's existence and their own power is at stake, there could be a bloodbath."

Gorbachev, the man whose name was so often invoked by the protesters, was careful throughout the fortieth anniversary celebration not to embarrass his hosts by openly upbraiding them for their lack of reforming zeal. Honecker was not so considerate in return. In a private meeting with the Soviet leader he reminded him that living standards in the USSR were lower than in the GDR. "Your problems are worse than ours," he insisted. Such talk could hardly have endeared Honecker to the Russian, and in a meeting with the Politbüro Gorbachev signaled his irritation by warning that "life punishes those who come too late." At least two Politbüro members, Egon Krenz and Günther Schabowski, got the impression that Gorbachev believed that Honecker ought to be ousted in the near future, a conclusion that they had already reached themselves.

Honecker's "punishment" for falling behind was not long in coming. The event that provided the immediate impetus for his ouster occurred not in East Berlin but in Leipzig, the old Saxon town that was becoming known as "the city of heroes." A mass demonstration of 50,000 marchers was announced for the night of October 9. Asked by his party colleagues how the regime should respond, Honecker provided no answer. He seemed irresolute, confused, and befuddled. Perhaps he believed that if he gave an order to shoot it would not be carried out. He certainly knew that the Soviets would not approve of a violent crackdown. In the end, he left the decision about how to handle the Leipzig situation to his defense minister, Heinz Keßler, and to the regional party bosses. When 50,000 Leipzigers set out on their march from the Nikolaikirche on the night of October 9, they had no idea how the authorities would react. Fearing the worst, Kurt Masur, the influential director of the Leipzig Gewandhaus Orchestra, urged both the marchers and the authorities to remain calm. As the march progressed, the police slowly melted back. There was no firing, no mass arrests. "We've won!" shouted the demonstrators. At this point, they did not realize how much they had won: their victory in the battle for Leipzig was a victory in the war for the future of Germany.

A week later Honecker was pushed from the position of power he had held for seventeen years. Having shown himself unable to contend effectively with any of the GDR's manifold problems—its sagging economy, emigration crisis, rebellious citizenry—he faced a hostile Politbüro at the group's meeting on October 17. His opponents had already laid the groundwork for his dismissal. When the SED veteran Willi Stoph proposed his removal from office, no one came to his defense. Egon Krenz, one of the key plotters against him, was appointed general secretary of the party in his place. For years Krenz had been known as Honecker's most loyal satrap. Now, by turning against the old man, he was acting just as Honecker had done in helping to bring down *his* patron, Walter Ulbricht, in 1971. But Honecker actually got the last laugh by sanctioning Krenz as his successor. This "Curse of the Pharaoh" undermined the new leader's effort to cast himself as a reformer, thereby guaranteeing that his tenure at the top would be very short indeed.

At the time of Honecker's fall no one could have known that the old Stalinist's proudest achievement, the Berlin Wall, would in effect go down with him. The three-week interregnum between the end of Honecker's reign and the fall of the

Wall was marked by escalating protest demonstrations against the new regime of Egon Krenz. The change in leadership obviously did not convince a large percentage of GDR citizens that the SED regime would introduce meaningful reforms without being compelled to do so. The largest demonstration to date occurred on November 4 at the Alexanderplatz in East Berlin. About 700,000 people crowded the vast square, brandishing hand-lettered signs with slogans like "Stay in the street and don't ease up!"; "Passports for everyone—a red card [soccer term for expulsion from the game] for the SED!" They heard speeches from representatives of a newly formed opposition group, Neues Forum, demanding a role in the political process. Jens Reich, a professor of molecular biology, appealed for "dialogue" with the government, though he cautioned that "Dialogue is not the main meal, only the appetizer." The writer Stefan Heym spoke excitedly of the fact that Germans were finally learning to "walk upright" after years of "clicking their heels" under the kaiser, the Nazis, and the SED. But walking upright, he added, was not enough; the German people had to learn to rule themselves. Members of the new government also spoke, trying their best to convince the people that significant changes were in the works. Markus Wolf, no longer wearing his mask of Stasi anonymity, delivered a short speech promising a cleanup of the domestic security forces. However, if the chorus of boos and catcalls was any indication, most people in the crowd considered a reformed Stasi a contradiction in terms.

For East Berlin the November 4 demonstration was a turning point. It suggested that the East German capital was finally coming into its own as a center of political protest and civic courage. Egon Krenz, the new East German leader, reaped the harvest of this popular awakening. With his set of big teeth and a mane of silver hair, he was widely caricatured in the suddenly iconoclastic East Berlin press as a Communist wolf disguised as Little Red Riding Hood's benevolent granny. He sought to gain support with promises of dialogue and a "market-oriented socialist planned economy," but no one, not even his SED colleagues, trusted him. The exiled singer Wolf Biermann described him aptly as "a walking invitation to flee the republic."

In fact, thousands of East Germans responded to the Krenz appointment by decamping to the West. On November 1, the day his government reopened the East German border with Czechoslovakia as a goodwill gesture, 23,000 people flooded out. Under pressure from the Czech government, the GDR embassy in Prague granted the refugees visas to travel on to the Federal Republic, which they promptly did. Word of this naturally got out, and within hours there was bumper-to-bumper Trabi traffic across Czechoslovakia to the Bavarian border. Irritated over this situation, Prague demanded that the GDR open its own borders with the FRG to free and unfettered travel. Unwilling to go this far, the Krenz government drafted new travel and visa regulations on November 6 that would allow citizens to leave the country for a month after getting approval by the state.

Smacking of desperation and bureaucratic foot-dragging, this measure was soundly rejected by the East German parliament, which, like the press, was suddenly determined to show its independence. In the wake of this unprecedented act of defiance, all the members of the Council of Ministers submitted their resignations, as did those of the Politbüro. During a chaotic meeting of the Central Committee on November 7, Krenz managed to retain his post as party boss, but Hans Modrow, one of Krenz's rivals, was named to the reconstituted Politbüro to keep an eye on him. Part of Modrow's attraction was that he was not part of the Berlin establishment. As head of the SED in Dresden, he had often stood up for that city against demands from East Berlin. For example, he had refused to send money and materials to the capital for its lavish 750th anniversary celebration. His stance won him the admiration of all the provincial politicians who secretly bristled at having to take their marching orders from the capital.

Reshuffling the government did nothing to stop the mass exodus, and on the morning of November 9 the regime came up with yet another set of travel regulations, which, by allowing folks to leave the country temporarily, was supposed to keep them from leaving for good. The new draft regulations stated that GDR citizens with valid passports could exit the country across *any* border, including that in Berlin. This concession was not quite as daring as it looked, however, because only about 4 million GDR citizens held passports, and it would probably take months for those who did not have passports to secure them. Nonetheless, the inclusion of Berlin among the borders to be opened was a momentous step. It would reduce the Berlin Wall from the world's most famous political barrier to little more than a speed bump on the route from East to West.

That evening Günter Schabowski held a press conference to discuss the government's program. The conference was televised live by GDR television, which in itself was unprecedented. Schabowski was a little unsure on the details of the new travel law because he had not been present at the meeting during which the plan was drafted. In the event, he said nothing about the impending changes until the session was almost over. Then, in response to a question from an Italian journalist about previous "failures" in government travel regulations, he announced, as if he were discussing some minor bureaucratic adjustment, that henceforth it would be possible for *every citizen* of the GDR to exit and reenter the country over *any* of its border crossings. When asked when this would take effect, he said "*ab sofort*" (immediately)." Did this new arrangement include East Berlin's border with West Berlin? he was asked. Looking at his notes, Schabowski replied: "Exits can occur at all GDR/BRD border crossings, including Berlin-West."

The Krenz regime had not intended for the new law to take effect *immediately*, but once Schabowski had announced this version of the regulations live to the world there was no way to reattach the original restrictions. In any case, it was extremely fitting that the new order was allowed to take effect on November 9, since it was on this date, seventy-one years before, that Philipp Scheidemann had peremptorily announced the kaiser's abdication from a window in the Reichstag. He had done so in order to prevent an even more radical alternative, namely the Communist-oriented republic envisaged by the Spartacists around Karl Liebknecht. Scheidemann and his SPD colleagues had proven incapable of controlling the torrent of events that soon swept over the fledgling Weimar Republic. The same fate would befall Schabowski and the new GDR rulers as they struggled desperately to keep their state afloat.

No sooner had Schabowski ended his press conference than East Berliners began streaming to the Wall. Guards at the various crossings suddenly found themselves besieged with demands that they throw open the gates: after all, the authorities had officially pronounced the border open. The guards, who knew nothing of the new order, naturally kept the barriers down. Exasperated, people began chanting "Open the Gate! The Wall must go!" Finally, at a little after 8:00 P.M., the command came to allow people to pass through the Wall. The gate at Bornholmer Strasse was the first to swing open, followed by those at Sonnenallee and Invalidenstrasse. Thousands surged through, some in their nightshirts. Many carried large plastic bags, as if off on a shopping spree. When the automobile-crossing at Checkpoint Charlie opened, a long line of Trabis rumbled West, honking and belching smoke. What those enthusiastic travelers did not realize was that the stamp they received on their documents that night meant that they had been *ausgebürgert* (denaturalized); had not subsequent developments been so dramatic, GDR citizens intending only to visit West Berlin (the majority of this group) might not have been allowed to return home.

On the other side of the Wall thousands of West Berliners were waiting, their arms laden with flowers, bottles of champagne, and toys for the kids. They greeted the easterners with hugs, kisses, and whacks on the back. They drummed on the roofs of the Trabis and thrust bottles of beer in the windows. When a bus advertising "Gorbachev Vodka" came in view, a huge cheer went up. Asked by reporters what they thought about this turn of events, virtually everyone shouted "Wahnsinn (crazy)." This was an understandable reaction, but, as Peter Schneider has noted, what was really crazy about this situation was not the opportunity to walk from one part of the city to another, but the impossibility of doing that simple thing for the past twenty-eight years.

The party next to the Wall soon turned into a party *on* the Wall, as hundreds of people scaled the barrier at the Brandenburg Gate and began dancing on the top. This was no mean feat, considering the narrowness of the space and the dancers' rather less than sober condition. Some folks celebrated by chipping away at the Wall with hammers, a gesture that would soon evolve into the lucrative business of selling "Pieces of the Wall" (or of any old cement structure that happened to be handy) to tourists. On that heady evening few revelers were inclined to ask themselves how the world's most formidable political barrier could have been transformed, in a matter of hours, into the world's most exuberant dance stage. We now know that the GDR regime had actually been thinking about bringing down the Wall earlier as a way of staying afloat economically. In light of the GDR's dire financial condition, a planning committee had proposed on October 24, 1989, to open the Berlin border in exchange for credits from Bonn. Krenz ultimately vetoed this idea, but the fact that it was seriously mooted points up the desperate straits of the regime. When we realize that the Berlin Wall had almost gone up for sale in the weeks prior to its fall, the events of November 9 seem a little more explicable, as does the fate of the GDR in the wake of Wall's demise.

Reunification

Just as the construction of the Berlin Wall in August 1961 had thrust the erstwhile German capital to the center of the world stage, so the Wall's fall in November 1989 focused all eyes on the divided city. Western news agencies rushed their top reporters to the Spree metropolis so that they might report "live from the Brandenburg Gate" on the collapse of the most important symbol of the Cold War. With the press rushing in, the politicians could not be far behind. West Berlin's mayor Walter Momper hastily organized a fete at the John-F.-Kennedy-Platz on November 10. The West Berlin CDU scheduled a rival ceremony for that same evening at the Gedächtniskirche. An infamous symbol of political division might be coming down, but the spirit of partisanship in West Berlin was alive and well.

Helmut Kohl was on a state visit to Poland when the Berlin Wall was breached. Recalling how Adenauer had lost favor with the West German electorate by remaining in Bonn when the Wall went up, Kohl decided to interrupt his Polish visit and fly to Berlin. Given the continuing Allied ban on West German flights into West Berlin and over GDR territory, this turned out to be something of an odyssey. Kohl's Bundeswehr plane had to fly over Sweden to Hamburg, where the chancellor boarded an American Air Force plane to fly on to Berlin. He did not arrive until the Kennedyplatz ceremony was well underway. When he finally got a chance to speak, he was shouted down by the largely pro-SPD crowd. Rowdy demonstrators also disrupted his speech that evening at the Gedächtniskirche. In the eyes of many leftist West Berliners, Kohl was an interloper bent on crashing their party for his own political purposes.

Former West Berlin mayor Willy Brandt, whose appearance at the Kennedyplatz ignited the wildest enthusiasm in that square since JFK's own visit in 1963, used this occasion to urge Berliners to regard their embrace at the Wall as the beginning of a larger reunion. "The fact that Berliners, and Germans in general, belong together manifests itself in a way that moves us and stirs us up," he shouted. "A great deal will now depend on whether we—we Germans on both sides—prove to be equal to this historical situation. . . . What is important is that [the Germans] develop a different relationship to one another, that they can meet in freedom and grow with one another." Mayor Momper, on the other hand, sounded a note of caution regarding the process of "growing together." Noting that many people were still fleeing the GDR, he entreated the East Germans "to consider whether they cannot now, after all, have more faith in the process of renewal and the process of reform in the GDR, whether they are not needed in the democratic awakening of the GDR. . . . Our desire is for the democratic movement in the GDR to run its own country, the second German state, as it sees fit. We Berliners support the reform process in the GDR with a passion and with solidarity."

Brandt's vision, not Momper's, prevailed. Pious hopes for a successful renewal of "the second German state" could not save the GDR. If Germany's first unification, as Bismarck famously stated, was forged by "blood and iron," its second union was forced by the implosion of its eastern half. In November 1989 over 130,000 East Germans, or almost 1 percent of the population of the GDR, moved west. Even those who remained showed little faith in the capacity of their state to create genuine democracy or prosperity. Nothing short of union with the West would do. Having earlier cried "Wir sind das Volk (We are the people)," they now cried "Wir sind ein Volk (We are one people)."

The SED government now sought desperately to save itself, and the GDR state, with an eleventh-hour makeover. A new cabinet under Hans Modrow, who took over as prime minister on November 13 (Krenz stayed on as general secretary), promised free elections in the near future. The "bloc parties," previously little more than fig leaves for one-party rule, were given the green light to function independently. The People's Parliament, using secret ballots for the first time, expelled Honecker and Mielke from its ranks. As he took his exit, the old Stasi boss had the bad grace to assure the East German people that he still "loved" them. Members of the new regime embarked on Round Table negotiations with dissident groups like New Forum and Democracy Now regarding the impending new order. They and the reformers talked enthusiastically about navigating a "third way" between communism and capitalism. These discussions, however, failed to generate much excitement among ordinary East Germans. Having seen the glitter of the capitalist West, many associated socialism as such with economic backwardness. "The third way," people joked, "is the way to the Third World."

The prospect of One German *Volk* was not uniformly welcomed by the powers that had defeated Germany in 1945 and presided over its division. After all, as the British historian Hugh Trevor-Roper had noted in June 1989, the "delicate balance of Europe" was based precisely on that division. British prime minister Margaret Thatcher reportedly observed the events in Germany with great "unease." She worried that a united Germany would be "much too large and powerful" for its own good, and, more importantly, for the good of its neighbors. French president François Mitterrand was equally discomforted by the thought of a united Germany. His stance reflected France's traditional distrust of its eastern neighbor, a wariness best summed up in François Mauriac's famous aperçu that the French loved Germany so much that they were glad there were two of them. Following the Wall's collapse, Mitterrand did all he could to thwart or delay the drive for German unification. He warned Foreign Minister Genscher that German unity might plunge Europe into a chaotic maelstrom reminiscent of 1913/14. In December 1989 he visited Moscow to enlist Gorbachev's help in keeping the Germans in their place. Gorbachev needed no French prodding: as soon as the Berlin Wall was breached he urged Chancellor Kohl not to do anything that might undercut the GDR government's efforts to stay alive through reforms and economic renewal. This process would take "much time," he cautioned.

Among the major foreign leaders whom Kohl consulted at that moment, only American president George Bush proved unambiguously positive about the developments in Germany. Like most Americans, he did not harbor that deep distrust of Germany that was second nature to many Western Europeans, Russians, and Poles. As he later wrote in his memoir, *A World Transformed*: "I was, of course, mindful of Germany's history of aggression, but I knew the country had done a lot to live down its Nazi past, to compensate for the horrors it had inflicted on Jews and others across Europe. . . . I did not believe that all present-day Germans should have to pay forever for what some of their countrymen had done in the past." Bush saw immediately that German unification might bring a strategic advantage to the West, namely, a shift of NATO's operational area significantly closer to the Soviet Union. When Kohl called him right after the Wall came down, Bush wished him "much luck and God's blessing."

Kohl knew that he would need all the luck he could get in the coming months. He was worried that unification might be hard to control given the "hereditary burden" with which the SED had saddled East Germany. He suggested privately that Germany would be best off if unification did not come until the end of the century. At the same time, however, he believed that certain intermediary steps might be initiated toward a kind of quasi unification. Taking up a proposal from Modrow for a "contractual community" between the two Germanys, Kohl put before the Bundestag on November 28 a Ten-Point Program calling for "confederative structures between the two states in Germany with a view to creating a federation." This step, his program stipulated, should be taken only after a democratic government had been freely elected in the GDR. Point Ten of the program looked toward German unification, but the timing was left vague: "With this comprehensive policy we are working for a state of peace in Europe in which the German nation can recover its unity in free self-determination. Reunification—that is regaining national unity—remains the political goal of the Federal government."

Its cautious language notwithstanding, Kohl's Ten-Point Program caused a tremendous sensation. Most of Germany's partners thought that the chancellor was moving much too fast. Thatcher and Mitterrand were apoplectic. German unification, announced the Iron Lady, was "not on the agenda." Gorbachev, who had just accused America's ambassador to Bonn of "acting like a German gauleiter" for having openly embraced German unification, now told a group of Russian students: "There are two German states. History saw to that. And this fact is generally accepted by the world community. . . . That is the reality, and we must work on the basis of that reality. . . . I do not think that the question of the reunification of these states is currently a pressing political question." President Bush, once again, did not echo the naysayers. Determined to bolster Kohl's position, he professed himself quite satisfied with the latter's initiative. "I feel comfortable," he told the chancellor. "I think we're on track."

For a growing number of East Germans, meanwhile, unification could not come too soon. They knew their state was bankrupt, and with the ongoing exodus conditions for those who remained were only getting worse. Now even basic foods were in short supply. For the easterners who considered rapid unity as the only way out, Chancellor Kohl, whom they began to call "our Helmut," emerged as a possible savior, a messiah wrapped in the West German flag. Their task was to convince Kohl that the time for unity was *now*, not ten years hence.

Pro-unification East Germans got their chance to deliver this message when Kohl paid a state visit to Prime Minister Modrow in Dresden on December 19, 1989. Huge crowds waving West German flags greeted the chancellor's plane at the airport. The people made a point of ignoring Modrow and cheering Kohl. For the chancellor, this reception was a revelation. As he later wrote, he now knew that "the GDR was at an end" and that unity had to come soon. He decided to deliver a major address on the German question in a place that could accommodate the thousands of East Germans who were descending on the Saxon capital. He chose the square in front of the bombed-out Frauenkirche, an appropriate selection given East German Protestantism's prominent role in the opposition. Thinking about his speech, he decided to avoid "nationalistic" bombast, for he worried that with any encouragement his audience might break out in a rousing chorus of "Deutschland, Deutschland über Alles." Once he stood before the sea of chanting people, however, he could not suppress an element of nationalist pathos. After extending greetings "from all your fellow citizens in the Federal Republic," he declared: "My goal remains, when the historical hour allows it, the unity of our nation. I know that we can reach this goal when we work toward it together." Later, with the thunderous chants still ringing in his ears, Kohl said to an aide: "I think that we'll achieve unity. It's coming. The people want it, it can't be stopped. This [GDR] regime is definitely at an end."

On December 22 Kohl struck another blow for German unity by presiding, along with Modrow and the mayors of West and East Berlin, over the official opening of the Brandenburg Gate to pedestrian traffic. Kohl had never before set foot in East Berlin. He had once tried to enter via Friedrichstrasse, only to be turned away as "unwanted." Now, as he stood at the historic gate, he declared that he would do all he could to promote German unity. He and Modrow each released a white dove while church bells rang, an orchestra with players from both east and west played Beethoven's Ninth, and East Germans waved GDR flags with holes cut in the middle where the state emblem had been. West Berlin mayor Walter Momper, now reconciled to rapid unification, declared: "Berlin is still divided, but the people are no longer separated and the city has regained its old symbol." A week later, on New Year's Eve, that august symbol was transformed into a giant jungle gym as hundreds of Berlin youths clamored up its sides and partied on the top, doing serious damage to the quadriga.

Although Kohl was well received in Berlin when he helped to open the Brandenburg Gate, the Spree city was not in the front rank of the rush to German unity. Ordinary Berliners on both sides of the now-derelict Wall were certainly excited over the prospect of unity, but the city's opinion-makers were often blasé or even hostile toward the project. It became fashionable among the leftist intelligentsia of West Berlin to condemn the easterners' longing for unification as a lamentable submission to the lure of Western materialism. Aware that the lowly banana was a symbol in the East of capitalist plenitude, West Berlin students brought bundles of the fruit to the Wall and threw them at easterners coming across to shop. Not having had to live under "real, existing socialism" themselves, the Western leftists were unhesitant to advise easterners to be content with their "purer" social system. Other Western intellectuals, taking a rather less condescending tack, rejected unification on the grounds that Germany, given its criminal past, did not deserve to be a single nation. A united Germany, it was claimed, would inevitably pose a danger to its neighbors. As Günter Grass put it in a *New York Times* piece on January 7, 1990:

> Our neighbors watch with anxiety, even with alarm, as Germans recklessly talk themselves into the will to unity. . . . There can be no demand for a new version of a unified nation that in the course of barely 75 years, though under several managements, filled the history books, ours and theirs, with suffering, rubble, defeat, millions of refugees, millions of dead, and the burden of crimes that can never be undone.

Elsewhere, Grass insisted that Germany's neighbors had every right to react negatively, "even hysterically," to the prospect of German unification, because "if we think about Germany and the German future, we have to think about Auschwitz."

In East Berlin, meanwhile, supporters of the SED regime, who had always constituted a significant force in the East German capital, strongly denounced the push toward unification. On December 19, 1989, 50,000 party members demonstrated for "a sovereign GDR, against reunification and a sellout" of their country. Two weeks later, on January 4, 1990, SED supporters and various pro-government groups marched to the Soviet War Memorial in Treptow Park, where they heard party leader Gregor Gysi denounce unification as a nefarious plot aimed at "ruining the chance for democratic socialism in the GDR." SED members, of course, had a personal stake in the GDR's survival, but in East Berlin it was not only they who opposed unification. Many reformist intellectuals (like some of their counterparts in the West) believed that socialism was morally superior to capitalism. In an interview, Stefan Heym insisted that the continued existence of a socialist state in Germany was "absolutely necessary for the socialist development in the whole world." The GDR now faced a crisis, he said, because its citizens had become fed up with the miserable conditions brought on by an inept leadership. However, it was not socialism per se that had "fallen on its face," but the form of Stalinism perfected by the GDR leaders. "The other, better form, in whose name so many courageous people have set down their ideas and laid down their lives, is still to come," he claimed. Contemplating the implications of reunification, a young East Berlin intellectual protested: "Go away, go away, leave my Wall where it is. . . . My God, what will happen if the West Germans come here to renovate and beautify everything, to put geraniums in the windows? Where am I supposed to go then? . . . It is so ugly, our Alex . . . , but it is *our Berlin*. . . . It would be so beautiful, an East Germany independent and democratic." Right after the Wall was breached, Robert Darnton, an American historian on sabbatical in Berlin, spoke with East Berlin intellectuals who were deeply worried about the new order of things. One of them advised: "Don't tear down the Wall. We need it as an intellectual barrier. It should be permeable, but it should stay up. One of the great mistakes in Berlin history was to tear down the customs wall in which the Brandenburg Gate was embedded in 1867. After that the tragedies of the modern age began."

A few years later, when the difficulties and dislocations of reunification had become painfully apparent, thousands of East Germans would find reasons to wax sentimental about the "good old GDR." There was a wave of nostalgia for things East German, from liberal abortion policies and secure jobs to the lowly Trabant, which became the chief symbol of a lost way of life. (Many West Berliners, for their part, would become just as nostalgic for their lost "isle of the blessed," where they had lived happily without having to worry too much about money, careers, or what was going on in the rest of the world. Even pre-1989 Kreuzberg fell under a haze of dewy-eyed commentary as the denizens of West Berlin's most famous alternative *Szene* recalled how wonderful life had been before the fall of the Wall.)

The orgy of nostalgia for the old East, however, was still a thing of the future in the early months of 1990, when whatever sympathy the GDR regime might have enjoyed was rapidly slipping away. Popular hostility toward the state focused on the Stasi, which Prime Minister Modrow unwisely tried to retain in a reformed and trimmed-down version. On January 12 he bowed to popular pressure and agreed to dissolve the organization, but the concession came too late. Three days later a mob stormed the Stasi headquarters in Normannenstrasse, smashing doors, trashing offices, and pitching furniture out windows. Taking advantage of the chaos, Stasi agents spirited some sensitive files out of the building by posing as demonstrators. Modrow rushed to the scene and appealed for order, but he was ignored; only when representatives of the new dissident factions posted guards at the doors was a measure of calm restored. The fall of East Berlin's Bastille proved to be a major milestone on the road—one is tempted to say the Autobahn—to East Germany's collapse.

Desperate for credibility with the citizenry, the SED now changed its name to Partei des demokratischen Sozialismus (Party of Democratic Socialism—PDS). The party's young and media-savvy leader, Gregor Gysi, offered a new face as well. But altered initials and a fresher look did not really add up to a new and more credible party. In its efforts to halt unification, moreover, the PDS could no longer count on help from Moscow, because by the beginning of 1990 the Soviets had reluctantly come to the conclusion that German unity was inevitable. Their primary goal now was to exert some influence on the unification process and, if possible, to profit from it. At the very least, they hoped to keep a united Germany out of NATO. If they could do this, the Atlantic alliance's eastern border would actually be shifted *farther* away from Moscow. The Soviets' new line on German unity was confirmed by Gorbachev on February 10, 1990, during a visit by Chancellor Kohl to Moscow. "Between the Soviet Union, the FRG, and the GDR, there are no differences of opinion about reunification and the people's right to strive for it," Gorbachev announced. Of course this was not quite correct, at least with respect to the GDR, but since when did the GDR have the right to define its own destiny?

Against a backdrop of economic implosion, erosion of public authority, and continuing depopulation (another 50,000 East Germans checked out in January), Prime Minister Modrow decided to move up the promised free elections to March 1990; that way, there might still be somebody around to vote. The main bloc parties—CDU, SPD, and FDP (Freie Demokratische Partei or Free Democratic Party)—entered the race with financial and logistical support from the West. The PDS, unlike the old SED, could no longer control the process from beginning to end. This meant that the end, for the first time in GDR history, was not predetermined.

The most aggressive campaigner turned out to be Helmut Kohl. Determined to achieve a victory for the East-CDU, which would amount to a victory for unification, Kohl stumped the GDR, promising "blooming landscapes" and "prosperity for all." Later, when things did not pan out as he had promised, he was accused of deliberately hoodwinking the credulous East Germans. It is more likely, however, that he was swept up in the euphoria of the moment. Interestingly, not one of his six campaign swings through East Germany included East Berlin. The East-SPD also campaigned hard, bringing in big guns from the West like Willy Brandt, Hans-Jochen Vogel, and Oskar Lafontaine. Unlike Kohl, they spent a great deal of time in East Berlin, the old SPD *Hochburg*. The Socialists were hindered, however, by divisions on the unity question: Brandt passionately favored it; Lafontaine did not.

When the East Germans went to the polls on March 18 they had an amazing twenty-four parties to choose from, ranging from the PDS on the left to the Kohl-backed "Alliance for Germany" on the right. There was even a Beer Drinkers' Union, which promised to protect eastern Germany's beer culture against imports from the West. The results of the voting confounded the pundits, most of whom had predicted an SPD win. Instead, the Alliance for Germany came out on top, winning almost an absolute majority. Obviously, many voters bought Kohl's promise of better times, expecting him, as one CDU partisan put it, "to help us quickly out of our mess." Apart from the SPD, the big losers were the small reform parties that had done so much to make this election possible; the Bündnis 90, for example, garnered only 2.9 percent of the vote. Bärbel Bohley, one of that party's candidates, complained bitterly that her countrymen had passed up the chance to create something new, opting instead for "money and bananas."

East Berlin did not contribute significantly to the victory for Kohl. The Alliance for Germany won only 21.6 percent of the vote there, compared to 35 percent for the SPD and 30 percent for the PDS. These results reflected the strength of the Communist establishment and the old socialist movement in the eastern half of the Spree metropolis. For pro-unity East Germans in other parts of the country, the vote in East Berlin confirmed their image of the GDR capital as a pampered, parasitic town, whose fat-bottomed *Bonzen* put their own interest above that of ordinary people and the nation as a whole.

The March 1990 election brought the beleaguered GDR yet another new government: a "grand coalition" of the CDU and SPD under the leadership of the East-CDU chief Lothar de Maizière. A descendant of the French Huguenots who had emigrated to Berlin in the late seventeenth century, de Maizière had stayed clear of entanglements with the former Communist rulers—or so people thought at the time—and seemed to be the right man to lead the GDR safely and smoothly into oblivion. Upon taking office he promised the "rapid and responsible realization of German unity after negotiations with the FRG under Article 23" of the *Grundgesetz* (basic law). This article allowed for the direct integration of the five states of the GDR into the FRG. Alluding to Hitler's incorporation of Austria into the Reich in 1938, as well as to the recorded message one hears in Germany indicating an out-of-service phone number, GDR patriots said of Article 23: "No *Anschluss* under this number."

But unification was coming, and another important step toward it occurred on July 1, 1990, when the East German currency gave way to the mighty D-mark. Bärbel Bohley's complaint that the March elections had been about money was not without validity: East Germans had become as contemptuous of their impotent ostmarks as they were of their flag; they wanted the D-mark, and they wanted it fast. Kohl realized that bringing Western currency to the GDR would signal a commitment to the East, just as importing D-marks to West Berlin in 1948 had shown a determination to save the city. Kohl also hoped that a change in currency would slow the East German exodus to the West. "If we don't want the people to come to the D-Mark," he said, "the D-Mark has to go the people." On February 6 he announced his intention of exploring a "currency union" with the GDR. The main question concerned the value at which the eastern currency should be converted. At the outset of the discussions, Federal Bank president Karl Otto Pöhl warned Kohl not to use currency as a lever for national unity. True politician that he was, however, the chancellor responded that "we should not approach this historic decision with a mercenary mind." As usual, Kohl prevailed. On July 1, 1990, the GDR got the D-mark, and the conversion rate was one to one.

A new Deutsche Bank outlet on the Alexanderplatz opened its doors at 12:00 noon, launching the alchemic process of converting Eastern lead to Western gold. To celebrate this "initial step toward unity," the bank manager gave the first customer through the door a bottle of champagne and a one hundred D-mark savings account. Flush with their new money, East Berliners talked excitedly about how they would spend it. Some planned elaborate vacation trips. Others thought in more modest terms: "Eating decently, visiting a disco or whorehouse, that's all possible now," enthused one man. Inevitably, there was a run on used Mercedeses—and, just as inevitably—a rash of accidents involving drivers unused to vehicles that actually accelerated when one stepped on the gas.

Amidst all the excitement, few realized that the monetary union might bring long-term challenges as well as instant rewards. Shoddy and unsophisticated eastern products, now priced in D-marks, could no longer compete with Western imports. Even domestically produced food was affected, as eastern shoppers suddenly turned up their noses at local cherries and apples in favor of fruit flown in from Washington State. Many companies had difficulty meeting their debt obligations and payrolls in the new currency; it was one thing to retain marginally productive workers when they were paid in ostmarks, quite another to do so when the wages were in D-marks. The GDR's Eastern European trading partners reduced imports from East Germany because the goods were now overpriced. It may indeed have been necessary to bring the D-mark east, but doing so at a parity of one to one turned out to be a crucial mistake.

While ostmarks disappeared into mine shafts, to join the Reichsmarks abandoned there in 1948, the Berlin Wall—that is, most of what was left of it after the *Mauerspechte* (Wall-peckers) had had their way with it—was dismantled by cranes.

"Wall-peckers" at work on the Berlin Wall, November 1989

Eighty-one colorful sections were sold at an auction in Monte Carlo in 1990; some of them fetched as much as 40,000 marks. Most of the rest were ground up for paving material. A block was presented to former President Ronald Reagan, who just three years before had urged Gorbachev to tear the structure down. Belatedly realizing that the Wall had value as an historical artifact, not to mention as a tourist attraction, city officials earmarked a 212-meter-long section at Bernauer Strasse for preservation. To protect it from the voracious peckers, a wire fence was built around it. The decision to create a permanent memorial there "to the victims of the German division" was delayed for a time because of resistance from the Church of St. Sophia, whose cemetery lay next to the Wall. The memorial that was ultimately installed, a dazzlingly clean section of concrete bordered by two bronze slabs, bears little resemblance to the original barrier. Aware of this deficiency, the city government under Eberhard Diepgen toyed with the idea of reconstructing a section of the "border defense system" in all its former horror—a kind of Disneyland of the Cold War.

As the Wall came down, so did all the additional trappings of the former border regime: watchtowers, guardhouses, dog-runs, light stanchions, and signal systems. The guards' hut at Checkpoint Charlie was removed in a special ceremony on June 22, 1990. British foreign secretary Douglas Hurd took this occasion to declare that, "at long last, we are bringing Charlie in from the cold."

The Checkpoint Charlie hut, which eventually went to a museum, proved easier to relocate than the thousands of guard dogs that had once patrolled the Berlin Wall and the inner-German border. After months of negotiation between East German officials and representatives of the West German Animal Protection Association, it was agreed that 2,500 former guard dogs would be sent to new homes in the West. News of this decision provoked howls of protest in the West German media, which warned that dogs raised under Stalinism would be unable to adjust to peaceable conditions in the West. Undoubtedly they would treat the mailman like a would-be escapee. The West German Shepherd Dogs Association, meanwhile, worried that a flood of East German *Schäferhunde* on the Western market would force down the price for locally bred dogs. East Germans were outraged over these complaints, insisting that their dogs were just as civilized as Western dogs. They agonized over stories that some of the dogs shipped to the West were being purchased by pimps looking for "killer beasts," or by New Yorkers who wanted trophy animals for their Fifth Avenue apartments, or, much worse, by Asians who regarded the pups as dinner items. The Wall dogs, East Germans said, were "the last victims of Stalinism."

Other signs of the changing times in the summer and fall of 1990 included the elimination of the restricted air corridors into Berlin and the dismantling of the American listening posts along the inner-German border. It is significant that these measures were undertaken by the Western powers, for it was they, and their former Russian allies, who had the final say on the question of German unification and the status of Berlin. The Germans could take some important steps toward unity on their own, but they could not become a fully sovereign and unified state without the acquiescence of the powers that had defeated them in 1945.

In February 1990 the powers agreed to a mechanism for negotiating the unity question: the "Two Plus Four Talks," involving the two Germanys along with the

Rotes Rathaus (Red City Hall), the seat of government for Greater Berlin

Americans, British, French, and Soviets. It soon became apparent that Britain and France were coming around to an acceptance of German unification, a development for which Helmut Kohl deserves most of the credit. To gain French approval, Kohl promised to push for a single European currency, a pet idea of Mitterrand's. At every opportunity the chancellor stressed the idea that German unification would be accompanied by—and be cocooned in—greater European unity. Just as West Germany had rearmed in the mid-1950s as an integral part of NATO and the Western European Union, so the two Germanys would now come together "in Europe's name."

The major question still to be resolved concerned Germany's place within the international security framework. Would a united Germany join NATO, declare its neutrality, or take some other course? Washington and Bonn insisted that unified Germany be a member of NATO, just as West Germany had been. The Soviets, as was noted above, hoped to keep Germany out of the Atlantic Alliance, preferring that the new nation assume a stance of neutrality. If this proved impossible, Russia was willing to countenance Germany's membership in *both* NATO *and* the Warsaw Pact, a very odd proposition.

Washington took the lead in pressuring Moscow to accept the NATO solution. When Gorbachev visited America for a summit meeting in late May 1990, Bush stressed to him that NATO would be a stabilizing force for the Germans, that it would help keep them in check. The Russian president countered with Moscow's dual alliance option, insisting that "if one anchor is good, two anchors are better." As an accomplished sailor, Bush knew something about anchors, and he also knew how to change tack. Aware that Gorbachev had often employed the rhetoric of national self-determination, he now asked his counterpart if he agreed that nations had the right to choose which alliances they might belong to, and, if so, whether Germany also had this right. To his astonishment, Gorbachev said yes, he agreed. Recognizing the significance of this agreement, Gorbachev's aides tried to get him to take it back. They did not understand that their president had already given up on the hope of keeping Germany out of NATO and was concerned now to extract rewards for his compliance in the form of loans and more favorable trade arrangements. True, the Soviets would have to pull their troops out of East Germany and Berlin, but Gorbachev hoped to receive compensation for that as well.

The final details of the unification package were worked out in various diplomatic meetings over the course of the next few weeks. Crucially, Bonn promised that after German reunification it would confirm the sanctity of the Oder-Neisse border with Poland, a guarantee that Kohl had hitherto avoided making for fear of alienating right-wing voters in the Federal Republic. Throughout these final negotiations, the East German delegation had little impact: the talks should have been called "One-plus-Four." A key moment came during a visit by Kohl to Gorbachev's home turf in the Caucasus Mountains in July. Moscow was insisting that Bonn pay for the withdrawal of Soviet troops from East Germany and Berlin and their relocation in the Soviet Union. The Germans had offered DM 8 billion, but Gorbachev wanted more, and threatened to sabotage German reunification if Moscow was rebuffed. In their Caucasus meeting the two men agreed on a figure of DM 12 million, combined with a credit of DM 3 billion. The Soviets would have four years in which to withdraw their troops, during which time no NATO troops could be stationed on former East German territory. The Western powers could keep their troops in West Berlin until the Soviets had fully withdrawn. Germany's own army, the Bundeswehr, would be reduced from about 400,000 men to 370,000. Kohl was

Oskar Lafontaine, Willy Brandt, Hans-Dietrich Genscher, Helmut Kohl, and Richard von Weizsäcker attending the German reunification ceremony at the Reichstag, October 3, 1990

understandably jubilant over this outcome: German unity was a done deal, and the price had not been exorbitant.

The final agreement on German unification was signed by the Two-Plus-Four foreign ministers at a ceremony in Moscow on September 12, 1990. With this gesture, the World War II victors gave up the rights over Germany that they had assumed in the Berlin Declaration of June 5, 1945, and the Potsdam Agreement of August 2, 1945. At long last, World War II was officially over. Agreement on Germany also signaled an unofficial end to the Cold War. At the signing ceremony, Soviet foreign minister Eduard Shevardnadze declared that there were no winners or losers in this settlement, but in truth this was a clear victory for the West and for a Western-oriented Germany. Another winner was Berlin, which of course had always been one of the main victims of the German division.

The Two-Plus-Four Treaty took effect on October 3, 1990, which Germany henceforth celebrated as its "Day of Unity." Significantly, the main ceremony was held in Berlin, Germany's once (and, as it would turn out, future) capital. The occasion was marked by restraint rather than hubris—a far cry from the triumphal scene in Versailles in 1871. Speakers at a gathering in the Philharmonie promised that a new Germany would not mean a new German nationalism. The official declaration of unity was issued at midnight at the Reichstag, a fitting choice given that building's weighty symbolism.

On December 2, 1990, Berliners elected the first unified city council since 1946. The results called into question the degree to which the city was really unified. The CDU won 47.8 percent of the vote in the west but only 24.3 percent in the east, giving it an overall total of 40.4. By contrast, the PDS garnered 24.8 percent in the east and a measly 1.3 percent in the west. Because of the PDS's strong showing in the east, the SPD did not win enough there to overcome the CDU's dominance in the more populous west; its overall total was 30.4. West Berlin Mayor Walter Momper (SPD), who had fervently hoped to become reunified Berlin's first chief executive, had to step aside for the CDU leader Eberhard Diepgen. As he took office, Diepgen promised a bright future for Berlin, but the stark division revealed by the electoral result constituted a danger sign. The new mayor also faced the difficult task of convincing Bonn to retain Berlin's generous federal subsidies now that the city was no longer a lonely outpost of Western democracy. As Momper put the matter: "Now he [Diepgen] has to bring us the bacon from Bonn, or he won't be able to fulfill the people's expectations."

Capital Question

The most contentious domestic issue raised by the unification of Germany involved the location of the new nation's seat of government. Should the principal power base remain in Bonn or move to Berlin? Berlin had always been the national capital *in principle*—Bonn being just a stand-in pending reunification—but, as everyone knew, the real capital was where the government was. Technically, the seat-of-government/capital question should not have come up at all, for according to an early parliamentary resolution governmental power was supposed to return to Berlin once political conditions permitted. A Bundestag resolution of November 3, 1949, which confirmed Bonn as West Germany's provisional capital, declared: "The leading organs of government will shift their seat of operations to the capital of Germany, Berlin, as soon as free, equal, and direct elections are held throughout Berlin and in the Soviet Occupation Zone." Throughout the period of division, leading West

German politicians paid lip service to this goal of "returning to Berlin." The fact of the matter, however, was that many West Germans had become content with Bonn as their seat of government and had no desire to see Berlin retrieve its earlier status. Bonn had brought safety and prosperity, they said; Berlin as national capital had brought nothing but war and misery. The "Bonner" were quite prepared to ignore the Bundestag's Berlin resolutions, or, if necessary, to pass a new law enshrining the Rhine city as united Germany's permanent capital. The pro-Berlin faction had most East Germans on its side, but the citizens of the "new states" had relatively little clout in the new Germany. If Berlin was indeed to become united Germany's principal power base, its partisans would have to triumph once again over a host of resentments and negative images attached to the Spree metropolis.

The debate over Bonn versus Berlin commenced shortly after the Wall came down and reached a dramatic climax in a historic Bundestag vote in the summer of 1991. Because the issue was seen as crucial to the nature and direction of the new nation, it galvanized the entire populace, becoming fodder for heated discussions in living rooms, university lecture halls, factory cafeterias, and newspapers across the country. Noted scholars did their best to put the matter in historical perspective. Advocates on both sides battled for the moral high ground, sometimes concealing lower motives such as economic interest and political advantage. (Pro-Bonn parliamentarians, for example, tended not to mention that their personal property holdings would probably lose value if the government moved to Berlin.) Although the debate had a partisan aspect from the beginning, the major parties ultimately split along regional and internal ideological lines. Old allies parted ways and new combinations emerged among some of the strangest political bedfellows in modern German history.

The Bonner had the initial advantage owing to inertia, geographical strengths, and the nature of German unification. The unification process, after all, had involved the absorption of East Germany into the Federal Republic. Did it not make sense then to keep the principal seat of government in Bonn, which, in contrast to the defunct GDR's former capital, continued to function as a center of power? Given all the challenges that the new nation faced just in pulling itself together, was it prudent to add the additional challenge of moving the seat of government? Unification was likely to be expensive: Would it be wise to escalate that cost with a capital transfer? Bonn was geographically close to the hubs of United Europe and NATO, while Berlin was on the eastern periphery of the European Union and even of the new Germany (in the old Reich, Berlin had been near the geographical center, 800 kilometers from Aachen in the west and 800 kilometers from Tilsit in the east, but in the new configuration it was just 90 kilometers from the Polish border). The Federal Republic's foreign partners had gotten used to Bonn as the seat of German power: why unsettle the situation with a return to Berlin?

Above all, why make such a move when the old power center was so freighted with heavy historical baggage? Bonn partisans needed hardly remind their fellow Germans—but they did so anyway—that Berlin had held sway during the rise of "militaristic Prussia," the disastrous *Weltpolitik* of the Second Reich, the failed democratic experiment of Weimar, the moral and political catastrophe of National Socialism, and the Stalinist dictatorship of the GDR. As Fritz Fischer, a historian famous for his work on imperial Germany's drive for world power, argued, Berlin was never "a capital of the heart" for the vast majority of Germans. He said that "a return to Prussia," would revive repressed memories of the horrors of Prussian-German history and awaken legitimate fears among Germans and foreigners alike. Adenauer had been right, Fischer said, to distrust the eastern-oriented megalopolis and to put his faith in Bonn, which symbolized "the tight connection between the Federal Republic, Western Europe, and America."

Of course, not all those who argued against Berlin focused on the same historical liabilities. Conservatives in the anti-Berlin faction emphasized the city's reputation for unruliness and "ungovernability." They recalled its communist agitators, radical students, and riotous *Chaoten*. Leftists and liberals opposed to Berlin, by contrast, recalled the city's function as the capital of Prussian authoritarianism. They were inclined to downplay the fact that Prussia and Berlin had also been centers of the German Enlightenment and democratic idealism in the pre-Bismarckian era, and bastions of beleaguered democracy in the Weimar period. Those who focused on Berlin as the capital of the Third Reich, meanwhile, tended to ignore the fact that it was not Berlin but Munich that had been the birthplace of Nazism and "capital of the movement."

Hammered by this barrage of criticism from their fellow Germans, Berliners seemed at first somewhat shell-shocked. Having just heard their town hailed as a harbinger of the new era of unity and freedom, they now saw it condemned as a prime symbol of the bad old times and thus unfit to serve as capital of a democratic Germany. Their initial response was to take shelter in trusty prejudices regarding the Bonner, whose attacks they loftily dismissed as the product of provincial small-mindedness. They also fell into self-pity, bewailing the fact that, as one Berlin journalist put it, "many Germans never liked Berlin," seeing it in the way that Americans saw New York City—"an evil place, even if lively and exciting."

Soon, however, the Berliners mounted a more forceful counterattack, replete with their own selective interpretations of the German past. Orchestrated by a hastily constructed lobby group called "Berlin as Capital," the campaign depicted the Spree city as a historic repository of liberty and tolerance, a refuge for unorthodox thinkers, and a paragon of antiauthoritarianism and resistance to tyranny. Berlin may have been the titular capital of the Third Reich, the Berliners argued, but it was never truly nazified and it put up more resistance to the Hitlerites than any other city. Berlin's historic commitment to freedom was all the more remarkable, the argument went on, because from the dark days of the Thirty Years War through the post–World War II division of Germany, this city had suffered tremendously. Although it could not be held responsible for Germany's unfortunate historical derailments, Berlin had had to pay more than its fair share of the penalties for these transgressions. Berlin's service to Germany, especially during the last trial-filled decades of division, justified its claim to being the true heart of the nation.

While these arguments betrayed a good measure of strategic amnesia, Berlin partisans had a point when they charged that the willful forgetting inherent in the opposition to the old capital was especially egregious. As historian Heinrich Winkler (who himself moved to Berlin to take a position at the Humboldt University) cogently stated: "Having their capital, in the full sense of the word, in Berlin would remind the Germans of a past which many people in Bonn prefer to envisage as an invention of the historians. For them, moreover, the ability to identify all historical transgressions with Berlin has always been conveniently exculpatory. . . . This method of detoxifying the German past would be harder to manage if Berlin were the capital."

The Bundestag decided to hold a vote on the capital question on June 20, 1991. The outcome was anyone's guess because the new nation's political class was as deeply divided on this issue as were the chattering classes in academia and the media. The CDU and CSU (Christian Social Union) leaned toward Bonn; the SPD was split down the middle; the FDP preferred Berlin, though not decisively; the Bündnis 90/Greens favored the Spree city, as did the PDS. The so-called Unity Treaty that had been drawn up in July 1990 contained no commitment on the future seat of government because the negotiators feared that a decision one way or the other could jeopardize passage of the treaty. The document merely stated: "The capital of Germany is Berlin. The question of the seat of government and parliament will be decided after the completion of unity."

Chancellor Kohl, who had been so decisive on the issue of German unification, proved, at least in the early phase of the debate, frustratingly indecisive on the seat-of-government question. For many months he said relatively little on the subject, leaving the nation to wonder on which side he would ultimately throw his formidable political weight. The Bonn contingent chose to believe that the chancellor was in its camp. This seemed a reasonable assumption, since Kohl's whole political career had been shaped by the "Bonn Republic," and he considered himself an heir of Adenauer. Although he lacked the old man's legendary hatred of Berlin, he, like so many West German conservatives, worried about the old capital's unruliness and leftist proclivities, of which he had gotten a powerful dose during his visit to the city following the Wall's initial opening. Moreover, he had the typical small-town German's horror of pulling up roots and moving to a new place, with all the "trauma" of buying a new house, finding a new school for the kids, making new friends, and—most wrenching of all—settling on a new *Stammkneipe* (favorite pub). On the other hand, Kohl well understood the importance of Berlin to the East Germans. He knew that they would see a decision to keep the federal government in Bonn as a slap in the face. If the "Ossis" (as the eastern Germans now came to be called) were to be successfully integrated into the Federal Republic, Germany's actual as well as titular capital would have to be located on the Spree. For Kohl, these considerations proved more compelling than his continuing reservations regarding the old capital. As the moment for the crucial Bundestag vote approached, therefore, he began lobbying within his own party for Berlin, hoping to line up enough CDU delegates to tip the balance.

While Kohl worked quietly behind the scenes for Berlin, President Richard von Weizsäcker came out openly and passionately for his native city. He had grown increasingly frustrated with CDU-backed suggestions that his own office, the largely ceremonial federal presidency, should represent the central government in Berlin while the chancellor's office, ministries, and parliament remained in Bonn. He wrote a memo to Kohl saying, "One thing must be absolutely clear: the presidency cannot serve as decoration for a so-called capital from which all the other governmental agencies are missing." Not satisfied that he had gotten his point across, Weizsäcker used a ceremony in the Nikolaikirche naming him as newly united

Berlin's first "honorary citizen" to push the old capital's cause. "Only in Berlin do we come from both sides but truly stand as one," he declaimed. Berliners, he went on, best understood what unification demanded because they had experienced the division more intensely than anyone else. "Here [in Berlin] is the place for a politically responsible leadership of Germany," he declared.

Weizsäcker was preaching to the choir on this occasion: the Nikolaikirche in Berlin was a far cry from the "Water Works" parliament in Bonn. On the eve of the parliamentary vote, Berlin's Mayor Diepgen pronounced himself "cautiously optimistic." He added, however, that if the vote went against Berlin the city would know how to "shape its own destiny, as it always has in the past." (Berlin in fact had never shaped its destiny without outside help.) Diepgen was placing his faith in the persuasive powers of Helmut Kohl, who, after having frustrated the mayor with his fence-sitting, promised to speak out in favor of Berlin.

As it happened, the chancellor did speak out for Berlin once the Bundestag debate got underway, but his speech was more folksy than forceful. He told how he had personally come to understand that Berlin was the "obvious capital," and he said that the government's move there offered the best hope for the rapid economic recovery of the east. The key speaker for the Berlin cause turned out not to be Kohl but his CDU colleague Wolfgang Schäuble. Although confined to a wheelchair as a result of injuries sustained in an assassination attempt, Schäuble had managed to get himself anointed "crown prince," the conservatives' best bet to replace old King Kohl once he finally vacated the throne. Now, in his Bundestag speech, Schäuble acted as if he already were the chancellor. He told his colleagues that the question they had to decide was not so much about jobs, moving costs, or regional power, but "the future of Germany." He reminded the delegates that they represented "the whole of Germany" in addition to their specific constituencies. Having found their country suddenly thrust back together, their task now was "to complete that unity." Yet it was not, he went on, only German unity that was at stake here, but the unity of Europe. Just as Germany meant more than West Germany, Europe meant more than Western Europe. Germany had managed to overcome its division because Europe also wished to be united. Therefore, a decision for Berlin amounted also to a decision to "overcome the division of Europe." Schäuble's appeal was so passionately put that a number of delegates later claimed that it was the decisive factor in the final vote.

Willy Brandt, the mayor of West Berlin when the Wall went up, also spoke forcefully about Berlin's mission now that the city was reunited. He too admonished his colleagues not to be guided by narrow considerations like personal comforts and moving costs when the demand of the hour was "to show solidarity with the east." He then went for the Bonners' jugular with a pointed historical comparison. Would anyone have expected France, he asked, to keep its government in idyllic Vichy once the end of foreign control over Paris allowed a return to the Seine? Not surprisingly, the implication that Bonn was Germany's Vichy inspired howls of protest from the Bonner, and even from Kohl. Undaunted, Brandt went on to belittle the Bonn contingent's proposal for a division of labor in which Berlin would remain Germany's "symbolic capital" while Bonn kept the real power. Germany, he said acidly, did not need "a separate capital for cocktail receptions." The old capital, having stood "as an outpost of freedom through difficult times," surely deserved more than "an honorary title devoid of real content."

Another eloquent appeal for Berlin came from the East German politician Wolfgang Thierse (SPD). The choice the Bundestag faced, he said, was "not between two cities." The deeper issue involved "the future social and political development of Germany," whose "completed unity" could be decisively advanced through a move to Berlin. At stake also was the relationship between east and west in Germany, the identity of the unified German state, Germany's relationship to its own history, and finally, Germany's understanding of the meaning of Europe.

Such pleas for the larger view may have influenced some delegates, but mundane matters of money, jobs, and domestic power relationships could not be wished away. Nor could the belief, harbored by many representatives, that Germany's federal traditions were more likely to be preserved by Bonn than by Berlin. The argument for Bonn was forcefully advanced by the Bavarian CSU politician Theodor Waigel, who also happened to be federal finance minister. Wearing his financial hat, Waigel pleaded for "a politics of just proportions" and economic caution. The integration of the new states was already imposing severe strains on the budget, he said. It was not "small-minded" when, along with the broader historical dimensions, one worried about the capacity of the federal government to function efficiently under the altered political and economic circumstances. Estimates for a move to Berlin stood between DM 30 and 40 billion, he announced, though some predicted twice that much. If sums like this were expended on a move to Berlin, spending on other items, such as social services, would have to be cut. It would be much more sensible, he concluded, to shift the presidential office to Berlin, and perhaps the Bundesrat, while keeping the rest of the government in Bonn.

There were many other speeches that day, and the delegates must have been relieved when, at 9:00 P.M., Bundestag President Rita Süssmuth started the voting on the five competing resolutions. In the crucial duel between the main Bonn and Berlin resolutions, the Berliners won by the narrow margin of eighteen votes, 338 to 320. To the parliament's credit, the voting was by no means on strict party lines. Schäuble's impassioned speech seems indeed to have had some impact on his own party, for the number of anti-Berlin votes in the CDU faction turned out to be fewer than in earlier counts. The party came down narrowly in favor of Bonn, 164 to 154. The SPD remained sharply divided, though tilting for Berlin at 126 to 110. With the largest parties so deeply split, the smaller groups had the decisive voice. The FDP voted 53 for Berlin, 26 for Bonn. The Bündnis 90/Greens went 6 to 2 in favor of Berlin, while the PDS came down 15 to 1 for the old capital. The Bavarian CSU, as expected, went solidly for Bonn.

Although relatively nonpartisan, the voting revealed an ominous division between east and west and a great deal of resistance to the prospect of a capital move. Delegates from the new eastern states, regardless of party, voted overwhelmingly for Berlin, while the majority of their western counterparts preferred Bonn. Moreover, given the ways in which internal German relations were to evolve in the next few years, it is safe to say that if the Bonn/Berlin vote had been held any later, the result would have been reversed.

A Wonderful Catastrophe

Cheers and clanging church bells on the Spree, howls of rage on the Rhine. "A Catastrophe for Bonn," wailed *Express*, a tabloid in the Rhine city. Angry demonstrators in Bonn's Marktplatz promised an "intifada" against the Bundestag's decision to move east. Noting that the national governmental train "still stands in the Bonn station," a local politician declared: "It is up to us to ensure that it never leaves."

In the end, the Bonner would prove unable to prevent the capital train from leaving for Berlin, but they would manage to delay the departure and substantially reduce the amount of baggage it carried east. For Berliners, Bonn's foot-dragging offered yet another reason for self-doubt. Their city was slated to become the new "capital of Europe," but they had cause to wonder whether Berlin would even become the full-fledged capital of Germany. "Berlin is on the razor's edge," declared the architect Hans Kollhoff. "It can be a great metropolis, or it can be a poverty zone. Both are possible."

Such fears notwithstanding, in the immediate aftermath of the Bundestag's historic vote, Berliners hailed a decision that promised to make their city a true national capital again, like Paris, London, Rome, and Madrid. In anticipation of this elevation of status, the town became the focal point of a short-lived investment boom reminiscent of the *Gründerjahre* following the first German unification in 1871. An American observer, Darryl Pinckney, made this parallel explicit when he wrote: "[Berlin] is once again the German Chicago, just like Mark Twain saw, a boom city, boiling over with secrets, deals, smugglers, entrepreneurs, contracts." Speculators from all over the world saw gold in the city's dilapidated buildings and vast empty spaces.

Some of the biggest and most aggressive players had moved in even before the city was officially reunited and designated the future seat of national government. Shortly before the Wall came down, Edzard Reuter, chief of Daimler-Benz, began negotiations to buy fifteen acres in the Potsdamer Platz from the Senate of West Berlin. In July 1990 Daimler bought the parcel for DM 92,873,550 (about $55 million), which real estate experts estimated was between one-third and one-seventh of the land's actual market value. When details of the deal became known, there was a great hue and cry. The Momper regime, people said, was selling off the symbolic heart of Berlin at a bargain-basement price to a company known to have worked hand-in-glove with the Nazis. In a typical Berlin gesture, members of the local leftist scene erected a gallows in the square and "hanged" a Mercedes star. A leading architectural reporter spoke of "the mistake of the century." City planners worried that the Daimler deal would set a precedent for future sales and undercut the possibility of coherent planning for the redevelopment of eastern Berlin. In response to the barrage of criticism, the Momper administration responded that the city had to be accommodating toward heavyweight corporations like Daimler, which in the past had been reluctant to invest in West Berlin. Local leaders also made much of the fact that Edzard Reuter was the son of Ernst Reuter, West Berlin's revered former mayor. Reuter himself argued that his company's decision to make a major commitment to Berlin would send an important message to the rest of German industry. His colleagues from other big firms, he confided, were following Daimler's Potsdamer Platz project "with the greatest interest," asking themselves, "Will large companies be welcome at all in the new Berlin? Or will Berlin remain little more than a *Kleingärtnerstadt* [small potatoes town], with a few cultural institutions?"

The concern that the Daimler sale might set a precedent proved warranted. Shortly after it was consummated, another large section of the Potsdamer Platz was purchased by the Sony Corporation, also at a bargain price. However, Sony's decision to build its European headquarters in Berlin, like Daimler-Benz's commitment, could be taken as a sign of faith in the city. Once the Mercedes and Sony logos were shining like beacons above a rebuilt Potsdamer Platz, could anyone doubt that Berlin was "back"?

In the meantime, the activities of the initial big investors, which also included American and French interests, ignited an explosion in real estate values and rents. Prices for choice properties in the city center had doubled following the Wall's opening, and they doubled again in the months following the Bundestag vote. Berlin suddenly went from having the lowest real estate costs of any major German city to vying with Frankfurt and Munich for the highest. By 1992, some commercial tenants were paying twice what they would for similar property on New York's Fifth Avenue. While this surge in prices was good news for Berliners with property to sell or rent out, it was bad news for old-line tenants, many of whom had been enjoying low rates because of rent-control. If Berlin's transformation was not to increase the gap between rich and poor, and between east and west, ways would have to be found to cushion the socioeconomic effects of unification.

This was not the only challenge that the city faced. Over the past forty years East Berlin had fallen drastically behind West Berlin in terms of infrastructure development. Telephone lines, sewers, public transportation networks, and road surfaces were all substandard. The task of renovating the east and knitting the two halves of the city back together was enormous—the urban equivalent of reconstructive surgery on a partly gangrenous patient. In this regard, Berlin was a microcosm of the new Germany. As *Der Spiegel* warned: "The test-case of Berlin will illustrate to even the most carefree and ignorant citizens of our land what national unity really means: a wonderful catastrophe."

The challenge soon became evident in a host of legal, political, and social dilemmas that complicated the process of unification. Among the trickiest of these problems was the welter of conflicting ownership claims attached to many factories, houses, and even vacant lots in eastern Berlin. In a fateful decision, the German government elected to restore ownership to those whose property had been confiscated by the Nazi or Communist regimes. (An alternative would have been to pay compensation, which is what the new Czech government did.) This meant that ownership issues had to be resolved before a property could legally be sold. Although the problem was hardly restricted to Berlin, the former capital was a veritable minefield of conflicting claims owing to its premier importance in the Communist and Nazi systems. By the summer of 1992 over 2 million claims had been filed throughout the former GDR, 200,000 of them in eastern Berlin alone.

Berlin's postunification boom, it quickly turned out, could not be sustained amidst all the doubts about the city's prospects. In addition to the problem of conflicting ownership claims, continuing resistance by the pro-Bonn lobby to the shift of central governmental institutions from the Rhine to the Spree undermined confidence in the capital-elect. According to the victorious Berlin resolution of June 20, 1991, the parliament was supposed to move east in four years. But later that year the Bundestag passed a new resolution establishing a commission to study the transfer based on "a division of labor between Bonn and Berlin." No time frame for the move was specified. The federal government, meanwhile, decided in December 1991 to relocate the chancellor's office to Berlin but also to divide the ministerial functions between Bonn and the new capital. Eight ministries (later changed to six) would retain their main offices in Bonn, including Defense, the largest. As further compensation for Bonn, eleven bureaucratic agencies already located in Berlin would be moved to the Rhine. As for the ministries slated to move east, Kohl's cabinet decided that the transfer could not be completed until the year 2000, with individual offices making the shift as their designated quarters became ready for occupancy. In an effort to expedite this process, the municipal government of Berlin proposed refurbishing existing structures that had served the GDR and/or the Nazis. Bonn, however, called for totally new buildings, whose construction would require more time, not to mention a lot more money. The inconsistency between Bonn's warnings about the high cost of a capital transfer and its demand for brand new government buildings was not lost on the Berliners. They spoke derisively of a "luxury move," suggesting that Bonn's insistence on new construction was designed to delay the transfer and to make it less palatable to the public.

The plan to shift capitals was in fact becoming increasing unpopular. A poll taken in early 1993 showed that 55 percent of the populace opposed the move, with only 39 percent in favor. The pro-Bonn faction voiced the hope that the next Bundestag, due to be elected in 1993, would reverse the parliament's decision to move. "I considered the decision to have been wrong at the time, and I still do," said Bonn's mayor, Hans Daniels. "You would have to be a prophet to say what the next parliament will decide," he added. For their part, Berliners complained that the efforts by the Bonner to postpone or cancel the move were having a negative effect on the local economy. As Mayor Diepgen put it, the campaign "makes investors uncertain and harms Berlin and the eastern states." As evidence for this, Diepgen pointed to the fact that of the eighty Japanese firms that had initially said they would establish branches in Berlin, only ten remained on board in 1993.

The Berliners themselves, however, were partly to blame for their city's failure to blossom economically in the wake of unification. Instead of focusing all their efforts on knitting the city together and creating an attractive climate for business, city officials divided their time between internecine battles over turf and all-too-ambitious schemes to elevate the city's profile.

Their biggest mistake in the early going was to waste valuable time and energy on a breathtakingly mismanaged campaign to win the Olympic Summer Games for Berlin in the year 2000. Of course, the last time Berlin had hosted the Olympics was in 1936, when Hitler had used the event to promote the Third Reich. Munich was the host in 1972, when eleven Israeli athletes were killed by Palestinian terrorists. Neither of these precedents was especially promising, but Berlin boosters were convinced that their city's recent history, especially its triumph over ideological division, gave it an excellent chance of getting the 2000 games. Its promotional scheme included a plan to refurbish the decaying Reichssportfeld as the main venue, which was probably not the best idea in terms of symbolism. In any event, the campaign quickly became mired in scandal and incompetence. The first head of the Berlin Olympic Committee, one Lutz Grüttke, was fired for fraud after just six months on the job. "It is sad that there is always such bad news from Berlin," lamented a spokesman for Daimler-Benz, one of the campaign's chief sponsors. Grüttke's successor, Nikolaus Fuchs, also got fired after it was revealed that the Berlin Committee had compiled dossiers on the private lives of International Olympic Committee members, complete with information on their drinking habits and sexual preferences. Optimistically, Fuchs had concluded that only seven IOC members were "not for sale." IOC president Juan Antonio Samaranch, who had previously described Berlin as a "strong candidate," now was reportedly opposed to the city. Berlin's bid was further weakened by lackluster support from the Kohl government, which thought that the future capital had enough on its plate without trying to host the Olympic Games. Many Berliners, in fact, thought this themselves, noting that their city was already a mess because of reconstruction. A leftist

"NOlympic" movement, meanwhile, argued that the games were nothing but a gift to the rich, paid for by the poor. For months on end this group sought to sabotage Berlin's bid by staging violent demonstrations and bombing buildings belonging to the campaign's sponsors. Although Mayor Diepgen claimed that "no other city would symbolize the Olympic ideal of peace and friendship" more effectively than Berlin, the IOC might be forgiven for thinking otherwise. In September 1993 it voted to give the games to Sydney, Australia. Berlin's botched bid had cost $100 million.

Berlin floundered economically also because reunification did not bring an end to some of the bad fiscal and administrative habits nourished during the division. The municipal bureaucracy, which had long been bloated in both east and west, did not trim down, at least in the first years after unification. True, some eastern officials with tainted political pasts were forced out (more on this later), but overall the merger of the two bureaucracies exacerbated problems of overstaffing. As in the past, officials who themselves ate copiously at the government trough spent lavishly on municipal amenities. Berlin was the only city in the world to have three major opera companies, three huge public universities, four symphony orchestras, and two city-run zoos. This would have been hard enough to fund even if generous subsidies continued to flow from the central governmental faucet, but—despite the best efforts of Diepgen—the subsidies from Bonn were scheduled to be phased out beginning in 1993.

There were problems on the private-sector front as well. Companies based in West Berlin, which had also been on the receiving end of generous federal subsidies, often failed to prepare adequately for the loss of that advantage. Moreover, with the collapse of the Soviet economic system in the early 1990s, West German firms with branches in Berlin found it expedient to move operations from there to places like Hungary and Czechoslovakia, where labor costs were lower and environmental regulations less stringent. After 1993 a substantial number of firms went out of business or left the city. The result was that the economy of western Berlin began to shrink within three years of unification, while unemployment and public indebtedness shot up. By 1996 the situation had deteriorated to the point that a new city treasurer, brought in from Hesse to help clean up the city's finances, ordered drastic cuts. To cope with an expected deficit of DM 32 billion over the next four years, she called for a hiring freeze, reductions in university staffing, and the scrapping of plans for a new east-west subway line.

A prominent early casualty of reunited Berlin's rapid transition from bloom to gloom was the lavishly renovated Friedrichstrasse, which, along with the Potsdamer Platz and the area around Checkpoint Charlie, constituted the most ambitious commercial redevelopment in the new Berlin. In 1994 great hopes attended the cornerstone-laying of the new complex, which was designed to house high-rent stores and offices. Mayor Diepgen was on hand to tout the "living big-city atmosphere" of the Spree metropolis. Representatives of the Societè Générale d'Enterprises, a French building concern that was backing the project, smiled broadly. And why not? Galeries Lafayette was building an 8,000-square-meter store, and this was just one of seventeen enterprises scheduled to open in the complex. Yet there were very good reasons for worry. Rents in the western part of the city were steadily dropping because the supply of retail and office space already exceeded demand. Some 25,000 square meters stood empty in the west as the project was launched. Could all this come to "a great crash?" asked Munich's *Süddeutsche Zeitung*, with undisguised schadenfreude. Two years later, when Galeries Lafayette opened its doors, there was indeed little to smile about. The floors were full of beautiful things but virtually devoid of customers. Other new enterprises on the street also lacked for trade. Their owners' only consolation, if one could call it that, was that things were bad all over the city. In 1995, according to a local trade group, Berlin's retailers experienced "one of the worst years since the war." Even the world-renowned KaDeWe, that mecca of consumerism in western Berlin, saw its sales drop 10 percent from their peak in 1992.

More important than Berlin's economic trials was its difficulty in living up to its promise as "workshop of unification." True, it certainly *looked* like a workshop. The town, especially its eastern part, crawled with bulldozers and road graders. A forest of cranes towered over Potsdamer Platz, once Europe's busiest square and now its largest construction site. (One of the Potsdamer Platz cranes, incidentally, had a bungee cord attached to it; for a mere one hundred marks one could take the plunge.) All the efforts to rejoin streets, reconnect utilities, and transform the east into a shining replica of the west, however, did little to pull the city together politically or socially. With the Berlin Wall now just a memory, the much-discussed "Wall in the Head" seemed to have become an even more formidable barrier to mutual understanding. Years earlier, Peter Schneider had heard a member of West Germany's mission in East Berlin muse: "Sometimes I think the Wall is the only thing that still keeps us Germans together." Now that the Wall was down, it was apparent that the man had a point.

The euphoria that accompanied the fall of the Wall, when thousands of easterners had swarmed into the west to be greeted with hugs and "welcome money," was more or less gone after two or three years of unification. During that short period West and East Germans discovered that the long years of separation had yielded different ways of thinking and acting. Mutually disillusioned, they began trafficking in negative stereotypes. Wessis, resenting the huge transfer payments from west to east (some DM 150 million per year), and the higher taxes these necessitated, decried the Ossis as dependent, shiftless, backward, and ungrateful. Earlier, West Germans had harbored a negative image of the GDR state but not of the people; now the people themselves were seen to be the problem. Ossis, for their part, found their western countrymen boastful, aggressive, and insensitive to the special problems they faced. They complained that the Wessis failed to acknowledge that the East had suffered much more than the West as a result of the settlement following World War II. In their eyes, the westerners were all too inclined to confuse the luck of political geography with talent and initiative.

In Berlin, the Wall in the Head was evident in a falling-off of movement between east and west. Rather than streaming to the west to shop, as they had in the immediate post-Wall era, East Berliners stayed home and even began buying eastern-made products again, which they now professed to find preferable to western goods. In 1993 only 9.3 percent of East Berliners said that they would live in West Berlin if given the chance; 7 percent of the West Berliners said they would go east. In the same year, a study of Berlin's youth scene revealed that contacts between eastern and western young people had not increased since 1990. Now, Ossis who drove their sputtering Trabis into western Berlin got hostile stares, or perhaps dog feces smeared on their windows. Rather than gifts of bananas, they got banana jokes, such as: "How do we know that Ossis are descended from apes? From all the bananas they eat." The easterners vented their indignation and humiliation in anti-western tabloids like *SuperIllu* and in a special rage hotline, *Wut-Telefon*. Following reports that western Berlin plasma banks were offering trifling sums for Ossi blood, the alternative newspaper *taz* ran the headline: "Western Vampires Suck East German Blood." Some easterners wore T-shirts that said, "I Want My Wall Back!" Tellingly, these shirts also sold well in the West.

The major source of resentment in the East derived from the nature of unification itself, which involved the wholesale imposition of Western institutions, values, and practices on the former GDR. While many East Berliners, especially at the beginning, were willing enough to adopt—or to try to adopt—Western ways, a sense of victimization soon took hold. Easterners claimed that they were being "colonized" by a West that was determined to extinguish everything that the GDR had stood for.

One of the first tasks that victors often undertake after absorbing a conquered territory is to replace objectionable place names with designations reflecting the altered political circumstances. As we have seen, Berlin had experienced several waves of name-changing over the course of its modern history, the most extensive being that following the Nazi defeat in 1945. Reunification brought another spate of rechristening, particularly in the east, which was littered with streets and squares named after Communist leaders, leftist heroes, and Third World Marxist martyrs. The legal tool for the name-changing was the 1985 West Berlin Strassengesetz, which was amended and extended to the entire city. It called for "the removal of those street names from the period 1945 to 1989 [honoring] active opponents of democracy and also intellectual-political precursors and defenders of Stalinist tyranny, the GDR regime and other unjust Communist regimes." Following these guidelines, authorities in united Berlin ordered seventy-five name changes in the eastern part of the city in the two years following German unification. Many of these changes were made by district councils and were not controversial. But as time went on, with more and more Communist heroes losing their places of honor on the municipal map, East Berliners with ties to the old system began to complain that the Wessis were trying to rob them of an important part of their collective identity.

The Berlin city council voted on May 16, 1991, to return Hermann-Matern-Strasse to its old designation of Luisenstrasse. This generated little resistance, for Matern had been the SED's chief inquisitor and enforcer of ideological conformity. At the same meeting, Otto-Grotewohl-Strasse, the former Wilhelmstrasse, was renamed Toleranzstrasse. This decision, however, did not last long, for the French pointed out that there was a similarly named street in Paris's red-light district, and it would not do to have the new capital's major governmental street associated with prostitution (enough people would make that link anyway). With Toleranzstrasse out, the council opted for Willy-Brandt-Strasse, but this choice was overridden by the senator for Traffic and Public Works, a CDU-man. He insisted on a return to Wilhelmstrasse, and, in 1993, Wilhelmstrasse it became. Meanwhile, the CDU delegates on the city council proposed to rename all streets and squares honoring Karl Marx, August Bebel, Karl Liebknecht, Rosa Luxemburg, and Clara Zetkin. The PDS and SPD balked at this, and the battle became so heated that the city authorities created an independent commission, which included noted historians, to advise them on these issues. The commission recommended that Communists who had died too soon to help bring Weimar down, or the GDR up, should not be purged, thus sparing Marx, Bebel, Luxemburg, and Liebknecht. Zetkin, however, remained fair game, since she had lived until 1933. Conservatives and moderate socialists on the commission pointed out that Zetkin, a dedicated Communist during the 1920s, had been an enemy of parliamentary democracy. Her street, which led from eastern Berlin to the Reichstag, occupied a very sensitive location. Thus in 1994 Clara-Zetkin-Strasse returned to its old name of Dorotheenstrasse, much to the dismay of local leftists, who held a protest rally decrying the "slander" of a great anti-Hitler activist and feminist crusader. Käthe Niederkirchner, a young Communist resistance fighter who had been murdered by the Nazis, was luckier. The street named after her in GDR days was not returned to its original designation—mainly because the previous name, Prinz-Albrecht-Strasse, now was synonymous with the Gestapo. However, because the Berlin municipal parliament had taken over the former Prussian House of Deputies, which is located on this street, the small piece of the road directly in front of the parliament was renamed Platz vor dem Abgeordnetenhaus. This way the Berlin legislators would not have the name of a Communist on their letterhead.

Throughout these struggles over nomenclature, the left accused the conservatives of hypocrisy, noting that several streets in western Berlin still bore the names of prominent generals and militarists, such as Moltke, Roon, and Richthofen. But the left was fighting a losing battle. In 1994 the senator for Traffic and Public Works struck again, returning Dimitroffstrasse (named after Georgi Dimitroff, head of the Comintern) to its previous designation, Danziger Strasse. This not only angered local leftists, who celebrated Dimitroff as the hero of the Reichstag fire trial, but alarmed the Poles, who worried that some Germans might imagine that restoring a street name was the first step toward regaining "lost territory" in the east. In a similar leap backwards, Marx-Engels Platz was returned to its old designation of Schlossplatz. Justifying this action, conservatives argued that it was hardly fitting for the square that had once harbored the royal palace (and might do so again, if a group of restorationists had their way) to carry the names of noted haters of the monarchy.

Monuments, like street names, often become bones of bitter contention following a change in regime. East Berlin had its full share of physical testimonials to communist heroism—a motley collection of pillars, busts, statues, and shrines, most of them as aesthetically unappealing as the neighborhoods in which they stood. Some inspired little affection even among GDR patriots and could be removed by the new powers in Berlin without much controversy. Few protested, for example, when the authorities ordered the elimination of the monuments to GDR border guards who had died at the Berlin Wall. It was quite otherwise with the proposed dismantling in 1991 of a sixty-three-foot-tall granite statue of Lenin, which had been dedicated by Walter Ulbricht in 1970 on Lenin's hundredth birthday. Claiming that it was totally unacceptable for Berlin to honor a "despot and murderer," the Diepgen government insisted that the statue be removed. A group of East Berliners, many of them residents of the Leninplatz neighborhood in Prenzlauer Berg where the statue stood, rallied to the defense of the monument on grounds that it was an integral part of GDR history. As one of them said: "For me, it's not about Lenin, but rather about demonstrating our power and not letting ourselves be pushed around." The easterners held protest demonstrations and draped the statue with a huge sash saying, "No Violence!" The PDS, meanwhile, demanded that if Lenin went, so must the Victory Column in West Berlin, which was equally "political." In the end, the Victory Column stayed and Lenin went—ignominiously broken up into pieces and deposited in a gravel pit. Leninplatz was then renamed Platz der Vereinten Nationen (United Nations Square), an ironic choice for a place that had now come to symbolize discord and division.

The fate of another GDR-commissioned monument, a huge bronze bust of the German Communist leader Ernst Thälmann, also became the focal point of an identity struggle in reunited Berlin. Unveiled by Honecker in 1986, the sculpture was a latter-day socialist equivalent of Wilhelm II's Siegesallee, a triumph of bombastic kitsch. (In a modern touch, Thälmann's nose was heated to prevent snow from accumulating there, but little could be done about the pigeons who left their signature on his bald head.) When the Berlin government proposed eliminating this monstrosity in 1993, a cry of protest went up from Ossis still smarting from their loss of Lenin. This time they managed to save their hero, largely because the bust was so big and solid that it would have cost too much to break down and cart away. The argument was also made that this work deserved preservation not as a political statement but as a classic example of GDR iconography—a historical relic of con-

Ernst Thälmann monument, covered in graffiti, 1994

siderable value. Those who found the monument offensive could always smear it with graffiti, which, in fact, they did not hesitate to do. By the mid-1990s Thälmann looked less heroic than pathetic—a perfect symbol for the defunct regime that had claimed him as one of its secular saints.

The removal of politically tainted street names and monuments was just the beginning of a much broader campaign to root out the remnants of the Marxist system in the former GDR. The new eastern states harbored tens of thousands of state-owned factories, stores, farms, and other assets that, in the eyes of united Germany's rulers, had no place in a free-market economy. Actually, this conclusion had already been reached by the Modrow government, which, in March 1990, had set up a privatization agency called the Treuhand to sell off some of the state-owned properties. Under East German administration, however, the Treuhand had managed to dispose of only 170 companies. After unification the agency came under the control of a government determined to make privatization a priority. The Treuhand quickly became the largest holding company in the world, with 8,000 companies,

40,000 plants, 6 million employees, and 62,000 square kilometers of farms, forests, and other real estate. Its holdings were particularly extensive in East Berlin, where it was the largest landlord. Appropriately, it set up shop in the city's largest office building, the former Nazi Air Ministry and "House of Ministries" in GDR days. Most of the staff were Wessis, as was the new director, Detlev Rohwedder, a former chief of Hoesch Steel and a legendary downsizer.

In selling off its state-owned factories, the Treuhand was supposed to commit the purchasers to retain as many workers as possible, but in many cases the buyers salvaged only the profitable parts of the operation and shut down the rest. Thousands of plants proved so outmoded, expensive to run, or destructive to the environment that they found no purchasers at all. They were kept open for a while with federal funds, but eventually most were simply closed down. As early as December 1991, 4 million East Germans were out of work, and millions more were underemployed. The Treuhand, which had been founded as the putative savior of GDR industry, became the most hated institution in the land. Rohwedder began receiving death threats on a daily basis, and in early 1991 he fell victim to a terrorist's bullet.

The murder of Rohwedder, of course, did not turn back the tide of privatization, which continued under his successor, Birgit Breuel, who led the Treuhand until its dissolution in late 1994. By that time, the former GDR, including eastern Berlin, which alone lost 150,000 manufacturing jobs, was substantially deindustrialized, with about half the adult population out of work. Assessing the role of the Treuhand, Christa Wolf wrote bitterly: "Isn't it a little uncanny how the work of two or three generations can just vanish into nothing—not by physical destruction, war, or bombs but in the middle of peacetime, by the stroke of a pen, by the inflexible magic word 'privatization'?"

In his satirical novel of post-Wall Berlin, *Schlehweins Giraffe*, Bernd Schirmer writes of a giraffe who has been *abgewickelt* (weeded out) from a Berlin zoo so strapped for funds that the weaker animals are fed to the stronger ones and superfluous specimens sold off to the public or to other zoos. The giraffe in question represents the millions of Ossis who after the *Wende* (the turnaround engendered by unification) suddenly found themselves deprived of their old cages and keepers, sold off to new owners—in essence devoured by their more powerful neighbors. The process of *Abwicklung* affected not only the redundant, but also the politically tainted: animals with the wrong spots, stripes, or colors. To weed these specimens out, the government of united Germany established a series of committees, consisting mostly of Wessis, that combed through the personnel lists of eastern German public institutions, including the army, police, universities, secondary schools, and research institutes. Like the Western Allies after the collapse of Nazism, the interrogators distributed questionnaires designed to identify people with problematical political pasts. As the former Communist capital—the central attraction of the GDR zoo—East Berlin came under particularly intense scrutiny.

In Berlin as elsewhere, weeding out known Stasi collaborators and SED time-servers proved the least controversial part of the purge. It was the marginal cases that caused the most problems, along with the dismissal of people who were simply seen as too old or intellectually calcified to adjust to the new environment. Rife as it was with condescension toward the "primitive" GDR, this process generated tremendous resentment in the eastern states. When queried by Western reviewers whether the employees of his institute had the linguistic skills to keep up with the latest English-language scholarship, one research director replied: "Look, it's not so simple. First we have to learn to eat with a knife and a fork, then maybe we can start on English." A group of *abgewickelte* economists from the East German Academy of Economics founded a cabaret in Berlin called Kartoon. A performer quipped in one of their skits: "We've got one thing in common with the government in Bonn: we haven't the foggiest idea of what we're doing at the moment."

One person's *Abwicklung* was another person's opportunity: the process created thousands of vacancies across the former GDR, and many of these spaces were filled with Wessis. The eastern universities were particularly attractive targets for job-hungry western academics. In the first years after unification hundreds of suddenly empty chairs were filled by Western scholars. Like missionaries, some of the newcomers hoped to help reshape the "desertlike" academic landscape in the east. As the premier university of the ex-GDR, Humboldt-Universität in Berlin attracted a host of academic stars from the west. Efforts to effect a rapid westernization of that institution, however, yielded bitter disputes, as representatives of the old guard fought tenaciously to defend their turf. The rector, Heinrich Fink, who had been appointed shortly before unification, declared his intention to "renew" the university as far as possible with existing personnel, rather than through a thorough purge. This did not sit well with the new senator for Science and Research, who supervised the Berlin universities. He ordered Fink's dismissal, citing as grounds the rector's collaboration with the Stasi during his tenure as a theology professor. Seeing Fink as the victim of a Wessi witch-hunt, many Humboldt students, professors, and eastern intellectuals rallied to his defense. Meanwhile, other academic personnel who were being *abgewickelt* appealed their dismissals in court. The august university, which many hoped would be an ideal meeting place between east and west, became instead an ideological battlefield.

So too did Berlin's literary landscape. The cause in this instance was not a formal purge but a widespread assault on the artistic reputation and personal character of a number of easterners following the opening of the Stasi files. Interestingly, pressure to throw open these files originated in the east, not in the west. Many GDR citizens believed that they had a right to know who had informed on them and what had been said. Officials of the federal government in Bonn, most notably Interior Minister Wolfgang Schäuble, warned that this could lead to an orgy of revenge-taking. Nevertheless, in 1991 the government passed a law that allowed access to personal files by the individuals upon whom the records were kept, but not to third parties. An independent commission was established to oversee this process. Its head was the former East German theologian Joachim Gauck, who (unlike Schäuble) believed that bringing the full scope of the Stasi crimes to light was necessary for collective healing. Of course, Gauck's agency did not have possession of everything the Stasi had collected, since some records had been shredded right after the Wall came down and others had been sold to the press by Stasi men looking to finance their retirement. The records under Gauck's purview, however, were voluminous, and many of them resembled shrapnel-filled letter-bombs, set to blow up in their viewer's face as soon as they were opened. The East German feminist Vera Wollenberger, for example, discovered that her husband had been spying on her for the Stasi for years. Not a few citizens who gained access to their files later came to regret their curiosity. Some blamed the messenger, accusing Gauck of rubbing the Ossis' noses in their sins, thereby aiding in the West's campaign of humiliation. No corner of East German life was left undamaged by the detonations in the Stasi files, but East Berlin's literary and intellectual community provided the most spectacular pyrotechnics.

The ugliness started when Wolf Biermann, the ex-East German songwriter and poet who had been expelled to the West in 1976, used the occasion of his Büchner prize speech in 1991 to attack some of his former colleagues for collaborating with the Stasi. He was toughest on a fellow poet named Sascha Anderson, who had been a cult figure in the Prenzlauer Berg literary scene in the late 1970s and early 1980s. Anderson was famous for writing supercool, obscure verse that vaguely attacked the system. It turned out, however, that he had also written much clearer lines for the benefit of the Stasi. Upon examining their files a number of his friends discovered that he had been diligently spying on them as a police informer. Biermann had been one of the targets. Now, in his Büchner speech, the singer referred to his former friend as "The untalented bullshitter Sascha-Asshole, a Stasi spy, who is still playing the son of the Muse hoping that his files will never show up." This blast itself became controversial, with some writers lining up on Biermann's side, others condemning him for his eagerness to pass judgment. Although few easterners defended Anderson for what he had done, most did not want him to become a posterboy in the West for two-faced Ossi intellectuals. Thus there were cries of outrage when Western tabloids equated Anderson and other Stasi informers with Gestapo stool pigeons. For his part, Anderson insisted that the Stasi had "never owned me." He also claimed, inconsistently, that he had been forced to spy or be killed.

Sascha Anderson had never been a major writer, but this was not true of Christa Wolf, whose exposure in 1993 in the German press as a sometime Stasi informer tore the Berlin literary community apart. Wolf had already come under fire three years earlier when she published a short autobiographical novel, *Was Bleibt* (What Remains), which told of her surveillance by the Stasi. The book had actually been written in 1979, but Wolf chose at that time to put it in a drawer. Its appearance in 1990 occasioned derision from some West German critics, who accused Wolf of delaying publication until it was safe to do so, while putting herself forward as a Stasi "victim." She was no victim, her critics said, but a "state poet" who had enjoyed all sorts of privileges. In early 1993, while Wolf was living in Santa Monica as a fellow of the Getty Center, *Der Spiegel* published details from her Stasi file that showed she had served as a police informer in Berlin from 1959 to 1962. Using the code name "Margarete," she had provided information on dissident writers who, as her Stasi control put it, "don't support the cultural policies of our party and government, or have succumbed to bourgeois tendencies." Wolf attempted to defend herself by characterizing the evidence as "thin stuff," but this hardly convinced her critics. Other writers, however, came to her defense. Günter Grass, though believing Wolf should have been more forceful in her criticism of the SED regime, condemned the attacks against her as a form of political scapegoating. He was also critical of the Gauck commission for leaking information from the Stasi files to the press. In a letter to Wolf, he wrote: "There is recognizably an attempt to use this episode, which lies more than twenty years in the past, to discredit the critical attitude which you demonstrated over decades, and to discredit your literary work along with it." Such support notwithstanding, Wolf emerged from this affair as severely damaged goods, soiled like the political legacy she still tried to defend. Commenting on the internecine bloodletting in Berlin's literary community, Peter Schneider opined: "The Wall has never been so high, nor worked so well, nor made everyone so crazy."

Literary figures like Wolf were not the only prominent easterners to be profoundly discredited by belated evidence of Stasi collaboration. A number of reformist politicians had their careers in post-Wall Germany derailed by such unwelcome revelations. Ibrahim Böhme, head of the eastern SPD and formerly a fixture in East Berlin's peace movement, disappeared from public life in 1990 after it was revealed that he had done some snooping for the Stasi. On the eve of his exposure, he was considered by many to be the strongest candidate for leadership of the GDR. The eastern-CDU leader, Lothar de Maizière, who had served as the GDR's last prime minister, was forced to resign his subsequent position in Kohl's cabinet because Stasi skeletons suddenly turned up in his closet. Accounts in the German press revealed that he had helped the police gather information on the East German Protestant church and on Bonn's legation in East Berlin. According to his Stasi contacts, "Czerny" (the code name he had selected) had been a very useful informant, "honest, loyal, and reliable." Manfred Stolpe (SPD), the post-unification minister-president of Brandenburg, similarly found himself under investigation for alleged Stasi collaboration during his tenure as a high official of the East German Federation of Protestant Churches. His was an exceptionally complicated case. Stasi files that surfaced in 1992 showed that he had attended numerous meetings with state security officers, but he insisted that his purpose on these occasions was solely to assist churchmen who had fallen afoul of the regime. He first denied, but later was forced to admit, that the Stasi had given him the code name "Secretary." The collaboration charges and his spirited defense ignited a bitter battle in the Brandenburg parliament over his fate. The CDU and Greens (who tended to be high-minded on these matters) demanded his ouster as prime minister; the SPD and PDS came to his defense. Stolpe survived this challenge, but the attacks on him continued, making him in the eyes of many Ossis yet another victim of "victor's justice." The PDS leader Gregor Gysi, who was himself under a cloud of suspicion for Stasi contacts, charged that the allegations against Stolpe were part of a plot by Bonn to disqualify former GDR leaders from high positions in united Germany.

Stolpe and his political colleagues were tried in the court of public opinion, not in a court of law, but there were plenty of formal trials involving former GDR leaders and security personnel in the years following the collapse of the East German state. Post-Wall Berlin became the central site of this judicial "reckoning with the past." As in earlier efforts of this kind, the results were on the whole unsatisfying. Many observers complained that the "big fish" were being allowed to swim free while smaller fry were hauled in and made to take the rap for the truly guilty. Some thought that the legal net was too finely meshed, others that it was not fine enough. In the end, the trials, like the opening of the Stasi files, impeded the healing process and exacerbated tensions between east and west.

According to the Unification Treaty, citizens of the former GDR could be tried for offenses that violated West German law, but punishment could not be imposed if the acts had been legal under East German codes. An exception to this last stricture, however, could be made in cases of such "extreme injustice" that the perpetrators must have known that they were violating international standards of human behavior. This of course was a recipe for legal confusion, not to mention political and social acrimony.

One of the early legal battles involved Erich Honecker, the former GDR dictator who had been instrumental in building the Berlin Wall and devising the measures to prevent escapes over the inner-German border. At first it did not look like Honecker would have to stand trial at all. On March 13, 1991, he had managed to fly to Moscow with Soviet assistance to avoid facing the charges that German prosecutors were drawing up against him. Bonn officially protested Russia's role in spiriting its old minion out of Germany, but Chancellor Kohl had undoubtedly known of Honecker's impending flight and was probably not sorry to see him go: after all, it could be highly embarrassing to try a leader whom the chancellor had personally welcomed in Bonn. By the spring of 1992, however, Kohl's government decided that a Honecker trial could be a useful way to show eastern Germans that there were no grounds for their growing *Ostalgie*. Reminded of Honecker's villainy, they might also be less inclined to condemn Kohl for failing to transform eastern Germany into a "blooming landscape." The new Russian government of Boris Yeltsin, anxious to shake off reminders of its own communist past, and hoping for additional loans from Bonn, proved willing to return Honecker to the Federal Republic. Thus in late 1992 he was flown back to Berlin and clamped in Moabit Prison, the same jail in which the Nazis had held him in the 1930s. While many

Ossis were glad to see him behind bars awaiting trial, there was considerable questioning, in both east and west, about the legitimacy of his arrest. To some, the treatment of Honecker looked more like vengeance than justice. Certainly he could no longer do any harm to anyone, save perhaps to those who had to listen to him endlessly protest his right to a tranquil old age. Moreover, medical tests revealed that he was suffering from cancer of the liver and stomach. Nonetheless, he was made to stand trial in November 1992 on charges of having ordered acts against life and liberty on the inner-German border. But after two months the trial was suddenly suspended on grounds of the defendant's ill health, and Honecker was once again given his freedom.

The former dictator's release prompted angry demonstrations in Berlin, mostly on the part of Ossis. The protesters were at a loss to understand how a man like Honecker, who had trampled on human rights, could successfully appeal his case on humanitarian grounds. Shortly after his release the old man flew to Chile to join his wife and daughter. Upon arrival in Santiago he was cheered by local leftists, who recalled with gratitude that the GDR had provided a refuge for some 5,000 Chileans fleeing the rightist dictatorship of General Augusto Pinochet.

Honecker's partner in crime, Erich Mielke, also found himself in Moabit Prison awaiting trial in the early 1990s. His lawyers claimed that he was mentally unfit to defend himself, and he certainly *seemed* senile, barking orders to imaginary inferiors on a toy telephone kindly supplied by his guards, and hiding under his bed when the prison psychologist arrived to interview him. After a while he recovered sufficiently to blame Honecker for whatever wrongs the GDR might have committed. In the end, the authorities determined that Mielke was competent to stand trial, but the charges proffered against him had nothing to do with his role as GDR minister of state security (the prosecution's case here seemed too weak); rather, he was tried for having murdered two policemen on Berlin's Bülowplatz way back in 1931. If Honecker's trial seemed questionable to some, the Mielke proceeding appeared doubly bogus, a misuse of the judicial process almost as egregious as Mielke's own perversion of the law as Stasi chief. The trial ended in October 1993 in a six-year jail sentence for Mielke, who was almost eighty-five when he began his term.

Markus Wolf, the Stasi's most brilliant foreign intelligence operative, was charged in 1992 with twelve counts of treason stemming from his work as head of East German Intelligence in the 1970s and 1980s. But the legitimacy of bringing Wolf to trial was debatable. Had he really done anything different than his West

German counterparts? Was not spying an accepted practice of a sovereign state? Was not his real offense simply that of making Bonn's counterspooks look bad? Foreign Minister Klaus Kinkel, who as a former head of West German Intelligence was particularly anxious to punish Wolf, lamely argued that the GDR spies had acted *offensively*, while FRG spies had acted only *defensively*. Wolf was brought to trial in September 1993. During the proceedings Kinkel made a brief appearance in court, and the encounter between these two former intelligence chiefs, one of them now a senior statesman, the other fighting to stay out of jail, struck Wolf as "in many ways symbolic of the trauma that East Germans were facing after unification. Their lives were on the slab, and the West held the scalpel for dissection." On December 6, 1993, the court found Wolf guilty and sentenced him to six years in prison. His lawyer, however, appealed the decision to the Federal Constitutional Court in Karlsruhe, which in May 1995 overturned the conviction on grounds that spying for the GDR did not amount to treason, since espionage was a normal activity for a sovereign state. The verdict put Wolf and other former GDR spies in the clear for the time being, but it remained possible that they could still be tried for espionage activities committed in third countries.

While Wolf could plausibly argue that he had not done anything his western counterparts had not also done, this defense was unavailable to those who had ordered and carried out killings at the Berlin Wall and inner-German border. As we have seen, Honecker was brought up on charges related to the *Schießbefehl* (shooting-order), as was General Heinz Keßler, head of the National Defense Council. (Later, so was Egon Krenz.) In Keßler's trial, it was shown that the GDR government had specifically authorized shooting as a last-resort measure to deter the "crime" of fleeing the country. East German officials, however, maintained that it was the Soviet Union, not the GDR, that had been responsible for the security procedures at the border.

As if unclear precisely where the order to shoot had originated, united Germany's legal authorities focused much of their attention on the low-level guards who had actually carried out the killings. This of course raised the objection that mere cogs in the machine were being made to bear most of the responsibility for the operation. Not surprisingly, the defendants argued that they were only following orders and that their acts had not been illegal under East German law. Nevertheless, in 1992 a Berlin court found two young border guards guilty of the shooting death of Chris Gueffroy, the last fatality at the Berlin Wall (February 6, 1989). The guard who had fired the fatal shots received a sentence of three-and-one-half years' imprisonment. In passing sentence, the court argued that an "intolerable disproportionality" existed between the "offense" of flight and the guards' lethal response.

The complaint that it was mainly the smaller fry who were being held accountable for the border shootings was addressed in 1996 by a trial in Berlin of six former generals of the East German army. Among the defendants was Klaus-Dieter Baumgarten, a former deputy defense minister. Charged with nineteen counts of manslaughter and attempted manslaughter, all six generals were found guilty and sentenced to prison terms of varying lengths. Baumgarten, who was accused of complicity in eleven killings and of signing orders to shoot fugitives, received the longest sentence: six and a half years. "This is a political verdict," said the general. He insisted that the border-security regime was a legal measure designed to thwart a Western invasion of East Germany.

Another well-publicized trial involved an officer of the East German Border Troops, Karl Bandemer, who commanded the 34th Border Regiment at the time of a particularly brutal murder at the Berlin Wall. According to trial testimony, on February 7, 1966, border guards opened fire on a construction worker named Willi Block as he tried to crawl through a coil of barbed wire. Hearing the shots, Bandemer rushed to the scene and discovered that the fugitive, though not yet wounded, was hopelessly caught in the wire. Rather than ordering his retrieval, Bandemer asked for an automatic pistol and opened fire on Block at a range of twenty meters. At least two border guards also fired. Over seventy rounds were expended, more than enough to dispatch Block. According to one witness, Bandemer bragged after the killing: "It takes the commander to come around to show the boys how these matters are handled." In his defense, Bandemer claimed that the fatal shots had actually come from the *western* side of the Wall. Although the court did not buy this, it found the defendant guilty only of second-degree manslaughter, and imposed a sentence of three years' imprisonment. Bandemer appealed the verdict on grounds of "legal error." At the time of his appeal—April 1997—only one sentence in the more than fifty cases involving shootings at the Wall had been definitively upheld after the exhaustion of all appeals.

Arrivals and Departures

In the mid-1990s Berlin presented a complicated and contradictory picture. The Wall was down, but the city remained deeply divided. Citizens on either side of the former barrier tended to read different newspapers, listen to different radio stations, even smoke different brands of cigarettes. In the 1995 elections for Berlin's House of Representatives, the PDS, or ex-Communists, became the strongest party in East Berlin with 38.3 percent of the eastern vote, while winning only 2.1 percent in the west. Great excitement over the town's new status as capital-elect was tempered by frustration over the inevitable changes that came with reunification and a new political mission. The city's extensive facelift belied economic stagnation, even decline. Companies and jobs were fleeing Berlin just as new migrants were pouring in from Eastern Europe. The city once again touted its openness and cosmopolitanism, but xenophobia and antiforeigner violence were one the rise. In 1996 the citizens of Brandenburg, reflecting old prejudices against Berlin, voted down an initiative to combine Brandenburg and Berlin into a single state, a measure that Mayor Eberhard Diepgen had claimed was necessary if the eastern region was to hold its own against the more powerful western states. Diepgen and other boosters spoke of Berlin as Europe's most happening city, but forty years of division and isolation had left a durable legacy of provincialism. Even some locals had to admit that the new Berlin might be more hype than hip. As one cabaret performer put it: "Berlin is like an old woman who dyes her hair and then thinks she is beautiful."

Prenzlauer Berg, the neighborhood in northeastern Berlin that had housed the most vibrant artistic "scene" in GDR days, developed a larger, trendier scene after the Wall came down. Western punks came over and squatted, while Kreuzberg artists and intellectuals, attracted by "the charm of the derelict," bought spacious apartments in the district's rundown but still-intact Wilhelmian-era *Mietskaserne*. Carpetbagging Wessis, along with a few entrepreneurial Ossis, opened a raft of new cafés and restaurants. The area around Kollwitzplatz was ground zero in this transformation. In the area's new cafés, which were carefully designed to look like old cafés, young people from all over the world congregated to eat ethnic food, drink overpriced wine and beer, and feel hip.

Many long-term residents were less than pleased by the "discovery" of Prenzlauer Berg. A neighborhood group protested the noisy intrusion of westerners and tourists. Locals spoke of being "forced out" by the newcomers. Dismissing their complaint, one of the café owners said that such malcontents "simply wanted the [Eastern] Zone back." Another source of grievance was the sudden escalation of rents in many of the housing units. Landlords who had reclaimed properties on the basis of prior ownership, or who had bought their buildings from the Treuhand,

Pasternak Café in Prenzlauer Berg, 1999

were anxious to make these units profitable. Because by law they could not substantially increase the rents paid by long-term tenants unless they made improvements to the dwellings, they did things like install new heating units in order to double the rent. One unscrupulous landlord sought to drive out his tenants out by manipulating the gas line in his building in order to produce small explosions. If a landlord needed assistance in getting rid of low-paying residents, he could call on *Entmietungspezialisten* (dislodging specialists) to do the job. As one entrepreneur explained: "A building is an economic unit and not a welfare office."

One of the trendiest new cafés in Prenzlauer Berg is called "Pasternak." Here one can catch a whiff of Russia without the bother, and the danger, of actually going there. Some of the Pasternak patrons are genuine Russians—members of a new Russian colony that had settled in the Spree city in the wake of the collapse of the Soviet Union. In 1995, 12,500 Russians were officially registered in Berlin, with perhaps three times that number present illegally. What was happening in the early 1990s was a smaller version of the huge Russian migration to Berlin in the 1920s. In the post-Wall influx, as in the post-1917 one, Russians made themselves at home by opening restaurants, bars, journals, and art galleries. Expatriates could listen to a Russian-language radio program that kept them abreast of news about their former homeland and the local émigré scene. In 1993 Patriarch Aleksy II, the spiritual leader of the Russian Orthodox Church, celebrated mass in a packed Berlin church. He was the first Orthodox patriarch to set foot on German soil. Russians with more worldly matters on their minds flocked to Charlottenburg to play and shop, just as they had in the 1920s. A number of boutiques on Fasanenstrasse, along with some appliance stores on Kantstrasse, catered specifically to wealthy Russians. Berliners suspected that the money behind these businesses came from the "Russian Mafia," which indeed had a strong presence in the city. The social center of the Russian community in post-Wall Charlottenburg was a café called "Hegel," located on fashionable Savignyplatz. It offered its patrons Slavic folksongs along with the inevitable vodka and borscht. If Pasternak was a piece of the new Berlin, Hegel was a slice of old Russia, a refuge from the rigors of fast-paced metropolitan life. "It's a different approach to life," averred the owner. "We drink more vodka, we appreciate music more, and we enjoy life more."

Many of the Russian New-Berliners were Jews. Berlin, in fact, was once again becoming a favored sanctuary for Russian and other Eastern European Jews who had become fed up with the persistent anti-Semitism in their homelands. By the mid-1990s the city's Jewish community counted about 10,000, by far the largest in Germany. The religiously inclined among them had four synagogues to choose from, representing the main traditions in Judaism. A Jewish cultural center stood next to the restored "New Synagogue," whose regilded dome dominated the Oranienburger Strasse on the edge of the old Scheunenviertel. A "Jewish Theater of Berlin" performed regularly (in Russian) at the Jewish Community Center in Fasanenstrasse.

It would be an exaggeration, however, to speak, as some Berliners did, of a "renaissance" of Jewish life in the once and future German capital. The Berlin Jewish contingent's size, while impressive by postwar German standards, was but a shadow of the 160,000-strong community of the 1920s. As before, Berlin's Jews were sharply divided between more established residents and new arrivals from the east. Many of the Russian-Jewish newcomers (in contrast to the *Ostjuden* a century earlier) were less interested in cultivating Jewish traditions than in integrating themselves as fast as possible into German society. In 1997 a much-publicized quarrel between two political factions within the local Jewish community became so embittered that Ignaz Bubis, head of the Central Council of Jews in Germany, called in a CDU politician from Frankfurt, Michel Friedman, to try to end the embarrassing "mud-fight" in Berlin. The city's political establishment, meanwhile, did little to assist newly arrived Jewish artists in their efforts to rebuild a viable cultural scene. As *Der Spiegel* observed: "Apparently no local politician has gotten it into his head that the unexpected and undeserved opportunity to revive Germany's Jewish cultural heritage requires special attention."

Rather than promoting a living Jewish culture, Berlin cultivated a nostalgia for the lost era of pre-Nazi Jewish vitality. Oranienburger Strasse, once lined with Jewish businesses, now became a kind of Jewish theme park. In addition to the New Synagogue, of which only the dome and front section—not the main sanctuary—were restored, there was an upscale kosher restaurant where tourists in search of an authentic Jewish experience could eat vegetarian blintzes and listen to piped-in klezmer music. A building nearby bore the sign, Kleiderfabrikation Goldstein, the work of a film crew making a TV movie about *Jüdisches Berlin*. Across the street stood a picturesquely dilapidated structure which had been turned into an avant-garde art center called Tacheles—Yiddish for "straight talking." The building in question had opened in 1909 as one of those grand iron and glass arcades that so fascinated turn-of-the-century flaneurs. In the 1920s it had served as an exhibition hall for futurist products made by the German Electric Company. Allied bombs and East German neglect had reduced it to a sagging hulk. The artists who "occupied" the place in 1990 with the battle cry, "Ideals are ruined, so we'll save the ruins," drew generous subsidies from the Berlin Senate. By the mid-1990s Tacheles had become a not-so-secret "secret tip" in all the guidebooks. A restaurant on the ground floor called "Café Zapata" promised a taste of the Mexican revolution, Berliner-*Szene* style, to package-tour groups bussed in from all over Europe.

Although generally welcoming its new Jewish residents, Berlin witnessed a number of anti-Semitic incidents in the years following the fall of the Wall. Neo-Nazis vandalized headstones in Jewish cemeteries and painted *Juden Raus!* on synagogues (which eventually were placed under twenty-four-hour police guard). Skinhead thugs declared that it was intolerable that Berlin, the "capital of the German Reich," should once again be attracting Jews from other parts of Europe. These actions were part of a much larger wave of right-wing antiforeigner violence washing over reunited Germany. In the fall of 1991 a group of skinheads, cheered on by lo-

Tacheles Art Center in Oranienburger Strasse

cal residents, attacked Vietnamese and Mozambican workers in a housing project in Hoyerswerda (in the former GDR). In the following summer thugs beat Gypsies and attacked the residents of an asylum center in the eastern port of Rostock. Many West Germans attributed these incidents to the postunification frustrations of the East Germans, but even worse outrages occurred in the "old states": the firebombing of a house in Mölln, near Hamburg, that killed a Turkish woman and her niece and granddaughter; the attack on a Turkish residence in Solingen that killed five women and children from a family who had been living in West Germany for twenty-five years.

The heart of Berlin's neo-Nazi scene was located in the eastern district of Lichtenberg, where the SED regime had built a number of vast prisonlike housing complexes. In GDR days the area had been a bastion of Communist loyalty, but in the last years of the regime it also harbored about 300 neo-Nazis. Many of the Lichtenberg skinheads had started out as hippies or punks but, when that form of protest seemed too timid, switched to Nazi slogans and symbols. According to Ingo Hasselbach, a veteran (and later critic) of the scene, he and his friends began spraying swastikas next to their circled "A's" for anarchism. "We didn't think much about what a swastika meant, but we knew it was the most forbidden of all symbols." Inspired by West German television documentaries on Nazi military campaigns in World War II, the skins ranged through the city in search of *Fidschis* (their term for Vietnamese guest workers) to terrorize and beat up. Admittedly, there were not very many *Fidschis* in East Berlin, but the boys did what they could. They also targeted the pacifist, reform-socialist crowd that congregated in Prenzlauer Berg. On the night of October 17, 1987, a gang of thugs armed with iron bars and chains stormed a pacifist rock concert at the Zionskirche. Hasselbach, who had recently served a prison term for publicly demanding that the Wall come down, was in on the attack. "We cleaned the church out," he boasted. "We hauled the punks out and beat them up." Revealingly, nearby police units were very slow to stop the Zionskirche bloodletting. Later, a Stasi official admitted that the GDR regime saw the skinhead gangs as a useful tool in their battle against the nascent reform movement.

When the Wall came down East Berlin's right-wingers began getting financial and organizational support from West German neo-Nazis, who saw the Ossi thugs as potential foot soldiers in their campaign to extend their influence to the east. Michael Kühnen, the leader of the West German Action Front of National Socialists, which was dedicated to "restoring the values of the Third Reich," helped out with cartons of Nazi literature, imperial war flags, camouflage outfits, switchblade knives, and steel-tipped Doc Marten boots, perfect for "sidewalk cracking," or stomping on the head of an opponent who had been knocked to the pavement. Kühnen and his lieutenants educated their Ossi charges about the "Auschwitz lie," the doctrine that the Holocaust had never happened. Kühnen elevated Hasselbach to "Führer" of the East German branch of his movement, and in early 1990 the new chief registered the National Alternative Berlin (NA Berlin) as East Germany's first radical-right party. The Berlin group could be more openly neo-Nazi than its West German parent because the Modrow government, anxious to show a democratic spirit, imposed few controls on the welter of new parties that sprang up after the fall of the Wall. As Hasselbach noted, "You could found the German Beer Drinkers' Union, or the National Party of German Assholes, if you wanted to." Within a matter of months the NA Berlin was one of the strongest radical-right parties in East Germany, with about 800 members. The group soon fractured, however, when it was disclosed that Kühnen was homosexual. One of Hasselbach's minions, a twenty-two-year-old hairdresser known as "Stinky," led a dissident antigay faction.

If Kühnen was in the vicinity, Stinky would shout, "Always keep your backs to the wall when the Führer comes!"

Kühnen encouraged the Eastern Nazis to think beyond the borders of the GDR and to join him in opposing the "Jew-controlled Bonn Republic." As the GDR crumbled, the Ossi skins became more aggressive, engaging in constant street battles with anarchists and leftist gangs. This was a new dimension for them, and very exciting. As Hasselbach wrote: "We were cutting loose in a way that was wilder than anything we'd ever imagined. It was an incredible feeling of freedom—roaming the streets, blowing up cars, and guarding our fortress against the anarchists, even if it did distract from the political work at hand." Of course, what was exhilarating for the skins was horrifying for the municipal authorities. Even Hasselbach admitted that the street battles were "costing Berlin the reputation it sought as a safe city, which it needed to become Europe's new cultural and business capital." In spring 1990 the city struck back by raiding the skins' headquarters in Weitlingstrasse, confiscating weapons and Nazi literature, jailing Hasselbach for five weeks, and throwing the NA Berlin off the electoral ballot for the May municipal elections.

These measures, really just slaps on the wrist, did nothing to cow the neo-Nazis. Following German unification and the decision to transfer the government to Berlin, the "National Alternative" became bolder than ever. Through Kühnen the group received support from elderly Nazi widows, who saw in these young thugs the advance guard of the Fourth Reich. With their widow-money the boys bought all manner of weaponry, including bazookas, machine guns, and grenades, from Russian soldiers in Berlin. The skins talked of destabilizing the democratic state through dramatic strikes and assassinations. Their hit list included Gregor Gysi, Ignaz Bubis, and even Helmut Kohl. Although these plans never got beyond the talking stage, the skins continued to attack foreigners in the streets. In 1990 they threw Molotov cocktails at a shelter for foreign workers in Lichtenberg. The police intervened only after considerable damage had been done. A few days later the city closed down the shelter.

The skinheads' brutal attacks on foreigners, and the Kohl government's inadequate countermeasures, generated a growing crescendo of negative publicity for newly united Germany. By 1992 the government began to take sterner measures, banning neo-Nazi groups and shutting down skinhead squats, including the one in Berlin's Weitlingstrasse. In the following year Bonn organized a giant rally against antiforeigner violence in Berlin. Some 300,000 citizens joined in this well-meaning demonstration, which took place on the anniversary of Reichskristallnacht. The event, however, turned out to be an embarrassing fiasco, both for Germany and for its future capital. About 300 leftists castigated the assembled dignitaries as "hypocrites" and pelted the main speaker, President Richard von Weizsäcker, with eggs, tomatoes, and paint bombs. When Helmut Kohl joined a march down Unter den Linden, he too was pelted with eggs. The demonstration ended in disarray, with Kohl stalking off in disgust. Commenting on the scene, the *New York Times* wrote: "[The rioters'] success in disrupting the largest demonstration in Berlin since German unification two years ago added to the growing crisis of confidence in German democratic institutions." Not surprisingly, this affair was grist in the mill for those many Germans who still regretted the decision to move the capital to the Spree metropolis. It was characteristic of Berlin, they said, that an intended demonstration against the radical right should turn out to be a showcase for the disruptive power of the radical left.

On June 18, 1994, Berlin witnessed another government-sponsored spectacle: a giant parade in honor of the Allied troops, whose departure from the city was scheduled to be completed by September of that year. An estimated 75,000 people watched soldiers from America, Britain, France, and Germany parade down Unter den Linden. Overhead flew a lone DC-3, representing the planes that had participated in the Berlin Airlift forty-six years before. The Russians had asked to be included in this event but were politely told by the German hosts that it would be better if they held their own good-bye ceremonies. The rebuff was hardly surprising, since the Kohl government and most citizens of western Berlin held Moscow responsible for the division of the city. Most eastern Berliners did so as well, and they had never exactly snuggled up to their Russian "protectors." On the other hand, many Ossis saw this snub of the Russians as yet another blow to their own self-esteem. As one commentator noted: "The residents of the GDR had to suffer a lot more during the division of Germany than [those of the FRG]; now even their conquerors were to get a second-class departure ceremony."

Although the departure of the Allied powers was another step in Berlin's return to "normalcy," and essential to its future role as national capital, many Berliners, especially of the older generation, watched the exodus with a certain sadness. "The Allies came as saviors and stayed on as protectors," said one seventy-seven-year-old lady. "They liberated us from one dictatorship and saved us from another one," she added. "Without [the Western Allies]," averred another oldster, "we'd all be Russians now." Sadder still over the Allied departure were the leaders of the city's various ethnic communities. As Douglas Jones, a U.S. State Department official, noted: "The withdrawal of Allied forces from Berlin filled ethnic community leaders with dread, because they had come to regard the Allies as protecting powers not from the Russians, but from the Germans."

The Russians bid their own farewell to Berlin in a ceremony on August 31, 1994. Historians noted that this was the biggest pullout ever by an army that had not been defeated in battle. Yet of course the pullout did signal a defeat of sorts, despite brave words about lasting friendship and future cooperation from Helmut Kohl and Boris Yeltsin. Spectators at the Soviet good-bye parade were few and far between. In addition to their war memorials, which the Germans promised to maintain, the Russians left behind barracks and other housing units stripped of window frames, toilet fixtures, and electrical outlets. They also left a legacy of environmental devastation in the form of toxic dumps and oil-soaked bases.

The final pullout of the Western Allied troops in September 1994, like the big parade in June, was at once festive and elegiac. Tens of thousands of Berliners turned out for countless good-bye parties, and many a tear was shed for the departure of "our good friends." To keep alive memories of the Allied presence in Berlin, and to educate future generations about the Western powers' role in the divided city, German officials established an Allied Museum at a former American base. The opening exhibition, entitled "More Than A Suitcase Remains—the Western Powers in Berlin 1944–1994," featured various *objets* of the Cold War era: a chunk of an eavesdropping tunnel dug under East Berlin in the 1950s; one of the Hastings cargo planes that flew in supplies in the airlift; a U.S. tank that had stood barrel to barrel with Russian armor when the Wall went up in 1961; and, pièce de résistance, the guards' hut from Checkpoint Charlie. There were also artifacts of the "abnormal normality" of everyday Allied life in the divided city: uniforms, street signs, Campbell's soup cans, candy wrappers.

The choice of a former American base for the Allied Museum was appropriate because the American impact on the town was by far the strongest. No major European city had become more Americanized than West Berlin. In addition to vast housing complexes and training facilities, the physical legacy left behind by the Americans included a golf course, yacht club, several schools, officers clubs, and

The Guard's House from Checkpoint Charlie at its new location in the Allied Museum

an array of McDonald's, Burger Kings, bagel shops, rib joints, diners, and other icons of the American Way of Life. For years Berlin had sponsored an annual Deutsch-Amerikanisches *Volksfest*, which drew in thousands, and it boasted an American-style football team, the Berlin Eagles. Of course, as we have noted, America's relationship with Berlin over the past half-century had hardly been tension-free. From the mid-1960s through the 1980s West Berlin had witnessed hundreds of anti-American demonstrations, many of them violent. Even the protests, however, were influenced by America's own counterculture, which provided the template for these actions. As for the new generation of Berliners coming of age in the 1990s, they saw America less as a savior, or as an oppressor, than as a giant pop-culture factory. A sixteen-year-old boy told an American reporter at the opening of the Allied Museum: "Just about everything we have that's fun comes from the United States. If it weren't for Americans, we wouldn't have baseball caps. We wouldn't have malls or fast-food shops or skateboards. Life just wouldn't be as good." Unlike the Russians, the Americans did not bequeath to Berlin a legacy of disemboweled buildings and polluted soil, but they certainly left behind plenty of junk.

Shortly before the America-dominated Allied Museum opened in Zehlendorf, a rival "German-Russian Museum" opened across town in Karlshorst, where the Soviet occupation had been based. The museum is located in the villa in which Field Marshal Keitel and Marshal Zhukov signed Germany's capitulation to the Soviets just before midnight on May 8, 1945. In 1968 the building was converted into the "Museum of the Unconditional Surrender of Fascist Germany in the Great Patriotic War, 1941–1945." The new facility, which opened in May 1995, fifty years after the capitulation, seeks to enshrine "common forms of memory," though it is doubtful that the Russians and Germans have much in common when it comes to interpretations of the past. Not surprisingly, the Karlshorst collection places considerable emphasis on the Second World War. A prize attraction is Hitler's campaign-map for the attack against Poland in 1939; a constantly running film clip shows Keitel driving across the destroyed Reich capital to the capitulation ceremony. The Karlshorst museum operates under combined German and Russian supervision, but this joint administration cannot disguise the fact that the institutionalized memory of Berlin's recent past, like the city itself, remains sharply divided.

The restored Reichstag building with its new high-tech dome. The Brandenburg Gate with its quadriga is in the foreground

THE BERLIN REPUBLIC

Every nation needs a center of power. The influence, the role, the pride, the self-confidence of a people, also their will-to-action, are reflected in their national capital and projected outward from that space.

—Arnulf Baring, "Eine Zukunft für unsere Vergangenheit" (1995)

On February 9, 1997, an old Wehrmacht hand grenade exploded in Berlin-Mitte, wounding five children. Three years earlier construction workers in the eastern district of Friedrichshain had struck and detonated an American bomb from World War II; the explosion killed three people and injured seventeen. These pieces of ordnance were among the tens of thousands of unexploded grenades, shells, and bombs lurking in Berlin's soil, waiting to claim belated victims. "The new capital," said a member of Berlin's fire department, "sits on one big time bomb."

Of course, unexploded bombs from World War II were only the most obvious relics of a dangerous past in the new German capital, whose landscape was haunted by a host of historical "ghosts." Many of these goblins were associated with the Nazi period, while others derived from the Prussian, imperial, Weimar, and post–World War II Stalinist eras. Those responsible for shaping post-Wall Berlin's renovation were not able simply to banish these spirits, much as some of them might have wished to do so; they had to find ways to live with their haunted past.

The fall of the Wall, the unification of Germany and Berlin, and the decision to move the seat of government from the Rhine to the Spree produced a dramatic physical transformation of the once and future German capital. There had been extensive rebuilding programs in both halves of the city during the forty-year division, but the post-Wall reconstruction was qualitatively more ambitious. No other city in modern times has witnessed such a far-reaching overhaul in so short a time. But Berlin's makeover was unique in spirit as well as in scale; given all those evil spirits in the firmament, the task presented a singular complex of political, psychological, and moral dilemmas.

In addition to dredging up political ghosts, the reconstruction of Berlin in the postunification era rekindled an old debate about the nature of the city. Was Berlin so lacking in coherent patterns of urban development and discernible aesthetic traditions that one could reshape it without paying much attention to the architectural past? "The only tradition in Berlin is that no phase of construction ever gave a damn about fitting in with the phase that went before," wrote the modernist architect, Christoph Langhof. Alternatively, was there a unifying aesthetic that needed to be respected? Here, two images of Berlin sharply collided: the city that "is always becoming and never is"; and the city that "already exists and need not be discovered anew."

New Teutonia

The battle for the architectural soul of the new Berlin began, appropriately enough, in the Potsdamer Platz, the once-bustling commercial hub that had become a gaping void as a result of World War II and the Wall. Over time the place had returned to nature, with rabbits multiplying in the weeds. It was as if, wrote the American architectural critic Paul Goldberger, "Times Square had been replaced by a chunk of the New Jersey Meadowlands." In Wim Wenders's classic film of 1980s West Berlin, *Himmel über Berlin*, an old man wanders across the western section of this wasteland, muttering, "It's got to be here somewhere. I can't find the Potsdamer Platz." When it came to ghosts of the past, this area had more than its share. In the vicinity of the Potsdamer Platz and the adjacent Leipziger Platz had stood Hitler's Neue Reichskanzlei and bunker, Roland Freisler's Volksgerichtshof, and Heinrich

Himmler's Gestapo and SS Headquarters. Spartacists had fought against the army here in 1919, and in 1953 Soviet tanks had formed a barrier at the sector border against rioting East German workers. When the Wall came down, Berliners hoped that the area would be the centerpiece of a renewal that was at once forward-looking and reverential—a leap into the future via a return to pre-Nazi vitality.

City leaders hoped this too, but in 1990 long-term planning took a back seat to aspirations for a quick burst of progress. As we have seen, the Momper government immediately sold off large sections of the square to Daimler-Benz and Sony. Other plots went to Hertie, a West German department store chain, and to Asean Brown Boveri (ABB), a multinational engineering firm. The companies all planned to develop major projects on their properties, and they were more interested in making a big commercial splash than in fitting in to some larger aesthetic design. Nor were they overly worried about the historical ghosts. As Daimler-Benz's cheerleading publicist explained to a visiting journalist, "Potsdamer Platz is a free land. It has no memory. It is a new country." To reinvent the square, the developers hired famous architects like Renzo Piano, Richard Rogers, José Moneo, and Arata Isozaki (Daimler-Benz); Helmut Jahn (Sony); and Giorgio Grassi (ABB). Daimler's Isozaki was especially enthusiastic about his assignment because Berlin perfectly fit his definition of a city as "a thing perpetually in a state of ruin." Echoing Albert Speer, Isozaki envisaged something like "ruin value" in the things he built. "For me," he said, "the moment of ecstasy is when everything that is built vanishes in a catastrophe." He and his colleagues saw the void in the middle of Berlin as a perfect place in which to build monuments to themselves.

It turned out, however, that the architects would not be allowed complete free rein. Stung by criticism that they were letting "a few fat cats' checkbooks" determine the fate of the Potsdamer Platz (and, by extension, the rest of Berlin-Mitte), city officials decided that there needed to be a unified developmental plan for the square. Volker Hassemer, senator for Urban Development and Environmental Protection, orchestrated a juried competition that in October 1991 awarded first prize to a plan submitted by two architects from Munich. It called for a continuation of Berlin's traditional height limit of thirty meters (Berlin was not to be "Frankfurtized" by a bunch of skyscrapers); the salvage of remaining historic structures; and a "mixed use" development that balanced retail, entertainment, office, and residential needs. The idea here was to ensure that the new Potsdamer Platz, like the Potsdamer Platz of old, functioned as a diverse and "living" part of the city.

One might question, of course, whether metropolitan liveliness could be planned at all. In the immediate context, however, the problem was how to reconcile the planners' ideals with those of the developers and architects. There ensued a wearisome series of negotiations that set the tone, and many of the standards, for the continuing debate on the development of the city. The municipal government's side in these negotiations was articulated by its new building commissioner, Hans Stimmann, who one commentator likened to Baron Haussmann, the rebuilder of Paris under Napoleon III. Those who believed that Berlin must continue to develop along traditional lines—whatever *they* were—could not have had a more forceful advocate. The stocky, white-haired Stimmann, who was born in Lübeck and trained as a mason, was convinced that there was indeed a core Berlin aesthetic, which he called the "classical modern," and he aimed to protect this ideal from its newest enemies: the horde of international architects who wanted to do for Berlin what they had done in places like Hong Kong and Toronto. Germany's metropolis was special, Stimmann insisted, and it had to be treated as such. "Berlin was totally destroyed by the bombs and after the war it was totally destroyed by the planners," he declared. "Berlin is the only city in the world where the inner city is empty. We must bring this city back so that when we look in the mirror, we will know that it is our face. If we look like Hong Kong or Tokyo, nobody will come. Berlin must look like Berlin." With his doctrine of "critical reconstruction" Stimmann found some influential allies, most notably the architect Josef Paul Kleihues, the architectural historians Vittorio Lampugnani and Dieter Hoffmann-Axthelm, and the publisher Wolf Jobst Siedler, who wrote frequently on the necessity of maintaining a sense of history and continuity in the Spree metropolis.

For proponents of a radically new Berlin, Stimmann was anathema. His critics called him "a demon for Prussian order" and condemned his vision of Berlin as "New Teutonia." The Polish-born American architect, Daniel Libeskind, who would design post-Wall Berlin's most innovative building, the Jewish Museum, had little patience with the rules laid down by the building commissioner's office. These regulations ignored, said Libeskind, Berlin's more recent tradition of breaking-with-tradition, of setting off in new directions. As examples of such daring modernity, Libeskind liked to cite Erich Mendelsohn's Columbushaus, Bruno Taut's Horseshoe Housing Estate, and Peter Behrens's AEG Turbine Factory. "There is an unnerving nostalgia for the past," he declared. Stimmann's rules constituted "the total erasure of fifty years of history of this city. It is going back to a time when things were not problematic, coupled with an authoritarian ideal of how to develop the city." Another Stimmann critic, the Frankfurt art historian Heinrich Klotz, echoed this charge of authoritarianism, to which he added megalomania. "Herr Stimmann and his allies claim that they are setting the world-standard for urban construction. Their blown-up metropolitan pretensions are simply embarrassing." After locking horns with Stimmann on the Potsdamer Platz plan, Rem Koolhaas, a noted Dutch architect, concluded that Berlin was simply not up to the task of setting urban-design standards for the rest of Germany and the world. "Berlin has become the capital at the very moment it is least able to take on the responsibility," he declared. The American critic, Goldberger, also doubted that Stimmann's Berlin was capable of breaking new ground: "What is troubling about the city's present architectural picture," he wrote, "is the sense that in post-Wall Berlin the very openness to new ideas and new forms that so long defined the city's culture is threatened by a desire to make Berlin too comfortable. It is as if the city had gone from oppression to smugness in one step." In the view of Richard Rogers, Berlin was "architecturally lost."

As might have been predicted, what resulted from the clash of visions over Potsdamer Platz was a series of compromises that left no one entirely satisfied. The architects were allowed to build somewhat higher than the general plan specified, and they were not forced to conform to a strict stylistic blueprint. On the other hand, they had to tone down some of their boldest conceits, abide by the mixed-use requirement, reduce intended space for parking, and preserve historical structures. In Daimler-Benz's case, this last stricture meant salvaging the Weinhaus Huth, a tavern-restaurant established in 1871 in which Theodor Fontane had been a regular, Himmler had held court, and Hitler's half-brother Alois had worked as head waiter in the 1930s. Sony had to preserve part of the facade and the "Kaisersaal" of the Grand Hotel Esplanade, which had been 90 percent destroyed in the war. To salvage this structure Sony went to the extraordinary length of building around the facade and moving the Kaisersaal seventy-five meters to the west. The old world would thus live on in the new, though as quaint museum pieces, rather like Augustus Pugin's "Medieval Room" in Joseph Paxton's Crystal Palace of 1851.

Potsdamer Platz in the mid-1990s was invariably described as "Europe's largest construction site," but in addition to being large the project was extremely challenging technically. Given Berlin's location above a giant aquifer, the builders created a sizable body of water as they dug foundations; divers worked sixty feet under the surface of this murky "lake," casting the concrete slabs on which the buildings would be propped. When the anchors were secured, pumps removed the ground water, but the pumpers had to be careful not to suck out too much lest they starve the trees in the neighboring Tiergarten. As they excavated, crews came across artifacts of Berlin's recent past: Schultheiß beer mugs, plates from the Café Josty, countless bomb fragments, and a "Stalin-Organ" rocket-launcher. One wonders what the workers, many of whom were Irish and Portuguese, made of these finds.

The square's relics may not have meant much to the workers, or for that matter, to the developers, but the topping-out of the construction in October 1996 was marked by a celebration that resembled nothing so much as a reconsecration. Daniel Barenboim, the new music director of the Staatsoper, used semaphore flags to conduct a ballet of construction cranes as they nodded and swung in time to the finale of Beethoven's Ninth Symphony, that ode to joy and universal brotherhood which had also been played at the reopening of the Brandenburg Gate. Most of the people who attended this strange ceremony probably were not aware that the Nazis had likewise used this music for special occasions, including a birthday celebration for Hitler in April 1942, when Goebbels proclaimed that "the sounds of the most heroic music of titans that ever flowed from a Faustian German heart should raise [the thought of serving and obeying the Führer] to a serious and devotional height."

As the buildings of the Potsdamer Platz slowly rose up from the sandy terrain, it became possible to get a sense of how the project would look when it was fully completed. Viewing the work in February 1999, when it was about two-thirds finished, the American critic Herbert Muschamp was less than overwhelmed. Although he found some of the individual buildings quite arresting, the complex as a whole, in his view, lacked distinctive power; it radiated a spectacular but not a specific modernism. "What Potsdamer Platz resembles," he wrote, "is an edge city; one of those private, development-driven urbanoid clusters that have sprouted up across the American landscape in recent years. It is reassuring that the new Potsdamer Platz is notably without nationalist expressions. The downside of this is that the place could be anywhere. Like other edge cities, it occupies a kind of nebulous international airport space." When it was completed a few months later, the Daimler-Benz portion of the project confirmed some of the critics' worst fears. With its collection of franchise establishments and cookie-cutter boutiques, it might just as well have been in Houston. Examining the complex in June 1999, the American urban sociologist, Saskia Sassen, sensed a lack of "social thickness"—an absence of diversity and complexity.

One way to lend specificity to a place is to attach to it names and symbols of historical significance. In 1997 the Potsdamer Platz promoters, with the backing of Berlin officials, decided to name a central plaza in the complex after one of Berlin's most glamorous daughters, Marlene Dietrich, who had died in 1992 in Paris at the age of ninety-one. Although Dietrich might not have been pleased to be so honored, it is perhaps fitting that she got such recognition, since heretofore her native city had been anything but generous toward her. The actress's decision to leave Berlin in 1930, to become an American citizen, and then to perform for Allied troops as they conquered Germany, earned her the reputation as a "traitor" in some Berlin circles. When she returned to Berlin in 1960 on a singing tour she drew bomb threats and protesters crying "Marlene, Go Home!" Her burial in 1992 in a Berlin cemetery next to her mother occasioned an outpouring of respect for her memory, but also some ugly complaints that the "foreign whore" was being allowed back in the city she had "rejected." In 1996 a Social Democratic official in the district gov-

Marlene-Dietrich-Platz in Potsdamer Platz, 1999

ernment of Schöneberg, where Dietrich was born, tried in vain to rename a local street, the Tempelhofer Weg, in her honor. Although the street in question was a dingy strip of auto-wrecking shops and recycling centers, the locals vehemently protested the plan. As one resident complained: "What did Dietrich do for us? She was always away." Other efforts to rename Berlin localities after Dietrich also failed. She finally found a place in the anonymous glitz of the new Potsdamer Platz primarily because there was no living constituency there to keep her away. As one commentator observed: "Only in this thoroughly synthetic space, where a poetic amnesia prevails, could the diva who for good reason stayed away from Germany finally find a home."

Potsdamer Platz was still just a jungle of cranes and scaffolds when the newly rebuilt Friedrichstrasse made its debut as post-Wall eastern Berlin's first major attempt at a commercial comeback. As we have seen, in economic terms the comeback was a flop, at least in its opening phase. But what about the aesthetic dimensions of the reconstruction? Friedrichstrasse boasts some impressive individual buildings. The most spectacular is Jean Nouvel's Galeries Lafayette, which updates the great Berlin department store tradition with new devices to bedazzle the customer. The main hall is dominated by glass cones in whose panels the shopping area is reflected. The result is an ever-changing kaleidoscope of luxury. On the whole, however, the Friedrichstrasse corridor seems antiseptic and bland. Most of its buildings, at least on the outside, do not make any significant design statements. Critics have blamed this on Stimmann's rules rather than on a lack of architectural talent, for the Friedrichstrasse reconstruction, like that of Potsdamer Platz, involved a number of international architects not known for their self-restraint. According to the Berlin journalist Gottfried Knapp, another source of the problem lay with the investors, for whom "the only acceptable building" was the traditional *Büropalast* (office palace), a structure with stores on the ground level, offices in the middle stories, and at the top a couple of luxury apartments for the mistresses of the real-estate barons. Thus, instead of "reviving the flair of Berlin-*Mitte*," as the street's promoters claimed, Friedrichstrasse managed merely to replicate the uninspiring commercial corridors found in most West German towns. All the hype notwithstanding, wrote Knapp, new Berlin's fabled avenue looked no better "than the pedestrian zones of Salzkirchen and Gelsengitter."

Bahnhof Friedrichstrasse, the storied train station that opened for business in 1882 and served for years as a central crosstown transit point, was also extensively rebuilt. Between 1961 and 1989 this station was the end of the line for most East Germans traveling on the westbound *S-Bahn* line; only the privileged few (or the burdensome old) with permission to go west used the terminal as a point of departure. For westerners (other than West Berliners) coming into East Berlin by *S-Bahn* or subway, this was the station where they had to detrain and obtain visas for their short-term stays in the city. Accordingly, the building was a Kafkaesque labyrinth of dingy stairwells, jerrybuilt hallways, temporary barriers, and passport-inspection cubicles, all patrolled by machine-gun-toting guards. Next to the main station was a shabby annex where travelers heading west were processed; for understandable reasons, this was known as the "Palace of Tears." With the reconstruction, which began in the early 1990s, all this changed. The place where GDR inspectors once stamped passports became a jeans store; the Palace of Tears was converted into a nightclub. Travelers could again walk from one part of the cavernous station to another; and, of course, the various trains, some 1,300 of them every day in the early 1990s, no longer had to reverse direction after arriving at the station. Bahnhof Friedrichstrasse was once again a major crossroads in the city, not the end of the line.

At the other end of Friedrichstrasse, near the intersection with Kochstrasse, stood the famous Checkpoint Charlie, which in the days of division had served as the principal crossing-point for foreigners between West Berlin and East Berlin. After the Wall came down the area around the dismantled checkpoint became the focal point of another major commercial redevelopment project in Berlin-Mitte, the so-called "American Business Center." In 1992 two Americans, the cosmetics baron Ronald Lauder, and Mark Palmer, formerly Washington's ambassador to Hungary, formed a partnership with a German real estate magnate, Abraham Rosenthal, to develop a large office complex on the site. "Once again, Americans and Germans extend their hands to build together," was the project's motto. These developers, too, hired star architects, most notably Philip Johnson, the grand old man of modern architecture. Johnson put up a giant billboard picture of himself on the property. (Later, in a reference to the famous kidnapping of John Paul Getty III, some Berlin anarchists stole the billboard and cut off Johnson's ear, which they sent to the developers with a note demanding a ransom for the return of the rest of the picture.) As construction progressed, the bottom dropped out of Berlin's commercial real estate market, prompting Lauder and Palmer to pull out. When the complex opened

The International Business center at Checkpoint Charlie, 1999

in 1997, only half its space could be rented. The name was quietly changed from American Business Center to International Business Center, but it probably should have been called the Rosenthal Center, since the German was left holding the bag. "As early as 1993 it was clear that Berlin was not going to become the jumping-off place for American business in Eastern Europe, as I had originally thought," admitted Rosenthal later. "I miscalculated."

Although economic vagaries, not faults in design, caused the Business Center's problems, the project was sharply criticized on aesthetic grounds as well. Johnson himself admitted that his building was a failure. He blamed this on Berlin's regulations, stating that no other city would have forced him to produce such a boring and mediocre design. Palmer, too, was disappointed that the complex lacked stylistic assertiveness, and he likewise faulted the regulations imposed on the project, "the small-town mentality of Stimmannism." Extrapolating from his experience at Checkpoint Charlie, Palmer drew unpromising conclusions for Berlin as a whole:

"Berlin could be the most important center in the world," he said in 1995, "but after being beaten down by the events of the past half-century, the Germans have become used to being self-effacing, not bold."

Back in the days when the Germans had not yet lost their taste for grand gestures, they had laid out the parts of central Berlin that would serve as their primary political stage in the modern era: the Pariser Platz, Schloßplatz, and the connecting avenue, Unter den Linden. Like the rest of Berlin-Mitte, these places had been heavily bombed in World War II, and then had suffered under Communist redevelopment schemes from the 1950s through the 1970s. With the fall of the Wall and the decision to transfer the capital to Berlin, something clearly had to be done with this crucial corridor. Given its historical and symbolic significance, there was strong sentiment in favor of a traditionalist reconstruction. But what exactly did "traditionalist" mean in a place like Berlin? And how should one proceed in those cases where the ghosts of the past threatened to overwhelm the good intentions of the present?

Pariser Platz, named in honor of Prussia's participation in the Allied victory over Napoleon in 1814, was often referred to as the "kaiser's reception room" after 1871. With the second unification it was due to become, in the words of Berlin's building senator Wolfgang Nagel, "the salon of the republic." But in the early 1990s this was a room with virtually no furniture. With the exception of the Brandenburg Gate and a section of the Prussian Academy of Arts, all its grand buildings were gone. Like so many vacant spaces in central Berlin, it now served as an ad hoc flea market, with Ossis peddling pieces of the Wall and other relics of the GDR. The Senate proposed that the square be rebuilt in a style "appropriate to the age." One critic derided this instruction as "a balloon without any air in it," but, as it turned out, the balloon was filled with some pretty heavy historical ballast.

The primary surviving structure on Pariser Platz, the Brandenburg Gate, had of course become *the* symbol of Berlin by the twentieth century. The Communists had restored it in the 1950s as a "gate of peace," piously eliminating the Prussian eagle and iron cross from the reconstituted quadriga on the top. During the years of division, when the monument was closed off by the Wall, it took on new symbolic meaning as the gate that wasn't. In addition to being Berlin's most prominent symbol, it became an icon of the Cold War. In the heady days of November 1989, it symbolized the end of Germany's, and Europe's, division. In 1991, reunited Berlin decided to replace the politically corrected 1958 quadriga with a remake of the version that had stood atop the gate between 1814 and 1945 (which itself was a revision of the original sculpture that Napoleon had stolen in 1806). But if one wanted to return the gate to its former glory and function as the portal of an enclosed square, it would also be necessary to reconstruct some or all of the buildings that had once surrounded it, beginning with the two August Stüler–designed palaces that had flanked it from 1844 until their destruction in the war. The contract for this project went to the Berlin architect Paul Josef Kleihues, who, true to the doctrine of "critical reconstruction," hued closely to the scale and volume of the Stüler buildings, while omitting most of their ornamental details. Kleihues also eliminated a series of arched windows that had harmonized with the facades of the two small wing-buildings attached to the gate. Unfortunately, these changes broke up the continuity of the original ensemble. Worse, the stark new "palaces," which looked more like fortresses, threatened to overpower the central edifice. In 1939 Albert Speer had planned to reduce the Brandenburg Gate to a traffic island by tearing down the small wing-buildings. Kleihues had no intention of diminishing the power of Berlin's most famous structure, but this, in effect, is exactly what his additions managed to accomplish.

Pariser Platz's other surviving, or partly surviving, structure, the Prussian Academy of Arts, had, like the Brandenburg Gate, traversed a complicated odyssey that mirrored the political vagaries of modern Berlin. Having moved into the neoclassical Palais Armin-Boitzenburg on the southeastern corner of the square in 1907, the Academy quickly became caught up in the culture wars of imperial Germany: artworks approved by the kaiser hung here, but so did works by Max Liebermann and Lovis Corinth. Heinrich Mann was elected president of the Academy in 1931—and dismissed from that position two years later by the Nazis. In 1937 Albert Speer expelled the Academy from the building and moved in his "General Directorship for the Reconstruction of the Reich Capital." It was here that Hitler's favorite toy, a thirty-meter-long model of "Germania," was installed. The model and the original part of the Academy building fell victim to Allied bombs during World War II; only an annex and connecting wing survived intact. With the creation of the GDR, artists belonging to the East German Academy of Arts took over the structure. Here the sculptor Fritz Cremer prepared his sketches for the heroic-Communist monument at Buchenwald. When the Wall went up, East German border guards commandeered the connecting wing, consigning the artists to the annex. The collapse of the GDR and unification of Germany brought a decision to rebuild this history-rich institution around its surviving structures. But should all dimensions of its history be acknowledged, or just the "worthy" parts? The architect Günter Behnisch, who won the contract, designed a glass-fronted building exuding "transparency" and "openness," but openness only to those aspects of the Academy's history that were "consistent" with its original function as a house of the muses. This did not include Albert Speer and the East German guards.

One of the buildings that had flanked Pariser Platz on its southern side was the famed Hotel Adlon, Berlin's grandest hostelry from its opening in 1907 to its sad end just after World War II, when drunken Red Army soldiers set fire to the parts of the structure that had survived Allied bombs. (The then proprietor, Louis Adlon, son of the founder, was deported to Russia and executed, apparently because the Soviets confused his title, "General-Director," with a military rank.) After the ruins were carted away, few Berliners imagined that they would ever see another version of this grand edifice, but in 1995 the corner stone was laid for a new hotel of the same name on exactly the same place. This time, however, the builders were different: the Kempinski chain and a group of international investors. There was considerable irony here, for at the turn of the century old Kempinski, fearing competition with his own hotel, had tried his best to prevent the Adlon from being built.

Building a major new hotel in mid-1990s Berlin was a great risk—Kempinski's director admitted that Berlin needed another big hotel "like a hole in the head"—so it was imperative to make this project stand out from the competition. The developers chose to do this by giving the hotel the look of its grand predecessor, while incorporating all the latest technical innovations, such as bulletproof windows and "steel-plated rooms for the celebrities." The architect, Rüdiger Patzschke, came up with a "tradition-oriented" design that so reeked of "period authenticity" that even Stimmann found it stifling. To critics who accused him of wallowing in the past, Patzschke replied: "We find the claim that contemporary architecture is the non-plus-ultra of design to be a narrow-minded misjudgment on the part of the representatives of the modern."

The new Hotel Adlon opened in June 1997, fifty-two years after its predecessor's destruction. The central foyer contains a fountain that had once graced the old building. The piano music featured in the main salon consists largely of teatime tunes from the 1920s. In another bow to the past, the Adlon boasts suites for visiting heads of state (along with adjoining space for their bodyguards) and a small balcony from which dignitaries can acknowledge the crowds below. The hotel's literature does not point out that it was from just such a balcony in the old Adlon that Nazi dignitaries watched the SA parade through the Brandenburg Gate on January 30, 1933.

The Hotel Adlon had stood next to the British embassy from 1907 to 1945. Such will be the case again in the new millennium, since the British are scheduled to open a new embassy on the same site in the year 2000. Berlin's government welcomed London's decision to build on this historic place as another crucial step in the Pariser Platz's phoenixlike rejuvenation. Like their neighbor, the Adlon, the British elected to employ a traditionalist and "restrained" design for their embassy.

France, whose stately embassy had graced the northern side of Pariser Platz, also made a commitment to return to its old site. However, when it came to the design of its new building, the French Foreign Ministry was not nearly so respectful of local standards as its British counterpart. The French had always been somewhat condescending toward Berlin, which tried so hard to be like Paris. Now, upon returning to the square named after their own capital, they were determined to remind the Germans that, though France might no longer be the Continent's leading power, it still set the tone in the realm of grand public construction. Their architect, Christian de Portzamparc, planned a striking structure featuring two-story-high windows in the facade. Upon unveiling this plan, Foreign Minister Hervé de Charette was careful to distinguish the French project from Kleihues's palaces and Patzschke's Adlon: "The buildings [on the square] are all stiff and tasteless," he said. "Our project will bring some French flair."

The United States, the other great Western power to have occupied a niche on Pariser Platz, was expected to join its allies in returning to its former location. Washington, after all, had been Berlin's most stalwart backer since the days of the airlift, and rebuilding on Pariser Platz would constitute an important gesture of support for the city. Yet America's return to the historic square was not a foregone conclusion. Washington worried that there might be too many restrictions, and too little space, at its old site. America's then ambassador to Germany, Richard Holbrooke, declared ominously in 1996: "It is our hope that we will be able to build at Pariser Platz, but we haven't made a final decision yet because we don't have the final German specifications. If the Germans can accommodate us, we'll end up there. But we are looking at alternative sites, and if we are faced with deal-breaking specifications, we'll go another way."

Holbrooke's comments alarmed and horrified the Berliners. Rüdiger Patzschke, the Adlon architect, fumed: "Nowhere else can you achieve what you can achieve at Pariser Platz. Plenty of countries would love to have their embassies there. It just wouldn't make sense for the Americans to go anywhere else. If they find the site too small or the rules too restrictive, they could put just their reception rooms and a few offices there. But to abandon the site altogether would not make sense."

Washington soon smoothed the Berliners' feathers by making a commitment to the Pariser Platz. Holbrooke, in fact, may have been bluffing in order to scare the Germans into imposing fewer restrictions. But no sooner had the decision been made to build at the old site than a new problem arose: a shortage of funds. Washington had planned to finance the construction of its new embassy from the sale of American-owned property in Germany, especially in West Berlin. The proceeds from these sales, however, were less than expected. The State Department therefore announced in 1997 that it was putting the new construction on hold; when its embassy moved to Berlin in 1999, it would make use of existing buildings, including the cramped former American embassy in East Berlin. In other words, because of its professed poverty, the richest country in the world was going to have to camp out in the German capital. Learning of this dire state of affairs, Berliners offered to take up a collection for Washington's new embassy. They said that America could think of such assistance as partial compensation for the Marshall Plan.

Chagrined by this turn of events, Washington insisted that it could find the funds to build an appropriate home on the Spree. The American embassy saga was not over yet, however, for a dispute over security measures put off construction once again. In the wake of terrorist attacks against its embassies in Kenya and Tanzania, Washington demanded security provisions for its future embassy in Berlin that sparked resistance from the Berlin Senate. The Americans insisted on a thirty-meter traffic- and pedestrian-free zone facing the open (western and southern) sides of its complex. This would require closing off two main avenues and rerouting the traffic. The Berlin Senate rejected the demand on grounds that, as one senator declared, the changes "would diminish the Brandenburg Gate and its environs." This response reflected a new attitude on the part of the Berliners toward their erstwhile "protective power." No longer was America's wish the locals' command. Once again, Washington threatened to build elsewhere in Berlin, though America's new ambassador, John Kornblum, was known to favor quarters, "preferably without windows," on Pariser Platz. Until the security issues could be resolved, the plot at Number 2 Pariser Platz remained empty, save for a small metal sign reading, "The once and future site of the American Embassy in Berlin."

Berlin's tradition-oriented planners and architects saw the Pariser Platz as a base from which to extend their influence down Unter den Linden to the city's other showplace square, the Schloßplatz. Like Pariser Platz, the Schloßplatz had been badly smashed up in the war, but, as we have seen, the old Hohenzollern Palace itself had survived partly intact until the Communists demolished it in 1950. The site was used for government-approved demonstrations and as a parking lot until the Honecker regime covered part of it with the GDR's own "palace," the Palast der Republik, in the mid-1970s.

Given the historic significance of the Schloßplatz and its missing and extant palaces, it was perhaps inevitable that the square's fate in the new Berlin would become the subject of heated debate. The Wall had barely come down when a call went up to demolish the GDR palace and to rebuild the old Hohenzollern Schloß in its place. The idea sparked spirited, albeit differentiated, resistance. Some of those who objected to rebuilding the old palace were quite prepared to tear down the newer one; other opponents of reconstruction were avid partisans of the existing GDR structure. There were thus "rival nostalgias" at work here, competing visions of the past that impeded any consensus about the future. And, as usual, the rival memories of Berlin were emblematic of conflicting collective identities and images of the German nation.

Those in favor of rebuilding the Hohenzollern Palace and tearing down the Palast der Republik had recourse to aesthetic, historical, and ideological arguments. The demolition of the Palast der Republik was easier to justify than the reconstruction of the old Schloß. The GDR building was undoubtedly ugly, and it stood at a pivotal location at the eastern end of the Linden, Berlin's most important avenue. Its presence there, argued one commentator, "blocks an urbane future for the socialist-usurped city center." Moreover, an inspection revealed that it was stuffed with asbestos, which made it a health hazard as well as an eyesore. Tearing it down could also be seen as belated revenge for the demolition of the old palace in 1950. Since the construction of the Palast had been meant to symbolize the triumph of communism, its destruction would symbolize that system's ultimate defeat in the Cold War. Finally, clearing away this relic of the GDR would eliminate a possible shrine for *Ostalgie.* In 1993 the Berlin Senate made a formal decision to tear down the Palast, though no specific demolition date was fixed.

This decision generated more opposition than the politicians had bargained for. Former citizens of the GDR, along with some sympathetic Wessis, mounted a petition campaign to save the Palast and flooded the newspapers with protests against the demolition plan. They insisted that the Palast had been less a repository of repression than "a site of popular amusement." Ossis recalled with fondness the hours they had spent in its restaurants, cafés, and bowling alley. They remembered it as one of the few places in East Berlin where an ordinary citizen could find clean public toilets and functioning East-West telephones. Admittedly, they conceded, the Palast was a little off-putting aesthetically, but no more so than most of the buildings thrown up in West Berlin during the 1960s and 1970s. Indeed, this faction contended, compared to West Berlin's International Congress Center, which was built at the same time, the Palast was downright "humane and friendly." As for the asbestos issue, this too was not just a Palast problem, since many western buildings were also filled with the stuff, and at any rate there were ways to get rid of it (and plenty of illegal Polish laborers to do the nasty work). The real "contamination," these folks said, had to do with the Palast's alleged pollution with GDR ideals, but it was precisely as a legacy of the former GDR, as a piece of municipal and national history, that the building should be retained. It was here, after all, that on August 23, 1990, the GDR had voted to join the Federal Republic. Berlin had precious few recent buildings of such singular historical importance, it was argued. To tear down this one would be to commit another of those offenses against history with which the city was all too familiar.

Even if the Palast der Republik were to be torn down as planned, rebuilding the old Hohenzollern Schloß in its place struck many observers as an outlandish, not to mention reactionary, idea. It would be much better, they argued, to put up a modern building on the site—a structure representative not of Berlin's feudal past but of its role as a trendsetter in architectural design. The opposition to reconstruction was also fueled by concern over the message that this action might send about the new Germany and its capital. The worry was not that the outside world would get the idea that the Germans wanted to bring back their monarchy, but that such a gesture could be interpreted as a revival of the German nationalist spirit.

That symbolic gestures involving Germany's monarchical past were capable of igniting widespread anxiety had become painfully evident in August 1991 when the body of Frederick the Great, who had once said that territorial expansion was "the first rule of government," was reburied at Sanssouci in nearby Potsdam. This reinterment was the end of a long odyssey for Frederick, who died in 1786. In his will the king had stated that he wished to be buried "without pomp or ceremony" at Sanssouci, but instead he was interred with great pomp at the Garrison Church in Potsdam. There he stayed until World War II. To protect the royal relic from Allied bombs, Göring moved the coffin in 1943 to a Berlin cellar, and two years later, to protect it from the advancing Russians, Hitler ordered it removed to a salt mine in Thuringia. The Americans found Frederick and placed him in a church in Marburg. In 1953 the king's Hohenzollern heirs moved him once again, this time to the family plot near Stuttgart. Finally, German unification prompted the family, some 205 years after Frederick's death, to grant him his last wish by interring him next to his beloved dogs in the soil of Sanssouci. The king's wish for simplicity, however, still eluded him. Helmut Kohl turned the reburial into a state occasion by insisting upon being present; the Bundeswehr sent an honor guard. The affair reminded some observers of the "Day of Potsdam" (March 21, 1933), when Hitler and Hindenburg bowed before Frederick's grave at the Garrison Church, thereby claiming an alliance between the Kaiserreich and the Third Reich. Kohl of course had no intention of signaling a revival of Frederick's expansionist ideals; rather, he simply wanted to "stand before our entire history." Nonetheless, his inept and controversial gesture, like his effort six years before to promote reconciliation with one of Germany's conquerors through a joint visit with President Ronald Reagan to the military cemetery at Bitburg, where Waffen-SS-men were buried, could not help but be misinterpreted.

Concerns about Germany's national image, combined with the other objections to a Schloß reconstruction, might have killed this idea immediately had it not found some influential supporters on the local and national levels. Once again Helmut Kohl made his influence felt as a champion and protector of Germany's national heritage. Believing (like Kaiser Wilhelm II) that Berlin needed a lot of historical ballast to keep it from floating off into a political cloud-cuckoo land, he offered his personal backing for the Schloß project. On the municipal front, Mayor Diepgen and the local CDU endorsed the scheme. One of Germany's best known journalists, Joachim Fest, used his pulpit at the *FAZ* to argue that the old palace, far from being a forbidding bastion of authoritarianism, had been an approachable, even folksy place whose courtyard was open to ordinary citizens. Wolf Jobst Siedler, the influential publisher, likened a possible Schloß reconstruction to Warsaw's restoration of its historic old city after World War II, and to Venice's rebuilding of its trademark Campanile in the early twentieth century. In his view, Berlin needed a reconstituted Schloß to bring coherence back to its devastated center. He pointed out that Schinkel's neoclassical Neues Museum had been designed to interact with the baroque facade of the old palace. The publisher could have countenanced a modern building that performed this function, but he had no faith that the modernists were capable of coming up with an appropriate design. Thus it was with "resignation" that he opted for a reconstruction of the old palace.

The figure who did the most to promote the idea of a palace reconstruction, Wilhelm von Boddien, came at his task with no such hesitation or regret. Interestingly, Boddien was not a local pillar of the community, not even a Berliner, but a Hamburg farm equipment magnate ("the John Deere of Germany") who described himself as a history buff and "Prussia-fan." Rather than simply talk up or write about a putative Schloß revival, he hit upon the idea of erecting a mock-up of the building's facade in order to show the Berliners, and visitors to the city, what they had been missing all these years. In 1993, at his direction, a trompe l'oeil canvas curtain painted to replicate the old palace's baroque facade went up next to the Palast der Republik, in whose gold-tinted windows the faux facade was gloriously reflected. The mock-up was itself a masterful piece of work, and it spoke much more eloquently for the Schloß than all the boosterish newspaper articles and speeches. As an additional promotional gambit, Boddien organized an exhibition on the Schloß that was housed in a temporary structure behind the facade. This exhibit allowed visitors to get a sense of how the palace had fit into the life of old Berlin, and how a reconstituted palace might serve the new Berlin. Boddien's promotional material made clear that he and other friends of the palace did not envisage a complete reconstruction, replete with the old royal interior. This would have been pointless, not to mention prohibitively expensive. (Boddien and his backers promised to raise private financing for the project.) In place of the old palace's warren of rooms, the new space might contain a hotel, library, ballrooms, and a conference center.

Mock-up of the Royal Palace, with the Palast der Republik in the background, 1994 (courtesy LBS)

As comments in the exhibition guest book made clear, Boddien's initiative generated a great deal of popular enthusiasm for a palace reconstruction. Of course, there was also plenty of hostile comment—arch comparisons of the mock-up to a Disneyesque piece of fakery, appropriate for a project that smacked of a royalist theme park. "The idea that the Germans should accept a building that was representative of the politics of royalist Prussia as a symbol of today's Germany is richly presumptuous," huffed one commentator. By the time the mock-up came down in 1994, however, polls suggested that the majority of Berliners favored rebuilding the old palace.

But of course Berlin was not rebuilt by polls. Even if Boddien and his friends could have raised all the money needed for their envisaged Schloß reconstruction (which was doubtful), the project still depended on the demolition of the Palast der Republik, and in 1995 the Berlin Senate reversed itself and decided to spare the GDR monstrosity, at least for the time being. The officials took this stance not only because of the protests against demolition, but because the city lacked the funds to tear down the Palast. This of course said a great deal about the realities of life in mid-1990s Berlin.

The fate of Berlin's two palaces remained in limbo as the federal government prepared to move to the Spree at the end of the decade. The new chancellor, Gerhard Schröder, professed support for a reconstruction of the Hohenzollern Palace on the site of the Palast der Republik because, as he said, the royal building was "simply prettier" than its Communist replacement, and people "need something for the soul." Michael Naumann, the new minister of culture, was also for a reconstruction, arguing that Berlin's historic center sorely lacked an appropriate architectural emblem; the missing palace was like "a torn-out molar." Neither Schröder nor Naumann, however, said anything about the public subsidies that would be necessary to supplement private funding for the project.

Left in limbo, too, was a proposal to erect a "Monument to German Unity" in the place where a huge equestrian statue of Wilhelm I had once stood, in front of the western facade of the Royal Palace. Wilhelm II had commissioned this statue in the 1890s as the "German National Monument," but many Germans had seen it simply as a monument to Hohenzollern hubris. The problem with the new proposal was that no one had a clear idea of how to represent German unity in a monument. (This had also been the case in the Kaiserreich.) Moreover, citizens of the eastern states objected to a German-unity monument on the grounds that Germany wasn't truly unified at all.

Another structure on the Schloßplatz that was reprieved from impending demolition was the GDR State Council Building. Completed by the Communists in 1964, this building, as noted above, contained in its facade the Royal Palace balcony from which Karl Liebknecht had proclaimed a socialist republic on November 9, 1918. Pending the completion in 2000 of a new Federal Chancellery in the Spreebogen (about which more below), the State Council Building, it was decided, could be pressed into service as the chancellor's Berlin office. It is ironic, but entirely typical of Berlin, that this hybrid house, historically linked to the emperors, Liebknecht, and Honecker, should also have been the temporary home of Helmut Kohl and Gerhard Schröder.

One part of former East Berlin that saw relatively little reconstruction in the decade after unification was the Alexanderplatz. True, the GDR-era signs atop the square's buildings were gone, the *S-Bahn* station was renovated, and the old Centrum department store was given a modest facelift by its new owner, the Kaufhof chain, but otherwise the area looked much as it had before the *Wende*. By day its shops catered largely to Ossis, by night it was overrun by bums and very aggressive rats. Nevertheless, Berlin's new rulers had hopes and plans for this place too, which after all was one of the most famous in the city. "The Alexanderplatz was once the heart, the pulsating heart, of this city," said Volker Hassemer, the senator for urban development. "A mystique surrounds this place, despite all that has been done to it." The unfortunate changes that had been imposed on the square by the Communists, however, were so thoroughgoing that it would take a great deal of time, effort, and money to undo them. Unlike Potsdamer Platz, the "Alex" was not an empty lot; it was encircled by buildings that were still in use, and at its center stood Berlin's tallest structure, the Television Tower. Hassemer envisaged a reconstructed square where Berliners "could again feel comfortable." But *which* Berliners? The senator was all too aware of the problem: "We want to send a message that says we hope to turn a square in the east into the central-point of the city. But in the east this is interpreted as 'Oh, so now they also want to steal our Alex, too.'" In 1999, ten years after the fall of the Wall, a sad sign hung in the Platz saying, "Wir waren das Volk (We were the people)."

As a first step toward an eventual reconstruction of the Alexanderplatz, a design competition was launched in April 1993. It was won by the Berlin architect Hans Kollhoff, who presented a plan that was anything but modest or backward-looking. His scheme, as originally formulated, called for a cluster of thirteen skyscrapers, the tallest of them 150 meters high. His model was Rockefeller Center, which he characterized as the "big-city architecture of the century." It may seem odd that this design, which flew in the face of the city's building regulations, could have been taken seriously by the judges, let alone have won first prize. The judges and municipal authorities, however, were prepared to take greater risks with the Alex because, as Stimmann himself admitted, "there was nothing left to reconstruct"; skyscrapers, in fact, would have the advantage of overwhelming, and thereby devaluing, the hated Television Tower. Moreover, according to Hassemer, a radically new square might reinforce Berlin's claim to belong among the great cities of the new millennium. Yet one had to ask, as did the GDR-trained architect Bruno Flierl, whether attempting to replicate Manhattan in Berlin would help endow the German city with an architectural identity of its own.

In any event, such dreams would have to wait. Kollhoff's plan called for the tearing down of much of the existing housing around the Alex, and when this became known, the Ossis protested en masse. Backpedaling, the Berlin Senate ordered that the demolition program be reduced and the number of skyscrapers be cut to four.

Continuing arguments about the plan led to repeated postponements of actual construction. If a new Alexanderplatz actually materializes in the coming years, and if Kollhoff's design lies at its core, at least one part of the new Berlin may indeed end up looking like Frankfurt—or, for that matter, like New York, Hong Kong, or Tokyo.

Home on the Spree

"First we shape buildings, then the buildings shape us," Winston Churchill once said of the Westminster parliament. As the Germans began to shape the structures that would house their government in Berlin, they were very mindful of the strong connections between architecture and politics. Governmental buildings everywhere carry representational and symbolic weight, but in the new Berlin this was doubly so, given old Berlin's history. Coming "home to the Spree" meant launching Germany's latest political drama on a stage still set with the props of several recent plays, most of them tragedies. Many people, Germans above all, worried that a return to Berlin would spur new delusions of grandeur.

When the German government made its decision to shift most of its functions to Berlin, it announced that it intended to build brand new quarters for the federal chancellor, the federal president, and for the ministries that would make the move. The buildings that had housed the Communist government in East Berlin were to be torn down. These decisions, however, soon fell victim to the economic realities of reunited Germany and to protest actions by an energetic conservation lobby in Berlin. Bowing to the protests, and hoping to cut costs, the government declared in February 1993 that, while the chancellor and president would still get new buildings, the ministries would move into existing structures, which would be renovated and expanded as necessary. Most of the existing buildings that were earmarked for ministerial service had been used by the Nazis or the Communists, and often by both. This obviously raised difficult issues of political symbolism. Klaus Töpfer, who as federal building minister from 1995 to 1998 oversaw much of the governmental construction in Berlin, was willing to confront this problem head-on. He declared that the buildings in which state-evil had been conducted should be retained as "sites of inescapable memory," so that would-be political criminals of the future "could never again entrench themselves behind bureaucratic desks." Nonetheless, in addition to hiring architects to renovate these haunted houses, the new occupants might have found it advisable to bring in an exorcist or two.

Certainly Klaus Kinkel, who served as foreign minister at the time when a new home in Berlin was selected for his agency, was in the market for some serious political detoxification. He found it "unworthy" that a high-profile institution like the Foreign Ministry should be resettled in the former Nazi Reichsbank, which, to make matters worse, had also housed the headquarters of the SED from 1959 to 1989. Before grudgingly accepting this decision, he had fought for a brand new building on the Schloßplatz. He wanted, he explained, an architectural setting that "did justice to the ministry's special concerns of political image in representing the Federal Republic of Germany abroad. . . . Future-oriented quarters for the Foreign Ministry in Berlin therefore require a new building."

The historical building that the Foreign Ministry inherited in Berlin is a long, curving, sandstone-sheathed behemoth that had taken the Nazis six years to build (1934–40). During the Third Reich the structure's facade was decorated with a frieze of muscled figures designed by Josef Thorak. Here Hjalmar Schacht and his colleagues worked out the financial dimensions of Germany's rearmament. The complex had survived the war relatively intact, and in 1950 the East German Finance Ministry had moved in after making some cosmetic changes and structural modifications. In 1959 the Central Committee of the SED, along with the Politbüro, took over the building, making it the power center of the GDR. Erich Honecker had an office on the second floor.

When united Germany's foreign minister (not Klaus Kinkel after all, but Joschka Fischer) took occupancy of his new quarters in 1999, his office stood in the same general area as Honecker's old suite. The plenary assembly room of the SED Central Committee became a conference room. "I think it's not at all bad for the federal government constantly to be conscious of living and working against the backdrop of a difficult history," said Fritjof von Nordenskjöld, the Foreign Ministry official overseeing the move to Berlin. However, Foreign Minister Fischer and his successors were not likely to be reminded very often of Schacht and Honecker, for extensive modifications and the addition of a whole new wing gave the complex a very different look and feel.

United Germany's Finance Ministry inherited an *Altbau* with an even more tainted pedigree than the Reichsbank: the former Nazi Aviation Ministry, which had mutated into the headquarters of the Soviet Military Administration for Germany (1945–49), then the House of Ministries of the GDR, and finally, after East Germany's collapse, the Treuhand Anstalt. The various agencies that this building housed over the years shared commitments to power and control—impulses reflected in the complex itself, which commands the corner of Wilhelmstrasse and Leipziger Strasse like a fortress. "All who approached here felt reduced in stature, whether they be ministerial officials or simple visitors," wrote Günter Grass in his historical novel of Berlin, *Ein Weites Feld* (Too Far Afield). The quarters from which Göring ran the Nazi air campaign, Russian generals ruled their occupation zone, GDR ministers ran their country into the ground, and the Treuhand bureaucrats sold off what remained, was modified repeatedly over the years without altering the sinister aspect. The Soviets removed the Nazi ornamentation and remodeled the main reception hall in Stalinist-baroque. The SED commissioned a mural to commemorate the building's status as the birthplace of the GDR. In 1992 the building was renamed "Detlev-Rohwedder-Haus" in honor of the Treuhand's first Western director, who was murdered by a terrorist.

Four years later work began on transforming the building into the Finance Ministry. As the construction crews tore out wall sections and ceiling panels, they came across yellowed copies of the SS magazine, *Das Schwarze Korps*, and the GDR union periodical, *Tribüne*. They also found a small bronze chest containing a document commemorating the completion of the building's structural frame "in the third year of freedom under the generous leadership of the Führer and Reichskanzler Adolf Hitler." Despite extensive renovations, some interior details from the original building were carried over into the new structure. These include the number-plaques for the row upon row of office doors and the aluminum banisters that Göring had personally designed as an homage to his beloved aircraft. Understandably, however, the new occupants preferred to highlight another aspect of the building's history: the presence there for a short time of the anti-Nazi resistance group, the Red Orchestra. During the renovation an exhibition on this group was installed in the lobby. In the interests of historical preservation, the occupants decided to retain the GDR-era mural glorifying the socialist state—which, however, they counterbalanced with a monument to the workers who had died in the uprising of 1953. Commenting in 1995 on the challenge that the designers faced in confronting this building's tangled past, Wolfgang Keilholz, the architect in charge of the renovation, said that he and his employers were obliged "to respect the fact that guilt emanated from this building. The user who will now occupy this building must know that.

And by occupying such a building one takes on an obligation, one that is greater than if one were just to tear down the building."

United Germany's Ministry of Labor also took on such an obligation, for this agency moved into what had once been Joseph Goebbels's Ministry of Popular Enlightenment and Propaganda. Unlike Göring, the Nazi propaganda minister had not commissioned a totally new building; rather, in 1933 his ministry had occupied the former Ordenspalais and two smaller buildings on the Wilhelmplatz. The main building had been built in 1737 and extensively remodeled by Schinkel one hundred years later. Finding it "out of date and obsolete," Goebbels ordered it redone in the "ocean-liner-style" he thought projected power and modernity. In 1937–38 the complex was expanded to include the former colonial ministry, while new wings extended Goebbels's empire to the Mauerstrasse one block east. The historic core of the complex was wrecked in the war, but some of the Nazi-era additions survived to become the GDR's Press Office and Ministry for Media Policy. Norbert Blüm (CDU), who was labor minister at the time his agency was consigned to this building, was horrified by the choice. He signaled his displeasure by refusing to visit the structure as it was undergoing the necessary renovations.

A different set of ghosts haunts the house that became united Germany's Economics Ministry. Originally hoping to move into the Prussian Herrenhaus (which instead was given to the Bundesrat), this ministry was shunted to a large structure on the Invalidenstrasse just to the east of where the Wall had run. Built in "Frederican-Baroque" style in 1903–5, this building served as the Kaiser-Wilhelm-Akademie für die Ausbildung von Militärärzten (Kaiser Wilhelm Institute for the Training of Military Physicians) before World War I. The poet Gottfried Benn received his training there. The Nazis had used the building as a courthouse, which was also its function during the early years of the GDR, when it was home to "Red Hilda" Benjamin, a relative of Walter Benjamin and East Germany's most zealous political prosecutor. At the height of her influence in the late 1950s, the West German press likened her to the Nazi hanging judge Roland Freisler. In the late 1960s the building was transformed into a government hospital that catered mainly to foreign diplomats, who were cared for by specially selected nurses; work crews remodeling the building in the 1990s discovered an entire room full of condoms.

As noted above, the Ministry of Defense's main office remains in Bonn, with a secondary office transferred to Berlin. The ministry's home on the Spree is the storied "Bendlerblock" on the Landwehr Canal. Having been constructed in 1911–14 for the Reichsmarineamt, this stately gray building housed Admiral von Tirpitz, orchestrator of imperial Germany's fateful naval race with Great Britain. After World War I it became the Reichswehr Ministry. Here, on February 3, 1933, Germany's top generals received Hitler and learned of his plans to expand Germany's "Lebensraum" (living space) to the east. The early campaigns of World War II were directed from this complex when it served as the headquarters of the Wehrmacht High Command. Also housed here were the offices of many of the military resisters against Hitler, including Count von Stauffenberg, who was executed in the Bendlerblock courtyard following the coup's failure. With the exception of a memorial to the resisters and a small museum (about which more below), extensive renovations to the complex obliterated all traces of the past.

Because the challenges of living with the ghosts of Berlin were made necessary by the Bundestag's decision to shift Germany's seat of government to the Spree, it is perhaps fitting that this body inherited the former capital's epitome of symbolically difficult buildings: the Reichstag. In actuality, some of that difficulty is undeserved, since neither the kaiser nor Hitler had had much to do with the place. Nonetheless, this war-scarred fossil was so laden with conflicting, mainly depressing, historical associations that many parliamentarians did not want to have anything to do with it. For them the site bore the uneradicable stink of grand pretensions and tragic failure. The building's very name was a problem, since "Reichstag" translates as "Imperial Diet." "We are not a German Reich but a Federation," protested Renate Schmidt (SPD), "and we want to underscore that federalism." In addition to its heavy symbolic baggage, the old building had the disadvantage of being architecturally inadequate for the demands of united Germany's parliament. The postwar renovations, such as they were, had not brought the structure up-to-date in terms of creature comforts and technical requirements. Günther Behnisch, the architect who had designed Germany's brand new and then promptly abandoned parliament building in Bonn, likened the Bundestag's decision to take over the Reichstag to the federal president's donning the kaiser's moth-eaten uniform in the 1990s. If it was to be put back into service as united Germany's parliament, the building would have to be extensively renovated and supplemented with additional structures.

The issue of the Reichstag's complicated historical associations could be dealt with in part through a new set of symbols, a reorientation of the building's imagery.

It so happened that a dramatic means of underscoring such a reorientation lay ready to hand. Since the early 1970s the Bulgarian-born artist Christo, whose favorite form of creative expression was wrapping up very big things in all manner of material, had been lobbying to "wrap" the Reichstag. He had been repeatedly rebuffed, most recently by Helmut Kohl, who feared that Christo secretly wanted to wrap *him*. Many politicians opposed the idea as an insult to the building's dignity. Wolfgang Schäuble protested that no other country would allow a structure of comparable historical importance to become the centerpiece of a conceptual art experiment. Would the British so disgrace Westminster, the Americans Capitol Hill, or the French the Palais Bourbon? Nevertheless, after the Wall came down Christo's plan found support among politicians who believed that through such a gesture the once and future parliament building could, so to speak, undergo a ritual rebirth: it could be wrapped as the Reichstag and unwrapped as the Bundestag. The CDU politician Heiner Geissler argued that "through Christo we get the chance to show the world Germany's tolerant and open-minded character." Christo himself suggested that the project would stimulate viewers to reflect on "what this building means to Europe, Germany, and many people around the world." With the backing of Mayor Diepgen and Bundestag president Rita Süssmuth, the plan was approved by a vote in the Bundestag on February 25, 1994.

As it turned out, the Reichstag-wrap was a huge public-relations coup for Berlin. Thousands of people came to view the old Prussian pile enveloped, like a rich bride, in a million square feet of silver-covered fabric. The cover-up made Berliners "see" the building again, just as the mock-up of the Hohenzollern Palace had made them revisualize that historic structure on its original site. When the wrapping came off in July 1995, the Reichstag was ready for its renovation.

But exactly what kind of renovation? A design competition in 1992/93 yielded very different answers to this question. Unable to select a clear winner, the jury awarded three first prizes: to the Dutchman Pi de Bruijn, the Spaniard Santiago Calatrava, and the Englishman Sir Norman Foster. Eventually, after further scrutiny and many heated discussions, Foster was given the contract to redesign Germany's most important building. The fact that he and the other finalists were all foreigners was quite telling. Clearly, the parliamentary officials had a fear of seeming too assertive, too "German" in the traditional sense. As the chairman of the Bundestag Building Committee admitted: "There was perhaps some anxiety that if we did it in a purely German manner we would have taken a whack."

The Reichstag "wrapped" by Christo, 1995

Foster, who had made his name by designing skyscrapers in Hong Kong and Frankfurt, won the Reichstag contract because his design seemed most likely to project the openness and transparency that were the cherished hallmarks of the modern German democracy. By matching the parliamentary building's new look with the principles and confident aspirations of its new tenants, Foster's Reichstag would show the world that the German government's return to Berlin meant neither an abandonment of the ideals of Bonn nor a relapse to the weaknesses of the pre-Bonn parliamentary order.

Once he began working in earnest on the renovation, however, Foster discovered that having a parliamentary committee as his boss meant having to entertain a dozen different concepts regarding the work at hand. Like Wallot, the original builder, he had to change his design repeatedly and accept countless compromises. His original design called for the existing structure to be surrounded by an outer framework of steel columns supporting a flat glass canopy. Foster explained that this accommodated "the need for a new symbol, a symbol that corresponds to our age, a new image of an open future." But some members of the Bundestag Building Commission objected that this design would make Germany's parliamentary headquarters look like a gas station or an airplane hangar. Forced to drop the canopy, Foster proposed a glass cylinder instead, which he said would suggest a "lighthouse of democracy." The SPD people liked this idea, but the CDU delegates on the commission insisted on a glass dome, which the original building had possessed. Originally, the conservatives wanted an exact replica of Wallot's dome, while the FDP favored a modern rounded dome, and the Greens stood for no dome at all. Eventually the CDU conceded that a remake of Wallot's dome would be too expensive and accepted a more modern version. Foster reluctantly complied and designed an inverted glass cup that suggested, according to different observers' imaginations, a half-egg, a space station, a greenhouse, a pimple ripe for popping, or Kohl's bald pate. Foster got his revenge by making the dome such a high-tech tour de force that it ended up costing much more than a Wallot-replica would have done. On the other hand, with its platform from which visitors could look down on the plenary hall below, the dome proved to be an effective symbol of political transparency. One could only hope that many Germans would

The Reichstag undergoing renovation, 1997

The Reichstag's new high-tech dome, 1999

visit their new house of democracy, since the overall price tag—DM 600 million, or $331 million—made it the most expensive public building in Berlin.

In order to reconfigure the Reichstag's interior for its new occupants, Foster gutted the place, completely doing away with the renovations introduced in the 1960s. In laying bare the original walls workers uncovered yet another "ghost" of Berlin's recent past: lots of graffiti left behind by the Russian soldiers who had occupied the building in 1945. "Glory to the Stalinist Falcons, Who Participated in the Storm on Berlin!" read one comment. "Death to the Germans!" read another. These were not the kind of decorations that most politicians would want in their parliament, and some conservatives urged that they be expunged. Foster, however, insisted that they be preserved, and in the end they were. As they go about their business, the parliamentary deputies will be confronted by constant reminders of the grim fate of the last German government to have ruled from Berlin.

The new Reichstag's interior contains positive historical symbols as well. Over Foster's objections, the deputies' seats were covered in the same bright periwinkle fabric used in Bonn, on the grounds that "German democracy was born on those seats." On the wall behind the speaker's rostrum hangs a large plastic representation of the German eagle, a replica of the rather corpulent one that had watched over the old Bundestag in Bonn. Foster had proposed a more athletic animal, one that looked as if it might actually be able to fly, but the parliamentarians insisted on retaining their "fat hen." No one should get the idea that the Berlin Republic was about to attack its neighbors.

Because the remodeled Reichstag was far too small to house the parliamentary offices and library, two new office blocks and a library were built in the immediate vicinity of the historic structure. The new buildings are connected to the old one by underground tunnels so that the delegates can go from one building to the other without ever having to face the elements, or, for that matter, the public. In the Berlin Republic, it seems, accessibility has its limits. The tunnels, along with a quick getaway route to the nearby Lehrter Bahnhof, will allow those delegates who have no use for Berlin to see as little as possible of their new home. With luck, they won't even have to know they're there.

Although still known popularly as the Reichstag, this is not the building's official designation. Fearing that this term suggested unseemly ambitions, a Bundestag committee came up with a new name: Deutscher Bundestag—Plenarbereich Reichstagsgebäude (German Federal Assembly—Plenary Area, Imperial Diet Building). No one, of course, will actually use this jawbreaker, but, like the "fat hen," it tells the world that the Berlin Republic's heart is in the right place.

Such reminders were perhaps well in order on the day the Bundestag took possession of its new Berlin home, April 19,1999. For the first time since World War II, German military forces were engaged in active combat, fighting alongside their NATO allies in the Balkans. At such a juncture, German leaders worried about the symbolism of moving back to a building closely associated with the outbreak of World War I. In his speech at the opening ceremony, Chancellor Schröder did not refer specifically to NATO's war against Serbia, but he was careful to disassociate the new Germany from the German government that had gone to war in 1914. United Germany's parliament might be meeting in the "Reichstag," he noted, but to equate this name with "Reich" would be "as senseless as equating Berlin with Prussian glory and German centralism." He added that it was the success of the "Bonn democracy" that had made "the Berlin Republic possible." Not all the parliamentary delegates, however, were as sanguine as the chancellor about what it might mean simultaneously to launch a new era in Berlin while pursuing a new war in Europe. Ludger Volmer, a Green Party member and Germany's deputy foreign minister, declared: "We are initiating our Berlin Republic in the midst of a European war, and I am one of the people responsible for a policy that leaves me no reason to be optimistic or happy."

The Reichstag is situated in the southeastern corner of the so-called Spreebogen (Spree Arc), a 150-acre plot created by a broad bend in the Spree River. Albert Speer had cleared this area to build the centerpiece of Hitler's envisaged "Germania"—a gargantuan Hall of the People that would hold 180,000 people and boast a dome sixteen times the size of Saint Peter's in Rome. From that building, a projected grand avenue—the "North-South Axis"—would slice across the city, intersecting with the "East-West Axis" near the Brandenburg Gate. Fortunately, the Hall of the People was never built—only part of the foundation was laid—and the Spreebogen remained a debris-strewn wasteland. Nothing was done with the area during the period of Berlin's division because it was earmarked as the site for a new administrative quarter once the German government returned to the Spree. As it turned out, of course, the returning government ended up taking over many of the old governmental buildings in Berlin-Mitte, leaving the Spreebogen reserved for the new complex that would house the Federal Chancellery and the necessary additional quarters for the Bundestag. (Originally, the Bundesrat was also scheduled to find a new home in the Spreebogen, but it did not decide to move to Berlin until 1996, and it therefore had to settle for the old Prussian Herrenhaus.) Because the Spreebogen complex involved the Berlin Republic's most important new construction, federal officials were determined to get its political symbolism right.

In 1992 Bonn launched an "International Urban Design Idea Competition for the Spreebogen." The term "international" was certainly apposite. A twenty-three-member jury made up of architects from seven countries, as well as of politicians from Bonn and Berlin, reviewed 835 submissions from forty-four nations. The entries, all submitted anonymously, came from as far afield as South Africa and Israel. As in the Potsdamer Platz reconstruction, the foreign competitors were excited at the prospect of doing something truly daring in the new Berlin. Entries from abroad featured futuristic skyscrapers, complexes of bunkers (not a good idea), and arrangements of oddly shaped megaliths. Many of the foreign architects, and a few of the German ones, had no inhibitions about projecting an aura of political power through their designs.

They should have known better. The German officials overseeing the competition were, as ever, worried about the political impression these buildings would make. "What are we saying to the world here?" they asked. "That we want to try to conquer it again?" Although most of the politicians were prepared to tolerate more flair in

Berlin than in Bonn, where the Chancellery resembled a provincial savings bank, they were determined that the Spreebogen complex should not be even remotely reminiscent of what Speer and Hitler had planned to do. Thus they wanted an overall design that was oriented east-west rather than north-south. They preferred to avoid the monumental neoclassicism typical of the public buildings in many democracies, since this style had also been favored by the Nazis. Instead of grandeur or majesty, they wanted buildings that projected modesty, openness, and accessibility. One of the foreign jury members, Karen Van Lengen, summed up this approach as follows: "They wanted to say, 'We're just this little country in Europe.' They're very sensitive about it because they know the world is watching." The French architect, Claude Vasconi, echoing the complaints of his counterparts at Potsdamer Platz and Checkpoint Charlie, believed that German timidity was ruining the chance for a significant architectural statement in the future capital. "Symbolism in architecture need not be synonymous with the Third Reich," he declared. "It's not everyday that one has the chance to rebuild a capital." Some of the foreign jury members became so fed up with what they regarded as Bonn's pusillanimity that they began referring to the politicians as "Bonbons" and "rednecks of the Rhine."

Of course, it was easy, and perhaps unfair, for foreign architects to chastise the Germans for hypersensitivity and overcautiousness in this matter. These critics did not have to live with historical memories of moral and political transgressions, which the rest of the world was more than happy to help the Germans keep alive. The reminders came in varying forms—reservations about German unification expressed by politicians like Thatcher and Mitterrand, the American "Holocaust" television series of the 1970s, books like Daniel Goldhagen's *Hitler's Willing Executioners*, jokes about the Germans' alleged inability to avoid periodically running off the rails. In this last category, one recalls the quip by the American comedian Jay Leno on the *Tonight Show* in 1990. "I'm sure that you have heard that Germany has been reunited. The only question now, I guess, is when it will go on tour again." While it may indeed have been true, as the foreign architects contended, that in its public architecture Germany erred on the side of caution, the Germans would certainly have garnered much greater criticism had they accepted designs that looked as if they might have come from the sketchbook of Albert Speer.

As it turned out, the sharply divided jury in the Spreebogen competition could not agree on a single winning entry, so it awarded two first prizes to two very different designs. One of them, by a trio of young architects who had been trained in the former GDR, involved a rectangular colonnaded structure of great formality and severity. When pictures of it were made public, many critics complained that it was far too Speer-like to be acceptable. The other first-place design, by the Berlin-based architectural team of Axel Schultes and Charlotte Frank, featured an east-west oriented *Band des Bundes* (Federal Strip), a linear ribbon of low-slung buildings broken up by a "Civic Forum" in the center. Reminiscent of the Mall in Washington, D.C., the strip extended from Moabit in the west to the Friedrichstadt in the east, crossing the Spree twice and thereby pulling together the two halves of the formerly divided city like a giant suture. This design won favor from Berlin's leaders, who liked its political symbolism. Some federal officials, on the other hand, worried that the effect was too monumental; they wanted something closer to the self-effacing look in Bonn. Helmut Kohl was not among these critics. Believing that the architecture of the Berlin Republic should convey a stronger sense of Germany's world importance (and believing too that he would be the first chancellor to rule from the new Chancellery), he eventually came down in favor of the Schultes design, which he hailed as "a successful combination of modesty and dignity." Kohl's intervention decided the matter, and on February 4, 1997, the chancellor personally presided over the groundbreaking ceremony for Schultes's Federal Strip.

Of course, Helmut Kohl did not turn out to be the first chancellor to rule from Berlin since Adolf Hitler—that distinction fell to Gerhard Schröder. The new Chancellery and the complex of which it is a part also turned out differently than the original design specified. According to Schultes's initial drawings, the Chancellery building was to feature large eyelike openings cut into its facade. Critics, including Mayor Diepgen, complained that these would bring back unwelcome memories of the Gestapo and the Stasi, whose "eyes" had been everywhere in the city. Schultes therefore reshaped the openings as half-ovals, rather like the half-moon glasses he favored. Another casualty was the "Civic Forum," the large public courtyard that was meant to suggest openness and accessibility. In truth, the government feared having a large public space directly adjacent to the main center of power. Obsession with security had been present even in idyllic Bonn, where it had produced a sizable no-go zone around the Chancellery and the "Chancellor's Bungalow." The security issue was much greater in Berlin, with its well-known propensity for disruptive demonstrations. In yet another change, the Federal Strip, of which the Chancellery constitutes the western end, was significantly foreshortened in the east, thereby undercutting its capacity symbolically to link the eastern and western halves of the city. This change was mandated partly for financial reasons. As the complex was being constructed, Germany was desperate to meet the fiscal preconditions for participation in the European Union's single currency plan. Among other requirements, countries wishing to join the Currency Union could not have a public deficit exceeding 3 percent of GDP. To avoid missing that target, expenditures on Berlin's reconstruction, including the Federal Strip, had to be reduced. There was also a political angle to the change. Extending the Strip into the Friedrichstadt would have required demolishing some apartment blocks and displacing their residents, a move problematic in itself, but especially so given Speer's extensive dislocation of Berliners during his own reconstruction of the city a half-century earlier. "The irony of Albert Speer's legacy," one commentator has written, "is that Berliners seem finally to believe in the power of architecture as much as he did."

The Politics of Memory

In attempting to "reckon with the past" through architecture, it was one thing for the rebuilders of Berlin to acknowledge the problematical pedigrees of certain historical buildings by preserving some of their features, quite another to establish memorials whose sole purpose was to remind future generations of what had transpired during their nation's darkest hour. Of course, all countries turn historically significant localities into shrines of national worship, where noble acts of triumph or sacrifice can be venerated. The challenge for Germany and Berlin was to give prominence to sites identified with crimes committed in the nation's name. Various efforts to do this had been undertaken in West Berlin and, to a much lesser degree, in East Berlin after the war. Official memory took different forms and bore different messages in the two halves of the city. Berlin, after all, was divided not just along the Cold War fault line, but also in terms of the remembrance of things past. In addition to having to decide what to do with the diverse memory sites that they inherited from the divided city, the authorities of reunited Berlin faced the question of whether more memorials were needed. As the post-Wall memory debate progressed, it soon became apparent that there was little agreement about how the once and future capital should visually acknowledge its role in the national catastrophe. More fundamentally, some began to ask whether the worst dimensions of the German past could properly be commemorated by physical memorials at all.

Crimes are perhaps most potently acknowledged at the scenes where they were committed. In the broad sense, all of Berlin, and for that matter all of Germany, could be viewed as a crime scene, but the former Reich capital had hundreds of specific sites that had been instrumental to the Hitler regime's criminality. In addition to the above-mentioned Nazi government buildings, many other structures related to the Third Reich survived the war relatively intact, and the vast majority of these bore no indication of their role in the terror. Only occasionally did one encounter the odd plaque or sign, such as the (hopelessly inadequate) one at the Wittenbergplatz *U-Bahn* station, which lists the main concentration camps as if they were travel destinations, or the sculpture at Tiergartenstrasse 4, where the Third Reich's euthanasia office was located.

Not surprisingly, the Germans preferred, especially in the early stages of the commemoration process, to focus on places where they could find something positive amidst all the horror. Hence the emphasis was on *resistance* to Nazi terror rather than on the terror itself. Berlin (both East and West) sought to highlight its role in the German resistance by naming streets after resisters and placing plaques on the houses where they had lived. In addition to such simple markers, there were also efforts to create more elaborate "memory sites," where the opposition to Nazi criminality could be contemplated in some detail.

The first such site in West Berlin was erected at Plötzensee, a prison used by the Nazis as an execution center for political prisoners and resisters. Almost 3,000 men and women, including hundreds of foreign nationals, were hanged or guillotined there during the Third Reich. The most prominent victims were German opponents to the regime. On December 22, 1942, eleven members of the Schulze-Boysen-Harnack group, known as the "Red Orchestra," were executed at the prison. As noted above, following the failed July 20, 1944, assassination attempt against Hitler, several participants in the plot were hanged at the prison. In 1952 the Senate of West Berlin turned the execution chamber into a memorial to the people who had died there, and, by extension, to all those who had sacrificed their lives opposing the Third Reich. Although the victims here were diverse, the emphasis in the exhibit—as in most of the Federal Republic's resistance commemorations—was on *conservative* opponents to Hitler. The Plötzensee memorial was also an integral part of Bonn's effort to employ the resistance legacy as a ticket of readmission to the civilized world. As President Theodor Heuss declared in a speech commemorating the tenth anniversary of the Twentieth of July plot: "The blood of the martyred resisters has cleansed our German name of the shame which Hitler cast upon it. [The resistance] is a gift to the German future." Since the early 1950s the story of the Twentieth of July assassination attempt has been told time and again, and Plötzensee has become a well-visited stop on the memory trail. With German unification it served as the place where the resisters' ideal of a morally responsible Germany could he highlighted.

Another major "memory site" focusing on the German resistance was installed in the Bendlerblock, where, as we have seen, Count Stauffenberg and some of the other military resisters were shot. A statue memorializing the resistance martyrs was erected in the courtyard in 1953. Interestingly, the sculptor who designed this idealized figure, Richard Scheibe, had also crafted heroic statuary for the Nazis. The name of the street on which the complex is located was changed in 1955 from Bendlerstrasse to Stauffenbergstrasse. As at Plötzensee, contemporary ideological issues colored interpretations of the past. In dedicating the Bendlerblock statue, West Berlin mayor Ernst Reuter coupled the Twentieth of July legacy with the uprising against the SED-regime that had just occurred in East Berlin. Reuter's gesture fit into the Federal Republic's campaign to portray the GDR as the principal legatee of the Third Reich—a mirror image of East German efforts to depict West German capitalists as the true heirs of Hitler. By the early 1980s ideological blinkers had been cast off sufficiently to allow a somewhat more inclusive interpretation of the resistance legacy. A small museum in the Bendlerblock that had originally been installed in the 1960s was expanded and revised to offer a more comprehensive picture of the German resistance, with the inclusion of noted Communists. Yet this very inclusiveness enraged conservatives, who insisted that Communists had no place in the resistance pantheon. Following unification, Defense Minister Volker Rühe demanded the removal from the exhibit of pictures of Walter Ulbricht and Wilhelm Pieck, who, he said, "merely replaced one unjust regime with another." Indignation, however, came from the other end of the political spectrum as well. On the eve of a celebration marking the fiftieth anniversary of the Twentieth of July plot, in July 1994, leftist students occupied the Bendlerblock museum in protest against what they saw as a dangerous veneration of reactionary militarists who had turned against Hitler only because he was losing the war.

A very different memorial, one concerned more with the perpetrators of Nazi terror than with the victims, was installed on the grounds of the SS and Gestapo headquarters in the former Prinz-Albrecht-Strasse. As we noted above, excavated ruins on the site and a small museum had been patched together there as a "Topography of Terror" on the eve of Berlin's 750th anniversary celebrations in 1987. The installation was primitive and makeshift, and its custodians encountered resistance to their efforts to construct a permanent study center at the site. Federal and local officials insisted that there was not enough money for the project. Obviously, they were uncomfortable with an undertaking that illustrated the Nazi terror's prominence in Berlin's political landscape. Although the "Topography of Terror" backers wanted improved facilities, they did not want changes so obtrusive as to obscure the site's quality as an "open wound" in the heart of the new Berlin. A design competition was launched in the early 1990s for renovations of the installations, but no substantial work was done. The place remained a powerful but confusing experience for most visitors, many of whom apparently expected to see more in the way of physical evidence of torture. The visitors' book contained comments like "Cool, but a bit tame on the gory bits." The fact that a preserved section of the Berlin Wall stood nearby was a further source of confusion; visitors could conclude that Hitler must have built the Wall. It is fitting, however, that relics of both the Nazi regime and the GDR stood cheek to jowl at this place: the point was not to conflate these two regimes, but to grasp Berlin's centrality to both.

A better-known site of Nazi criminality is the Villa Wannsee, or "Haus am Wannsee," though only one significant political event took place there, the so-called Wannsee Conference (January 20, 1942), at which various bureaucratic details of the Holocaust were discussed. Adolf Eichmann's record of the conference was discovered in 1947, but it took another forty-five years to "give this place its history back," as Mayor Diepgen put it in his remarks at the opening of a documentation center at the site on January 20, 1992. The Soviet and American military authorities who had commandeered the villa after the war made nothing of its history, nor did the German officials who used it as a children's recreation center from 1952 to 1988. In the 1960s the West Berlin government even turned down an offer of $5 million from the World Jewish Congress to establish a documentation center in the house. The Berlin Senate said that it feared attracting neo-Nazis to the site, but it is more likely that it feared a backlash from right-wing voters. Finally, in the late 1980s, the West Berlin authorities came to understand that it was more damaging politically to ignore the villa's history than to acknowledge it, and the work that culminated in the documentation center began. The exhibit that was installed in the house is a cross between a museum and a memorial, which, like all such hybrid constructs, presents a problem in itself. As Ian Buruma has commented: "You can remember the Holocaust through art, through ceremony, or through analysis and discourse, but you cannot do all this at the same time, or in the same place."

The Villa Wannsee lies not far from the freight train station at Grunewald from which some 50,000 Berlin Jews were shipped to the concentration camps. The vast majority never returned. Like the infamous villa, this place received no acknowledgment of its historical role in the killing process for many years after the war. In 1973 a private group erected a plaque at the loading ramps, but the plaque was often defaced and twice stolen. Shortly before the *Wende*, the West Berlin government commissioned a modest memorial for the site; unveiled in 1991, it consists of a concrete slab imprinted with walking human forms. Two years later, the local head of the national railway system—the same organization that had contracted with the SS to transport Jews to the camps at a bargain rate—announced that the ramps would be torn down and replaced by a cleaning facility for high-speed Intercity-Expreßzug (intercity express, ICE) trains. Upon learning of this plan, Jewish groups vehemently protested. Jerzy Kanal, the head of the Berlin Jewish Community, noted that there were still Jews living in Berlin who had been deported from Grunewald. Local newspapers decried the planned "ramp to the train-wash." Claiming that he had not known of the Grunewald station's history, the railway chief agreed to forego the cleaning facility and to work with the Central Council of German Jews to construct "a worthy memorial" and historical exhibit at the site.

If the memorials and "memory sites" in the former West Berlin testify to the hesitancy, tortuousness, and ambiguity of the commemoration process, this is doubly true of the sites that were established in the East. To the extent that the GDR government wrestled with the legacy of National Socialism at all, it was mainly to interpret the crimes of the Nazis as the consequences of a crusade by "monopoly capitalism" against the Communists, who were portrayed as both Nazism's primary victims and as its heroic conquerors. If the leftist resisters happened to be Jewish, this was downplayed or ignored. Only in the 1980s did the GDR regime begin to acknowledge the fate of the Jews under Nazism with commemorative sites in East Berlin. Monuments or plaques were placed at the Jewish cemeteries at Weißensee and Schönhauser Allee and at the deportation site at Grosse Hamburger Strasse. Yet even this belated effort was half-hearted and spotty. A small monument in the Lustgarten dedicated to the Communist resister Herbert Baum failed to mention his

Monument to the deportation of Berlin's Jews at Grunewald Station

Jewish origins, and the location on the Rosenstrasse where demonstrations by non-Jewish wives had led to the release of their Jewish husbands was acknowledged only after German unification.

A typical example of GDR memory politics was the memorial erected at the Sachsenhausen concentration camp in Oranienburg, about twenty-five miles north of Berlin. As with the larger memorial at Buchenwald near Weimar, this exhibit focused almost exclusively on the Communist prisoners and Red Army POWs. The plight of the Jews who were incarcerated there was hardly mentioned. Moreover, beyond installing their tendentious museum, the GDR authorities did little to preserve the camp's buildings and facilities, which were allowed slowly to rot away. Even worse was the situation at the women's camp at Ravensbrück, where the National People's Army built a base on the grounds.

After unification, the federal government and the state of Brandenburg announced plans to thoroughly restore the Sachsenhausen site, but little was done beyond a partial revision of the exhibits. In 1992 neo-Nazi vandals burned some of the Jewish barracks at the camp. Due to a lack of funds, the foundation responsible for the site was unable either to repair this damage or to prevent further deterioration of the property. At several places on the grounds visitors were

Monument to the Rosenstrasse Women's Protest, 1999

warned away from buildings by signs reading, "Caution! Danger of Collapse. No Trespassing." The custodians were also unable to hire guides to conduct tours or to adequately catalog the new material donated to the camp on the occasion of the fiftieth anniversary of its liberation in 1995. "This is an authentic site, a place where the evil was actually perpetrated," said the foundation's director. "It is a place that horrifies even people who have read many books about the Holocaust. When the federal government moves to Berlin in a few years, it will become more important than ever. But we don't have the resources to do what needs to be done here."

A lack of resources was not a problem at the Neue Wache, which in the first half of the twentieth century stood as Germany's main shrine to its fallen soldiers—a German version of Britain's Cenotaph and France's Tomb of the Unknown Soldier. Upon being absorbed into the commemorative culture of reunited Germany, this hallowed structure became embroiled in a revealing struggle over how the new nation should memorialize the victims of military violence and political tyranny in the era between 1914 and 1945.

The Neue Wache, which stands on Unter den Linden next to the former Prussian Arsenal (now the German Historical Museum), is a small but striking neoclassical building designed by Schinkel in 1818 to celebrate Prussia's victory over

Napoleon. Until 1918 it served as the headquarters of the Palace Guard. In 1931 it was converted by the architect Heinrich Tessenow into a memorial for the German dead of World War I, with an unknown-soldier tomb in the shape of an altar, as well as a large gold and silver wreath that recalled the *corona civica* awarded by the Roman Senate to the Republic's heroic soldiers. The Nazis co-opted this shrine, adding a cross on the back wall as "a symbol of the Christian Volk in the new Reich." As part of their own co-optation of national symbolism, the East Germans rededicated the Neue Wache in 1960 as a "Memorial to the Victims of Fascism and Militarism." In front of the building they established a permanent honor guard, whose members goose-stepped into position. (Tourists were always astonished at this sight, associating the goose step with Nazi militarism, but in fact this was an old Prussian maneuver and thus part of the GDR's appropriation of Prussian symbolism.) In 1969 the East Germans redesigned the building's interior, adding a Tomb of the Unknown Resistance Fighter and urns containing ashes from the concentration camps and World War II battlefields.

With the collapse of the GDR and the dissolution of the National People's Army in 1990, the Neue Wache was closed, its fate uncertain. Three years later, however, Chancellor Kohl decided that this structure should be pressed into service once again as a place of memory—this time as the central memorial for all the victims of both world wars, as well as for "the victims of racial persecution, resistance, expulsion, division, and terrorism." In other words, this was to be a one-stop-covers-all memorial, a kind of supermarket of commemoration sites. As Kohl noted, state visitors wishing to lay a wreath at a sacred site could absolve that obligation here through a single gesture. And for the Germans themselves, he said, the Neue Wache offered a version of the "nation united in mourning."

But this was just the problem. As many critics noted, the Kohl plan conflated victims and perpetrators, honoring them all equally and indiscriminately. The concept did not distinguish between people who had been killed by the Hitler regime and leading Nazis (like Roland Friesler) who had been victims of the Allied bombing. Since the main thing about victims is their lack of responsibility for their fate, Kohl seemed to be suggesting that the Germans of the Hitler era, virtually all of whom were victims in this scheme, lacked responsibility for the Reich's crimes. Of course, the chancellor certainly did *not* mean to suggest this, but in his push to redefine Germany's relationship with its painful history and to take account of the entire past rather than just the grimmest moments, he showed himself, as he had at Bitburg

Enlarged version of Käthe Kollwitz's pietà in the Neue Wache, 1999

and Frederick the Great's reburial, surprisingly ham-handed in the complicated arena of historical symbolism.

The controversy surrounding the Neue Wache was further compounded by the renovation plan proposed by Kohl. In place of Tessenow's stone tomb, the chancellor proposed an enlarged replica of Käthe Kollwitz's pietà, her sculpture of a mother mourning her dead son. Critics, including leading members of Berlin's Jewish community, objected that as a Christian symbol this was hardly appropriate for the millions of Jews who had died at the hands of the Nazis. Moreover, the sculpture specifically referred to the loss of dead sons and thus did not encompass the millions of women who had died in World War II. Finally, Kollwitz herself had been a pacifist. Was it appropriate to place a work of hers in a former Prussian guardhouse?

Despite a barrage of criticism from historians, Jewish groups, various leftist and pacifist organizations, and the local art community, Kohl held fast to his plan. On "National Mourning Day" (November 14, 1993), the chancellor personally presided over the reopening of the Neue Wache. The monument had been restored essentially as he had proposed. An enlarged pietà reposed somberly beneath an opening in the ceiling that allowed sunlight to fall on the figure. The only significant change to Kohl's original concept was a bronze plaque beside the entrance that named the specific victim-groups being memorialized. The long list, a Who's Who of Nazi victims, did not include Waffen-SS men, but this did not prevent some folks from leaving flowers inscribed to the memory of SS officers killed in the war. Moreover, the last-minute addition of the inclusive plaque failed to make the memorial more palatable to most of its critics. Protesters shouting "murderers are not victims" attended the opening ceremony, which was pointedly boycotted by Berlin's Jewish leader, Jerzy Kanal, and by the city's senator for cultural affairs, Ulrich Roloff-Momin.

The controversy surrounding the Neue Wache, acrimonious as it was, paled in comparison to the bitter debate over a commemorative site that did not yet exist: a national monument in Berlin to all the Jews murdered by the Nazis in the Holocaust. A plan to create such a site surfaced in 1988, shortly before the Wall came down. It was spearheaded by a television talk-show hostess named Lea Rosh. Originally, Rosh wanted to locate the proposed memorial on the former Gestapo/SS grounds, thereby displacing the "Topography of Terror" exhibit. When Germany and Berlin became unified, however, Helmut Kohl offered Rosh and her backers an even more prominent space, a five-acre site just south of the Brandenburg Gate. Like Rosh, Kohl believed that such a monument would help Germany atone for its greatest crime.

This plan immediately came under fire for a host of reasons. Berlin, as has been noted, possesses a number of sites which had figured prominently in the Holocaust. Many critics of the Rosh concept believed that it would be better to focus Germany's commemorative and atonement efforts on "active museums" like the Sachsenhausen camp, the "Topography of Terror" exhibit, and the Wannsee villa. As it happened, the site offered by Kohl for the Holocaust memorial was close to a number of Nazi-era bunkers that lay buried under mounds of sand. In 1990 construction workers digging in the area found remains of the underground shelters for Hitler's drivers, replete with eerie scenes from Nazi mythology. Later, Goebbels's bunker and remnants of the Führerbunker (whose location was known, but kept secret) were unearthed as well. City officials insisted upon reburying all these sites, but proponents of the active-museum concept argued that they should be preserved as crime scenes, like the Topography of Terror. It would be a travesty, they said, if the proposed Holocaust memorial displaced actual sites of evil. Then there were those many citizens who were simply fed up with efforts by Berlin and Bonn to memorialize the Holocaust and thereby perpetuate Germany's sense of guilt and obligation. As a character in Michael Kleeberg's novel, *Ein Garten im Norden* (1998), complains: "They've thrown enough of our tax money away on this crap. It's high time to draw a line under the past!" In the early 1980s Alfred Dregger, a right-wing Christian Democrat, called for all Germans "to come out of Hitler's shadow," to make their nation "normal." A very different objection came from left-wing Berlin intellectuals, who argued that Germany had no "right" to the memory of the Nazis' victims. This memory, they said, belonged exclusively to those who had suffered; furthermore, they said, having the sufferers' pain "honored" next to the Brandenburg Gate would only add to the confusion between victims and perpetrators.

Whether or not they worried about this confusion, some of the victims of the Nazi terror had their own objections to the Rosh project. The Nazis, as we know, had targeted a number of groups besides Jews in their mass killing, and survivors from these groups, such as Gypsies (called Sinti and Roma in Germany), homosexuals, and the mentally disabled, complained about being left out of Rosh's scheme. If they were to be excluded from the Holocaust memorial, these groups wanted memorials of their own. The Sinti-Roma agitated for a spot at the Brandenburg Gate, so as to be on an equal footing with the Jews, but in 1993 the Berlin Senate vetoed this idea. Homosexual groups likewise agitated for a separate memorial, which spawned a quarrel within Berlin's gay community, since some of its members believed that the commemoration should focus exclusively on the roughly 50,000 gay men who had been persecuted under National Socialism, while others wanted to include lesbians, who were not specifically targeted by the Nazis. The memorial's possible location also inspired a dispute. Some wanted it in the Nollendorfplatz, a meeting point for Berlin gays in the 1990s (and Christopher Isherwood's old haunt in the early 1930s), where there was already a triangle-shaped plaque reading: "Beaten to death, silenced to death—to the homosexual victims of Nazism." Another faction insisted on having the monument near the Brandenburg Gate. Such close proximity to the proposed Jewish memorial, however, provoked opposition from local officials, who worried that it would suggest an "equality of oppression."

In response to the criticism of an exclusivity in Germany's politics of memory, backers of a memorial specifically for Jews argued that what was being memorialized was not only the loss of millions of lives, but the destruction of "a thousand-year culture belonging to the heart of Europe," as Peter Radunski, Berlin's Senator for Science, Research, and Culture, put it. The unspoken implication here, of course, was that the loss of Jewish creativity through the Holocaust represented a far more significant blow to German culture than did that of the other groups.

Some of those who attacked the Holocaust memorial plan also attacked Rosh herself, who unquestionably offered an inviting target. Decked out in her trademark jeweled bifocals and raspberry-colored suits, she appeared on countless talk shows, hers and others, touting her project. She did not say "There's no business like Shoah business," but to her detractors she seemed to be exploiting the Holocaust for purposes of self-promotion. It hardly helped that Rosh is herself only part Jewish—her mother's father was a Berlin Jew—and that she had changed her name from Edith to Lea. The name-change exposed her to accusations of "Jewish envy"—of wanting to assume for herself the role of persecuted victim.

The most trenchant criticism of Rosh's project, however, had to do with the very idea of trying to capture the *problematique* of the Holocaust in the capital of the perpetrators via a physical monument. Theodor Adorno said famously that after Auschwitz there could be no more poetry. Could a piece of art, a symbolic representation in marble or brick, adequately convey the shame felt—if indeed it was always felt—by the perpetrators and their heirs fifty years after the fact? To some degree, of course, the objection of lack-of-punch applies to all commemorative monuments. "There is nothing in the world as invisible as a monument," wrote the Austrian novelist Robert Musil. Are monuments not in actuality more often abettors to forgetting than aids to remembering? By locating memory in a thing that is easily passed by and ignored, do not monuments allow us to let that memory lapse from our active consciousness? As sites of official observance, do they not often become, as the Germans say, "wreath-dumping places," where politicians can perfunctorily absolve the tired rituals of their profession? And, aside from the politicians, are not monuments most loved by pigeons, who leave their signatures all over their surfaces? (André Malraux once advised a writer friend never to become so famous that he was honored with a monument, for that would mean a future of being shat upon.) But—and this is the main point—if all the difficulties of preserving or representing memory in a monument apply to relatively trivial or painless acts of commemoration, would this not be much more the case in the act of "remembering" the Holocaust? Andreas Nachama, a spokesman for Berlin's Jewish Community, declared that the Holocaust memorial idea represented "an impossible assignment."

Despite all the criticism of her plan, Rosh pushed forward, and in 1995 a design competition for a National Holocaust Memorial in Berlin was sponsored by the municipal authorities and the federal government. The competition attracted 528 entries, most of them convincing illustrations of the perils of trying to capture the Holocaust in an all-encompassing monument. One of them proposed an immense Ferris wheel equipped with freight cars like the ones in which Jews had been transported to the camps. Its designer explained that this would reflect "the tension between hope and hopelessness, between carnival and genocide." Another entry proposed a giant oven, burning around the clock. Exactly what it would burn was not specified. Yet another called for erecting a blood-filled container 130 feet tall and 100 feet wide. Daniel Libeskind proposed an arrangement of raw-concrete walls 21 meters high and 115 meters long, which he entitled "Breath of Stone." Then there was a Star of David sculpture crowned by a broken heart symbolizing German remorse. Another star-design featured a garden bordered in yellow flowers to evoke the yellow stars the Jews were forced to wear in the Third Reich.

Some of the entries, it should be admitted, reflected an understanding of the drawbacks of all representational memorialization. There were a number of anti-monument proposals that seemed to have been inspired by a famous antimonument in Hamburg, which consisted of a metal tube covered with people's comments that slowly shrank into an underground silo, thereby symbolizing the element of forgetting inherent in the process of remembering. Among the antimonument proposals for the Holocaust memorial was a block-long series of bus stops, where people could board buses to former concentration camps. (This was not a bad idea, since the authorities of Oranienburg refused to institute a bus line from the town's train station to Sachsenhausen.) Another, rather less promising, entry suggested grinding up the Brandenburg Gate into fine powder, like crematorium ash, and sprinkling it over the memorial grounds.

The winning design, which was backed by Lea Rosh and her supporters, consisted of a football field–sized tombstone garnished with eighteen boulders brought to Berlin from Masada in Israel, where Jewish zealots had committed suicide rather than surrender to the Romans in the first century A.D. The boulders were meant to symbolize the small rocks placed by mourners on Jewish gravestones. (The symbolism was somewhat confusing, however, since the Jews who died in the Holocaust had hardly committed suicide.) In addition to the boulders, the tombstone would have engraved on its surface the names of all the officially recorded victims of the Holocaust, some 4.2 million of them. The idea for this apparently derived from the Vietnam Memorial in Washington D.C., though of course it was rather more ambitious.

Even many who favored a Holocaust memorial heaped criticism on this design. Not only was it bombastic and kitschy, it would, as Ignaz Bubis objected, heighten the victims' anonymity rather than personalize their fate. "The name of Moses Rabbinowitch would appear a thousand times," he pointed out. In the face of this barrage of criticism Kohl personally vetoed the selection and ordered a new competition.

In 1997 the government commissioned a second contest, this time by invitation only. The jury now included a distinguished American Jewish scholar, James E. Young, who had written an influential book called *The Texture of Memory: Holocaust Memorials and Meaning.* Interestingly, Young belonged to the school that was highly skeptical of monuments in general, and Holocaust monuments in particular. Yet eventually he and the other members of the jury found a proposal that they liked by the design team of Peter Eisenman and Richard Serra—a giant labyrinth of 4,000 concrete pillars on an undulating concrete field. The idea here was to pull visitors into a punishing maze: Not only would they be forced to "remember" the Holocaust; they'd have to remember how to get out. "Here there is no goal, no end, no path," explained the artists. Young called this "the Venus fly trap of Holocaust memorials."

Conceptually intriguing though it was, this design had a lot of problems. Parents might bring their kids there to permanently ditch them. People would undoubtedly climb up on the pillars to get their orientation, then fall off and hurt or even kill themselves. Was it appropriate for a Holocaust memorial to claim new victims? Once again Kohl intervened, demanding that the designers rework their proposal. Serra refused and dropped out. Eisenman modified the design by reducing the number of pillars and shortening their height. His amended creation was much less menacing: a kind of Holocaust-Lite.

Kohl and his advisers liked this version better, but by now the chancellor had an election to face, and there was considerable sentiment in Germany against erecting a new Holocaust memorial at all in the future capital. The Social Democrats had adopted this stance, and their candidate, Gerhard Schröder, was ahead in the polls. Kohl therefore put the project on hold until after the elections.

Kohl of course lost that election, leaving Germany not only with a new chancellor, but with the irony that the man who had done the most to shape the planning for the new capital would not be leading the government when it moved to Berlin in 1999. As for the Holocaust memorial, Schröder opposed it on grounds that it was "backward-looking," and thus little help to the new Germany's need to "move on." During an address delivered on the occasion of the sixtieth anniversary of Reichskristallnacht at the New Synagogue in Berlin, Schröder said that the Germans must "look ahead without forgetting what happened." He added that reunited Germany had come of age and felt "neither superior nor inferior to anyone." The chancellor's comments, when combined with novelist Martin Walser's highly publicized complaint that the Holocaust was being used a "tool of intimidation" to induce "merely a compulsory exercise," signaled to some observers a dangerous turn in German thinking. "Intellectual nationalism is spreading," warned Ignaz Bubis, German Jewry's chief spokesman, "and it is not free of an understated anti-Semitism."

Stung by such criticism, Schröder quickly declared that he would subject the Holocaust memorial to further review. In January 1999 he approved yet another design, which combined Eisenman's toned-down maze with a research center for scholars and a "House of Remembrance" featuring a 65-foot-high "Wall of Books." The books, a million tomes in all, would be open to consultation by scholars, thereby accommodating the idea that the Holocaust memorial should not be just a thing to gaze at, or to get lost in, but an "interactive" center of education and research. Michael Naumann, Schröder's minister of culture, declared himself satisfied with the new arrangement. "All statements pro and con have been taken care of," he said. "This is a superb synthesis. It is not a compromise."

Of course, this solution *was* a compromise, like virtually everything else in the new Berlin. Final approval awaited a vote in the Bundestag, which came on June 25, 1999. After more than a decade of debate, Germany had finally agreed to build a memorial in Berlin to the 6 million Jews killed in the Holocaust. "We are not building this monument solely for the Jews," said Wolfgang Thierse, the speaker of the parliament. "We are building it for ourselves. It will help us confront a chapter in our history."

A memorial devoted to the Holocaust is not the same thing as a museum devoted to the Holocaust. Some people thought that Germany ought to have such a museum, but this need had already been brilliantly addressed by the Holocaust Museum in Washington, D.C. Instead of a museum focusing specifically on the Holocaust, Germany's new capital ended up getting the "Jewish Museum," which examines the role of Jews in German life, particularly in Berlin. Yet in many ways this institution is really about the Holocaust, too; its design is as discomforting as the original Eisenman/Serra Holocaust memorial proposal, and its principal purpose is to get people to reflect on the tortuous relationship between Germans and Jews that culminated in Auschwitz. Moreover, like the Holocaust memorial, it stimulated great controversy, and it very nearly did not get built at all.

The idea for a museum devoted to Germany's and Berlin's Jews was first floated in the late 1980s, and a design competition was held in 1988, the year before the Wall came down. According to the specifications, the building in question was to be an extension of the existing Berlin Museum on Lindenstrasse in Kreuzberg. The competition was won by the Polish-born American architect Daniel Libeskind, who shortly thereafter moved his practice from Berlin to Los Angeles out of frustration over Hans Stimmann's conservative building codes. Libeskind's winning design, which with a few modifications was the one that actually got built, proposed a zigzag structure resembling a lightning bolt, or a distorted Star of David. Its interior contains a main passageway leading to a Chamber of Reflection

Garden of Exiles at the Jewish Museum, 1999

resembling a chimney, as well as Caligari-like slanted walls, vertigo-inducing shafts, and empty spaces that the architect calls "voids," which are meant to draw attention to the vacuum in Berlin left by the disappearance of tens of thousands of its Jews.

As soon as the project was announced, it came under fire from a number of quarters. Christian Democrats on the city council insisted that the undertaking be postponed because there were more pressing demands on the municipal budget, such as Berlin's Olympic Games bid. Members of the board of the Berlin Museum questioned whether the city needed another Jewish center, since millions of marks had just been spent to restore the New Synagogue in former East Berlin. Some Jewish leaders, citing the city's influx of impoverished Eastern European Jews, argued that the money could be better spent on social programs for the newcomers. "We need schools, apartments, teachers, assistance," said Mario Offenberg, the leader of Berlin's Conservative Adass Jisroel congregation. "Only then can we think of museums." Bowing to these objections, the city council voted in 1991 to put off construction for five years, which many took to be a polite form of cancellation. Libeskind was among them: "I don't think anyone believes this project will get built if there is a five-year delay," he said.

By the mid-1990s construction had finally commenced on the Jewish Museum, but the project remained under fire, and it might not have been completed had not W. Michael Blumenthal come to the rescue in 1997 as the museum's first director. In some ways Blumenthal seemed an unlikely choice. He was not a German citizen and he had no experience in museum administration. But in fact his background—and even more his personal skills—suited him perfectly for the job. Born in Oranienburg in 1926, he had grown up in Berlin and fled with his family to Shanghai in 1939 to escape Hitler's persecution. Moving to America in 1947, he went on to become an adviser to Presidents Kennedy and Johnson, and finance minister under President Jimmy Carter. This was a man who knew about money—how to raise it and how to spend it. As an American, he had a useful impatience with German pedantry and title-mania, telling astounded Germans not to call him "Dr. Blumenthal," since he "didn't know how to repair sick stomachs." Most importantly, as a partial outsider who commuted between Berlin and Princeton, Blumenthal could more effectively mediate between the feuding factions in Berlin's Jewish community than an insider.

On January 23, 1999, the Jewish Museum, though still empty, opened for inspection with a spectacular fund-raising dinner. One might have thought that few

Germans, even well-heeled ones, would pay DM 25,000 ($14,800) a table to sit in an empty building. But many of Germany's leaders, including Chancellor Schröder and three of his cabinet ministers, showed up, as did an array of bankers and corporation executives. This led one commentator to label the opening "the first glittering prelude to the Berlin Republic." Blumenthal's promotional skills undoubtedly had something to do with this. So, perhaps, did a desire on the part of the bankers and executives, whose organizations were facing charges of having exploited slave labor during the war, to polish their image. But it also seems probable that the bitter controversy surrounding the Holocaust memorial, with all its talk of "moving on" and being "neither better nor worse" than any other nation, prompted some soul-searching among Germany's political and economic leaders. What better place than in a museum, and in a Jewish Museum at that, for the national elite to make manifest that the new Germany would not attempt to "draw a line under the past?"

Berlin 2000

The agonizing debate about how to deal with Germany's past in the new capital reflected a deeper quandary about national identity in the late 1990s—two-thirds of a century after the founding of the Third Reich, a half-century since the German division, and a decade since the fall of the Berlin Wall. Although many Germans worried about how the transfer of their capital from Bonn to Berlin would be perceived abroad, the move was actually more unsettling at home than outside Germany, for it made the question of the new nation's "normality" all the more pressing. The shift to Berlin signaled the final end of the Federal Republic's provisionality and limited sovereignty. Did this mean that Germany could act just like any other nation when it came to matters of national pride and the articulation of national interests? Assessing the predicament of the impending "Berlin Republic" in 1997, the American scholars Andrei Markovits and Simon Reich were confident that the country would remain democratic, but were less certain that it would find a way to act responsibly and consistently on the world stage. "In the context of national power," they wrote, "Germany's self-understanding remains murky. Germany vacillates between an overbearing projection of power (mainly, though not exclusively, in the realm of the economy) and a reticence about admitting that power; the country's identity remains uncertain and ill-defined in the area of power as it is crystal clear in the domain of democracy."

It is too early to tell how the experience of ruling from Berlin will affect German foreign policy. Very probably, being back in the traditional capital—if one can use the word "traditional" for an experience that lasted only seventy-four years—will heighten the Germans' desire to behave like a "normal" nation when it comes to the projection of power. At the same time, however, it will make an "escape from the past"—should that be anyone's intention—even harder to manage than was the case when quiet little Bonn, the town "without a history" (in Adenauer's phrase), set the tone. The "ghosts of Berlin" will see to that.

But even if these spirits were not dutifully hovering over the old Reichshauptstadt, waving their sheets like caution flags, the new capital is not the sort of place to inspire illusions of grandeur. Germany might be a powerful nation, but Berlin is not the political and economic center of gravity it once was. The decentralization of power and influence that began with the German division will be altered somewhat by the move to Berlin, but not as much as opponents to the shift have suggested. With six ministries and fully two-thirds of the central government's 25,000 bureaucrats staying in Bonn, the Rhineland city will remain a significant player in German politics. Frankfurt, home of the new European Central Bank, will continue to be Germany's (and the Continent's) financial center, Hamburg will still be a major force in publishing, Stuttgart will remain the capital of cars, and Munich, despite much hand-wringing about "Der Sieg der Saupreussen," will remain an important cultural center and power broker in national politics.

Moreover, the beginning of the governmental move to Berlin in the late 1990s did not manage to pull the city out of the economic doldrums that had set in after the reunification boomlet. In 1998 Berlin's economy actually declined by 0.3 percent, registering the worst performance of any German region. Bankruptcies were about double the national rate. Industrial production continued to fall, while the unemployment rate climbed to 18 percent, almost eight points higher than the national average. Some 275,000 Berliners were receiving public assistance. Of the top hundred companies listed on the Dax, the Frankfurt-based stock exchange, not one decided to shift its headquarters to Berlin. The only Dax-30 company to have its main office in the capital was Schering, which had been in Berlin since its foundation. Berlin was rebuilding the old Lehrter Bahnhof to become Europe's largest train station, but the city was anything but a hub of air transportation. By 1998 the number of intercontinental flights to Berlin had declined from fifteen to three: Ulan

Bator, Singapore, and Havana. Lufthansa had reduced its flights to the city, and the big American airlines had stopped flying there altogether. To help the city adjust to its new responsibilities, the European Union promised DM 2 billion in aid for the period from 2000 to 2006, but as a condition for the aid it demanded that Berlin finally put its economic house in order and offer a plan for sustained renewal. Lamentably, the town's political establishment showed no signs of being able to come up with such a plan, nor did it work to stimulate initiative in the private sector by stripping away the outdated business regulations that had stifled initiative for years. "Leere Kassen, leere Köpfe (empty treasury, empty heads)" is the harsh phrase that one local expert employed to sum up Berlin's political-economic situation in late 1999.

United Berlin's cultural scene—as often in the past—provided something of an exception to this empty-headed theme: once again a wealth of cultural offerings constituted the city's strongest suit. Reunification allowed the old/new capital to consolidate, rationalize, refocus, and renovate its cultural institutions, which had previously been split between East and West. In this domain, at least, few would deny that the new Berlin was a genuine *Weltstadt.*

For Berlin's vaunted art museums, reunification meant reuniting collections that had been dispersed during the war and then arbitrarily divided by politics. No longer was it necessary, as it had been during the Cold War, to make complicated exchanges—cultural equivalents of the famous spy swaps—to reassemble key collections or to return well-known treasures to their original locations. Shortly after the *Wende* parts of the Pergamum Altar that had been stored in West Berlin were reinstalled on the altar's frieze in the Pergamum Museum on Museum Island. The 3,350-year-old bust of Queen Nefertiti, which had also been held hostage in West Berlin, was reunited with the bust of her husband, King Akhnaton, in the Bode Museum. A collection of French impressionist paintings that Westerners had feared was lost, but which in actuality had been hidden away in East Berlin, rejoined the city's other impressionists in the National Gallery. Adolf Menzel's dispersed oeuvre was likewise brought together again in the same institution. Meanwhile, the severely dilapidated buildings on Museum Island, which now fell under the control of the well endowed Stiftung preussischer Kulturbesitz, could be refurbished and equipped with the technical devices necessary to preserve and protect their precious holdings.

The former Museum for German History on Unter den Linden required another form of renovation: as the GDR's principal historical museum, it had combined traditional displays of armor, costumes, and documents with tendentious exhibits celebrating the Socialist Fatherland, including its infamous "Anti-Fascist Protective Barrier." The structure in which the museum was housed, the old Prussian Zeughaus (Armory), was itself of historical importance, having been built by King Friedrich I of Prussia to hold his kingdom's arms and war booty. Accordingly, it was covered in triumphant war deities and other bellicose motifs. Fortunately, the East Germans did not "demilitarize" the building when they appropriated it for their own use. Their claimed stewardship over German history was of course a source of irritation in the West. To trump the Communists in this domain, Helmut Kohl ordained in the mid-1980s that West Berlin must have a museum of its own focusing on the history of Germany up to 1945 (a museum devoted exclusively to the history of the Federal Republic was built in Bonn). The fall of the Wall, however, brought a change of plans: now Kohl's government decided to take over and revamp the East Germans' museum on Unter den Linden rather than to build a brand new structure in the capital. Without consulting with officials in Berlin, Kohl commissioned the Chinese-American architect I. M. Pei to renovate the Zeughaus and to design an annex for traveling exhibits. The chancellor clearly hoped that Pei would do for Berlin's musty old historical museum what he had done for the Louvre in Paris and the National Gallery in Washington, D.C. What "worked" in Paris and Washington, however, does not seem to have worked so well in Berlin. The new facility has not yet opened, but already it is possible to see that Pei's brand of bland modernism does not harmonize with the classical-martial style of the original building.

In the early to mid 1990s, before the German Historical Museum was closed for its renovations, a number of exhibitions were mounted there that reflected the changed political order in Bonn and Berlin. Although they were well received by the public, some professional historians found them hardly less tendentious than the old East German displays. Moreover, these historians asked, was it legitimate for the government to try to generate a common or homogenized idea of the German past through carefully arranged objects and images? One critic suggested that the new museum amounted to a *Geschichtsaufbereitungsanlage*—a historical processing plant.

Just as divided Berlin had had duplicate national galleries—Mies van der Rohe's New National Gallery in West Berlin's Kulturforum and F. A. Stüler's National Gallery on Museum Island—the divided city was also home to duplicate state libraries—Hans Scharoun's Staatsbibliothek in the Kulturforum and the old Prussian

Staatsbibliothek on Unter den Linden. Like the city's art treasures, its book collections had been scattered during the war and then (partially) reassembled in separate quarters on opposite sides of the political divide. For example, the autograph score of Beethoven's Eighth Symphony, once held in its entirety in the Unter den Linden complex, came to be split between that facility, the "Stabi" in West Berlin, and a library in Poland. German reunification allowed all three movements of Beethoven's work to be reunited in the temperature-controlled vault of Staatsbibliothek in the Kulturforum. Once similar technical features have been added to the Unter den Linden facility, the city's entire collection of musical scores, maps, children's books, and pre-1956 publications will be housed there, while the more modern collections will go to the Kulturforum.

While it proved fairly simple to rearrange Berlin's book and manuscript collections to avoid duplication of services, this was not the case with its great musical ensembles, which were accustomed to performing exactly what they wanted when they wanted. After reunification Berlin's three opera companies and four major symphony orchestras had to compete for the same state subsidies and discriminating audiences. As in the heady days of Weimar, Berlin hardly seemed big enough for its galaxy of conductors and opera stage directors, which included Claudio Abbado (Karajan's replacement) at the Philharmonic; Vladimir Ashkenazy at the Radio Symphony Orchestra; Daniel Barenboim at the Staatsoper Unter den Linden; Götz Friedrich at the Deutsche Oper; and Harry Kupfer at the Komische Oper. To prevent these titans from stepping on each other's toes, performances had to be carefully scheduled—and sometimes revised. Thus the Deutsche Oper delayed a new production of Wagner's *Parsifal* so as not to undercut Barenboim's debut with the same work at the Staatsoper in 1992. (It is safe to say that Furtwängler would never have done this for Karajan, or Karajan for anyone else.) Of course, Berlin's musical public profited from this embarrassment of riches, but some former fans could not enjoy the plenty. Because seat prices in the east now matched those in the west, many easterners suddenly found themselves shut out of their favorite venues. "Sadly, I'm going to have to give this up," complained an aging eastern pensioner during the intermission in Offenbach's *Tales of Hoffmann* at the Staatsoper. "The seat prices have become as steep as the stairs!" For many culture-loving Ossis, the freedom that came with the fall of the Wall meant, among other things, the freedom henceforth to derive their cultural enrichment chiefly from the tiny screen at home.

While higher ticket prices may have added to the new "wall" running through reunited Berlin, they did not prevent the city from becoming a greater cultural magnet for the rest of the country, and indeed for the entire world. Much more than in the days of division, Berlin in the 1990s became a regular stop for cultural tourists from abroad. Visitors who had once come to see the Wall now stood in line for tickets to the Philharmonie and the Staatsoper.

Reunited Berlin also became *the* place to go for Germany's hip younger generation. According to a *Der Spiegel* poll in September 1994, the nation's youth preferred the Spree metropolis over all other German cities as a getaway destination. Every summer thousands of young people descended on Berlin's Tiergarten area to participate in the so-called "Love Parade," a bacchanalian orgy of street-dancing, beer, drugs, rave music, and open-air sex. Not surprisingly, such an affair had its detractors, especially among residents of the Tiergarten district, who complained bitterly of being invaded by an army of beer-swilling, whistle-blowing, dope-ingesting louts, who trampled the vegetation in the park and left tons of garbage in their wake. When outraged residents pleaded with city officials to shift this onslaught to a less vulnerable location, such as the Avus speedway or the old Olympic grounds, the event's sponsors, fearing for their profits, countered that the Love Parade was a "political demonstration" and off-limits to official tampering. Self-serving though the organizers' argument undoubtedly was, the Love Parade had become too much a fixture in the new Berlin to banish to the suburbs. Moreover, for all its offensive qualities, this celebration of youthful hedonism was rather less ominous in its implications then many of the other demonstrations that had transpired in this historic district.

In April 1999 the new Berlin made its debut on the stage of international diplomacy by hosting the European Union summit. Chancellor Schröder had expressly asked that the conference be moved from Brussels to Berlin so that the new German capital could show what it could do. And that it did. The police escort conducting France's president Jacques Chirac to a meeting in the restaurant Zur Letzten Instanz in the eastern part of the city got lost en route. A power outage put the press center out of business for two hours. There were so many security officials from so many different agencies that, in their confusion, the officials arrested each other. "The Germans," said Bernard Demange, the spokesperson for the French embassy in Bonn, "are becoming ever more French, while the French are becoming more German."

While the European Union (EU) chiefs were meeting in Berlin's Intercontinental Hotel, next to the zoo, a cabaret show entitled "Die Berliner Republik" opened at the nearby Volksbühne. In this send-up of the new Germany, the country's first chancellor to rule from Berlin lived in a dumpy 1960s-era bungalow filled with flea-market furniture. As his first order of business, the Schröderlike character abandoned his capital for Africa, searching for the Ring of the Nibelungen, the "true German spirit," and the capacity to fear. "I'm so afraid because I have no fear," he confessed.

The main fear that the rest of the world harbors about the Berlin Republic is not that it might soon run off the rails, but that it might take too long to get properly on track. One of the principal rationales behind the shift of the capital to Berlin was the hope that this would help the new eastern German states achieve a level of prosperity and productive capacity similar to that in the West, thereby allowing Germany to overcome the debilities attached to reunification and resume its role as the "economic locomotive of Europe." Ten years after the fall of the Wall, the East could boast some bright spots, such as Dresden and Jena, which were becoming centers of the high-tech industry, but in general the region was still far from pulling its own weight, and there was talk of its becoming a permanent drag on the German (and hence the European) economy—a kind of German *Mezzogiorno*. If the former GDR was like a "colony of pensioners," consuming goods with the help of subsidies but not producing enough on its own, could Berlin, a city which itself had long lived on subsidies, help to pull it out of this condition?

Economic indices, of course, can improve as well as decline, and one could only hope that with time Berlin would shake off the bad habits acquired during the long division and play the more dynamic role that most Germans, and most of the rest of the world, wished it to play. One could only hope, too, that the city would find ways to dismantle its "Wall in the Head"—that formidable barrier to cooperation and understanding. As the German government made its move to Berlin, this debility seemed as acute as ever. In the municipal elections of October 10, 1999, one month after Berlin became the official capital of reunited Germany, the PDS gained its largest victory yet, largely at the expense of Schröder's sagging SPD. As in earlier elections, the PDS recorded its gains almost exclusively in eastern Berlin, where it won approximately 40 percent of the vote. In the western districts of the city, meanwhile, the CDU generated its best showing since World War II by winning 48.9 percent of the tally. While this election, like a series of earlier SPD defeats, represented a setback for Schröder's moderate reformist course, it was also a setback for Berlin, which needed a modicum of political consensus to deal with its many pressing problems.

It would be remiss, however, to conclude an assessment of Berlin at this historic juncture by focusing exclusively on the many problems that continue to bedevil this perennially troubled city. As we noted above, the Spree metropolis is once again attracting the nation's youth—and not just for weekend visits or the annual Love Parade. An influx of young writers, artists, filmmakers, and art dealers is collectively fashioning one of Europe's most vital avant-garde scenes. Once staid Berlin-Mitte is awash in new art galleries. The newcomers are attracted by a sense of excitement, an edginess, that can be found nowhere else in Germany. Even jaded old-time residents are delighted by the fact that Berlin is getting another chance to become a great world metropolis. The city that some thought might become the "capital of the twentieth century"—and which ended up instead being identified with that era's many horrors—might yet become, if not the capital of the twenty-first century, one of the most dynamic and progressive centers of the new age. "[Berlin] will be a great city of the next century, but it still has to be created," declared Karl Kaiser in 1999, whose German Institute for Foreign Affairs had just made the move from Bonn to the new capital. "And I think that it is the open-endedness that creates this strong sense of intrigue."

Whether or not Berlin soon rivals New York, London, Paris, or Tokyo on the world stage, it is unlikely to remain as self-effacing in its capital role as did Bonn. While Bonn was a suitable, even ideal, capital for a fledgling democracy trying to find its way in a suspicious world, Berlin is in a better position to represent the German state as it seeks to realize the full potential of its democratic maturity and national reunification. Far from departing from the principles of the "Bonn Republic," the "Berlin Republic" can perfect and extend those ideals.

The "old" Federal Republic, contrary to Helmut Kohl's claims, was always a land of immigrants, but it was easier to deny this reality in the Bonn era than is the case with multiethnic Berlin as the capital. Just in time for the move to Berlin, Germany took the first step toward a long overdue revision of its citizenship laws, which heretofore were based almost exclusively on bloodlines. The new law, passed in May 1999, allows any child born in Germany with at least one parent resident in the country for eight years to gain automatic German citizenship. Such an individual can maintain dual citizenship until age twenty-three, then must decide which citizenship to keep. The principal beneficiary of this change is Germany's well-established Turkish community, which has always been especially prominent in Berlin. Of course, the new law will not mean an end to prejudices or social discrimination, in Berlin or elsewhere, but it does represent a significant shift in the country's view of itself.

In the Bonn Republic, Germany's governments kept a wary eye on Eastern Europe even while making strategic economic investments in the region. From the outset, Bonn's primary concern was to keep the Federal Republic firmly anchored in the European and Atlantic West. Adenauer's foreign policy was dominated by reconciliation with France and the establishment of strong ties with America. With Berlin as its capital, Germany will maintain its strong Western ties, but it will also look more to the east. Indeed, if the Federal Republic is to realize its full potential as a major European power, it will have to take the lead in integrating those parts of the Continent that are not yet members of the EU into a broader European framework. Here, too, preliminary steps have already been taken. Whereas the old Federal Republic mended fences in the first instance with its neighbors to the west, united Germany has taken measures to improve its relations with Poland. Polish-German ties will undoubtedly be strengthened by having the German capital in Berlin, which is only fifty miles from the Polish border.

The core of the Bonn Republic was the conservative Catholic southwest and even more conservative Bavaria. National unification began the shift away from that core, and it made possible the previously unimaginable victory of a "Red-Green" coalition in 1998. The move to Berlin carries this gravitational shift further and provides the setting for a new, more "experimental" style of German leadership, both at home and abroad. None of the top leaders in the Schröder government hail from Berlin, but they seem more at home on the Spree than on the Rhine. Schröder himself was a leftist student leader in the 1960s before reinventing himself as a centrist "new Socialist." As minister-president of Lower Saxony he became quite cozy with big business, sitting on the board of Volkswagen and bailing out a steel mill at a cost

The "New Berliner" Chancellor Gerhard Schröder at the Brandenburg Gate, August 25, 1999

of nearly $1 billion. Partial to Cuban cigars and Italian suits, he was always impatient with stuffy Bonn, considering himself a man for "new beginnings." Where better to launch new beginnings than from a city that has always been more than happy to toss away the old in favor of something new?

Joschka Fischer, Germany's new foreign minister, is likewise a former radical turned pragmatist. In his protest-filled youth he was briefly incarcerated for rioting. He remains willing to challenge established doctrine, whether it be the pacifist and noninterventionist shibboleths of his own Green Party, or the deference to Washington, NATO, and Brussels typical of Bonn's foreign policy in the old days. Like Schröder, Fischer is excited by the prospect of ruling from Berlin, seeing the place more as a city of the future—European and global—than as a frightening relic of the bad old German past. There is, he says, "no negative genius" lurking in Berlin; it will not stir the nationalist in the German soul. "Fears about Berlin will remain only that—fears," he says confidently. The Berlin Republic will not revert to centralized nationalism, he adds, because Germans have become "passionate federalists," and also because the nation-state itself has lost much of its power under the influences of Europeanization and globalization. "The nation state in Europe is now a thing of the past, no more than a virtual reality," he insists. Of course, this is not quite accurate, but it is certainly true that in the age of expanding European unity, multinational corporate mergers, the Internet, and the "Global Village," the traditional nation-state is a much-diminished force.

Precisely because nation-states have lost some of their clout, however, national identity, expressed partly in terms of patriotic symbolism, remains important. For obvious reasons, expressions of patriotic sentiment have been difficult for the Germans during the past fifty years. In an effort to find an acceptable alternative to traditional flag-waving patriotism, the West German philosopher Jürgen Habermas once proposed a "constitutional patriotism"—reverence for the ideals expressed in the Grundgesetz. But this is a rather bloodless concept, incapable of generating much popular enthusiasm. Germany may not be able to act as a fully "normal" nation for the foreseeable future, but with time it will have to evolve a viable sense of national patriotism distinct from chauvinism. With the fall of the Third Reich now over a half-century in the past, it is reasonable to expect that the Germans might become more comfortable in their own skins. Of course, a transfer of capitals cannot alone accomplish this coming to terms with the national self. Nonetheless, it might just be that Berlin, the city where the Germans have experienced the peaks and depths of their national experience, can help to show the way.

NOTES

Introduction

Page

xvii "Siamese city": The term is employed by Peter Schneider in his seminal novel of divided Berlin, *The Wall Jumper* (New York, 1983), 5.

xviii "abuse of power": "'Parvenu Polis' and 'Human Workshop': Reflections on the History of the City of Berlin," *German History* 6:3 (December 1988), 242.

xxi "born in Berlin": Quoted in Jules Huret, *Berlin um Neunzehnhundert*, translated by Nina Knoblich (Berlin, 1987 [1909]), 13.

xxi "months in Berlin": Ibid., 14.

xxiii from the Hanseatic League: "700 und 50 Jahre Berlin. Zur Geschichte einer deutschen Metropole," in Thomas Ludwig, ed., *Berlin. Geschichte einer deutschen Metropole* (Munich, 1986), 277.

xxiv "first duty": Ibid., 278.

xxiv "king has betrayed us!": Quoted in Günter Richter, "Zwischen Revolution und Reichsgründung," in Wolfgang Ribbe, ed., *Geschichte Berlins. Zweiter Band. Von der Märzrevolution bis zur Gegenwart* (Munich, 1987), 615.

xxv "air of the world city": Alberti quoted in Gordon A. Craig, *The Germans* (New York, 1982), 274.

xxvi lack of historical memory: Laurenz Demps, "Von der preussischen Residenzstadt zur hauptstädtischen Metropole," in Werner Süß and Ralf Rytlewski, eds., *Berlin. Die Hauptstadt. Vergangenheit und Zukunft einer europäischen Metropole* (Berlin, 1999), 17.

xxvi "merciless progress": Arthur Eloesser, *Die Strasse meiner Jugend* (Berlin, 1987 [1907]), 7.

xxvi "dreams of the Twenties": Quoted in Wolf von Eckardt and Sander L. Gilman, *Bertolt Brecht's Berlin. A Scrapbook of the Twenties* (Lincoln, Neb., and London, 1993), xi.

Chapter 1

1 "a *Weltstadt*": Lord Frederick Hamilton, *My Yesterdays* (Garden City, N.Y., 1930), 13.

1 "your own devices": Quoted in "Die Mauer in den Herzen," *Die Zeit*, Jan. 31, 1992.

2 "for a patriotic heart": Rudolf Vierhaus, ed., *Das Tagebuch der Baronin Spitzemberg* (Göttingen, 1960), 127.

3 "turmoil so calmly": Quoted in Ruth Glatzer, ed., *Berlin wird Kaiserstadt. Panorama einer Metropole* (Berlin, 1993), 32.

3 "never forget this day": Quoted in Hannah Pakula, *An Uncommon Woman. The Empress Frederick* (New York, 1995), 290.

3 "thrice as wide as Broadway"; "has ever seen": Quoted in ibid., 289–290.

4–5 "view of the Pariser Platz"; "was truly astounding": Glatzer, *Berlin wird Kaiserstadt*, 28, 31

5 domination of national life: Reiner Pommerin, *Von Berlin nach Bonn. Die Alliierten, die Deutschen und die Hauptstadtfrage nach 1945* (Cologne/Vienna, 1989), 4–5.

6 "this old Prussian lady": Ludovica Hesekiel, *Von Brandenburg zu Bismarck. Roman aus der Gegenwart*, 2 vols. (Berlin, 1873), II, 260. Quoted in Katherine Roper, *German Encounters with Modernity: Novels of Imperial Berlin* (Atlantic Highlands, N.J., 1991), 44.

7 "the same as unhappiness": Theodor Fontane, *Briefe in zwei Bänden*, 2 vols. (Munich, 1981), II, 130.

7 matters of the soul: See Klaus Bergmann, *Agrarromantik und Grossstadtfeindlichkeit* (Meisenheim am Glan, 1970).

7 "metropolis of the German spirit": Quoted in Fritz Stern, *Gold and Iron. Bismarck, Bleichröder, and the Building of the German Empire* (New York, 1979), 500.

7 "stink of civilization": Quoted in Otto Pflanze, *Bismarck and the Development of Germany. Volume II, The Period of Consolidation 1871–1880* (Princeton, 1990), 35.

7 "charming though you are": Ibid., 289.

7 "industrially and politically": Quoted in Walter Nelson, *The Berliners. Their Saga and Their City* (New York, 1969), 79.

7 "travel to meetings": Quoted in Bernd Sösemann, "Exerzierfeld und Labor deutscher Geschichte. Berlin im Wandel der deutschen und europäischen Politik zwischen 1848 und 1933," in Werner Süß and Ralf Rytlewski, eds., *Berlin. Die Hauptstadt. Vergangenheit und Zukunft einer europäischen Metropole* (Berlin, 1999), 107.

8 "other part of his body": Quoted in Glatzer, *Berlin wird Kaiserstadt*, 54.

8 "unhoused guests": Pommerin, *Von Berlin nach Bonn*, 7.

8 on the Wilhelmplatz: For a discussion of government buildings on the Wilhelmstrasse, see Laurenz Demps, *Berlin-Wilhelmstrasse. Eine Topographie preussisch-deutscher Macht* (Berlin, 1994), 125–164.

9 "never managing to be": Karl Scheffler, *Berlin—Ein Stadtschicksal* (Berlin, 1910), 219.

9 Brandenburg, East Prussia, and Silesia: Hans O. Modrow, *Berlin 1900* (Berlin, 1936), 106; Paul Goldschmidt, *Berlin in Geschichte und Gegenwart* (Berlin, 1910), 383–384. See also Hsi-huey Liang, "Lower-Class Immigrants in Wilhelmine Berlin," *Central European History* 3 (March–June, 1970), 94–111.

9 irreverence and caustic wit: Paul Mendes-Flohr, "The Berlin Jew as Cosmopolitan," in Emily D. Bilski, ed., *Berlin Metropolis: Jews and the New Culture, 1890–1918*. Exhibition Catalog (Berkeley, 1999), 15–31; Peter Gay, "Encounter with Modernism. German Jews in Wilhelmian Culture," in Peter Gay, *Freud, Jews and Other Germans* (New York, 1978), 93–164.

9 "Berlin-Jewish symbiosis": See especially Peter Gay, "The Berlin-Jewish Spirit. A Dogma and Some Doubts," in Gay, *Freud, Jews*, 169–188. See also W. Michael Blumenthal, *The Invisible Wall* (Washington, D.C., 1998).

9 were not modernists: See Gay, "The Berlin-Jewish Spirit"; and Peter Paret, "Modernism and the 'Alien Element' in German Art," in Bilski, ed., *Berlin Metropolis*, 34.

10 limits on height: On the attempts to control Berlin's growth in the 1860s, see Brian Ladd, *Urban Planning and Civic Order in Germany* (Cambridge, Mass., 1990), 80–83.

10 east of the old city: The classic study on the Mietskasernen is Werner Hegemann, *Das steinerne Berlin* (Berlin, 1930). See also Albert Südekum, *Grossstädtisches Wohnungselend* (Berlin, 1908); and the photographic volume, Gesine Asmus, ed., *Hinterhof, Keller und Mansarde: Einblicke in Berliner Wohnungselend 1901–1920* (Reinbek bei Hamburg, 1982).

11 "every nook and cranny": Quoted in Gisela Heller, *Unterwegs mit Fontane in Berlin und der Mark Brandenburg* (Berlin, 1993), 31.

11, 12 "mind and will"; "boxes for habitation": Glatzer, *Berlin wird Kaiserstadt*, 76, 80.

12 "the civilized world": Peter de Mendelssohn, *Zeitungsstadt Berlin* (Berlin, 1959), 69.

13 "a Judas goat"; "the market woman": Quoted in Gordon A. Craig, *Germany 1866–1945* (New York, 1978), 81.

13 in exclusively Christian hands: Blumenthal, *Invisible Wall*, 217–218.

13 "continually increasing influence": Henry Vizetelly, *Berlin under the New Empire*, 2 vols. (New York, 1968), I, 63.

13 "Lucullan feasts": Blumenthal, *Invisible Wall*, 221.

14 "a respectable prince"; "among plutocratic parvenus": Stern, *Gold and Iron*, 281, 165.

14 comings and goings: On Strousberg, see ibid., 358–366; Blumenthal, *Invisible Wall*, 221–224.

14 "air of the new": Quoted in Demps, *Berlin-Wilhelmstrasse*, 143.

16 "without a lover": Georg Brandes, *Berlin als deutsche Reichshauptstadt. Erinnerungen aus den Jahren 1877–1883* (Berlin, 1989), 11.

16 "frightfully small-townish": Quoted in Pierre-Paul Sagave, *1871. Berlin-Paris. Reichshauptstadt und Hauptstadt der Welt* (Frankfurt, 1971), 27–28.

16 "pitiful hovels"; "assaulted the senses": Kastan quoted in Glatzer, *Berlin wird Kaiserstadtt*, 34.

17 "plumage of a peacock"; "Paris, or London": Tissot quoted in ibid., 35–36.

17 "English and French capitals"; "extension and improvement": Vizetelly, *Berlin,* I, 77, 19. For studies of English and French perspectives on imperial Berlin, see Anne Orde, "Das Bild Berlins in englischen Reisebüchern," in Gerhard Brunn und Jürgen Reulecke, eds. *Metropolis Berlin. Berlin als deutsche Hauptstadt im Vergleich europäischer Hauptstädte 1871–1939* (Bonn, 1992), 272–291; Cécile Chombard-Gaudin, "Frankreich blickt auf Berlin 1900–1939," in ibid., 367–407.

18 "civilization until after 1870": August Bebel, *Aus meinem Leben. Zweiter Teil* (Berlin, 1946), 125.

18 "tracked one's steps": Vizetelly, *Berlin*, I, 14.

18 "foulest smelling capitals"; "external foes": Quoted in Ladd, *Urban Planning*, 53.

18–19 "hideous stench": Quoted in Glatzer, *Berlin wird Kaiserstadt*, 38.

19 "slovenliness itself"; "tight and stiff"; "foot in it": Jules Laforgue, *Berlin. The City and the Court* (New York, 1996), 211–214.

19 "to the martial elements": Vizetelly, *Berlin*, I, 316.

20 "ridiculous and barbaric": Brandes, *Berlin als Reichshauptstadt*, 9.

20 "from his regiment": Charles Hardinge, *Old Diplomacy* (London, 1947), 25.

20 "in the Ark"; "led astray here": Vizetelly, *Berlin*, II, 287, 293.

21 "to soil themselves": Laforgue, *Berlin*, 158–159.

21 banks of the Spree: *Berliner Volks-Zeitung*, Feb. 9, 1873.

22 "squaring of the circle": Friedrich Spielhagen, *Sturmflut*, in *Sämmtliche Werke*, Vol. XIII, Part I (Leipzig, 1886), 47. Quoted in Fritz Stern, *The Failure of Illiberalism* (New York, 1972), 31.

22 "system of corruption": Craig, *Germany*, 82.

22 "fruit and milk vendors": Glatzer, *Berlin wird Kaiserstadt*, 94.

23 "to us poor Christians": Quoted in Stern, *Gold and Iron*, 501–502.

23 "our misfortune": Walter Boehlich, *Der Berliner Antisemitismusstreit* (Frankfurt, 1965), 12.

24 "not live to see": Quoted in Gerhard Masur, *Imperial Berlin* (New York, 1989), 115.

24 "*Judenwirtschaft*": Stern, *Gold and Iron*, 502.

24 "readily available means": Theodor Fontane, *L'Adultera. Sämtliche Werke. Romane, Erzählungen, Gedichte*, II (Munich, 1962), 29. Quoted in Harold James, *A German Identity 1790–1990* (New York, 1989), 75.

24 "left drowning": Quoted in Stern, *Failure of Illiberalism*, 36.

25 "undesirable elements"; come to Berlin: Stern, *Gold and Iron*, 526.

25 "abstain from the election"; "Reich and government": Ibid., 529.

26 "ancient folly": Quoted in Peter G. J. Pulzer, *The Rise of Political Anti-Semitism in Germany and Austria* (New York, 1964), 337–338.

27 "alongside the streets": Quoted in Cyril Buffet, *Berlin* (Paris, 1993), 231.

27 "clean sand over it": Mark Twain, "The German Chicago," in Charles Neider, ed., *The Complete Essays of Mark Twain* (Garden City, N.Y., 1963), 93.

28 "with which to cope"; "arrogance and overbearingness": Quoted in Pflanze, *Bismarck*, II, 247.

28 "race in the world"; along the way: Ibid., 248–249. See also Eberhard Kolb, ed., *Europa und die Reichsgründung: Preussen-Deutschland in der Sicht der grossen europäischen Mächte, 1860–1880, Historische Zeitschrift. Beiheft 6* (Munich, 1980).

29, 30 "principal entrance"; "exchange of regimentals"; "imperial visitors": Vizetelly, *Berlin*, I, 219–221.

30 "of the vanquished"; "Austrian Kaiser"; "be distinguished": Ibid., 22–27.

31 "amused to hear"; "than anything else": Quoted in Pakula, *Uncommon Woman*, 301.

31 "than they are": Quoted in Pflanze, *Bismarck*, II, 259.

31 "some doomed city": Vizetelly, *Berlin*, I, 231.

32 come up in the world: Brandes, *Berlin als Reichshauptstadt*, 178.

33 "to relieve herself" : Bismarck in conversation with Julia Grant. Quoted in William S. McFeely, *Grant. A Biography* (New York, 1981), 471.

33 "by the Congress"; "better than its reputation": Brandes, *Berlin als Reichshauptstadt*, 178.

34 "ordinary and tasteless": Vierhaus, ed., Spitzemberg *Tagebuch*, 172.

34 "from overwork"; "out of gnats"; "of presiding": Quoted in Pflanze, *Bismarck*, II, 438, 53.

35 "go to Kissingen"; "buried before midnight": Quoted in Pakula, *Uncommon Woman*, 349.

36 "to wear under them": Quoted in Stern, *Gold and Iron*, 409.

36 "a colonial policy"; "map of Africa": Quoted in Thomas Pakenham, *The Scramble for Africa, 1876–1912* (New York, 1991), 203.

37 "no neighbors at all": Quoted in Stern, *Gold and Iron*, 411.

38 "get away with anything": Quoted in Adam Hochschild, *King Leopold's Ghost* (Boston, 1988), 83.

39 "careful solicitude"; "carved up Africa": Pakenham, *Scramble*, 254.

40 "So much for Philosophy": Quoted in McFeely, *Grant*, 469.

40 "being shot at": Quoted in Pflanze, *Bismarck*, II, 392.

40 "Precisely so": Quoted in McFeely, *Grant*, 469.

41 "must be struck": Bebel quoted in Vizetelly, *Berlin*, II, 437.

41 "aims of Social Democracy"; "get anything done"; "by liberalism": Quoted in Pflanze, *Bismarck*, II, 395, 402.

42 "between the social classes"; "endangered districts": Quoted in ibid., 413–414.

42 "an industrial exhibition": Brandes, *Berlin als Reichshauptstadt*, 168–169.

42 "of the times"; "sent you here"; "yellow coat"; "for the future": Quoted in Glatzer, *Berlin wird Kaiserstadt*, 254–263.

43 "rather go under"; "smallness"; with his whip; "off a revolution": Ibid., 264–265, 267, 269.

45 "that rules Berlin"; "press of Berlin": Moritz Busch, *Bismarck: Some Secret Pages of His History* (London, 1898), 3 vols., II, 470–472.

Chapter 2

47 "possible in Berlin": Quoted in Rolf Stremmel, *Modell und Moloch. Berlin in der Wahrnehmung deutscher Politiker vom Ende des 19. Jahrhunderts bis zum Zweiten Weltkrieg* (Bonn, 1992), 54.

47 "Silicon Valley of its day": Sir Peter Hall, *Cities in Civilization* (New York, 1998), 377.

48 "consciousness regarding itself": Wolf Jobst Siedler, "Die traditionelle Traditionslosigkeit. Notizen zur Baugeschichte Berlins" in Manfred Schlenke, ed., *Preussen, Versuch einer Bilanz: Ausstellung Katalog* (Reinbek bei Hamburg, 1981), 311.

48 "venerable beside it": Mark Twain, "The German Chicago," in Neider, ed., *Complete Essays*, 88.

48 "rapidity of its growth": Charles Huard, *Berlin comme je l'ai vu* (Paris, 1907), 33.

48 "city of Parvenus": Walther Rathenau, "Die schönste Stadt der Welt," in Jürgen Schutte and Peter Sprengel, eds. *Die Berliner Moderne 1885–1914* (Stuttgart, 1987), 100–101.

48 "youngest European great city": Arthur Eloesser, *Die Strassen meiner Jugend* (Berlin, 1987), 31.

48 eastern Europeans: Gerhard Brunn, "Metropolis Berlin," in G. Brunn and Jürgen Reulecke, *Metropolis Berlin. Berlin als deutsche Hauptstadt im Vergleich europäischer Hauptstädte 1871–1939* (Bonn, 1992), 21.

49 "German non-culture": Karl Scheffler, *Berlin—Ein Stadtschicksal* (Berlin, 1910), 121.

49 "surrogates and imitations"; "a shoreless future": Eloesser, *Strasse*, 77–80.

49 "lack of historical interest": Karl Baedeker, *Berlin and Its Environs: Handbook for Travellers* (Leipzig, 1903), 51.

49 collapse of moral integrity: Roper, *German Encounters*, 127–145. On attitudes toward Berlin in German literature at the turn of the century, see also Viktor Zmegac, "Für und gegen Berlin in der literarischen Kultur der Jahrhundertwende," in Klaus Siebenhaar, ed., *Das poetische Berlin. Metropolenkultur zwischen Gründerzeit und Nationalsozialismus* (Wiesbaden, 1992), 69–84.

49 "reign among us": Quoted in Roper, *German Encounters*, 200.

49 "and steam boilers"; "of his youth": Max Kretzer, *Meister Timpe* (Stuttgart, 1976), 28, 64.

50 capital's nightlife: John H. Zammito, "Der Streit um die Berliner Kultur 1871 bis 1930," in *Jahrbuch für die Geschichte Mittel- und Ostdeutschland.* Band 35 (Berlin, 1986), 238.

50 "spiritual emptiness": Quoted in Andrew Lees, "Critics of Urban Society in Germany, 1854–1914," *Journal of the History of Ideas* 40:1 (Jan.-March 1979), 71.

51 "ought to be now": Quoted in Pakula, *Uncommon Woman*, 476.

52 "chivalry in Berlin": Quoted in ibid., 471.

53 "young men in it": Quoted in John C. G. Röhl and Nicolaus Sombart, eds., *Kaiser Wilhelm II. New Interpretations* (Cambridge and New York, 1982), 47.

53 "offer you a fountain": Michael Erbe, "Berlin im Kaiserreich," in Wolfgang Ribbe, ed., *Geschichte Berlins. Zweiter Band. Von der Märzrevolution bis zur Gegenwart* (Munich, 1987), 761.

54 "blood of my subjects": Quoted in Otto Pflanze, *Bismarck and the Development of Germany, Volume III. The Period of Fortification* (Princeton, 1990), 358.

55 "with incomparable success": Ibid., 373.

55 "constantly being added": Vierhaus, ed., Spitzemberg *Tagebuch*, 275–276.

55 "fast-changing economy and society": Pflanze, *Bismarck*, III, 419–420.

56 relax, not to mourn: Alfred Kerr, *Wo liegt Berlin? Briefe aus der Reichshauptstadt 1895–1900* (Berlin, 1997), 408.

57 "side of my ancestors": Quoted in Pflanze, *Bismarck*, III, 428.

57 "beautiful city in the world": Scheffler, *Berlin*, 138.

57 "put on their clothes": Quoted in Lamar Cecil, *Wilhelm II, Volume II. Emperor and Exile (1900–1941)* (Chapel Hill, 1996), 23.

58 "have something": Kerr, *Wo liegt Berlin?*, 5.

59 "impression of emptiness": Avenarius, "Der Dom," quoted in Ruth Glatzer, ed., *Berliner Leben 1870–1900. Erinnerungen und Berichte* (Berlin, 1963), 52.

59 Protestantism would replace Catholicism: Thomas Parents, "Rom, Berlin und Köln," in Hans Wilderotter, ed., *Hauptstadt. Zentren, Residenzen, Metropolen in der deutschen Geschichte* (Cologne, 1989), 389.

59 "leadership of Europe": Michael S. Cullen, "Der Reichstag und Schloss Bellvue," in ibid., 340.

59 "wanted to be": Michael S. Cullen, *Der Reichstag. Die Geschichte eines Monuments* (Stuttgart, 1990), 38.

60 "narrow back street": Theophil Zolling, *Bismarcks Nachfolger* (Berlin, 1885), 517–518. Quoted in Roper, *German Encounters*, 225.

60 "ape house of the Reich"; "Pickpockets": Cullen, *Reichstag*, 32, 314–317.

61 "could be made to be ugly": Quoted in Cecil, *Wilhelm II*, II, 42–43.

61 "made of marble": Quoted in Anthony Read and David Fisher, *Berlin Rising* (New York, 1994), 126.

61 "crawling back on all fours": Quoted in Röhl and Sombart, *Kaiser Wilhelm II*, 31.

62 "a loyal subject": Heinrich Mann, *Der Untertan* (Berlin, 1947), 93, 55.

62 second shot: Alson J. Smith, *A View of the Spree* (New York, 1962), x–xii.

63 "instead of to debase": Ernst Johann, ed., *Reden des Kaisers* (Munich, 1966), 211.

63 "revolution of humanity": Quoted in Masur, *Imperial Berlin*, 244. On imperial Berlin's theater scene, especially the contribution of Jews to it, see Peter Jelavich, "Performing High and Low: Jews in Modern Theater, Cabaret, Revue, and Film," in Bilski, ed., *Berlin Metropolis*, 208–235.

64 "champagne and caviar": Quoted in Peter Jelavich, *Berlin Cabaret* (Cambridge, Mass., 1993), 63.

64 "strives to realize": Quoted in Cecil, *Wilhelm II*, II, 47.

64 "practical and upright": Quoted in Jelavich, *Berlin Cabaret*, 63. On Reinhardt, see also Jelavich, "Performing High and Low," 213–223.

65 "just been written": Quoted in Dieter Glatzer and Ruth Glatzer, eds., *Berliner Leben 1900–1914. Eine Historische Reportage aus Erinnerungen und Berichte* (Berlin, 1986), 2 vols., I, 485–486.

65 the Berlin Philharmonic: Walther Kiaulehn, *Berlin. Schicksal einer Weltstadt* (Munich, 1980), 268–269. See also Ronald Taylor, *Berlin and Its Culture* (New Haven, 1997), 205–207; and Michael Farr, *Berlin! Berlin! Its Culture, Its Times* (London, 1992), 127–128.

65 "with all haste": Quoted in Kiaulehn, 272.

66 "Wagner is too noisy"; "commonplace conductor": Quoted in Cecil, *Wilhelm II*, II, 46.

66 "to bite me": Ibid., 45.

67 "a vulgar fellow": Quoted in Masur, *Imperial Berlin*, 239.

68 part of the court set himself: On Menzel, see Kiaulehn, *Berlin*, 289–295; Taylor, *Berlin and Its Culture*, 174–176.

68 "on your conscience, old Menzel": Brandes, *Berlin als Reichshauptstadt*, 136.

69 wholesome and uplifting art: On Werner, see Peter Paret, *The Berlin Secession. Modernism and Its Enemies in Imperial Germany* (Cambridge, Mass., 1980), 15–20; Anton von Werner, *Erlebnisse und Eindrücke 1870–1890* (Berlin, 1913).

69 "throw them out!"; "out to anyone": Quoted in Paret, *Berlin Secession*, 50, 43. On Liebermann, see also Peter Paret, "Modernism and the 'Alien Element'," in Bilski, ed., *Berlin Metropolis*, 35–38; Emily D. Bilski, "Images of Identity and Urban Life: Jewish Artists in Turn-of-the-Century Berlin,"

in ibid., 103–106; and Chana C. Schütz, "Max Liebermann as a 'Jewish' Painter: The Artist's Reception in His Time," in ibid., 146–163.

71 "hideous than it already is": Quoted in Cecil, *Wilhelm II*, II, 39.

71 "chests of deserving men"; trees blue: Farr, *Berlin!*, 121.

71 Berlin Secession: In addition to Paret, see Marion F. Deshmukh, "Art and Politics in Turn-of-the-Century Berlin. The Berlin Secession and Kaiser Wilhelm II," in Gerald Chapple and Hans H. Schulte, eds., *The Turn of the Century: German Literature and Art, 1890–1915* (Bonn, 1981), 463–473.

72 "soul of the German nation"; "today's classics": Quoted in Paret, *Berlin Secession*, 160, 156.

73 "infinite love"; "big city night": Quoted in Charles W. Haxthausen, "Images of Berlin in the Art of the Secession and Expressionism," in Kelly Morris and Amanda Woods, eds., *Art in Berlin 1815–1989* (Atlanta, 1989), 68. On Meidner, see also Bilski, "Images of Identity," in Bilski, ed., *Berlin Metropolis*, 123–127.

73 "dehumanized world"; "what is seen": Ibid., 73–76.

74 "in Gothic countries": Brandes, *Berlin als Reichshauptstadt*, 45.

74–75 "most odious hostility": Quoted in Caroline Moorehead, *Lost and Found: The 9,000 Treasures of Troy* (New York, 1994), 197.

76 "all German citizens": Ibid., 199.

76 "von Moltke and myself": Quoted in David A. Traill, *Schliemann of Troy. Treasure and Deceit* (New York, 1995), 214.

76 treasure-house of ancient plunder: Suzanne L. Marchand, *Down from Olympus. Archaeology and Philhellenism in Germany, 1750–1970* (Princeton, 1996), 188–189.

76–77 "of foreign origin"; "less prominent place": Quoted in Cecil, *Wilhelm II*, II, 40.

77 Cézanne painting: Emily D. Bilski, "Introduction," in Bilski, ed., *Berlin Metropolis*, 3.

77 "not to *him*": Quoted in Paret, *Berlin Secession*, 161.

77 "raises my bile": Quoted in Masur, *Imperial Berlin*, 226.

78 quarantine or disinfecting: On Virchow, see Gerhard Hiltner, *Rudolf Virchow* (Stuttgart, 1970).

79 "with such institutions": Jules Huret, *Berlin um Neunzehnhundert* (Berlin, 1997), 247–248.

79 Paul Ehrlich: On Ehrlich, see Fritz Stern, *Einstein's German World* (Princeton, 1999), 13–34.

79 "golden age of German physics": Quoted in ibid., 39.

79–80 Virchow versus Bismarck: Hiltner, *Virchow*, 43–46.

80 "political animal"; "Regiment of the Guards": Quoted in Masur, *Imperial Berlin*, 110, 99.

80 "as was its predecessor": Quoted in Cecil, *Wilhelm II*, II, 59.

80 "new triumph of science": Quoted in Stern, *Einstein's German World*, 38.

81 "obstacle to the exhibition": Quoted in Masur, *Imperial Berlin*, 126.

81–82 Industrial Exhibition of 1896: On this, see Jochen Boberg, Tilman Fichter, and Eckhart Gillen, *Die Metropole. Industriekultur in Berlin im 20. Jahrhundert* (Munich, 1896), 16–27.

82–83 urban transportation: On Berlin's transportation system, see ibid., 31–51; and Hans Kollhoff, "The Metropolis as a Construction: Engineering Structures in Berlin, 1871–1914," in Josef Paul Kleihues and Christina Rathgeber, eds., *Berlin/New York. Like and Unlike* (New York, 1993), 47–58.

84 "by the evening sun": Quoted in Kollhoff, "The Metropolis," 52.

85 automobiles in Berlin: See Glatzer and Glatzer, eds., *Berliner Leben 1900–1914*, I, 125–128.

85 Zeppelins: see Peter Fritzsche, *A Nation of Fliers. German Aviation and the Popular Imagination* (Cambridge, Mass., 1992), 19–20.

85 "apparent impossibilities": Quoted in Glatzer and Glatzer, eds., *Berliner Leben 1900–1914*, II, 228.

85 "to get a better view": Ibid., 229.

86 "He is manoli": Bernt Engelmann, *Berlin. Eine Stadt wie keine andere* (Göttingen, 1991), 196.

86 "bringer of light"; "most important city": Quoted in Joachim Schlör, *Nachts in der grossen Stadt. Paris, Berlin, London 1840 bis 1930* (Munich, 1994), 68–69.

86 *Wildness und Weltstadt:* Gottfried Korff and Reinhard Rürup, eds., *Berlin, Berlin. Die Ausstellung zur Geschichte der Stadt* (Berlin, 1987), 465.

86 "soaps and toothbrushes": Franz Hessel, *Ein Flaneur in Berlin* (Berlin, 1984), 32–33.

87 "elevated lifestyle": Quoted in Korff and Rürup, eds., *Berlin, Berlin*, 466.

87 "city of show windows": Quoted in Peter Fritzsche, *Reading Berlin 1900* (Cambridge, Mass., 1996), 154.

87 "fill the streets?"; "a bewildering mess": Quoted in ibid., 153, 172.

87 could pass up: Kiaulehn, *Berlin*, 222.
87–88 "glass-covered counters": Huret, *Berlin um Neunzehnhundert*, 59.
88 "elegance for all"; "with the little lady": Quoted in Kiaulehn, *Berlin*, 225.
88 day's headlines: On Berlin's newspapers, see ibid., 477–504; Fritzsche, *Reading Berlin*; and Peter de Mendelssohn, *Zeitungsstadt Berlin* (Berlin, 1982).
88 "the way it really is"; crossroads in Europe; "Catch Hennig": Fritzsche, *Reading Berlin*, 63–74, 160.
90 arranged a pardon: On the Voigt episode, see Wolfgang Heidelmayer, ed., *Der Fall Köpenick* (Frankfurt am Main, 1968); and the Carl Zuckmayer play, "Der Hauptmann von Köpenick."
90 "amounted to anything": Glatzer and Glatzer, eds., *Berliner Leben 1900–1914*, II, 613.
91 "don't you think?": Quoted in Hedda Adlon, *Hotel Adlon* (Munich, 1993).
92 "half-museum, half-living room": Quoted in Korff and Rürup, *Berlin, Berlin*, 205.
92 "bespectacled men at their sides": Huret, *Berlin um Neunzehnhundert*, 62.
92 36 percent Russians: Korff and Rürup, *Berlin, Berlin*, 205.
93 "all over again": Huret, *Berlin um Neunzehnhundert*, 67.
93 "most enticing nights": Hans Ostwald, ed., *Grossstadtdokumente*, Band 30 (Berlin, n.d.), 15.
93 "almost completely disappeared"; "dominate the milieu": Quoted in Schlör, *Nachts*, 107, 109.
94 Heinze case: See Richard Evans, "Prostitution, State and Society in Imperial Germany," *Past and Present* 70 (Feb. 1976), 119.
94, 95 "down the street"; "fair game"; "have survived": Ostwald, *Grossstadtdokumente*, 17–19, 28.
95 Ringvereine: Read and Fisher, *Berlin Rising*, 175–176.
96 "rest of the world": Ostwald, *Grossstadtdokumente*, 23–24.
96 "houses and humanity": Magnus Hirschfeld, *Berlins drittes Geschlecht* (Berlin, 1991), 18.
96 "how they live"; "Amerika-Franzl"; "strong sympathy"; "indecent occurred": Ibid., 13, 21, 48, 52.
97 two thousand male prostitutes: See Modris Eksteins, *Rites of Spring. The Great War and the Birth of the Modern Age* (Boston, 1989), 83.
98 Eulenberg case: See Kiaulehn, *Berlin*, 514–516; Cecil, *Wilhelm II*, II, 112–116; Isabel V. Hull, *The Entourage of Kaiser Wilhelm II* (New York, 1982), 105–145.
98 "cleared or stoned": Quoted in Cecil, *Wilhelm II*, II, 115–116.
99 "in an iron grip": Quoted in Korff and Rürup, *Berlin, Berlin*, 333.
100 cases of emergency: G. A. Ritter and Jürgen Kocka, *Deutsche Sozialgeschichte 1870–1914. Dokumente and Skizzen* (Munich, 1982), 144–147.
100 "my work mechanically": Quoted in ibid., 152–153.
101 "paid for each piece": Quoted in Korff and Rürup, *Berlin, Berlin*, 335.
101 Home and Work Show: Ibid., 336.
101 unable to conceive children; "cradle of her child": Rosemary Orthmann, *Out of Necessity. Women Working in Berlin at the Height of Industrialization* (London and New York, 1991), 170–171.
102 "nothing but a broodhen": Quoted in Cecil, *Wilhelm II*, II, 6–7.
102 "the day after": Georg Hermann, *Kubinke* (Gütersloh, 1967), 8–9. Quoted in Fritzsche, *Reading Berlin*, 117.
102–103 "needles sticking out": Quoted in Fritzsche, *Reading Berlin*, 119.
103 workers in imperial Germany: See Kiaulehn, 169–214; Eduard Bernstein, ed., *Die Geschichte der Berliner Arbeiterbewegung* (Berlin, 1924).
103–104 SPD electoral successes: Erbe, "Berlin im Kaiserreich," in Ribbe, ed., *Geschichte Berlins, II*, 770–775.
106 "exotic colorful bird": Elzbieta Etinger, *Rosa Luxemburg* (Boston, 1986), 76.
107 "be gunned down": Quoted in Jay Winter and Blaine Baggett, *The Great War and the Shaping of the Twentieth Century* (New York, 1996), 31.
107 "exclusive use of traffic": Quoted in Thomas Lindenberger, *Strassenpolitik. Zur Sozialgeschichte der öffentlichen Ordnung in Berlin, 1900 bis 1914* (Bonn, 1995), 11.

Chapter 3

110 "become a world-empire": Quoted in Malcolm Carroll, *Germany and the Great Powers* (New York, 1975), 378.

110 "German impudence": Quoted in Friedrich Thimme, "Die Kruger Depesche," *Europäische Gespräche*, 1924, 213.

110 "unfortunate impression": Sir Sidney Lee, *King Edward VII*, 2 vols. (New York, 1925–27), I, 724–725.

110 "wants to fight": Quoted in J. C. G. Röhl, *Germany without Bismarck* (Berkeley, 1967), 166.

110 "jumpy" fellow: Quoted in Cecil, *Wilhelm II*, II, 95.

110 gift of Frederick the Great statue: Nathan Miller, *Theodore Roosevelt. A Life* (New York, 1992), 389.

111 "failure in history": Quoted in Robert K. Massie, *Dreadnought. Britain, Germany, and the Coming of the Great War* (New York, 1991), 106.

111 make a splash: For a comprehensive study of Anglo-German enmity, see Paul M. Kennedy, *The Rise of the Anglo-German Antagonism* (London, 1980).

111 "a little boy": Quoted in Lamar Cecil, "History as family chronicle: Kaiser Wilhelm II and the dynastic roots of the Anglo-German antagonism," in Röhl and Sombart, eds., *Kaiser Wilhelm II*, 105.

111 "to the *Botokunden*": Ibid., 107.

111 "compel that recognition": Quoted in Theodor Schiemann, *Deutschland und die Grosse Politik*, 2 vols. (Berlin, 1902–15), I, 11–12.

111 "future on the water": Quoted in Michael Balfour, *The Kaiser and His Times* (Boston, 1964), 206.

112 "butt-ends of [their] rifles": Alfred von Tirpitz, *My Memoirs*, 2 vols. (New York, 1970), I, 134.

112 Naval bills: See Eckart Kehr, *Battleship Building and Party Politics in Germany, 1894–1901* (Chicago, 1973).

113 grounds of the Berlin Zoo: Korff and Rürup, eds., *Berlin, Berlin*, 292.

114 "aimed at us": Massie, *Dreadnought*, 601.

114 "mad as hatters": Norman Rich and M. H. Fisher, eds., *Friedrich von Holstein. The Holstein Papers: The Memoirs, Diaries and Correspondence of Friedrich von Holstein*, 4 vols. (New York, 1955), I, 207. See also Terence F. Cole, "The Daily Telegraph Affair and its Aftermath: the Kaiser, Bülow, and the Reichstag, 1908–1909," in Röhl and Sombart, eds., *Kaiser Wilhelm II*, 249–268.

115 "in a madhouse": Vierhaus, ed., Spitzemberg *Tagebuch*, 489.

115 "ruler of this people": Quoted in Cole, "The Daily Telegraph Affair," 263.

115 "Jewish press carnival": Quoted in Cecil, *Wilhelm II*, II, 140.

115 "safeguarding constitutional responsibilities": Bernard, Fürst von Bülow, *Memoirs of Prince von Bülow*. 4 vols. (Boston, 1931), II, 423.

116 "I am neither"; "He can't do it": Quoted in Konrad H. Jarausch, *The Enigmatic Chancellor: Bethmann-Hollweg and the Hubris of Imperial Germany* (New Haven, 1973), 66–70.

116 "work out fine": Quoted in Cecil, *Wilhelm II*, II, 147.

116 firmly onto his string: Paul M. Kennedy, "The Kaiser and German Weltpolitik," in Röhl and Sombart, eds. *Kaiser Wilhelm II*, 155.

116 "extremely relieved"; "little popguns": Quoted in Cecil, *Wilhelm II*, II, 154, 163.

117 "the German sword": *Reichstag Verhandlungen*, XII, Leg. Per. II, Session 7718 (Nov. 9, 1911). See also Bernadotte E. Schmitt, *England and Germany, 1740–1914* (Princeton, 1916), 338.

117 "matter with the Hohenzollerns?": Quoted in Cecil, *Wilhelm II*, II, 165.

118 "coffin of German prestige": *National Zeitung*, Nov. 5, 1911.

118–119 "a more fortunate result": Quoted in Gordon A. Craig, *Germany 1866–1945*, 330–331.

119 "I hate the Slavs": Quoted in Cecil, *Wilhelm II*, II, 176.

119 "more precarious than ever": Alan Clark, ed., *'A Good Innings.' The Private Papers of Viscount Lee of Fareham* (London, 1974), 121.

120 "whole thing off": Quoted in Read and Fisher, *Berlin Rising*, 156.

120 "heels of that rabble": Quoted in Cecil, *Wilhelm II*, II, 168.

120 "remain at home": Theodor Wolff, *Der Kreig des Pontius Pilatus* (Zurich, 1934), 328.

121 "to my subjects"; "deadly serious hour": Quoted in Eksteins, *Rites of Spring*, 56–57.

121 "Long Live Social Democracy": Jeffrey Verhey, "The Spirit of 1914. The Myth of Enthusiasm and the Rhetoric of Unity in World War I," Ph.D. Dissertation, Berkeley, 1991, 141.

121 "still alive": Quoted in Cecil, *Wilhelm II*, II, 205.

122 "cool decisiveness": Quoted in Peter Grupp, *Harry Graf Kessler 1868–1937* (Munich, 1995), 163.

122 "reached its high point": Quoted in Eksteins, *Rites of Spring*, 60.

122 "German sword to victory": Quoted in Verhey, "Spirit of 1914," 32.

123 "demanded by duty": Quoted in Eksteins, *Rites of Spring*, 61.
123 prospect of war: James W. Gerard, *My Four Years in Germany* (New York, 1917), 133–134.
123 "dinner in St. Petersburg": Winter and Baggett, *Great War*, 59.
124 bacon at Waterloo: Cecil, *Wilhelm II*, II, 208.
124 apologized profusely: Gerard, *My Four Years*, 138–139.
124 "such dangerous people"; "lost their senses": Quoted in Verhey, "Spirit of 1914," 179–180.
125 "willingness for sacrifice": Quoted in Stremmel, *Modell*, 55.
126 war games in the streets: Felix Gilbert, *A European Past* (New York, 1988), 28.
126 "son of my wife": Käthe Kollwitz, *Briefe an den Sohn 1904 bis 1945* (Berlin, 1992), 96.
127 "show his patriotism": Quoted in Verhey, "Spirit of 1914," 203.
127 bursting with happy crowds: Ibid., 202.
127 "too high a price": Quoted in Hellmut von Gerlach, ed., *Die grosse Zeit der Lüge: Der erste Weltkrieg und die deutsche Mentalität (1871–1921)* (Bremen, 1994), 2. Belinda Davis's new study, *Home Fires Burning: Food, Politics, and Everyday Life in World War I Berlin* (Chapel Hill, 2000) appeared too recently to be consulted for this book.
128 first two weeks of the war: Jay Winter and Jean-Louis Robert, *Capital Cities at War. Paris, London, Berlin, 1914–1918* (Cambridge, 1997), 139.
129 other parts of the Reich: Ibid., 58–66; Ernst Kaeber, *Berlin im Weltkriege. Fünf Jahre städtischer Kriegsarbeit* (Berlin, 1921), 1–20.
129 "concentrated in Berlin?": Quoted in Stremmel, *Modell*, 98.
129 Rathenau: On Rathenau's contribution, see Wolfgang Kruse, "Kriegswirtschaft und Gesellschaftvision. Walther Rathenau und die Organisierung des Kapitalismus," in Hans Wilderotter, ed., *Die Extreme berühren sich. Walther Rathenau 1867–1922* (Berlin, 1993), 151–168; Gerald D. Feldman, *Army, Industry, and Labor in Germany* (Princeton, 1966).
131 female work-force: Winter and Robert, *Capital Cities*, 188.
131 motormen: Gerard, *My Four Years*, 407; see also Kaeber, *Berlin im Weltkriege*, 2.
131 "socialist principles": Quoted in Feldman, *Army*, 104.
132 "orgy of interest politics": Ibid., 150.
132 "during the entire war": Adlon, *Hotel Adlon*, 81.
132 "bread was unpalatable": Gilbert, *European Past*, 32.
133 profit for themselves: "Marmelade statt Butter?" *Berlin Lokal-Anzeiger*, Oct. 19, 1919.
134 "their hollow breasts": Quoted in Dieter Glatzer and Ruth Glatzer, eds., *Berliner Leben 1914–1918. Eine historische Reportage aus Erinnerungen und Berichten* (Berlin, 1983), 265.
134 "next meal will be": Evelyn Blücher von Wahlstatt, *An English Wife in Berlin* (New York, 1920), 158.
134 "picking them clean": Quoted in Stremmel, *Modell*, 95.
134 "eating shit for dessert": Quoted in Robert Scholz, "Ein unruhiges Jahrzehnt: Lebensmittelunruhen, Massenstreiks und Arbeitslosen-Krawalle in Berlin 1914–1923," in Manfred Gallus, ed., *Pöbelexzesse und Volkstumulte in Berlin. Zur Sozialgeschichte der Strasse (1830–1980)* (Berlin, 1984), 83.
134 "discourse in Berlin": Ibid., 85.
135 "these difficult times": Ibid., 87.
136 "Truly a Weltstadt": Quoted in Stremmel, *Modell*, 235. See also A. Joachimsthaler, *Korrektur einer Biographie. Adolf Hitler 1908–1920* (Munich, 1989), 170–171.
136 "mistakes and dark sides": Stremmel, *Modell*, 235.
136 "fields of grain": Harnack quoted in Gerard, *My Four Years*, 147–148.
137 "Manifesto of the Ninety-three": See Jürgen von Ungern-Sternberg and Wolfgang von Ungern-Sternberg, *Der Aufruf 'An der Kulturwelt!'* (Stuttgart, 1996), 72–73.
137 "Manhattan Project": Fritz Stern, *Dreams and Delusions* (New York, 1987), 65.
137 "then, however, regularly": Quoted in ibid., 63.
138 "live in Berlin": Quoted in Ronald W. Clark, *Einstein. The Life and Times* (New York, 1971), 168.
138 "speak out for peace"; "cessation of hostilities": Ibid., 181; also Stern, *Einstein's German World*, 115–118.
139 "one excitement to another": *Berlin Börsen-Courier*, Dec. 9, 1915. Quoted in Jelavich, *Berlin Cabaret*, 119.
139 "darling, darling army": Quoted in Helga Bemmann, *Claire Waldoff* (Frankfurt am Main, 1994), 97.
139 "one enemy alone": Quoted in Jelavich, *Berlin Cabaret*, 119.

139 "lead in fashion questions": Quoted in Verhey, "Spirit of 1914," 120.
140 "of their fellow citizens": Jelavich, *Berlin Cabaret*, 121.
141 "Frau General": Quoted in Bemmann, *Claire Waldoff*, 100–101.
141 "whores and champagne"; "unpatriotic bastards"; in the trenches: Quoted in Jelavich, *Berlin Cabaret*, 124.
142 "existence with impunity": Quoted in Paret, *Berlin Secession*, 235.
142 "Roman Eagle"; Iron Cross: Ibid., 238, 240–243.
143 "banality in life": Robert Hughes, *Nothing If Not Critical* (New York, 1990), 167.
143 "Courbet of the cannibals": Ibid., 168.
144 "sign of their fate": Quoted in Clark V. Poling, "The City and Modernity: Art in Berlin in the First World War and Its Aftermath," in Morris and Woods, eds. *Art in Berlin 1815–1989*, 84.
144 "arrived there": George Grosz, *An Autobiography* (New York, 1983), 94.
144 cretinous thugs: Beth Irwin Lewis, *George Grosz. Art and Politics in the Weimar Republic*, rev. ed. (Princeton, 1991), 21–23.
145 "side by side": Grosz, *Autobiography*, 102.
145 "smells of shit": Quoted in Frank Whitford, "The Many Faces of George Grosz," in *The Berlin of George Grosz. Drawings, Watercolours and Prints 1912–1930*. Royal Academy of Arts, London (New Haven, 1997), 7.
145 Widmung an Oskar Panizza: Ibid.
146 "war Dada da"; "aimless of the world unite": Quoted in Eksteins, *Rites of Spring*, 210.
146 "Art is shit": Quoted in Lewis, *George Grosz*, 57.
146 "by a long shot": Karl Riha, ed., *Dada Berlin. Texte, Manifeste, Aktionen* (Stuttgart, 1977), 17.
146 distribution of resources: Ingo Materna and Jans-Joachim Schreckenbach, eds., *Dokumente aus geheimen Archiven. Band 4, 1914–1918. Berichte des Berliner Polizeipräsidenten zur Stimmung und Lage der Bewölkerung in Berlin 1914–1918* (Weimar, 1987), 166–167.
147 "we want turnips"; "influence as here": Quoted in Scholz, "Unruhiges Jahrzehnt," 93.
148 to a rapid end; "fateful" development: Materna and Schreckenbach, *Dokumente*, 172, 208–209.
148 "the Russian revolution": Quoted in J. P. Nettl, *Rosa Luxemburg* (Oxford, 1969), 420.
148 the strike leaders: Materna and Schreckenbach, *Dokumente*, 193.
149 "during the war": Quoted in Robert Asprey, *The German High Command at War* (New York, 1991), 331.
150 for generous donations: Gilbert, *European Past*, 31.
150 "stage powerful demonstrations"; "with the authorities": Materna and Schreckenbach, *Dokumente*, 234–235, 239.
151 control over the masses: Feldman, *Army*, 449.
151 "come this summer": Materna and Schreckenbach, *Dokumente*, 271.
152 "to dark pessimism": Quoted in Asprey, *High Command*, 402.
152 at the latest: Materna and Schreckenbach, *Dokumente*, 279.
152 "anything less than hopeful": Blücher, *English Wife*, 245.
152 going to happen: Cecil, *Wilhelm II*, II, 273.
153 "have served us": Quoted in Winter and Baggett, *Great War*, 307.
153 "representatives of the German people": Quoted in Cecil, *Wilhelm II*, II, 283.
153 push him from power; in attendance: Ibid., 288, 353–354.
154 "to the capital"; "schoolboys": Harry Kessler, *In the Twenties. The Diaries of Harry Kessler* (New York, 1971), 5, 7.
155 "tasteless way of the times": Blücher, *English Wife*, 294.
155 "great German Republic": Philipp Scheidemann, *Memoiren*. 2 volumes (Dresden, 1928), II, 310–314.

Chapter 4

157 "kinds of debauchery!": Klaus Mann, *The Turning Point* (New York, 1984), 86.
157 "crisis in modern civilization": Stephen Spender, "Life Wasn't a Cabaret," *New York Times Magazine*, Oct. 30, 1979, 24.

157 "Hauptstadt of vice": Quoted in John J. White, "Sexual Mecca, Nazi Metropolis, City of Doom: The Pattern of English, Irish and American Reactions to the Berlin of the Interwar Years," in Derek Glass, Dietmar Rösler, and John J. White, eds., *Berlin. Literary Images of A City. Eine Grossstadt im Spiegel der Literatur* (Berlin, 1989), 183.

157–158 "puppies [were] virgins": Stephen Spender, *The Temple* (London, 1988), 185.

158 "seemed to be trump": W. E. Süskind, "Raymund," *Neue Rundschau*, I (1927), 374. Quoted in Gerald D. Feldman, *The Great Disorder. Politics, Economics, and Society in the German Inflation 1914–1924* (New York, 1993), 3.

158 "available was bad": Quoted in Scholz, "Unruhiges Jahrzehnt," 99.

159 "our power": Quoted in Henning Köhler, "Berlin in der Weimarer Republik," in Ribbe, ed., *Geschichte Berlins*, II, 806.

159 "is carried out": Quoted in Otto Friedrich, *Before the Deluge. A Portrait of Berlin in the 1920s* (New York, 1986), 32.

160 "into the Christmas night"; "Byzantine conditions": Kessler, *In the Twenties*, 41–43.

162 "lack of heat and light": Ernst Troeltsch, *Die Fehlgeburt einer Republik. Spektator in Berlin 1918 bis 1922* (Frankfurt am Main, 1994), 15.

162, 163 "Hallisches Ufer"; "nothing has happened": Kessler, *In the Twenties*, 54–60.

163 corpse of Rosa Luxemburg: Gilbert, *European Past*, 14.

163 "murders of the Gestapo": Köhler, "Berlin in der Weimarer Republik," 809.

164 "Der Geist von Berlin": *Schwäbische Merkur*, Jan. 10, 1919, quoted in Anton Kaes, Martin Jay, and Edward Dimendberg, eds., *The Weimar Republic Sourcebook* (Berkeley, 1994), 414–415. For a study of perspectives on Berlin in the German press of the Weimar era, see Michael Bienert, *Die eingebildete Metropole. Berlin im Feuilleton der Weimarer Republik* (Stuttgart, 1992).

164 "confuse us on this score": Heinrich Winkler, "Alle lieben Berlin . . . ," *Die Zeit*, May 3, 1991.

165 "nothing will be spared": "Dadaisten gegen Weimar," in *Tendencies of the Twentieth Century*. Exhibition Catalog (Berlin, 1977), 3/180.

165–166 "workers kept quiet": Alfred Döblin, *Der deutsche Maskenball von Linke Poot* (Freiburg, 1972), 289–290.

166 "dismal place the morgue is": Quoted in Friedrich, *Before the Deluge*, 52.

166 "victory at home"; "preponderant mood": Kessler, *In the Twenties*, 86, 83.

167 "these fetters": Quoted in Friedrich, *Before the Deluge*, 54.

169 "totally black": Käthe Kollwitz, *Die Tagebücher* (Berlin, 1989), 458.

169 "not a bank robber": Quoted in Richard Hanser, *Putsch! How Hitler Made Revolution* (New York, 1970), 226.

170 "cancer and appendicitis": Family Journal No. 8, Edwin Rogers Embree Papers, Yale University.

170 "into question": Troeltsch, *Die Fehlgeburt*, 125.

170 "rule the hour": *Deutsche Allgemeine Zeitung*, July 29, 1923. Quoted in Köhler, "Berlin in der Weimarer Republik," 838–839.

173 dropped to 670; ballooned to 7368: Feldman, *Great Disorder*, 505.

173 "attacks on the French Embassy": Lord d'Abernon to Foreign Office, Jan. 14, 1923, Public Record Office, FO 371, 8703/726.

174 "so funny sometimes": Quoted in Friedrich, *Before the Deluge*, 124.

175 "steeped in nicotine": Ilya Ehrenburg, *Memoirs: 1921–1941* (New York, 1963), 10.

177 "the Flying Dutchman": Quoted in Friedrich, *Before the Deluge*, 133.

177 "twenty marks left": William White, ed., *By-Line, Ernest Hemingway* (New York, 1967), 46.

177 "bought boys cheap": Phillip Herring, *Djuna. The Life and Work of Djuna Barnes* (New York, 1995), 97–98.

177 "struggling German writers": Malcolm Cowley, *Exile's Return* (New York, 1951), 133.

178 "Nigger Republic of Liberia": Hans Ostwald, *Sittengeschichte der Inflation* (Berlin, 1931), 99.

178 "We are loving America": Ibid., 100.

178 "one American penny": Quoted in Von Eckardt and Gilman, *Bertolt Brecht's Berlin*, 17.

178 "a much rawer place": Köhler, "Berlin in der Weimarer Republic," 841.

179 475 Swiss francs: Ibid.

179 a fine price: Ostwald, *Sittengeschichte*, 25.

179 "from its misery": Quoted in Jelavich, *Berlin Cabaret*, 156.

179 "as no one else": Quoted in Alex de Jonge, *The Weimar Chronicle* (New York, 1978), 162.

180 "announcements to the public": Michael Bienert, ed., *Joseph Roth in Berlin: Ein Lesebuch für Spaziergänger* (Cologne, 1996), 199.

180 "wanton sexual chaos": Thomas Wehrling, "Die Verhurung Berlins," Das Tage-Buch 1 (November 6, 1920), 1381–1383. Quoted in Kaes, Jay, and Dimendberg, eds., *Weimar Sourcebook*, 721.

180 "student Willy": Hans Pollak, *Tatort Mulackritze. Berliner Unterwelt in den zwanziger Jahren* (Berlin, 1993), 119–120.

180 "extra money": Stefan Zweig, *The World of Yesterday* (New York, 1943), 238.

180 "functioned like men": Josef von Sternberg, *Fun in a Chinese Laundry* (New York, 1965), 288.

180 "international film star": Quoted in Friedrich, *Before the Deluge*, 128.

181 "in comparison with the Germans": Stephen Spender, *European Witness* (New York, 1946), 238.

181 all up on the floor: Robert McAlmon, *Distinguished Air/Grim Fairy Tales* (Paris, 1925), 11–25.

182 50 million mark bills; only 145,000 people: Köhler, "Berlin in der Weimarer Republik," 839–840.

182 ugly anti-Semitic undertones: On the Scheunenviertel rioting, see Trude Maurer, *Ostjuden in Deutschland 1918–1933* (Hamburg, 1936), 329–334.

182 "East over Germany": Bienert, ed., *Roth in Berlin*, 73–77.

184 "pogrom"; "widespread misery"; "signal to German Jewry": Maurer, *Ostjuden*, 335–344.

184 "coming storm": *Völkischer Beobachter*, Nov. 8, 1923.

185 "a metropolis of brain power": Quoted in Anton Gill, *A Dance between Flames. Berlin between the Wars* (London, 1993), 187.

185 "was to yield": Carl Zuckmayer, *Als wär's ein Stück von mir* (Frankfurt am Main, 1969), 263.

185 "his back on Berlin"; "most amusing"; "claims of publicity": Quoted in Clark, *Einstein*, 227, 256–259.

186 "that dirty Jew": Quoted in Friedrich, *Before the Deluge*, 215.

186–187 to live in Germany: Andrew Field, *VN. The Life and Art of Vladimir Nabokov* (New York, 1986), 71–72.

187 "stepmother of Russian cities": Ehrenburg, *Memoirs*, 22. For a collection of Russian writing about Weimar Berlin, see Fritz Mierau, *Russen in Berlin 1918–1933* (Leipzig, 1987). See also Karl Schlögel, *Berlin Ostbahnhof Europas. Russen und Deutsche in ihrem Jahrhundert* (Berlin, 1998); and Christiane Landgrebe and Cornelie Kister, *Flaneure, Musen, Bohemiens. Literatenleben in Berlin* (Berlin, 1998), 126–146.

187 "Rumania, or Holland": Quoted in Martin Lüdke, "Vladimir Nabokov," in Günther Rühle, *LiteraturOrt Berlin* (Berlin, 1994), 135.

187 "decaying mammoth village": Kafka to Grete Bloch, April 8, 1914, in Franz Kafka, *Letters to Felice* (London, 1974), 381.

188 Kafka in Berlin: See Peter-André Alt, "Franz Kafka," in Rühle, ed., *LiteraturOrt Berlin*, 141–145.

188 "and enough money": Quoted in Michael Horowitz, *Ein Leben für die Zeitung. Der rasende Reporter Egon Erwin Kisch* (Vienna, 1985), 59.

188 "imaginative than objectivity": Egon Erwin Kisch, *Der rasende Reporter* (Berlin, 1955), viii.

188 in May 1933: Erhard Schüte, "Egon Erwin Kisch," in Rühle, ed., *LiteraturOrt Berlin*, 127.

189 "a thousand social steps": Bienert, ed., *Roth in Berlin*, 65–66.

189 "and mean us": Quoted in Malcolm Bradbury, ed., *The Atlas of Literature* (London, 1996), 184.

189 "someone of our kind": Franz Hessel, *Ein Flaneur in Berlin* (Berlin, 1984), 9. On Hessel, see Anke Gleber, *The Art of Taking a Walk* (Princeton, 1999), 63–128; Hermann Kähler, *Berlin, Asphalt und Licht. Die Grosse Stadt in der Literatur der Weimarer Republik* (Berlin, 1986), 170–180.

190 "fate of the Jews": Franz Hessel, *Heimliches Berlin* (Frankfurt am Main, 1982), 137.

190 "simply do not exist": Matheo Quinz, "Das Romanische Café," *Der Querschnitt* 6 (1926), 608. Quoted in Kaes, Jay, and Dimendberg, eds., *Weimar Sourcebook*, 416.

191 "passing by the pool": Ibid.

191 "drank their daily coffee": Quoted in Jürgen Schebera, *Damals im Romanischen Café* (Braunschweig, 1988), 30.

191 "egg, soft-boiled": Quoted in Von Eckardt and Gilman, *Bertolt Brecht's Berlin*, 41.

192 "breathtaking shamelessness": Quoted in Klaus Völker, "Bertolt Brecht," in Rühle, ed., *LiteraturOrt Berlin*, 116.

192 "grind each other down": Ibid., 117.

192 "that eyes dream": Quoted in Frederic Ewen, *Bertolt Brecht. His Life, His Art, His Times* (New York, 1992), 100.
193 "is not possible": Bertolt Brecht, *Gesammelte Werke.* 20 Bände. Edited by Elisabeth Hauptmann (Frankfurt, 1967), I, 187.
193 "a Jesuit seminarian": Zuckmayer, *Als wär's ein Stück von mir*, 321.
193 "any of his lovers": Quoted in John Fuegi, *Brecht & Co.* (New York, 1994), 92.
193 "is chopped beef": Völker, "Bertolt Brecht," 119.
193 "classical theater of Reinhardt": Quoted in Patrick McGilligan, *Fritz Lang. The Nature of the Beast* (New York, 1997), 51–52.
193–194 and fire department: Karl Prümm, "Die Stadt ist der Film," in Peter Alter, ed., *Im Banne der Metropolen. Berlin und London in den zwanziger Jahren* (Göttingen, 1993), 111–130.
195 "something quite new": Quoted in Bärbel Schrader and Jürgen Schebera, *The "Golden" Twenties* (New Haven, 1988), 90.
195 "sense of horror": Ibid.
195 "bit a lovely girl": Ehrenburg, *Memoirs*, 11.
196 "made on his crew"; "sparrow that's molting": Quoted in McGilligan, *Fritz Lang*, 64–65, 85.
197 "Menschheit bester Teil": Ibid., 91.
197 "more American than the Americans": Quoted in Thomas Saunders, *Hollywood in Berlin. American Cinema and Weimar Germany* (Berkeley, 1994), 89.
198 film *Metropolis*: McGilligan, *Fritz Lang*, 104.
199 "Who is the most Beautiful?": Quoted in Barbara McCloskey, *George Grosz and the Communist Party* (Princeton, 1997), 55.
199–200 "Machine Art of Tatlin": Ibid. 69.
200 "equipped for maneuvers": Quoted in Whitford, "The Many Faces of George Grosz," 10.
200 "keep their hands off art": Quoted in McCloskey, *George Grosz*, 80.
200 "you are an artist": Quoted in Von Eckardt and Gilman, *Bertolt Brecht's Berlin*, 13.

Chapter 5

204 "Amerikanismus und Bolshevismus": Quoted in Boberg, Fichter, and Gillen, *Die Metropole*, 190.
204 "where it is dark": Quoted in Kaes, Jay, and Dimendberg, eds., *Weimar Sourcebook*, 419–420.
206–207 "rapid pace of work": Quoted in Korff and Rürup, eds., *Berlin, Berlin*, 461.
207 "surrounding Einstein's universe": Quoted in Gill, *A Dance between Flames*, 177.
207 a Manhattan transfer: Fritz Neumeyer, "Manhattan Transfer: The New York Myth and Berlin Architecture in the Context of Ludwig Hilberseimer's High-Rise City," in Kleihues and Rathgeber, eds., *Berlin/New York*, 318.
208 "a new nocturnal existence": *"Berlin Wirbt!" Metropolenwerbung zwischen Verkehrsreklame und Stadtmarketing 1920–1945. Ausstellung Katalog* (Berlin, 1995), 16.
209 "Jeder einmal in Berlin": Ibid., 13.
209 refused to attend: Köhler, "Berlin in der Weimarer Republik," 856.
210 "is concentrated there"; for the painting: Ibid., 852, 855.
210 "an intellectual core": Christoph Stölzl, ed., *Die Zwangziger Jahre in München. Ausstellungskatalog* (Munich, 1979), 98.
211 beer-besotted population: *Münchner Neueste Nachrichten*, Sept. 21, 1924.
211 "apostle of Americanism": Quoted in Boberg, Fichter, and Gillen, *Die Metropole*, 190.
211 "babylonian mongrelism": Quoted in Martin Geyer, *Verkehrte Welt* (Göttingen, 1998), 273.
211 "of their orchestras": Quoted in Josephine Baker and Jo Bouillon, *Josephine* (New York, 1977), 58.
211 "number of gifts": Quoted in Jean-Claude Baker and Chris Chase, *Josephine* (New York, 1993), 124.
211 "hardly be contained"; "grotesque orgies": Quoted in Jelavich, *Berlin Cabaret*, 171.
211–213 "have come to pass"; "European culture": Ibid., 170.
213 "Amerikanische Jazz-Tanzkapelle": Quoted in Michael H. Kater, *Different Drummers. Jazz in the Culture of Nazi Germany* (New York, 1992), 16.
213 "energy, efficiency, productivity": Quoted in Jelavich, *Berlin Cabaret*, 180.

214 "magnificently simple music"; "intellectual ownership": Quoted in Von Eckardt and Gilman, *Bertolt Brecht's Berlin*, 88.

214 "cacophonic garbage"; "spirit of music"; "can relax"; "respectable backdrop": Ibid., 108–111.

215 "hope for the new Europe": Bruno Walter, *Theme and Variations* (New York, 1947), 256.

215 "barbarism closed in": Ibid., 268.

215 "symposium of the minds"; "unmagical of theaters": Ibid., 268–269.

216 "everywhere one looks"; "Obermusikjude": Quoted in Peter Heyworth, *Otto Klemperer: His Life and Times*. 2 vols. (Cambridge, 1993–96), I, 261.

217 "monument to ruins"; "must be shut": Ibid., 281, 283.

217 expressing displeasure: Sam H. Shirakawa, *The Devil's Music Master. The Controversial Life and Career of Wilhelm Furtwängler* (New York, 1992), 47–48.

218 with the German government: Secretary of State, Jan. 4, 1927, National Archives, Washington, D.C., 366, Roll 79.

218 collective shut down; short run: John Willet, *Art and Politics in the Weimar Period. The New Sobriety 1917–1933* (New York, 1996), 149–151, 190–191.

219 Weltbühne: On the journal, see István Deák, *Weimar Germany's Left-Wing Intellectuals. A Political History of the Weltbühne and its Circle* (Berkeley, 1968).

219 rejected as ridiculous: Peter Gay, *Weimar Culture* (New York, 1968), 74.

219 Tucholsky: The best biography of Tucholsky is Michael Hepp, *Kurt Tucholsky. Biographische Annäherungen* (Reinbek bei Hamburg, 1993).

220 "a German provincial city": Kurt Tucholsky, "Berlin! Berlin!" *Gesammelte Werke in 10 Bänden* (Reinbek bei Hamburg, 1975), II, 130.

220 "conflicts, and shortcomings": Quoted in Matthias Eberle, "Otto Dix und die Neue Sachlichkeit," in C. Joachimides, N. Rosenthal, W. Schmied, eds., *Deutsche Kunst im 20. Jahrhundert* (Munich, 1986), 447. See also Wieland Schmied, "Post-Expressionism: Notes on Dada, Neue Sachlichkeit, and Bauhaus," in Kleihues and Rathgeber, eds., *Berlin/New York*, 341–355.

222 "was *very* interesting": Quoted in Michael Peppiatt, *Francis Bacon. Anatomy of an Enigma* (New York, 1996), 28–29.

222 Döblin: On Döblin, see David B. Dollenmayer, *The Berlin Novels of Alfred Döblin* (Berkeley, 1988).

222–223 "no end to it": Alfred Döblin, *Berlin Alexanderplatz*. Translated by Franz Jonas (New York, 1993), 5–7.

224 "better than mine": Ibid., 60–61.

224–225 "of imminent collapse": Erich Kästner, *Fabian. Die Geschichte eines Moralisten* (Munich, 1994), 99.

225 "plunge into this?": Joseph Goebbels, *Die Tagebücher von Joseph Goebbels. Sämtliche Fragmente*, ed. Elke Fröhlich, 4 vols. (Munich, 1987), I, 205.

225–226 "as a fish needs water": Quoted in Ralf Georg Reuth, *Goebbels* (New York, 1993), 81.

226 "off the streets": Quoted in Dieter Schütte, *Charlottenburg* (Berlin, 1988), 87.

226 "soil that reckoning": Quoted in Reuth, *Goebbels*, 91.

226 "only the Israelites": Quoted in Kaes, Jay, and Dimendberg, eds., *Weimar Sourcebook*, 500.

227 "or village untouched": Joseph Goebbels, *Kampf um Berlin* (Munich, 1934), 11. On the Nazi Party in Berlin at the time of Goebbels's arrival, see Martin Broszat, "Die Anfänge der Berliner NSDAP 1926/27," *Vierteljahrshefte für Zeitgeschichte*, 8. Jg. (1960), 85–117.

227 "immense bat-shadow of home": Quoted in Richard Davenport-Hines, *Auden* (New York, 1995), 88.

227 "grubby old men"; "uncartesian world of Berlin": Ibid., 87.

227 "under police control": Peppiatt, *Bacon*, 29.

227–228 Auden and Isherwood: For a study of these English writers' encounter with Berlin, see Norman Page, *Auden and Isherwood. The Berlin Years* (New York, 1998).

227–228 "as I was doing": John Lehmann, *In the Purely Pagan Sense* (London, 1985), 44.

228 "to bed together": Davenport-Hines, *Auden*, 97.

228 "mass of bruises": Quoted in Humphrey Carpenter, *W. H. Auden. A Biography* (London, 1993), 90.

228 "will be good"; "were shaking": Ibid., 86.

229 "Berlin meant boys": Christopher Isherwood, *Christopher and His Kind* (New York, 1976), 2.

229 "working-class foreigner"; "masquerade of perversions"; "the entire nation": Ibid., 3, 29, 4.

229 "suitable viewer appeared"; "distasteful customs"; "potent ingredients": Ibid., 16, 29, 43.

230–231 "a bankrupt middle class": Christopher Isherwood, *Goodbye to Berlin* (Harmondsworth, England, 1945), 7.
231 "luggage of her lodgers": Ibid., 8.
231 "synonym for stupidity": Quoted in Paul Bowles, *Without Stopping. An Autobiography* (New York, 1972), 109–111; Christopher Sawyer-Lauçanno, *An Invisible Spectator* (New York, 1989), 100–102.
231 Hamilton: On Gerald Hamilton, see Isherwood, *Christopher and His Kind*, 72–78; also Gerald Hamilton, *Mr. Norris and I* (London, 1956).
232 "Deutschland Erwache!": Stephen Spender, *World Within World* (London, 1951), 130.
232 "friction, and sparks": Quoted in Willet, *Art and Politics*, 177.
232–233 Sklarek scandal: Köhler, "Berlin in der Weimarer Republik," 868–875.
233 "become a circus director": Quoted in Stremmel, *Modell*, 146.
233 "boldest dreams": Quoted in Reuth, *Goebbels*, 109.
233 "establish a dictatorship": Kessler, *In the Twenties*, 367–368.
234 liability for the nation: British Embassy Report, Jan. 27, 1930, Public Record Office, FO 371, 14357/934.
236 "also need a face?": Quoted in Steven Bach, *Marlene Dietrich. Life and Legend* (New York, 1992), 107–108.
236 "your pubic hair": Ibid., 113.
237 "corrupting kitsch": Ibid., 141.
237 "spirit never dead": Quoted in Reuth, *Goebbels*, 113.
238 Kreuzberg and Köpenick: Christian Engeli and Wolfgang Ribbe, "Berlin in der NS-Zeit," in Ribbe, ed., *Geschichte Berlins*, II, 990; see also Reuth, *Goebbels*, 120.
238 "lounging about and demonstrating": Kessler, *In the Twenties*, 399–400.
239 "prudent thing to do": Bella Fromm, *Blood and Banquets* (New York, 1990), 27.
239 "on their seats, shrieking": Leni Riefenstahl, *A Memoir* (New York, 1995), 62.
240 Berlin Schutzpolizei: See Hsi-huey Liang, *The Berlin Police Force in the Weimar Republic* (Berkeley, 1970), 91. See also Modris Eksteins, "War, Memory, and Politics: The Fate of the Film *All Quiet on the Western Front*," *Central European History*, Vol. 13 (1980), 60–80.
240 "anything like it": Quoted in Reuth, *Goebbels*, 125.
240 "not a cent more": Zuckmayer, *Als wär's ein Stück von mir*, 379–380.
240 "serious music is on the way": Quoted in Heyworth, *Klemperer*, I, 383.
241 "future time": Quoted in Alan Balfour, *Berlin. The Politics of Order 1737–1989* (New York, 1990), 65.
241 fate of Bauhaus: Willet, *Art and Politics*, 208; Elaine S. Hochman, *Architects of Fortune. Mies van der Rohe and the Third Reich* (New York, 1990), 73–105.
241 "espionage and treason": Quoted in Deak, *Weimar Germany's Left-Wing Intellectuals*, 190–192.
241 "cannot support that": Quoted in Heyworth, *Klemperer*, I, 378.
242 stodgy and backward looking: David Clay Large, *Where Ghosts Walked: Munich's Road to the Third Reich* (New York, 1998), 202–206.
242 "pigsty in Munich"; "I'll back you": Reuth, *Goebbels*, 127, 130.
242 "élan of the SA"; who looked Jewish: Ibid., 130, 137.
244 "he's a hat": Quoted in Craig, *Germany*, 561.
244 "orders of their superior": Fromm, *Blood and Banquets*, 55.
245 "chivalry": Henry Ashby Turner, Jr., *Hitler's Thirty Days to Power* (Reading, Mass., 1996), 12; Ian Kershaw, *Hitler, 1889–1936: Hubris* (New York, 1999), 373–374.
245–246 "hammer-and-sickle": Grosz, *Autobiography*, 245.
246 "stay in Paris"; "must appease them": Arthur Koestler, *Arrow in the Blue* (New York, 1952), 245.
246 "kindly nod": Ibid., 253–254.
247 "tacked on to it"; "never see it again": Quoted in Clark, *Einstein*, 447, 452.
247–248 "shames one's correctitude": Quoted in Kaes, Jay, and Dimendberg, eds., *Weimar Sourcebook*, 425–426.
248 323,000 in September: Engeli and Ribbe, "Berlin in der NS-Zeit," 905.
248 "the Underground Railway": Quoted in Friedrich, *Before the Deluge*, 354.
248–249 "still-dripping geraniums"; "liberated life": Daniel Guéran, *The Brown Plague. Travels in Late Weimar and Early Nazi Germany* (Durham, N.C., 1994), 68.
249 "half clown": Ibid., 63.

250 "rejection of bourgeois methods"; "revolutionary struggle"; "incredible tension": Quoted in Reuth, *Goebbels*, 155–156.
251 traditional beggars: *Vossische Zeitung*, Oct. 10, 1932.
252 regain power himself; "hold [the Nazis] off": Fromm, *Blood and Banquets*, 62–63, 68.
253 "Later? Vanished!": Quoted in Turner, *Hitler's Thirty Days*, 1–2.

Chapter 6

255 "happy and clean city": Quoted in *Berlin Wirbt!*, 18.
255 "spiritually in flight": Hermann Ullmann, *Flucht aus Berlin?* (Jena, 1932), 7.
256 "on the Jew Republic"; "won a battle": Quoted in Turner, *Hitler's Thirty Days*, 110.
257 "never defeat us": *Völkischer Beobachter*, Jan. 22–23, 1933.
258 "over the box": Zuckmayer, *Als wär's ein Stück von mir*, 384–385.
258 "German loyalty": André François-Poncet, *The Fateful Years* (London, 1949), 43.
258 "Foreign Minister as well": Kessler, *In the Twenties*, 441–442.
258 "he'll squeal": Quoted in Turner, *Hitler's Thirty Days*, 147.
258 "out of here alive": Albert Wucher, *Die Fahne Hoch* (Munich, 1963), 159.
259 "collective delirium": Theodor Düsterberg, *Die Stahlhelm und Hitler* (London, 1949), 41.
259 "prolonged applause": Adlon, *Hotel Adlon*, 260.
259 "wants to vomit": Quoted in Bert Engelmann, *Berlin. Eine Stadt wie keine andere* (Göttingen, 1991), 250.
259 "prisoners at Tannenberg": Fromm, *Blood and Banquets*, 76.
259 "in your country?": Quoted in Reuth, *Goebbels*, 164.
260 Göring directive: Hans-Norbert Bukert, Klaus Matußek, Wolfgang Wippermann, "*Machtergreifung*" *Berlin 1933* (Berlin, 1982), 65.
260 "exterminate, that's all": Quoted in Joachim C. Fest, *Hitler* (New York, 1974), 392.
260–261 Reichstag fire: See Ulrich von Hehl, "Die Kontroverse um den Reichstagsbrand," *Vierteljahrshefte für Zeitgeschichte*, 36. Jg. (1988), 259–280; Eckhard Jesse, "Der Reichstagsbrand—55 Jahre danach," *Geschichte in Wissenschaft und Unterricht* 1988/4, 195–219; Martin Broszat, "Zum Streit um den Reichstagsbrand," *Vierteljahrshefte für Zeitgeschichte*, 8. Jg. (1960), 275–279.
261 "God-given signal": Quoted in Sefton Delmer, *Trail Sinister* (London, 1961), 189.
262 "hell to pay"; "appointed by parliament": Quoted in Craig, *Germany*, 577, 578.
262 "society in the world": Quoted in Walter Leo, *Die Steine reden noch* (Berlin, 1987), 47.
263 "wobbly heads": Quoted in Bukert, Matußek, and Wippermann, *Machtergreifung*, 66.
264 "manual labor": Rumboldt to Foreign Office, May 3, 1933, PRO, FO 371, 16723/4091.
264 Köpenicker Blutwoche: Bukert, Matußek, and Wippermann, *Machtergreifung*, 67.
264 "the national revolution": Quoted in Kurt Schilde and Johannes Tuchel, *Columbia-Haus. Berliner Konzentrationslager 1933–1936* (Berlin, 1990), 31–32.
264–265 "the work-ethic": Quoted in Bukert, Matußek, and Wippermann, *Machtergreifung*, 67.
265 "loyalty and iron solidarity": Quoted in Korff and Rürup, eds., *Berlin, Berlin*, 529.
265 until 1940: On Lippert, see his memoir, Julius Lippert, *Im Strom der zeit, Erlebnisse und Eindrücke* (Berlin, 1942).
265–266 "law, and church": Franz von Papen, *Memoirs* (London, 1952), 305–307.
266 Night of the Long Knives: On this, see Kershaw, *Hitler*, 512–522; Heinz Höhne, *Mordsache Röhm. Hitlers Durchbruch zur Alleinherrschaft, 1933–1934* (Reinbek bei Hamburg, 1984); Kurt Gossweiler, *Die Röhm-Affäre* (Cologne, 1983); David Clay Large, *Between Two Fires. Europe's Path in the 1930s* (New York, 1990), 101–137.
267 "have happened here": William E. Dodd, Jr., *Ambassador Dodd's Diary, 1933–1938* (New York, 1941), 118.
267 "streets of Berlin": Ibid., 127.
267 "animals I hope": Ivone Kirkpatrick, *The Inner Circle* (London, 1959), 90.
267 "enemies of the state": Max Domarus, ed., *Reden und Proklamationen 1932–1945/Hitler*, 2 vols. (Wiesbaden, 1973), I, 421.

268 "not be soft": Quoted in Andreas Dorpalen, *Hindenburg and the Weimar Republic* (Princeton, 1964), 480.
268 "young National Socialist movement": Quoted in Fest, *Hitler*, 475.
268 "looked in their uniforms": Isherwood, *Christopher and His Kind*, 124.
268 "social deviants": On the Nazi persecution of homosexuals, see Burkhard Jellonnek, *Homosexuelle unter dem Hakenkreuz. Die Verfolgung von Homosexuellen im Dritten Reich* (Paderborn, 1990).
268 "be responsible?": Isherwood, *Christopher and His Kind*, 122.
269 close-to-the-soil values: See Stremmel, *Modell*, 232–241.
269 "Mecca or Rome": Quoted in Bergmann, *Agrarromantik*, 357.
269 "always liked Berlin"; "today's resources": Werner Jochmann, ed., *Monologe im Führer Hauptquartier 1941–1944/Adolf Hitler* (Hamburg, 1980), 100–101.
270 a major purge: On the Nazi campaign against Berlin's free press, see Engeli and Ribbe, "Berlin in der NS-Zeit," 940–942; De Mendelssohn, *Zeitungsstadt Berlin*, 324–422.
270 "unser Unglück": Engeli and Ribbe, "Berlin in der NS-Zeit," 941.
270 reverse this decision: John V. H. Dippel, *Bound Upon a Wheel of Fire* (New York, 1996), 132.
270 "last a generation"; "tightrope walking": Quoted in Deak, *Weimar Germany's Left-wing Intellectuals*, 214–215.
272 reading the Jewish press: Dippel, *Bound*, 88–89, 127–128.
272 direct Nazi control: Engeli and Ribbe, "Berlin in der NS-Zeit," 942.
272 Berlin-on-the-Pacific: See Lawrence Weschler, "Paradise: The Southern California Exile of Hitler's Cultural Exiles," in Stephanie Barron, ed., *Exiles and Émigrés. The Flight of European Artists from Hitler* (Los Angeles, 1997), 341–357; Salka Viertel, *The Kindness of Strangers* (New York, 1969); Anthony Heilbut, *Exiled in Paradise. German Refugee Artists and Intellectuals in America from the 1930s to the Present* (New York, 1983).
273 "literary subversion": On the book burnings, see Hermann Haarmann, Walter Huder, Klaus Siebenhaar, *'Das war ein Vorspiel nur'... Bücherverbrennung in Deutschland 1933: Voraussetzungen und Folgen* (Berlin, 1983); Hans-Wolfgang Strätz, "Die studentische 'Aktion wider den undeutschen Geist' im Frühjahr 1933," *Vierteljahrshefte für Zeitgeschichte*, 16. Jg. (1968), 347–372.
273 "Jewish hyper-intellectualism": Quoted in Haarmann, Huder, and Siebenhaar, "Vorspiel," 46.
273 Reichskulturkammer: For a study of this institution, see Alan E. Steinweis, *Art, Ideology, and Economics in Nazi Germany. The Reich Chambers of Music, Theater, and the Visual Arts* (Chapel Hill, 1993).
274 "inner emigration": Taylor, *Berlin's Culture*, 269–272.
274 Hans Fallada: On Fallada, see Klaus Farin, *Hans Fallada 'Welche sind, die haben kein Glück'* (Berlin, 1993); Reinhard K. Zachau, *Hans Fallada als politischer Schriftsteller* (New York, Bern, 1990).
274 "un-German" imagery: On Benn, see Werner Rübe, *Provoziertes Leben. Gottfried Benn* (Stuttgart, 1993).
274 Jünger and Nazis: see Thomas Nevin, *Ernst Jünger and Germany. Into the Abyss, 1914–1945* (Durham, 1996), 75–133.
275 "humble Party member": Quoted in Taylor, *Berlin's Culture*, 267.
276 "transitory wealth": Mann, *Turning Point*, 281–282.
276 too gloomy: Taylor, *Berlin's Culture*, 267.
277 "will be back": Quoted in Hans Bunge, "Brecht im zweiten Weltkriege," *Neue deutsche Literatur* X (1962), No. 3, 37.
277 girlie shows: Jelavich, *Berlin Cabaret*, 240.
277 "of the cinematic art": Quoted in Reuth, *Goebbels*, 195.
277 "as the primary school": Quoted in Taylor, *Berlin's Culture*, 267.
278 47 percent of the directors: McGilligan, *Fritz Lang*, 175.
278 "without brain": Billy Wilder, *Der Prinz von Wales geht auf Urlaub* (Berlin, 1996), 23.
278 "crazy nightlife of the bars": Quoted in Kevin Lally, *Wilder Times. The Life of Billy Wilder* (New York, 1996), 19.
278 "even without Hitler": Quoted in ibid., 59.
279 "who understands us": Quoted in Reuth, *Goebbels*, 194.
279 doctor's casting couch: Geza von Cziffra, *Es war eine rauschende Ballnacht: Eine Sittengeschichte des deutschen Films* (Frankfurt, 1987), 141–143.

280 pure entertainment pictures: Bärbel Dalichow and Axel Geiss, eds., *Filmstadt Babelsberg* (Berlin, 1994), 47.

281 "aspects of the German cinema"; "without falsifying them": Riefenstahl, *Memoir*, 137, 160.

281 "a healthy one": Quoted Taylor, *Berlin and its Culture*, 275.

282 Academy of Arts expulsions: Hildegard Brenner, *Ende einer bürgerlichen Kunst-Institution. Die politische Formierung der Preussischen Adakemie der Künste ab 1933* (Stuttgart, 1972), 23–26.

282 "like Köllwitz paints her": Quoted in Catherine Krahmer, ed., *Käthe Kollwitz* (Reinbek bei Hamburg, 1981), 113.

282 in his private residence: Jonathan Petropoulos, *Art as Politics in the Third Reich* (Chapel Hill, 1996), 25.

283 "freedom of art": Quoted in ibid., 45.

283 Ausstellung entartete Kunst: See Stephanie Barron, ed., *Degenerate Art: The Fate of the Avant-Garde in Nazi Germany* (Los Angeles, 1984).

283 adopted hometown: Large, *Ghosts*, 232.

283 "denied traditional autonomy": Peter Raabe, *Die Musik im Dritten Reich* (Regensburg, 1936), 9.

283 "to each other": Quoted in Michael H. Kater, *The Twisted Muse. Musicians and Their Music in the Third Reich* (New York, 1997), 75–76.

284 "events in Germany": Quoted in ibid., 93.

284 "back in Berlin": Quoted in Heilbut, *Exiled in Paradise*, 150. On Weill in exile, see Ronald Sanders, *The Days Grow Short. The Life and Music of Kurt Weill* (Los Angeles, 1980), 196–395.

284 "giant mortuary": Quoted in Kater, *Muse*, 79.

285 "friend Stefan Zweig": Quoted in Josef Wulf, *Musik im Dritten Reich* (Frankfurt, 1983), 197–198.

285 "a matter of survival"; "justified": *Vossische Zeitung*, April 11, 1933.

286 "musicians of the present": Quoted in Shirakawa, *Devil's Music Master*, 153.

287 "art institutes of the new Reich": *Völkischer Beobachter*, Dec. 7, 1934.

287 "appointed by him": Quoted in Wulf, *Musik*, 378.

287 Karajan: On Karajan's meteoric career, see Berndt W. Wessling, *Herbert von Karajan. Eine kritische Biographie* (Munich, 1994).

288 "arrogant fop": Robert Kraft, "The Furtwängler Enigma," *New York Review of Books*, Oct. 7, 1993, 10.

288 NSRSO: See Kater, *Muse*, 33–34.

288 "in the jazz band"; "works of German composers": Quoted in Kater, *Drummers*, 29, 44.

288–289 "Golden Seven"; "prohibitions and decrees": Quoted in ibid., 52–56, 57.

290 "*we* were": Peter Gay, *My German Question. Growing Up in Nazi Berlin* (New Haven, 1998), 111.

291 "have any more Jews!": Fromm, *Blood and Banquets*, 103.

292 who was a Jew: On the anti-Semitic measures, see Engeli and Ribbe, "Berlin in der NS-Zeit," 952–960; Hans Gerd Sellenthin, *Geschichte der Juden in Berlin und des Gebäudes Fasanenstrasse 79/80* (Berlin, 1959), 70–90; Helmut Genschel, *Die Verdrängung der Juden aus der Wirtschaft im Dritten Reich* (Göttingen, 1966).

292 "with great interest": Quoted in Arnd Krüger, *Die Olympische Spiele 1936 und die Weltmeinung* (Berlin, 1972), 53.

293 threatened boycott: Duff Hart-Davis, *Hitler's Games: The 1936 Olympics* (New York, 1986), 10.

293 "athlete in history": Quoted in Richard D. Mandell, *The Nazi Olympics* (New York, 1971), 76.

295 permission from him: Hans-Georg Stümke and Rudi Finkler, *Rosa Winkel, rosa Listen* (Reinbek bei Hamburg, 1981), 252.

295 "practical than New York": Mandell, *Nazi Olympics*, 140.

295 "Adolf Hitler!": *Berlin Wirbt!*, 18.

295 "White House"; "have added"; "government money": Dodd, *Diary*, 340–343.

296 "die Juden zu brei": Quoted in Krüger, *Die Olympische Spiele*, 229.

296 "front for the general visitors": William L. Shirer, *Berlin Diary* (New York, 1941), 65.

297 foreign press reports: Jürgen Bellers, ed., *Die Olympiade Berlin 1936 im Spiegel der ausländischen Presse* (Münster, 1986), 232–233; 20–21, 51–52.

297 "invent one"; "ever been built"; "I yelled": Quoted in David Herbert Donald, *Look Homeward. A Life of Thomas Wolfe* (New York, 1988), 385, 386.

298 "man of the hour in Germany": Quoted in Mandell, *Nazi Olympics*, 227.

298 "experienced such passion": Riefenstahl, *Memoir*, 199.

298 *Olympia*: For an analysis of the film, see Cooper C. Graham, *Leni Riefenstahl and Olympia* (Metuchen, N.J., 1986).

298 "forced themselves": Quoted in Reuth, *Goebbels*, 219.

299 "collect his thoughts": Quoted in ibid. On the anniversary, see Engeli and Ribbe, "Berlin in der NS-Zeit," 972; and Gerhard Weiss, "Panem et Circenses: Berlin's Anniversaries as Political Happenings," in Charles W. Haxthausen and Heidrun Suhr, eds., *Berlin: Culture and Metropolis* (Minneapolis, 1991), 244–246.

300 "Germania": See Hans J. Reichardt and Wolfgang Schäche, *Von Berlin nach Germania. Ausstellungskatolog* (Berlin, 1986); Barbara Miller Lane, *Architecture and Politics in Germany 1918–1945* (Cambridge, Mass., 1968).

300 "traitorous elements": Quoted in Rudy Koshar, *Germany's Transient Pasts. Preservation and National Memory in the Twentieth Century* (Chapel Hill, 1998), 164.

300 "a sublime metropolis": Quoted in Hochman, *Architects of Fortune*, 259.

301 "hang the expense": Quoted in David Irving, *Göring. A Biography* (New York, 1990), 153.

301 "a zero": Quoted in Gitta Sereny, *Albert Speer: His Battle with Truth* (New York, 1995), 140.

303 "politics"; "from the Communists"; "dusty bureaucrats": Albert Speer, *Inside the Third Reich* (New York, 1970), 17, 22, 53.

304 "stone abutments"; "law of ruins": Ibid. 55–56.

304 "greatest of all plans"; "Paris and Vienna"; "about that"; "soap company": Ibid., 73, 75, 102.

305 "master of the world": Jochmann, ed., *Monologe*, 101–102.

305 "move out"; "only by war": Speer, *Inside the Third Reich*, 75.

306 "horrible sexual degenerate": Denis Mack Smith, *Mussolini* (New York, 1982), 185.

306 "history themselves"; "loose upon it": François-Poncet, *Fateful Years*, 246.

307 "delirious joy": Shirer, *Berlin Diary*, 149.

307 Niemöller resistance: Engeli and Ribbe, "Berlin in der NS-Zeit," 961.

308 Catholics and Nazism in Berlin: Ibid., 964–968; Cécile Lowenthal-Hensel, *50 Jahre Bistum Berlin. Menschen und Ereignisse 1930–1945* (Berlin, 1980).

308 "from the grass roots": John Cornwell, *Hitler's Pope: The Secret History of Pius XII* (New York, 1999), 7.

309 Polish Jew expulsions: Leni Yahil, *The Holocaust: The Fate of European Jewry, 1932–1945* (New York, 1991), 109.

310 "spontaneous anti-Jewish riots": Goebbels, *Die Tagebücher*, III, 1281.

310 "crystal night": See Walter H. Pehle, ed., *November 1938: From 'Reichskristallnacht' to Genocide* (New York, 1991).

310 "torn records"; "desired and expected purpose": Quoted in Dippel, *Bound*, 245.

311 "army of vandals"; "by a hurricane": Gay, *My German Question*, 133–135.

312 "degradation ritual": Marion A. Kaplan, *Between Dignity and Despair. Jewish Life in Nazi Germany* (New York, 1998), 122.

312 "the German nightmare": Gay, *My German Question*, 134.

312 "for God's sake": Inge Deutschkron, *Outcast. A Jewish Girl in Wartime Berlin* (New York, 1989), 35–36.

312 "disturbed by the events": Quoted in Reuth, *Goebbels*, 240–241.

312 "do things like that"; "private property": Quoted in Read and Fisher, *Berlin Rising*, 217.

313 "can be sure of that": Quoted in Daniel Jonah Goldhagen, *Hitler's Willing Executioners. Ordinary Germans and the Holocaust* (New York, 1996), 101.

313 "airhead Goebbels": Quoted in Richard Breitman, *The Architect of Genocide. Himmler and the Final Solution* (New York, 1991), 53.

313 "a nice bloodletting": Quoted in Reuth, *Goebbels*, 241.

313 "ghetto decree"; 75,000 remained: Engeli and Ribbe, "Berlin in der NS-Zeit," 958.

314 "alive in Germany": Quoted in Dippel, *Bound*, 248.

315 "the German tempo": Quoted in Brian Ladd, *The Ghosts of Berlin. Confronting German History in the Urban Landscape* (Chicago, 1997), 129.

316 "final shipwreck": Sir Nevile Henderson, *Failure of a Mission. Berlin 1937–1939* (New York, 1940), 223.

316 "not be bloodless": Quoted in Fest, *Hitler*, 572; See also Martin Gilbert and Richard Gott, *The Appeasers* (London, 1964), 164.
316 air raid drill and rationing: Engeli and Ribbe, "Berlin in der NS-Zeit," 996–997.
317 spontaneous celebrations: Shirer, *Berlin Diary*, 185.

Chapter 7

320 "newsboys were shouting": Shirer, *Berlin Diary*, 197.
320 "into a romantic": Ruth Andreas-Friedrich, *Berlin Underground 1938–1945* (New York, 1989), 49.
320–321 "no war hysteria"; "war after all": Shirer, *Berlin Diary*, 200–201, 207.
321 "degeneration into obscenity": Quoted in Hans-Dieter Schäfer, ed., *Berlin im Zweiten Weltkrieg* (Munich, 1991), 15.
322 "in zero weather": George F. Kennan, *Memoirs 1925–1950* (Boston, 1967), 107.
322 "our nation aright": Andreas-Friedrich, *Berlin Underground*, 54.
322 Dick-und-Doof: Hans-Dieter Schäfer, *Das gespaltene Bewußtsein. Über Deutsche Kultur und Lebenswirklichkeit 1933–1945* (Munich, 1982), 129.
322 "thousand-year existence": Shirer, *Berlin Diary*, 333.
323 from the masses: Ibid., 451–452; René Juvet, *Ich war dabei . . . 20 Jahre Nationalsozialismus, 1923–1943, Ein Tatsachenbericht* (New York, 1944), 106–108.
324 "would hold out": Quoted in William Manchester, "Undaunted by Odds," *Military History Quarterly* (Spring 1988), 88.
324 "place to hit them": Quoted in ibid., 95.
325 "shouting 'Heil Hitler'": Quoted in Peter Fritzsche, "Air Conditioning Germany," *Military History Quarterly* (Spring 1996), 26.
325–326 "do to a house"; "live in this town"; "people here"; "massacre the population": Shirer, *Berlin Diary*, 489, 486–487, 490–491.
326 Berlin defenses: Martin Middlebrook, *The Berlin Raids* (Harmondsworth, England, 1990), 25–26.
327 "freeze on my body": Ibid., 26.
328 "such a large city": Ibid., 46. See also Richard Overy, *Why the Allies Won* (New York, 1995), 120; also Gerhard L. Weinberg, *A World at Arms* (New York, 1994), 578.
329 "bombenlose Nacht": Howard K. Smith, *The Last Train from Berlin* (New York, 1942), 62.
329 "four hours' sleep": Marie Vassiltchikov, *Berlin Diaries 1940–1945* (New York, 1988), 28–29.
330 "newspaper by it": Harry W. Flannery, *Assignment to Berlin* (New York, 1942), 227–28.
330 "Casserole Day": Vassiltchikov, *Berlin Diaries*, 36.
330 "Johnnies": Smith, *Last Train*, 127.
330 "prey to delusions": Domarus, ed., *Reden und Proklamationen*, II, 1714.
330 "has just been subtracted": Quoted in Buffet, *Berlin*, 342.
331 attack the Soviet Union: Gerhard L. Weinberg, *Germany, Hitler, and World War II* (New York, 1995), 160–162.
331–332 "nation on earth"; space for him; "all seven floors": Smith, *Last Train*, 115–135.
332 "complaint was forthcoming": Flannery, *Assignment*, 261.
333 "Jew cities": Quoted in Reuth, *Goebbels*, 275.
333 "as we would wish it"; "large number of Jews"; revamping of Berlin": Quoted in ibid., 277, 298.
333 Star of David: Kurt Jakob Ball-Kaduri, "Berlin wird Judenfrei. Die Juden in Berlin in den Jahren 1942/43," *Jahrbuch für die Geschichte Mittel- und Ostdeutschlands*. Bd. 22 (1973), 201.
334 were drastically reduced: Hans Günther Adler, *Der verwaltete Mensch: Studien zur Deportation der Juden aus Deutschland* (Tübingen, 1974), 50–51.
334 "and self-torture"; "at the butcher's": Deutschkron, *Outcast*, 65, 98.
334 "out of place here": Quoted in Reuth, *Goebbels*, 299.
335 "processing of the transport": Deutschkron, *Outcast*, 114.
335 "or other impositions": Quoted in Wolfgang Wippermann, *Steinerne Zeugen. Stätten der Judenverfolgung in Berlin* (Berlin, 1982), 60.
336 "Technocrats of Death"; "further into the East": Quoted in ibid., 17.
337 watched the transports depart: Kaplan, *Between Dignity and Despair*, 198.

337 "befallen their fellow citizens": Ibid.

337 "tortures, and gassings": Andreas-Friedrich, *Berlin Underground*, 83.

337 "terribly little to help": Ursula von Kardorff, *Berliner Aufzeichnungen 1942 bis 1945* (Munich, 1992), 44.

338 "to handle filthy Jews": Quoted in Nathan Stoltzfus, *Resistance of the Heart. Intermarriage and the Rosenstrasse Protest in Nazi Germany* (New York, 1996), 183.

338 "is to be 'Jew-free'": Andreas-Friedrich, *Berlin Underground*, 90.

338 "become free of Jews": Quoted in Stoltzfus, *Resistance of the Heart*, 212.

338 *Judenfrei:* Quoted in Kaplan, *Between Dignity and Despair*, 232.

339 deportation figures: Peter Wyden, *Stella* (New York, 1992), 189–190.

339 "ranks were thinning"; "happening in their streets": Deutschkron, *Outcast*, 111, 123–124.

340 until the Nazi collapse: For a compelling account of the underground lives of the Jewish survivors in Berlin, see Leonard Gross, *The Last Jews in Berlin* (New York, 1982).

340–341 "no visible damage"; "victim of the Jews": Quoted in Wyden, *Stella*, 152, 254–255.

342 Baum Group: See Wolfgang Wippermann, *Die Berliner Gruppe Baum und der jüdische Widerstand* (Berlin, 1981).

342 Rosenstrasse protest: See Stoltzfus, *Resistance of the Heart.*

342–343 "from them again"; "husbands back"; "extremely dangerous": Quoted in ibid., 213, 235, 237.

344 need for ground invasion: Arthur Harris, *Bomber Offensive* (London, 1947), 73–76.

344 "German war effort": Quoted in Overy, *Why the Allies Won*, 117.

344 mockup of Berlin apartments: "Angriff auf 'German Village,'" *Der Spiegel* 41/1999, 238–243.

345 Berlin soldiers' death figures: Stoltzfus, *Resistance of the Heart*, 196–197.

345 "storm, break loose!": Quoted in Reuth, *Goebbels*, 316.

346 signs of defeatism: Marlis G. Steinert, *Hitler's War and the Germans* (Athens, Ohio, 1977), 186.

346 "on the defensive": Ian Kershaw, *The 'Hitler Myth': Images and Reality in the Third Reich* (Oxford, 1987), 187.

346 "do so anymore": Kardorff, *Berliner Aufzeichnungen*, 62–63.

346 August 23/24, 1943 raid: Middlebrook, *Berlin Raids*, 71–72.

346 November/December, 1943 raids: Ibid., 123–139. See also Earl R. Beck, *Under the Bombs. The German Home Front, 1942–1945* (Lexington, Ky., 1986).

347 "what happens next": Engeli and Ribbe, "Berlin in der NS-Zeit," 1015.

348 final weeks of agony: Wessling, *Karajan*, 98.

348 "preserve its good humor"; DTU: Quoted in Kater, *Drummers*, 124, 168.

349 face of adversity: Linda Schulte-Saxe, "Retrieving the City as *Heimat*: Berlin in Nazi Cinema," in Haxthausen and Suhr, eds., *Berlin*, 177–180.

349 not fit to serve: Martin Kitchen, *Nazi Germany at War* (London, 1995), 270.

349 *Kolberg:* Anton Kaes, *From Hitler to Heimat. The Return of History as Film* (Cambridge, Mass., 1989), 2–4.

349 *Das Leben Geht Weiter*: Kitchen, *Nazi Germany at War*, 275.

350 "All clear!": Andreas-Friedrich, *Berlin Underground*, 139–140.

350 "a magnificent spectacle": Speer, *Inside the Third Reich*, 288.

351 "Soldiers Hall in Berlin": Ibid., 298.

352 "in the first place?": Andreas-Friedrich, *Berlin Underground*, 140.

352 complexity of the capital: Beatrix Herlemann, "Der deutsche kommunistische Widerstand während des Krieges," *Beiträge zum Widerstand 1933–1945*. Nr. 35, Gedenkstätte deutscher Widerstand, Berlin, 1989.

352 "to get the verdict changed": Quoted in Michael Balfour, *Withstanding Hitler* (London, 1988), 211.

352 July 20, 1944: The classic study of the German resistance is Peter Hoffmann, *The History of the German Resistance 1933–1945* (Cambridge, Mass., 1977). For a different perspective, see Theodore S. Hamerow, *On the Road to the Wolf's Lair: German Resistance to Hitler* (Cambridge, Mass., 1997). Berlin's place in the resistance is treated in Peter Steinbach, "Zwischen Bomben und Gestapo—Berlin als Reichshauptstadt," in Hannelore Horn, *Berlin als Faktor nationaler und internationaler Politik* (Berlin, 1988), 23–44.

355 were yet to come: Joachim Fest, *Staatsstreich: Der lange Weg zum 20. Juni* (Berlin, 1984), 8.

355 Eisenhower's Berlin strategy: Stephen E. Ambrose, *Eisenhower and Berlin, 1945. The Decision to Halt at the Elbe* (New York, 1967), 17–37.
355 take the German capital: Norman Gelb, *The Berlin Wall* (New York, 1986), 20.
356 "other fellows take over": Quoted in Ambrose, *Eisenhower and Berlin*, 89.
356 "controls Europe": Quoted in Gelb, *Berlin Wall*, 22.
356 "let him take Berlin": Quoted in John Keegan, "Berlin," *Military History Quarterly* (Winter 1990), 77. See also Christopher Duffy, *Red Storm on the Reich. The Soviet March on Germany* (New York, 1991), 297.
357 Hitler's bunker: Anthony Read and David Fisher, *The Fall of Berlin* (New York, 1993), 222.
357 "go down fighting": Quoted in Keegan, "Berlin," 73.
358 "the last bullet": Quoted in Engeli and Ribbe, "Berlin in der NS-Zeit," 1022.
358 "could not escape": Kardorff, *Berliner Aufzeichnungen*, 119.358
359 "why should the dead?"; "he'll have company": Schäfer, ed., *Zweiter Weltkrieg*, 295, 289.
359 alcohol and morphine: Douglas Botting, *From the Ruins of the Reich. Germany 1945–1949* (New York, 1985), 64.
360 Speer plan to kill Hitler: Speer, *Inside the Third Reich*, 429–431.
361 summarily executed: Reuth, *Goebbels*, 356.
361 "die without honor": Quoted in Reinhard Rürup, ed., *Berlin 1945. Eine Dokumentation* (Berlin, 1995), 32.
362 "kept in hiding": Quoted in Norman M. Naimark, *The Russians in Germany. A History of the Soviet Zone of Occupation 1945–1949* (Cambridge, Mass., 1995), 80.
362 "sent you here"; "Fascist lair": Quoted in ibid., 77.
363 "service to the German people": Ada Petrova and Peter Watson, *The Death of Hitler* (New York, 1995), 36.
363 Hitler's and Braun's deaths: account here based largely on ibid.
363 Goebbels' and family's death: Reuth, *Goebbels*, 360–363.
364 "a businesslike manner": Quoted in Hugh Trevor-Roper, *The Last Days of Hitler* (New York, 1962), 265.
365 "claimed any more victims": Quoted in Hans-Norbert Burkert, Klaus Matußek, Doris Obschernitzski, *Zerstört, Besiegt, Befreit. Der Kampf um Berlin bis zur Kapitulation 1945* (Berlin, 1985), 176.
365 Hitler's corpse identification: Petrova and Watson, *Death of Hitler*, 56.
367 Hitler sightings: see Donald M. McKale, *Hitler. The Survival Myth* (New York, 1981).
367 "Living God": "Hitler Is Alive?" *Weekly World News*, Nov. 21, 1989.

Chapter 8

369 "goods are hot!": Quoted in Lally, *Wilder Times*, 177.
371 "role in my childhood": Gilbert, *European Past*, 5.
371 "bike from you yet?": Margret Boveri, *Tage des Überlebens. Berlin 1945* (Frankfurt, 1966), 109–110.
373 "Führer and Chancellor": Ruth Andreas-Friedrich, *Battleground Berlin. Diaries 1945–1948* (New York, 1990), 23–26.
374 "were to meet": Ladd, *Ghosts of Berlin*, 194.
374 "symbols of abundance and fertility": Anonymous, *A Woman in Berlin* (New York, 1955), 70.
374 unable to protect her: Andreas-Friedrich, *Battleground*, 16–17.
376 fabled Western metropolis: For accounts of Red Army rapine in Berlin, see Naimark, *The Russians in Berlin*, 69–140; and Erich Kuby, *The Russians and Berlin 1945* (London, 1965), 260–288.
376 "aren't over yet": Andreas-Friedrich, *Battleground*, 36.
376 electrical generating capability: Philip Windsor, *City on Leave. A History of Berlin 1945–1962* (London, 1963), 35–38.
377 cultural removals: Naimark, *The Russians in Berlin*, 175–178; Moorehead, *Lost and Found*, 276–282; Lynn H. Nichols, *The Rape of Europa. The Fate of Europe's Treasures in the Third Reich and the Second World War* (New York, 1994), 361–364.
379 "city of progress": Wolfgang Leonhard, *Child of the Revolution* (Chicago, 1985), 318.

381–382 "tense and demoralized"; "You now mayor"; "in our control"; "got our deputy": Ibid., 298, 302, 303, 315.
383 "odor of death": Robert Murphy, *Diplomat Among Warriors* (New York, 1964), 257.
383 "time and history": Ibid., 259.
383 "our occupation zone": Lucius Clay, *Decision in Germany* (New York, 1950), 15.
384 "all the arrangements": Quoted in Richard Brett-Smith, *Berlin '45. The Grey City* (London, 1966), 48.
384 "are not human": Hans Speier, *From the Ashes of Disgrace. A Journal of Germany 1945–1955* (Amherst, Mass., 1981), 26.
384 "urgently each night": Andreas-Friedrich, *Battleground*, 65.
384 "for the Germans": Quoted in Brett-Smith, *Berlin '45*, 44.
384 requisitioning 125 homes: Botting, *Ruins*, 215.
384 "best French champagne": Curt Riess, *Berlin Berlin! 1945–1953* (Berlin, n.d.), 64.
384 "a paradise": Ibid.
385 "girls the moon": Quoted in Alexandra Richie, *Faust's Metropolis* (New York, 1998), 640.
385 "more rarely—marriage": George Clare, *Before the Wall. Berlin Days 1946–1948* (New York, 1990), 70.
385 "Sherman, Jenghis Khan": Quoted in David McCullough, *Truman* (New York, 1992), 415.
386 "ours to them": Quoted in ibid., 403.
387 "population throughout Germany": Windsor, *City on Leave*, 28.
387 Europe and Germany: On the Potsdam Conference, see Charles L. Mee, Jr., *Meeting At Potsdam* (New York, 1975).
388 "inhabited by a fifth": Botting, *Ruins*, 513.
389 "carried anyone away": Quoted in Dagmar Barnouw, *Germany 1945. Views of War and Violence* (Bloomington, 1996), 91.
390 smokes at PX: Speier, *Ashes*, 26.
390 Clay's wife; "a couple thousand bucks": Quoted in Botting, *Ruins*, 229–230.
390 "glass of crystal": Speier, *Ashes*, 27.
390 came of the threats: Jörg Roesler, "The Black Market in Postwar Berlin and the Methods Used to Contain It," *German History* 7:1 (April 1989), 96.
390 for their freedom: See Tom Bower, *The Pledge Betrayed* (New York, 1982); and Bower, *The Paperclip Conspiracy: The Battle for the Spoils and Secrets of Nazi Germany* (London, 1987).
391 applicants too closely: Clare, *Before the Wall*, 47.
392 "the German renewal": Quoted in Wolfgang Schivelbusch, *In a Cold Crater. Cultural and Intellectual Life in Berlin 1945–1948* (Berkeley, 1988), 63.
392 "in the next twenty years": Quoted in Dalichow and Geiss, eds., *Filmstadt Babelsberg*, 67.
393 "Hit or miss": Clare, *Before the Wall*, 82.
394 mood of the Berliners: See Joseph Hoppe, "Frolic at Five—Mehr als ein Soldatensender," in Tamara Domentat, ed., *Coca-Cola, Jazz und AFN. Berlin und die Amerikaner* (Berlin 1985), 118–127.
394 RIAS: See Herbert Kundler, *RIAS Berlin. Eine Radio-Station in einer geteilten Stadt* (Berlin, 1994).
394 Free University: See James F. Tent, "The Free University of Berlin: A German Experiment in Higher Education 1948–1961," in Jeffrey M. Diefendorf, et al., eds., *American Policy and the Reconstruction of West Germany, 1945–1955* (New York, 1993), 237–256.
394 "all the greater": Quoted in Schivelbusch, *Cold Crater*, 30.
395 "on cultural directives"; "cultural axis": Quoted in ibid., 31.
395 "nothing to begin from": Spender, *European Witness*, 236.
395 "Stay here!": Quoted in Shirakawa, *Devil's Music Master*, 340.
395 "can say as much?": Quoted in Taylor, *Berlin and Its Culture*, 291.
396 "cherished by all peoples": *Berlin Wirbt!*, 23.
396 "more alive than Paris": Quoted in Schivelbusch, *Cold Crater*, 22.
396 flee back to America: Fritz Kortner, *Aller Tage Abend* (Munich, 1959), 560.
396 Brecht complaint: "Ein Ort für die Ewigkeit," *Der Tagesspiegel*, Sept. 1, 1994.
396 "noise": Suhrkamp to Kracauer, Jan. 30, 1946. Quoted in Schivelbusch, *Cold Crater*, 23..
396 "will not last": Furtwängler to Helmut Grohe, Feb. 12, 1947. Quoted in ibid.
396 "charred remains": Elisabeth Langgässer, quoted in ibid.
396 "golden hunger years": For a survey of this period, see Hans Borgelt, *Das war der Früling von Berlin* (Munich, 1980).

397 "saddle on a cow": Anne McElvoy, *The Saddled Cow* (London, 1993).
397 fusion of east-SPD and KPD: Naimark, *Russians in Berlin*, 275–284.
398 "Russian lovers": Andreas-Friedrich, *Battleground Berlin*, 136.
399 "people just disappeared": Clare, *Before the Wall*, 229.
400 Stalin's plans for Germany: See R. C. Raack, "Stalin Plans His Post-War Germany," *Journal of Contemporary History* 28 (1993), 53073, especially 62–63; Dietrich Staritz, "The SED, Stalin, and the German Question: Interests and Decision-Making in Light of New Sources," *German History* 10 (1992), 274–289, especially 277. For a recent study of Germany in the Cold War, see W. R. Smyser, *From Yalta to Berlin. The Cold War Struggle over Germany* (New York, 1999).
400 "routine questions"; "dramatic suddenness": Quoted in David Clay Large, "The Great Rescue," *Military History Quarterly* (Spring 1997), 16.
402 lair of the Bear: See Charles F. Pennacchio, "The East German Communists and the Origins of the Berlin Crisis," *East European Quarterly* 24 (September, 1995), 292–313.
402 "pyramids of skulls": Frank L. Howley, *Berlin Command* (New York, 1950), 197.
402 leakiest blockade: William Stivers, "The Incomplete Blockade: Soviet Zone Supply of West Berlin, 1948–49," *Diplomatic History* 21:4 (Fall 1997), 569–602.
402–403 "fight for freedom"; "full of danger": Quoted in Large, "Rescue," 17.
403–404 "no time at all"; "hell of a fix"; "air strength"; "as it developed": Quoted in ibid., 17–18.
405–406, 408 "you beat him"; "relieve the distress"; "when birds walked"; "blockade is ended": Quoted in ibid., 18–20.
408–409 "Russians the airlift"; "trains are moving": Quoted in ibid., 20–21.
409 "Americans against the Russians": Quoted in Volker Koop, *Kein Kampf um Berlin? Deutsche Politik zur Zeit der Berlin Blokade 1948/49* (Bonn, 1988), 13.
409 Berlin after all: Ibid.
411 "enemy of the sea": Quoted in Dennis L. Bark and David R. Gress, *A History of West Germany. Vol. 1: From Shadow to Substance* (Oxford, 1989), 321.
412 "Mongolian": Arnulf Baring, *Aussenpolitik in Adenauers Kanzlerdemokratie* (Munich, 1969), 53.
412 "a pagan city": Quoted in Reiner Pommerin, *Von Berlin nach Bonn*, 45.
412 "east is occupied"; "[Wilhelm Hoegner]": Quoted in ibid., 47, 51.
414 "deference to reality": John Le Carré, *A Small Town in Germany* (New York, 1983), 17.
414 "mission in a cornfield": Quoted in Michael Z. Wise, *Capital Dilemma. Germany's Search for a New Architecture of Democracy* (New York, 1988), 24.
414 "it was a beginning": Quoted in ibid., 23.
415 East Berlin street names: See Maoz Azaryahu, "Street Names and Identity: The Case of East Berlin," *Journal of Contemporary History* 21:4 (October 1986), 581–604; Dirk Verheyen, "What's in a Name? Street Name Politics and Urban Identity in Berlin," *German Politics and Society* 15:3 (Fall 1997), 44–72.
417 also very poor: See Günter Braun, "Der Wiederaufbau Berlins—Eine Stadt auf dem Weg zu neuen Aufgaben," in Industrie und Handelskammer zu Berlin, ed., *Berlin und seine Wirtschaft* (Berlin, 1987), 223–230.
417 "engagement of Bonn for Berlin": Quoted in Windsor, *City on Leave*, 135.
418 building rivalry: See Bruno Flierl, *Berlin baut um—Wessen Stadt wird die Stadt?* (Berlin, 1998), 27; Josef Paul Kleihues, "From the Destruction to the Critical Reconstruction of the City: Urban Design in Berlin after 1945," in Kleihues and Rathgeber, eds., *Berlin/New York*, 395–409.
418 a utopian dream: See Jeffry M. Diefendorf, *In the Wake of War. The Reconstruction of German Cities after World War II* (New York, 1993), 191–194; Ladd, *Ghosts of Berlin*, 177–178.
420 "national consciousness of the people": Quoted in Jörn Düwel, "Berlin: Planen im Kalten Krieg," in Marita Gleiss, ed., *1945, Kriegs, Zerstörung, Aufbau: Architecten und Stadtplanung 1940–1960* (Berlin, 1995), 208.
420 Stalinallee: See Ladd, *Ghosts of Berlin*, 181–188; Tilo Köhler, *Unser die Strasse—Unser der Sieg. Die Stalinalle* (Berlin, 1993).
421 in Western hands: "Zuhause unter Fremden," *Süddeutsche Zeitung*, July 17/18, 1999.
421 "can find expression": Quoted in Ladd, *Ghosts of Berlin*, 56.
422 "unglorious past": Quoted in Wise, *Capital Dilemma*, 43.
423 "point for German reunification": Quoted in Cullen, *Reichstag*, 403.

423 cultural barbarism: Wolf Jobst Siedler, *Die gemordete Stadt* (Berlin, 1978); "Scheußliche neue Schönheit," *Süddeutsche Zeitung*, Aug. 24/25, 1985.

423 Hansaviertel: Ladd, *Ghosts of Berlin*, 188–189; Kleihues, "From the Destruction," 399–400.

424 "shown in our city": "Als die Welt noch überschaubar war," *Der Tagesspiegel*, June 6, 1999.

424 "all the horrors began": Ibid.

425 expelled from their homes: On the border installations, see David Shears, *The Ugly Frontier* (New York, 1970).

425 emigration from the GDR: See David E. Murphy, Sergei A. Kondrashev, and George Bailey, *Battleground Berlin. CIA vs. KGB in the Cold War* (New Haven, Conn., 1997), 156.

425 "low work norms": Carola Stern, *Walter Ulbricht. Eine politische Biographie* (Berlin, 1963), 140.

426 "will of the masses": Ibid., 144.

427 rescinding of norm increases: On this and other details of the uprising, see Arnulf Baring, *Uprising in East Germany* (Ithaca, 1972).

428 "all the Russians dead": Quoted in Richie, *Faust's Metropolis*, 685.

429 absence of support from intelligentsia: See "In der Gaststätte 'Rüberzahl' ruft der Brigadier zum Streik auf," *Süddeutsche Zeitung*, June 19, 1993.

429 "Socialist Unity Party of Germany": Quoted in Fuegi, *Brecht*, 543–544.

429 "and elected another?": Quoted in ibid., 549.

430 "face of the German working class": Quoted in "Ich habe der Arbeiterklasse ins Antlitz geschaut," *Der Tagesspiegel*, June 17, 1993.

431 "enjoyment of prosperity": Stern, *Failure of Illiberalism*, 217.

433 Stasi: For a recent history of this organization, see John O. Koehler, *Stasi. The Untold Story of the East German Secret Police* (Boulder, Col., 1999). The best study is David Childs and Richard Popplewell, *The Stasi. The East German Intelligence and Security Service* (London, 1996).

433 Wolf: On Markus Wolf, see his memoir, *Man Without a Face. The Autobiography of Communism's Greatest Spymaster* (New York, 1997); also Markus Wolf, *Die Troika* (Düsseldorf, 1989); and Leslie Colitt, *Spymaster* (Reading, Mass., 1995).

434 "went through Berlin": Quoted in Peter Grose, *Gentleman Spy. The Life of Allen Dulles* (New York, 1994), 397.

434 Gehlen Organization: See Reinhard Gehlen, *Der Dienst. Erinnerungen 1942–1971* (Mainz, 1971); Mary Ellen Reese, *General Reinhard Gehlen: The CIA Connection* (Fairfax, Va., 1990).

435 "always a traitor"; "die for the Federal Republic": "Ich habe mich ergeben," *Der Spiegel*, Dec. 21, 1955, 11. See also David Clay Large, "A 'Gift to the German Future?' The Anti-Hitler Resistance and West German Rearmament," *German Studies Review* 7:3 (October 1984), 301.

435 "revenge for 1945": Wolf, *Man Without a Face*, 80.

436 as soon as he could: Otto John, *Twice Through the Lines* (New York, 1972).

436 "mystery play": Murphy, Kondrashev, and Bailey, *Battleground Berlin*, 185.

436 "damaged goods on us": Wolf, *Man Without a Face*, 82.

436 "Operation Gold": On this, see Murphy, Kondrashev, and Bailey, *Battleground Berlin*, 205–237; "Operation Gold," *Der Spiegel*, 39/1997, 82–85.

436 "came to Berlin": Quoted in Grose, *Gentleman Spy*, 397.

437 "unguarded and exposed": Wolf, *Man Without a Face*, 91.

438 "capital of the GDR": Gelb, *Berlin Wall*, 47.

438 "land it is situated": Quoted in Ann Tusa, *The Last Division. A History of Berlin 1945–1989* (Reading, Mass., 1997), 116.

438 "occupiers in West Berlin": Quoted in ibid.

439 "are wholly illogical": John Lewis Gaddis, *We Now Know: Rethinking Cold War History* (New York, 1997), 141.

439 "will fly automatically": Quoted in Kai Bird, *The Color of Truth. McGeorge Bundy and William Bundy: Brothers in Arms* (New York, 1998), 204.

439 "Germany cannot stand": Quoted in ibid. For Khrushchev's position on Berlin, see also Douglas Selvage, "Khrushchev's November 1958 Ultimatum: New Evidence from the Polish Archives," in *Cold War Flashpoints. Bulletin of the Cold War International History Project* (Winter 1988) 200–203.

439	threat of nuclear war: See William Burr, "Avoiding the Slippery Slope: The Eisenhower Administration and the Berlin Crisis, November 1958–January 1959," *Diplomatic History* 18:2 (Spring 1984), 177–205.
439	"atomized than communized": Quoted in Tusa, *The Last Division*, 175.
440	"use of nuclear weapons" "not for Berlin!": Quoted in Gaddis, *We Now Know*, 141.
440	"twice in this century": Quoted in Tusa, *The Last Division*, 175.
441	"holocaust and humiliation": Quoted in Michael R. Beschloss, *The Crisis Years. Kennedy and Khrushchev 1960–1963* (New York, 1991), 174.
441	"testicles of the West": Quoted in Gelb, *Berlin Wall*, 3.
442	"including the corridors"; "hands off Berlin"; "contractual rights": Quoted in Beschloss, *The Crisis Years*, 216, 177.
442–443	"in the world"; "*your problem*"; "force a change"; "be at stake"; "another think coming": Quoted in ibid., 217–227.

Chapter 9

445	"political constructs collide": Peter Schneider, *The Wall Jumper* (New York, 1983), 3–4.
446	"application of these measures": Quoted in Kai-Axel Aanderud, *Die eingemauerte Stadt* (Recklingshausen, 1991), 42.
448	"cemented shut": Quoted in ibid., 43.
448	construction of the Wall: For a narrative history of the Berlin Wall, see Peter Wyden, *Wall. The Inside Story of Divided Berlin* (New York, 1989); on Honecker's role, see "Das Mauer-Komplott," *Die Zeit*, Aug. 16, 1991; "Gipsbrei für die Rattenlöcher," *Der Spiegel* 33/1991, 102–112.
449	"to build a wall": Quoted in Aanderud, *Die eingemauerte Stadt*, 29.
449, 451	"right to do"; "without anesthesia": Quoted in ibid., 36, 49.
451	marching into West Berlin: Willy Brandt, "Berlin, die Mauer und der Prozess der Entspannung," in Eberhard Diepgen, ed., *750 Jahre Berlin. Anmerkungen, Erinnerungen, Betrachtungen* (Berlin, 1987), 42.
451	"without improving it": Quoted in Aanderud, *Die eingemauerte Stadt*, 50.
451–452	"anything about this?"; "of their jail": Quoted in Beschloss, *Crisis Years*, 272, 278.
452	dispersed the attackers: Gelb, *Berlin Wall*, 178.
453	*Ostpolitik* of the 1970s: Brandt, "Berlin," 42–43.
454	"bleeding to death": Willy Brandt, *People and Politics. The Years 1960–1975* (Boston, 1976), 37.
454	"filled with wild animals": Aanderud, *Die eingemauerte Stadt*, 93.
454	"Deeds, Not Words"; "does not stand alone": Beschloss, *Crisis Years*, 284.
455	"inside it are free": Quoted in Peter Conrad, *Modern Times, Modern Places* (New York, 1998), 341.
456	"would have broken loose"; "runaway tank": Beschloss, *Crisis Years*, 333, 334.
456	"inclinations of General Clay": Ibid., 369.
457	wave of the future: McElvoy, *Saddled Cow*, 81.
457	sources of opposition: See Richard L. Merritt, "East Berlin as a Metropolis," in Margy Gerber, ed., *Studies in GDR Culture and Society* 8, (Lanham, Md., 1988), 16–22. See also Manfred Rexin, "Ost-Berlin als DDR Hauptstadt," in Gerd Langguth, ed., *Berlin vom Brennpunkt der Teilung zur Brücke der Einheit* (Cologne, 1990), 70–86.
459	"costs the state 150,000 marks": Craig R. Whitney, *Spy Trader* (New York, 1993), 65.
459	"Western influenced": Holger Kuhle, "Auferstanden aus Ruinen: Der Alexanderplatz," in Bernd Wilczek, ed., *Berlin, Hauptstadt der DDR 1949–1989. Utopie und Realität* (Baden-Baden, 1995), 54.
459	"size and beauty": Ibid., 56.
460	"escape to freedom"; "stay in West Berlin": Wolfgang Ribbe, "Berlin zwischen Ost und West," in Ribbe, ed., *Geschichte Berlins*, II, 1100.
461	"family of nations": Brandt, *People and Politics*, 72.
462	"Aryan": Quoted in Beschloss, *Crisis Years*, 606.
462	"another Hitler?": Quoted in Gelb, *Berlin Wall*, 226.
463	"come to Berlin!"; "friend of the Germans": Quoted in Beschloss, *Crisis Years*, 606–07.
464	"economic bridge": Braun, "Wiederaufbau," in *Berlin und seine Wirtschaft*, 213.

464 West Berlin economy: See Joachim Nawrocki, "Berliner Wirtschaft. Wachstum auf begrenztem Raum," in Dieter Baumeister, ed., *Berlin-Fibel. Berichte zur Lage der Stadt* (Berlin, 1975), 247–320; Richard L. Merritt and Anna J. Merritt, *Living with the Wall. West Berlin, 1961–1985* (Durham, N.C., 1985), 136–148.

465 corruption in West Berlin: See Mathew D. Rose, *Berlin. Hauptstadt von Filz und Korruption* (Munich, 1997); Peter Bölke, *Geschäfte mit Berlin* (Munich, 1973).

466 big city *am Tropf:* Peter Bender, "Die Absurdität Berlins," *Der Spiegel* 20/1981, 40–41.

466 influx of foreigners: John Borneman, *Belonging in the Two Berlins. Kin, State, Nation* (Cambridge, 1992), 206–207.

467 Turks in West Berlin: See Heidrun Suhr, "Fremde in Berlin: The Outsiders' View from the inside Haxthausen and Suhr, eds., *Berlin*, 225–238; Günter Grass, "In Kreuzberg fehlt ein Minarett," in Hans Werner Richter, ed., *Berlin, Ach Berlin* (Munich, 1981), 116–118; Aras Ören, *Gefülslosigkeiten: Reisen von Berlin nach Berlin* (Frankfurt, 1986).

467 "mutton, thyme, and garlic": Aras Ören, *Was will Niyazi in der Naunynstrasse?* (Berlin, 1973), 21.

467 "Kreuzberg purdah": Suhr, "Fremde," 227.

467 "lock-down room": "Führt euch anständig auf, dann könnt ihr bleiben," *Der Tagesspiegel*, Dec. 22, 1995.

468 "to the smell": "Jetzt besteht die Gefahr des Tohuwabohus," *Der Spiegel*, 42/1984, 85.

468 "to a Turkish speaker": Adam Lebor, *A Heart Turned East* (New York, 1998), 188.

468 "it's your problem": Quoted in ibid., 190–191.

469 "The Glittering Thing": "Das Glitzerding," *Der Spiegel*, 41/1966, 41–60.

470 "new rising from old": Quoted in Richie, *Faust's Metropolis*, 800.

471 comparative cultural spending: Wilhelm A. Kewenig, "Berlin—The Cultural Metropolis of Germany?" in Gerhard Kirchhoff, ed., *Views of Berlin* (Boston, 1989), 240–241; Jane Kramer, *The Politics of Memory: Looking for Germany in the New Germany* (New York, 1996), 117–118.

471 Kulturforum: See "Kämpfer für Kunst und Demokratie," *Der Tagesspiegel*, April 9, 1995.

472 "in a new relationship": Quoted in Balfour, *Berlin—The Politics of Order*, 215.

473 "concrete cells": Ian Fleming, *Thrilling Cities* (London, 1963), 137.

474 "past grows luxuriantly": Schneider, *Wall Jumper*, 5–6.

474 half-century after Hitler: Kramer, *Politics of Memory*, 7.

474 Karajan and Philharmonie: Herbert von Karajan, "Dirigent für Berlin," in Diepgen, ed., *750 Jahre Berlin*, 157–158; Wolfgang Stresemann, "Berlin as a Music Center," in Kirchhoff, ed., *Views of Berlin*, 194–195.

474 theatrical scene in West Berlin: Joachim Werner Preuss, "Berlin as Theater Center," in Kirchhoff, ed., *Views of Berlin*, 216–226.

475 "spontaneous internationalism": François Bondy, "Berlin's cultural Message—Some Reflections," in Martin J. Hillenbrand, ed., *The Future of Berlin* (Montclair, N.J., 1980), 270.

477 "sense since the war": Quoted in Taylor, *Berlin and Its Culture*, 318.

477 other half as more "foreign": Quoted in Peter Nöldechen, "Uwe Johnson," in Rühle, ed., *Literatur-Ort Berlin*, 179.

477 Film in West Berlin: See Ronald Holloway, "Filmstadt Berlin," in Kirchhoff, ed., *Views of Berlin*, 203–215.

479 "for the Communist call": Greil Marcus, *Lipstick Traces. A Secret History of the 20th Century* (Cambridge, Mass., 1989), 74.

479 emotional train-wreck: Victor Bockris, *Lou Reed. The Biography* (New York, 1995), 217–221.

479 David Bowie and Iggy Pop in Berlin: Christopher Sandford, *Bowie. Loving the Alien* (New York, 1998), 160–164.

480 "true Berlin": See Gerhard Weiss, "Panem et Circenses," in Haxthausen and Suhr, eds., *Berlin*, 247–251; Geoffrey J. Giles, "Berlin's 750th Anniversary Exhibitions," *German History* 6:2 (August 1988), 164–170.

480 "the Allied bombing"; "with the perpetrators": Korff and Rürup, eds., *Berlin, Berlin*, 6.

480 "Topography of Terror": See Ladd, *Ghosts of Berlin*, 160–169; Reinhard Rürup, ed., *Topography of Terror. A Documentation* (Berlin, 1989).

483 anti-Americanism: See Dan Diner, *America in the Eyes of the Germans* (Princeton, 1996), 105–149.

483 "napalm and poison gas": Quoted in Stefan Aust, *Der Baader-Meinhof-Komplex* (Munich, 1989), 41.

484 anti-Shah demonstration: See ibid., 49–53.
484 "first political murder": Quoted in Terence Prittie, *The Velvet Chancellors. A History of Post-War Germany* (London, 1979), 148–149.
484 "in Iran every day": Heinrich Albertz, *Blumen für Stukenbrock. Biographisches* (Stuttgart, 1981), 246.
485 "hard to take psychologically": Quoted in Ulrich Chaussy, *Die drei Leben des Rudi Dutschke* (Berlin, 1993), 169–170.
486 "all over the world": Quoted in ibid., 8.
487 Bachmann-Dutschke correspondence: Ibid., 275–281.
487 "also pulled the trigger": Aust, *Baader-Meinhof-Komplex*, 65.
487 employed by the BfV: Chaussy, *Die drei Leben*, 253.
488 "Hochburg der K-Gruppen": Borneman, *Belonging*, 254.
488 "failed revolution": Klaus Hübner, *Einsatz. Erinnerungen des Berliner Polizeipräsidenten 1969–1987* (Berlin, 1997), 186.
488 "allowed to exist": Quoted in Aust, *Baader-Meinhof-Komplex*, 68.
488 "must arm ourselves": Quoted in Dennis L. Bark and David R. Gress, *A History of West Germany Vol. 2: Democracy and Its Discontents* (Oxford, 1989), 134.
489 Baader escape: Jillian Becker, *Hitler's Children: The Story of the Baader-Meinhof Terrorist Gang* (Philadelphia, 1977), 101.
489 murder of Drenckmann: Hübner, *Einsatz*, 271.
489 "since Rosa Luxemburg": Quoted in Becker, *Hitler's Children*, 283.
490 "Kommando Ulrike Meinhof": Aust, *Baader-Meinhof-Komplex*, 435.
490 "organizations of the world": Quoted in ibid., 535.
491 by their own hand: Ibid., 586–587.
491 "PX parking lot": Henrik Bering, *Outpost Berlin. The History of the American Military Forces in Berlin, 1945–1994* (Chicago, 1995), 223.
491 La Belle bombing: Domentat, ed., *Coca-Cola*, 168–178.
491 false identity papers: "Die seltsame Kumpanei von Stasi und RAF," *Süddeutsche Zeitung*, Feb. 15/16, 1997.
492 "against the Nazis"; "Germany under Hitler": Wolf, *Man Without a Face*, 277, 279.
493 "Rauhaus": Ian Walker, *Zoo Station. Adventures in East and West Berlin* (New York, 1988), 161–162.
493 squatters' movement": See Ribbe, "Berlin zwischen Ost und West," 1108–1109; Bernd Sonnewald and Jürgen Raabe-Zimmermann, "Die 'Berliner Linie' und die Hausbesetzer Szene," in *Politologische Studien*, 27 (Berlin, 1983).
494 Lenné-Dreieck: See Axel Steinhage and Thomas Flemming, *Berlin 1945–1989. Jahr für Jahr. Die Ereignisse in der geteilten Stadt* (Berlin, 1995), 266.
494 Maxwell's: See Kramer, *Politics of Memory*, 1–50.
495 "separation virus": Peter Schneider, *Couplings* (New York, 1996), 9.
495 "the case of war?": Quoted in Bering, *Outpost*, 222.
496 "part of us": Quoted in Michael Simmons, *Deutschland und Berlin. Geschichte einer Hauptstadt 1871–1990* (Berlin, 1990), 285.
496 "never forget that": Quoted in McElvoy, *Saddled Cow*, 82.
498 Luther's rehabilitation: Robert F. Goeckel, "The Luther Anniversary in East Germany," *World Politics* 37 (October 1984), 112–33.
499 exhumation of Goethe: "The Sorrows of Goethe," *New York Times*, March 19, 1999.
499 Prussian revival: See I. R. Martin, "The Changing Image of Prussia in the German Democratic Republic," *German Life and Letters* 37:1 (1983), 57–70.
500 "international musical world": "Im Grunde ein Wunder," *Der Weltspiegel*, June 26, 1994.
500 "its history and culture": Quoted in Weiss, "Panem et Circenses," 249.
500 Dom restoration: "Die Heimkehr des verlorenen Sohnes," *Süddeutsche Zeitung*, June 4, 1993.
500 Nikolaiviertel: See Ladd, *Ghosts of Berlin*, 44–47.
501 "typical workers' neighborhood": Ibid., 108.
503 "Palazzo Prozi": "Vom Palast der Republik zum Ballast der Bundesrepublik?" *Der Tagesspiegel*, March 27, 1993.
503 "weht er Mauern fort": Ibid.
504 act as they did: Timothy Garton Ash, *The File. A Personal History* (New York, 1997).

504 a Stasi informer: Peter Schneider, *The German Comedy. Scenes of Life after the Wall* (New York, 1991), 114.

506 banana joke: Clemens de Wroblewski, "Hauptstadt Berlin. Ein Witz," in Wilczek, ed., *Hauptstadt der DDR*, 247.

506 "double contrast": Timothy Garton Ash, *In Europe's Name. Germany and the Divided Continent* (New York, 1993), 200.

507 "Nischengesellschaft": Hans-Joachim Maaz, *Behind the Wall. The Inner Life of Communist Germany* (New York, 1993), xv.

507 "We'll finish the job": Timo Zilli, *Folterzelle 36* (Berlin, 1993), 36, 8.

507 95,847 marks a head: Whitney, *Spy Trader*, 168–169.

508 three billion marks: Ibid., xxxv.

508 "firm position of socialism": Quoted in McElvoy, *Saddled Cow*, 150.

508 more restraint: "Scharfmaul und Prahlhaus," *Die Zeit*, Sept. 27, 1991.

509 Biermann expulsion: See Horst Domdey, "Der Anfang vom Ende. 1976, Wolf Biermanns Ausbürgerung," in Wilczek, ed., *Berlin—Hauptstadt der DDR*, 175–191.

510 "state he supported": Quoted in "Deutschland im Herbst," *Der Tagesspiegel*, Nov. 15, 1996.

510 "spirit of reflection": Quoted in McElvoy, *Saddled Cow*, 152.

510 "will be crushed": Quoted in Domdey, "Der Anfang vom Ende," 181.

511 Distel Cabaret: "Nichts mehr gegeben," *Der Tagesspiegel*, Oct. 31, 1993.

512 "Are Communists Allowed to Dream?": Taylor, *Berlin and its Culture*, 358.

512 East Berlin Rock: See Peter Wicke, "Der King vom Prenzlauer Berg. Vom Mythos des Rock in einer sozialistischen Metropole," in Wilczek, ed., *Berlin—Hauptstadt der DDR*, 236–246.

513 "our working-class youth": Quoted in Richie, *Faust's Metropolis*, 753.

514 "Die Mauer muss weg": Quoted in Steinhage and Flemming, *Berlin 1945–1989*, 263.

514 one and the same: On the Prenzlauer Berg scene, see Klaus Michael, "Prenzlauer Berg. Streifzüge durch eine Kulturlandschaft," in Wilczek, ed., *Berlin—Hauptstadt der DDR*, 192–215; Philip Brady, "'Wir hausen im Prenzlauer Berg': On the Very Last Generation of GDR Poets," in Walter Pape, ed., *1870/71–1989/90. German Unifications and the Change of Literary Discourse* (Berlin/New York, 1993), 278–301.

514 "end for the GDR": Quoted in "Deutschland im Herbst," *Der Tagesspiegel*, Nov. 15, 1996.

514 negotiations with the GDR: Ash, *In Europe's Name*, 38.

515 "blood and iron": *Die Zeit*, July 10, 1987.

515 "Brandenburg Gate remains closed": U.S. Department of State, *Documents on Germany 1944–1985* (Washington, D.C., 1985), 1415.

Chapter 10

517 "one city again": Eberhard Diepgen, ed., *Erlebte Einheit. Ein deutsches Lesebuch* (Berlin, 1985), 8.

518 "fearless East Germans": "For the Wall's Fall, East Germans Are Given Their Due," *New York Times*, Nov. 10, 1999.

518 "elder statesman": Quoted in McElvoy, *Saddled Cow*, 191–192.

519 "opposing alliances": Quoted in Bark and Gress, *A History of West Germany. Vol. 2: Democracy and Its Discontents*, 499.

520 "by the regime": Quoted in McElvoy, *Saddled Cow*, 193.

521 refused to disperse: On the Leipzig demonstrations, see Charles S. Maier, *Dissolution. The Crisis of Communism and the End of East Germany* (Princeton, 1997), 135–146; Wolf-Jürgen Grabner, Christiane Heinze, and Detlef Pollack, eds., *Leipzig im Oktober. Kirchen und alternative Gruppen im Umbruch der DDR. Analysen aur Wende* (Berlin, 1990).

522 "Europe as a whole": Quoted in Hans-Hermann Hertle, *Chronik des Mauerfalls* (Berlin, 1996), 71.

522 "regret at their departure": Quoted in ibid., 74.

523 another one hundred years: On East Berlin's relatively small role in the early phase of the 1989 revolution, see Wolfgang Templin, "Gesamt-Berlin—Eine Fiktion?" in Werner Süß and Ralf Rytlewski, eds., *Berlin. Die Hauptstadt* (Berlin, 1999), 334–337.

523 "uncertainty, even fear": G. Jonathan Greenwald, *Berlin Witness. An American Diplomat's Chronicle of East Germany's Revolution* (University Park, Pa., 1995), 169.
524 "Don't panic": Quoted in ibid., 171.
524 "to be here"; "matter of morality": Ulrike Bresch, ed., *Oktober 1989. Wider den Schlaf der Vernunft* (Berlin, 1990), 49, 9.
524 "could be a bloodbath": Greenwald, *Berlin Witness*, 176–177.
524 "worse than ours": Quoted in Maier, *Dissolution*, 155.
525 reached themselves: Günter Schabowski, *Das Politbüro* (Reinbek bei Hamburg, 1990), 71–111.
525 "We've won!": McElvoy, *Saddled Cow*, 200–201; Maier, *Dissolution*, 156–157; "Wende und Ende des DDR Staates (3)," *Der Spiegel*, 41/1999, 77–109.
525 "Curse of the Pharaoh": Maier, *Dissolution*, 158.
526 November 4 rally in East Berlin: Greenwald, *Witness*, 242–248; Harold James and Marla Stone, eds., *When the Wall Came Down. Reactions to German Unification* (London/New York, 1992), 125–129.
526 "flee the Republic": Quoted in McElvoy, *Saddled Cow*, 203–204.
528 "including Berlin-West": Quoted in Hertle, *Chronik*, 141–148.
528 take place on November 9: Among the myriad accounts of this intoxicating moment, see, in addition to the above-cited works, Hedda Angermann, ed., *Aufbrüche. Dokumentation zur Wende in der DDR* (Munich, 1991).
529 past twenty-eight years: Schneider, *German Comedy*, 37.
529 proposed demolition of Wall for credits: Hertle, *Chronik*, 92–103.
530 Kohl trip to West Berlin: Klaus Dreher, *Helmut Kohl. Leben mit Macht* (Stuttgart, 1998), 455–457.
530 "grow with one another": Quoted in James and Stone, eds., *When the Wall Came Down*, 42.
530 "and with solidarity": Quoted in ibid., 47–48.
531 Round Table discussions": Maier, *Dissolution*, 168–184; Konrad H. Jarausch, *The Rush to German Unity* (New York, 1994), 75–94.
531 "delicate balance of Europe": Hugh Trevor-Roper, "On the Unification of Germany," *The Independent*, June 17, 1989. For an analysis of Western reactions to German unification, see Gert-Joachim Glaessner and Ian Wallace, eds., *The German Revolution of 1989: Causes and Consequences* (Oxford, 1992).
531 "too large and powerful": Margaret Thatcher, *The Downing Street Years* (New York, 1993), 792–796.
532 "much time": Quoted in Dreher, *Kohl*, 460. For an excellent recent study of German-Russian relations at the time of German reunification and beyond, see Angela E. Stent, *Russia and Germany Reborn. Unification, the Soviet Collapse, and the New Europe* (Princeton, 1999).
532 "done in the past": George Bush and Brent Scowcroft, *A World Transformed* (New York, 1998), 187.
532 American position on German unification: See Gerald R. Kleinfeld, "Die Verwirklichung des Unwahrscheinlichen: Amerikanische Aussenpolitik und deutsche Wiedervereinigung," in Wolfgang-Uwe Friedrich, ed., *Die USA und die deutsche Frage* (Frankfurt, 1991), 369–390. See also Charles Maier, "Reflections on the Day of German Unity," in ibid., 449–454.
532 "God's blessing": Quoted in Dreher, *Kohl*, 458.
532–533 "creating a federation"; "goal of the Federal government": Quoted in James and Stone, eds., *When the Wall Came Down*, 33–41.
533 "not on the agenda"; "pressing political question": Quoted in Philip Zelikow and Condoleeza Rice, *Germany Unified and Europe Transformed* (Cambridge, Mass., 1995), 124.
533 "on track": Quoted in ibid.
534 "definitely at an end": Dreher, *Kohl*, 489–497.
534 "regained its old symbol": Walter Momper, *Grenzfall. Berlin im Brennpunkt deutscher Geschichte* (Munich, 1991), 236.
535 "think about Auschwitz": *Die Zeit*, February 10, 1990.
535 "sellout" of their country; "socialism in the GDR": Quoted in Jarausch, *Rush*, 91.
535 "still to come"; "independent and democratic": Quoted in James and Stone, eds., *When the Wall Came Down*, 142, 62.
535 "modern age began": Quoted in Robert Darnton, *Berlin Journal 1989–1990* (New York, 1991), 77.
536 "isle of the blessed": "Bedenke, das du tot warst," *Die Zeit*, April 5, 1991. For more on West Berlin nostalgia, see "Wenn die Sumpfbüten welken," *Frankfurter Allgemeine Zeitung*, July 28, 1994.
536 new face: For Gysi's view of unification, see Gregor Gysi, *Einspruch! Gespräche, Briefe, Reden* (Berlin, 1992); and G. Gysi and Thomas Falkner, *Wir brauchen einen dritten* Weg (Hamburg, 1990).

537–538 "to strive for it"; "prosperity for all"; "out of our mess": Quoted in Jarausch, *Rush*, 109, 124–125.
538 "money and bananas": Quoted in ibid., 117.
538 "under Article 23": "Grosse Koalition steht," *Die Welt*, April 10, 1990.
538 Election results: Brigitte Walz, Anke Notle, and Uwe Prell, eds., *Berlin Handbuch. Das Lexikon der Bundeshauptstadt* (Berlin, 1992), 1342.
539 "go to the people"; "with a mercenary mind"; "all possible now": Quoted in Jarausch, *Rush*, 109, 137–138.
539 fate of the Wall: See "Weg, weg, weg," *Der Spiegel*, 28/1999, 42–45.
541 Two-Plus-Four negotiations: See ibid., 271–327; Dreher, *Kohl*, 527–535; Horst Teltschik, *329 Tage. Innenansichten der Einigung* (Berlin, 1991).
541 guard dogs: See Schneider, *German Comedy*, 207–212.
543 "two anchors are better": Quoted in Zelikov and Rice, *Germany Unified*, 276–277.
545 December 1990 elections: "Es geht eine Glatze," *Der Spiegel*, 51/1990, 87.
545 "the people's expectations": Ibid.
545 "the Soviet Occupation Zone": Quoted in Reiner Pommerin, "Die Hauptstadt: 'Der Bundestag versammelt sich alsdann in Berlin . . . '" in Udo Wengst, ed., *Historiker betrachten Deutschland. Beiträge zum Vereinigungsprozess und zur Hauptstadtdiskussion* (Bonn, 1992), 217.
546 capital debate: On this issue, see ibid. and Helmut Herler, ed., *Die Hauptstadtdebatte* (Bonn, 1991).
547 "Western Europe, and America": Fritz Fischer, "Rückkehr nach Preussen?" in Wengst, *Die Historiker betrachten Deutschland*, 246–251.
548 "lively and exciting": *New York Times*, Nov. 1, 1991.
548 true heart of the nation: See contributions by Gerhard Keiderling, Peter von Oertzen, and Hagen Schulze in Wengst, *Historiker betrachten Deutschland.*
548 "if Berlin were the capital": "Alle lieben Berlin . . . " *Die Zeit*, May 3, 1991.
549 "completion of unity": Quoted in Dreher, *Kohl*, 577.
549 "agencies are missing": "Rollenspiel um die Hauptstadt," *Die Zeit*, March 22, 1991.
550 "responsible leadership of Germany"; "in the past": Quoted in Dreher, *Kohl*, 579–581.
550 "obvious capital": *Berlin-Bonn. Die Debatte. Alle Bundestagsreden vom 20. Juni 1991* (Cologne, 1991), 85–87.
550 "division of Europe": Ibid., 52–55.
551 "of real content": Ibid., 62–67.
551 "not between two cities": Ibid., 29–37.
551 "politics of just proportions": Ibid., 68–72.
552 "it never leaves": "Ein Päckchen für Bonn," *Der Spiegel*, 32/1991, 81.
553 "Both are possible": "Berlin, Crowned Germany's Capital, Still Fears for its Future," *New York Times*, Nov. 1, 1998.
553 "smugglers, entrepreneurs, contracts": Quoted in Katherine Roper, "Imagining the German Capital: Berlin Writers in the Two Unification Eras," in Pape, ed., *German Unifications*, 184.
553 actual market value: Kramer, *Politics of Memory*, 107.
553 "mistake of the century": "Berlin-Potsdamer Platz," *Die Zeit*, Aug. 10, 1990.
553 "a few cultural institutions": Ibid.
554 real estate boom: See "Der drückt sich durch," *Der Spiegel*, 32/1991, 26–29; "Wiedergewonnene Normalität," *Süddeutsche Zeitung*, March 26, 1993.
554 effects of unification: "Ökonomische Grenzen in einer vereinigten Stadt," *Neue Züricher Zeitung*, May 23, 1995.
554 "a wonderful catastrophe": "Eine wunderbare Katastrophe," *Der Spiegel*, 26/1991, 18–30; see also "Vereinte Stadt mit Doppelkopf," *Die Zeit*, Sept. 21, 1990. For a searing indictment of Berlin's politics and society since reunification, see Uwe Rade, *Hauptstadt der Verdrängung. Berliner Zukunft zwischen Kiez und Metropole* (Berlin, 1997).
555 "luxury move": Peter Jochen Winters, "Berlin-Umzug und die deutsche Einheit," *Deutschland Archiv*, 27. Jg. (February 1994), 113–116; "Wir haben verloren," *Der Spiegel*, 45/1997, 32–33.
555 "I still do": "Berliners Object to Doubts over New Capital," *New York Times*, Feb. 14, 1993.
556 "bad news from Berlin": "Picture Is Dimming for Games in Berlin," *New York Times*, July 14, 1992.
556 "not for sale": Ibid.
557 "NOlympic" movement: "Protests and Bombs Greet Olympic Bid," *New York Times*, Sept. 19, 1993.
557 "peace and friendship": Ibid. See also "Olympia 1936-Olympia 2000," *Der Tagesspiegel*, Dec. 13, 1992.

557 beginning in 1993: "Berlin Feels the Pinch of Living with a Budget," *International Herald Tribune*, April 1, 1996.
558 "a great crash?": "Riskante Geschäfte mit der Eins-A-Lage," *Süddeutsche Zeitung*, April 5, 1994.
558 "since the war": "Berlin Is Deep in Red Territory," *International Herald Tribune*, March 6, 1996.
558 "us Germans together": Schneider, *German Comedy*, 4.
559 would go east; since 1990: "Die Baustelle der Wiedervereinigung," *Die Zeit*, Oct. 8, 1993.
559 "bananas they eat": Quoted in Katie Hafner, *The House at the Bridge. A Story of Modern Germany* (New York, 1995), 125.
559 "Suck East German Blood": Schneider, *German Comedy*, 163.
560 "unjust Communist regimes": Quoted in Dirk Verheyen, "What's in a Name? Street Name Politics and Urban Identity in Berlin," *German Politics and Society*15:3 (Fall 1997), 44.
560 their collective identity: "With 2 Sets of Heroes, It's Hard to Name Streets," *New York Times*, Dec. 1, 1994; "Lenin soll Platz und Strasse verlieren," *Die Welt*, Sept. 2, 1991.
560 Otto-Grotewohl-Strasse/Wilhelmstrasse: "Warum nicht Müler?" *Die Zeit*, June 26/28, 1991.
561 Zetkinstrasse: "With 2 Sets of Heroes"; also Ladd, *Ghosts of Berlin*, 211.
562 "despot and murderer"; "pushed around": Quoted in Ladd, *Ghosts of Berlin*, 197.
562 Thälmann monument: Ibid., 201–203. On GDR monuments, see also Martin Schönfeld, "Erhalten-Zerstören-Verändern? Diskussionsprozesse um die politische Denkmäler der DDR in Berlin," *Kritische Berichte*, 1/1991, 39–43.
563 Treuhand: See, inter alia, Jarausch, *Rush*, 151–152.
564 "magic word 'privatization'?": Christa Wolf, *Parting from Phantoms. Selected Writings 1990–1994* (Chicago, 1997), 31.
564 *abgewickelt*: Bernd Schirmer, *Schlehweins Giraffe* (Frankfurt, 1992).
565 "can start on English": Quoted in Maier, *Dissolution*, 307.
565 "doing at the moment": Quoted in John Tagliabue, "What Divides Berlin Now?" *New York Times Magazine*, April 7, 1991, 60.
566 an ideological battlefield: On Abwicklung and the Fink case, see Maier, *Dissolution*, 302–311; "Die DDR in uns," *Der Spiegel*, 50/1991, 18–24.
566 collective healing: See "Interview mit Joachim Gauck," *Deutschland Archiv* 28:11 (November 1995), 1228–1232.
566 Stasi for years: On Wollenberger's case and the horrors of the Stasi files, see Vera Wollenberger, *Virus der Heuchler. Innenansicht aus Stasi-Akten* (Berlin, 1992).
567 "files will never show up": Wolf Biermann, *Der Stürz des Dädalus, oder Eizes für die Eingeborenen der Fidschi-Inseln über den IM Judas Ischariot und den Kuddelmudd* . . . (Cologne, 1992), 56.
567 "never owned me": Quoted in Stephen Kinzer, "East Germans Face Their Accusers," *New York Times Magazine*, April 12, 1992, 50.
567 literary community: See Thomas Anz, ed., *"Es geht nicht um Christa Wolf": Der Literaturstreit im vereinten Deutschland* (Munich, 1991); Karl-Heinz J. Schoeps, "Intellectuals, Unification, and Political Change 1990: The Case of Christa Wolf," in Pape, ed., *German Unifications*, 252–277.
567 "state poet": See the contributions by Marcel Reich-Rainicki, Ulrich Greiner, and Hans Noll in ibid.
567 "succumbed to bourgeois tendencies": "Die ängstliche Margarete," *Der Spiegel*, 4/1993, 160.
568 "work along with it": Grass letter in Wolf, *Parting from Phantoms*, 208.
568 "everyone so crazy": Schneider quoted in Kramer, *Politics of Memory*, 191.
568 "honest, loyal, and reliable": "Ehrlich, treu, zuverlässig," *Der Spiegel*, 50/1990, 30–38; "Menschlich bewegt," *Der Spiegel*, 52/1990, 20–23.
568 positions in united Germany: "Menschlich bewegt," 20.
569 Honecker case: See "Moabiter Satyrspiele," *Der Spiegel*, 3/1993, 76–77.
570 welcome in Chile: "Glücklich und zufrieden," ibid., 78–79.
570 Mielke case: McElvoy, *Saddled Cow*, 100–101; Schneider, *German Comedy*, 113.
571 "scalpel for dissection": Wolf, *Man Without a Face*, 339.
571 Keßler trial: Maier, *Dissolution*, 320.
572 "intolerable disproportionality": See ibid., 321; also Robert Alexy, Mauerschützen. *Zum Verhältnis von Recht, Moral, und Strafbarkeit* (Göttingen, 1993).
572 "a political verdict": "Six Generals in Germany Are Sentenced," *New York Times*, Sept. 11, 1996.

572 "matters are handled": "Ein Offizier, der wußte, was er wollte," *Süddeutsche Zeitung*, April 26, 1997.
572 all appeals: Ibid.
573 2.1 percent in the west: Hartmut Häußermann, "Berlin: Lasten der Vergangenheit und Hoffnungen der Zukunft," *Aus Politik und Zeitgeschichte*, 17/1997 (April 18, 1997), 10–11.
573 durable legacy of provincialism: For a highly critical appraisal of Berlin's intellectual life in the mid-1990s, see Michtild Küpper, "Einheitsschmerzen, Einheitsträume," *Neue Züricher Zeitung*, May 23, 1995.
573 "thinks she is beautiful again": "Berlin Flourishes Again, but Difficulties Arise," *Wall Street Journal*, April 1, 1995.
573 "charm of the derelict": "Der Charm des Maroden," *Der Spiegel*, 15/1998, 48–50; "Berlin's Vital Café Culture," *New York Times*, Feb. 20, 1994.
573 "wanted [Eastern] zone back": "Der Charm des Maroden," 48.
574 "not a welfare office": "Renditenjägern mit Wildermanieren," *Süddeutsche Zeitung*, May 20, 1992.
574 present illegally: "Russian Artists Flocking to Berlin," *New York Times*, Jan. 17, 1995.
575 "Russian Mafia": "They're Coming Again! Russians Relish Germany," *New York Times*, Nov. 30, 1995.
575 "enjoy life more": Ibid.
575 Jewish influx: "Aus aller Herren Länder," *Der Tagesspiegel*, July 22, 1996.
576 "mud-fight": "Streit in der Synagoge," *Der Spiegel*, 9/1997, 84–85.
576 "requires special attention": "Ausgerechnet ein Jude," *Der Spiegel*, 16/1994, 180.
576 Oranienburger Strasse and Tacheles: "Ab jetzt soll's Freude sein," *Der Spiegel*, 11/1997, 54–57; "Ruine im Biersumpf," *Der Spiegel*, 20/1997, 182–185.
576 *Juden raus!:* "German Paradox: Alongside Healing, New Flames," *New York Times*, May 8, 1990.
578 "most forbidden of symbols": Ingo Hasselbach with Tom Reiss, "How Nazis Are Made," *New Yorker*, Jan. 8, 1996, 39.
578 "beat them up": Quoted in Martin A. Lee, *The Beast Reawakens* (Boston, 1997), 242.
578 "values of the Third Reich": Quoted in ibid., 197.
578–579 "if you wanted to"; "the Führer comes!"; "work at hand" "business capital": Hasselbach, "How Nazis are Made," 42–47.
580 "German democratic institutions": "350,000 in Germany Protest Violence Against Immigrants," *New York Times*, Nov. 9, 1992.
580 "second-class departure ceremony": "Wer sagt zum Abschied 'Do swidanja'?" *Der Tagesspiegel*, Feb. 8, 1994.
581 "from another one"; "all be Russians now": "Allied Soldiers March to Say Farewell to Berlin," *New York Times*, June 19, 1994.
581 "from the Germans": Quoted in Lee, *Beast*, 386.
581 biggest pullout ever: "Russian Troops Bid 'Auf Wiedersehen' to Germany," *New York Times*, Sept. 1, 1994.
581 Allied Museum: "Fertighaus der Geschichte," *Süddeutsche Zeitung*, Sept. 5, 1994.
582 "wouldn't be as good": "The G.I.'s Legacy: Basketball and Sweet Memories," *New York Times*, Sept. 27, 1994.
583 "common forms of memory": "Gemeinsames Erinnern?" *Süddeutsche Zeitung*, May 12, 1995; "Ein Fundstück aus dunkler Geschichte," *Fokus*, 4/1993, 78–79.

Chapter 11

585 "one big time bomb": "Warten auf den grossen Knall," *Der Spiegel*, 9/1999, 77–80.
586 "that went before": "Try a little tenderness," *The Economist*, Mar. 30, 1996, 91.
586 "not to be discovered anew": "Die Baustelle der Wiedervereinigung," *Die Zeit*, Oct. 8, 1993.
586 "New Jersey Meadowlands": Paul Goldberger, "Reimagining Berlin," *New York Times Magazine*, Feb. 5, 1995, 45.
587 "a new country": Peter Conrad, "Rebuilding Berlin," *New Yorker*, April 28/May 5, 1997, 225.
587 "vanishes in a catastrophe": Ibid., 223.

587 "living" part of the city: "Platz für Berlin," *Die Zeit*, Oct. 18, 1991.
588 under Napoleon III: "Ein Baron Haussmann unserer Tage," *Süddeutsche Zeitung*, Sept. 21, 1993.
588 "must look like Berlin": Quoted in Goldberger, "Reimagining Berlin," 47.
588 continuity in the Spree metropolis: For Siedler's view, see his essay collection, *Phoenix im Sand. Glanz und Elend der Hauptstadt* (Berlin, 1998).
588 "New Teutonia": "Heimatkunde für Neuteutonia," *Der Spiegel*, 42/1994, 48–59.
589 "develop the city": Quoted in Goldberger, "Reimagining Berlin," 48.
589 "are simply embarrassing": Quoted in "Heimatkunde für Neuteutonia," 48.
589 "take on the responsibility": "The Capital Builders," *The Economist*, Nov. 9, 1991, 20.
589 "smugness in one step": Goldberger, "Reimagining Berlin, 49.
589 "architecturally lost": "Architektonisch ist Berlin verloren," *Süddeutsche Zeitung*, July 9, 1994.
590 "and devotional height": Quoted in David B. Dennis, *Beethoven in German Politics, 1870–1989* (New Haven, 1996), 168.
590 "international airport space": "Once Again, A City Rewards the Walker," *New York Times*, April 11, 1999.
591 "social thickness": "Das seltsame Gefühl, nicht in Berlin zu sein," *Der Tagesspiegel*, June 6, 1999.
591 "Marlene, Go Home!"; "find a home": "Heim in die Pfütze," *Der Spiegel*, 32/1997, 96–99; also "Marlene's Street of Dreams? To the Barricades!," *New York Times*, Dec. 16, 1996.
592 "Salzkirchen und Gelsengitter": "Wie in Gelsengitter die Fussgängerzone," *Süddeutsche Zeitung*, April 19, 1995.
593 Bahnhof Friedrichstrasse: "Langsam heilt die tiefe Narbe," *Die Zeit*, March 29, 1999; also Ladd, *Ghosts of Berlin*, 15–16.
594 "I miscalculated": "Mauerstrasse ist nicht Wall Street," *Süddeutsche Zeitung*, May 8, 1998.
595 "not bold": Quoted in Goldberger, "Reimagining Berlin," 48.
595 "salon of the republic"; "without air in it": "Was wird aus dem Pariser Platz?" *Die Zeit*, Feb. 25, 1994.
595 Brandenburg Gate: Ladd, *Ghosts of Berlin*, 72–81; "Glanzvolle Geschichte, ungewisse Zukunft," *Der Tagesspiegel*, Feb. 24, 1994; also Willmuth Arenhövel and Ralf Bothe, *Das Brandenburger Tor: Eine Monographie* (Berlin, 1991).
596 Prussian Academy of Arts: "Lästige Zeugen," *Süddeutsche Zeitung*, May 10, 1995.
597 Hotel Adlon: "Das Vermächtnis des schönen Gigolo," *Süddeutsche Zeitung*, May 17, 1995.
598 "some French flair": Quoted in Christian Bahr and Günter Schneider, *Hauptstadtbau* (Berlin, 1997), 18.
599 "go another way"; "not make sense": Quoted in "Flurry Raised on Embassy in New Berlin," *New York Times*, Feb. 10, 1996.
599 shortage of funds: "Is U.S. Too Poor to Join New Germany's Fun?" *New York Times*, April 7, 1997.
600 "preferably without windows": "Am besten, ohne Fenster," *Der Spiegel*, 5/1999, 46–47; "Germans Are Balking at U.S. Embassy Blueprint," *New York Times*, Oct. 28, 1999.
600 "rival nostalgias": Ladd, *Ghosts of Berlin*, 59.
600 "socialist-usurped city center": "Monotone Klotzigkeit," *Frankfurter Allgemeine Zeitung*, Feb. 4, 1995.
601 no date was fixed: "Das Schloß als Symbol," *Der Spiegel*, 29/1998, 158–163.
601 "popular amusement"; "humane and friendly": "Ein wahres Volkshaus," *Frankfurter Allgemeine Zeitung*, Feb. 4, 1995.
602 reburial of Frederick the Great: "Aktion Sarg und Asche," *Der Spiegel*, 33/1991, 28–47.
603 "resignation": Siedler, *Pheonix im Sand*, 116–132.
603 von Boddien: See "Das Schloß als Symbol."
604 "richly presumptuous": "Die Fassaden-Lüge, *Süddeutsche Zeitung*, Aug. 8/9, 1998.
605 "simply prettier": "Milliarde für die Seele," *Der Spiegel*, 6/1999, 17.
605 truly unified at all: "Nationaldenkmal, Ten Years After," *Süddeutsche Zeitung*, May 20/21. 1998.
606 "has been done to it"; "feel comfortable": "Das malträtierte Herz der Stadt," *Süddeutsche Zeitung*, March 20/21, 1993.
606 "architecture of the century": "Die planerische Zukunft Berlins," *Süddeutsche Zeitung*, Nov. 12, 1994.
606 "left to reconstruct": "Capital gains," *The Economist*, Feb. 19, 1994, 99.

606 identity of its own: Bruno Flierl, *Berlin baut um—Wessen wird die Stadt?*, 105–106.
607 "buildings shape us": Quoted in "Die Macht der Mauern," *Der Spiegel*, 22/1998, 57.
607 "behind bureaucratic desks": Quoted in ibid., 54.
608 "require a new building": Quoted in Wise, *Capital Dilemma*, 92.
608 "a difficult history": Quoted in ibid., 93.
609 like a fortress: "Das Monstrum von Mitte," *Süddeutsche Zeitung*, Oct. 28, 1988.
609 "simple visitors": Günter Grass, *Ein weites Feld* (Munich, 1998), 66.
609 "Reichskanzler Adolf Hitler": "Macht der Mauern," *Der Spiegel*, 22/1998, 57.
610 "tear down the building": Quoted in Wise, *Capital Dilemma*, 107.
610 "out of date and obsolete": Quoted in Reuth, *Goebbels*, 173.
610 one block east: Demps, *Wilhelmstrasse*, 219–222.
610 Bendlerblock: "Macht der Mauern," 68; Ladd, *Ghosts of Berlin*, 149–151.
611 "underscore that federalism": Quoted in "The Reichstag: Just a Chamber of Bad Memories?" *New York Times*, July 31, 1991.
611 kaiser's uniform: Wise, *Capital Dilemma*, 121.
612 "open-minded character": Quoted in Ladd, *Ghosts of Berlin*, 94.
612 "around the world": "Christo Is Ready to Wrap the Reichstag," *New York Times*, Jan. 7, 1993.
614 "open future": Quoted in ibid. See also "Dem Volke Staat zeigen," *Der Spiegel*, 8/1993, 28–30.
614 dome debate: "Dom des Volkes," *Der Spiegel*, 15/1999, 44–48.
615 Reichstag graffiti: See ibid., and "Verordnete Geschichtsvergessenheit," *Der Tagesspiegel*, July 8, 1999.
615 "born on those seats": Quoted in Jane Kramer, "Living with Berlin," *New Yorker*, July 5, 1999, 58.
616 Reichstag name: "What's in a name?" *The Economist*, April 17, 1999, 55.
616 "Berlin republic possible"; "optimistic or happy": Quoted in "With Smoked Salmon and Beer, Berlin Greets Parliament," *New York Times*, April 20, 1999.
617 "conquer it again?": Quoted in "Macht der Mauern," *Der Spiegel*, 22/1998, 69.
618 "world is watching"; "rebuild a capital": Quoted in Wise, *Capital Dilemma*, 60, 61.
618 "rednecks of the Rhine": Ellen Posner, "Hell's Capital," *Atlantic Monthly*, July 1944, 95.
618 Spreebogen competition: Wise, *Capital Dilemma*, 65–67.
619 "modesty and dignity": Quoted in ibid., 72.
619 Federal Chancellery: Ibid., 72–79.
620 "as much as he did": Kramer, "Living with Berlin," 54.
620 remembrance of things past: See Peter Reichel, *Politik mit der Erinnerung. Gedächtnisorte im Streit um die nationalsozialistische Verganenheit* (Munich, 1995), 173–175.
621 Plötzensee: See Ladd, *Ghosts of Berlin*, 151–152; Peter Steinbach, "Vermächtnis oder Verfälschung? Erfahrungen mit Ausstellungen zum deutschen Widerstand," in Gerd R. Überschar, *Der 20. Juli 1944. Bewertung und Rezeption des deutschen Widerstandes gegen das NS-Regime* (Cologne, 1994), 171–178.
622 "gift to the German future": Theodor Heuss, *Gedenkrede zum 20. Juli 1944* (Tübingen, 1954), 30.
622 Bendlerblock museum: Reichel, *Politik mit der Erinnerung*, 227, 231; see also Steinbach, "Vermächtnis," 171–173.
623 Topography of Terror: See the exhibition catalog edited by Rürup, *Topography of Terror*; also Ladd, *Ghosts of Berlin*, 160–169; Reichel, *Politik mit der Erinnerung*, 196–202; and "Verletzungen am Denk-Ort," *Süddeutsche Zeitung*, Dec. 16, 1992.
623 Villa Wannsee: See Reichel, *Politik mit der Erinnerung*, 193–96; "Berlin Villa, From War to Peace," *New York Times*, June 26, 1997; Eberhard Diepgen, "Erinnern für die Zukunft" (Berlin, 1992), 5.
624 "in the same place": Ian Buruma, *The Wages of Guilt. Memories of War in Germany and Japan* (New York, 1994), 238.
624 "ramp to the train-wash": "Stark belastet," *Der Spiegel*, 30/1993, 76.
626 "No trespassing": "Cutbacks Drawing a Curtain on a Holocaust Site," *New York Times*, Nov. 4, 1995.
627 "in the new Reich": George L. Mosse, *Fallen Soldiers. Reshaping the Memory of the World Wars* (New York, 1990), 97.
627 Neue Wache: See Reichel, *Politik mit der Erninnerung*, 231–246; Ladd, *Ghosts of Berlin*, 217–224; Wise, *Capital Dilemma*, 145–146; Wolf Jobst Siedler, "Wo Preussen am preußischsten war," *Die Zeit*, Dec. 3, 1993; "Stellen die Toten den Termin?", *Berliner Zeitung*, Nov. 11, 1993.
628 Kollwitz pietà: "Dem Schmerz eine Richtung," *Der Tagesspiegel*, March 19, 1993.

629	"murderers are not victims": "Ohne Militärparade und Glockenlaut," *Frankfurter Allgemeine Zeitung*, Nov. 12, 1993.
629	bunker discoveries: "Düstere Bunker der Geschichte, *Frankfurter Allgemeine Zeitung*, Nov. 12, 1993; "Braune Suppe im Boden," *Der Spiegel*, 8/1998, 28–29; "An Inconvenient Bit of History in Berlin," *San Francisco Chronicle*, Feb. 1, 1995; "Hitler's Bunker Unearthed," *San Francisco Chronicle*, Oct. 16, 1999.
630	"a line under the past": Michael Kleeburg, *Ein Garten im Norden* (Berlin, 1998), 85.
630	"out of Hitler's shadow": Quoted in Buruma, *Wages*, 244.
630	"equality of oppression": "A Memorial to Gay Pain of Nazi Era Stirs Debate," *New York Times*, Feb. 6, 1997; "Zigeuner ohne Lobby," *taz*, Nov. 18, 1993.
630	"to the heart of Europe": Quoted in "Auf der Höhe der Zeit," *Der Spiegel*, 48/1997, 66.
630	Rosh criticism: See Kramer, *Politics of Memory*, 257–293; "Vom Mahnmal zum Wahnmal," *Der Spiegel*, 35/1998, 170–181; Michael Z. Wise, "Totem and Taboo," *Lingua Franca*, Dec/Jan., 1999, 38–46.
631	"invisible as a monument": Quoted in Wise, "Totem," 39.
631	"impossible assignment": Quoted in "Auf der Höhe der Zeit," 67.
632	"between carnival and genocide": Wise, *Capital Dilemma*, 149.
633	"a thousand times": Quoted in ibid., 150.
633	"Venus fly trap": Quoted in Wise, "Totem," 40.
633	after the elections: Ibid., 41–44.
634	"not a compromise": "Schröder Backs Design for a Vast Berlin Holocaust Memorial," *New York Times*, Jan. 18, 1999.
634	"chapter in our history": "Berlin Holocaust Memorial Approved," *New York Times*, June 26, 1999.
635	built at all: "In Berlin, Project for Jewish Display in Doubt," *New York Times*, Aug. 7, 1991; see also Reichel, *Politik mit der Erinnerung*, 258–260.
636	"think of museums"; "five-year delay": "In Berlin, Project" *New York Times*, Aug 7, 1991.
636	"repair sick stomachs": "Pendeln zwischen die Welten," *Der Spiegel*, 39/1997, 60–63.
637	"prelude to the Berlin Republic": "Remembrance of Jewish times past," *The Economist*, Jan. 30, 1999.
637	"domain of democracy": Andrei S. Markovits and Simon Reich, *The German Predicament* (Ithaca, 1997), 203.
638	power broker in German politics: "A Cinderella of a City, And It's Nearly Midnight," *New York Times*, Jan. 14, 1997.
638	Berlin's economy: See "Berlin's blues," *The Economist*, April 3, 1999, 58; "A New Berlin? Not So Fast," *International Herald Tribune*, Oct. 29, 1998.
639	"Leere Kassen": "Leere Kassen, Leere Köpfe," *Süddeutsche Zeitung*, Sept. 28, 1999.
639	museum reorganization: Farr, *Berlin! Berlin!*, 190–191; Werner Knopp, "Berlin—Stadt der Museen," in Werner Süß, ed., *Hauptstadt Berlin. Band 2: Berlin im vereinten Deutschland* (Berlin, 1995), 551–561.
640	*Geschichtsaufbereitungsanlage*: The critic is Benekikt Erenz. See Reichel, *Politik mit der Erinnerung*, 256. On Pei's design for the German Historical Museum, see Wise, *Capital Dilemma*, 135–141.
641	library reorganization: See Farr, *Berlin! Berlin!*, 193.
642	cultural tourism in the new Berlin: Ulrich Roloff-Momin, "Kulturstandort Berlin," in Süß, ed., *Hauptstadt Berlin*, II, 543–550.
642	Love Parade controversy: "Anwohner—Love Parade auf die Avus," *Der Tagesspiegel*, Oct. 30, 1999.
643	"becoming more German": "Start mit Blackout," *Der Spiegel*, 13/1999, 28.
643	"I have no fear": "Scheitern als Close," *Der Spiegel*, 12/1999, 252–253.
643	economy in the east: See "The Berlin Republic. A Survey of Germany," *The Economist*, Feb. 6, 1999.
643	East Berlin election: "Former Communists Surge in Berlin Municipal Voting," *New York Times*, Oct. 11, 1999.
644	"strong sense of intrigue": Quoted in "So In, So Very Berlin: A Capital Seeks Its Identity," *New York Times*, Sept. 26, 1999.
645	from the Polish border: Arnulf Baring, "Die Berliner Republik," *Aus Politik und Zeitgeschichte*, 33/1999, 9.
646	"no negative genius": "Germany's Pragmatic Ex-Radical Thinks Globally," *New York Times*, Jan. 28, 1999.

INDEX

A NOTE ON THE AUTHOR

David Clay Large, professor of history at Montana State University, is a specialist in modern German history. Among his books are *Germans to the Front: West German Rearmament in the Adenauer Era; Where Ghosts Walked: Munich's Road to the Third Reich;* and *Between Two Fires: Europe's Path in the 1930s.* He divides his time between Bozeman, Montana, and San Francisco, California.

A NOTE ON THE TYPE

This book was typset in Caslon 540, a typeface derived from William Caslon's eighteenth century types. The popularity of these types led to a practically endless range of Caslon copies; among them Caslon 540, from American Type Founders in 1902, and Caslon 3, a slightly bolder face also from ATF in 1905, which was later modified for use with Intertype and Linotype technologies. Both designs have the warm, solid, straightforward style that has made Caslon popular for over 200 years; these Caslons, however, have shorter descenders, and higher contrast, features that enable them to hold up better with the faster presses and the new varieties of paper introduced at the turn-of-the-century.

CPSIA information can be obtained
at www.ICGtesting.com
Printed in the USA
LVHW021524201218
601212LV00007B/261